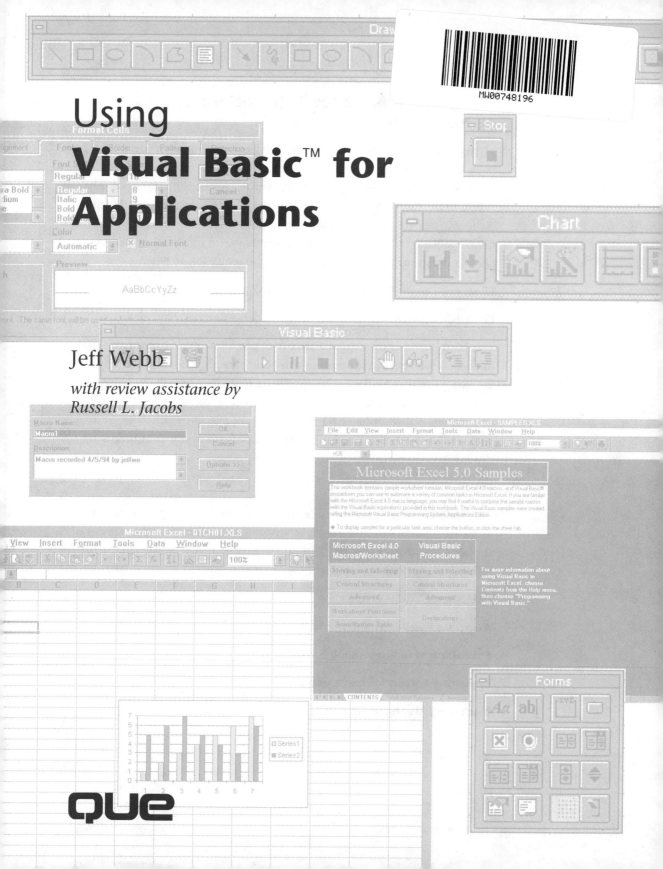

Using
Visual Basic™ for Applications

Jeff Webb

with review assistance by
Russell L. Jacobs

que

Using Visual Basic for Applications

Copyright © 1994 by Que® Corporation

Library of Congress Catalog Number: 94-66726

ISBN: 1-56529-725-3

96 95 94   6 5 4 3 2

Interpretation of the printing code: The rightmost double-digit number is the year of the book's printing; the rightmost single-digit number, the number of the book's printing. For example, a printing code of 94-1 shows that the first printing of the book occurred in 1994.

Publisher: David P. Ewing

Associate Publisher: Michael Miller

Publishing Manager: Joseph B. Wikert

Managing Editor: Michael Cunningham

Marketing Manager: Greg Wiegand

Credits

Publishing Manager
Brad R. Koch

Acquisitions Editor
Angela J. Lee

Acquisitions Coordinator
Patricia J. Brooks

Product Director
C. Kazim Haidri

Production Editors
Lynn Northrup
Linda Seifert

Copy Editors
Danielle Bird
Geneil Breeze
Noelle Gasco
Lorna Gentry
Chuck Hutchinson
Patrick Kanouse
Andy Saff
Kathy Simpson

Editorial Assistant
Michelle R. Williams

Technical Editor
Deirdre Maloy

Book Designer
Paula Carroll

Cover Designer
Dan Armstrong

Production Team
Steve Adams
Angela Bannan
Cameron Booker
Dan Caparo
Stephen Carlin
Kim Cofer
Karen Dodson
Carla Hall
Michael Hughes
Clint Lahnen
G. Alan Palmore
Nanci Sears Perry
Linda Quigley
Michael Thomas
Marcella Thompson
Tina Trettin
Donna Winter
Lillian Yates

Composed in *Stone Serif* and *MCPdigital* by Que Corporation

Dedication

For my son, the actor.

About the Author

Jeff Webb was a senior member of the BASIC documentation team at
Microsoft. He worked on BASIC PDS, QBASIC, OLE Automation, and all
versions of Visual Basic. He contributed to many books and help systems,
notably: *Visual Basic Reference; OLE 2 Programmer's Reference (Creating Program-
mable Applications);* and *Programming Integrated Solutions with Microsoft Office.*
Currently, he runs Wombat Technology in Seattle, WA.

Acknowledgments

I owe special thanks to the folks at Que and Microsoft for helping bring this book to completion. In particular, Lynn Northrup and Russ Jacobs deserve gold medals for doing everything they could to finish this book ahead of schedule. Lynn kept her sense of humor and understood all but one of my jokes—that's the best batting average I've seen. Russ took on a lot of extra work near the end of the project. I owe them both a great deal.

Thanks also to Deirdre Maloy, the technical editor on the book, who kept me honest with the Mac users.

I'd also like to acknowledge the help of Drew Fletcher, Glenn Hackney, and Steven Mitchell, all from Microsoft. They helped me work through some of the more obscure details of Visual Basic in Excel and were always forthcoming with new information. I hope this book furthers their goal of making Visual Basic the most useful programming language of our time.

Finally, I'd like to thank the core team in the Basic writing group at Microsoft for making me feel welcome during my tenure there. Ship it!

Trademark Acknowledgments

All terms mentioned in this book that are known to be trademarks or service marks have been appropriately capitalized. Que cannot attest to the accuracy of this information. Use of a term in this book should not be regarded as affecting the validity of any trademark or service mark.

Visual Basic is a trademark of the Microsoft Corporation.

Screen Reproductions in this book were created using Collage Complete from Inner Media, Inc., Hollis, New Hampshire.

We'd Like To Hear From You!

As part of our continuing effort to produce books of the highest possible quality, Que would like to hear your comments. To stay competitive, we *really* want you, as a computer book reader and user, to let us know what you like or dislike most about this book or other Que products.

You can mail comments, ideas, or suggestions for improving future editions to the address below, or send us a fax at (317) 581-4663. For the on-line inclined, Macmillan Computer Publishing now has a forum on CompuServe (type **GO QUEBOOKS** at any prompt) through which our staff and authors are available for questions and comments. In addition to exploring our forum, please feel free to contact me personally on CompuServe at 74143,1574 to discuss your opinions of this book.

Thanks in advance—your comments will help us to continue publishing the best books available on computer topics in today's market.

Christopher Haidri
Product Development Specialist
Que Corporation
201 W. 103rd Street
Indianapolis, Indiana 46290
USA

Contents at a Glance

Contents

18 Using Additional Display Controls   679

19 Sending and Receiving Mail   735

20 Advanced Topics   749

Appendixes **785**

A Trappable Errors **787**

B Table of Key Codes **797**

C Table of Intrinsic Constants **809**

D Style Guidelines for Professional-Quality Code **831**

Introduction

With so many great software packages available, why should anyone but professional software developers learn to program? Won't software applications continue to become more sophisticated, until programming is a thing of the past? When using application or operating system commands, your interaction is controlled by the design of the system. Well-designed systems seem natural, with boundless capabilities, but sooner or later you'll find their limits, and the system will never learn to breach them.

When programming, you learn to collaborate with your computer. Systems are as simple or sophisticated as you choose to make them. The limits are determined only by your ability to express yourself and, of course, by the power of your hardware. Learning to program makes using a computer more like a conversation with a friend and less like filling out a form. This human/machine interaction can be frustrating, enjoyable, and eventually addictive.

Visual Basic is the most powerful interactive programming language available for personal computers. I say this without qualification because you can do more in less time with more fun using Visual Basic than you can using C, C++, Pascal, FORTRAN, or Lisp. I've worked in these languages and know that they have things to recommend them—but in a work, time, fun analysis, Visual Basic comes out clearly on top.

The Past, Present, and Future

When I started work at Microsoft, Windows was just that annoying utility you had to start before you could run Excel; power users knew the command line, and power programmers knew assembly language or C. I was immediately assigned to an obscure project named Basic PDS. There I saw a team of fanatically devoted folks hell-bent on one thing: beat Borland. Sales numbers of their Turbo products versus our Microsoft products were regularly posted, and there was a fair amount of paranoia that "The Competition" would discover our plans.

Soon after we shipped the leanest, fastest Basic development environment ever devised, Borland withdrew from the Basic market. Also around that time, Windows 3.0 shipped—we watched the Microsoft stock price climb and started struggling with a thing called the Windows API. A couple of guys on the team had a wild idea: they'd take the macro language being developed for a database product we were working on and ship it as a Windows version of Basic. Management pronounced it "opportunistic" (a good thing). While marketing struggled with a name, Bill Gates called it "Visual Basic."

Visual Basic blew away all the sales projections. Finally, there was an easy way to create Windows applications! When our friend at Borland, Phillipe Kahn, likened Visual Basic to "crack cocaine," we knew we'd finally won. The expression "just write a VB app to do it" worked its way into the Microsoft lingo and became generalized. Need to paint your house? Write a VB app to do it.

Though Visual Basic started as a database macro language, it became a stand-alone tool with few ties to applications. To complete Bill Gates' vision, Microsoft needed a way to reunite Visual Basic and applications. Visual Basic couldn't just be shoved into each application as a macro language; it had to remain an open programming tool that could operate *between* applications as an integrating layer.

When you say "integration" at Microsoft, people expect you to exclaim "Ole!" More properly, Object Linking and Embedding (OLE) is Microsoft's long-promoted standard for including one application's documents in another. On the simplest level, OLE provides a way to exchange data between applications. The Visual Basic group undertook the task of extending OLE so that you could exchange commands as well as data. These extensions were dubbed *OLE Automation* and released with OLE, version 2.0.

Excel is the first application to fully implement OLE Automation, and it's also the first to include Visual Basic for Applications. Visual Basic for Applications completes Visual Basic's destiny—finally, there's an easy way to program applications!

Of course, that's not the end. Visual Basic will be part of all the Microsoft Office applications. Additional applications from Microsoft and other companies are becoming VB-programmable through the OLE 2.0 standard. Soon, you will be able to control all the applications on your desktop using Visual Basic.

But why stop there? OLE 2.0 defines a standard for Remote Process Control (RPC), in effect letting you control other computers from a single desktop.

This is more than just an opportunity to wreak some havoc over the network—it's a chance to distribute tasks and control numerous devices (including printers, phones, faxes, and copiers) from your PC.

Who knows—maybe someday I'll even be able to program my VCR!

On Programming Style

I won't tell you how to program if you don't tell me how to write. (Just kidding.) I've got opinions on what is clear and what isn't clear, and I voice such opinions occasionally in this book. *Good programming style* ultimately is whatever best suits your needs and the needs of those around you.

Declaring all your variables before you use them is a good idea. Another good idea is to use prefixes to identify the data types of variables and functions. Most of the example code in this book follows these guidelines; however, what is clearest in code is not always clearest on the page. For instance, it is awkward to wade through reams of variable declarations before getting to the code discussed in surrounding text. So, I've compromised in some places. Appendix D is devoted to the subject of programming style in detail.

Syntax Conventions

Most books on programming use some variance of the syntax conventions used here. This type of syntax is called Backus-Naur Form (BNF). The following table shows the BNF notation when discussing functions, statements, methods, and properties:

Formatting	Description
Abs(x)	Terms shown in this typeface indicate key words, such as objects, properties, methods, statements, and functions. This typeface is also used for procedure and variable names in text.
italic	Italic indicates items that you must provide, such as the names of objects and arguments. The names used in method arguments are the same ones that Excel uses to identify those arguments.
[]	Square brackets enclose optional items.
[item1 ¦ item2]	This indicates a choice between two items.

Throughout this book, exact syntax for methods and properties is introduced in the format

Application. ActivateMicrosoftApp

Application. ActivateMicrosoftApp (*index*)

where the larger, shaded line indicates the name of the method or property, and the second line contains its full syntax. If the syntax is lengthy and must wrap to additional lines, a special character (_) appears at the end of each incomplete line to indicate that the syntax continues.

How This Book Is Organized

This book is divided into three parts:

- Chapters 1-4 explain the fundamentals of programming with Visual Basic for Applications.

- Chapters 5-20 describe specific programming tasks and include references to Excel's objects, properties, and methods.

- Appendixes A-E include tables of special information that applies to more than one programming topic.

Here is a brief overview of what you will learn in each chapter or appendix:

Chapter 1, "Programming with Excel," shows how to use the Visual Basic programming tools to record, modify, and run procedures in Excel. This chapter also shows how to step through a procedure, locate and fix mistakes, and get on-line Help.

Chapter 2, "Using Visual Basic," explains the fundamental programming structures in Visual Basic and shows you how to use them. These fundamental structures include procedures, loops, variables, arrays, and error handlers.

Chapter 3, "Performing Tasks with Visual Basic," shows how to use the Visual Basic statements, functions, and operators to work with various types of data.

Chapter 4, "Using Objects," shows how Excel's objects are organized and describes how to use Excel's objects, properties, and methods to perform common programming tasks.

Chapter 5, "Controlling the Excel Application," explains how to use the Application object to control Excel. This chapter also describes how to run procedures automatically when Excel starts, opens, or closes a file.

Chapter 6, "Controlling Excel Files," explains how to use the Workbook and AddIn objects to open and manipulate files in Excel.

Chapter 7, "Controlling the Excel Display," explains how to use the Window and Pane objects to control the placement and appearance of Excel windows.

Chapter 8, "Using Sheets," explains how to use the Sheets collection as well as Worksheet, Chart, and Module objects to manipulate the sheets in an Excel workbook.

Chapter 9, "Working with Ranges of Cells," explains the various ways you can get and use Range objects to work with the cells in a worksheet. This chapter also demonstrates programming tasks that use ranges of cells, such as searching and replacing, and getting and setting cell values.

Chapter 10, "Linking and Embedding," explains how to use the Picture and OLEObject objects to link and embed objects from other workbooks or other applications.

Chapter 11, "Printing and Displaying Results," explains how to print objects and how to use the Style, Border, Font, and PageSetup objects to control the on-screen and printed appearance of objects.

Chapter 12, "Getting and Manipulating Stored Data," explains how to use the PivotTable object and the Object Database Connectivity (ODBC) add-in to view data stored in worksheets and external databases.

Chapter 13, "Creating Charts," describes the objects used to create and manipulate charts, and explains how to work with multiple chart groups.

Chapter 14, "Controlling Charts," describes how to work with axes, legends, and points in a series. This chapter also explains how to customize the appearance of both 2-D and 3-D charts, and how to add drop lines, trendlines, grid lines, error bars, and other objects to charts.

Chapter 15, "Creating Graphics," explains the objects that you can draw on charts and worksheets. Drawing objects include Arcs, Lines, Rectangles, Ovals, and Pictures.

Chapter 16, "Customizing Menus and Toolbars," explains the Menu and Toolbar objects and describes how to customize menus and toolbars. This chapter also describes how to distribute customized menus and toolbars to other users.

Chapter 17, "Creating and Displaying Dialog Boxes," explains the Dialog and DialogSheet objects and describes how to display built-in Excel dialog boxes, as well as how to create and display your own custom dialog boxes.

Chapter 18, "Using Additional Display Controls," explains additional dialog control objects that Excel provides, including `EditBoxes`, `ListBoxes`, `OptionButtons`, and `CheckBoxes`. This chapter also covers using the `ScrollBar` and `Spinner` objects.

Chapter 19, "Sending and Receiving Mail," explains the `RoutingSlip` and `Mailer` objects and describes how to distribute workbooks using electronic mail. This chapter also describes how to distribute and install add-ins, templates, and toolbars using electronic mail.

Chapter 20, "Advanced Topics," describes how to create and display on-line Help; create add-ins; use Excel from Visual Basic, version 3.0; and use dynamic-link libraries (DLLs).

Appendix A, "Trappable Errors," lists the trappable error codes and describes strategies for trapping and handling errors.

Appendix B, "Table of Key Codes," lists the special key codes used for `SendKeys` and the ANSI character codes used by the `Chr` and `Asc` functions.

Appendix C, "Table of Intrinsic Constants," lists the built-in constants by category and gives their values.

Appendix D, "Style Guidelines for Professional-Quality Code," lists prefixes used to identify the data types and scope of variables and describes professional coding practices that lead to more reliable, readable Visual Basic code.

Appendix E, "Using Function, Property, and Method Data Types," lists the data types of values returned from Visual Basic functions and Excel properties and methods. This appendix also describes how to use data types to conserve memory and verify results.

Part I

VBA Programming

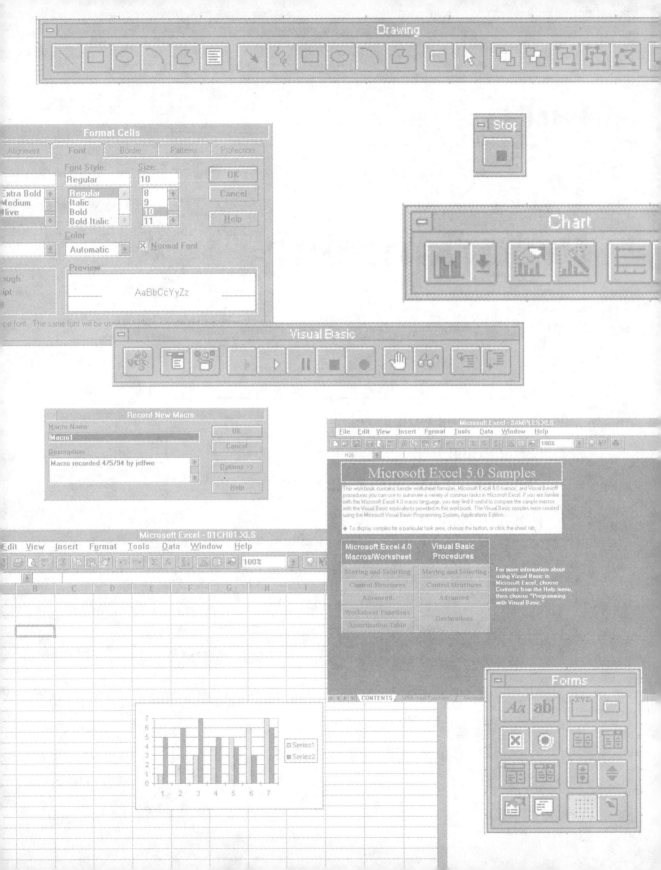

Chapter 1

Programming with Excel

For many years, applications have included macro languages that let you automate various everyday tasks by writing scripts. Although many of these macro languages were powerful, they suffered from some fatal flaws:

■ Each language was different. Even within applications sold by one company, no two macro languages were alike. This made it hard to move from application to application or to reuse your learning as you moved among applications.

■ Macro languages were usually tied to the user interface—when the user interface changed, so did the language. You had to relearn with every new release.

■ As applications grew, the languages became more complicated and less understandable.

■ There was no easy way to use one application from another application, and absolutely no way to run one application's macros from another application.

Visual Basic for Applications solves each of these problems in turn:

■ Visual Basic is a de facto Windows programming standard with over 300,000 users worldwide. Visual Basic for Applications remains true to the Visual Basic standard, and Microsoft is preparing to ship it with all its Office applications. Excel is the first application to include Visual Basic.

■ Visual Basic for Applications uses a standard "core language" and objects provided by the application. These objects embody fundamental features of the application, so they aren't likely to change.

■ Objects group features into a hierarchy that is more understandable than a "flat" macro language consisting of thousands of possible commands.

■ Visual Basic for Applications can call other Visual Basic for Applications programs, even if they are written in another application. Support for working with multiple applications at once is built in to Visual Basic for Applications at the most fundamental level.

Visual Basic for Applications is much more than a macro language in Excel; it is a *programming language* you can use to create applications, solve business problems, and automate everyday tasks using Excel and other applications as building blocks.

In this chapter, you learn how to do the following:

■ Use objects to control aspects of Excel.

■ Record and modify Visual Basic procedures.

■ Run procedures.

■ Understand the internal workings of a procedure by stepping through it and watching variables.

■ Get on-line Help in Visual Basic for Applications.

Working with Objects

Visual Basic uses *objects* to get information and perform actions in Excel. Objects are the building blocks of the Excel application; they include visible aspects of Excel, such as worksheets, and invisible concepts, such as page setup (see fig. 1.1). For a complete description of Excel's objects and how you use them, see Chapter 4.

Some examples of objects include:

Object	Description
Application	A running copy of Excel
Workbook	An entire workbook—one Excel file
Chart	A graphic chart in a workbook
Worksheet	An entire worksheet in a workbook
Range	A single cell or range of cells on a worksheet

Range   Application

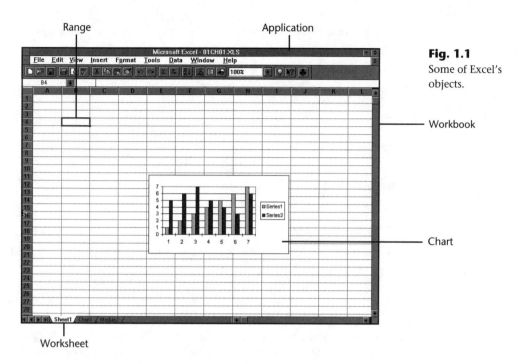

Fig. 1.1
Some of Excel's
objects.

Workbook

Chart

Worksheet

Excel has about 80 objects in all. Each object lets you control a different feature of Excel. For example, suppose you have an object that represents cell A1
on a worksheet (see fig. 1.2).

Range ("A1")

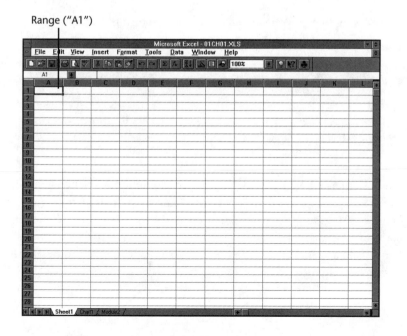

Fig. 1.2
Cell A1.

Cell A1 is a Range object in Excel. Each cell on a worksheet is a Range object, and these objects may also include more than one cell. For example, Range("A1:B4") includes the cells in the range A1:B4.

Using Visual Basic for Applications, you can do these things with an object:

- Set the values of the object's properties (see the definition of properties that follows). The following code line inserts a formula in the cell:

    ```
    Range("A1").Formula = "Sum(B1, C1, C3)"
    ```

- Return the values of the object's properties. The following code line gets the numeric value of the cell:

    ```
    x = Range("A1").Value
    ```

- Invoke the object's methods. The following code line selects the cell:

    ```
    Range("A1").Select
    ```

In general, *properties* control the appearance of objects and *methods* perform actions on objects. In practice, this distinction is less clear. The real difference between properties and methods is semantic: properties can appear on the left or right side of an equal sign (=); methods can appear only on the right side.

The following line uses the Value property to set the value of cell A1:

```
Range("A1").Value = 97
```

The following line uses the Address method to return the address of cell A1:

```
x = Range("A1").Address()
```

> **Note**
>
> Because the difference between properties and methods is less important than the task each property or method performs, this book groups properties and methods together when describing objects.

Each object has many different properties and methods—the Range object alone has 88 methods and 46 properties! Some of these properties and methods are common to other objects, but most of them are unique to the Range object. Excel has about 1,400 unique properties and methods you can use with Visual Basic for Applications. Fortunately, Excel does a couple of things to make learning how to program easier.

- First and most important, you can record your actions in Excel using Visual Basic. You can then look at and replay the code Excel generated for those actions.

- Second, Excel lets you step through code one line at a time. Because you can see the effect of each line as it executes, you can quickly associate actions with properties and methods.

- Finally, Excel provides context-sensitive on-line Help for most of the Visual Basic language elements. The Help for some of these elements is weak or unenlightening, but often the Help can be useful. The Help for the Visual Basic core language (fundamental statements like Do...Loop, If...Then, Dim, and so on) is especially good. Visual Basic's core language is common to all applications and is included in a separate library (VBAEN.DLL for the U.S. version) that will be shared by other applications as they incorporate support for Visual Basic.

Recording Code

Recording is the best way to learn how to write code for Excel. Everyone I know who programs Excel uses recorded code to learn how to do specific tasks.

To record Visual Basic code in Excel:

1. Open a workbook and select a sheet to start recording from. You can start recording anywhere, even with no workbook open, but since Excel records all your actions (such as opening a file), you'll want to get to the most convenient point before starting the recorder.

2. Choose **T**ools, **R**ecord Macro, **R**ecord New Macro. Excel displays the Record New Macro dialog box (see fig. 1.3).

Fig. 1.3
The Record New Macro dialog box.

3. You can change where Excel places the code and other recording options by clicking the Options button. Clicking Options displays the record options on the Record New Macro dialog box (see fig. 1.4).

Fig. 1.4
The Record New
Macro dialog box
with options.

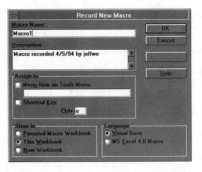

Use the Assign To options to add the recorded procedure to the Tools
menu and to assign a shortcut key to run the recorded code.

Use the Store In options to choose a location in which to store the recorded code. The Personal Macro Workbook is the file PERSONAL.XLS.
Recorded code in this workbook is available from all other workbooks.

Use the Language options to record the code in the Visual Basic language or in the Excel 4.0 macro language. This option is provided for
compatibility with Excel 4.0.

4. Click OK. Excel creates a new module, starts recording your actions, and
displays the Stop Recording toolbar (see fig. 1.5).

Fig. 1.5
The Stop Record-
ing toolbar.

5. Perform the actions you want to record, and click the Stop button when
you're done. Excel stops recording.

Tip
Your recorded
code will be
cleaner if you
walk through
the actions you
want to per-
form before you
start recording.
Otherwise, you
may record
mistakes the
first time.

Analyzing Recorded Code

To see the code that Excel recorded, click the tab of the module sheet that
Excel created—usually Module1. A Visual Basic module is much like any other
sheet in Excel, except it does not contain cells or a grid. Instead, modules
contain blocks of code called *procedures* (see fig. 1.6).

Excel records your actions with a great deal of detail. Methods that take arguments include all the arguments, even if you use the default settings. Excel
methods have *named arguments*; that is, each argument has a name and a
setting.

Comments

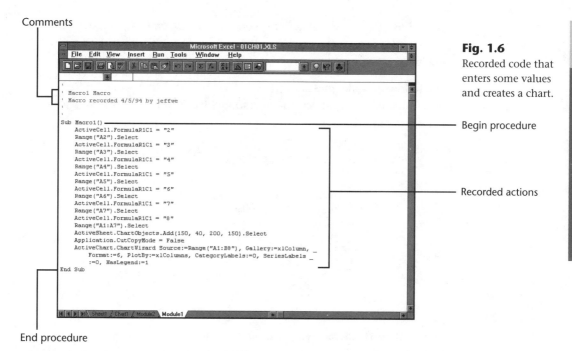

Fig. 1.6
Recorded code that enters some values and creates a chart.

Begin procedure

Recorded actions

End procedure

In the following code lines, Source, Gallery, Format, and so on are the names of arguments, and Range("A1:B8"), xlColumn, 6, and so on are the settings:

```
ActiveChart.ChartWizard Source:=Range("A1:B8"), Gallery:=xlColumn, _
    Format:=6, PlotBy:=xlColumns, CategoryLabels:=0, SeriesLabels _
    :=0, HasLegend:=1
```

The preceding code creates a chart from a range of cells. Long statements like this one are continued over multiple lines using a space and an underscore (_). Although the preceding statement takes three lines, it executes as a single statement. The line-continuation characters make the code more readable.

Tip
The Excel documentation often refers to procedures as *macros*. The two terms mean the same thing, though *macro* often also refers to Excel 4.0 macros.

Modifying Code

Although recorded code is very useful for learning Excel, it is not always the best code for what you want to do. For one thing, it tends to be very specific, dealing with one worksheet or range of cells. Also, it doesn't repeat actions effectively unless you run the code multiple times.

To perform these types of actions, you must add Visual Basic decision making and looping constructions. To modify code, simply edit the procedure in the module.

The following code lines show a recorded procedure that was modified to act on all the worksheets in a workbook. **Bold** lines were added, and ~~strikethrough~~ lines were removed.

```
' Macro2 Macro
' Macro recorded 4/5/94 by jeffwe
' Modified to format all sheets.
' Sub Macro2()
    ' For each worksheet in the workbook...
    For Each sht In Worksheets
        sht.Activate
        Range("A1").Select
        ActiveCellSelection.AutoFormat Format:=xlClassic1, _
        Number:=True, Font:=True,
            Alignment:=True, Border:=True, Pattern:=True, _
            Width:=True
    Next sht
End Sub
```

The lines `Modified to format all sheets` and `For each worksheet in the workbook` are added comments to explain changes and describe actions. Comments don't affect the task being performed; they are included for instructive value.

The line `For Each sht In Worksheets` is an added `For...Each` statement, so the code acts on each worksheet in the workbook. `For...Each` statements are described in greater detail in Chapter 2.

The line `sht.Activate` activates each sheet in the workbook. `Activate` is a method common to many objects and is described in Chapter 4.

The line `Range("A1").Select` is replaced by the line `sht.Activate`. Since the next line uses the active cell, you can save a step by deleting `Range("A1").Select`.

Using the active cell, rather than the current selection, allows you to delete the line `Range("A1").Select` and save a step. This isn't absolutely necessary, but it is more efficient.

The recorded code autoformats the active sheet. The modified code activates each sheet in the workbook and autoformats it. You don't have to activate an item to change it—the following lines show further changes that autoformat the sheets without activating them.

```
' Macro2 Macro
' Macro recorded 4/5/94 by jeffwe
' Modified to format all sheets without activating
' Sub Macro2()
        ' For each worksheet in the workbook...
        For Each sht In Worksheets
                sht.Activate
                ' Remove default arguments, to make this clearer.
                sht.UsedRange.ActiveCell.AutoFormat Format:=xlClassic1, _
                Number:=True, Font:=True, _
                    Alignment:=True, Border:=True, Pattern:=True, _
                    Width:=True
        Next sht
End Sub
```

The lines **Modified to format all sheets without activating, For each worksheet in the workbook,** and **Remove default arguments, to make this clearer** are added comments to explain the code.

The line **For...Each sht in Worksheets** is an added For...Each statement, as in the previous example.

The line **sht.Activate** is removed, and the line that follows uses UsedRange rather than ActiveCell to get a range from each sheet, so it's no longer necessary to activate each sheet. This line also changes ActiveCell to sht.UsedRange and removes default arguments (all but Format). UsedRange returns a range containing all the used cells in each worksheet—this saves you from activating each worksheet. UsedRange is described in greater detail in Chapter 9. Removing the default arguments from AutoFormat makes the task that the code is performing clearer.

As you can see, little of the recorded code remains. Still, the original recording is a useful "leg-up" on figuring out where to start.

Correcting Mistakes

When you type a line in a module and press Enter, Visual Basic checks to see if you have entered the line correctly. If it recognizes a term in the line, it capitalizes it according to its internal libraries. If it detects an error or any missing information, it colors the line red and displays an error message (see fig. 1.7).

This type of error is called a *syntax error* because the line did not conform to the syntax that Visual Basic expected. You can get additional information about the error by clicking the Help button in the error message dialog box. To correct the error, click OK and change the line accordingly.

Fig. 1.7

A syntax error in
Visual Basic.

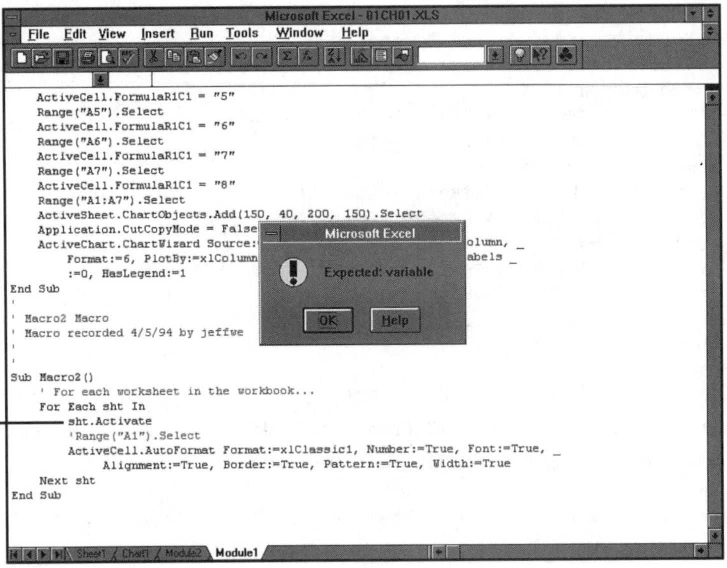

Line with error ————

Some errors can't be detected immediately when you enter them. A common
example is calling another procedure you haven't yet defined (see fig. 1.8).
Visual Basic lets you write procedures in any order, so it can't detect this
problem until it compiles your code before running it.

This type of error is called a *compile-time error,* because it occurs when the
code is compiled into a form that the computer can execute. To correct the
problem, click OK and check the procedure name. You may have mistyped
the name or not yet created the procedure.

In the example shown in figure 1.8, the SortRows() procedure could not be
found. This was a simple typing error; changing the name to SortRow() fixes
the problem.

> **Note**
>
> Visual Basic compiles all the code in your module when you run a procedure.
> Compile-time errors may occur in other procedures as well as in the one you are
> trying to run.

The last type of error can't be detected until you try to run a procedure.
A typical example of this type of error is using a property or method with
the wrong object (see fig. 1.9).

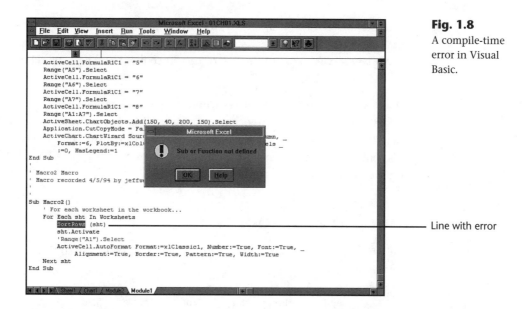

Fig. 1.8
A compile-time error in Visual Basic.

Line with error

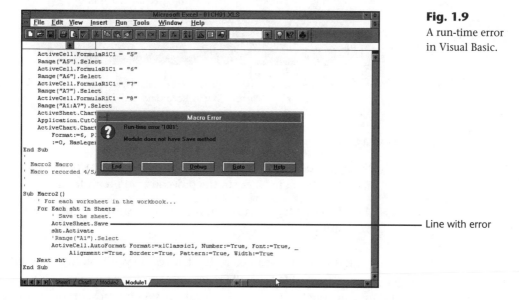

Fig. 1.9
A run-time error in Visual Basic.

Line with error

This type of error is called a *run-time error,* because it occurs while the computer is running the code. To correct this problem, click the Goto button and correct the line of code.

In the example shown in figure 1.9, the line `ActiveSheet.Save` fails because `Sheet` objects do not have a `Save` method. To fix this problem, delete the line. Add `ActiveWorkbook.Save` to the end of the procedure to save the workbook (the intended action).

Not all run-time errors are mistakes. There are some situations when you expect these types of errors to occur and you need to detect the error in your code. This process is called *error handling.* Error handling uses the `On Error` statement to trap and take actions on specific types of errors. See Chapter 2 for more information on error handling.

Running Procedures

Excel provides a Visual Basic toolbar to help you run code or step through code (see fig. 1.10).

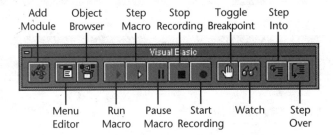

Fig. 1.10
The Visual Basic toolbar.

To run a procedure from a module, follow these steps:

1. Display a module by clicking the Modules tab in the workbook, and place the cursor anywhere in the procedure you want to run.

2. Click the Run Macro button on the Visual Basic toolbar or press F5. Excel runs the procedure.

If you are trying to run recorded code, chances are you'll receive an error message. Recorded code generally relies on a specific worksheet being active. Since modules don't include cells, they don't support most of the actions that worksheets do. An error often occurs when you try to run recorded procedures while displaying a module.

Tip
Find a worksheet's name on the tab at the bottom of the sheet.

To fix this problem, add a line of code to the beginning of the procedure that activates a worksheet. The following line activates the worksheet named `"Sheet1"`:

```
Sheets("Sheet1").Activate
```

Alternatively, you can run the procedure while the worksheet is active. To run a procedure while a worksheet is displayed, follow these steps:

1. Choose **T**ools, **M**acro. Excel displays the Macro dialog box (see fig. 1.11).

2. Double-click the name of the procedure to run. Excel runs the procedure.

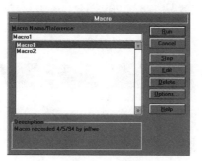

Fig. 1.11
The Macro dialog box.

You can't run Function procedures or procedures that take arguments directly from the Macro dialog box. To run a Function procedure or to provide arguments to a procedure, create a Sub procedure that calls the procedure you want to run.

The following lines show a Test() Sub procedure that provides an argument and displays the result from the function FindPrime().

```
Sub Test()
    MsgBox FindPrime(200)
End Sub

Function FindPrime(n)
    n = Int(n)
    If n <= 1 Then FindPrime = 1
    For i = 2 To n / 2
        If (n Mod i) = 0 Then
            FindPrime = FindPrime(n - 1)
            Exit Function
        End If
    Next i
    FindPrime = n
End Function
```

Stepping Through Code

Use the Debug window to step through and analyze procedures you've written or recorded. To step through a procedure, follow these steps:

1. Display a module, and place the cursor anywhere in the procedure you want to step through.

2. Click the Step Macro button on the Visual Basic toolbar or press F8. Excel displays the Debug window (see fig. 1.12).

Watch pane tab

Fig. 1.12
The Visual Basic
Debug window.

Immediate pane ———

Code pane ———

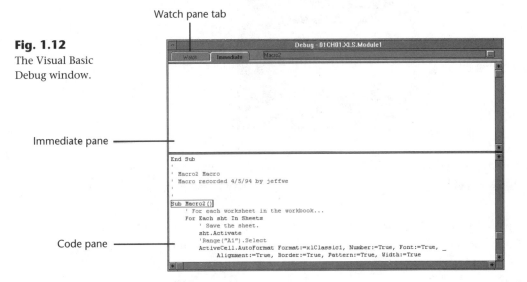

3. Press F8 or click the Step Into button on the Visual Basic toolbar to run the next line of code. As you execute each line, Excel scrolls through the procedure in the Code pane and puts a border around the next line.

   As each line executes, Excel performs the action indicated by the line of code. If an error occurs, Excel halts execution and displays an error dialog box.

4. When you run the last line of a procedure, Excel closes the Debug window.

> **Note**
>
> The Step Into (F8) and Step Over toolbar buttons let you run lines of code when the Debug window is displayed. Step Over runs a procedure call as a single line, rather than "stepping in" to the called procedure.

When there is an error in the Code pane, use the Immediate pane to work through that line until you correct the error. You can't change code in the Code pane of the Debug window, but you can try out individual lines of code by typing them in the Immediate pane.

To run lines of code in the Immediate pane, follow these steps:

1. Press F8 to display the Debug window.

2. Click in the Immediate pane, and type some code. For example:

   ```
   Worksheets(1).Activate
   ```

3. When you press Enter, Excel executes the line. In this case, Excel activates the first worksheet.

You can use the Immediate pane to test out a line of code. When you get the line right, you can copy the line to the Clipboard, and then close the Debug window and paste the line into your module.

Viewing Variables

While the Debug window is displayed, you can view the values of variables in the active procedure by using the Watch pane. The Watch pane displays changes in the value of variables as your procedure executes; this can help you locate problems in your code that are producing unexpected results.

To view the value of a variable in the Watch pane, follow these steps:

1. Step through the procedure until you get to the point where the variable you want to view is used.

2. Select the variable in the Code pane and click the Watch button, or press Shift+F9. Excel displays the Instant Watch dialog box (see fig. 1.13).

3. The instant watch displays the value of the variable. If the variable hasn't received a value yet, it displays a value of Empty. To add the variable to the Watch pane, click Add.

4. To view the value of variables in the Watch pane, click the Watch tab in the Debug window. Excel displays the Watch pane (see fig. 1.14).

5. As you step through your procedure, Excel updates the values in the Watch pane. When control passes to another procedure, Excel displays the value Out of context.

Fig. 1.13
The Instant Watch
dialog box.

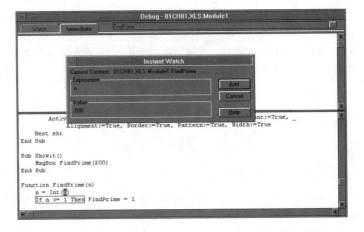

Variables with watches   Procedure where the variable is defined

Fig. 1.14
The Watch pane.

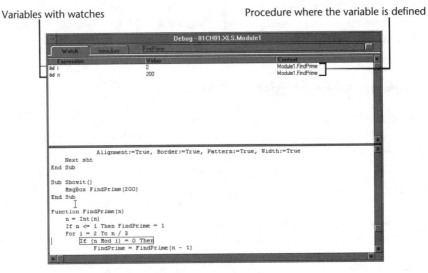

You can view the values of expressions the same way you view variables. An *expression* is any set of variables, constants, and operations that results in a value. The following expression has the value True or False:

```
(n Mod i) = 0
```

Expressions can include Visual Basic functions or methods. The following expression returns the tangent of the variable x:

```
Tan(x)
```

Another tool for viewing expressions is the Immediate pane of the Debug window. To view the value of an expression in the Immediate pane, type a question mark (?) followed by the expression. The following line displays the approximate value of Pi (3.14159265358979):

```
?4 * Atn(1)
```

Unlike the Watch pane, you can cut and paste values from the Immediate window into your code.

> **Note**
>
> The ? (question mark) is shorthand for Print in Visual Basic. You can use Print in your procedure to send output to the Immediate pane. When you use Print in a module, you must qualify it with the object Debug, for example, Debug.Print i. This tells Visual Basic to print the value of i to the Debug window.

Pausing Code at a Location

You may want to run your code and stop it at some point before it ends, to look at variables or to try out different lines of code. You can stop a procedure at a specific line by inserting a *break point*.

To insert a break point, follow these steps:

1. Move the cursor to the line of code on which you want to stop.

2. Click the Toggle Breakpoint button or press F9. Excel highlights the line by making its background red.

When you run the procedure, Excel stops at the break point and displays the Debug window. This happens whether you run the procedure from a module or from a worksheet, so be sure to remove all break points before distributing your procedures to other people.

To remove a break point, follow these steps:

1. Move the cursor to the line containing the break point.

2. Click the Toggle Breakpoint button or press F9. Excel clears the highlighting for the line and removes the break point.

You can't set break points on lines that are not executable. *Executable statements* are those that perform actions in Excel, such as selecting a cell or creating a chart. Statements that are not executable include comments and variable declarations; you can't set break points on these lines.

Restarting and Stopping Code

After your code is paused, either by using a break point or by stepping through a procedure, you can resume execution by clicking the Resume Macro button or by pressing F5.

To end the procedure without resuming, click the Stop button or close the Debug window by double-clicking the window's Control Box.

You can't undo actions that were performed by a procedure unless you take special steps in your code. See Chapter 5 for information on the OnUndo and OnRepeat properties.

Viewing Objects and Inserting Code with the Object Browser

You can view many of the functions and statements Visual Basic provides and all of the objects, properties, and methods Excel provides by using the Object Browser.

To use the Object Browser, follow these steps:

1. In a module, click the Object Browser toolbar button or press F2. Excel displays the Object Browser dialog box (see fig. 1.15).

Fig. 1.15
The Object
Browser dialog
box.

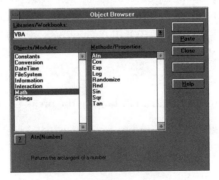

2. Click the down arrow on the Libraries/Workbooks drop-down list to
   display the component you currently have loaded. The Excel library
   contains all of the objects, properties, and methods in Excel. The VBA
   library contains most of the functions and statements in Visual Basic's
   core language.

   Select a library to use by clicking one of the names in the list. Excel
   displays the library's elements in the Objects/Modules and Methods/
   Properties lists.

3. Select a category or object from the Object/Modules list and an item
   from the Methods/Properties list. (The titles of these lists are misleading
   because the items they display do not always match their titles.) Excel
   displays the syntax and description of the item at the bottom of the
   dialog box.

4. Click Paste to paste the item into the module. Click the ? button to see
   the on-line Help for the selected item.

The Object Browser dialog box also displays the procedures in all the workbooks and add-ins that have references. A workbook has a reference if it is
loaded in Excel or if it has a reference established in the References dialog
box.

To add a reference to a workbook or add-in, follow these steps:

1. Display a module.

2. Choose **T**ools, **R**eferences. Excel displays the References dialog box
   (see fig. 1.16).

Fig. 1.16
The References
dialog box.

3. Click the Browse button to select a workbook or add-in. Excel displays
   the Browse dialog box (see fig. 1.17).

Fig. 1.17

The Browse dialog box.

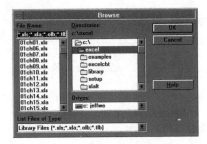

4. Select a file to reference and click OK. Excel adds the file to the References dialog box and puts an X beside the file name, indicating that you have a reference to that workbook or add-in.

After you have a reference to a workbook or add-in, you can use the procedures it contains. Use the Object Browser dialog box to view the procedures a workbook or add-in provides.

Getting Help

Interaction with the programmer has been the key feature of Visual Basic since it was created over 30 years ago. Context-sensitive Help is a natural extension of that interactivity. In many ways, Visual Basic leads all other programming languages in its approach to Help.

To get Help on an item in Visual Basic, follow these steps:

1. Select the item, and press F1. If there is Help available for the item, Excel displays the appropriate Help. For example, if you select InStr in the following line and press F1, Excel displays the on-line Help (see fig. 1.18).

        If **InStr**(UCase(Answer), "Y") Then

2. If a term is used in both Visual Basic and Excel, Excel displays a dialog box that lets you choose the topic to view. For example, if you select Open in the following line and press F1, Excel displays the Basic Help dialog box (see fig. 1.19).

        Open filename For Input As #1

3. Choose the item to display by double-clicking it.

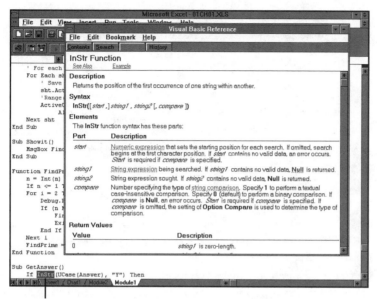

Fig. 1.18
On-line Help for
the Visual Basic
InStr function.

Select InStr and press F1 to get Help.

Fig. 1.19
The Basic Help
dialog box.

Select Open and press F1 to get Help.

If Excel can't find a topic for the item you select, it displays the Help Table of
Contents. To find a topic from there, click one of the links such as Keywords
by Task (see fig. 1.20).

Fig. 1.20
Keywords by Task
Help.

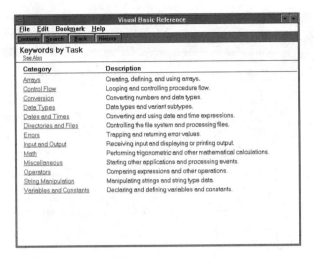

The Keywords by Task topic helps you locate the correct Visual Basic statement or function for a specific programming task, such as creating an array or changing the contents of a string.

Alternatively, you can search through an index of terms by clicking the Search button in the Help window. After you click the Search button, the Search dialog box appears (see fig. 1.21).

Fig. 1.21
The Search dialog
box.

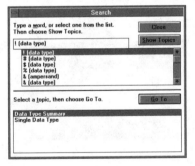

The Search dialog box works like a book index: you select a term from the first list by scrolling and double-clicking. The topics for that term are displayed in the second list. Double-click a topic to go to that topic.

Although Excel's Help is extensive, you may notice the following problems:

■ You might run out of memory. If you run more than a few applications while working with Excel, you may get Out of Memory messages when you try to use Help. In this case, shut down one of the other applications and try again.

■ The Help might not be helpful. The Help for objects in Excel consists of lists of the object's properties and methods. Though this is useful, it doesn't tell you how to use the objects or what each is for. This book tries to remedy that problem by describing how to use every property and method for each of Excel's objects.

■ The examples might seem trivial. The best way to learn programming is by example; unfortunately, most of the examples in Excel's Help are only one line long and don't show a context or explain why you would use the example code. Again, this book tries to fill that void by offering more detailed examples and explaining the purpose of each example.

■ You may not find the topic you want. Excel divides most of its Help into two files: VBA_XL.HLP and MAINXL.HLP. When you request Help from a module, Excel displays VBA_XL.HLP, which includes Help for all of Excel's statements, functions, objects, properties, and methods. When you request Help from a worksheet, Excel displays MAINXL.HLP, which includes Help for all of Excel's user-interface features, such as menus, toolbars, and procedures. Search does not work across more than one file, so you may have to open the other file before you can find the topic you want.

> **Note**
>
> In general, the Help topics for the Visual Basic core language are more complete than those for Excel's objects, properties, and methods. The Visual Basic core language has been around for quite a while and the Help has the benefit of a lot of practical experience. Excel's objects, properties, and methods are new with version 5.0 of Excel.

Excel's Visual Basic Samples

Excel provides quite a few programming examples in SAMPLES.XLS. These examples show you how to perform a variety of programming tasks and give the Excel 4.0 macro language equivalents for some tasks. It's a good idea to look at this file regardless of your level of experience. By default Excel installs SAMPLES.XLS in the \EXCEL\EXAMPLES directory (see fig. 1.22). The examples in SAMPLES.XLS are described in Table 1.1.

Fig. 1.22
The SAMPLES.XLS
Contents sheet.

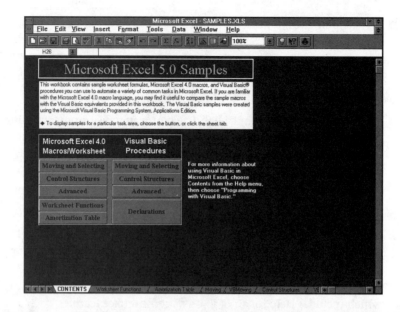

Table 1.1 SAMPLES.XLS procedures

Category	Procedure
Visual Basic control structures	VB_Do_Loop
	VB_Do_Until
	VB_For_Next_Array
	VB_Main_Function(Time_Called:=)
	VB_Main_Procedure
	VB_Multiple_Condition_Testing
	VB_While_Next_UsingSelect
Working with Range objects	VB_Resize_Selection_Using_Offset
	VB_Selecting_Edges_Of_Range
	VB_Sort_Database
	VB_Variable_Move

Category	Procedure
Calling other applications and using the Windows API	VB_API_Call_GetPrivateProfileString
	VB_API_Call_Play_WAV_File
	VB_Branch_Example
	VB_Call_Extract
	VB_Distance(X1:=, Y1:=, X2:=, Y2:=)
	VB_ExtractWordFormFields
	VB_GetVerInfo(sFileName:=)
	VB_GetWindowsDirectory
	VB_GotoSamplesSheet ButtonNo:=
	VB_Launch_Word_API(AppPath:=)
	VB_MS_Query_Fetch
	VB_Redimension
	VB_VersionBrowser
	VB_Word_QuickPrint
Windows API function declarations	GetFileVersionInfo(szFile:=, handle:=, cbBuf:=, lpvData:=)
	GetFileVersionInfoS(szFile:=, handle:=, cbBuf:=, lpvData:=)
	GetFileVersionInfoSize(szFile:=, dwVerHnd:=)
	GetModuleFileName(hinst:=, lpszFilename:=, cbFileName:=)
	GetModuleHandle(App:=)
	GetPointer(scr:=, dest:=)
	GetPrivateProfileString (lpApplicationName:=, lpKeyName:=, lpDefault:=, lpReturnedString:=, nsize:=, lpFileName:=)
	GetWindowsDirectory(lpbuffer:=, nsize:=)
	lstrcpy(lpszString:=, LpStr:=)
	sndPlaySound WavFile:=, wFlags:=
	VerLanguageName(uLang:=, lpszLang:=, cbLang:=)
	VerQueryFixInfo(lpvBlock:=, lpszSubBlock:=, lplpBuf:=, lpcb:=)
	VerQueryValue(lpvBlock:=, lpszSubBlock:=, lplpBuf:=, lpcb:=)

Chapter 2

Using Visual Basic

Visual Basic has evolved since version 1.0 was released in 1991. Visual Basic for Applications includes new features and some improvements to the core language. This chapter walks you through creating your first procedure in Visual Basic and covers the fundamental programming structures. It also covers some new ground by discussing object-oriented programming with Visual Basic's new Property procedures.

So put on your hunting boots and let's program!

In this chapter, you learn how to do the following:

- Write procedures.
- Repeat actions in code.
- Control the flow of code.
- Add procedures to the Tools menu.
- Create methods and properties.
- Declare variables.
- Create and use arrays.
- Trap and skin errors.

Your First Procedure

Visual Basic code is stored in workbooks (*.XLS files) as *modules*. Each module contains *procedures*—blocks of Visual Basic code that you can run from Excel. When you record code, Excel creates a module, adds it to your workbook, and writes your recorded actions to a procedure named Macro1(). When you want to start writing code on your own, you must add a module to the workbook.

To add a module to a workbook, follow these steps:

1. Click the right mouse button on a sheet tab. Excel displays a pop-up menu (see fig. 2.1).

Fig. 2.1
The pop-up menu used to create a module.

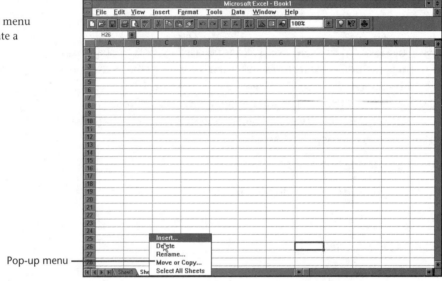

Pop-up menu

2. Select Insert. Excel displays the Insert dialog box (see fig. 2.2).

Fig. 2.2
The Insert dialog box.

3. Double-click Module. Excel creates a new module sheet (see fig. 2.3).

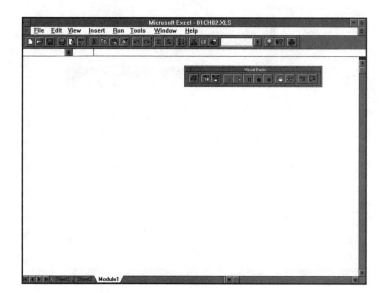

Fig. 2.3
A new module
sheet.

VBA Programming

You create procedures by typing in a module. Procedures have a certain form, which you must use for Excel to understand where the procedure begins and ends. Type the following lines in a module:

```
' My first procedure.
Sub ShowTime()
    Application.DisplayStatusBar = True
    Application.StatusBar = Now
End Sub
```

If you make a mistake and Excel can't understand one of the lines, Excel displays an error message and highlights the line with red. Go back and check the line and fix any errors. When you're finished, the procedure should look like figure 2.4.

To run the procedure, click any line in the procedure and press F5. Your procedure displays the date and time in Excel's status bar. ShowTime() uses two of the Application object's properties: DisplayStatusBar makes sure the Excel status bar is showing on-screen; StatusBar sets the text to display in Excel's status bar—in this case, the date and time returned by Visual Basic's Now function.

The Application object has many other properties and methods, and Excel has many other objects with their own properties and methods. Don't worry about those for now (or, if you insist, turn to Chapter 4, "Using Objects," for an overview of Excel's objects).

Fig. 2.4

Anatomy of the
ShowTime( )
procedure.

Comment ⌐

Procedure ─
definition

Statements ⌐
identify the
actions to be
performed.

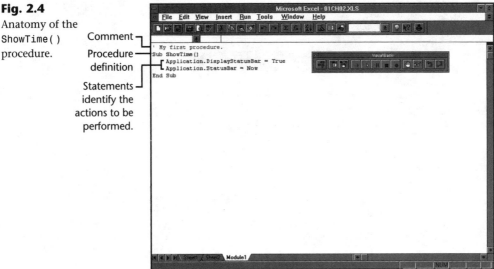

Adding a Procedure to a Menu

It is easy to run ShowTime( ) from a module. To run ShowTime( ) from a worksheet, you'll want to add the procedure to a menu.

To add a procedure to the Tools menu, follow these steps:

1. Choose **T**ools, **M**acro. Excel displays the Macro dialog box (see fig. 2.5).

Fig. 2.5

The Macro dialog
box.

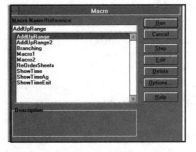

2. Select the procedure name (in this case, ShowTime), and click the Options button. Excel displays the Macro Options dialog box (see fig. 2.6).

3. Mark the Menu Items on Tools Menu check box, and then type Show Time in the text box below the check box. Click OK when you are done.

VBA Programming

Fig. 2.6
The Macro
Options dialog
box.

4. Click Close in the Macro dialog box.

Excel adds the menu item Show Time to the Tools menu (see fig. 2.7).

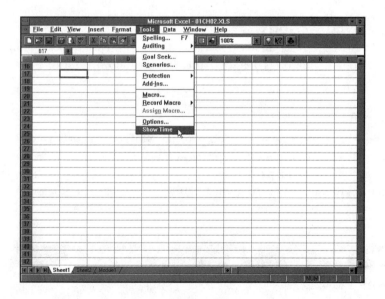

Fig. 2.7
The new Show
Time menu item.

To run the ShowTime() procedure, choose Tools, Show Time.

Controlling Program Flow

When you run ShowTime(), you'll notice that it updates the date and time once. That's OK for the date, but not too useful for the time. To update the time continuously, you need to add a loop. *Loops* are one of the four types of control-flow statements Visual Basic provides.

Type of control	Visual Basic statements
Repeating (looping)	Do...Loop While...Wend For...Next For Each
Descision making	If...Then...Else Select Case...End Select
Exiting or pausing	DoEvents Exit End Stop
Branching	Call Go Sub...Return Goto

Repeating Actions

Visual Basic's Do...Loop and While...Wend statements repeat tasks indefinitely or until some condition is met. Do...Loop has the following form:

```
Do [While condition ¦ Until condition]
    one or more Visual Basic statements...
Loop [While condition ¦ Until condition]
```

The Visual Basic statements in a loop execute while condition is True or until it becomes True. You can test condition at the top of the loop (Do While...), at the bottom of the loop (Loop While...), or not at all. Testing at the bottom guarantees the statements contained in the loop will execute at least once. Not testing causes the statements to repeat forever—this is called an *infinite loop*.

Note

While...Wend has a similar form to Do...Loop and is functionally equivalent. It is easier and more straightforward to stick to one form or the other. This book uses Do...Loop.

To see how loops work, try one out with ShowTime(). Add the lines shown in **bold** to your procedure.

```
' My first procedure.
Sub ShowTime()
    Do
            Application.DisplayStatusBar = True
            Application.StatusBar = Now
    Loop
End Sub
```

> **Note**
>
> Notice that statements in a Do...Loop are indented an extra tab space. It is tradi-
> tional to indent statements contained in any control-flow structure to show their
> relationship to each other and the rest of the procedure. This is a good habit to
> develop early.

When you run ShowTime(), the time is updated continuously in the status bar,
but your system seems frozen—you can't make selections or type in any of
the windows. This is because Excel is running your procedure *continuously*—
every spare instant is being devoted to showing the time. This is what an
infinite loop does.

To break out of the infinite loop, press Ctrl+Break. Excel displays the Macro
Error dialog box (see fig. 2.8). Click End to end your procedure.

Fig. 2.8
The Macro Error
dialog box.

Obviously, infinite loops are not a very "user-friendly" programming practice. To end the loop in a more appropriate fashion, use a While or Until
condition. To see how conditions work, add a While condition to ShowTime().
The new lines are shown in **bold**.

```
' My first procedure.
Sub ShowTime()
    ' Set a time to stop, five seconds from now.
    StopTime = Now + TimeValue("00:00:05")
    Do While Now < StopTime
            Application.DisplayStatusBar = True
            Application.StatusBar = Now
    Loop
End Sub
```

ShowTime() now runs for five seconds and then ends.

Tip
Notice the new
comment added in
this step. Always
comment your loop
and decision-mak-
ing conditions.
Comments don't
make the code run
any better, but they
help you under-
stand the task being
performed.

Use For...Next when you want to repeat an action a specific number of times rather than when a condition is met. For...Next has this form:

```
For counter = start To end [Step increment]
      one or more Visual Basic statements...
Next [counter]
```

To see how For...Next works, add this procedure to a module and press F5 to run:

```
' Add up the numbers in a range.
Sub AddUp()
      For iCount = 1 To 100
            n = n + iCount
      Next iCount
      ' Display the result.
      MsgBox n
End Sub
```

Tip

You don't have to use *counter* with Next, but it makes your code slightly more readable if you include it.

You can experiment by adding a Step value to skip numbers or count backward by using a negative *increment*. For example:

```
' Add up the numbers in a range.
Sub AddUp()
      ' Counts backward by 2s.
      For iCount = 1 To -100 Step -2 ' Use negative Step to count _
      backward.
            n = n + iCount
      Next iCount
      ' Display the result.
      MsgBox n
End Sub
```

For Each is a variation on For...Next that is designed to work with arrays and collections of objects. It has the following form:

```
For Each element In [array ¦ collection]
      one or more Visual Basic statements...
Next [element]
```

To try out For Each, add these lines to a module:

```
' Add up the numeric values in a selected range of cells.
Sub AddUpRange()
      ' For each cell in the selected range...
      For Each rngCount In Selection
            ' Add the values together.
            n = n + Val(rngCount)
      Next rngCount
      ' Display the result.
      MsgBox n
End Sub
```

To see how For Each works, select a range of cells on a worksheet and run AddUpRange(). The procedure loops for each of the cells in the selection, retrieving its value and adding it to the total. In this case, the counter rngCount is a Range object. You can use any of the object's properties and any methods on rngCount in the statements in the loop.

As you might realize, For...Each is very important when working with groups of objects—it makes it easy to perform global operations on objects in any group. For...Each also makes it clear what group you are performing actions on. When working with collections and arrays, For...Each is a big improvement over For...Next.

Exiting Loops

It is not always convenient to wait until a loop ends on its own, so you can use an Exit statement to end the loop immediately. Exit lets you add or supersede the ending condition of a loop.

For example, this Exit Do (shown in bold) ends the ShowTime() loop at noon.

```
Sub ShowTime()
    ' Set a time to stop, five seconds from now.
    StopTime = Now + TimeValue("00:00:05")
    Do While Now < StopTime
        Application.DisplayStatusBar = True
        Application.StatusBar = Now
        ' Exit at noon.
        If TimeValue(Now) = TimeValue("12:00:00") Then Exit Do
    Loop
End Sub
```

Similarly, Exit For ends a For...Next or For Each loop. This change to AddUpRange() ends the loop when the procedure encounters an empty cell.

```
' Add up the numeric values in a selected range of cells.
Sub AddUpRange()
    ' For each cell in the selected range...
    For Each rngCount In Selection
        ' If the cell is empty, end the loop and return to display the total.
        If IsEmpty(rngCount) Then Exit For
        ' Add the values together.
        n = n + Val(rngCount)
    Next rngCount
    ' Display the result.
    MsgBox n
End Sub
```

It is common to use Exit in conjunction with If...Then, as shown in the preceding example. The next section explains more about using If...Then.

Making Decisions

Visual Basic's `If...Then...Else` statement chooses an action, depending on a condition. In its simplest form, `If...Then...Else` looks like this:

```
If condition Then statement1 [Else statement2]
```

This short form is good for statements that fit on one line. It is more common to use block `If...Then...Else` statements because they let you run more code and look clearer in code. The block `If...Then...Else` statement has this form:

```
If condition1 Then
    choice 1: one or more Visual Basic statements...
[ElseIf condition2
    choice 2: one or more Visual Basic statements...]
[Else
    choice 3: one or more Visual Basic statements...]
End If
```

When an `If...Then...Else` statement executes, Visual Basic checks the value of `condition1`. If it is any value other than 0, Visual Basic runs the subsequent lines of code. If the value is 0, Visual Basic skips to `ElseIf` and checks the value of `condition2`. Again, if it's not 0, Visual Basic runs the subsequent lines, otherwise it skips to `Else` and runs those lines.

`ElseIf` and `Else` are optional. If you omit them, and the `condition1` is 0, Visual Basic skips to `End If` and continues on.

To see how `If...Then...Else` works, add these lines to the `AddUpRange()` procedure created earlier. The new lines are shown in **bold**.

```
' Add up the numeric values in a selected range of cells.
Sub AddUpRange()
    ' If the active sheet isn't a worksheet, then activate a _
      worksheet.
    If TypeName(ActiveSheet) <> "Worksheet" Then
        Worksheets(1).Activate
    End If
    For Each rngCount In Selection
        ' If the cell contains a number, add it.
        If IsNumeric(rngCount) Then
            n = n + rngCount
        ' Else the cell text, so concatenate it.
        Else
            temp = rngCount & ", " & temp
        End If
    Next rngCount
    MsgBox temp & n
End Sub
```

These changes enhance AddUpRange() two ways. First, you no longer have to select a worksheet before running AddUpRange(). Second, AddUpRange() no longer ignores cells that contain text; instead, it concatenates all the text values it finds.

Select Case is similar to If...Then...Else, except it lets you choose between many more *condition* values. Select Case has the following form:

```
Select Case condition
    Case value1
        choice 1: one or more Visual Basic statements...
    Case value2
        choice 2: one or more Visual Basic statements...
    Case valuen
        choice n: one or more Visual Basic statements...
    [Case Else
        choice else: one or more Visual Basic statements...]
End Select
```

When a Select Case statement executes, Visual Basic checks the value of *condition* and then compares it to the values in each Case line. When *condition* matches *value*, Visual Basic runs the subsequent lines of code. If *condition* doesn't match any *value*, it skips to Case Else and runs those lines.

You can have any number of Case lines and you can include more than one value on each line. You can even include a range of values by using the To clause.

Select Case is commonly used to evaluate returned constant values and error codes. In both situations, there are usually three or more possible return values and using an If...Then...Else statement would be awkward.

Another common use of Select Case is evaluating the type of object returned by the TypeName function. The ReOrderSheets() procedure shows a Select Case statement used to move sheets in a workbook so that they are grouped together by type—worksheets come first, then charts, followed by modules and dialog sheets.

```
Sub ReOrderSheets()
    ' For each sheet in a workbook...
    For Each shtCount In Sheets
        ' Group the different types of sheets together.
        Select Case TypeName(shtCount)
            Case "Worksheet"
                iWrk = iWrk + 1
                shtCount.Move after:=Sheets(iWrk)
            Case "Chart"
                iChrt = iChrt + 1
                shtCount.Move after:=Sheets(Worksheets.Count + iChrt)
```

```
                        Case "Module"
                                iMod = iMod + 1
                                shtCount.Move after:=Sheets _
                                (Worksheets.Count + Charts.Count + iMod)
                        Case "DialogSheet"
                                iDlg = iDlg + 1
                                shtCount.Move after:=Sheets _
                                (Worksheets.Count + Charts.Count _
                                        + Modules.Count + iDlg)
                End Select
        Next shtCount
End Sub
```

As you can see in ReOrderSheets(), the Sheets collection contains different types of objects. There are several collections that contain more than one type of object; these collections are often used with Select Case: Selection, DrawingObjects, and GroupObjects.

Branching to Procedures, Subroutines, or Lines

Visual Basic lets you direct the flow of execution to other procedures, subroutines, or lines of code. This is sometimes called *branching,* and it is often used in conjunction with decision making statements, like If...Then and Select...Case.

The Call statement calls a procedure. The following procedure calls the ShowTime() procedure:

```
Sub Branching()
        Call ShowTime
End Sub
```

You can omit the word Call without changing the effect. For example:

```
Sub Branching()
        ShowTime
End Sub
```

Omitting Call is the more common form. When the ShowTime line executes, control transfers to the first line of the ShowTime() procedure. When the last line of ShowTime() runs, control returns to the Branching() procedure and the next line executes—in this case, End Sub.

In earlier versions of Visual Basic, Call was restricted to Sub procedures. Now, you call use Call with Function and Sub procedures. If a procedure is a Function, Visual Basic throws away the return value.

Gosub...Return branches to subroutine within a procedure. *Subroutines* are blocks of code, usually at the end of a procedure, identified by a line label. Goto branches directly to a line label in the procedure. The practice of branching to line labels within a procedure is best reserved for error handling (discussed in "Handling Errors" later in this chapter). If you are already familiar with these statements and like them, by all means continue using them. If you are new to Visual Basic, you are better off learning about using procedures to direct program flow.

Organizing Tasks into Procedures

All code must be part of a procedure to run in Visual Basic. Procedures identify the blocks of code that perform the specific tasks. Visual Basic has two types of procedures:

■ Sub procedures perform tasks that do not return a result. Excel always records code as Sub procedures. Sub procedures show up in the Macro dialog box, so you can run them from worksheets and from menu selections (see fig. 2.9).

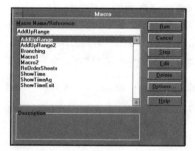

Fig. 2.9
Sub procedures are listed in the Macro dialog box.

■ Function procedures perform tasks that return a result. Excel lists Function procedures in the User Defined category of the Function Wizard—Step 1 of 2 dialog box (see fig. 2.10). On worksheets, you can use Function procedures in formulas of cells.

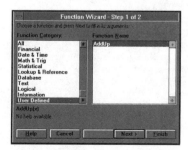

Fig. 2.10
Function procedures are listed in the Function Wizard—Step 1 of 2 dialog box.

Sub procedures have this form:

```
Sub procedurename ([arguments])
     one or more Visual Basic statements
End Sub
```

Function procedures are very similar:

```
Function procedurename ([arguments]) [As datatype]
     one or more Visual Basic statements
     ' Assign the value to return before ending:
     procedurename = return value
End Function
```

The first line of a procedure (Sub... or Function...) is called the *procedure definition*. The procedure definition names the procedure and describes what arguments it takes and the value it returns if any.

The placeholder *arguments* is a list of data items that are passed in to a procedure. Arguments are discussed in the next section.

Passing Arguments to Procedures

Recorded procedures, and most of the procedures in this book up to this point, do not take arguments. In real life, however, most procedures take one or more arguments. Arguments provide the data that a procedure works on.

The RunCubeRoot() and CubeRoot() procedures show an argument in action as in this example:

```
Sub RunCubeRoot()
     X = CubeRoot(200)
End Sub

' Find cube root by approximation.
Function CubeRoot(n)
     Dim X As Single, X1 As Single, X2 As Single
     ' Make first two guesses.
     X1 = 0: X2 = n
     ' Loop until difference between guesses is less than _
     .00000000000001.
     Do Until Abs(X1 - X2) < 0.00000000000001
          X = (X1 + X2) / 2
          ' Adjust guesses.
          If X * X * X - n < 0 Then
               X1 = X
          Else
               X2 = X
          End If
     Loop
     CubeRoot = X
End Function
```

First, `RunCubeRoot()` passes the value `200` to `CubeRoot()` as the argument `n`. `CubeRoot()` uses the value of `n` (`200`) in its calculations and returns the cube root of `200`.

To call `CubeRoot()` from the formula in a cell, enter this formula:

```
=CubeRoot(200)
```

You can also use cell references and other functions. For example:

```
=CubeRoot(Sum(A1:A5))
```

Specifying Data Types

In all these cases, the value entered in the parentheses is passed in to `CubeRoot()`. In its preceding form, `CubeRoot()` accepts any value you pass to it. For example:

```
Sub RunCubeRoot()
    X = CubeRoot("some text")
End Sub
```

Even though `"some text"` isn't something that has a cube root, the procedure still tries to figure it out, finally causing a "Type mismatch" error. To catch these types of errors as early as possible, declare a type for the argument in the procedure definition. The following line accepts numeric values for the argument `n`:

```
Function CubeRoot(n As Integer)
```

If you try to pass a string to this version of `CubeRoot()`, you'll get a "Type mismatch" error as soon as you try to run the procedure.

The return value of a function can also have a data type. For example:

```
Function CubeRoot(n As Integer) As Single
```

This means that `CubeRoot()` accepts an integer and returns a single-precision number (a number with a decimal place). There are many other data types available in Visual Basic. They are discussed in the "Creating Variables and Constants" section later in this chapter.

Passing Arguments by Reference or by Value

Besides data types, you can also specify *how* Visual Basic passes arguments to a procedure. By default, Visual Basic passes a *reference* to the argument. Any changes to the argument are reflected in the variable that was passed in as the argument.

Changing the value of a passed-in argument is very useful. The following procedure shows how you can convert the `CubeRoot()` function into a `Sub` procedure. Instead of returning a value directly, it changes the passed-in argument to a cube root (shown in bold).

```
' Change a number to a cube root of itself.
Sub CubeRoot(n)
      Dim X As Single, X1 As Single, X2 As Single
      ' Make first two guesses.
      X1 = 0: X2 = n
      ' Loop until difference between guesses is less than _
        .00000000000001.
      Do Until Abs(X1 - X2) < 0.00000000000001
            X = (X1 + X2) / 2
            ' Adjust guesses.
            If X * X * X - n < 0 Then
                  X1 = X
            Else
                  X2 = X
            End If
      Loop
      ' Set n to the result (Cube Root of n)
      n = X
End Sub
```

Because `CubeRoot()` is now a `Sub`, you call it slightly differently:

```
Sub RunCubeRoot()
      ' Pick a number
      iValue = 200
      ' Convert the number to its own cube root.
      CubeRoot(iValue)
      ' Display the new value.
      MsgBox iValue
End Sub
```

There are times when you *don't* want a procedure to be able to change an argument. To prevent changes, use the `ByVal` keyword. If you change the procedure definition of `CubeRoot()` as follows, the value of `iValue` does not change when you call `CubeRoot()`.

```
Sub CubeRoot(ByVal n)
```

When you pass arguments by value, Visual Basic makes a temporary copy of the variable and passes the copy rather than the original. When the procedure ends, Visual Basic throws the copy away—any changes are discarded.

Optional Arguments

In previous versions of Visual Basic, you had to provide all of the arguments to a procedure or you would get an "Argument count mismatch" error. Now, you can create optional arguments by using the `Optional` keyword.

Optional arguments make procedures more flexible because they can receive or return any number of values. Using optional arguments in a procedure involves two steps:

1. Specify the argument as Optional in the procedure definition.

2. Check if the argument is missing before using it in the procedure code.

Average() demonstrates how to declare and test optional arguments. CallAverage() demonstrates calling a procedure with the second argument omitted.

```
Sub CallAverage()
    ' Call Average and omit the second argument.
    Msgbox Average(1, , 3)
End Sub

' Average some numbers.
Function Average(x, Optional y, Optional z)
    ' The number of values to average (initial setting).
    iCount = 3
    ' If a number is omitted, use 0 and decrement the number of values.
    If IsMissing(y) Then y = 0 : iCount = iCount - 1
    If IsMissing(z) Then z = 0 : iCount = iCount - 1
    Average= (x + y + z) / iCount
End Sub
```

If you omit the If IsMissing... lines, you get a "Type mismatch" error when you try to add one of the missing arguments.

Optional works well when you want one or two optional arguments, but if you want a large number of optional arguments, use Paramarray. By changing optional arguments to a parameter array, you can call Average() with any number of arguments:

```
Sub CallAverage()
    ' Call Average with an arbitrary number of arguments.
    Msgbox Average(1,2,3,6,12,42,109)
End Sub

' Add up some numbers.
Function Average(ParamArray x())
    ' Using each element in the array x()...
    For Each vCount In x
        ' Add the value to a running total.
        temp = temp + vCount
    Next vCount
    ' Return the average.
    Average = temp / (UBound(x) + 1)
End Function
```

When you use `Paramarray` there are several points to remember:

- The argument is an array and must appear with empty parentheses in the procedure definition—in this case, `x()`.

- You can't omit intervening arguments with `Paramarray`. For example, you can't call `Average()` like this:

```
Msgbox Average(1, , 3)          ' Invalid with Paramarray!
```

- You also can't combine `Optional` and `Paramarray`.

- `Paramarray` must be the last argument in the procedure definition.

Hiding Procedures from Other Workbooks

Sometimes you want to prevent procedures from being widely available. This is common when creating add-ins to distribute to other users. Some procedures may be "internal" to the workings of the add-in, while others may be for general consumption.

To prevent others from using a procedure, declare it as `Private`. `Private` procedures can only be called from within the module where they are defined.

To make a procedure private, prefix the procedure definition with the `Private` keyword. For example:

```
Private Sub CallAverage()
    ' Call Average with an arbitrary number of arguments.
    Msgbox Average(1,2,3,6,12,42,109)
End Sub
```

Alternatively, you can make all the procedures in a module private by using the `Option Private Module` statement at the module level.

```
' Make all procedures in this module private by default
Option Private Module

' This procedure is private
Sub CallAverage()
    ' Call Average with an arbitrary number of arguments.
    Msgbox Average(1,2,3,6,12,42,109)
End Sub
```

To make a procedure in a private module available, prefix the procedure definition with the `Public` keyword. For example:

```
' Make all procedures in this module private by default
Option Private Module
```

```
' This procedure is now public
Public Sub CallAverage()
     ' Call Average with an arbitrary number of arguments.
     Msgbox Average(1,2,3,6,12,42,109)
End Sub
```

Using Recursion

Recursion occurs when a procedure calls itself to solve a problem. Although it is possible to solve problems without recursion, you can save some code and have some fun if you understand how it works.

The FindPrime() procedure, as follows, returns the largest prime number that is less than n (the passed-in argument). If n is not prime to begin with, FindPrime() subtracts 1 from n and calls itself again (recursion).

```
Function FindPrime(n)
     ' If n is less than 1, then return 1.
     If n <= 1 Then FindPrime = 1
     ' Check if n is prime.
     For i = 2 To n / 2
          ' If n is evenly divisible it's not prime...
          If (n Mod i) = 0 Then
               ' Subtract 1 from n and call FindPrime again (Recursion).
               FindPrime = FindPrime(n - 1)
               Exit Function
          End If
     Next i
     FindPrime = n
End Function
```

You can watch recursion at work by stepping through FindPrime() in the Debug window. Other practical uses for recursion include performing binary searches and calculating factorials. Situations where a problem needs to be broken into successively smaller pieces is a candidate for recursion. Be careful, though, recursion can cause "Out of memory" errors in some situations. For more information, see Appendix E, "Using Function, Property, and Method Data Types."

Creating Your Own Methods and Properties

You can use module names when calling procedures in Visual Basic. For example, the following line displays the result of the Average() function in Module1.

```
MsgBox Module1.Average(1, 12, 31, 44, 15)
```

VBA Programming

The preceding line is syntactically identical to Excel's Average function:

```
MsgBox Application.Average(1, 12, 31, 44, 15)
```

In fact, a module's procedures are equivalent to an object's methods; to create module properties, use one of the following three special procedures:

- The Property Get procedure returns the value of a property.

- The Property Let procedure assigns the value of a property.

- The Property Set procedure sets the property to a reference to an object.

Packaging your modules as objects with properties and methods is a natural way to expand the capabilities of Visual Basic for Applications.

Creating Read/Write Properties

Properties can have one type, or all three types, of property procedures. Usually, they have both a Property Get and Property Let procedure. The following pair of property procedures define the NumLock property.

```
'''''''''''''''''''''''''''''''''''''''''''''''''''''''''''''''''
' Module Keyboard
'
' Declare Windows API calls used to get and set keyboard states.
' Declare Sub GetKeyboardState Lib "USER" (lpKeyState As Any)
' Declare Sub SetKeyboardState Lib "USER" (lpKeyState As Any)
' The index for the NumLock key in the 256-byte lpKeyState array.
Const VK_NUMLOCK = &h90

' Returns the state of the NumLock key: True = on, False = Off
Property Get NumLock() As Boolean
    ' Create an array to hold key states (256 bytes = 128 inte-
gers)
    Dim lpbKeyState(128) As Integer
    ' Get key state settings.
    GetKeyboardState lpbKeyState(0)
    ' Check the VK_NUMLOCK element of the array.
    If (lpbKeyState(VK_NUMLOCK / 2)) Then
        NumLock = True
    Else
        NumLock = False
    End If
End Property

' Changes the state of the NumLock key: True = on, False = off
Property Let NumLock(bState As Boolean)
    ' Create an array to hold key states (256 bytes = 128 inte-
gers)
    Dim lpbKeyState(128) As Integer
    ' Get key state settings.
    GetKeyboardState lpbKeyState(0)
```

```
' If the current state is the same as the bState, then no _
  change needed.
If lpbKeyState(VK_NUMLOCK / 2) And bState Then Exit Property
' Otherwise, set the correct value in the array.
If bState Then
     lpbKeyState(VK_NUMLOCK / 2) = 1
Else
     lpbKeyState(VK_NUMLOCK / 2) = 0
End If
' Set the keyboard state.
SetKeyboardState lpbKeyState(0)
End Property
```

The line `Declare Sub GetKeyboard State Lib` declares the Windows API functions that the `NumLock` property uses to get and set the state of the `NumLock` key. For more information on using Windows API functions and other functions in DLLs, see Chapter 20, "Advanced Topics."

The `Get` property procedure for the `NumLock` property calls the Windows API function `GetKeyboardState` to determine whether the `NumLock` key is on or off. The `NumLock` property returns True if the `NumLock` key is on, False if it is off.

The `Let` property procedure for the `NumLock` property calls the Windows API function `GetKeyboardState` to determine whether the `NumLock` key is on or off. It then compares that setting to the passed-in setting (`bState`) and if the two settings don't match, it uses the Windows API function `SetKeyboardState` to change the `NumLock` key setting.

Notice that the `Get` and `Let` procedures for a property have the same name, in this case `NumLock`. This lets Visual Basic know that they define the behavior for a single procedure.

Use a property procedure the same way you use object properties. The following lines display the `NumLock` key state and then turn the `NumLock` key on.

```
Sub UseNumLock()
     ' Get property
     MsgBox Keyboard.NumLock
     ' Set property.
     Keyboard.NumLock = True
End Sub
```

Creating a Read-Only or Write-Only Property

To create a read-only property, create a `Property Get` procedure for the property. Omit the `Property Let` procedure. The following code shows a read-only `SystemDirectory` property that returns the Windows system directory:

```
' Environmental Windows functions
Declare Function GetSystemDirectory Lib "KERNEL" (ByVal lpBuffer As
String, _
```

```
                ByVal nSize As Integer) As Integer

    Property Get SystemDirectory() As String
        Dim lpBuffer As String * 256
        iLen = GetSystemDirectory(lpBuffer, 256)
        If iLen Then
            SystemDirectory = Mid$(lpBuffer, 1, iLen)
        Else
            SystemDirectory = ""
        End If
    End Property
```

You can read the new `SystemDirectory` property, but you can't set it. The assigment statement below causes a "Procedure type mismatch" error.

```
    Sub TestSystemDirectory()
        ' Display SystemDirectory
        MsgBox SystemDirectory
        ' Set SystemDirectory (causes procedure type mismatch error)
        SystemDirectory = "c:\win\system"
    End Sub
```

A "Procedure type mismatch" error is not a trappable error. That is, you can't handle such an error in code. To be a little kinder to your users, define a `Property Let` procedure which triggers an error, as shown here.

```
    Property Let SystemDirectory(s As String)
        ' Error 1000 is the same error that Excel displays when you _
          try to set a read-only property.
        Error 1000
    End Property
```

You can trigger any error value with the `Error` statement. I've chosen `Error 1000` because this is the error code that Excel returns when you try to assign a value to one of its read-only properties.

To create a write-only property, define a `Property Let` procedure and omit (or return an error for) the `Property Get` procedure. Write-only properties are far less common than read-write and read-only properties.

Creating Object Properties

Excel has many properties that return objects. For example, the `Worksheet` object's `UsedCells` property returns a `Range` object containing all the cells on the worksheet that contain data. It is sometimes useful to create your own properties that return objects—for example, you may want to create a `NumericCells` property which returns a `Range` object containing all the cells on a worksheet that contain numeric data.

Properties that contain objects have `Property Get` and `Property Set` procedures. As you might expect, working with objects is more complicated than setting or returning simple values. The following procedures demonstrate four common operations.

- Create() shows how to create an embedded Word document. It calls the Basic() Property Set procedure to initialize the Basic property.

- Property Set SetBasic() sets the mobjBasic object variable. Both the variable and the Property Set procedure are private—they are not available to other modules. If you want to allow users to Set the object variable themselves, remove the Private keyword.

- Property Get Basic() returns the mobjBasic object variable. Using Property Get functions to provide access to private variables like mobjBasic is quite common. This provides a level of control over the variable.

- Property Let Basic() allows users to set the object variable using assignment syntax rather than Set. This procedure delegates to the private SetBasic() procedure and may be omitted.

The following procedure is defined in a module named Document. It shows how to create a property that sets and returns an object. The Create() procedure creates a new Word 6.0 embedded document. Unlike the OLEObjects Add method, Create() allows you to specify the size and location of the object. Create() uses the SetBasic property to keep track of the WordBasic object for the document it created.

```
''''''''''''''''''''''''''''''''''''''''''''''''''''''''''''''''''
' Document module
' Internal variable for WordBasic object.
Private mobjBasic As Object

Function Create(x1, y1, x2, y2) As Object
    ' Add a Word object to the current sheet.
    With ActiveSheet.OLEObjects.Add("Word.Document.6", , False, False)
        ' Set the position and size.
        .top = x1
        .left = y1
        .Width = x2 - x1
        .Height = y2 - y1
        ' Set the Basic property of the Word object
        Set Document.SetBasic = _
ActiveSheet.OLEObjects(.Index).Object.Application.WordBasic
        ' Return the object that was created (same behavior as _
        Excel's Add methods)
        Set Create = ActiveSheet.OLEObjects(.Index)
    End With
End Function
```

The following code shows how to define a property that sets an object reference. The `SetBasic()` procedure checks if the passed-in object (`obj`) is a `WordBasic` object using the `TypeName` function. If it is, it updates the private module-level variable `mobjBasic`, otherwise it triggers an error.

```
Private Property Set SetBasic(obj As Object)
    ' Check if this is a WordBasic object.
    If TypeName(obj) = "wordbasic" Then
        Set mobjBasic = obj
    Else
        Error 1005
    End If
End Property
```

Notice that the `SetBasic()` is private. This prevents it from being used outside the `Document` module. This prevents `mobjBasic` from being inadvertantly changed outside of this module.

The `Basic()` `Get` property function returns the object reference maintained in the private, module-level variable `mobjBasic`. If `mobjBasic` doesn't contain a valid object reference, the `Basic` property returns an error.

```
Property Get Basic() As Object
    ' If there is an object in mobjBasic.
    If IsEmpty(mobjBasic) = False Then
        ' Return the WordBasic object.
        Set Basic = mobjBasic
    Else
        ' No current object, trigger "Unable to get property" _
          error (same as Excel uses).
        Error 1006
    End If
End Property
```

The `Basic()` `Let` property function sets the object reference maintained in the private, module-level variable `mobjBasic` by calling the private property procedure `SetBasic()`. This provides a slightly more user-friendly way to assign an object variable, because it doesn't require the user to use the `Set` statement.

```
' Optional, allow users to assign an object to the object variable.
Property Let Basic(obj As Object)
    ' Delegates to SetBasic().
    Set SetBasic = obj
End Property
```

The `TestObject()` procedure demonstrates how to use the `Property Get Basic` procedure:

```
Sub TestObject()
    Worksheets(1).Activate
    ' Create an embedded document.
```

```
        With Document.Create(1, 1, 100, 100)
            .Activate
            ' Get the Basic property and call Word's Insert method.
            .Basic.Insert "Some text"
        End With
    End Sub
```

The `SetObject()` procedure demonstrates how to use the `Property Let Basic` procedure to set an object reference with assignment instead of using the `Set` statement:

```
    Sub AssignObject()
        ' Set an object reference using property assignment.
        Basic = OLEObjects(1).Object.Application.WordBasic
    End Sub
```

You may or may not want to let users create object references using assignment. This depends on whether you feel it is clearer to allow assignment, require the `Set` statement, or prohibit setting a reference altogether.

Creating Variables and Constants

By default, Visual Basic creates the storage for variables automatically, the first time you use them. This means you aren't required to declare variables before using them, as you are required to do in C and certain other languages.

Automatically created variables are of the type `Variant`. Variants are special in that they can contain any type of data: strings, numbers, Boolean values, errors, arrays, or objects. Variants freely conform to any value you assign them. Sometimes this poses a problem, however.

Often, you want to know exactly what type of data you are working with. To do this, you must declare the variable using a `Dim` statement. `Dim` has this form:

```
    Dim variablename As datatype
```

Visual Basic has the following data types that you can use with `Dim`:

Data type	Range of values
Boolean	True (−1) or False (0)
Integer	−32,768 to 32,767

(continues)

Data type	Range of values
Long	–2,147,483,648 to 2,147,483,647
Single	–3.402823E28 to –1.401298E–45 for negative values; 1.401298E–45 to 3.402823E38 for positive values
Double	–1.79769313486232E308 to –4.94065645841247E–324 for negative values; 4.94065645841247E–324 to 1.79769313486232E308 for positive values
Currency	–922,337,203,685,477.5808 to 922,337,203,685,477.5807
Date	January 1, 1000 to December 31, 9999
Object	Any object reference
String	Strings may range in length from 0 to approximately 65,535
Variant	Any numeric value up to the range of a Double or any character text

If a variable exceeds the range of its data type, you get an `Overflow` error (error code 6). This lets you know the data is the wrong type for the variable. The `TooBig()` procedure demonstrates the overflow error:

```
Sub TooBig()
    Dim int As Integer
    int = 32768          ' Overflow!
End Sub
```

You can fix this by using a larger data type, such as `Long`:

```
Sub TooBig()
    Dim int As Long
    int = 32768          ' No Overflow
End Sub
```

Making Variables Available to Other Procedures, Modules, and Workbooks

When you declare a variable in a procedure, it is local to that procedure. That is, other procedures can't change its value. To let other procedures get at the value of a variable, you have to declare the variable at the *module level*. Module-level variables appear at the top of a module, before any `Sub` or `Function` statements.

Which procedures can access the variable is determined by how the variable is declared, as shown in the following table.

Keyword	Declared at	Variable is
`Dim`	Procedure	Available only to procedure
`Dim`	Module	Available to all procedures in module
`Private`	Module	Available to all procedures in module (same as `Dim`)
`Option Private Public`	Module	Available to all procedures in all modules of the current workbook
`Public`	Module	Available to all procedures in all modules of all workbooks

If a variable is declared at both the module and procedure levels, the procedure-level variable is used while you are in the procedure and the module-level variable is used in all other procedures.

The following lines demonstrate a variable declared at the module and procedure level. First run `Proc1()`, a message box displays 5 (the value at the procedure level). Next run `Proc2()`, and a message box displays 0 (the value at the module level).

```
Dim x As Integer

Sub Proc1()
    Dim x As Integer
    x = 5
    ' Displays 5 (local variable).
    MsgBox x
End Sub

Sub Proc2()
    ' Displays 0 (module variable).
    MsgBox x
End Sub
```

Requiring Variable Declaration

Although automatic variables make it easier to write code, they also make it easier to make mistakes. For example, the following procedure displays an empty message box because of a simple typing mistake:

```
Sub Automatic()
    Dim sMyText As String
    sMyText = "This is something to show."
    MsgBox MyText            ' Oops, typo! Displays empty message.
End Sub
```

Variable name spelling errors are some of the hardest bugs to track down because they aren't obvious. To catch this type of error before it happens, turn off Visual Basic's automatic variable creation.

To turn off automatic variables add an `Option Explicit` statement at the module level:

```
Option Explicit

Sub Automatic()
    Dim sMyText As String
    sMyText = "This is something to show."
    MsgBox MyText            ' Oops, typo! Displays empty message.
End Sub
```

Now, when you try to run the procedure, Visual Basic flags `MyText` and displays an error message, `Variable not defined`.

Defining Constants

Constants are values that don't change. It is a good idea to use a constant, rather than a variable, for any value that doesn't change. This prevents accidental changes to the value. Use the `Const` statement to define a constant. The following line creates the constant `Red`:

```
Const Red = &H0000FF
```

You can use constants as part of any expression. For example, this line sets the interior of a range using the constant `Red`:

```
Range("a1").Interior.Color = Red
```

Creating User-Defined Types

User-defined types are made up of one or more data types. To create a data type, use the `Type...End Type` statement. `Type...End Type` has this form:

```
Type typename
    element1 As datatype
    element2 As datatype
    elementn As datatype
End Type
```

`Type...End Type` can only be used at the module level. These lines declare the user-defined data type `MyType`:

```
Type MyType
     iCode As Integer
     sName As String
     dDate As Date
End Type
```

To use a user-defined type, declare a variable as the type and assign values to the elements of the type as in this example:

```
Sub UserType()
    ' Declare a variable MyVar
    Dim MyVar As MyType
    ' Assign values to its elements.
    MyVar.iCode = 2624
    MyVar.sName = "Wombat Tech"
    MyVar.dDate = Now
End Sub
```

To pass an argument of user-defined type to a procedure, declare the argument as the user-defined type. The `PassIt()` procedure receives an argument of type `MyType`:

```
Sub PassIt(myRec As MyType)
     MsgBox myRec.sName
End Sub
```

Creating and Using Arrays

Arrays contain a series of variables. Each variable is called an *element* of the array and is identified by an *index*. Arrays can have one or more dimensions. There are three ways to create an array:

Statement or function	Task
Dim	Creates an array
Redim	Creates an array that can be resized
Array	Creates a resizable one-dimensional array using a list of values

`Dim` and `Redim` declare arrays without assigning values. The following line creates a one-dimensional array that can contain 20 strings:

```
Dim sNames(1 to 20) As String
```

To create an array with more than one dimension, specify the size of each dimension. The following line declares a two-dimensional array:

```
Dim iValues(1 To 20, 1 To 20) As Integer
```

Use Redim to create arrays that can be resized. You can't use Redim at the module level. To make a resizable array available to other procedures, declare it with Dim but don't specify a range. The following lines create a resizable array, assign some values to the elements in the array, and then resize the array.

```
' Create resizable array.
Dim iResizable() As Integer

Sub UseArray()
    ' Size the array (erases any previous elements)
    ReDim iResizable(1 To 10)
    ' Assign some values to array elements.
    For iCount = 1 To 10
        iResizable(iCount) = iCount * iCount
    Next iCount
    ' Resize the array (preserve any previous elements)
    ReDim Preserve iResizable(1 To 20)
    ' Display one of the elements.
    MsgBox iResizable(5)
End Sub
```

The first Redim sets the initial size of the array. The second Redim resizes the array. The Preserve clause in the second Redim preserves the values that are already in the array. If the Preserve clause is omitted, the existing elements would be erased.

The Array function creates an array from a list of values. The following line creates an array with four elements:

```
vNames = Array("Jeff", "Tim", "Jay", "Don")
```

Array assigns an array to a variable of the type Variant. This is slightly different than an array declared with Dim or Redim, but you can still use all the array functions with Variant arrays.

These functions are often used to manipulate arrays:

Statement or function	Task
LBound	Returns the lower bound of the array—usually 0 or 1
UBound	Returns the upper bound of the array
For Each...Next	Performs operations on each element of the array

Handling Errors (Trapping and Skinning)

Not all errors are mistakes. There are some situations when you expect errors to occur and need to detect the error in your code. This process is called *error handling*. Error handling uses the On Error statement to trap and take actions on specific types of errors.

Error handling is primarily a three-step process:

1. Use an On Error statement to start handling errors.

2. Write code to test for errors.

3. Turn off error handling.

On Error has the following three forms:

Statement	Task
On Error Goto *handler*	Jumps to the line label named *handler* when an error occurs
On Error Resume Next	Continues execution at the next line after an error occurs
On Error Goto 0	Stops handling errors

The following lines show error handling using On Error Goto:

```
' Opens a file for Input. Returns file number if successful, 0 if _
  failure.
Function iOpenFile(sFilename As String) As Integer
    Dim iFilenumber As Integer, iTries As Integer
    ' Turn on error handling.
    On Error GoTo iOpenFileErr
    ' Get a free file number.
    iFilenumber = FreeFile()
    ' Open file. We don't know if the file exists yet, so might _
      cause an error.
    Open sFilename For Input As iFilenumber
    ' Return file number so user can manipulate file.
    iOpenFile = iFilenumber
    ' Important! Turn off error handling.
    On Error GoTo 0
    ' Clear status bar.
    Application.StatusBar = ""
    ' Important! Exit procedure before the error handler.
    Exit Function
' Label identifies error handler. This label must be unique to the _
  workbook.
iOpenFileErr:
```

```
' Classic way to do this: Select Case on the error code, with _
  a Case statement
' for each possibility.
Select Case Err
    Case 52, 53, 75, 76 ' Bad file name or number, file not _
    found, or path error.
            ' Display a status message indicating the error.
            Application.StatusBar = "File not found."
            ' Prompt the user for the file to open.
            sFilename = Application.GetOpenFilename _
            (, , "Choose file to open")
            ' If the user chose Cancel...
            If sFilename = "False" Then
                    ' Return 0 to indicate that the function didn't _
                      open a file.
                    iOpenFile = 0
                    ' Turn off error handling and exit.
                    On Error GoTo 0
                    Exit Function
            End If
    Case 55 ' File already open by VB for an incompatible _
              read/write access.
            ' This shouldn't happen, but if it does, return 0 _
              and exit.
            iOpenFile = 0
            On Error GoTo 0
            Exit Function
    Case 67 ' Too many files are open
            Application.StatusBar = "Too many files or _
            applications open."
            MsgBox "Close one or more files or applications and _
            try again."
            iOpenFile = 0
            On Error GoTo 0
            Exit Function
    Case 70 ' Permission denied.
            Application.StatusBar = "Permission denied."
            MsgBox "You can't open " & sFilename & _
                    ". It requires a password or is in use by _
                    another application."
            iOpenFile = 0
            On Error GoTo 0
            Exit Function
    Case 71 ' Disk not ready.
            ' Keep track of the number of tries.
            iTries = iTries + 1
            ' Let the user try twice, but don't beat them over _
              the head.
            If iTries < 3 Then
                    Application.StatusBar = "Can't read from drive."
                    MsgBox "Make sure the disk is inserted and the _
                    drive door is closed."
            ' Fail after second try -- maybe the user changed _
```

```
                    his/her mind.
                Else
                    iOpenFile = 0
                    On Error GoTo 0
                    Exit Function
                End If
            Case Else
                ' Report the error, so you can fix it.
                MsgBox "An unanticipated error occurred. _
                Please report " & _
                    "the following information to AppBug: " & Chr$(10) & _
                    "Procedure: iOpenFile" & Chr$(10) & _
                    "Error: " & Err & Error()
                iOpenFile = 0
                On Error GoTo 0
            Exit Function
        End Select
        ' You must tell Visual Basic to return after handling the error.
        Resume
    End Function
```

The following lines show error handling using `On Error Resume Next`:

```
    Sub PollingDemo()
        ' Start polling for errors.
        On Error Resume Next
        ' This line returns error 1004 if an outline can't be created.
        Selection.AutoOutline
        ' If there was an error...
        If Err Then
            ' Alert user of the error.
            Application.Statusbar = "Can't create outline on this selection."
            Beep
            ' Important! Reset error back to 0.
            Err = 0
        End If
        ' Turn off error trapping.
        On Error GoTo 0
    End Sub
```

The error handling process is described in further detail in Appendix A, "Trappable Errors."

Chapter 3

Performing Tasks with Visual Basic

Computers were originally developed as tools for calculating ballistic trajectories. Though computers have changed a lot since then, their fundamental role is still crunching data. This chapter describes the finer points of crunching using Visual Basic.

In this chapter, you learn how to do the following:

- Express yourself in Visual Basic.

- Perform operations within expressions.

- Work with numbers, strings, and dates.

- Use data files.

- Interact with users and other applications.

Creating Expressions

An *expression* is a group of items that yield a value. That value might be a number, a string, True, False, a date, or any other type of data. Expressions can be made up of any combination of functions, operators, variables, and constants.

All expressions can be grouped based on the type of value they return:

- Numeric expressions evaluate to a number.

- String expressions evaluate to a string of text.

- Logical expressions evaluate to True or False.

- Date expressions evaluate to a date or time.

- Object expressions evaluate to a reference to an object.

Table 3.1 lists some examples of different types of expressions.

Table 3.1 Assorted types of expressions		
Type of expression	**Example**	**Value**
Numeric	`1+1`	2
	`Abs(-12)`	12
	`x^2 + y \ z`	Depends on values of variables.
String	`"Some text"`	`"Some text"`
	`"Some text " & "some more"`	`"Some text some more"`
	`Mid(sVar, 1, 20)`	The first 20 characters of sVar.
Logical	`True`	−1
	`x = y`	True if x and y are equal, otherwise False.
	`iVar And &HFF`	The low-order byte from iVal.
Date	`Now`	The current date and time.
	`DateValue(12, 15, 1989)`	My son's birthday.
Object	`ActiveSheet`	Sheet object that currently has focus.
	`GetObject _ (,"Excel.Application")`	A running instance of Excel.

The rest of this chapter explains how to form expressions using Visual Basic statements, functions, and operators.

Using the Visual Basic Operators

Operators are the glue used to create expressions. Table 3.2 shows the operators that are available in Visual Basic.

Table 3.2 Visual Basic operators		
Category	**Operator**	**Task**
Numeric	^	Raises a number to a specified power.
	-	Makes a number negative.
	*	Multiplies two numbers.
	/	Divides two numbers.
	\	Divides two numbers and returns an integer (no fraction).
	Mod	Divides two numbers and returns the remainder as an integer.
	+	Adds two numbers.
	-	Subtracts two numbers.
	=	Assigns one value to another.
Strings	&	Concatenates two strings.
Numeric and string comparison	=	Returns True if two values are the same.
	<>	Returns True if two values are different.
	<	Returns True if the value on the left is less than the value on the right.
	>	Returns True if the value on the left is greater than the value on the right.
	<=	Returns True if the value on the left is less than or equal to the value on the right.
	>=	Returns True if the value on the left is greater than or equal to the value on the right.
	Like	Returns True if two strings are similar.
Logical	Not	Returns the logical negation of an expression.
	And	Returns the logical conjunction of two expressions.
	Or	Returns the logical or bit-wise disjunction of two expressions.
	Xor	Returns the logical exclusion of two expressions.
	Eqv	Returns the logical equivalence of two expressions.
	Imp	Returns the logical implication of two expressions.
Object comparison	Is	Compares two objects to see if they are the same.

Order of Operations

For those who are new to programming, mathematical operations might seem backward in Visual Basic. For example:

```
x = 1 + 2..' rather than 1 + 2 = x
```

This is the way programming languages express operations. The calculation is read from left to right and operations with the highest *precedence* are performed first. Table 3.3 shows operations by order of precedence.

Table 3.3 Operator order of precedence				
Numeric	**String**	**Numeric/string comparison**	**Logical**	**Object comparison**
^		= [4]	Not	
- [1]		< >	And	
*, /		<	Or	
\		>	Xor	
Mod		<=	Eqv	
+, - [2]		>=	Imp	
	&	Like		Is
= [3]	= [3]	= [3]	= [3]	= [3]

[1]*Negation, as in* -1.

[2]*Subtraction, as in* 2 - 1.

[3]*Assignment, as in* x = 1 + 1.

[4]*Comparison, as in* If x = y Then ....

Assignment (the equal sign, =) has the lowest order of precedence. In other words, = is the last operation performed in a calculation. The expression x = 1 + 2 tells Visual Basic to add 1 and 2, then assign the value to x.

You can change the order of evaluation by enclosing an expression in parentheses. The following line squares 1, then subtracts it from y and assigns the value to x:

```
x = y - 1^2            ' Probably a mistake!
```

The following line subtracts 1 from y, squares the result and assigns the value to x:

```
x = (y - 1)^2            ' Change order of evaluation.
```

Joining Strings

Both & and + can be used to join two strings. However, & *forces* the variables to be treated as strings. Since Variant variables can change their type, always use & when joining strings.

Books on programming often use the word *concatenation* when referring to joining strings together. Concatenate is really just a fancy word for join.

The JoinStrings() procedure shows the difference between + and & when used with Variants:

```
Sub JoinStrings()
    x = 123
    y = "456"
    z = x + y          ' Result is 579
    sz = x & y          ' Result is "123456"
End Sub
```

Performing Comparisons

Comparisons are often used with decision-making statements like If...Then and as conditions within loops. In general, comparison expressions are either True or False. However, they can also be Null if part of the expression is Null.

The CubeRoot() procedure, shown in the following listing, demonstrates numeric comparison in action. When the expression Abs(X1 - X2) < 0.00000000000001 becomes True, the loop ends. If the expression X * X * X - n < 0 is True, then X is assigned to X1, otherwise X is assigned to X2.

```
' Find cube root by approximation.
Function CubeRoot(n)
    Dim X As Single, X1 As Single, X2 As Single
    ' Make first two guesses.
    X1 = 0: X2 = n
      ' Loop until difference between guesses is less than _
        .00000000000001.
    Do Until Abs(X1 - X2) < 0.00000000000001
        X = (X1 + X2) / 2
        ' Adjust guesses.
        If X * X * X - n < 0 Then
            X1 = X
        Else
            X2 = X
        End If
    Loop
    CubeRoot = X
End Function
```

You can use the comparison operators with strings as well as numbers. Three of the comparison operators are used most with strings: =, <>, and `Like`.

Use = and <> to see whether two strings are the same. Both operators compare the strings character by character and are case-sensitive. For example, the following comparison is False because c is uppercase in the second string:

```
"abc" = "abC"
```

`Like` lets you do less-than-exact comparisons. This comparison is True, because Visual Basic ignores case by default when using `Like`:

```
"abc" Like "abC"
```

You can change this behavior by adding an `Option Compare Binary` statement to the module level. If you add the following line to the module level, the line in the preceding example becomes False:

```
Option Compare Binary
```

The real power of `Like` is in its pattern-matching. Table 3.4 shows how to use pattern-matching characters with `Like`.

Table 3.4 Pattern-matching characters used with *Like*

Character	Description	Examples	Result
*	Wildcard	"aBBBa" Like "a*a"	True
[]	List	"F" Like "[A-Z]"	True
[!]	Not in list	"F" Like "[!A-Z]"	False
#	Single number	"a2a" Like "a#a"	True
		"aM5b" Like "a[L-P]#[!c-e]"	True
?	Single character	"BAT123khg" Like "B?T*"	True
		"CAT123khg" Like "B?T*"	False

Use `Like` to screen the data a user enters. `GetSSN()` gets a Social Security number from the user using one of two formats. If the number isn't entered correctly, the user is prompted again:

```
Function GetSSN()
    Do
        vResult = InputBox("Enter your Social Security Number:")
        ' User pressed Cancel.
        If vResult = "" Then Exit Do
```

```
        If vResult Like "###-##-####" Then
            ' Remove hyphen
            vResult = Mid(vResult, 1, 3) & Mid(vResult, 5, 2) _
            & Mid(vResult, 8, 4)
            Exit Do
        ElseIf vResult Like "#########" Then
            ' No need to remove hyphens.
            Exit Do
        ' User enters some invalid data.
        Else
            ' Display message.
            MsgBox "Please enter the number again."
        End If
    Loop
    ' Return the number or "" if Cancelled.
    GetSSN = vResult
End Function
```

Using Logic

Logical operators are often used to combine comparisons in decision-making statements like If...Then. Logical expressions are either True, False, or Null.

Logical comparisons have this form:

```
result = exp1 operator exp2
```

The following example shows two comparision statements joined using an And statement. Both conditions must be True for the message box to display.

```
If (x > y) And (a > c) Then MsgBox "Both are True"
```

The following example shows two comparisions joined using an Or statement. Either condition must be True for the message box to display.

```
If (x > y) Or (a > c) Then MsgBox "Either or both are True"
```

The result of logical operations is most clearly shown by a truth table. Table 3.5 shows the results of all logical operations.

Table 3.5 Logical operator truth table

Operator	exp1	exp2	Result
And	True	True	True
	True	False	False
	True	Null	Null
	False	True	False
	False	False	False
	False	Null	False

(continues)

VBA Programming

Table 3.5 Continued			
Operator	**exp1**	**exp2**	**Result**
	Null	True	Null
	Null	False	False
	Null	Null	Null
Eqv	True	True	True
	True	False	False
	False	True	False
	False	False	True
Imp	True	True	True
	True	False	False
	True	Null	Null
	False	True	True
	False	False	True
	False	Null	True
	Null	True	True
	Null	False	Null
	Null	Null	Null
Not	True	N/A	False
	False	N/A	True
Or	True	True	True
	True	False	True
	True	Null	True
	False	True	True
	False	False	False
	False	Null	Null
	Null	True	True
	Null	False	Null
	Null	Null	Null
XOr	True	True	False
	True	False	True
	True	Null	Null
	False	True	True

Operator	exp1	exp2	Result
	False	False	False
	False	Null	Null
	Null	True	Null
	Null	False	Null
	Null	Null	Null

Performing Bit-Wise Comparison

The logical operators are also used to compare the individual bits in two expressions. This is called *bit-wise comparison*.

Bit-wise comparision is most commonly used to get a number of results from a single value. In the following code, the `iFont` argument in `FormatCell()` holds information about two kinds of font attributes.

```
' Module-level code
Const IFONT_BOLD = &hff
Const IFONT_NORMAL = &h0
Const IFONT_ITALIC = &hff00

Sub Test()
    ' Set formatting.
    miFont = IFONT_BOLD + IFONT_ITALIC
    ' Call FormatCell
    FormatCell IFONT_BOLD + IFONT_ITALIC
End Sub

Sub FormatCell(iFont As Integer)
    ' If iFont contains a Bold setting
    If iFont And IFONT_BOLD Then
        ActiveCell.Font.Bold = True
    Else
        ActiveCell.Font.Bold = False
    End If
    If iFont And IFONT_ITALIC Then
        ActiveCell.Font.Italic = True
    Else
        ActiveCell.Font.Italic = False
    End If
End Sub
```

The results of bit-wise comparison are most clearly shown by a table. Table 3.6 shows the results of comparison operations using this form:

```
result = exp1 operator exp2
```

Table 3.6 Bit-wise comparison table			
Operator	**Bit in exp1**	**Bit in exp2**	**Bit in result**
And	0	0	0
	1	0	1
	0	1	1
	1	1	1
Eqv	0	0	1
	0	1	0
	1	0	0
	1	1	1
Imp	0	0	1
	0	1	1
	1	0	0
	1	1	1
Not	1	N/A	0
	0	N/A	1
Or	0	0	0
	0	1	1
	1	0	1
	1	1	1
Xor	0	0	0
	0	1	1
	1	0	1
	1	1	0

Comparing Objects

You can't use objects with numeric or string comparison operators. For example, the following If statement causes error 1000

```
Sub CompareObjects()
    Set x = ActiveSheet
    Set y = x
    If x = y Then MsgBox "These are the same"
End Sub
```

To compare two objects, use the `Is` statement. The `CompareObjects()` procedure shown in the following code now runs correctly, displaying the message box:

```
Sub CompareObjects()
    Set x = ActiveSheet
    Set y = x
    If x Is y Then MsgBox "These are the same"
End Sub
```

Notice, however, that the two variables must be set to each other, as in the line `Set y = x`. The following version of `CompareObjects()` does not display the message box, even though `x` and `y` both refer to the active sheet:

```
Sub CompareObjects()
    Set x = ActiveSheet
    Set y = ActiveSheet
    If x Is y Then MsgBox "These are the same"
End Sub
```

Working with Numbers

Visual Basic provides a number of functions and statements for performing common mathematical operations. Excel provides a larger number of math functions, many of which duplicate those found in Visual Basic. This section covers only the Visual Basic math functions.

Table 3.7 lists the math and numeric functions provided by Visual Basic.

Table 3.7 Math and numeric functions and statements

Category	Function or statement	Task
General calculations	Abs	Returns the absolute value of a number.
	Exp	Returns the exponent of a number.
	Log	Returns the natural logarithm of a number.

(continues)

Table 3.7 Continued

Category	Function or statement	Task
	Sgn	Returns the sign of a number.
	Sqr	Returns the square root of a number.
Random numbers	Randomize	Initializes the random number generator.
	Rnd	Returns a random number as a fraction between 0 and 1.
Numeric conversions	CBool	Converts a value to the Boolean data type.
	CCur	Converts a value to the Currency data type.
	CDate	Converts a value to the Date data type.
	CDbl	Converts a value to the Double data type.
	CInt	Converts a value to the Integer data type.
	CLng	Converts a value to the Long data type.
	CSng	Converts a value to the Single data type.
	CStr	Converts a value to the String data type.
	CVar	Converts a value to the Variant data type.
	CVErr	Converts a value to the Variant data type with the subtype Date.
	Str	Converts a number to a string.
	Fix	Removes the fractional part of a real number.
	Hex	Converts a decimal number to hexidecimal.
	Int	Removes the fractional part of a real number.
	Oct	Converts a decimal number to octal.
Trigonometry	Atn	Returns the arc tangent of an angle expressed in radians.
	Cos	Returns the cosine of an angle expressed in radians.
	Sin	Returns the sine of an angle expressed in radians.
	Tan	Returns the tangent of a ratio.

Generating Random Numbers

Use the Rnd() function to generate random numbers in a specified range. By default, Rnd() generates the same sequence of numbers each time you run it. To avoid this, use Randomize before you call Rnd().

RandomDigit() returns a random number between 0 and 9:

```
Function RandomDigit() As Integer
    ' Initialize random number generator.
    Randomize
    ' Return random number in the range.
    RandomDigit = Int((9 - 0 + 1) * Rnd + 0)
End Function
```

Because Rnd() returns a number between 0 and 1, you have to perform some calculations to get a number in the desired range. The formula for generating random numbers in a range is:

```
Int((upperbound - lowerbound + 1) * Rnd + lowerbound)
```

Converting Values

Visual Basic automatically converts data from one type to another as long as the assigned value fits in the variable. This process is called *coercion*.

The CoerceValues() procedure in the following code shows how Visual Basic automatically coerces a value from one data type to another:

```
Sub CoerceValues()
    ' Declare variable of two different types.
    Dim iValue As Integer, sngValue As Single
    ' Assign a value.
    sngValue = 99.9
    ' Coerce the value to an integer (rounds to 100).
    iValue = sngValue
End Sub
```

Use manual coercion when you want to be explicit in code. You perform coercion manually by using the data type conversion functions. The following version of CoerceValues() performs the same conversion as shown above:

```
Sub CoerceValues()
    ' Declare variable of two different types.
    Dim iValue As Integer, sngValue As Single
    ' Assign a value.
    sngValue = 99.9
    ' Coerce the value to an integer (rounds to 100).
    iValue = CInt(sngValue)
End Sub
```

Besides converting data types, you can also convert numbers between decimal (base-10, the default), hexidecimal (base-16), and octal (base-8). To use a hexidecimal or octal number in code, add a &H or &O prefix to the number. To display a number in hexidecimal or octal notation, use the Hex and Oct functions.

Hexidecimal numbers are often used when making Windows API calls and when creating bit-masks or defining RGB colors. For example, the following line defines a constant RGB value for purple:

```
Const PURPLE = &hFF00FF
```

Using Trigonometric Functions

Visual Basic's trigonometric functions use radians, rather than degrees, to indicate angles. Radians are useful for polar coordinate systems, but most of us are more used to working with degrees.

To convert degrees to radians, multiply degrees by Pi/180 as shown in the following example:

```
Const PI = 3.14159265

Function DegreesToRadians(degrees)
    DegreesToRadians = degrees * (PI / 180)
End Function
```

To convert radians to degrees, multiply radians by 180/Pi as shown in the following example:

```
Function RadiansToDegrees(radians)
    RadiansToDegrees= radians * (180 / PI)
End Function
```

You can use the Visual Basic trigonometric functions to derive more complex functions, as listed in Table 3.8.

Table 3.8 Derived trigonometric functions	
Trigonometric function	**Derived equation**
Secant	1 / Cos(X)
Cosecant	1 / Sin(X)
Cotangent	1 / Tan(X)
Inverse Sine	Atn(X / Sqr(-X * X + 1))
Inverse Cosine	Atn(-X / Sqr(-X * X + 1)) + 1.5708
Inverse Secant	Atn(X / Sqr(X * X - 1)) + Sgn((X) -1) * 1.5708

Trigonometric function	Derived equation
Inverse Cosecant	Atn(X / Sqr(X * X - 1)) + (Sgn(X) - 1) _ * 1.5708
Inverse Cotangent	Atn(X) + 1.5708
Hyperbolic Sine	(Exp(X) - Exp(-X)) / 2
Hyperbolic Cosine	(Exp(X) + Exp(-X)) / 2
Hyperbolic Tangent	(Exp(X) - Exp(-X)) / (Exp(X) + Exp (-X))
Hyperbolic Secant	2 / (Exp(X) + Exp(-X))
Hyperbolic Cosecant	2 / (Exp(X) · Exp(-X))
Hyperbolic Cotangent	(Exp(X) + Exp(-X)) / (Exp(X) - Exp (-X))
Inverse Hyperbolic Sine	Log(X + Sqr(X * X + 1))
Inverse Hyperbolic Cosine	Log(X + Sqr(X * X - 1))
Inverse Hyperbolic Tangent	Log((1 + X) / (1 - X)) / 2
Inverse Hyperbolic Secant	Log((Sqr(-X * X + 1) + 1) / X)
Inverse Hyperbolic Cosecant	Log((Sgn(X) * Sqr(X * X + 1) +1) / X)
Inverse Hyperbolic Cotangent	Log((X + 1) / (X - 1)) / 2
Logarithm to base *n*	Log(X) / Log(*n*)

VBA Programming

Working with Strings of Text

Much of the data you receive from users comes in as strings of text. Visual
Basic provides a number of functions and statements for performing tasks
such as:

- Comparing two strings to see if they are the same or for sorting.

- Converting strings to numbers or numbers to strings.

- Formatting output.

- Getting and changing parts of a string.

- Creating strings of repeating characters.

Table 3.9 lists the functions that Visual Basic provides for working with strings of text.

Table 3.9 String functions		
Category	**Function or statement**	**Task**
Comparison	StrComp	Compares one string to another.
	InStr	Finds a substring within a longer string.
	Option Compare	Sets string comparison rules.
Conversion	Asc	Converts a single character to its ANSI value.
	Chr	Converts a number to a character with the corresponding ANSI value.
	Val	Converts a string to a numeric value.
Formatting	Format	Formats text, numbers, and dates as strings.
	LCase	Returns a string in lowercase.
	LSet	Left-justifies a string.
	RSet	Right-justifies a string.
	UCase	Returns a string in uppercase.
Manipulation	Left	Returns a number of characters from the left side of a string.
	LTrim	Removes blank spaces from the left side of a string.
	Mid	Returns a number of characters from any position within a string.
	Right	Returns a number of characters from the right side of a string.
	RTrim	Removes blank spaces from the right side of a string.
	Trim	Removes blank spaces from the right and left sides of a string.
Repeating characters	Space	Creates a string containing blank spaces.
	String	Creates a string containing a repeated character.

Performing Comparisons

Use InStr to find a character or string within another string. InStr is also a
valuable tool for testing the contents of a string.

The TabsToSpaces() procedure, shown in the listing below, uses InStr to locate the Tab character (Chr(9)) and as a test in an If statement. Because InStr
returns 0 if the substring is not found, the variable iTabLocation serves a dual
purpose.

```
Sub TabsToSpaces(sSource)
    Do
        ' Find a tab character in a line.
        iTabLocation = InStr(sSource, Chr(9))
        ' If a tab was found...
        If iTabLocation Then
            ' Replace the tab with four spaces.
            sSource = Mid(sSource, 1, iTabLocation - 1) & _
            Space(4) & _
                Mid(sSource, iTabLocation + 1)
        End If
    ' Repeat until no more are found.
    Loop While iTabLocation
End Sub
```

Use StrComp when comparing values for sorting. The SortArray() procedure
shown in the following listing uses StrComp to compare the strings in an array
and put them in order.

```
' Sorts an array of strings by swapping elements.
Sub SortArray(sWord)
    iFirst = LBound(sWord)
    iLast = UBound(sWord)
    ' If only one element, exit.
    If iFirst = iLast Then Exit Sub
    ' Make a pass for each element of the array.
    For iTimes = iFirst To iLast
        sTemp = sWord(iTimes)
        ' Check sTemp against each element, if out of order, _
        then swap values.
        For iCount = iFirst To iLast
            If StrComp(sTemp, sWord(iCount)) = -1 Then
                ' Swap values.
                sTemp = sWord(iCount)
                sWord(iCount) = sWord(iTimes)
                sWord(iTimes) = sTemp
            End If
        Next iCount
    Next iTimes
End Sub
```

By default, StrComp compares the text of the two strings and ignores case. To
change this default, use the Option Compare Binary statement:

```
Option Compare Binary          ' Use case-sensitive comparisons
```

Converting Characters to or from Numbers

Use the Chr() function to create a character from an ANSI value. This is useful for adding whitespace characters to a string. Unfortunately, Chr() can't be used in constant expressions, so you must define these characters as variables. The following lines of code show commonly used variable definitions for whitespace characters:

```
' Common whitespace characters.
TAB = Chr(9)          ' Tab character.
LF = Chr(10)          ' Line feed.
CR = Chr(13)          ' Carriage return.
```

Similarly, the Asc() function returns the ANSI value of a character. This is useful for hashing stored passwords so they can't be read by others. *Hashing* is computer lingo for encoding something so it can't be easily read.

The sHash() procedure shown in the following listing converts a password into a randomly hashed string using a user ID. Since user IDs are unique, each password can be uniquely hashed. Encode() generates a random ANSI based on the source character and the user ID.

```
Private Function sHash(sPass, iUser) As String
    ' For each character in sPass
    For iCount = 1 To Len(sPass)
        ' Generate a hashed character.
        sChar = Chr(Encode(Asc(Mid(sPass, iCount, 1)), iUser))
        ' Build the hashed string backwards.
        sTemp = sChar + sTemp
    Next
    sHash = sTemp
End Function

' Encode the character by adding a random number between _
  50 and 100.
Private Function Encode(Item, iUser)
    Encode = Item + (Int(Rnd(-iUser) * (100 - 50 + 1)) + 50)
End Function
```

The sDehash() and Decode() procedures shown in the following listing decode a hashed password. These two sets of functions use a simple hashing method, which you can make more complex for greater security.

```
Private Function sDehash(sPass, iUser) As String
    ' For each character in sPass
    For iCount = 1 To Len(sPass)
        sChar = Chr(Decode(Asc(Mid(sPass, iCount, 1)), iUser))
        ' Build the decoded string backwards.
        sTemp = sChar + sTemp
    Next
    sDehash = sTemp
End Function
```

```
' Decode the character by subtracting a random number between _
  50 and 100.
' Since Rnd is seeded with -iUser, the same value is generated _
  each time.
Private Function Decode(Item, iUser)
    Decode = Item - (Int(Rnd(-iUser) * (100 - 50 + 1)) + 50)
End Function
```

Formatting Text, Numbers, and Dates as Strings

Visual Basic provides the `LCase()` and `UCase()` functions to change the case of a string. With the introduction of `Like` and `StrComp`, these functions have become less important for performing comparisons. They are still useful for formatting strings, however.

The following lines of code change text to lowercase in a selected range:

```
Sub LowerCase()
    For Each rng In Selection
        rng.Value = LCase(rng.Value)
    Next rng
End Sub
```

Notice that you don't have to check whether a cell contains text or numbers. Changing the case of a `Variant` number does not cause an error or affect the value of the `Variant`.

Use the `Format()` function to display text, numbers, and dates in a specific format. The following line displays the first three characters of the current weekday:

```
MsgBox Format(Now, "ddd")
```

The `Format` function has this general form:

```
Format(data [, formatstring])
```

The argument *formatstring* is either a predefined, named format, or a user-defined format string. Table 3.10 shows the named formats Visual Basic provides. Table 3.11 lists the format characters you can use to build your own format strings.

Table 3.10 *Format* function named formats

Category	Named format	Description
Numeric	"General Number"	Returns a number as is, with no thousands separator.

(continues)

Table 3.10 Continued

Category	Named format	Description
	`"Currency"`	Returns a number with thousands separator; encloses negative numbers in parentheses; includes two digits to the right of the decimal separator.
	`"Fixed"`	Returns a number with at least one digit to the left and two digits to the right of the decimal separator.
	`"Standard"`	Returns a number with thousands separator, at least one digit to the left and two digits to the right of the decimal separator.
	`"Percent"`	Returns a number multiplied by 100 with a percent sign (%) appended to the right; includes two digits to the right of the decimal separator.
	`"Scientific"`	Uses standard scientific notation.
	`"Yes/No"`	Returns "No" if number is 0; otherwise, returns "Yes".
	`"True/False"`	Returns "False" if number is 0; otherwise, returns "True".
	`"On/Off"`	Returns "Off" if number is 0; otherwise, returns "On".
Date/time	`"General Date"`	Returns a date and/or time. For real numbers, returns a date and time (for example, 4/3/93 05:34 PM); if there is no fractional part, returns only a date (for example, 4/3/93); if there is no integer part, returns time only (for example, 05:34 PM).
	`"Long Date"`	Returns a date according to your system's long date format.
	`"Medium Date"`	Returns a date using the medium date format appropriate for the language version of the host application.
	`"Short Date"`	Returns a date using your system's short date format.
	`"Long Time"`	Returns a time using your system's long time format: includes hours, minutes, seconds.
	`"Medium Time"`	Returns a time in 12-hour format using hours and minutes and the AM/PM designator.
	`"Short Time"`	Returns a time using the 24-hour format (for example, 17:45).

Table 3.11 _Format_ function format characters		
Category	**Character**	**Description**
String	@	Includes a character or a space. If the string has a character in the position where the @ appears in the format string, includes it; otherwise, includes a space in that position. Placeholders are filled from right to left unless there is an ! character in the format string.
	&	Character placeholder. If the string has a character in the position where the & appears, includes it; otherwise, includes nothing. Placeholders are filled from right to left unless there is an ! character in the format string.
	<	Forces lowercase. Includes all characters in lowercase format.
	>	Forces uppercase. Includes all characters in uppercase format.
	!	Forces left-to-right fill of placeholders. The default is to fill from right to left.
Numeric	None	No formatting. Includes the number with no formatting.
	0	Digit placeholder. If the expression has a digit in the position where the 0 appears in the format string, includes it; otherwise, includes a zero in that position.
	#	Digit placeholder. If the expression has a digit in the position where the # appears in the format string, includes it; otherwise, includes nothing in that position.
	.	Decimal placeholder.
	%	Percentage placeholder. The expression is multiplied by 100. The percent character (%) is inserted in the position where it appears in the format string.
	,	Thousands separator.
	:	Time separator. In some locales, other characters may be used to represent the time separator. The time separator separates hours, minutes, and seconds when time values are formatted.
	/	Date separator. In some locales, other characters may be used to represent the date separator. The date separator separates the day, month, and year when date values are formatted.

(continues)

Table 3.11 Continued		
Category	**Character**	**Description**
	E- E+ e- e+	Scientific format. If the format expression contains at least one digit placeholder (0 or #) to the right of E-, E+, e-, or e+, the number is included in scientific format and E or e is inserted between the number and its exponent. The number of digit placeholders to the right determines the number of digits in the exponent. Use E- or e- to place a minus sign next to negative exponents. Use E+ or e+ to place a minus sign next to negative exponents and a plus sign next to positive exponents.
	- + $ ( ) space	Includes a literal character. To include a character other than one of those listed, precede it with a backslash (\) or enclose it in double quotation marks (" ").
	\	Includes the next character in the format string. Many characters in the format expression have a special meaning and can't be included as literal characters unless they are preceded by a backslash.
	"ABC"	Includes the string inside double quotation marks. To include a string in format from within code, you must use Chr(34) to enclose the text.
Date/Time	:	Time separator.
	/	Date separator.
	c	Includes the date as ddddd and includes the time as ttttt, in that order. Includes only date information if there is no fractional part to the date serial number; includes only time information if there is no integer portion.
	d	Includes the day as a number without a leading zero (1-31).
	dd	Includes leading zero (01-31).
	ddd	Includes the day as an abbreviation (Sun-Sat).
	dddd	Includes the day as a full name (Sunday-Saturday).
	ddddd	Includes a date as a complete date (including day, month, and year), formatted according to your system's short date format setting.
	dddddd	Includes a date serial number as a complete date (including day, month, and year), formatted according to the long date setting recognized by your system.

Category	Character	Description
	w	Includes the day of the week as a number (1 for Sunday through 7 for Saturday).
	ww	Includes the week of the year as a number (1-53).
	m	Includes the month as a number without a leading zero (1-12). If m immediately follows h or hh, the minute rather than the month is included.
	mm	Includes the month as a number with a leading zero (01-12). If m immediately follows h or hh, the minute rather than the month is included.
	mmm	Includes the month as an abbreviation (Jan-Dec).
	mmmm	Includes the month as a full month name (January-December).
	q	Includes the quarter of the year as a number (1-4).
	y	Includes the day of the year as a number (1-366).
	yy	Includes the year as a 2-digit number (00-99).
	yyyy	Includes the year as a 4-digit number (1000-9999).
	h	Includes the hour as a number without leading zeros (0-23).
	hh	Includes the hour as a number with leading zeros (00-23).
	n	Includes the minute as a number without leading zeros (0-59).
	nn	Includes the minute as a number with leading zeros (00-59).
	s	Includes the second as a number without leading zeros (0-59).
	ss	Includes the second as a number with leading zeros (00-59).
	ttttt	Includes a time as a complete time (including hour, minute, and second), formatted using the time separator defined by the time format recognized by your system. A leading zero is included if the leading zero option is selected and the time is before 10:00 A.M. or P.M. The default time format is h:mm:ss.

(continues)

Table 3.11 Continued		
Category	**Character**	**Description**
	AM/PM	Uses the 12-hour clock and includes an uppercase AM with any hour before noon; includes an uppercase PM with any hour between noon and 11:59 P.M.
	am/pm	Uses the 12-hour clock and includes a lowercase AM with any hour before noon; includes a lowercase PM with any hour between noon and 11:59 P.M.
	A/P	Uses the 12-hour clock and includes an uppercase A with any hour before noon; includes an uppercase P with any hour between noon and 11:59 P.M.
	a/p	Uses the 12-hour clock and includes a lowercase A with any hour before noon; includes a lowercase P with any hour between noon and 11:59 P.M.
	AMPM	Uses the 12-hour clock and includes the AM string literal as defined by your system with any hour before noon; includes the PM string literal as defined by your system with any hour between noon and 11:59 P.M. AMPM can be either uppercase or lowercase, but the case of the string included matches the string as defined by your system settings.

Getting Parts of Strings

Use Mid to get and replace parts of strings. SpacesToUnderscores() replaces the spaces in a string with underscores:

```
Sub SpacesToUnderscores(sSource)
    Do
        ' Find a space character in a line.
        iLocation = InStr(sSource, Chr(32))
        ' If a space was found...
        If iLocation Then
            ' Replace the space with underscore.
            Mid(sSource, iLocation, 1) = "_"
        End If
    ' Repeat until no more are found.
    Loop While iLocation
End Sub
```

Mid can also return a part of a string. The procedure sBaseName() returns the base name (the portion before the period) of a DOS file, as shown in the following example:

```
Function sBaseName(sSource) As String
        ' Find the period in the filename.
        iLocation = InStr(sSource, ".")
        ' If a period was found...
        If iLocation Then
            ' Get the base name.
            sBaseName = Mid(sSource, 1, iLocation - 1)
        Else
            ' Otherwise, return the whole name.
            sBaseName = sSource
        End If
End Function
```

Repeating Characters

Use the Space() and String() functions to create strings of repeating characters. The following code creates an empty string 256 characters long:

```
sEmpty = Space(256)
```

The following code creates a string of 256 exclamation marks (for points you *really* feel strongly about):

```
sWhoa = String(256, "!")
```

Working with Dates and Times

The Date data type makes it easy to work with dates and times. Dates are double-precision numbers. The whole part of the number represents the date, and the fractional part represents the time. For example, the following code displays tomorrow's date:

```
MsgBox "Tomorrow is " & DateValue(Now + 1)
```

Similarly, the following code sets the system clock back one hour:

```
Time = Timevalue(Now - 1/24)
```

Visual Basic provides a number of functions and statements for working with dates and times, as shown in Table 3.12.

Table 3.12 Date and time functions and statements

Category	Function or statement	Task
Current	Date	Sets or returns the system date.
	Now	Returns the current date and time.

(continues)

	Table 3.12 Continued	
Category	**Function or statement**	**Task**
	Time	Sets or returns the system time.
	Timer	Returns the number of seconds since midnight (used for timing processes).
Date manipulation	DateSerial	Returns a Date value for a day, month, and year expressed as numbers separated by commas.
	DateValue	Returns a Date value for a date and/or time usually expressed as a string.
	Day	Returns the day of the month from a date. The returned day is a number between 1 and 31.
	Month	Returns the month from a date. The returned month is a number between 1 and 12.
	Weekday	Returns the weekday from a date. The returned weekday is a number between 1 and 7.
	Year	Returns the year from a date. The returned year is a number between 1000 and 9999.
Time manipulation	Hour	Returns the hour from a time. The returned number is between 0 and 23.
	Minute	Returns the minute from a time. The returned number is between 0 and 59.
	Second	Returns the second from a time. The returned number is between 0 and 59.
	TimeSerial	Returns a Date value for an hour, minute, and second expressed as numbers separated by commas.
	TimeValue	Returns a Date value for a time usually expressed as a string.

Working with Data Files

Most of the files you work with in Excel are workbook files (*.XLS). Occasionally, you may want to create a file with a custom format, instead of using one of the Excel formats. These custom files let you store and retrieve records of information in much the same way as you retrieve data from a database.

Using data files involves three basic steps:

1. Open the file using the Open statement.

2. Read or write data using Input, Print, Write, Get, or Put statements.

3. Close the file using the Close statement.

Table 3.13 lists the Visual Basic statements and functions you use to create and access data files.

Note

Excel's GetOpenFilename and GetSaveAsFilename methods display dialog boxes to get file names from the user. Though they aren't part of Visual Basic per se, they are much too useful to ignore here. I use them throughout this section.

Table 3.13 Data file functions and statements

Category	Function or statement	Task
Accessing files	Close	Closes an open file.
	FileAttr	Returns the attributes of an open file.
	FileCopy	Makes a copy of a file.
	FreeFile	Returns a number that can be used as a file handle by the Open statement.
	Lock...Unlock	Controls access to all or part of an open file.
	LOF	Returns the length of an open file in bytes.
	Open	Opens a file and assigns it a file handle.
	Reset	Closes all open files.
Attributes of files	FileDateTime	Returns a Date value indicating when the file was created or modified.
	FileLen	Returns the length of a file in bytes.
	GetAttr	Returns the attributes of a file, directory, or volume label on disk.
	SetAttr	Changes the attributes of a file, directory, or volume label on disk.

(continues)

Table 3.13 Continued

Category	Function or statement	Task
Manage drives	ChDir	Sets the current directory.
	ChDrive	Sets the current drive.
	CurDir	Returns the current directory.
	MkDir	Creates a directory.
	RmDir	Removes a directory.
Manage files	Dir	Finds a file in a directory.
	Kill	Deletes a file.
	Name	Renames a file.
Position in file	EOF	Returns True if the file cursor is at the end of a file.
	Seek	Sets or returns the position of the file cursor in an open file.
	Loc	Returns the position of the file cursor in an open file.
Read data	Get	Reads data from an open binary or random-access file and places it in a variable.
	Input #	Reads records from an open sequential file and places them in variables.
	Line Input #	Reads a line from an open sequential file and places it in a variable.
Write data	Print #	Writes a line to an open sequential file.
	Put	Writes data to an open binary or random-access file.
	Spc	Inserts a number of blank spaces in a line to write to a sequential file.
	Tab	Skips to a specific column position when writing data to a sequential file.
	Width #	Sets the width of lines written to a sequential file.
	Write #	Writes records, separated by commas, to a sequential file.

Creating Reports with Sequential Files

Sequential files are the simplest type of data file. They consist of text lines, and each line is terminated with a carriage return and line-feed characters. You write data to and read data from a sequential file one line at a time.

Sequential files are easy to view and print. For this reason, they are generally used for reports and text data, such as README.TXT files.

When opening a sequential file, the Open statement has this form:

```
Open filename For [Input ¦ Output ¦ Append] As filenumber
```

The placeholder *filename* is the name of the file to open. The name should include drive and directory information if the file isn't in the current directory; for example, C:\TEMP\TEMP.TXT. The placeholder *filenumber* is a number used to identify the open file in subsequent lines. The Visual Basic FreeFile function returns a unique number that can be used as *filenumber*.

The For clause provides three types of access. Use Input to read a file; Output to write to a file, overwriting any existing file; and Append to write to a file, appending any existing information in the file.

The ReadWords() procedure shows how to open and read a sequential file. ReadWords() opens the file and reads one character at a time, putting each word into a separate array element. When done, ReadWords() returns the new array. An example of ReadWords() follows:

```
Function ReadWords(Filename) As Variant
    ReDim WordArray(1500)
    TempChar = ""
    CharNumber = 0
    ' Get a valid file number.
    iFileNum = FreeFile
    Open Filename For Input As iFileNum
    Do Until EOF(1)
        TempChar = Asc(Input(1, iFileNum ))
        ' Word delimiters
        If TempChar = 32 Or TempChar = 13 Or TempChar = 9 Or _
        TempChar = 10 Then
            ' Start new word unless at beginning
            If CharNumber <> 0 Then
                CharNumber = 0
                WordNumber = WordNumber + 1
                ' If the array is full, make it bigger.
                If WordNumber = UBound(WordArray) Then
                    ReDim Preserve WordArray _
                    (UBound(WordArray) + 500)
                End If
            End If
        End If
```

```
                    Else
                        ' Characters to add to word
                        WordArray(WordNumber) = WordArray(WordNumber) + _
                        Chr(TempChar)
                        CharNumber = CharNumber + 1
                    End If
            Loop
            Close iFileNum
            ' Trim off remaining elements.
            ReDim Preserve WordArray(WordNumber)
            ' Return the array of words.
            ReadWords = WordArray
        End Function
```

The WriteWords() procedure shows how to open and write to a sequential file. WriteWords() opens the file and writes each element in an array to the file as a line. An example of WriteWords() follows:

```
        Sub WriteWords(WordArray, Filename)
            ' Get a valid file number.
            iFileNum = FreeFile
            ' Open the file for writing.
            Open Filename For Output As iFileNum
            For TempIndex = 0 To UBound(WordArray) - 1
                ' Write each word to the file.
                Print iFileNum , WordArray(TempIndex)
            Next TempIndex
            ' Close the file.
            Close iFileNum
        End Sub
```

You can combine ReadWords(), WriteWords(), and SortArray() (described earlier) to create a sorted list of all the words in a file, as shown in the following SortFile() procedure. The SortFile() procedure uses Excel's File Open and File Save As dialog boxes to get the file name.

```
        Sub SortFile()
            ' Use Excel's File Open dialog to get the filename to read.
            WordArray = ReadWords(Application.GetOpenFilename)
            ' Sort the words from the file.
            SortArray WordArray
            ' Use Excel's File Save As dialog to get the filename to _
                write.
            WriteWords WordArray, Application.GetSaveAsFilename
        End Sub
```

Storing and Retrieving Data with Random-Access Files

Though sequential files are easy to use, they aren't well suited for storing and retrieving structured data. *Random access* lets you read and write a file using data structures called *records*. The term *random access* arises from the fact that you use these types of files to get records from any location in the file, rather than one line at a time as with sequential files.

When opening a random-access file, the Open statement has this form:

```
Open filename For Random [Access access lock] As filenumber Len = _
recordlength
```

As with sequential files, the placeholder *filename* is the name of the file to open. The placeholder *filenumber* is a number used to identify the open file in subsequent lines.

The Access *access* clause provides three types of access. Use Read to read a file; Write to write to a file; and Read Write to read or write to the file (this is the default). Use *lock* to control the access other processes can have to the file. Possible settings are: Shared (default), Lock Read, Lock Write, and Lock Read Write. The Len = *recordlength* clause specifies the length of a single record.

Records have a fixed format, usually determined by a Type...End Type statement. For example:

```
Type EmployeeRec
    FName As String * 20
    MInitial As String * 1
    LastName As String * 20
    ID As Integer
    Password As String * 8
End Type
```

The EmployeeRec type definition describes the structure of an employee record. The WriteFile() procedure shown in the following listing uses this structure to write records from a worksheet to a random-access file.

```
Sub WriteFile()
    ' Declare variable with the correct type.
    Dim CurrentRecord As EmployeeRec
    ' Get a filename to open.
    Filename = Application.GetSaveAsFilename
    ' Get a valid file number.
    iFileNum = FreeFile
    ' Open the file for random access.
    Open Filename For Random As iFileNum  Len = Len(CurrentRecord)
    ' Write records from the active worksheet to a file.
    Do
        iCount = iCount + 1
        With ActiveSheet
            ' Stop at the first blank cell in column 1
            If IsEmpty(.Cells(iCount, 1)) Then Exit Do
            ' Read each value into a field in the record
            CurrentRecord.FName = .Cells(iCount, 1). _
            Characters(1, 20).text
```

```
                              CurrentRecord.MInitial = .Cells(iCount, 2). _
                              Characters(1, 1).text
                              CurrentRecord.LastName = .Cells(iCount, 3). _
                              Characters(1, 20).text
                              CurrentRecord.ID = .Cells(iCount, 4).Value
                              CurrentRecord.Password = .Cells(iCount, 5). _
                              Characters(1, 8).text
                              ' Write the record to the file.
                              Put iFileNum , iCount, CurrentRecord
                      End With
                Loop
                ' Close the file.
                Close iFileNum
        End Sub
```

ReadFile() reads the random-access file created by WriteFile() and displays the records in the active worksheet. For example:

```
        Sub ReadFile()
                Sheets(1).Activate
                Dim CurrentRecord As EmployeeRec
                ' Get a filename
                Filename = Application.GetOpenFilename
                ' Get a valid file number.
                iFileNum = FreeFile
                ' Open the file for random access
                Open Filename For Random As iFileNum Len = Len(CurrentRecord)
                Do Until EOF(1)
                        iCount = iCount + 1
                        ' Read record.
                        Get iFileNum, iCount, CurrentRecord
                        ' Display it in the worksheet.
                        With ActiveSheet
                                .Cells(iCount, 1) = CurrentRecord.FName
                                .Cells(iCount, 2).Value = CurrentRecord.MInitial
                                .Cells(iCount, 3).Value = CurrentRecord.LastName
                                .Cells(iCount, 4).Value = CurrentRecord.ID
                                .Cells(iCount, 5).Value = CurrentRecord.Password
                        End With
                Loop
                ' Close the file
                Close iFileNum
        End Sub
```

By default, random-access files are open for both read and write access. This is different from sequential files, which can only be open for one type of access at a time.

Using Binary File Access

Sequential files access a file one line at a time; random-access files access a file one record at a time. Binary-access files access files one *byte* at a time. This is the lowest-level type of access you can use.

```
        Open filename For Binary [Access access lock] As filenumber
```

As with sequential files, the placeholder *filename* is the name of the file to open. The placeholder *filenumber* is a number used to identify the open file in subsequent lines.

The Access *access* clause provides three types of access. Use Read to read a file; Write to write to a file; and Read Write to read or write to the file (this is the default). Use *lock* to control the access other processes can have to the file. Possible settings are: Shared (default), Lock Read, Lock Write, and Lock Read Write.

Binary access is quite powerful and versatile, but you have to be careful. Variables used with Get and Put must match the Len clause exactly. The LoadFile() procedure shown in the following listing uses binary access to load the entire contents of a file into a string variable. You must reserve the correct amount of space in the string before you can write to the variable.

```
Function LoadFile(FileName) As String
    Dim strBuffer As String
    ' Get a valid file number.
    iFileNum = FreeFile
    ' Open the file for binary access.
    Open FileName For Binary As iFileNum
    ' Reserve the correct amount of space in a variable.
    strBuffer = Space$(FileLen(FileName))
    ' Load the contents of the file into the variable.
    Get iFileNum, 1, strBuffer
    ' Close the file
    Close iFileNum
    ' Return the file contents
    LoadFile = strBuffer
End Function
```

The WriteFile() procedure shown in the following listing writes a string to a file using binary access:

```
Sub WriteFile(FileName, strBuffer As String)
    ' Get a valid file number.
    iFileNum = FreeFile
    ' Open the file for binary access.
    Open FileName For Binary As iFileNum
    ' Load the contents of the file into the variable.
    Put iFileNum, 1, strBuffer
    ' Close the file
    Close iFileNum
End Sub
```

LoadFile() and WriteFile() can be used together to tranform the contents of a file. The ChangeFile() procedure reads the contents of a file into a string variable, changes all tabs in the file to spaces, then writes the data back to the file, as in the following example.

```
Sub ChangeFile()
    Dim strBuffer As String
    ' Get a filename to open.
    FileName = Application.GetOpenFilename
    ' Load the contents of the file into a string.
    strBuffer = LoadFile(FileName)
    ' Change tabs to spaces (this procedure is defined earlier)
    TabsToSpaces strBuffer
    ' Write the file back to disk
    WriteFile FileName, strBuffer
End Sub
```

Changing File Attributes

Use the FileDateTime() function to find out when a file was created or changed. The bCompareFiles() procedure compares the dates of two files. If InstallFile is newer than ExistingFile, the procedure returns True; if not, the procedure prompts the user.

```
Function bCompareFiles(InstallFile, ExistingFile) As Boolean
    If FileDateTime(ExistingFile) > FileDateTime(InstallFile) Then
        bCompareFiles = MsgBox ("Existing file newer than _
        install file. Overwrite " & _
        ExistingFile & "?", vbYesNo)
    Else
        bCompareFiles = True
    End If
End Function
```

You can modify the read/write, hidden, and archive attributes of files on disk using GetAttr and SetAttr. The procedure MakeReadWrite() uses GetAttr and SetAttr to change the read/write attribute of a file:

```
Sub MakeReadWrite()
    FileName = Application.GetOpenFilename
    If GetAttr(FileName) And vbReadOnly Then
        SetAttr FileName, vbNormal
    End If
End Sub
```

Changing Drives and Directories

Tip
The ChDir state-
ment accepts a
drive letter, but
doesn't change to
that drive. You
must use ChDrive
to switch to a
different drive.

Both the GetOpenFilename and GetSaveAsFilename methods may change the current drive and directory. You can also use CurDir, ChDir, and ChDrive to keep track of and change directories.

The GetFileName() procedure shown in the following listing returns a file name using the GetOpenFilename method, but retains the current directory and drive settings, regardless of what file was selected.

```
Function GetFileName()
    ' Get the current directory and drive.
    TempDir = CurDir()
```

```
      ' Get a filename (may change current drive/directory.
      FileName = Application.GetOpenFilename
      ' Switch back to the original drive
      ChDrive Mid(TempDir, 1, 1)
      ' Switch back to the original directory.
      ChDir TempDir
      ' Return the filename
      GetFileName = FileName
   End Function
```

Checking Results

When programming Excel, there are many situations when you have to check the result of an operation to determine whether it succeeded. The Is*type* functions let you test result values before you take an action that might otherwise result in an error. Is*type* functions include IsArray, IsDate, IsEmpty, IsError, IsMissing, IsNull, IsNumeric, and IsObject. These and other result-checking functions are described in Table 3.14.

Similarly, TypeName and VarType are useful in determining the type of variant or object that was returned from an operation. TypeName is particularly useful, because not all objects support the same methods.

The following line exits a function if a passed-in argument is not an array—such a line would be a useful addition to the SortArray() procedure:

```
      If IsArray(WordArray) = False Then Exit Function.
```

Similarly, the following TypeName function checks if the active sheet is a worksheet:

```
      If TypeName(ActiveSheet) <> "Worksheet" Then Exit Sub
```

Table 3.14 Result-checking functions

Category	Function or statement	Task
Boolean tests	IsArray	Returns True if a variable contains an array.
	IsDate	Returns True if a variable contains a Date value.
	IsEmpty	Returns True if a variable has not been initialized.
	IsError	Returns True if a variable contains an error value.

(continues)

	Table 3.14 Continued	
Category	**Function or statement**	**Task**
	IsMissing	Returns True if an optional argument has been omitted.
	IsNull	Returns True if a variable contains no valid data.
	IsNumeric	Returns True if a variable contains numeric data.
	IsObject	Returns True if a variable contains a reference to an object.
Type tests	TypeName	Returns the name of a variable's data type.
	VarType	Returns a value indicating the data type of a variable.

Interacting with Users and Applications

The core Visual Basic language provides Beep, InputBox, and MsgBox for alerting and interacting with users. These three items are well used but unexciting staples for displaying and getting simple messages:

```
MsgBox "Yet another message box"
```

The reason the core language provides so little for user-interaction is because Excel provides so much. Excel even provides its own InputBox method! This is the way it should be; Excel gives you the building blocks for creating applications—there should be no need to reinvent the wheel (except for InputBox, of course).

In fact, you're not even limited to Excel's building blocks. Visual Basic lets you reach into the toy chests of other applications. By interacting with other applications, you can integrate tasks like record keeping, invoicing, sales analysis, and annual reports. The rest of this chapter discusses two ways to interact with other applications.

Table 3.15 describes the functions and statements that Visual Basic provides for interacting with users and applications.

Table 3.15 User and application interaction functions and statements		
Category	**Function or statement**	**Task**
Interact with users	Beep	Sounds a beep.
	InputBox	Displays a dialog box to get data from the user.
	MsgBox	Displays a dialog box containing a message to the user.
Interact with other applications	DoEvents	Yields the current process to allow other applications to process events.
	SendKeys	Sends keystrokes to an application.
Run other applications	Appactivate	Activates a running application.
	CreateObject	Starts an OLE application and returns an object you can use in Visual Basic code.
	GetObject	Returns an object from a running OLE application. You can use the returned object in Visual Basic code.
	Shell	Runs an application.

Interacting with OLE Applications

Applications that support *OLE Automation* provide objects that Visual Basic can use from Excel. OLE Automation is part of the Object Linking and Embedding (OLE) standard developed at Microsoft. OLE Automation was developed within the Visual Basic group to make it possible to program one application from another. At this writing, three widely distributed applications support OLE Automation:

- Microsoft Excel, version 5.0

- Microsoft Word, version 6.0

- Shapeware Visio (a business graphics and drawing application), version 2.0

Other software companies are working hard to support this new standard.

Working with OLE Automation applications is a three-step process:

1. Establish a reference to the application using `CreateObject` or `GetObject`.

2. Use the other application's object by invoking methods and properties—the same as you do with Excel.

3. Close the reference to the object by setting it to `Nothing` when you are done.

The following `WordBasic()` procedure shows you how to establish a reference to Microsoft Word, use `WordBasic` methods to create and modify a document, and then close the reference.

```
Sub WordBasic()
    Dim wdBasic As Object
    ' Starts Microsoft Word and creates the object.
    Set wdBasic = CreateObject("Word.Basic")
    ' Microsoft Word starts with no active document, so you must
    ' create a new document or open an existing one.
    wdBasic.FileNew
    ' Insert some text in the document.
    For i = 0 to 2
        wdBasic.Insert "Vigorous writing is concise."
    Next i
    ' Save the document.
    wdBasic.FileSaveAs "EBWHITE.DOC"
    ' Clear the variable. This line quits Word if Word was not
    ' already running when CreateObject was executed.
    Set wdBasic = Nothing
End Sub
```

What You Need to Know About OLE

Computers are supposed to make your work easier, so why do the people who work on them keep coming up with new three-letter acronyms that need to be explained? This is one of the great paradoxes of our time, however it keeps me employed, so I won't complain.

Object Linking and Embedding (OLE) was developed so that you can combine data from different applications in a single document. The terms *linking* and *embedding* refer to where the data is stored. An Excel worksheet might include an embedded Word document—embedded means that the Word document is stored in the Excel workbook. That same worksheet might contain a link to data in another workbook, perhaps stored on a network drive—the linked data appears in the current worksheet, but it is actually stored somewhere else.

You might not want to think about where items are stored, but the distinction between linking and embedding is important. Linked items show live data—if the source changes, you will see that change in the linked object on your worksheet. Embedded objects are local to your workbook—though you can change the data in embedded objects, the changes are only visible in your workbook.

In Excel, you create OLE linked and embedded objects by choosing Insert, Object.

OLE Automation is part of the OLE standard that allows Visual Basic to get at another application's objects. Using OLE Automation, another application's objects seem just like Excel's objects (except, of course, they perform different tasks). You use GetObject and CreateObject to work with OLE Automation objects.

Creating applications that implement OLE and OLE Automation is beyond the scope of this book. If you're interested in doing this, please read:

- *Inside OLE 2,* by Kraig Brockschmidt, Microsoft Press, 1994.

- *OLE Programmer's Reference,* Volume 1 (OLE Objects), Microsoft Press, 1994.

- *OLE Programmer's Reference,* Volume 2 (OLE Automation), Microsoft Press, 1994.

Tips for OLE

When you use OLE Automation, remember these points:

- If multiple instances of an application are running, CreateObject and GetObject return the most recently run instance that is visible.

- An application may quit if the object variable loses scope or is set to Nothing. An application may not prompt you to save changes and work may be lost. For this reason, it is a good idea to use Public variables for OLE Automation object references.

- GetObject without a first argument always fails with Microsoft Word. Most applications support this form of GetObject to return a reference to their object only if they are already running. Microsoft Word does not support this behavior.

■ Most applications start with no documents loaded. Many methods fail unless you open a document.

Interacting with NonOLE Applications

Some applications do not support OLE Automation. Nevertheless, some interapplication communication is always possible. The easiest way to communicate with applications that do not support other mechanisms is by sending keystrokes.

When you send keystrokes to another application, it appears to the other application that the user is typing at the keyboard. For example, this statement sends the keys 4, 5, and 6 as if they were typed at the keyboard:

```
SendKeys "456"
```

These keystrokes aren't sent until your Visual Basic code stops executing or when the DoEvents statement is called. However, you can force the keys to be sent immediately:

```
SendKeys "456", True
```

Passing True for the optional second argument on the call to SendKeys causes Visual Basic to yield, allowing the keystrokes to be processed, before continuing with the rest of your code.

Keystrokes that you send go to the active application. If you do not activate another application, your macro sends keystrokes to Excel. Use the AppActivate statement to send keystrokes to another application. For example, if the Windows Notepad application is running, this statement activates it:

```
AppActivate "Notepad"
```

If the application is not already running, you must start it with the Shell function before you can activate it and send keystrokes to it. For example:

```
Shell "NOTEPAD.EXE"
```

You may want to send characters that you cannot simply type into a string, such as Tab, F1, and Enter. To send these characters, you send the name of the key surrounded by brace characters ({}). For example, to send the keystrokes for Tab, F1, and Enter, use this statement:

```
SendKeys "{TAB}{F1}{enter}"
```

These special keys are listed in Appendix B, "Table of Key Codes."

Chapter 4

Using Objects

You can think of Excel's objects as being similar to the objects you encounter in the real world—bicycles, toasters, and radios are all objects you use to perform tasks. Real-world objects have features, such as color, size, and weight. They also often have uses, such as getting to work, toasting a bagel, or listening to National Public Radio.

Just like real-world objects, Excel objects also have features (called *properties*) and uses (called *methods*). Excel provides 77 individual objects. Each object encapsulates some aspect of Excel. Each of Excel's objects has its own set of properties and methods. Table 4.1 compares some real-world objects to Excel objects (not all of the features and uses of each object are shown).

Table 4.1 Real-world versus Excel objects

Object type	Object	Features (properties)	Uses (methods)
Real world	Bicycle	Color Size Weight Number of speeds	Transportation Recreation Conversation piece
	Toaster	Color Size Weight Darkness setting	Toasting
	Radio	Color Size Weight	Receiving radio broadcasts Tuner setting Volume setting

(continues)

Table 4.1 Continued

Object type	Object	Features (properties)	Uses (methods)
Excel	Application	Caption Height Width Top Left	Calculate Save Quit
	Window	Height Width Top Left	Activate Close
	Range	Height Width Top Left Value	Copy Select

In this chapter, you learn how to do the following:

■ Work with objects using properties and methods.

■ Refer to objects in code.

■ Find the right object to perform specific tasks.

■ Use properties and methods that are common to most objects.

■ Use properties and methods that don't require an object (called *global* properties and methods).

■ Use Excel 4.0 macro functions in Visual Basic.

Using Properties and Methods

A typical Excel object has about 40 different properties and methods. A few of these are common to almost all objects, but most embody some unique aspect of the object. Tables 4.2 and 4.3 show the properties and methods for the Range object (a Range object is one or more cells on a worksheet). Though Range has about 130 properties and methods in all, only about two dozen (shown in **bold**) apply to the most common, everyday tasks.

Table 4.2 Range object properties

Column	Orientation
ColumnWidth	OutlineLevel
Count	PageBreak
Creator	ParentConsolidate
Font	PivotField
Formula	PivotItem
FormulaArray	PivotTable
FormulaHidden	PrefixCharacter
FormulaLocal	**Row**
FormulaR1C1	**RowHeight**
FormulaR1C1Local	ShowDetail
HasArray	SoundNote
HasFormula	**Style**
Height	Summary
Hidden	**Text**
HorizontalAlignment	Top
Interior	UseStandardHeight
Left	UseStandardWidth
LocationInTable	**Value**
Locked	VerticalAlignment
Name	Width
NumberFormat	WrapText
NumberFormatLocal	

Table 4.3 Range object methods

Activate	AutoFit
Address	AutoFormat
AddressLocal	AutoOutline
AdvancedFilter	BorderAround
Application	Borders
ApplyNames	**Calculate**
ApplyOutlineStyles	**Cells**
Areas	Characters
AutoFill	**CheckSpelling**
AutoFilter	**Clear**

(continues)

Table 4.3 Continued

ClearContents	Item
ClearFormats	Justify
ClearNotes	ListNames
ClearOutline	NavigateArrow
ColumnDifferences	Next
Columns	NoteText
Consolidate	**Offset**
Copy	Parse
CopyPicture	PasteSpecial
CreateNames	Precedents
CreatePublisher	Previous
CurrentArray	**PrintOut**
CurrentRegion	PrintPreview
Cut	Range
DataSeries	RemoveSubtotal
Delete	**Replace**
Dependents	Resize
DialogBox	RowDifferences
DirectDependents	Rows
DirectPrecedents	Run
End	**Select**
EntireColumn	Show
EntireRow	ShowDependents
FillDown	ShowErrors
FillLeft	ShowPrecedents
FillRight	**Sort**
FillUp	SortSpecial
Find	SpecialCells
FindNext	SubscribeTo
FindPrevious	Subtotal
FunctionWizard	Table
GoalSeek	TextToColumns
Group	Ungroup
Insert	Worksheet

Properties set or return information about the state of an object, such as the width of a column of cells. In code, properties have the following form:

```
object.property[ = setting]
```

The following line of code changes the column width for cells `A1:B4`:

```
Range("A1:B4").ColumnWidth = 12
```

Methods perform actions on an object, such as printing a range of cells. In code, methods have the following form:

```
object.method [(arguments)]
```

The following line of code prints the range of cells A1:B4:

```
Range("A1:B4").PrintOut
```

Sometimes, the distinction between what should be a property and what should be a method is less than clear. For example, should hiding something be a `Hide` method or a `Hidden` property? For `Range`, the answer is `Hidden` property. For `DialogSheet` objects, the answer is `Hide` method. And for most other objects, the answer is "None of the above" (most objects use the `Visible` property).

It's easier to not worry about the semantic differences between properties and methods and instead focus on the syntactic differences:

- Properties can appear on either side of an equal sign. You can set (assign to) or return (assign from) a property.

- Methods can only appear on the right side of an equal sign. You can only return (assign from) methods.

Setting and Returning Properties Values

There are two types of properties:

- *Read/write properties* have values that you can set or return. For example, the `ColumnWidth` property of a range can be used on the right or left side of an equal sign:

  ```
  Range("A1").ColumnWidth = Range("A1").ColumnWidth + 10
  ```

- *Read-only properties* only return values. For example, the `Column` property can only be used on the left side of an equal sign:

  ```
  CurrentColumn = Range("A1").Column
  ```

> **Tip**
> When a property appears to the left of an equal sign, you are writing to it. When a property appears on the right side, you are reading from it.

In Chapters 5-20, Part II, "Programmer's Reference," the syntax of read/write properties includes the equal sign. For example, this is the syntax line you see for `ColumnWidth`:

```
range.ColumnWidth [= width]
```

This tells you that you can set or return the width of a range of cells.

The syntax of read-only properties does not include the equal sign. The following is the line you see for `Column`:

```
range.Column
```

This tells you that you can't set the column number of a range.

Returning Values from Methods

All methods return a value, but you may not always be interested in the return value. For example, `Select` selects a range of cells and returns True if the selection was successful. Because selecting cells either succeeds or causes an error, you don't usually keep the result of `Select`. Visual Basic lets you "throw away" the return value by not assigning the result to a variable. For example:

```
Range("A1:B4").Select           ' Ignores the return value.
```

Tip

Select omits parentheses, while Address includes them. When you want to throw away the return value of a method, omit parentheses. When you want to return the value, include parentheses.

In some cases, the whole purpose of a method is to retrieve a value. For example, the `Address` method returns the cell address of a range in a specified format:

```
CurrentAddress = Selection.Address(ReferenceStyle:=R1C1)
```

The `Select` method takes no arguments; `Address` takes as many as five arguments. In syntax, arguments are listed by name. The following is the syntax line you see for `Address` in the reference sections of this book:

```
range.Address ([RowAbsolute], [ColumnAbsolute], [ReferenceStyle], _
   [External], [RelativeTo])
```

When you use `Address`, you can include none or all of the arguments shown in the preceding line. You also have the option of including the name of each argument. The preceding example uses the argument named `ReferenceStyle`, but you could just as easily omit the name and indicate the position of the argument instead:

```
CurrentAddress = Selection.Address(, , R1C1)
 ' Include third argument.
```

Tip

Named arguments use := to separate the argument name from its value.

This is called using *positional arguments*. Positional arguments are identified by their position in the argument list, rather than the name of the argument. It's a good idea to always use named arguments for methods that take more than one argument—it makes it easier to read the code later on.

Returning Objects from Methods

Most methods return values, but some methods return objects. Objects require some special treatment. For example, you can't assign an object to a variable using the equal sign. Instead, you must use the Set statement:

```
Set rngOffset = Range("A1:A4").Offset(1,1)
```

Because Offset returns a Range object, omitting Set assigns the error value 2015 (xlErrNA) to rngOffset. This causes error 13, Type Mismatch, if rngOffset is not a Variant, as shown in the following code:

```
rngOffset = Range("A1:A4").Offset(1,1)      ' Returns Error 2015!
```

If the Range contains only one cell, you can omit Set without an error, but the returned value reflects the value in the cell rather than the cell itself, as shown in the following code:

```
rngOffset = Range("A1").Offset(1,1)  ' Returns the value of cell A1
```

This is because the Range object has a default property—the Value property. When you use an object on the right side of an equals statement but don't specify a property or method, Visual Basic uses the default property for the object.

Methods that return objects can also be used as part of any object expression. The following line of code sets the Bold property of the Font object in the Range object returned by Offset:

```
Range("A1:A4").Offset(1,1).Font.Bold = True
```

To learn more about object expressions, read the following section.

Tip
Not all objects provide default properties, and when they do, it isn't always the Value property. It's not a good idea to rely on default properties when writing code.

Referring to Objects

Objects in Excel are organized into a hierarchy. Figure 4.1 shows an abbreviated view of how these objects are arranged.

Each object exists somewhere in the application's hierarchy of objects. At the top of this hierarchy is an Application object. Any changes you make to the Application object affect the entire application. For example, the following line closes all open workbooks and quits Excel:

```
' Close the application.
Application.Quit
```

Fig. 4.1

Excel's object
hierarchy.

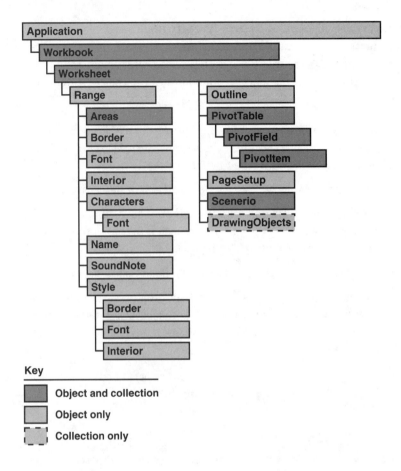

The Application object contains other large objects. For example, you can use the following code to refer to *all* the workbooks that are currently loaded in Microsoft Excel:

```
Application.Workbooks
```

Notice that Workbooks is plural because it refers to a collection of workbooks. A *collection* is an array of objects. For example, the following DisplayNames() procedure displays the names of each of the currently loaded workbooks:

```
Sub DisplayNames()
    For Each wrkCount In Application.Workbooks
        ' Display the name of each workbook.
        MsgBox wrkCount.FullName
    Next x
End Sub
```

If you want to retrieve just one workbook from the collection, you can use the `Item` method. The following code refers to the first workbook:

```
Application.Workbooks.Item(1)
```

You won't often see the `Item` method in code. That's because it's the default method for all collections. In other words, you can omit the word `Item` and still get the same effect:

```
Application.Workbooks(1)           ' Same as previous line.
```

Most collections accept a number or a string with `Item`. It is most common to use the `Name` property of an object to identify it in the collection:

```
Application.Workbooks("BOOK1.XLS")   ' Use name rather than number.
```

Each workbook contains a collection of worksheets, and each worksheet contains a range of cells. In code, referring to a specific cell could look like this:

```
Sub GetACell()
    ' Refers to cell A1 on Sheet1 in the first workbook.
    Application.Workbooks("BOOK1.XLS").Worsheets("Sheet1").Range("A1"). _
    Value = 42
End Sub
```

That's pretty complicated, but here are some shortcuts you can use:

- **Activation.** Visual Basic works on the active item when an object isn't qualified.

- **`With...End With`.** This statement lets you use the properties and methods of a specific object in a single block.

- **Using object variables.** You can use the `Set` statement to create an object variable that refers to a specific object.

- **Defaults.** As mentioned earlier in this chapter, you can omit default property and method names like `Item` and `Value`.

Using the Active Object

When working in Excel, you usually have a workbook open and a worksheet displayed. In this situation, the workbook you are working in is called the *active workbook*. The worksheet that is displayed is called the *active worksheet*.

If you have more than one worksheet displayed on-screen, the worksheet that contains the cursor (where text or data will next be inserted) is the active worksheet. If you have more than one workbook displayed on-screen, the workbook that contains the active worksheet is the active workbook.

> **Note**
>
> Active objects are sometimes said to have focus. *Having focus* means that the object will receive the next user action, such as typing or choosing a menu action.

Visual Basic uses the active workbook and active worksheet if you don't specify a particular workbook or worksheet. The following code selects cell A1 in the active worksheet of the active workbook:

```
Range("A1").Select
```

Use the `Activate` method to change the active sheet or workbook. The following code activates `Sheet2` in a workbook:

```
Sheets("Sheet2").Activate
```

You can tell what sheet or workbook is active by using the activation methods. These methods return the currently active object, as shown in Table 4.4:

Table 4.4 Methods for finding the active object	
Method	**Returns the active**
ActiveCell	Cell
ActiveChart	Chart
ActiveDialog	Dialog sheet
ActiveMenuBar	Menu bar
ActivePrinter	Name of the active printer (not an object)
ActiveSheet	Sheet of any type
ActiveWindow	Window
ActiveWorkbook	Workbook
Selection	Selected range of cells

These methods return `Nothing` if there is no active item of that type. For example, if the active sheet is a module, there is no active cell. To check if an object exists, use the `TypeName()` function. The `ShowActive()` procedure displays the address of the active cell:

```
Sub ShowActive()
    If TypeName(ActiveCell) = "Range" Then
        MsgBox ActiveCell.Address
    End If
End Sub
```

Using the *With...End With* statement

Use With ... End With to set an implied object in a block of code. In the following lines of code, the FormatA1() procedure changes the formatting properties of cell A1 on the active sheet:

```
Sub FormatA1()
    With Application.ActiveSheet.Cells(1,1)
        .Bold = True
        .ColumnWidth = 40
    End With
End Sub
```

With...End With has the following form:

```
With object
    .property statments
    .method statements
End With
```

Any executable Visual Basic statements can be used inside With...End With, but property and method statements can omit the object name. To use a property or method of another object inside With...End With, simply include the name of that object (as shown in **bold** below). For example:

```
Sub FormatA1()
    With Range("A1")
        .Bold = Range("A2").Bold
        .ColumnWidth = 40
    End With
End Sub
```

Creating Object Variables

An *object variable* is a variable that refers to an object. Object variables are different from other types of variables because you must use Set when initializing them. For example:

```
Set rngActive = ActiveCell
```

The variable rngActive contains the address of the object, rather than the actual object. You can declare object variables as specific object types, such as Range, Workbook, or Window, or you can use the general object data type. The following code shows a declaration for a Worksheet object variable:

```
Dim wrkActive As Worksheet
```

If you try to set an object other than a worksheet to `wrkActive`, you will get a "Type mismatch" error (error code 13).

Object variables are useful for keeping track of a specific object. The `ReSelect()` procedure records the current selection in an object variable, changes the current selection, then reselects the original selection:

```
Sub ReSelect()
    ' Declare an object variable.
    Dim rngSelect As Range
    ' Initialize the object variable
    Set rngSelect = Selection
    ' Change the current selection
    For Each rngCount In Selection
        ' Select each cell.
        rngCount.Select
    Next rngCount
    ' Reselect the original range.
    rngSelect.Select
End Sub
```

Finding the Right Object for the Job

The trick to programming with Excel is finding the right object for the task you want to perform. Some choices are obvious, such as using a `Range` object when working with cells. Others are not so obvious, such as using a `PivotTable` to access data stored in a database. For this reason, it important to have an overview of how the objects in the Excel object hierarchy are organized.

The objects provided by Microsoft Excel can be divided into the following categories:

- *Top-level objects* control the Excel application, the files it loads, and the windows it displays.

- *Workbook objects* let you access the parts of a workbook—mainly the different sheets it contains and items that are saved with the workbook, such as routing slips.

- *Worksheet objects* describe the elements in a Microsoft Excel worksheet. These include ranges, embedded objects, and other elements that appear on the worksheet.

- *Charting objects* include objects used to create and modify charts, such as data series, legends, and axes.

- *Drawing objects* include objects that can be "drawn" on a worksheet or chart. These objects are displayed on the Drawing toolbar.

- *Menu and toolbar objects* let you access Excel's built-in menus and toolbars. These objects also let you create your own toolbars and menus.

- *Dialog box objects* let you display Excel dialog boxes and create your own custom dialog boxes that respond to user events.

Top-Level Objects

Figure 4.2 shows the Excel objects that control the appearance and display of the Excel application. Table 4.5 describes those objects and lists their collections (if any).

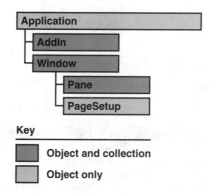

Fig. 4.2
Excel's top-level objects.

Table 4.5 Excel's top-level objects		
Object	**Collection**	**Description**
Application		Controls the entire Excel application and performs tasks such as quitting Excel, getting information about the user's system, displaying dialog boxes, and prohibiting user actions.
AddIn	AddIns	Provides access to extensions to Microsoft Excel. You can write these extensions in Visual Basic.
Window	Windows	A window displayed by Microsoft Excel.
Pane	Panes	One of two possible window regions.
PageSetup		Contains the printer attributes used to print an object.

VBA Programming

Workbook Objects

Figure 4.3 shows the objects that can be contained in a workbook. In Excel, each loaded file (*.XLS) is a Workbook object. Table 4.6 describes those objects and lists their collections (if any).

Fig. 4.3
Workbook objects
hierarchy.

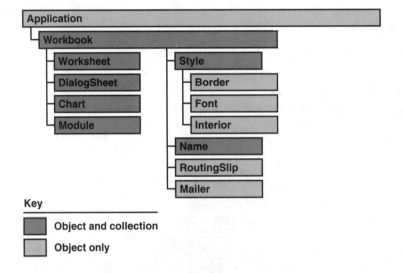

Table 4.6 Excel's workbook objects hierarchy		
Object	**Collection**	**Description**
Workbook	Workbooks	Use workbooks to open new files and perform operations on all the files currently open in Excel.
Module	Modules	A sheet that can contain Visual Basic code. Module objects don't support most of the properties and methods that worksheets do. However, you can use Module objects to archive Visual Basic code as text files and reload those files using Visual Basic.
Name	Names	A user-defined name for range, drawing object, or scenario.
	Sheets	The worksheets, modules, chart sheets, dialog sheets, and module sheets in a workbook.
Style	Styles	A named set of formatting attributes that determine how the contents of a cell are displayed.

Object	Collection	Description
Interior		The interior region of a drawing object.
Border	Borders	The border of an object in a sheet.
Font		Contains the attributes of the text font in an object.
RoutingSlip		Contains information used to send a workbook through electronic mail to one or more recipients.
Mailer		Contains information used to send a workbook through electronic mail using Macintosh PowerTalk.

Worksheet Objects

Figure 4.4 shows the objects that can be contained in a worksheet. Table 4.7 describes those objects and lists their collections (if any).

Some of the objects, like Style, are repeated in other places in the object hierarchy. Style is described in the Workbook hierarchy rather than here because styles are saved with the workbook, rather than with the worksheet.

Table 4.7 Excel's worksheet objects hierarchy		
Object	**Collection**	**Description**
Worksheet	Worksheets	Contains the cells and drawing objects on a worksheet.
OLEObject	OLEObjects	Linked or embedded objects in a worksheet or chart.
Outline		Controls the characteristics of a worksheet's outline.
Scenario	Scenarios	A named set of cells within a workbook.
Range		A set of cells in a worksheet. Ranges may or may not be contiguous.
	Characters	The collection of alphanumeric characters in the value of an object. Use the Characters collection to format portions of the text in an object.

(continues)

Table 4.7 Continued		
Object	**Collection**	**Description**
	Areas	Contains the Range objects in a multiple selection.
SoundNote		Contains audible information that is attached to a cell in a worksheet, such as a voice annotation.
PivotField	PivotFields	A column of data from the source of a pivot table.
PivotItem	PivotItems	A data element from the source of a pivot table.
PivotTable	PivotTables	A table in a worksheet that is used to summarize and view data from other worksheets or external databases.

Fig. 4.4
Worksheet objects
hierarchy.

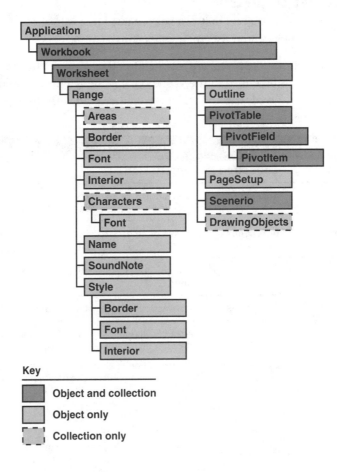

Charting Objects

Figure 4.5 shows the objects used when creating and formatting charts.
Table 4.8 describes those objects and lists their collections (if any).

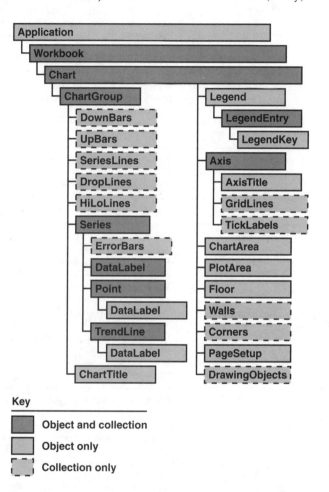

Fig. 4.5
Charting objects
hierarchy.

Table 4.8 Excel's charting objects hierarchy		
Object	**Collection**	**Description**
Axis	Axes	The horizontal or vertical axis of a chart.
AxisTitle		The title of one of the axes in a chart.

(continues)

Table 4.8 Continued

Object	Collection	Description
Chart	Charts	A chart. The `Chart` object is the top-level object among the charting objects; it contains all the other charting objects.
ChartArea		The on-screen area that contains the chart.
ChartGroup	ChartGroups	A set of series plotted as a single chart type in a chart. Simple charts contain one `ChartGroup` object.
ChartTitle		The title of a chart.
	Corners	The corners of a 3-D chart.
DataLabel		A label of a point within a series.
	DownBars	The down bars on a `ChartGroup` object.
	DropLines	The drop lines on a `ChartGroup` object.
	ErrorBars	The error bars on a series.
Floor		The floor of a 3-D chart.
	Gridlines	The grid lines in a chart.
Legend		Contains the attributes of the legend for a chart.
LegendEntry	LegendEntries	The entry in a chart legend for a single series.
LegendKey		Contains the formatting attributes for a legend entry.
	HiLoLines	Contains the attributes for the high-low lines on a chart group.
PlotArea		Contains the attributes of the area on which a chart is drawn.
Point	Points	A point within a series.
Series	SeriesCollection	A set of data plotted as a single color in a chart.
	SeriesLines	Contains the attributes for the lines between series in a stacked bar or stacked column chart group.
	TickLabels	Contains the attributes for the labels that appear along the axis of a chart.

Object	Collection	Description
Trendline	Trendlines	Contains the attributes for a trendline of a series.
	UpBars	Contains the attributes of the up bars of a chart group.
	Walls	Contains the attributes of the walls of a 3-D chart.

Drawing Objects

Drawing objects are those you create using the Drawing and Forms toolbars. The objects on the Forms toolbar are listed with the dialog boxes section of this chapter in Table 4.11, because they are usually placed on dialog sheets.

Figure 4.6 shows the objects used when drawing on a worksheet, chart, or dialog sheet. Table 4.9 describes those objects and lists their collections (if any).

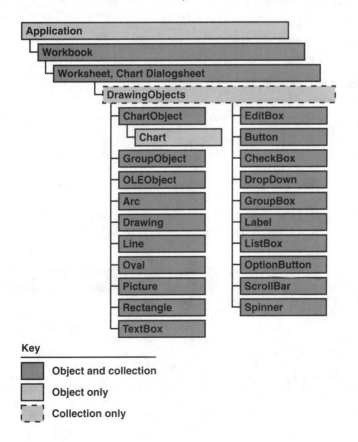

Fig. 4.6
Drawing objects hierarchy.

VBA Programming

Table 4.9 Excel's drawing objects hierarchy

Object	Collection	Description
Arc	Arcs	A graphic arc drawn on a sheet.
Drawing	Drawings	A graphic free-form drawing on a sheet.
	DrawingObjects	The collection of drawing objects on a single sheet.
GroupObject	GroupObjects	A collection of drawing objects that are grouped together using the Group method.
Line	Lines	A graphic line drawn on a sheet.
Oval	Ovals	A graphic oval drawn on a sheet.
Picture	Pictures	A picture or linked object on a sheet.
Rectangle	Rectangles	A graphic rectangle drawn on a sheet.
TextBox	TextBoxes	A text box on a sheet. Text boxes are the worksheet equivalent of edit boxes on a dialog sheet.

Menu and Toolbar Objects

Use the Menu and Toolbar objects to:

- Add items to existing menus and toolbars.

- Remove or change items on existing menus and toolbars.

- Create new menus and toolbars.

Figure 4.7 shows the objects used when working with menus and toolbars. Table 4.10 describes those objects and lists their collections (if any).

Table 4.10 Excel's menu and toolbar objects hierarchy

Object	Collection	Description
Menu	Menus	A menu in a menu bar, such as the File menu.
MenuBar	MenuBars	A set of top-level menu items in Microsoft Excel, such as the Worksheets menu bar.
MenuItem	MenuItems	An item in a menu, such as the Open command in the File menu.

Object	Collection	Description
Toolbar	Toolbars	A built-in or user-defined toolbar in Microsoft Excel, such as the Drawing toolbar.
ToolbarButton	ToolbarButtons	A button on a toolbar.

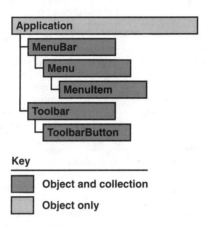

Fig. 4.7
Menu and toolbar objects hierarchy.

VBA Programming

Dialog Box Objects

Use the dialog box objects to display Excel's built-in dialog boxes and to create and display your own custom dialog boxes. Figure 4.8 shows the objects used when creating and displaying dialog boxes. Table 4.11 describes those objects and lists their collections (if any).

The drawing objects listed in this table (those objects that appear on the Forms toolbar) may also be used on worksheets and charts, as well as dialog sheets.

Table 4.11 Excel's dialog box objects hierarchy		
Object	**Collection**	**Description**
Dialog	Dialogs	A dialog box that is provided by Microsoft Excel as a built-in element of the user interface.
DialogSheet	DialogSheets	A sheet containing a custom dialog box.
Button	Buttons	A graphic button on a worksheet, chart, or dialog sheet.

(continues)

Object	Collection	Description
Table 4.11 Continued		
CheckBox	CheckBoxes	A check box on a sheet.
DialogFrame		The border of a dialog box. The DialogFrame object determines the location and size of a custom dialog box.
DropDown	DropDowns	A drop-down list box on a sheet.
EditBox	EditBoxes	Text boxes on a dialog sheet.
GroupBox	GroupBoxes	A frame that groups dialog sheet objects such as option buttons.
Label	Labels	Text that cannot be edited that is displayed on a sheet.
ListBox	ListBoxes	A scrollable list.
OptionButton	OptionButtons	An option button on a sheet.
ScrollBar	ScrollBars	A scroll bar on a sheet.
Spinner	Spinners	A miniature scroll bar on a sheet.

Common Properties and Methods

All of Excel's objects have the Application, Creator, and Parent properties.

■ The Application property returns "Microsoft Excel" for all objects. This property is intended as a way of identifying objects that come from other applications via OLE Automation.

■ The Creator property returns the number 1480803660 for all objects. This is the numeric equivalent of the Application property.

■ The Parent property returns the next higher object in the object hierarchy. The parent of the Application object is the Application object itself.

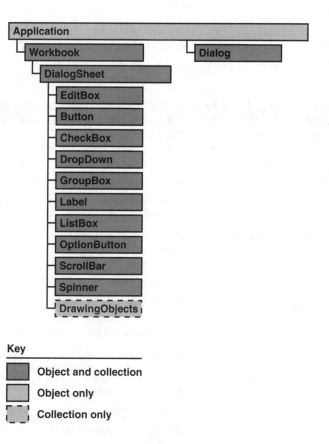

Fig. 4.8
Dialog box objects
hierarchy.

Key

Object and collection

Object only

Collection only

When programming in Excel, the Application and Parent properties are not
particularly useful—you can usually assume that objects come from Excel and
that the identity of the parent of an object is usually not an issue. The Parent
property, however, can be used to explore Excel's object hierarchy. In the
following code, the ShowParents() procedure calls FindParents() to build an
object hierarchy from a selected object using the Parent property:

```
Sub ShowParents()
    FindParents Selection, objpath
    MsgBox objpath
End Sub

Sub FindParents(obj, objpath)
    ' If you reach the Application object, end recursion.
    If TypeName(obj) <> "Application" Then
        FindParents obj.Parent, objpath
    End If
    ' As each procedure returns from recursive call, build the _
      object path.
    objpath = objpath & " > " & objpath
End Sub
```

Besides `Application`, `Creator`, and `Parent`, Excel has about a dozen more properties that appear with many objects. The properties and methods shown in Table 4.12 are useful in most general programming situations.

Table 4.12 Common properties and methods		
Category	**Property**	**Task or method**
General	Activate	Activates an object by switching the focus to it.
	Caption	Sets or returns the text that appears on an object.
	Value	Sets or returns the numeric or string value of an object. This is often the default property of an object.
Appearance	Height	Sets or returns the height of an object in points.
	Left	Sets or returns the horizontal position of an object in points.
	Top	Sets or returns the vertical position of an object in points.
	Visible	True if the object is visible; False if it is hidden.
	Width	Sets or returns the width of an object in points.
Collections	Add	Adds an object to a collection. Add is often used to create new objects.
	Count	Returns the number of objects in a collection.
	Index	Returns the numeric index of objects in a collection.
	Item	Returns a single object from a collection of objects.
Names and titles	Application	Returns "Microsoft Excel."
	Creator	Returns 1480803660.
	Name	Returns the name of an object. Names are often used with the Item method to retrieve objects from a collection.
	Parent	Returns the next-higher object in Excel's object hierarchy.
Printing	PrintOut	Prints an object.
	PrintPreview	Shows a print preview of an object.

Activating and Obtaining Values from Objects

Use the Activate method to move around in a workbook. Activate applies to the following objects:

Chart	Pane
ChartObject	Range
DialogSheet	Window
MenuBar	Workbook
Module	Worksheet
OLEObject	

When you activate an object, Excel displays that object and gives it focus. The following code activates the first sheet in a workbook:

```
Sheets(1).Activate
```

Use the Caption property to set or return the text displayed in an object. The following objects have Caption properties:

Application	EditBox
AxisTitle	GroupBox
Button	Label
Characters	Menu
ChartTitle	MenuBar
CheckBox	MenuItem
DataLabel	OptionButton
DialogFrame	TextBox
DrawingObjects	Window
DropDown	

The following code sets the title in the Excel title bar:

```
Application.Caption = "Now this is power!"
```

Use the Value property to get data from objects. The following objects have Value properties:

Application	PivotField
Borders	PivotItem
CheckBox	PivotTable
DropDown	Range
ListBox	ScrollBar
Name	Spinner
OptionButton	Style

Value is usually the default property for an object. If an object doesn't have data associated with it, Value returns the name of the object. The following code displays the name of the first style in a workbook:

```
MsgBox ActiveWorkbook.Styles(1).Value
```

Changing the Size, Location, and Appearance of Objects

Height and Width determine the size of an object and Left and Top determine its position. All measurements in Excel are in points. A point is 1/72 of an inch.

The following objects have Height, Width, Left, and Top properties:

Application	Drawing
Arc	DrawingObjects
Button	DropDown
ChartArea	EditBox
ChartObject	GroupBox
CheckBox	GroupObject
DialogFrame	Label

Legend	Range
Line	Rectangle
ListBox	ScrollBar
OLEObject	Spinner
OptionButton	TextBox
Oval	Toolbar
Picture	Window
PlotArea	

You can only set these properties for objects that you can normally move or resize in the Excel user interface. For example, if Excel is maximized, you can't change its height or width. In the following code, the procedure HalfHigh() sets the height of the Excel application to half of its former size:

```
Sub HalfHigh()
    ' Make sure Excel is not maximized.
    Application.WindowState = xlNormal
    ' Change its Height setting.
    Application.Height = Application.Height / 2
End Sub
```

Use the Visible property to hide or show objects. The following objects have a Visible property:

Application	DropDown
Arc	EditBox
Arcs	GroupBox
Button	GroupObject
Chart	Label
ChartObject	Line
CheckBox	ListBox
DialogSheet	Module
Drawing	Name
DrawingObjects	OLEObject

OptionButton	Sheets
Oval	Spinner
Picture	TextBox
PivotItem	Toolbar
Rectangle	Window
ScrollBar	Worksheet

Caution

Use caution when using the `Visible` property with the `Application` object—it will make Excel disappear!

The following code hides Excel:

```
Application.Visible = False
```

Note

Excel continues to run while it is hidden, but you can't switch to it or close it, even from the Windows task list. If you find yourself in this situation, the easiest solution is to close the running (hidden) copy of Excel and restart Windows.

Collection Properties and Methods

Almost all collections in Excel have these three properties and methods:

- `Add` creates a new object and adds it to the collection.

- `Count` returns the number of objects that are in the collection.

- `Item` returns an object from a collection using the object's name or index.

In addition, most objects that belong to a collection have an `Index` property that returns the object's order in the collection.

The `Add` method is different for almost every collection in Excel. It is described in the reference section for each object in this book. `Count`, `Item`, and `Index` are very consistent, however.

The following code displays the number of worksheets in a workbook:

```
MsgBox Worksheets.Count
```

This code displays the index of the active sheet:

```
MsgBox ActiveSheet.Index
```

Printing Objects

It might surprise you that Excel doesn't have a `Print` method. That's because Visual Basic reserves the word `Print` and uses it to print to the Debug window. To print an object in Excel, use the `PrintOut` or `PrintPreview` methods. The following objects have `PrintOut` and `PrintPreview` methods:

```
Chart

DialogSheet

Module (has PrintOut method only)

Range

Sheets

Window

Workbook

Worksheet
```

The following code previews the print output for the active workbook:

```
ActiveWorkbook.PrintPreview
```

Global Properties and Methods

The common properties and methods described in the preceding section are available with many different objects. This section is about the properties and methods that are global in Excel. *Global* properties and methods are those that can be used without specifying an object.

So far in this book, you've seen lines of code like the following used without much explanation:

```
ActiveCell.Value = 42
```

It's obvious that the line sets the value of the active cell, but how does Excel *get* the active cell? ActiveCell is actually a global method. That is, you can use the ActiveCell method without qualifying it, as shown in the following code:

```
Application.ActiveCell.Value = 42
```

All global properties and methods belong to the Application object. They are described here rather than with the Application object because they are generally used without the Application qualifier. When programming with Excel, these properties and methods seem like built-in keywords that aren't attached to any particular object.

All of the properties and methods listed in Table 4.13 can be used without specifying an object. Each of these methods and properties are discussed in greater detail later in this book.

Table 4.13 Global properties and methods

Category	Property or method	Task
Activation	ActiveCell	Returns the active cell on the active sheet.
	ActiveChart	Returns the active chart sheet.
	ActiveDialog	Returns the active dialog sheet.
	ActiveMenuBar	Returns the currently displayed menu bar.
	ActivePrinter	Returns the name of the current printer.
	ActiveSheet	Returns the active sheet (may be a worksheet, module, chart, or dialog sheet).
	ActiveWindow	Returns the active window.
	ActiveWorkbook	Returns the active workbook.
	Selection	Returns the currently selected objects (may be a range, one or more drawing objects, or any other set of items that can be selected).
Ranges of cells	Cells	Returns one or all of the cells in a worksheet.
	Columns	Returns one or all of the columns of cells in a worksheet.
	Evaluate	Converts the name of a range to a reference to that range.
	Intersect	Returns the shared cells in two or more ranges that overlap.

Category	Property or method	Task
	Range	Returns a range of cells.
	Rows	Returns one or all of the rows of cells in a worksheet.
	Union	Joins two or more ranges into a single range.
Workbooks and windows	Calculate	Recalculates all open workbooks.
	AddIns	Returns one or all of the add-ins that are available to Excel.
	Windows	Returns one or all of the windows currently displayed for Excel.
	Workbooks	Returns one or all of the workbooks that are currently loaded.
Sheets	Charts	Returns one or all of the chart sheets in a workbook.
	DialogSheets	Returns one or all of the dialog sheets in a workbook.
	Excel4IntlMacro Sheets	Returns one or all of the international macro sheets in a workbook.
	Excel4MacroSheets	Returns one or all of the macro sheets in a workbook.
	Sheets	Returns one or all of the sheets in a workbook (includes all sheet types).
	ThisWorkbook	Returns the workbook that contains the procedure that is currently running.
	Worksheets	Returns one or all of the worksheets in a workbook.
	Modules	Returns one or all of the module sheets in a workbook.
	Names	Returns one or all of the Name objects defined in a workbook. Name objects are defined names, such as those used for ranges of cells.
Menus and toolbars	MenuBars	Returns one or all of the menu bars that are available (built-in and custom).
	ShortcutMenus	Returns one or all of the shortcut menus that are available (built-in and custom).
	Toolbars	Returns one or all of the toolbars that are available (built-in and custom).
Sending	DDEAppReturnCode	Returns the last DDE return code received.

(continues)

Table 4.13 Continued

Category	Property or method	Task
Keystrokes and DDE	DDEExecute	Runs a command via DDE.
	DDEInitiate	Begins a DDE session with another application.
	DDEPoke	Sends data to an application via DDE.
	DDERequest	Receives data from an application via DDE.
	DDETerminate	Ends a DDE session with another application.
	SendKeys	Sends keystrokes to a running application.
Running macros	ExecuteExcel4Macro	Runs an Excel 4.0 macro or worksheet function.
	Run	Runs a Visual Basic procedure or worksheet function.

Using Excel 4.0 Macro Worksheet Functions

Many of the macro worksheet functions introduced in Excel version 4.0 are available Application object methods in Visual Basic. Use these methods as you would any method. For example:

```
x = Application.Fact(10)          ' Return the factorial of 10.
```

The worksheet functions that Excel provides in Visual Basic can be grouped into nine categories:

- Numeric functions

- Trigonometric functions

- Date/time function (only one of these is provided)

- Statistical functions

- Financial functions

- String functions

- Reference and look-up functions

- Database and list management functions

- Result-checking functions

Many of these functions are very useful and can save you a great deal of effort over writing the task using Visual Basic alone. Unfortunately, Excel does not install on-line Help for these functions by default. You may have to run Excel's Setup program again to install the file MACROFUN.HLP.

Table 4.14 contains the Visual Basic numeric functions.

Table 4.14 Numeric worksheet functions	
Function	**Task**
Ceiling	Rounds a number to the nearest integer or to the nearest multiple of significance.
Combin	Returns the number of combinations for a given number of objects.
CountIf	Counts the number of nonblank cells in a range that meet the given criteria.
Even	Rounds up a number to the nearest even integer.
Fact	Returns the factorial of a number.
Floor	Rounds down a number toward zero.
Ln	Returns the natural logarithm of a number.
MDeterm	Returns the matrix determinant of an array.
MInverse	Returns the matrix inverse of an array.
MMult	Returns the matrix product of two arrays.
Odd	Rounds up a number to the nearest odd integer.
Power	Returns the result of a number raised to a power.
Product	Multiplies the supplied arguments.
Roman	Converts an Arabic numeral to Roman, as text.
Round	Rounds a number to a specified number of digits.
RoundDown	Rounds down a number toward zero.

(continues)

VBA Programming

Table 4.14 Continued	
Function	**Task**
RoundUp	Rounds up a number away from zero.
Sum	Adds the supplied arguments.
SumIf	Adds the cells specified by a given criteria.
SumProduct	Returns the sum of the products of corresponding array components.
SumSq	Returns the sum of the squares of the arguments.
SumX2MY2	Returns the sum of the difference of squares of corresponding values in two arrays.
SumX2PY2	Returns the sum of squares of corresponding values in two arrays.
SumXMY2	Returns the sum of squares of differences of corresponding values in two arrays.

Table 4.15 contains the Visual Basic trigonometric functions.

Table 4.15 Trigonometric worksheet functions	
Function	**Task**
Acos	Returns the arccosine of a number.
Acosh	Returns the inverse hyperbolic cosine of a number.
Asin	Returns the arcsine of a number.
Asinh	Returns the inverse hyperbolic sine of a number.
Atan2	Returns the arctangent from x- and y-coordinates.
Atanh	Returns the inverse hyperbolic tangent of a number.
Cos	Returns the cosine of a number.
Cosh	Returns the hyperbolic cosine of a number.
Degrees	Converts radians to degrees.
Log	Returns the logarithm of a number to a specified base.
Log10	Returns the base-10 logarithm of a number.

Function	Task
Pi	Returns the value of Pi.
Radians	Converts degrees to radians.
Sinh	Returns the hyperbolic sine of a number.
Tanh	Returns the hyperbolic tangent of a number.

Table 4.16 contains the date/time function (only one of these is provided in Visual Basic).

Table 4.16 Date/time worksheet function	
Function	**Task**
Days360	Calculates the number of days between two dates based on a 360-day year.

Table 4.17 lists Visual Basic's statistical functions.

Table 4.17 Statistical worksheet functions	
Function	**Task**
AveDev	Returns the average of the absolute deviations of data points from their mean.
Average	Returns the average of the supplied arguments.
BetaDist	Returns the cumulative beta probability density function.
BetaInv	Returns the inverse of the cumulative beta probability density function.
BinomDist	Returns the individual term binomial distribution probability.
ChiDist	Returns the one-tailed probability of the chi-squared distribution.
ChiInv	Returns the inverse of the one-tailed probability of the chi-squared distribution.
ChiTest	Returns the test for independence.
Confidence	Returns the confidence interval for a population mean.

(continues)

Table 4.17 Continued

Function	Task
Correl	Returns the correlation coefficient between two data sets.
Count	Counts how many numbers are in the list of arguments.
Covar	Returns covariance, the average of the products of paired deviations.
CritBinom	Returns the smallest value for which the cumulative binomial distribution is less than or equal to a criterion value.
DevSq	Returns the sum of squares of deviations.
ExponDist	Returns the exponential distribution.
FDist	Returns the F probability distribution.
FInv	Returns the inverse of the F probability distribution.
Fisher	Returns the Fisher transformation.
FisherInv	Returns the inverse of the Fisher transformation.
Forecast	Returns a value along a linear trend.
Frequency	Returns a frequency distribution as a vertical array.
FTest	Returns the result of an F-test.
GammaDist	Returns the gamma distribution.
GammaInv	Returns the inverse of the gamma cumulative distribution.
GammaLn	Returns the natural logarithm of the gamma function, G(x).
GeoMean	Returns the geometric mean.
Growth	Returns values along an exponential trend.
HarMean	Returns the harmonic mean.
HypGeomDist	Returns the hypergeometric distribution.
Intercept	Returns the intercept of the linear regression line.
Kurt	Returns the kurtosis of a data set.
Large	Returns the k-th largest value in a data set.
LinEst	Returns the parameters of a linear trend.
LogEst	Returns the parameters of an exponential trend.

Function	Task
LogInv	Returns the inverse of the lognormal distribution.
LogNormDist	Returns the cumulative lognormal distribution.
Max	Returns the maximum value in a list of arguments.
Median	Returns the median of the given numbers.
Min	Returns the minimum value in a list of arguments.
Mode	Returns the most common value in a data set.
NegBinomDist	Returns the negative binomial distribution.
NormDist	Returns the normal cumulative distribution.
NormInv	Returns the inverse of the normal cumulative distribution.
NormSDist	Returns the standard normal cumulative distribution.
NormSInv	Returns the inverse of the standard normal cumulative distribution.
Pearson	Returns the Pearson product moment correlation coefficient.
Percentile	Returns the k-th percentile of values in a range.
PercentRank	Returns the percentage rank of a value in a data set.
Permut	Returns the number of permutations for a given number of objects.
Poisson	Returns the Poisson distribution.
Prob	Returns the probability that values in a range are between two limits.
Quartile	Returns the quartile of a data set.
Rank	Returns the rank of a number in a list of numbers.
RSq	Returns the square of the Pearson product moment correlation coefficient.
Skew	Returns the skewness of a distribution.
Slope	Returns the slope of the linear regression line.
Small	Returns the k-th smallest value in a data set.
Standardize	Returns a normalized value.

(continues)

Table 4.17 Continued	
Function	**Task**
StDev	Estimates standard deviation based on a sample.
StDevP	Calculates standard deviation based on the entire population.
StEyx	Returns the standard error of the predicted *y*-value for each *x* in the regression.
TDist	Returns a student's *t*-distribution.
TInv	Returns the inverse of a student's *t*-distribution.
Trend	Returns values along a linear trend.
TrimMean	Returns the mean of the interior of a data set.
TTest	Returns the probability associated with a student's *t*-test.
Var	Estimates variance based on a sample.
VarP	Calculates variance based on the entire population.
Weibull	Returns the Weibull distribution.
ZTest	Returns the two-tailed *P*-value of a *z*-test.

Table 4.18 shows Visual Basic's financial functions.

Table 4.18 Financial worksheet functions	
Function	**Task**
Db	Returns the depreciation of an asset for a specified period using the fixed-declining balance method.
Ddb	Returns the depreciation of an asset for a specified period using the double-declining balance method or some other method you specify.
Fv	Returns the future value of an investment based on periodic, constant payments and a constant interest rate.
Ipmt	Returns the interest payment for an investment for a given period.
Irr	Returns the internal rate of return for a series of cash flows.
MIrr	Returns the internal rate of return where positive and negative cash flows are financed at different rates.

Function	Task
NPer	Returns the number of periods for an investment.
Npv	Returns the net present value of an investment based on a series of periodic cash flows and a discount rate.
Pmt	Returns the periodic payment for an annuity.
Ppmt	Returns the payment on the principal for an investment for a given period.
Pv	Returns the present value of an investment.
Rate	Returns the interest rate per period of an annuity.
Received	Returns the amount received at maturity for a fully invested security.
Sln	Returns the straight-line depreciation of an asset for one period.
Syd	Returns the sum-of-years' digits depreciation of an asset for a specified period.
Vdb	Returns the depreciation of an asset for a specified or partial period using a declining balance method.

Table 4.19 lists the Visual Basic string functions.

Table 4.19 String worksheet functions	
Function	**Task**
Clean	Removes all nonprintable characters from text.
Find	Finds one text value within another (case-sensitive).
Fixed	Formats a number as text with a fixed number of decimals.
Proper	Capitalizes the first letter in each word of a text value.
Replace	Replaces characters within text.
Rept	Repeats text a given number of times.
Search	Finds one text value within another (not case-sensitive).
Substitute	Substitutes new text for old text in a text string.
Trim	Removes spaces from text.

Table 4.20 contains the Visual Basic look-up and reference functions.

Table 4.20 Look-up and reference worksheet functions	
Function	**Task**
Choose	Chooses a value from a list of values.
HLookup	Looks in the top row of an array and returns the value of the indicated cell.
Index	Uses an index to choose a value from a reference or array.
Lookup	Looks up values in a vector or array.
Match	Looks up values in a reference or array.
Offset	Returns a reference offset from a given reference.
Transpose	Returns the transpose of an array.
VLookup	Looks in the first column of an array and moves across the row to return the value of a cell.

Table 4.21 lists the Visual Basic database and list management functions.

Table 4.21 Database and list management worksheet functions	
Function	**Task**
DAverage	Returns the average of selected database entries.
DCount	Counts the cells containing numbers from a specified database and criteria.
DCountA	Counts nonblank cells from a specified database and criteria.
DGet	Extracts from a database a single record that matches the specified criteria.
DMax	Returns the maximum value from selected database entries.
DMin	Returns the minimum value from selected database entries.
DProduct	Multiplies the values in a particular field of records that match the criteria in a database.
DStDev	Estimates the standard deviation based on a sample of selected database entries.

Function	Task
DStDevP	Calculates the standard deviation based on the entire population of selected database entries.
DSum	Adds the numbers in the field column of records in the database that match the criteria.
DVar	Estimates variance based on a sample from selected database entries.
DVarP	Calculates variance based on the entire population of selected database entries.
Subtotal	Returns a subtotal in a list or database.

Table 4.22 lists the result-checking functions.

Table 4.22 Result-checking worksheet functions	
Function	**Task**
CountBlank	Counts the number of blank cells in a range.
IsErr	Returns True if the value is any error value except #N/A.
IsError	Returns True if the value is any error value.
IsLogical	Returns True if the value is a logical value.
IsNA	Returns True if the value is the #N/A error value.
IsNonText	Returns True if the value is not text.
IsNumber	Returns True if the value is a number.
IsText	Returns True if the value is text.

Using Macro Worksheet Functions Not Available as Methods

Some worksheet functions are not available as methods. For the most part, these are functions that duplicate Visual Basic statements or functions, such as ABS and TAN. However, some of the functions are very useful—particularly the engineering functions.

To use one of these functions, call it with the `ExecuteExcel4Macro` method. The following code returns the result of Bessel function Kn(x):

```
x = Application.ExecuteExcel4Macro("BESSELK(1, 9)")
```

These worksheet functions are not available as methods:

ABS	COUPDAYBS
ACCRINT	COUPDAYS
ACCRINTM	COUPDAYSNC
ADDRESS	COUPNCD
AMORDEGRC	COUPNUM
AMORLINC	COUPPCD
AREAS	CUMIPMT
ATAN	CUMPRINC
BESSELI	DATE
BESSELJ	DATEVALUE
BESSELK	DAY
BESSELY	DEC2BIN
BIN2DEC	DEC2HEX
BIN2HEX	DEC2OCT
BIN2OCT	DELTA
CELL	DISC
CHAR	DOLLAR
CODE	DOLLARDE
COLUMN	DOLLARFR
COLUMNS	DURATION
COMPLEX	EDATE
CONCATENATE	EFFECT
CONVERT	EOMONTH

ERF	IMSQRT
ERFC	IMSUB
ERROR.TYPE	IMSUM
EXACT	INDIRECT
EXP	INFO
FACTDOUBLE	INT
FVSCHEDULE	INTRATE
GESTEP	ISBLANK
HEX2BIN	ISEVEN
HEX2DEC	ISODD
HEX2OCT	ISREF
HOUR	LCM
IMABS	LEFT
IMAGINARY	LEN
IMARGUMENT	LOWER
IMCONJUGATE	MDURATION
IMCOS	MID
IMDIV	MINUTE
IMEXP	MOD
IMLN	MONTH
IMLOG10	MROUND
IMLOG2	MULTINOMIAL
IMPOWER	N
IMPRODUCT	NA
IMREAL	NETWORKDAYS
IMSIN	NOMINAL

NOW	SQRTPI
OCT2BIN	T
OCT2DEC	TAN
OCT2HEX	TBILLEQ
ODDFPRICE	TBILLPRICE
ODDFYIELD	TBILLYIELD
ODDLPRICE	TEXT
ODDLYIELD	TIME
PRICE	TIMEVALUE
PRICEDISC	TODAY
PRICEMAT	TRUNC
QUOTIENT	TYPE
RAND	UPPER
RANDBETWEEN	VALUE
RIGHT	WEEKDAY
ROW	WORKDAY
ROWS	XIRR
SECOND	XNPV
SERIESSUM	YEAR
SIGN	YEARFRAC
SIN	YIELD
SQLREQUEST	YIELDDISC
SQRT	YIELDMAT
SQRTPI	

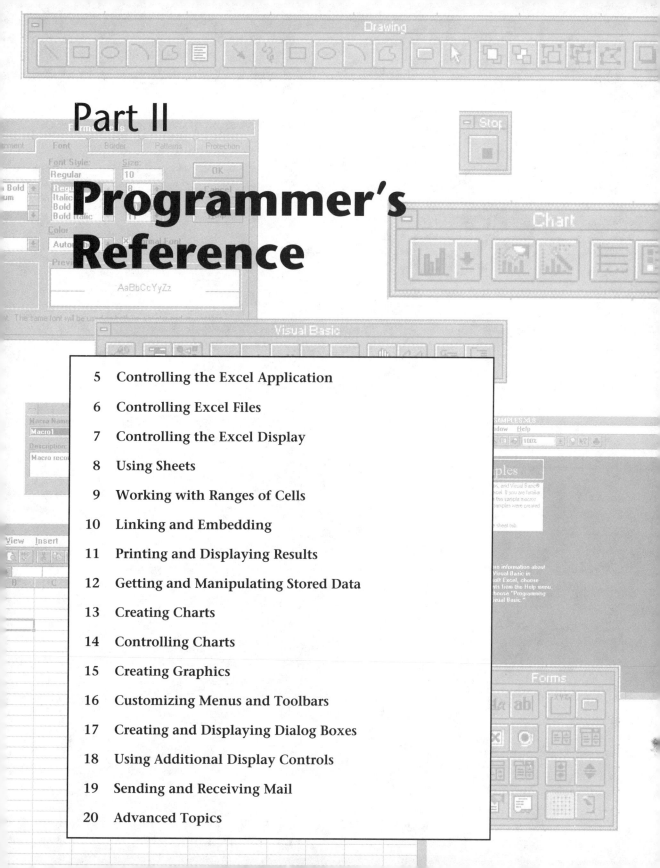

Part II

Programmer's Reference

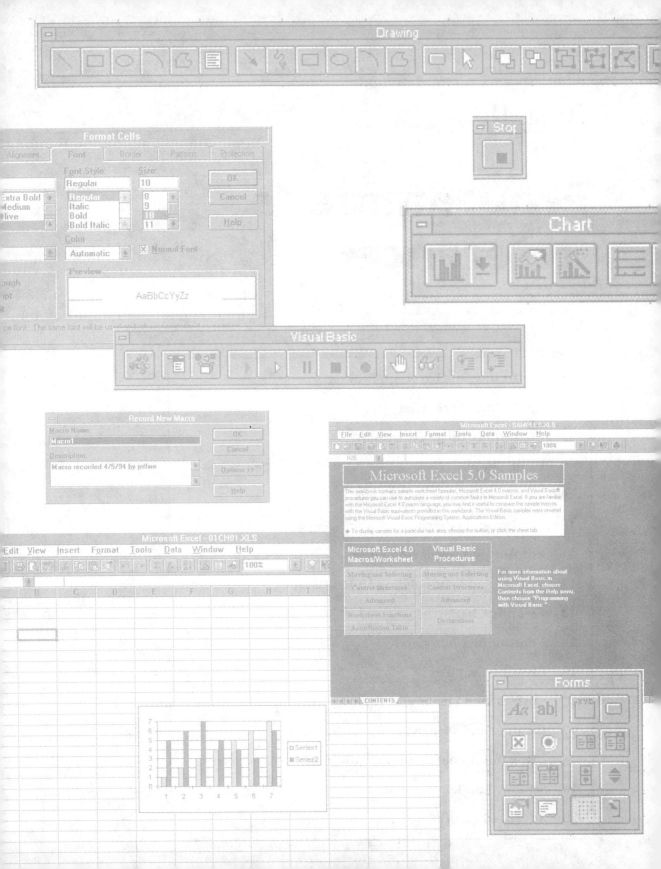

Chapter 5

Controlling the Excel Application

The `Application`, `Workbook`, `Window`, and `AddIn` objects control the main aspects of how Excel starts up and behaves. The `Application`, `Workbook`, `Window`, and `AddIn` objects are top level in that they control aspects of the current Excel session, file, display, and add-in features, respectively. This chapter discusses the `Application` object in detail. In Chapter 6, "Controlling Excel Files," you learn about `Workbook` objects; and in Chapter 7, "Controlling the Excel Display," you learn about `Window` objects and `AddIn` objects.

In this chapter, you learn how to do the following:

- Use Excel to load a file automatically.

- Run a procedure automatically.

- Quit Excel and save changes.

- Display Excel dialog boxes and get information from the user.

- Obtain system settings and modify Excel's option settings.

The `Application` object, `Workbook` object, and `Window` object are shown in figure 5.1.

Fig. 5.1
Top-level objects.

Application object —

Workbook object —

Window objects —

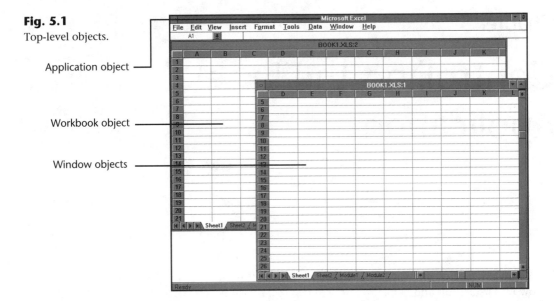

Loading Files Automatically

Excel automatically loads the files it finds in its startup directory. By default, this directory is \EXCEL\XLSTART. You can't easily change the name of the startup directory once Excel is installed, but you can add the name of another directory to search.

Excel always loads the files in XLSTART first, then it searches any alternate startup directory you specify. To add an alternate startup directory, follow these steps:

1. Choose **T**ools, **O**ptions.

2. From the Options dialog box, choose the General tab.

3. In the Alternate Startup File Location text box, type the name of the alternate startup directory to search.

4. Click OK.

> **Note**
>
> Excel loads all the files it finds in the startup and alternate startup directories, regardless of what types of files they are. Excel loads Word documents, text files, and temporary files, and performs any appropriate conversions.

Running Procedures Automatically

In Excel there are some predefined procedures that run automatically when certain actions take place. These procedures have special names that identify the action that triggers them:

- `Auto_Open` runs whenever Excel loads a specific file. Use `Auto_Open` to create a custom configuration for a file. This is a good way to control the display of that file or to prompt for data when the file is loaded. You can also use `Auto_Open` to "lock in" a configuration so that it's always the same on startup—a good idea when configuring a workstation used by many different people.

- `Auto_Close` runs whenever Excel closes a specific file. Use `Auto_Close` to validate data, handle file sharing, or restore previous configurations.

- `Auto_Activate` runs whenever a specific sheet receives focus (becomes the active sheet). Use `Auto_Activate` to control the display of windows. For example, you may want to ensure that a certain sheet is always maximized when it is active.

> **Note**
>
> *Focus* refers to the active window, dialog box, worksheet, input field, or other control(s) that receives keyboard input. It is sometimes referred to as input focus.

- `Auto_Deactivate` runs whenever focus leaves a specific sheet. Use `Auto_Deactivate` to validate data and restore the display if the display was changed during `Auto_Activate`.

Of course, you can use any of these automatic macros to perform any task that you can code in Visual Basic. These suggestions are intended to give you some idea of each procedure's usefulness.

> **Note**
>
> Excel only runs automatic procedures when a user event causes an action. If a procedure causes an action, the automatic procedures only run if you use the `RunAutoMacros` method to "force" the automatic procedures.

Creating *Auto_Open* and *Auto_Close* Procedures

Each file can have one Auto_Open and one Auto_Close procedure. Like any other procedure, these automatic procedures are stored in files. The following example shows typical actions of an Auto_Open procedure:

```
' Runs whenever this file is opened.
Sub Auto_Open()
    ' Maximize Excel.
    Application.WindowState = xlMaximized
    ' Display sheet 1.
    Sheets("Sheet1").Activate
End Sub
```

As soon as you open a file, the Auto_Open procedures for that file become active. If you open two workbooks with different Auto_Open procedures, each procedure runs in turn.

Creating *Auto_Activate* and *Auto_Deactivate* Procedures

Each sheet can have its own Auto_Activate and Auto_Deactivate procedures. This means that a file can contain many Auto_Activate and Auto_Deactivate procedures. To assign an Auto_Activate or Auto_Deactivate procedure to a sheet, define a name for it by following these steps:

1. Display the sheet to receive the procedure by clicking its sheet tab.

2. Choose **I**nsert, **N**ame **D**efine.

3. In the Names in **W**orkbook text box, type a line with the form *sheetname*!Auto_Activate or *sheetname*!Auto_Deactivate. *sheetname* is the name of the sheet as it appears on the sheet's tab. For example, the full line might be called Sheet1!Auto_Activate.

4. In the **R**efers to text box, type the name of the procedure to run. The procedure can be named anything, but it's a good idea to use an obvious name, such as =Sheet1OnActivate.

5. Click OK.

The next example shows the code you might write for the Auto_Activate and Auto_Deactivate procedures assigned to Sheet1:

```
' Runs when sheet 1 receives focus.
Sub Sheet1OnActivate()
    ' Maximize the sheet.
    Application.DisplayFullScreen = True
    ' Turn off gridlines.
    ActiveWindow.DisplayGridlines = False
End Sub
```

```
' Runs when sheet 1 loses focus.
Sub Sheet1OnDeactivate()
    ' Restore the normal view.
    Application.DisplayFullScreen = False
    ' Turn on gridlines if they are available.
    If ActiveSheet.Type = xlWorkbook Then
        ActiveWindow.DisplayGridlines = True
    End If
End Sub
```

Running Procedures Automatically When Excel Starts

You can combine Excel's automatic file loading with the Auto_Open procedure feature to create a procedure that runs whenever Excel is started, not just when a file is loaded. To do this, simply create a file containing an Auto_Open procedure and save it in the \EXCEL\XLSTART or alternate startup directory.

Running Procedures When Other Actions Occur

Many objects in Excel can run procedures when an action occurs. To detect these actions, you assign a procedure name to an event property or method for the object. For example, the following line of code runs the procedure GoHome at 6:00 p.m.:

```
Application.OnTime ("18:00:00", GoHome)
```

Table 5.1 lists the actions that objects can detect. Foe more information on detecting these actions, look up the property or method by name in the reference sections in Chapters 5-20 of this book.

Tip

When there are several files in the startup directory, it's hard to tell which file loads first. It's therefore wise to have only one file in the startup directory with an Auto_Open procedure.

II

Programmer's Reference

Table 5.1 Actions that Excel can detect		
Property or method	**Found with these objects**	**Occurs when**
OnAction	Arc, Arcs, Button, Buttons, CheckBox, CheckBoxes, DialogFrame, Drawing, Drawings, DrawingObject, DropDown, DropDowns, EditBox, EditBoxes, GroupBox, GroupBoxes, GroupObject, GroupObjects, Line, Lines, ListBox, ListBoxes, OLEObject, OLEObjects, OptionButton, OptionButtons, Oval, Ovals, Picture, Pictures,	The object receives focus. An object may receive focus because of a user action, such as clicking, or because a procedure activates the object.

(continues)

Table 5.1 Continued

Property or method	Found with these objects	Occurs when
	Rectangle, Rectangles, Scrollbar, Scrollbars, Spinner, Spinners, TextBox, TextBoxes, ToolbarButton	
OnCalculate	Application, Worksheet	The object recalculates because of a user action.
OnData	Application, Worksheet	The object receives data through an OLE link or a DDE conversation.
OnDoubleClick	Application, Chart, DialogSheet, Worksheet	The user double-clicks an object. The OnDoubleClick property replaces the default behavior of double-clicking the object.
OnEntry	Application, Worksheet	Data is entered in the formula bar or in a cell.
OnKey	Application	The user presses a specific key. The OnKey method takes two arguments: *key* and *procedure*.
OnRepeat	Application	Microsoft Excel repeats the last edit.
OnSheetActivate	Application, Chart, DialogSheet, Module, Workbook, Worksheet	The object receives focus. An object may receive focus because of a user action, such as clicking the sheet tab, or because a procedure activates the sheet.
OnSheetDeactivate	Application, Chart, DialogSheet, Module, Workbook, Worksheet	The object loses focus. An object may lose focus because of a user action, such as clicking another sheet tab, or because a procedure activates a different sheet.
OnTime	Application	A specific time occurs. The time is determined by your system's internal clock.

Property or method	Found with these objects	Occurs when
OnUndo	Application	Executes the specified procedure when Microsoft Excel restores the last edit.
OnWindow	Application, Window	The object's window receives focus because of a user action. The OnWindow property *does not* respond when a procedure, OLE, or DDE event activates the window.

If two objects detect the same action, only one procedure is run. For example, if the application and a worksheet both have an OnData property set and the worksheet receives data, only the worksheet's procedure is run.

Customizing the Excel Application

The Application object represents the running copy of Excel. It is the top-level object for all of Excel. Use the Application object to control the entire Excel application and to perform tasks such as the following:

- Quitting Excel and saving the current workspace.

- Getting information about the user's system.

- Displaying dialog boxes that query the user for information.

- Prohibiting user actions.

- Managing Excel's lists and formats.

Quitting and Saving the Workspace

Quitting the Excel application from Visual Basic is very simple. Use the following line of code:

```
Application.Quit
```

Excel lets you save the names and arrangement of open files in a workspace file. By default, the file is named RESUME.XLW. You can save settings to this file at any time using the Save method:

```
Application.Save
```

Tip
The Workbook object also has a Save method. Use Save with workbooks to save changes to workbooks rather than to workspaces.

Using the Save method makes it easy to pick up where you left off. You can specify a file name with Save—this creates a unique file that you can open to reload all the files in this workspace:

```
Sub SaveSpaceBeforeQuitting()
    ' Open AUTOWORK.XLW from the File menu to reopen all files.
    Application.Save("AUTOWORK.XLW")
    Appication.Quit
End Sub
```

Obtaining System Settings

Many of the Application object's properties return some sort of information about the user's system. For example, the following code displays the name of the user's operating system (Windows or Macintosh):

```
MsgBox Application.OperatingSystem
```

Other properties return arrays of settings. For example, the following code displays all of the international settings on a worksheet:

```
Sheets("Sheet1").Range("A1:AS1") = Application.International
```

System information also includes what files are installed with Excel. Since such lists vary in size and content, you need to do more work to retrieve their values. The following code shows a typical way of displaying values from a property that returns a variable-sized array:

```
Sub ListConverters()
    Dim iRows As Integer, vConverters As Variant, rngConverters As Range
    ' Get the array of file converters.
    vConverters = Application.FileConverters
    ' Check if any converters are installed.
    If IsEmpty(vConverters) Then
        MsgBox "No converters are installed."
        Exit Sub
    End If
    ' Find out how many rows are needed to display.
    iRows = UBound(vConverters, 1)
    ' Display the array in three columns on Sheet1.
    With Sheets("Sheet1")
        .Range(.Cells(1, 1), .Cells(iRows, 3)).Value = vConverters
        .Range(.Cells(1, 1), .Cells(iRows, 3)).AutoFormat
    End With
End Sub
```

Getting Information from the User

The most direct way to get information from the user is to use an input box. For example:

```
vUserData = InputBox("Enter some data.")
```

Excel has its own InputBox method that you can use instead of Visual Basic's. Excel's input box lets you easily validate what was entered. The following code displays an InputBox that accepts only formulas:

```
vUserFormula = Application.InputBox("Enter a date:", type:=0)
```

You can also get information using Excel's Open and Save As dialog boxes. For example, the following code retrieves a file name using the standard Open dialog box, but does not open the file:

```
vFilename = Application.GetOpenFilename
```

Finally, you can display any of Excel's built-in dialog boxes using the Dialogs method. For example:

```
Application.Dialogs(xlDialogOpen).Show
```

The preceding line displays the Open dialog box, but unlike GetOpenFilename, it actually opens the file that the user chooses. See Chapter 17, "Creating and Displaying Dialog Boxes," for more information on using dialog boxes.

Preventing Interruptions by the User

Turning off user edits is useful if you are performing a long task in a procedure and you don't want the user to interrupt it. For example:

```
Sub RebuildDataTables()
    'Turn off user edits (prevents interruptions)
    Application.Interactive = False
    ' Turn off screen updating to speed up the job.
    Application.ScreenUpdating = False
    ' Build tables...
    ' Notify user of what you are doing:
    Application.StatusBar = "Rebuilding tables..."
        ' Code omitted here...
    ' All done!
    Application.StatusBar = "Tables complete! Resume your work."
    ' Turn user edits and screen updating back on.
    Application.Interactive = True
    Application.ScreenUpdating = True
End Sub
```

Be sure to turn edits back on when you're done!

It's a good idea to use the status bar to indicate progress when performing long tasks that lock out edits.

II

Programmer's Reference

Managing Lists and Chart Formats

You use the `AddChartAutoFormat` and `AddCustomList` methods of the `Application` object to create new chart formats and lists. Lists are used by the `AutoFill` feature of Excel. For example:

```
Sub DemoCustomList()
    ' Create a custom list from an array.
    Application.AddCustomList Array("Me", "Myself", "And I")
    With Sheets("Sheet1")
        ' Insert an item from the list in a cell.
        .Cells(1, 1).Value = "Me"
        ' Autofill range A1:A15 with items from the list.
        .Cells(1, 1).AutoFill .Range("A1:A15")
    End With
End Sub
```

Since it's at the top, the `Application` object has many more properties and methods than other objects. A *property* is a value representing the status, behavior, or value of an object for that property. A *method* is a procedure that performs a task, such as setting a property, or opening a file.

Table 5.2 lists the properties and methods of the Excel application. Properties and methods shown in **bold** are described in the reference section that follows this table. Nonbold items are common to most objects and are described in Chapter 4, "Using Objects."

Table 5.2 Application properties and methods

ActivateMicrosoftApp	**Calculation**
ActiveCell	**Caller**
ActiveChart	**CanPlaySounds**
ActiveDialog	**CanRecordSounds**
ActiveMenuBar	Caption
ActivePrinter	**CellDragAndDrop**
ActiveSheet	**Cells**
ActiveWindow	**CentimetersToPoints**
ActiveWorkbook	**Charts**
AddChartAutoFormat	**CheckSpelling**
AddCustomList	**ClipboardFormats**
AddIns	**ColorButtons**
AlertBeforeOverwriting	**Columns**
AltStartupPath	**CommandUnderlines**
Application	**ConstrainNumeric**
AskToUpdateLinks	**ConvertFormula**
Build	**CopyObjectsWithCells**
Calculate	Creator
CalculateBeforeSave	**CustomListCount**

CutCopyMode

DataEntryMode

DDEAppReturnCode

DDEExecute

DDEInitiate

DDEPoke

DDERequest

DDETerminate

DefaultFilePath

DeleteChartAutoFormat

DeleteCustomList

Dialogs

DialogSheets

DisplayAlerts

DisplayClipboardWindow

DisplayExcel4Menus

DisplayFormulaBar

DisplayFullScreen

DisplayInfoWindow

DisplayNoteIndicator

DisplayRecentFiles

DisplayScrollBars

DisplayStatusBar

DoubleClick

EditDirectlyInCell

EnableCancelKey

EnableTipWizard

Evaluate

Excel4IntlMacroSheets

Excel4MacroSheets

ExecuteExcel4Macro

FileConverters

FindFile

FixedDecimal

FixedDecimalPlaces

GetCustomListContents

GetCustomListNum

GetOpenFilename

GetSaveAsFilename

Goto

Height

Help

IgnoreRemoteRequests

InchesToPoints

InputBox

Interactive

International

Intersect

Iteration

LargeButtons

Left

LibraryPath

MailLogoff

MailLogon

MailSession

MailSystem

MathCoprocessorAvailable

MaxChange

MaxIterations

MemoryFree

MemoryTotal

MemoryUsed

MenuBars

Modules

MouseAvailable

MoveAfterReturn

Name

Names

NextLetter

OnCalculate

OnData

OnDoubleClick

OnEntry

OnKey

OnRepeat

OnSheetActivate

OnSheetDeactivate

OnTime

OnUndo

OnWindow

OperatingSystem

OrganizationName

Parent

Path

PathSeparator

PreviousSelections

PromptForSummaryInfo

Quit

(continues)

Table 5.2 Continued

Range	ThisWorkbook
RecordMacro	Toolbars
RecordRelative	Top
ReferenceStyle	TransitionMenuKey
RegisteredFunctions	TransitionMenuKeyAction
RegisterXLL	TransitionNavigKeys
Repeat	Undo
ResetTipWizard	Union
Rows	UsableHeight
Run	UsableWidth
Save	UserName
ScreenUpdating	Value
Selection	Version
SendKeys	Visible
SetDefaultChart	Volatile
Sheets	Wait
SheetsInNewWorkbook	Width
ShortcutMenus	Windows
ShowToolTips	WindowsForPens
StandardFont	WindowState
StandardFontSize	Workbooks
StartupPath	Worksheets
StatusBar	

Application.ActivateMicrosoftApp

Application.ActivateMicrosoftApp (*index*)

Switches focus from Excel to the application indicated by *index*. If the application is not running, then it is started. *index* has these values: xlMicrosoftWord, xlMicrosoftPowerPoint, xlMicrosoftMail, xlMicrosoftAccess, xlMicrosoftFoxPro, xlMicrosoftProject, and xlMicrosoftSchedulePlus.

Note

In the section that follows, parameters for properties and methods that appear in brackets are optional and should be included only if needed.

[Application.]ActiveCell

Returns a Range object containing the currently active cell. If more than one cell is selected, this is the cell in the upper left corner of the selection.

[Application.]ActiveChart

Returns the Chart object of the currently active chart if a chart sheet has focus, otherwise returns Nothing.

[Application.]ActiveDialog

Returns the DialogSheet object of the currently active dialog if a dialog sheet has focus, otherwise returns Nothing.

[Application.]ActiveMenuBar

Returns the MenuBar object of the currently displayed menu bar.

[Application.]ActivePrinter

[Application.]ActivePrinter [= *printername*]

Sets or returns the name of the printer to which workbooks print. Use the PrintOut method to print to the printer.

[Application.]ActiveSheet

Returns the Worksheet, Chart, or Module object of the currently active sheet. If no sheet is active, returns Nothing.

[Application.]ActiveWindow

Returns the Window object of the currently active window.

[Application.]ActiveWorkbook

Returns the Workbook object of the currently active workbook. If no workbooks are loaded, returns Nothing.

Application.AddChartAutoFormat

Application.AddChartAutoFormat *Chart, Name, [Description]*

Adds an automatic chart format to the list of available formats.

Argument	Description
Chart	A chart object on which to base the new automatic style.
Name	A name for the new format.
Description	A description of the format.

Application.AddCustomList

Application.AddCustomList *ListArray [ByRow]*

Adds a custom list to the Custom Lists tab in the Options dialog box.

Argument	Description
ListArray	A range or array that includes the list items. List items must be text; other types are ignored.
ByRow	True if items are a row in the range; False if they are a column. The default is False.

[Application.]AddIns

[Application.]AddIns ([*Index*])

Index indicates the name or number of the AddIn object to return from the Add-Ins collection. If omitted, returns the collection of AddIns that are currently available to Excel.

Application.AlertBeforeOverwriting

Application.AlertBeforeOverwriting [= True | False]

True displays a message box before saving a new file using an existing file name; False turns off this behavior. The default is True.

Application.AltStartupPath

Application.AltStartupPath [= *path*]

Sets or returns the path name of a secondary directory to search for startup files. The StartupPath property sets or returns the name of the primary directory that is searched. The default is Null.

Application.AskToUpdateLinks

Application.AskToUpdateLinks [= True | False]

True prompts before updating when you open a file that contains links; False updates the links automatically, without prompting. The default is True.

Application.Build

Returns the build number of Excel (undocumented).

[Application.]Calculate

Recalculates all open workbooks.

Application.CalculateBeforeSave

Application.CalculateBeforeSave [= True | False]

True recalculates cells before saving a workbook; False saves without calculating. The default is True.

Application.Calculation

Application.Calculation [= xlAutomatic | xlManual | xlSemiautomatic]

xlAutomatic automatically recalculates cells; xlManual recalculates only when the user chooses Calc Now (F9); xlSemiautomatic automatically recalculates all cells except data tables.

II

Programmer's Reference

Application.Caller

Returns the information about how the procedure was started as described below:

Procedure started from	Return value
Another procedure	The Caller property of the calling procedure. Does not return information about the call relationship between procedures.
Formula in one or more cells	A range specifying the cell or cells.
Auto_Open, Auto_Close, Auto_Activate, or Auto_Deactivate	The name of the workbook.
Menu item	An array of three elements specifying the command's position number, the menu number, and the menu bar number.
Drawing object	The name of the object.
Button on a toolbar	An array of two elements specifying the tool position number and the name of the toolbar.
OnDoubleClick/OnEntry properties	The name of the object with the property setting.
Tools Macro dialog box	Run-time error xlErrRef (2023).

Application.CanPlaySounds

Returns True if a sound card is installed; False if it is not installed.

Application.CanRecordSounds

Returns True if a sound card with a recording feature is installed; False if it is not installed.

Application.CellDragAndDrop

Returns True if Excel's drag-and-drop editing feature is on; False if it is off.

[Application.]Cells

[Application.]Cells ([*RowIndex*], [*ColumnIndex*])

Returns a range object containing a single cell, a row of cells, a column of cells, or all the cells in a worksheet.

Argument	Description
RowIndex	The number of the row of cells to return.
ColumnIndex	The number of the column of cells to return. For example, column D is column number 4.

If `RowIndex` and `ColumnIndex` are omitted, `Cells` returns the collection of all cells in the workbook.

The following line of code selects cell D6 on the active worksheet:

```
ActiveSheet.Cells(6,4).Select
```

Application.CentimetersToPoints

Application.CentimetersToPoints (*Centimeters*)

Returns the number of points in the measurement `Centimeters`.

[Application.]Charts

[Application.]Charts ([*Index*])

`Index` indicates the name or number of the `Chart` object to return from the `Charts` collection. If omitted, returns the collection of `Charts` in the active workbook.

[Application.CheckSpelling]

[Application.CheckSpelling] ([*word*], [*CustomDictionary*], [*IgnoreUppercase*], [*AlwaysSuggest*])

Checks the spelling of one or more words in the active workbook.

II

Programmer's Reference

Argument	Description
Word	The word to check. If omitted, Excel checks all words in the active workbook.
CustomDictionary	A string indicating the file name of the custom dictionary to examine if the word is not found in the main dictionary. If omitted, the currently specified dictionary is used. The default is None.
IgnoreUppercase	True ignores the spelling of words in all uppercase characters; False checks the spelling of all words. The default is False.
AlwaysSuggest	True displays a list of suggested alternate spellings when an incorrect spelling is found; False prompts user for correct spelling. The default is False.

The following code checks the spelling of all the cells in a workbook:

```
Application.CheckSpelling
```

Application.ClipboardFormats

Returns a one-dimensional array listing the data formats currently on the Clipboard. Formats are indicated by the following constants:

xlClipboardFormatBIFF	xlClipboardFormatDIF
xlClipboardFormatBIFF2	xlClipboardFormatDspText
xlClipboardFormatBIFF3	xlClipboardFormatEmbeddedObject
xlClipboardFormatBIFF4	xlClipboardFormatEmbedSource
xlClipboardFormatBinary	xlClipboardFormatLink
xlClipboardFormatBitmap	xlClipboardFormatLinkSource
xlClipboardFormatCGM	xlClipboardFormatLinkSourceDesc
xlClipboardFormatCSV	xlClipboardFormatMovie

xlClipboardFormatNative

xlClipboardFormatObjectDesc

xlClipboardFormatObjectLink

xlClipboardFormatOwnerLink

xlClipboardFormatPICT

xlClipboardFormatPrintPICT

xlClipboardFormatRTF

xlClipboardFormatScreenPICT

xlClipboardFormatStandardFont

xlClipboardFormatStandardScale

xlClipboardFormatSYLK

xlClipboardFormatTable

xlClipboardFormatText

xlClipboardFormatToolFace

xlClipboardFormatToolFacePICT

xlClipboardFormatVALU

xlClipboardFormatWK1

Application.ColorButtons

Application.ColorButtons [= True | False]

True if the toolbar buttons are color; False if they are monochrome.

[Application.]Columns

[Application.]Columns ([*Index*])

Returns the column specified by *Index*. If omitted, returns all the columns in a worksheet. The following line of code selects column C in the active worksheet:

```
ActiveSheet.Columns(3).Select
```

Application.CommandUnderlines

Application.CommandUnderlines [= xlOn | xlOff | xlAutomatic]

This is always xlOn in Windows. Command underlines are the underlines that appear under letters in menu items to indicate the accelerator key (for example, the **F**ile menu). On Macintosh, xlOff turns off menu name underlines, and xlAutomatic turns underlines on only when the menu is active.

Application.ConstrainNumeric

Application.ConstrainNumeric [= True | False]

For Pen Windows, True limits handwriting recognition to numbers and punctuation.

Application.ConvertFormula

Application.ConvertFormula (*Formula, FromReferenceStyle, [ToReferenceStyle], [ToAbsolute], [RelativeTo]*)

Returns a string containing the converted formula.

Argument	Description
Formula	The formula to convert, in text format.
FromReferenceStyle	xlA1 if *Formula* uses A1 cell addresses; xlR1C1 if *Formula* uses R1C1 cell addresses.
ToReferenceStyle	xlA1 if the return value uses A1 cell addresses; xlR1C1 if the return value uses R1C1 cell addresses. The default is *FromReferenceStyle*.
ToAbsolute	Specifies whether rows, columns, or both use absolute or relative references in the returned formula. Values are: xlAbsolute, xlAbsRowRelColumn, xlRelRowAbsColumn, and xlRelative. The default is xlRelative.
RelativeTo	The cell to make references relative to. The default is the current selection point.

Application.CopyObjectsWithCells

Application.CopyObjectsWithCells [= True | False]

True if drawing objects are included in selections for cut, copy, extract, and sort operations. The default is True.

Application.CustomListCount

Returns the number of custom and built-in lists. There are four built-in lists, so this number is never less than 4. You can see custom and built-in lists from the Custom Lists tab of the Options dialog box.

Application.CutCopyMode
Application.CutCopyMode [= True | False]

Returns xlCut if Excel is in Cut mode; xlCopy if Excel is in Copy mode. Setting this property to True or False cancels the cut or copy operation. On the Macintosh only, setting this to True also copies the selection to the Clipboard.

Application.DataEntryMode
Application.DataEntryMode [= xlOn | xlOff | xlStrict]

xlOn if Excel is in Data Entry mode; xlOff if it is not in data entry mode; and xlStrict if Excel is in Data Entry mode, but you can't use Esc to exit.

Application.DefaultFilePath
Application.DefaultFilePath [= *path*]

Sets or returns the default file path Excel uses to open files.

Application.DeleteChartAutoFormat
Application.DeleteChartAutoFormat (*Name*)

Deletes an automatic chart format. *Name* specifies the chart to delete.

Application.DeleteCustomList
Application.DeleteCustomList (*ListNum*)

Deletes a custom list from the Custom Lists tab of the Options dialog box. *ListNum* indicates the index of the item to delete as displayed in the the Custom Lists list box. *ListNum* must be greater than 4, since there are four standard lists included with Excel that you can't delete. If *ListNum* is greater than the number of available lists, Excel does not delete a list and returns False.

> **Note**
>
> The Excel documentation says DeleteCustomList returns an error if the list does not exist, but that is incorrect.

Application.Dialogs

Application.Dialogs [(*Index*)]

Returns a collection of Excel's built-in dialog boxes. You can choose from among the dialog boxes using the *Index* argument. *Index* accepts the following values:

xlDialogActivate	xlDialogCopyPicture
xlDialogActiveCellFont	xlDialogCreateNames
xlDialogAddChartAutoformat	xlDialogCreatePublisher
xlDialogAddinManager	xlDialogCustomizeToolbar
xlDialogAlignment	xlDialogDataDelete
xlDialogApplyNames	xlDialogDataLabel
xlDialogApplyStyle	xlDialogDataSeries
xlDialogAppMove	xlDialogDefineName
xlDialogAppSize	xlDialogDefineStyle
xlDialogArrangeAll	xlDialogDeleteFormat
xlDialogAssignToObject	xlDialogDeleteName
xlDialogAssignToTool	xlDialogDemote
xlDialogAttachText	xlDialogDisplay
xlDialogAttachToolbars	xlDialogEditboxProperties
xlDialogAttributes	xlDialogEditColor
xlDialogAxes	xlDialogEditDelete
xlDialogBorder	xlDialogEditionOptions
xlDialogCalculation	xlDialogEditSeries
xlDialogCellProtection	xlDialogErrorbarX
xlDialogChangeLink	xlDialogErrorbarY
xlDialogChartAddData	xlDialogExtract
xlDialogChartTrend	xlDialogFileDelete
xlDialogChartWizard	xlDialogFillGroup
xlDialogCheckboxProperties	xlDialogFillWorkgroup
xlDialogClear	xlDialogFilterAdvanced
xlDialogColorPalette	xlDialogFindFile
xlDialogColumnWidth	xlDialogFont
xlDialogCombination	xlDialogFontProperties
xlDialogConsolidate	xlDialogFormatAuto
xlDialogCopyChart	xlDialogFormatChart

xlDialogFormatCharttype

xlDialogFormatFont

xlDialogFormatLegend

xlDialogFormatMain

xlDialogFormatMove

xlDialogFormatNumber

xlDialogFormatOverlay

xlDialogFormatSize

xlDialogFormatText

xlDialogFormulaFind

xlDialogFormulaGoto

xlDialogFormulaReplace

xlDialogFunctionWizard

xlDialogGallery3dArea

xlDialogGallery3dBar

xlDialogGallery3dColumn

xlDialogGallery3dLine

xlDialogGallery3dPie

xlDialogGallery3dSurface

xlDialogGalleryArea

xlDialogGalleryBar

xlDialogGalleryColumn

xlDialogGalleryCustom

xlDialogGalleryDoughnut

xlDialogGalleryLine

xlDialogGalleryPie

xlDialogGalleryRadar

xlDialogGalleryScatter

xlDialogGoalSeek

xlDialogGridlines

xlDialogInsert

xlDialogInsertObject

xlDialogInsertPicture

xlDialogInsertTitle

xlDialogLabelProperties

xlDialogListboxProperties

xlDialogMacroOptions

xlDialogMailLogon

xlDialogMailNextLetter

xlDialogMainChart

xlDialogMainChartType

xlDialogMenuEditor

xlDialogMove

xlDialogNew

xlDialogNote

xlDialogObjectProperties

xlDialogObjectProtection

xlDialogOpen

xlDialogOpenLinks

xlDialogOpenMail

xlDialogOpenText

xlDialogOptionsCalculation

xlDialogOptionsChart

xlDialogOptionsEdit

xlDialogOptionsGeneral

xlDialogOptionsListsAdd

xlDialogOptionsTransition

xlDialogOptionsView

xlDialogOutline

xlDialogOverlay

xlDialogOverlayChartType

xlDialogPageSetup

xlDialogParse

xlDialogPasteSpecial

xlDialogPatterns

xlDialogPivotFieldGroup

xlDialogPivotFieldProperties

xlDialogPivotFieldUngroup

xlDialogPivotShowPages

xlDialogPivotTableWizard

xlDialogPlacement

xlDialogPrint

xlDialogPrinterSetup

xlDialogPrintPreview

xlDialogPromote

xlDialogProtectDocument

xlDialogPushbuttonProperties

xlDialogReplaceFont

xlDialogRoutingSlip

xlDialogRowHeight

xlDialogRun

xlDialogSaveAs

xlDialogSaveCopyAs

xlDialogSaveNewObject

xlDialogSaveWorkbook

xlDialogSaveWorkspace

xlDialogScale

xlDialogScenarioAdd

xlDialogScenarioCells

xlDialogScenarioEdit

xlDialogScenarioMerge

xlDialogScenarioSummary

xlDialogScrollbarProperties

xlDialogSelectSpecial

xlDialogSendMail

xlDialogSeriesAxes

xlDialogSeriesOrder

xlDialogSeriesX

xlDialogSeriesY

xlDialogSetControlValue

xlDialogSetPrintTitles

xlDialogSetUpdateStatus

xlDialogShowDetail

xlDialogShowToolbar

xlDialogSize

xlDialogSort

xlDialogSortSpecial

xlDialogSplit

xlDialogStandardFont

xlDialogStandardWidth

xlDialogStyle

xlDialogSubscribeTo

xlDialogSubtotalCreate

xlDialogSummaryInfo

xlDialogTable

xlDialogTabOrder

xlDialogTextToColumns

xlDialogUnhide

xlDialogUpdateLink

xlDialogVbaInsertFile

xlDialogVbaMakeAddin

xlDialogVbaProcedureDefinition

xlDialogView3d

xlDialogWindowMove

xlDialogWindowSize

xlDialogWorkbookAdd

xlDialogWorkbookCopy

xlDialogWorkbookInsert

xlDialogWorkbookMove

xlDialogWorkbookName

xlDialogWorkbookNew

xlDialogWorkbookOptions

xlDialogWorkbookProtect

xlDialogWorkbookTabSplit

xlDialogWorkbookUnhide

xlDialogWorkgroup

xlDialogWorkspace

xlDialogZoom

[Application.]DialogSheets

[Application.]DialogSheets ([*Index*])

Index indicates the name or number of the DialogSheet object to return from the DialogSheets collection. If omitted, returns the collection of DialogSheets in the active workbook.

Application.DisplayAlerts

Application.DisplayAlerts [= True | False]

True if Excel displays messages to the user; False if messages are not displayed.

Application.DisplayClipboardWindow

Application.DisplayClipboardWindow [= True | False]

For the Macintosh only. True if the Clipboard window is displayed; False if it is not displayed.

Application.DisplayExcel4Menus

Application.DisplayExcel4Menus [= True | False]

True if Excel version 4.0 menus are displayed; False if version 5.0 menus are displayed.

Application.DisplayFormulaBar

Application.DisplayFormulaBar [= True | False]

True if the formula bar is displayed; False if it is not displayed.

Application.DisplayFullScreen

Application.DisplayFullScreen [= True | False]

True if Excel is displayed full screen (the full-screen item on the View menu); False if it is not displayed full screen.

Application.DisplayInfoWindow

Application.DisplayInfoWindow [= True | False]

True if the Info window is displayed; False if the window is not displayed. The Info window displays notes and formulas for a cell.

Application.DisplayNoteIndicator

Application.DisplayNoteIndicator [= True | False]

True if the note indicator is displayed; False if it is not displayed. The note indicators appear as small dots in the upper right corner of a cell.

Application.DisplayRecentFiles

Application.DisplayRecentFiles [= True | False]

True if recently opened files are displayed on the file menu; False if they are not displayed. The default is True.

Application.DisplayScrollBars

Application.DisplayScrollBars [= True | False]

True if horizontal and vertical scroll bars are displayed; False if they are not displayed. The default is True.

Application.DisplayStatusBar

Application.DisplayStatusBar [= True | False]

True if the status bar at the bottom of the screen is displayed; False if it is not displayed. The default is True.

Application.DoubleClick

Performs a double-click at the current selection point.

Application.EditDirectlyInCell

Application.EditDirectlyInCell [= True | False]

True if you can edit directly in cells; False if you cannot edit directly in cells. The default is True. Editing in a cell means that you can select portions of the data in the cell from the worksheet, rather than from the formula bar.

Application.EnableCancelKey

Application.EnableCancelKey [= xlDisabled | xlErrorHandler | xlInterrupt]

`xlDisabled` prevents the user from stopping a running Visual Basic procedure by pressing Ctrl+Break, Command+Period (Macintosh), or Esc. `xlErrorHandler` causes these key combinations to invoke a trappable error (error code 18). The default is `xlInterrupt`.

Application.EnableTipWizard

Application.EnableTipWizard [= True | False]

True if the TipWizard is running; False if it is not running. The default is True.

[Application.]Evaluate

[Application.]Evaluate (*name*)

Returns the `Range` object specified by *name*. The argument *name* may be an address or a named range. The `Evaluate` method is the same as enclosing a name in square brackets. The following code sets the value of cell A1:

```
[A1].Value = 42
```

[Application.]Excel4IntlMacroSheets

[Application.]Excel4IntlMacroSheets ([*Index*])

Index indicates the name or number of the `Excel4IntlMacroSheet` object to return from the `Excel4IntlMacroSheets` collection. If omitted, returns the collection of `Excel4IntlMacroSheets` in the active workbook.

[Application.]Excel4MacroSheets

[Application.]Excel4MacroSheets ([*Index*])

Index indicates the name or number of the `Excel4MacroSheet` object to return from the `Excel4MacroSheets` collection. If omitted, returns the collection of `Excel4MacroSheets` in the active workbook.

II

Programmer's Reference

Application.FileConverters

Returns an array listing the installed file converters. The array has two dimensions. The upper bound of the first dimension corresponds to the number of converters that are installed. The second dimension has three elements: the name of the converter, the path and file name of the converter, and the file extension or file type (Macintosh) of the files to convert.

Returns Empty if no converters are installed.

Application.FindFile

Displays the Excel Find File dialog box.

Application.FixedDecimal

Application.FixedDecimal [= True | False]

True formats subsequent entries as fixed-decimal numbers; False turns off this behavior. The number of decimal places is determined by the FixedDecimalPlaces property. The default is False.

Application.FixedDecimalPlaces

Application.FixedDecimalPlaces [= *number*]

Sets or returns the number of decimal places used when the FixedDecimal property is set to True. The default is 2.

Application.GetCustomListContents

Application.GetCustomListContents (*ListNum*)

Returns an array containing the elements of a custom list from the Custom Lists tab of the Options dialog box. *ListNum* indicates the index of the item to delete as displayed in the Custom Lists list box. *ListNum* 1 to 4 indicate the four standard lists included with Excel. If *ListNum* is greater than the number of available lists, GetCustomListContents returns False.

> **Note**
>
> The Excel documentation says GetCustomListContents returns an error if the list does not exist, but that is not correct.

Application.GetCustomListNum

Application.GetCustomListNum (*ListArray*)

Returns the list number (`ListNum`) of a custom or built-in list. `ListArray` is an array or range containing all items on the list. The comparison ignores case. Returns False if the list is not found.

Application.GetOpenFilename

Application.GetOpenFilename ([*FileFilter*], [*FilterIndex*], [*Title*], [*ButtonText*])

Displays Excel's Open File dialog box and returns a file name; does not open the selected file in Excel.

Argument	Description
FileFilter	A file filter string to use in the List Files of Type drop-down list in the dialog box.
	In Windows, each filter has two parts: the text to display and the type of files to display. To display multiple types of files, separate the types with semicolons; for example, "Text files, *.txt, Excel files, *.xls;*.xla;*.xl5." The default is "All files (*.*), *.*."
	In Macintosh, this string is made up of the special Macintosh file type codes separated by commas; for example, "TEXT,XLA,XLS4." The default is all file types.
FilterIndex	The index of the FileFilter to use by default when the dialog box is displayed (Windows only, ignored by Macintosh). The default is 1.
Title	The title to be displayed in the dialog box. The default is Open.
ButtonText	The text to be displayed on the Open button in the dialog box (Macintosh only). The default is Open.

Application.GetSaveAsFilename

Application.GetSaveAsFilename ([*InitialFilename*], [*FileFilter*], [*FilterIndex*], [*Title*], [*ButtonText*])

Displays Excel's File Save As dialog box and returns the file name entered by the user. Does not save the file.

Argument	Description
InitialFilename	The name to be displayed in the File Name text box in the dialog box. The default is the active workbook name.
FileFilter	A file filter string to use in the List Files of Type drop-down list in the dialog box.
	In Windows, each filter has two parts: the text to display and the type of files to display. To display multiple types of files, separate the types with semicolons; for example, "Text files, *.txt, Excel files, *.xls;*.xla;*.xl5." The default is "All files (*.*), *.*."
	In Macintosh, this string is made up of the special Macintosh file type codes separated by commas; for example, "TEXT,XLA,XLS4." The default is all file types.
FilterIndex	The index of the FileFilter to use by default when the dialog box is displayed (Windows only, ignored by Macintosh). The default is 1.
Title	The title to be displayed in the dialog box. The default is Save As.
ButtonText	The text to be displayed on the Open button in the dialog box (Macintosh only). The default is Open.

Application.Goto

Application.Goto *Reference* [*Scroll*]

Moves the selection point to the range or Visual Basic procedure indicated by *Reference*.

Argument	Description
Reference	The range object or the name of the procedure to go to. For example: `Sheets("Sheet1").Range(Cells(1,1), Cells(2,2))` selects cells A1:B2 on Sheet 1; `Auto_Open` displays the `Auto_Open` procedure and moves the cursor to the second line of the procedure; and "Inventory Data" selects the range named Inventory Data. If the range or name does not exist, `Goto` returns an error.
Scroll	True if the window should scroll so the selection is displayed in the upper right-hand corner of the window. False if the selection should be displayed anywhere in the window. The default is True.

[Application.]Help

[Application.]Help ([*HelpFile*], [*HelpContextID*])

Displays topics from on-line Help files (*.HLP).

Argument	Description
HelpFile	The name of the Help file to display.
HelpContextID	The context ID of the topic to display.

The following code displays the worksheet functions index from Excel's Visual Basic Help file:

```
Application.Help "vba_xl.hlp", &H18061
```

When the Help file is displayed, Help has focus but the Excel procedure continues to execute.

Application.IgnoreRemoteRequests

Application.IgnoreRemoteRequests [= True | False]

True prevents Excel from responding to DDE requests; False accepts DDE requests. The default is False.

Application.InchesToPoints

Application.InchesToPoints (*Inches*)

Returns the number of points in the measurement *Inches*.

Application.InputBox

Application.InputBox (*Prompt,*[*Title*], [*Default*], [*Left*], [*Top*], [*HelpFile*], [*HelpContextID*], [*Type*])

Displays an input box and returns the data entered by the user. False if the user chooses Cancel. Differs from the InputBox statement by offering data validation for Excel data types through the *Type* argument.

II

Programmer's Reference

Argument	Description
Prompt	The message to display as a prompt to the user.
Title	The title to display in the input box. The default is " ".
Default	The value to return to if the user does not enter data. The default is " ".
Left	The horizontal position of the input box on the screen. Measured in points from the left edge of the screen to the right edge of the input box.
Top	The vertical position of the input box on the screen. Measured in points from the top edge of the screen to the top edge of the input box.
HelpFile	The name of a help file containing a help topic for this input box.
HelpContextID	The context ID of a help topic to display for this input box. If *HelpFile* and *HelpContextID* are present, the input box appears with a Help button. Otherwise, no Help button is displayed.
Type	A number indicating the type of Excel data returned from the input box:

Number	Return value
0	Formula
1	Number
2	Text
4	Boolean (True/False)
8	Array of data from a range of cells or reference to cells
16	Error value
64	Array of data from a range of cells

If the user enters data that can't be interpreted as the specified type, Excel displays a message box and lets the user try again. The default is 2 (Text).

To accept multiple types of data, add the *Type* values together. For example:

```
vAnswer = Application.InputBox(Prompt:="Enter a number or string:",
Type:=1+2)
```

Using *Type* 8 or 64 returns arrays when used with the assignment operator (=). For example:

```
Sub IterateOverCells()
     Dim iColumns As Integer, iRows As Integer, i As Integer, j As
Integer, vAnswer As Variant
     vAnswer = Application.InputBox(Prompt:="Enter a range in A1
format:", Type:=8)
     If IsArray(vAnswer) Then
          iRows = UBound(vAnswer, 1)
          iColumns = UBound(vAnswer, 2)
          'Select each cell in range, one at a time.
          For i = 1 To iRows
              For j = 1 To iColumns
                   ' This is where you'd perform operations on
                     each cell.
                   ActiveSheet.Cells(i, j).Select
              Next j
          Next i
     ElseIf vAnswer = False Then
          ' User chose Cancel, so exit.
          Exit Sub
     Else
          ' Input was a single-cell range. vAnswer is the value of
            that cell.
          iRows = 0
          iColumns = 0
     End If
End Sub
```

To return a reference to a range of cells, use the Set statement and *Type* 8. You must trap errors when doing this, since the user may choose Cancel. Cancel would return False rather than a Range object, which would cause error 424 (object required) on the Set statement. There is no other way to test for Cancel in this case. For example:

```
Sug SelectReference()
     ' Trap possible error if user chooses Cancel.
     On Error Resume Next
     ' Set the variable to refer to the range returned by InputBox.
     Set vResult = Application.InputBox(Prompt:="Enter a range in
A1 format:", Type:=8)
     ' User pressed cancel.
     If Err <> 0 Then
          ' Turn off error trapping.
          On Error Goto 0
          ' Exit procedure.
          Exit Sub
     End If
     ' Turn off error trapping.
     On Error Goto 0
     ' Select the range.
     vResult.Select
End Sub
```

II

Programmer's Reference

Application.Interactive

Application.Interactive [= True | False]

True prevents Excel from responding to user actions such as typing or clicking the mouse; False accepts user actions. The default is False.

Application.International

Returns a single-dimension array containing 45 elements. These elements indicate international settings.

Array element	Indicates
xlCountryCode	Number indicating the country version.
xlCountrySetting	Number indicating the current country setting in the Microsoft Windows Control Panel, or the country number as determined by your Apple system software.
xlDecimalSeparator	Decimal separator.
xlThousandsSeparator	Zero or thousands separator.
xlListSeparator	List separator.
xlUpperCaseRowLetter	Uppercase row letter (for R1C1 references).
xlUpperCaseColumnLetter	Uppercase column letter.
xlLowerCaseRowLetter	Lowercase row letter.
xlLowerCaseColumnLetter	Lowercase column letter.
xlLeftBracket	Character used instead of the left bracket ([) in R1C1 relative references.
xlRightBracket	Character used instead of the right bracket (]).
xlLeftBrace	Character used instead of the left brace ({) in array literals.
xlRightBrace	Character used instead of the right brace (}).
xlColumnSeparator	Character used to separate columns in array literals.
xlRowSeparator	Character used to separate rows.
xlAlternateArraySeparator	Alternate array item separator to use if the current array separator is the same as the decimal separator.

Array element	Indicates
xlDateSeparator	Date separator (/ in U.S.).
xlTimeSeparator	Time separator (: in U.S.).
xlYearCode	Year symbol in number formats (y in U.S.).
xlMonthCode	Month symbol (m).
xlDayCode	Day symbol (d).
xlHourCode	Hour symbol (h).
xlMinuteCode	Minute symbol (m).
xlSecondCode	Second symbol (s).
xlCurrencyCode	Currency symbol ($).
xlGeneralFormatName	Name of the general number format.
xlCurrencyDigits	Number of decimal digits to use in currency formats.
xlCurrencyNegative	Indicates the currency format for negative currencies: 0 = ($x) or (x$) 1 = -$x or -x$ 2 = $-x or x-$ 3 = $x- or x$ Note: The position of the currency symbol is determined by xlCurrencyBefore.
xlNoncurrencyDigits	Number of decimal digits to use in noncurrency formats.
xlMonthNameChars	Number of characters to use in month names.
xlWeekdayNameChars	Number of characters to use in weekday names.
xlDateOrder	Indicates the date order: 0 = month-day-year 1 = day-month-year 2 = year-month-day
xl24HourClock	True if using 24-hour time; False if using 12-hour time.
xlNonEnglishFunctions	True if displaying functions in language other than English.

II

Programmer's Reference

(continues)

Array element	Indicates
xlMetric	True if using the metric system; False if using the English measurement system.
xlCurrencySpaceBefore	True if adding a space before the currency symbol.
xlCurrencyBefore	True if the currency symbol precedes the currency values; False if the currency symbol follows the currency values.
xlCurrencyMinusSign	True if using a minus sign for negative numbers; False if using parentheses.
xlCurrencyTrailingZeros	True if trailing zeros are displayed for zero currency values.
xlCurrencyLeadingZeros	True if leading zeros are displayed for zero currency values.
xlMonthLeadingZero	True if a leading zero is displayed in months when months are displayed as numbers.
xlDayLeadingZero	True if a leading zero is displayed in days.
xl4DigitYears	True if using 4-digit years; False if using 2-digit years.
xlMDY	True if the date order is Month-Day-Year when dates are displayed in the long form; False if the date order is Day-Month-Year.
xlTimeLeadingZero	True if the leading zero is shown in the time.

[Application.]Intersect

[Application.]Intersect (*Arg1*, *Arg2*, [*Argn...*])

Returns the Range object containing the overlapping region of two or more ranges.

Argument	Description
Arg1	The first Range object to intersect.
Arg2	The second Range object to intersect.
Argn	Any number of additional Range objects to intersect.

Application.Iteration

Application.Iteration [= True | False]

True causes Excel to use iteration to calculate formulas that refer to themselves (a circular reference); False causes an error on circular references. The default is False.

Excel uses the MaxChange and MaxIterations properties to control the number of calculations performed during iteration.

Application.LargeButtons

Application.LargeButtons [= True | False]

True if Excel's toolbar buttons are large (about twice the standard size); False if toolbar buttons are standard size. The default is False.

Application.LibraryPath

Returns the path of the directory Excel searches when looking for add-ins at startup.

Application.MailLogoff

Ends a MAPI Mail session. If no MAPI session exists, causes an error.

Application.MailLogon

Application.MailLogon ([*Name*], [*Password*], [*DownloadNewMail*])

Closes any existing MAPI mail sessions and creates new session, starting the Microsoft Mail spooler. Returns True if mail is started successfully; False otherwise.

Argument	Description
Name	User name for the mail session.
Password	User password.
DownloadNewMail	True downloads new mail immediately. The default is False.

Application.MailSession

Returns a string containing the hexadecimal MAPI identification number.
Returns Null if there is no active session.

Application.MailSystem

Returns the mail system installed on your machine: `xlNoMailSystem`, `xlMAPI`,
or `xlPowerTalk`.

Application.MathCoprocessorAvailable

Returns True if a math coprocessor is installed on your machine; False if it is
not installed.

Application.MaxChange

Application.MaxChange [= *number*]

The maximum amount of change allowed in resolving circular references
when using iteration. Excel stops recalculating a circular reference when the
amount of change between the old and new values is less than `MaxChange`, or
when the number of calculations exceeds `MaxIterations`.

Application.MaxIterations

Application.MaxIterations [= *number*]

The maximum number of calculations performed when resolving circular
references using iteration.

Application.MemoryFree

Returns the number of bytes of memory available for Excel to use.

Application.MemoryTotal

Returns the number of bytes of memory installed on your system.

Application.MemoryUsed

Returns the number of bytes of memory currently used by Excel. This number
does not include the amount of memory used by DLLs that Excel uses.

[Application.]MenuBars
[Application.]MenuBars (*Index*)

Index indicates the name or number of the MenuBar object to return from the MenuBars collection. If omitted, returns the collection of MenuBars in the active workbook. Built-in menu bars are identified by the following constants:

Constant	Returns this menu bar
xlWorksheet	Worksheet, macro sheet, and dialog sheet
xlChart	Chart
xlModule	Visual Basic module
xlNoDocuments	No documents open
xlInfo	Info Window
"Shortcut Menus 1"	General worksheet, module, and toolbar shortcut menus
"Shortcut Menus 2"	Drawing object and dialog sheet shortcut menus
"Shortcut Menus 3"	Charting shortcut menus
xlInfo	Info Window
xlWorksheet4	Excel version 4.0 worksheet menu bar
xlChart4	Excel version 4.0 chart menu bar
xlWorksheetShort	Excel version 3.0 short worksheet menu
xlChartShort	Excel version 3.0 short chart menu

[Application.]Modules
[Application.]Modules (*Index*)

Index indicates the name or number of the Module object to return from the Modules collection. If omitted, returns the collection of Modules in the active workbook.

Application.MouseAvailable

Returns True if a mouse is installed; False if it is not installed.

Application.MoveAfterReturn

Application.MoveAfterReturn [= True | False]

True moves the selection off the current cell when the user presses Enter; False does not move the selection.

[Application.]Names

[Application.]Names (*Index*)

Index indicates the name or number of the Name object to return from the Names collection. If omitted, returns the collection of Names in the active workbook.

Application.NextLetter

Opens the oldest unread message in the In Tray (Macintosh with PowerTalk mail only).

Application.OnCalculate

Application.OnCalculate [= *procedurename*]

Sets or returns the name of a procedure to run when worksheets recalculate. Setting this property for a worksheet overrides the Application setting.

Application.OnData

Application.OnData [= *procedurename*]

Sets or returns the name of a procedure to run when Excel receives DDE or OLE-linked data. Setting this property for a worksheet overrides the Application setting.

Application.OnDoubleClick

Application.OnDoubleClick [= *procedurename*]

Sets or returns the name of a procedure to run when the user double-clicks anywhere on a worksheet, chart, dialog box, or module. Setting this property for a worksheet, chart, dialog box, or module object overrides the Application setting.

Application.OnEntry

Application.OnEntry [= *procedurename*]

Sets or returns the name of a procedure to run when the user enters data in a cell. Setting this property for a worksheet overrides the Application setting.

Application.OnKey

Application.OnKey *Key*, [*Procedure*]

Sets the name of a procedure to run when a key is pressed.

Argument	Description
Key	The key or key sequence that runs the procedure.
Procedure	The name of the procedure to run. If omitted, pressing the specified key no longer runs the procedure; any Excel-defined behavior for the key is restored.

Key is usually the name of the key as it appears on the keyboard; for example, the "u" key. Special keys have the following codes:

Key name	Key code
BACKSPACE	"{BACKSPACE}" or "{BS}"
BREAK	"{BREAK}"
CAPS LOCK	"{CAPSLOCK}"
CLEAR	"{CLEAR}"
DELETE or DEL	"{DELETE}" or "{DEL}"
DOWN arrow	"{DOWN}"
END	"{END}"
ENTER (numeric keypad)	"{ENTER}"
ENTER	"~" (tilde)
ESC	"{ESCAPE}" or "{ESC}"
HELP	"{HELP}"

(continues)

Key name	Key code
HOME	"{HOME}"
INS	"{INSERT}"
LEFT arrow	"{LEFT}"
NUM LOCK	"{NUMLOCK}"
PAGE DOWN	"{PGDN}"
PAGE UP	"{PGUP}"
RETURN	"{RETURN}"
RIGHT arrow	"{RIGHT}"
SCROLL LOCK	"{SCROLLLOCK}"
TAB	"{TAB}"
UP arrow	"{UP}"
F1 through F15	"{F1}" through "{F15}"

You can combine keys using these special codes:

Key to combine with	Special code
SHIFT	"+"
CTRL	"^"
ALT or OPTION	"%"
COMMAND	"*"

Application.OnRepeat

Application.OnRepeat *Text, Procedure*

Sets the name of a procedure to run when the user chooses **E**dit, Redo (**u**).

Argument	Description
Text	Text to be displayed in place of the Redo menu item. This typically describes the action to repeat.
Procedure	The name of the procedure to run.

The Redo menu item is automatically reset after each edit. You should use the OnRepeat method as the last statement of procedures you want to let the user repeat. Otherwise, edits caused by the procedure may reset the Redo menu item.

Application.OnSheetActivate

Application.OnSheetActivate [= *procedurename*]

Sets or returns the name of a procedure to run when the user double-clicks anywhere on a worksheet, chart, dialog box, or module. Setting this property for a worksheet, chart, dialog box, or module object overrides the Application setting.

Application.OnSheetDeactivate

Application.OnSheetDeactivate [= *procedurename*]

Sets or returns the name of a procedure to run when the user activates a worksheet, chart, dialog box, or module. Setting this property for a worksheet, chart, dialog box, or module object overrides the Application setting.

Application.OnTime

Application.OnTime *EarliestTime, Procedure,* [*LatestTime*], [*Schedule*]

Sets the name of a procedure to run at a specified time.

Argument	Description
EarliestTime	The earliest time you want to run the specified procedure.
Procedure	The name of the procedure to run.
LatestTime	The latest time you want to run the specified procedure. The default is any time in the future.
Schedule	True adds the procedure to the list of procedures to run at specified times; False clears previously scheduled procedures. The default is True.

Application.OnUndo

Application.OnUndo *Text, Procedure*

Sets the name of a procedure to run when the user chooses **E**dit, **U**ndo.

Argument	Description
Text	Text to be displayed in place of the Undo menu item. This text typically describes the action to undo.
Procedure	The name of the procedure to run.

The Undo menu item is automatically reset after each edit. You should use the OnUndo method as the last statement of procedures you want to let the user undo. Otherwise, edits caused by the procedure may reset the Undo menu item.

Application.OnWindow

Application.OnWindow [= *procedurename*]

Sets or returns the name of a procedure to run when the user switches to a new window. Setting this property for a Window object overrides the Application setting.

Application.OperatingSystem

Returns a string containing the name and version number of the operating system.

Application.OrganizationName

Returns a string containing the name of the user's organization, as entered during Excel's installation process.

Application.Path

Returns the name of the directory where Excel is installed.

Application.PathSeparator

Returns "\" in Windows; ":" on the Macintosh.

Application.PreviousSelections

Application.PreviousSelections (*index*)

Returns one of the four last-selected ranges entered in the Go To dialog box (the Go To selection from the Edit menu). *Index* may be a whole number between 1 and 4. Other values cause an error.

Application.PromptForSummaryInfo

Application.PromptForSummaryInfo [= True | False]

True prompts for file summary information before new files are saved; False turns off this feature. The default is True.

Application.Quit

Exits Excel.

[Application.]Range

[Application.]Range ([*Cell1*], [*Cell2*])

Returns a range of cells.

Argument	Description
Cell1	The upper left cell of the range.
Cell2	The lower right cell of the range.

Excel has three forms of the Range method: cell references, strings, or square brackets. All three of the following lines of code select the same range of cells on the active sheet:

```
Range(Cells(1, 1), Cells(4, 4)).Select
Range ("A1:D4")
[a1:d4].Select
```

Application.RecordMacro

Application.RecordMacro [*BasicCode*], [*XlmCode*]

Sets the code Excel records if you turn on the macro recorder, then run this procedure.

Argument	Description
BasicCode	The code to record for the Visual Basic language.
XlmCode	The code to record for the Excel 4.0 macro language.

Typically, you will want to use your procedure name for *BasicCode*. For example:

```
Application.RecordMacro "FORMATS.XLA!ReformatSheet"
```

Application.RecordRelative

Returns True if macros are recorded using relative cell addresses; False if macros are recorded using absolute addresses. Relative cell addresses are recorded starting from the ActiveCell and offset to position the selection point. The default is False.

Application.ReferenceStyle

Application.ReferenceStyle [= xlA1 | xlR1C1]

xlA1 displays cell addresses using a letter for the column and number for the row (A1, B2, Z99, and so on). xlR1C1 uses numbers for both column and row (R1C1, R2C2, R26C99, and so on). The default is xlA1.

Application.RegisteredFunctions

Returns an array listing the registered DLL functions (code resources on the Macintosh). The array has two dimensions. The upper bound of the first dimension corresponds to the number of DLL functions that are registered. The second dimension has three elements: the name of the DLL, the name of the function, and the return values and number and type of arguments for the function. The following example demonstrates the use of RegisteredFunctions.

```
Sub ListRegisteredFunctions()
    Dim iRows As Integer, vFunctions As Variant
    ' Get the array of registered functions.
    vFunctions = Application.RegisteredFunctions
    ' Check if any functions are registered.
    If IsNull(vFunctions) Then
        MsgBox "No functions are registered."
        Exit Sub
    End If
    ' Find out how many rows are needed to display.
    iRows = UBound(vFunctions, 1)
    ' Display the array in three columns on Sheet1.
    With Sheets("Sheet1")
        .Range(.Cells(1, 1), .Cells(iRows, 3)).Value = vFunctions
        .Range(.Cells(1, 1), .Cells(iRows, 3)).AutoFormat
    End With
End Sub
```

Application.RegisterXLL

Application.RegisterXLL [*Filename*]

Loads an XLL file in Excel and registers the functions it contains. Returns
True if successful; False otherwise.

Application.Repeat

Repeats the last edit.

Application.ResetTipWizard

Resets the TipWizard so that previously shown tips are once more displayed.
The TipWizard stops showing a tip after it has been displayed a few times.

[Application.]Rows

[Application.]Rows ([*Index*])

Index indicates the number of the row to return. If omitted, returns all the
rows on the active worksheet. The following line of code selects the fourth
row on the active worksheet:

```
Rows(4).Select
```

Application.Save

Application.Save [*Filename*]

Saves the current workspace as *Filename*. The default for *Filename* is RESUME.XLW.

Application.ScreenUpdating

Application.ScreenUpdating [= True | False]

True if Excel updates the visual display; False if the display does not change. Setting this property to True speeds up tasks and hides actions from the user. Be sure to set this property back to True before returning control to the user. The default is True.

[Application.]Selection

Returns the currently selected object or objects. Returns Nothing if no objects are selected. Selections are usually a single, rectangular range of cells, but they may include multiple ranges and drawing objects that appear on sheets. Use the Select method to select an object in code.

Application.SetDefaultChart

Application.SetDefaultChart [*FormatName*]

Sets the name of a chart format to use by default when creating new charts. The default for *FormatName* is xlBuiltin.

[Application.]Sheets

[Application.]Sheets ([*Index*])

Index indicates the name or number of the Sheet object to return from the Sheets collection. If omitted, returns the collection of Sheets in the active workbook. The Sheets collection includes Worksheet, Chart, and Module Sheet objects.

Application.SheetsInNewWorkbook

Application.SheetsInNewWorkbook [= *number*]

Sets or returns the number of worksheets Excel creates when you create a new workbook. The default is 16.

[Application.]ShortcutMenus

[Application.]ShortcutMenus (*Index*)

Index indicates the name or number of the shortcut Menu object to return from the Menus collection. If omitted, returns the collection of shortcut Menus in the active workbook. Built-in shortcut menus are identified by the following constants:

Constant	Returns this shortcut menu
xlAxis	Chart Axis
xlButton	Button
xlChartSeries	Chart Series
xlChartTitles	Chart Titles
xlColumnHeader	Column
xlDebugCodePane	Debug Code Pane
xlDesktop	Desktop
xlDialogSheet	Dialog Sheet
xlDrawingObject	Drawing Object
xlEntireChart	Entire Chart
xlFloor	Chart Floor
xlGridline	Chart Gridline
xlImmediatePane	Immediate Pane
xlLegend	Chart Legend
xlMacrosheetCell	Macro Sheet Cell
xlModule	Module
xlPlotArea	Chart Plot Area
xlRowHeader	Row
xlTextBox	Text Box
xlTitleBar	Title Bar
xlToolbar	Toolbar

(continues)

Constant	Returns this shortcut menu
xlToolbarButton	Toolbar Button
xlWatchPane	Watch Pane
xlWorkbookTab	Workbook Tab
xlWorksheetCell	Worksheet Cell

Application.ShowToolTips

Application.ShowToolTips [= True | False]

True if tool tips are displayed; False if they are not displayed. The default is True.

[Application.]StandardFont

[Application.]StandardFont [= *name*]

Sets or returns the name of the font to use in worksheet cells by default. The default is "Arial."

Application.StandardFontSize

Application.StandardFontSize [= *size*]

Sets or returns the default font size in points. The default is 10.

Application.StartupPath

Returns the path of the Excel startup directory; for example, C:\EXCEL\XLSTART.

Application.StatusBar

Application.StatusBar [= *text*]

Sets or returns the text displayed in the status bar.

[Application.]ThisWorkbook

Returns the Workbook object of the workbook in which the currently running procedure resides. The following code displays the name of the workbook in which a procedure is stored:

```
MsgBox ThisWorkbook.Name
```

[Application.]Toolbars

[Application.]Toolbars (*Index*)

Index indicates the name or number of the Toolbar object to return from the Toolbars collection. If omitted, returns the collection of Toolbars in the active workbook. Built-in toolbars are identified by the name that appears in the Toolbars dialog box.

The following code hides the standard toolbar in Excel:

```
Toolbars("Standard").Visible = False
```

Application.TransitionMenuKey

Application.TransitionMenuKey [= *key*]

Sets or returns a key you can use as an alternate to the Alt key for activating menus. The alternate menu key is not active when you are editing a module. The default is "/".

Application.TransitionMenuKeyAction

Application.TransitionMenuKeyAction [= xlLotusMenus | xlExcelMenus]

Sets or returns the action taken when you press the transition menu key (usually "/"). xlLotusMenus displays Lotus 1-2-3 Help when you press the key; xlExcelMenus activates the Excel menu bar when you press the key. The default is xlExcelMenus.

Tip

The Transition properties correspond to the items displayed in the Transition tab in the Options dialog box.

Application.TransitionNavigKeys

Application.TransitionNavigKeys [= True | False]

True activates the alternate navigation shortcut keys; False deactivates these keys. The default is False.

Application.Undo

Removes the last edit.

[Application.]Union

[Application.]Union (Arg1, Arg2, [Argn])

Joins two or more Range objects, and returns the resulting Range object.

Argument	Description
Arg1	The first Range object to join.
Arg2	The second Range object to join.
Argn	Any number of additional Range objects to join.

A range may contain multiple regions if it is a multiple selection or if it is a union of several ranges. The following range has three regions:

```
rngMulti = Union([a1:d4], [e2:f3], [g1])
```

Use the Areas method of the Range object to get contiguous ranges from within a union of ranges.

Application.UsableHeight

Returns the height that can be used by a window in Excel. Measurement is in points.

Application.UsableWidth

Returns the width that can be used by a window in Excel. Measurement is in points.

Application.UserName

Application.UserName [= *text*]

Sets or returns the name of the current user as entered during Excel's setup.

Application.Version

Returns the version number of Excel.

Application.Volatile

Application.Volatile [*Volatile*]

Setting *Volatile* to True recalculates cells when the procedure changes calculations in cells; False recalculates cells only when a cell value changes. The default is True if *Volatile* is omitted.

Application.Wait

Application.Wait *Time*

Pauses Excel until `Time`. Excel displays the wait cursor until `Time` and can't perform edits while Excel is paused, although users can switch to other applications.

[Application.]Windows

[Application.]Windows ([*Index*])

`Index` indicates the name or number of the `Window` object to return from the `Windows` collection. If omitted, returns the collection of `Windows` that are currently displayed.

Application.WindowsForPens

Returns True if Excel is running under Pen Windows; False otherwise.

[Application.]WindowState

[Application.]WindowState [= *setting*]

Sets or returns Excel's Windows display. Can be one of the following settings: `xlNormal`, Excel is not maximized or minimized; `xlMaximized`, maximizes Excel (Windows only); or `xlMinimized`, minimizes Excel (Windows only). Maximizing Excel maximizes all windows on the Excel desktop.

[Application.]Workbooks

[Application.]Workbooks ([*Index*])

`Index` indicates the name or number of the `Workbook` object to return from the `Workbooks` collection. If omitted, returns the collection of `Workbooks` that are currently open.

[Application.]Worksheets

[Application.]Worksheets (*Index*)

`Index` indicates the name or number of the `Worksheet` object to return from the `Worksheets` collection. If omitted, returns the collection of `Worksheets` in the active workbook.

II

Programmer's Reference

Chapter 6

Controlling Excel Files

A workbook is a file in Excel. Use the Workbooks collection to open new files or to perform operations on all the files currently open in Excel. Use the Workbook object to get information about or to perform operations on a single open file.

In this chapter, you learn how to do the following:

- Open and save files.

- Protect files.

- Use Workbook properties and methods.

Opening and Saving Files

You create a new file by adding it to the Application's Workbooks collection. The following line of code creates a new workbook:

```
Application.Workbooks.Add
```

Similarly, you open an existing file using the Open method:

```
Application.Workbooks.Open "c:\excel\myfile.xls"
```

When Excel creates or opens a workbook, it adds it to the collection of currently open workbooks. You can choose from the Workbooks collection in a number of ways. The following example shows different ways to select and save workbooks:

```
Sub DemoSaving()
    ' Save the workbook that currently has focus.
    ActiveWorkbook.Save
    ' Save a workbook by name.
    Workbooks("BOOK1.XLS").Save
```

Tip
When you want to save a workbook under a new name, use the SaveAs method to create the clone under the new name.

```
      ' Save each workbook in turn.
      For Each wrk In Workbooks
            wrk.Save
      Next wrk
  End Sub
```

Protecting Files

File protection prevents users from changing data or changing the display. You can *lock down* a workbook at a number of levels using the Protect method. Lock down refers to restricting file access. Protecting a workbook in this manner allows for a more secure system. The following line of code creates a password for the current workbook and prevents changes to the order of the worksheets and display of the windows:

```
ActiveWorkbook.Protect password:="wombat", structure:=True, _
windows:=True
```

Similarly, you can permit changes using Unprotect:

```
ActiveWorkbook.Unprotect password:="wombat"
```

The Workbook object and Workbooks collection have specific properties and methods, which are listed in Table 6.1. Properties and methods shown in **bold** are described in the reference section that follows this table. Nonbold items are common to most objects and are described in Chapter 4, "Using Objects."

Table 6.1 Workbook and Workbooks properties and methods	
Activate	**DeleteNumberFormat**
ActiveSheet	DialogSheets
Add[2]	**DisplayDrawingObjects**
Application	Excel4IntlMacroSheets
Author	Excel4MacroSheets
ChangeFileAccess	**FileFormat**
ChangeLink	**ForwardMailer**
Charts	**FullName**
Close	**HasMailer**
Colors	**HasPassword**
Comments	**HasRoutingSlip**
Count[2]	Item[2]
CreateBackup	**Keywords**
Creator[1]	**LinkInfo**
Date1904	**LinkSources**

Mailer	**Routed**
Modules	**RoutingSlip**
Name	**RunAutoMacros**
Names	**Save**
NewWindow	**SaveAs**
OnSheetActivate	**SaveCopyAs**
OnSheetDeactivate	**Saved**
Open2	**SaveLinkValues**
OpenLinks	**SendMail**
OpenText2	**SendMailer**
Parent	**SetLinkOnData**
Path	Sheets
PrecisionAsDisplayed	**Styles**
PrintOut	**Subject**
PrintPreview	**Title**
Protect	**Unprotect**
ProtectStructure	**UpdateFromFile**
ProtectWindows	**UpdateLink**
ReadOnly	**UpdateRemoteReferences**
ReadOnlyRecommended	Windows
Reply	Worksheets
ReplyAll	**WriteReserved**
Route	**WriteReservedBy**

[1] *Applies to the Workbooks collection.*

[2] *Applies to the Workbooks collection and the Workbook object.*

workbook.Author

workbook.Author [= *name*]

Sets or returns the name of the workbook's author, as displayed in the workbook's file summary information.

workbook.ChangeFileAccess

workbook.ChangeFileAccess (*Mode*, [*WritePassword*], [*Notify*])

Changes how you are accessing the current file. Changing access may reload the file.

Argument	Description
Mode	`xlReadWrite` or `xlReadOnly`.
WritePassword	The file's password. The default is no password.
Notify	True if Excel displays a message when the file can't be accessed; otherwise False. The default is True.

workbook.ChangeLink

workbook.ChangeLink (*Name, NewName, [Type]*)

Changes the source of an Excel link. The links changed can be an Excel, DDE, or OLE link.

Argument	Description
Name	The formula of the link in the workbook.
NewName	The new file name to link to.
Type	`xlExcelLink` if the link is from another Excel workbook; `xlOLELink` if the link is from another application. The default is `xlExcelLink`.

workbook.Close

workbook.Close ([*SaveChanges*], [*Filename*], [*RouteWorkbook*])
workbooks.Close

Closes one workbook (first syntax line) and workbooks. Close closes all workbooks.

Argument	Description
SaveChanges	True to save changes to disk; False to ignore changes. The default displays prompt if file has changed.
Filename	The name of the file to save. The default is to save as the workbook name.
RouteWorkbook	True routes the workbook to the next recipient; False does not. The default prompts user whether to route.

Ignored if the workbook's HasRoutingSlip property is False or if its Routed property is True.

workbook.Comments

workbook.Comments [= *comments*]

Sets or returns comments, as displayed in the workbook's file summary information.

workbook.CreateBackup

Returns True if the previous version of the file is renamed with the BAK file extension every time you save the file. To turn this behavior on or off, use the SaveAs method.

workbook.Date1904

workbook.Date1904 [= True | False]

True if all dates are calculated from January 2, 1904; False if they are calculated from January 1, 1900. The default is False.

workbook.DeleteNumberFormat

workbook.DeleteNumberFormat (*NumberFormat*)

Deletes a number format from the Format Codes list on the Numbers tab of the Format Cells dialog box. NumberFormat is the index of the format in the list.

workbook.DisplayDrawingObjects

workbook.DisplayDrawingObjects [= *xlAll* | *xlPlaceholders* | *xlHide*]

xlAll displays all drawing objects; xlPlaceholders shows placeholder frames instead of the drawing; xlHide does not display drawings. The default is xlAll.

workbook.FileFormat

Returns the file format of the workbook, as determined by the following constants:

xlAddIn	xlNormal
xlCSV	xlSYLK
xlCSVMac	xlTemplate
xlCSVMSDOS	xlText
xlCSVWindows	xlTextMac
xlDBF2	xlTextMSDOS
xlDBF3	xlTextPrinter
xlDBF4	xlTextWindows
xlDIF	xlWK1
xlExcel2	xlWK1ALL
xlExcel3	xlWK1FMT
xlExcel4	xlWK3
xlExcel4Workbook	xlWK3FM3
xlIntlAddIn	xlWKS
xlIntlMacro	xlWQ1

The Far East version of Excel has these additional formats:

    xlExcel2FarEast

    xlWJ2WD1

    xlWorks2FarEast

workbook.ForwardMailer

Macintosh with PowerTalk mail system only. Creates a mailer for forwarding a workbook based on the mailer received with the workbook. A workbook can only be forwarded if it has first been received. If no mailer was received (the workbook was not received through mail), an error is generated. This method only creates a mailer; use the SendMailer method to actually send the workbook. This method generates an error when used in Windows.

workbook.FullName

Returns the file name and path of the workbook file.

workbook.HasMailer

workbook.HasMailer [= True | False]

Macintosh with PowerTalk mail system only. True if the workbook has a mailer; False otherwise. Setting HasMailer to True creates a mailer. The default is False.

workbook.HasPassword

workbook.HasPassword [= True | False]

workbook.HasRoutingSlip

workbook.HasRoutingSlip [= True | False]

True if the workbook has a routing slip; False otherwise. Setting HasRoutingSlip to True creates a routing slip. The default is False.

> **Note**
>
> A routing slip is an object with its own methods and properties. These methods and properties include recipients, creator, delivery, and status, among others. An object of this class is used to define the parameters for sending a workbook to another person or group of people.

workbook.Keywords

workbook.Keywords [= *comments*]

Sets or returns keywords for the file, as entered in the workbook's file summary information.

workbook.LinkInfo

workbook.LinkInfo (*Name, LinkInfo, [Type], [EditionRef]*)

Used for OLE or DDE links. Returns 1 if the link is updated automatically; 2 if the link is updated manually. For editions, returns the edition date.

Argument	Description
Name	The formula that describes the link, as returned by the LinkSources method.
LinkInfo	For OLE or DDE links use xlUpdateState. For editions, use xlEditionDate.
Type	For OLE or DDE links, use xlOLELinks. For editions, use xlPublishers or xlSubscribers.
EditionRef	For OLE or DDE links, omit. For editions, specify the edition reference in R1C1 format. This argument is required if there are multiple publishers or subscribers with the same workbook name.

workbook.LinkSources

workbook.LinkSources ([*Type*])

Returns an array of formulas that describe the links in a workbook. *Type* is xlOLELinks for OLE and DDE links, xlExcelLinks for links to other workbooks, xlPublishers for edition publishers, or xlSubscribers for edition subscribers.

workbook.Mailer

Macintosh with PowerTalk mail system only. Returns the Mailer object attached to a workbook.

workbook.NewWindow

Creates a new window for the workbook.

workbook.OnSheetActivate

workbook.OnSheetActivate [= *procedure*]

Sets or returns the name of a procedure to run when a worksheet in the workbook receives focus.

workbook.OnSheetDeactivate

workbook.OnSheetDeactivate [= *procedure*]

Sets or returns the name of a procedure to run when a worksheet in the workbook no longer has focus.

workbooks.Open

***workbooks*.Open (*Filename*, [*UpdateLinks*], [*ReadOnly*], [*Format*], [*Password*], [*WriteResPassword*], [*IgnoreReadOnlyRecommended*], [*Origin*], [*Delimiter*], [*Editable*], [*Notify*], [*Converter*])**

Argument	Description
Filename	The path and name of the file to open.
UpdateLinks	0 does not update links; 1 updates only links from other workbooks; 2 updates only links from other applications; 3 updates all links. The default displays a dialog box prompting user.
ReadOnly	True to open for read-only access; False to open for read-write. The default is False.
Format	Specifies the column separator to use when opening a text file. 1, tabs; 2, commas; 3, spaces; 4, semicolons; 5, nothing (text goes in one cell); 6, character specified by *Delimiter* argument. The default is 1.
Password	The password required to open the file. The default prompts user if password is required.
WriteResPassword	The password required to make changes to the file. The default prompts user if password is required.
IgnoreReadOnlyRecommended	True does not display Excel's Read Only Recommended dialog box. False displays the dialog box if the file was saved as Read Only Recommended. The default is False.
Origin	xlWindows if the file is a text file from the Windows operating system; xlMacintosh if it is from the Macintosh; xlMSDOS if it is from DOS. Omit if the file is not a text file. The default is the current operating system.
Delimiter	The character in the text file that indicates a new column in a row of data. Required if *Format* is 6.
Editable	For Excel 4.0 add-ins only. True displays the add-in in a window and does not run Auto_Open macros; False hides the add-in. The default is False.

(continues)

II

Programmer's Reference

Argument	Description
Notify	True notifies the user when the file is available for the requested access specified in the *ReadOnly* argument. False causes Open to fail if the file is not available for the specified access. The default is False.
Converter	The index of the converter to try first when opening the file. If the converter does not match the file type, each converter is tried in turn. The index of a converter corresponds to the converter's first-dimension index in the array returned by `Application.FileConverters`.

workbook.**OpenLinks**

workbook.**OpenLinks (*Name*, [*ReadOnly*], [*Type*])**

Opens the linked documents in their source application.

Argument	Description
Name	The name of the link as returned by the `LinkSources` property. Use an array of names to open more than one linked document at a time.
ReadOnly	True if the linked document is opened for read-only access; False otherwise. The default is False.
Type	For Excel workbook links, use `xlExcelLinks`. For OLE or DDE links, use `xlOLELinks`. For editions, use `xlPublishers` or `xlSubscribers`.

workbooks.**OpenText**

workbooks.**OpenText (*Filename*, [*Origin*], [*StartRow*], [*DataType*], [*TextQualifier*], [*ConsecutiveDelimiter*], [*Tab*], [*Semicolon*], [*Comma*], [*Space*], [*Other*], [*OtherChar*], [*FieldInfo*])**

Opens a text file and converts text fields to cells in a workbook.

Argument	Description
Filename	The name of the file to open.
Origin	xlWindows if the file is from the Windows operating system; xlMacintosh if it is from Macintosh; xlMSDOS if it is from DOS. The default is the current operating system.
StartRow	Line at which to start reading the text file. The default is the beginning of the file.
DataType	xlDelimited if text fields are separated by a delimiting character; xlFixedWidth if each line in the file has the same width and the text fields have fixed begin and end character positions in the file.
TextQualifier	Valid only if *DataType* is xlDelimited. xlDoubleQuote if text data is enclosed in quotation marks; xlSingleQuote if it is enclosed in single quotation marks; xlNone if text is not enclosed in punctuation. The default is xlDoubleQuote.
ConsecutiveDelimiter	Valid only if *DataType* is xlDelimited. True if consecutive delimiters (such as Tabs) are interpreted as one delimiter; False if not. The default is False.
Tab	Valid only if *DataType* is xlDelimited. True if the delimiter is the Tab character; False otherwise. The default is False.
Semicolon	Valid only if *DataType* is xlDelimited. True if the delimiter is a semicolon; False otherwise. The default is False.
Comma	Valid only if *DataType* is xlDelimited. True if the delimiter is a comma; False otherwise. The default is False.
Space	Valid only if *DataType* is xlDelimited. True if the delimiter is a space; False otherwise. The default is False.
Other	Valid only if *DataType* is xlDelimited. True if the delimiter is specified by the *OtherChar* argument; False otherwise. The default is False.
OtherChar	Valid only if *DataType* is xlDelimited. The character that separates text fields in the file. The default is none.
FieldInfo	Valid only if *DataType* is xlFixedWidth. An array of two-element arrays, each of which describes the data type of a column to create when interpreting the text file. The following list shows valid values for the *FieldInfo* parameter.

When opening fixed-length text files, *FieldInfo* describes the start position of each column to read and the data type of that column. Data types have these codes:

Code	Interprets column as
1	General data
2	Text
3	MDY date
4	DMY date
5	YMD date
6	MYD date
7	DYM date
8	YDM date
9	Skip this column

For example:

```
ActiveWorkbook.OpenText("MYDATA.TXT", DataType:=xlFixedWidth, _
    FieldInfo:=Array(Array(0,1), Array(10,2), Array(45,9),
Array(47,4)
```

This line of code describes three columns of data: Characters 1 through 10 are interpreted as general data, characters 10 through 45 are text, 45 through 47 are skipped, and 47 to the end of the line are interpreted as a DMY date.

workbook.Path

Returns the path of the workbook file. The returned path does not include the final path separation character; for example, "C:\EXCEL\SAMPLES."

workbook.PrecisionAsDisplayed

workbook.PrecisionAsDisplayed [= True | False]

True if calculations use the displayed values of cells; False if calculations use the stored value of cells. The default is False.

workbook.Protect

workbook.Protect ([*Password*], [*Structure*], [*Windows*])

Prevents changes to a workbook.

Argument	Description
Password	Specifies a password the user must enter to unprotect a workbook. The default is None.
Structure	True prevents changes to the order of the worksheets; False allows changes. The default is False.
Windows	True prevents changes to the display and arrangement of windows; False allows changes. The default is False.

workbook.ProtectStructure

Returns True if the order of the worksheets in the workbook is protected; False otherwise. The default is False.

workbook.ProtectWindows

Returns True if the display and arrangement of windows in the workbook are protected; False otherwise. The default is False.

workbook.ReadOnly

Returns True if the workbook is read-only; False otherwise. The default is False.

workbook.ReadOnlyRecommended

Returns True if the workbook is read-only recommended; False otherwise. The default is False.

workbook.Reply

Macintosh with PowerTalk mail system only. Creates a copy of the workbook and a mailer for replying to the person who originally sent the workbook. Valid only if the workbook was received through mail.

workbook.**ReplyAll**

Macintosh with PowerTalk mail system only. Creates a copy of the workbook and a mailer to send to the sender and recipients of the workbook. Valid only if the workbook was received through mail.

workbook.**Route**

Returns True if the workbook has been routed on; False if it has not been routed on or if the workbook does not have a routing slip.

workbook.**Routed**

Routes the workbook to the next recipient on the workbook's routing slip, then sets the Routed property to True. Valid only if HasRoutingSlip is True and Routed is False.

workbook.**RoutingSlip**

Returns a routing slip object for the workbook. Valid only if HasRoutingSlip is True; otherwise causes an error.

workbook.**RunAutoMacros**

workbook.**RunAutoMacros (*Which*)**

Runs one of the automatic macros for the workbook. Which determines the macro to run: xlAutoOpen, xlAutoClose, xlAutoActivate, or xlAutoDeactivate.

workbook.**Save**

Saves the current workbook to disk using its existing file name.

workbook.**SaveAs**

workbook.**SaveAs ([*Filename*], [*FileFormat*], [*Password*], [*WriteResPassword*], [*ReadOnlyRecommended*], [*CreateBackup*])**

Saves a workbook to disk and sets the workbook's file properties.

Argument	Description
Filename	The name of the file to save the workbook as. The default is to the current file name.
FileFormat	A constant that determines the format of the file to save. See the FileFormat property for a list of these constants. The default is xlNormal.
Password	A password the user must enter to open the file. The default is None.
WriteResPassword	A password the user must enter to open the file for write access. The default is None.
ReadOnlyRecommended	True causes Excel to display a message recommending read-only access when the file is opened for write access; False causes Excel not to display the message. The default is False.
CreateBackup	True to save the previous version of the file using the BAK extension; False to save only the current version. The default is False.

workbook.**SaveCopyAs**

workbook.**SaveCopyAs ([*Filename*])**

Creates a copy of the current workbook file. The file is saved as *Filename*. If omitted, the user is prompted for a file name.

workbook.**Saved**

workbook.**Saved [= True | False]**

True if there have been no changes to the file since it was last saved; False otherwise. Setting this property to True after edits may cause Excel to discard edits when the file is closed.

workbook.**SaveLinkValues**

workbook.**SaveLinkValues [= True | False]**

True saves a copy of the values from cells linked from other workbooks with this workbook; False discards the linked values when the file is closed, but reloads them when the link is reestablished—as when opening the file. The default is True.

workbook.SendMail

workbook.**SendMail** (*Recipients*, [*Subject*], [*ReturnReceipt*])

Sends a workbook as an electronic mail message.

Argument	Description
Recipients	Text specifying the mail name of the person to receive the workbook, or an array of names if more than one person is to receive the workbook.
Subject	Text to place in the Subject line of the mail message.
ReturnReceipt	True to receive notification when the message is received; False otherwise. The default is False.

workbook.SendMailer

workbook.**SendMailer** ([*FileFormat*], [*Priority*])

Macintosh with PowerTalk mail system only. Sends a workbook as a PowerTalk mail message.

Argument	Description
FileFormat	The file format of the workbook to send. See the FileFormat property for a list of constants. The default is xlNormal.
Priority	xlNormal for normal priority; xlHigh for urgent messages; xlLow for low priority. The default is xlNormal.

workbook.SetLinkOnData

workbook.**SetLinkOnData** (*Name*, [*Procedure*])

Specifies the name of a procedure to run when a DDE or OLE link is updated.

Argument	Description
Name	The formula of the link, as returned by the LinkSources method.
Procedure	The name of the procedure to run. The default is None.

workbook.**Styles**

workbook.**Styles ([*Index*])**

Returns one or all the styles defined for a workbook. *Index* specifies the style object to return. If omitted, returns the Styles collection.

workbook.**Subject**

workbook.**Subject [= *text*]**

Sets or returns the subject text saved with a workbook's summary information.

workbook.**Title**

workbook.**Title [= *title*]**

Sets or returns a descriptive title for the file, as entered in the workbook's file summary information.

workbook.**Unprotect**

workbook.**Unprotect ([*Password*])**

Changes a protected workbook to unprotected (changes allowed). *Password* is required if the workbook protection was set using a password.

workbook.**UpdateFromFile**

Updates a read-only workbook from its source file.

workbook.**UpdateLink**

workbook.**UpdateLink ([*Name*], [*Type*])**

Updates one or more links in a workbook.

Argument	Description
Name	The name of the link as returned by the LinkSources property. Use an array of names to open more than one linked document at a time. The default is all links.
Type	For Excel workbook links, use xlExcelLinks. For OLE or DDE links, use xlOLELinks. The default is xlExcelLinks.

workbook.UpdateRemoteReferences

workbook.UpdateRemoteReferences [= True | False]

True updates all OLE and DDE links from other applications; False does not update links. The default is False.

workbook.WriteReserved

Returns True if the workbook has a write reserve password. Use the `FileSaveAs` method to set this property. The default is False.

workbook.WriteReservedBy

Returns the name of the user who currently has write permission to the file.

Chapter 7

Controlling the Excel Display

A window is the fundamental display unit in Excel. Use the Windows collection to create new windows and to arrange all the currently open windows. Use the Window object to close, scroll, or switch between windows.

In this chapter, you learn how to do the following:

- Open and close a window.

- Scroll a window in any direction.

- Switch between windows.

- Use Window and Windows properties and methods.

- Use Pane and Panes objects.

- Use AddIn and AddIns objects.

Opening and Closing a Window

You open a new window using the NewWindow method. NewWindow creates the window and adds it to the Windows collection. Use the Close method to close a window. For example:

```
Sub DemoOpenClose()
    ' Create a new window.
    ActiveWindow.NewWindow
    ' Tile the windows.
    Windows.Arrange
    ' Display the number of windows.
    MsgBox "There are " & Windows.Count & " open windows."
```

```
        ' Close the first window.
        Windows(1).Close
        ' Close the active window.
        ActiveWindow.Close
    End Sub
```

Scrolling a Window

You can scroll a window in any direction using the `LargeScroll` and
`SmallScroll` methods. The following line of code scrolls a window four rows
down and three columns to the right:

```
        ActiveWindow.SmallScroll down:=4, toright:=3
```

Working with a window is often frustrating, because many methods and
properties fail if the window is not displaying a worksheet or macro sheet.
The previous code line is a good example—if you try to run it from a module,
it causes an error. To avoid this, test the contents of a window before using
the window's methods or properties. For example:

```
    Sub Scroll(Down, ToRight)
        ' Test if window is displaying a Module (Module doesn't have _
          a Type property)
        For Each modTest In Application.Modules
            If modTest.Name = ActiveSheet.Name Then Exit Sub
        Next
        ' Test if window is displaying a worksheet.
        If ActiveSheet.Type = xlWorksheet Then
            ActiveWindow.SmallScroll down:=Down, toright:=ToRight
        End If
    End Sub
```

As an alternative, you can use error trapping to test for success or failure. For
example:

```
    Sub Scroll(Down, ToRight)
        ' Turn on error trapping.
        On Error Resume Next
        ActiveWindow.SmallScroll down:=Down, toright:=ToRight
        ' If the method failed, then sound a beep.
        If Err <> 0 Then
            ' Take action (could substitute something else).
            Beep
            ' Reset Err code.
            Err = 0
        End If
        ' Turn off error trapping.
        On Error GoTo 0
    End Sub
```

Switching Between Windows

Use the `Activate` method to switch between windows in Excel. There are several forms you can use:

```
Sub DemoSwitching()
    ' Switch to next window.
    ActiveWindow.ActivateNext
    ' Switch to first window.
    Windows(1).Activate
    ' Switch to window that has the caption book1.xls:2
      (error if it doesn't exist)
    Windows("book1.xls:2").Activate
End Sub
```

The `Window` object and `Windows` collection have specific properties and methods, which are listed in Table 7.1. Properties and methods shown in **bold** are described in the reference section that follows this table. Nonbold items are common to most objects and are described in Chapter 4, "Using Objects."

Table 7.1 Window and Windows properties and methods

Activate	**GridlineColorIndex**
ActivateNext	Height
ActivePrevious	Index
ActiveCell	Item[2]
ActiveChart	**LargeScroll**
ActivePane	Left
ActiveSheet	**NewWindow**
Application[1]	**OnWindow**
Arrange[2]	**PageSetup**
Caption	**Panes**
Close	Parent[1]
Count[2]	PrintOut
Creator[1]	PrintPreview
DisplayFormulas	**ScrollColumn**
DisplayGridlines	**ScrollRow**
DisplayHeadings	**ScrollWorkbookTabs**
DisplayHorizontalScrollBar	**SelectedSheets**
DisplayOutline	Selection
DisplayRightToLeft	**SetInfoDisplay**
DisplayVerticalScrollBar	**SmallScroll**
DisplayWorkbookTabs	**Split**
DisplayZeros	**SplitColumn**
FreezePanes	**SplitHorizontal**
GridlineColor	**SplitRow**

(continues)

Table 7.1 Continued

SplitVertical	Visible
TabRatio	**VisibleRange**
Top	Width
Type	**WindowNumber**
UsableHeight	WindowState
UsableWidth	**Zoom**

[1]*Applies to the Windows collection.*
[2]*Applies to the Windows collection and the Window object.*

*window.*ActivateNext

Switches focus to the next window listed in the Window menu. When the last window is reached, calling the ActivateNext method will cycle to the first window in the Window menu.

*window.*ActivatePrevious

Switches focus to the last window listed in the Window menu.

*window.*ActivePane

Returns the Pane object that currently has focus. The Pane and Panes objects are fully explained later in this chapter.

*windows.*Arrange

windows.Arrange ([*ArrangeStyle*], [*ActiveWorkbook*], [*SyncHorizontal*], [*SyncVertical*])

Arranges all of the currently open windows or window icons.

Argument	Description
ArrangeStyle	xlTiled tiles windows; xlCascade overlaps windows; xlHorizontal tiles windows horizontally; xlVertical tiles windows vertically; xlIcons arranges window icons (Windows only). The default is xlTiled.
ActiveWorkbook	True arranges only the windows for the active workbook; False arranges all windows. The default is False.

Argument	Description
SyncHorizontal	True synchronizes horizontal scrolling so all windows scroll together. Ignored if *ActiveWorkbook* is False. The default is False.
SyncVertical	True synchronizes vertical scrolling so all windows scroll together. Ignored if *ActiveWorkbook* is False. The default is False.

window.**DisplayFormulas**

window.**DisplayFormulas [= True | False]**

True displays formulas, instead of values, for the window; False does not. Causes error if window is not displaying a worksheet. The default is False.

window.**DisplayGridlines**

window.**DisplayGridlines [= True | False]**

True displays grid lines for the window; False otherwise. Causes error if window is not displaying a worksheet, dialog sheet, or macro sheet. The default is True.

window.**DisplayHeadings**

window.**DisplayHeadings [= True | False]**

True displays row and column headings for the window; False does not. If the window is not currently displaying a worksheet or a macro sheet, calling DisplayHeadings will generate an error. The default is True.

window.**DisplayHorizontalScrollBar**

window.**DisplayHorizontalScrollBar [= True | False]**

True displays a horizontal scroll bar for the window; False does not. The default is True.

window.**DisplayOutline**

window.**DisplayOutline [= True | False]**

True displays the outline bar in the left margin of the window; False hides the outline bar. Causes error if window is not displaying a worksheet or macro sheet. The default is False.

*window.***DisplayRightToLeft**

*window.***DisplayRightToLeft [= True | False]**

This option is only available in the Arabic and Hebrew versions of Excel. True if window displays text right to left; False otherwise.

*window.***DisplayVerticalScrollBar**

*window.***DisplayVerticalScrollBar [= True | False]**

True displays a vertical scroll bar for the window; False does not. The default is True.

*window.***DisplayWorkbookTabs**

*window.***DisplayWorkbookTabs [= True | False]**

True displays the workbook tabs at the bottom of the window; False hides the tabs. The default is True.

*window.***DisplayZeros**

*window.***DisplayZeros [= True | False]**

True displays zero values in cells; False does not display zero values. Causes error if window is not displaying a worksheet or macro sheet. The default is True.

*window.***FreezePanes**

*window.***FreezePanes [= True | False]**

True prevents the resizing of panes in a window and prevents the scrolling of the upper left-most pane; False allows panes to be resized and scrolled. Setting this property to True while only one pane is displayed splits the window into four equal panes. The default is False.

*window.***GridlineColor**

*window.***GridlineColor [= *color*]**

Sets or returns the color of the grid lines in a window. *Color* is expressed as an RGB color value. Causes error if window is not displaying a worksheet, dialog sheet, or macro sheet. The default is RGB(0,0,0) (black).

window.**GridlineColorIndex**

window.**GridlineColorIndex** [= *colorindex*]

Sets or returns the color of the grid lines in a window. *ColorIndex* is expressed as an index into the color palette. Causes error if window is not displaying a worksheet, dialog sheet, or macro sheet. The default is xlAutomatic.

window.**LargeScroll**

window.**LargeScroll** ([*Down*], [*Up*], [*ToRight*], [*ToLeft*])

Scrolls the window a multiple number of visible ranges at one time.

Argument	Description
Down	Number of visible ranges to scroll down. The default is 0.
Up	Number of visible ranges to scroll up. The default is 0.
ToRight	Number of visible ranges to scroll to the right. The default is 0.
ToLeft	Number of visible ranges to scroll to the left. The default is 0.

If the window can't scroll as many ranges as specified, the window scrolls as far as possible in that direction.

window.**NewWindow**

Creates a new window and adds it to the Windows collection.

window.**OnWindow**

window.**OnWindow** [= *procedure*]

Sets or returns the name of a procedure to run when the window receives focus.

window.**PageSetup**

Returns the PageSetup object for the window. Use the returned PageSetup object to control the printing and layout attributes of the worksheet in the active window.

The following line of code sets the center header to print with the sheet in the active window:

```
ActiveWindow.PageSetup.CenterHeader = ActiveWorkbook.FullName
```

window.Panes

window.Panes ([*Index*])

Returns one or all of the Pane objects displayed in a window. *Index* specifies the number of the pane to return. If *Index* is omitted, returns the Panes collection object.

> **Caution**
>
> The Panes collection doesn't work with the For Each statement. The value(s) returned from the Panes method is either a specific pane or all panes, making the use of the For Each statement impossible.

window.ScrollColumn

window.ScrollColumn [= *columnnumber*]

Sets or returns the number of the column that appears next to the left edge of the window.

window.ScrollRow

window.ScrollRow [= *columnnumber*]

Sets or returns the number of the row that appears next to the top edge of the window.

window.ScrollWorkbookTabs

window.ScrollWorkbookTabs (*Sheets* | *Position*)

Scrolls the tab display at the bottom of the window. You must specify *Sheets* or *Position*, but not both arguments.

Argument	Description
Sheets	The number of tabs to scroll. Positive numbers scroll right; negative numbers scroll left.
Position	Use xlFirst to scroll to first tab; use xlLast to scroll to last tab.

*window.*SelectedSheets

Returns a collection which contains all the currently selected sheets in a window.

*infowindow.*SetInfoDisplay

*infowindow.*SetInfoDisplay ([*Cell*], [*Formula*], [*Value*], [*Format*], [*Protection*], [*Names*], [*Precedents*], [*Dependents*], [*Note*])

Sets the information displayed in the Info window. Using this method with other windows causes an error.

Argument	Description
Cell	True displays the cell address; False hides the address. The default is True.
Formula	True displays the cell formula; False hides the formula. The default is True.
Value	True displays the cell value; False hides the value. The default is False.
Format	True displays the cell format information; False hides the format information. The default is False.
Protection	True displays the cell protection status; False hides the protection status. The default is False.
Names	True displays any names assigned to the cell; False hides name information. The default is False.
Precedents	xlDirect displays the addresses of all cells included in the selected cell's formula; xlAll displays the addresses of all cells used when calculating the value of the selected cell; xlNone hides this information. The default is xlNone.
Dependents	xlDirect displays the addresses of all cells whose formulas include the selected cell; xlAll displays the addresses of all cells whose value depends on the value of the selected cell; xlNone hides this information. The default is xlNone.
Note	True displays a note for the cell; False hides the note. The default is True.

II

Programmer's Reference

*window.*SmallScroll

*window.*SmallScroll ([*Down*], [*Up*], [*ToRight*], [*ToLeft*])

Scrolls the window a multiple number of cells or rows at a time.

Argument	Description
Down	Number of cells to scroll down. The default is 0.
Up	Number of cells to scroll up. The default is 0.
ToRight	Number of cells to scroll to the right. The default is 0.
ToLeft	Number of cells to scroll to the left. The default is 0.

If the window can't scroll as many cells as specified, the window scrolls as far as possible in that direction.

*window.*Split

*window.*Split [= True | False]

True splits the window horizontally. When set, the split box is placed at the bottom of the first row. Causes error if window is not displaying a worksheet or macro sheet. The default is False.

*window.*SplitColumn

*window.*SplitColumn [= *columnposition*]

Sets or returns the position of the vertical split box in columns. Causes error if window is not displaying a worksheet or a macro sheet. The default is 0.

*window.*SplitHorizontal

*window.*SplitHorizontal [= *pointposition*]

Sets or returns the position of the horizontal split box in points. Causes error if window is not displaying a worksheet or a macro sheet. The default is 0.

*window.*SplitRow

*window.*SplitRow [= *rowposition*]

Sets or returns the position of the horizontal split box in rows. Causes error if window is not displaying a worksheet or a macro sheet. The default is 0.

*window.*SplitVertical

window.SplitVertical [= *pointposition*]

Sets or returns the position of the vertical split box in points. Causes error if window is not displaying a worksheet or macro sheet. The default is 0.

*window.*TabRatio

window.TabRatio [= *ratio*]

Sets or returns the ratio between the width of the window's tab display and vertical scroll bar. The default is 0.75.

*window.*Type

Returns a constant that identifies the type of window: xlChartInPlace, the edit window for an embedded chart; xlChartAsWindow, the edit window for a chart sheet; xlWorkbook, a workbook window; xlInfo, an Info window; or xlClipboard, the Clipboard window (Macintosh only).

*window.*VisibleRange

Returns the range of cells in the display area of the window.

Note

The VisibleRange may not be accurate if the window is obscured by other windows. The range value contained in the VisibleRange property holds only those cells that can be seen. If this property is checked while a dialog box obscures part of the window, the range value would be inaccurate.

*window.*WindowNumber

Returns the position of the window in the Window menu.

*window.*Zoom

window.Zoom [= **True** | **False** | *percentage*]

True sizes the current selection to fill the window; False restores the normal view; *percentage* zooms the display by a certain percentage. Causes error if window is not displaying a worksheet, chart sheet, or macro sheet. The default is False.

II

Programmer's Reference

The *Pane* and *Panes* Objects

A *pane* is a portion of a window that displays a worksheet. Worksheets have two panes if they are split; otherwise they have one (the default). Use the Panes collection to specify the pane of a window that has been split. Use the Pane object to obtain information about, activate, or scroll a pane.

You create a second pane by calling the Split method on a Window object containing a worksheet. Windows displaying other types of sheets don't support the Split method. For example:

```
Sub SplitWindow()
    ' Turn on error trapping.
    On Error Resume Next
    ' Attempt to split window.
    ActiveWindow.Split
    ' If it failed, then this is not a work or macro sheet.
    If Err <> Then
        MsgBox "Can't split this window"
        Err = 0
    Else
        ' Switch to the next pane.
        ActiveWindow.Panes(2).Activate
    End If
    On Error Goto 0
End Sub
```

You can also create a second pane manually by dragging the split box.

The Pane object and Panes collection have specific properties and methods, which are listed in Table 7.2.

Table 7.2 Pane and Panes properties and methods

```
Activate
Application
Count
Creator
Index
Item
LargeScroll
Parent
ScrollColumn
ScrollRow
SmallScroll
VisibleRange
```

The *AddIn* and *AddIns* Objects

Add-ins are special files that add features to Excel. Use the Add-Ins collection to add new add-ins to Excel. Use the AddIn object to remove an installed add-in or to get information about an add-in.

The following code displays a list of the add-ins currently available for use in Excel:

```
Sub ListAddins()
     Dim sAddinList As String, addNext As Addin
     ' Builds a list of the AddIns currently available.
     For Each addNext In Application.AddIns
          If addNext.Installed = True Then
               sAddinList = sAddinList & addNext.Title & " "
          End If
     Next addNext
     MsgBox "These addins are available for use: " & sAddinList
End Sub
```

To call a function from an add-in, use the function name. The following line of code calls the AddVisioToolBars procedure in an installed add-in:

```
AddVisioToolbars
```

The AddIn object and AddIns collection have specific properties and methods, which are listed in Table 7.3. Properties and methods shown in **bold** are described in the reference section that follows this table. Nonbold items are common to most objects and are described in Chapter 4, "Using Objects."

Table 7.3 AddIn and AddIns objects properties and methods
Add
Application
Author
Comments
Count[2]
Creator[1]
FullName
Installed
Item
Keywords
Name
Parent
Path
Subject
Title

[1]*Applies to the AddIns collection.*
[2]*Applies to the AddIns collection and the AddIn object.*

II

Programmer's Reference

addins.Add

addins.Add (*FileName*, [*CopyFile*])

Makes an add-in available to Excel and adds its title to the Add-Ins dialog box. The add-in is not loaded in Excel until its `Installed` property is set to True.

Argument	Description
FileName	The file specification for the add-in.
CopyFile	True copies the add-in file to Excel's library directory; False does not copy the file. If omitted, Excel prompts the user.

addin.Installed

addin.Installed [= True | False]

True loads the add-in; False unloads the add-in. The default is False.

Chapter 8

Using Sheets

Excel workbooks contain multiple pages, or *sheets*. Each sheet has a tab at the bottom that lets you easily flip back and forth between pages by clicking the desired tabs. There are several different kinds of sheets (see fig. 8.1):

- *Worksheets* contain cells in which you can enter data and formulas. They are the most common type of sheet in a workbook.

- *Chart sheets*, as you might expect, contain charts. Charts can also be embedded in worksheets.

- *Module sheets* contain Visual Basic code. Because you are reading this book, you'll probably see many of these.

- *Dialog sheets* contain custom dialog boxes. Excel includes special dialog box editing tools that you use to create these.

- *Excel4Macro sheets* and *Excel4IntlMacro sheets* contain Excel version 4.0 type macros. The old macro language used functions entered in cells. This is very different from the way Visual Basic procedures are written. Visual Basic functions are written into separate sheets and not directly into worksheet cells.

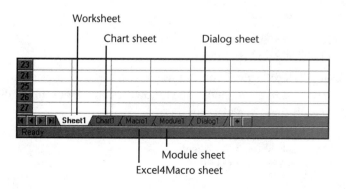

Fig. 8.1
Types of sheets.

This chapter explains how to create and manipulate the different sheets available in Excel; along the way, the chapter covers the Sheets, Worksheet, Module, Outline, and Scenario objects.

In this chapter, you learn how to do the following:

- Create different types of sheets.

- Copy, delete, and move sheets.

- Insert data, charts, drawings, and embedded objects in a worksheet.

- Manipulate views of data on worksheets using outlines and pivot tables.

- Save Visual Basic code to text files.

- Load Visual Basic code from text files.

- Set up variable data using scenarios.

Manipulating Sheets in a Workbook

The Sheets collection contains all the sheets in a workbook. Use the Sheets collection to select individual sheets and to perform tasks such as copying and deleting sheets or changing their order.

Accessing Sheets

The most common way to access a sheet is to use the ActiveSheet method. The following line of code displays the name of the currently active sheet:

```
MsgBox ActiveSheet.Name
```

Similarly, you can use a number or a name with the Sheets object to access a specific sheet:

```
' Activates the first sheet.
Sheets(1).Activate

'Activates the sheet named "Sheet3"
Sheets("Sheet3").Activate
```

Because Sheets is a collection, you can use it with For Each to perform operations on each sheet in a workbook. The following code, for example, displays the name of each sheet in a workbook:

```
Sub ShowNamesOfSheets()
     For Each shtNext In Sheets
          MsgBox shtNext.Name
     Next shtNext
End Sub
```

> **Note**
>
> The sheets are numbered in order from 1 to *n*, with *n* the last sheet. You can refer to the sheets by their number or name (appearing on the sheet tab). All workbooks open with a default of 16 sheets; this number can be altered by adding or removing sheets.

Determining Sheet Types

The Sheets collection contains *all* types of sheets—worksheets, modules, dialog sheets, chart sheets, and macro sheets. Not all operations are valid on all types of sheets. For example, modules don't contain cells, so you'll get an error if you try to select a range in a module.

When working with the Sheets collection, it's very important to make sure you have the right type of sheet before you act. To determine the type of a sheet, use the TypeName function and the Type property. Unfortunately, the Type property isn't available on Module, Chart, or Dialog sheets. For example:

```
Sub ShowTypeofSheet()
    Select Case TypeName(ActiveSheet)
        Case "Worksheet"
            If ActiveSheet.Type = xlWorksheet Then
                MsgBox "This sheet is a worksheet!"
            ElseIf ActiveSheet.Type = xlExcel4MacroSheet Then
                MsgBox "This sheet is a macro sheet!"
            Else
                MsgBox "This sheet is an international macro _
                sheet!"
            End If
        Case "Module"
            MsgBox "This sheet is a module!"
        Case "Chart"
            MsgBox "This sheet is a chart sheet!"
    End Select
End Sub
```

After you know what type of sheet you have, it is safe to perform tasks that are specific to that type of sheet. For example:

```
Sub ClearWorksheet()
    If TypeName(ActiveSheet) = "Worksheet" Then
        ' Clear all cells.
        ActiveSheet.UsedRange.Clear
    End If
End Sub
```

II

Programmer's Reference

Copying and Deleting Sheets

As with most objects, you add sheets using the collection object and delete sheets using the individual object. For example:

```
' Add a single worksheet using defaults.
Sheets.Add

' Delete a specific sheet (the first one).
Sheets(1).Delete
```

It might surprise you, but `Sheets.Copy` copies *all* the sheets in a workbook. This makes sense if you remember this rule: Use the collection to act on all sheets, and use a single object to act on one sheet. Here are two examples:

```
' Create a copy of the current workbook
Sheets.Copy

' Create a copy of the current sheet and place the copy before _
the current one.
ActiveSheet.Copy Before:=ActiveSheet
```

Moving Sheets

You can move sheets within the current workbook. The following line of code moves the current sheet one tab lower in the sheet order:

```
ActiveSheet.Move Before:=ActiveSheet.Previous
```

The following line of code moves the current sheet one tab higher in the sheet order:

```
ActiveSheet.Move After:=ActiveSheet.Next
```

`Sheets` have specific properties and methods, which are listed in Table 8.1. Properties and methods shown in **bold** are described in the reference section that follows this table. Nonbold items are common to most objects and are described in Chapter 4, "Using Objects."

Table 8.1 Sheets properties and methods	
Add	Item
Application	**Move**
Copy	Parent
Count	PrintOut
Creator	PrintPreview
Delete	Select
FillAcrossSheets	Visible

sheets.Add

sheets.Add ([*Before*], [*After*], [*Count*], [*Type*])

Creates a new worksheet or macro sheet and adds it to the Sheets collection.

Argument	Description
Before	The sheet object before which to insert the new sheet; for example, Sheets("Sheet1").
After	The sheet object after which to insert the new sheet. Don't specify both *Before* and *After*.
Count	The number of sheets to add. The default is 1.
Type	xlWorksheet to add a worksheet; xlExcel4MacroSheet to add a macro sheet; xlExcel4IntlMacroSheet to add an international macro sheet. The default is xlWorksheet.

The following line of code adds a worksheet to the current workbook:

```
Sheets.Add
```

The next line adds a macro sheet and inserts it before the first sheet in the current workbook:

```
Sheets.Add Before:=Sheets(1), Type:=xlExcel4MacroSheet
```

sheets.Copy

sheets.Copy ([*Before*], [*After*])

Creates a copy of the current sheet.

Argument	Description
Before	The sheet object before which to insert the new sheets; for example, Sheets("Sheet1").
After	The sheet object after which to insert the new sheets. Don't specify both *Before* and *After*.

If both *Before* and *After* are omitted, Copy creates a new workbook to contain the sheets. The following code creates a copy of the current workbook:

```
Sheets.Copy
```

Programmer's Reference

II

To copy an individual sheet, use a single sheet object. The next code creates a copy of the active worksheet and adds it to the Sheets collection:

```
ActiveSheet.Copy Before:=Sheets(1)
```

sheets(index).**Delete( )**

Deletes the specified sheet. Prompts the user before deleting. The following line of code deletes Sheet1 in the current workbook:

```
Sheets("Sheet1").Delete
```

sheets.**FillAcrossSheets**

sheets.**FillAcrossSheets (*Range*, [*Type*])**

Copies the contents and/or formulas in a range of cells to the same range on other worksheets.

Argument	Description
Range	The range to copy to all worksheets.
Type	xlAll to copy formulas and values of cells; xlContents to copy the values only; xlFormulas to copy formulas only. The default is xlAll.

The following code copies the currently selected range to all other sheets in the current workbook:

```
Sheets.FillAcrossSheets Selection
```

sheets(index).**Move**

sheets(index).**Move ([*Before*], [*After*])**

Changes the order of sheets in a workbook.

Argument	Description
Before	The sheet object before which to move the new sheet; for example, Sheets("Sheet1").
After	The sheet object after which to move the sheet.

You must specify either *Before* or *After*, but not both. The following code moves sheet 1 after sheet 4:

```
Sheets("sheet1").Move After:=Sheets("Sheet4")
```

Working with Individual Worksheets

Worksheets are the backbone of Excel. Use the Worksheets collection to create new worksheets and perform tasks on all worksheets. Use the Worksheet object to perform the following tasks:

- Access ranges of cells.

- Add drawings, charts, and other objects.

- Change views on data.

- Control changes to data.

Working with Cells in a Worksheet

The Worksheet object lets you access ranges of cells in three ways:

- Use the Cells method to access all cells in a worksheet.

- Use the UsedRange property to access all cells containing data.

- Use the Range method to access an arbitrary range of cells.

The following code shows how to perform actions on all the cells in a worksheet:

```
Sub IterateOverCells()
      Dim rng As Range, iCount As Integer
      ' Get each cell in the worksheet, one at a time.
      For Each rng In ActiveSheet.Cells
           ' Assign value to a cell (any operation could go here).
           rng.Value = iCount
           iCount = iCount + 1
           If iCount > 1000 Then Exit For
      Next rng
End Sub
```

> **Note**
>
> Although there is a Cells method, there is no such thing as a Cell object. The smallest unit is a Range object. A range may contain just one cell.

The UsedRange property is very useful for getting at all the cells that have values. Because it's more specific than the Cells collection, UsedRange can speed up operations that you want to perform on all existing cell values. For example, you can speed up IterateOverCells by replacing the code

```
For Each rng In ActiveSheet.Cells
```

with

```
For Each rng In ActiveSheet.UsedRange
```

The Range method is probably the most frequently used method in Excel. It is so commonly used that Excel provides three different forms—cell references, strings, or square brackets. Each of the following lines of code selects the same range of cells:

```
ActiveSheet.Range(Cells(1, 1), Cells(4, 4)).Select
ActiveSheet.Range ("A1:D4").Select
[a1:d4].Select
```

Inserting Charts, Drawings, and Other Objects

Worksheets can contain many different types of embedded objects:

- Chart objects

- Drawing objects

- Form objects

- OLE objects

Figure 8.2 shows the toolbars used to insert Chart, Drawing, and Form objects into a worksheet.

Fig. 8.2
Toolbars used for inserting objects.

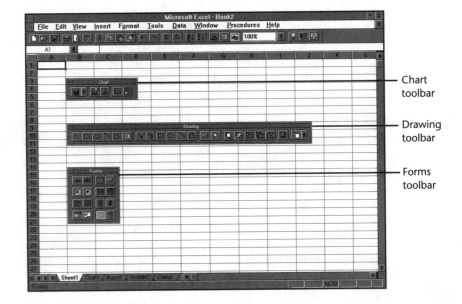

Chart toolbar

Drawing toolbar

Forms toolbar

Inserting Charts

To insert a chart on a worksheet, use the Add method on the worksheet's ChartObjects collection, then assign one or more data series to the chart. The easiest way to assign data series is by using the ChartWizard method. The ChartWizard method modifies the properties of a chart. The following code creates a quick bar chart from all the data on a worksheet:

```
Sub QuickChart()
    Dim chrtobj As ChartObject
    ' Add a chart object to the worksheet.
    Set chrtobj = ActiveSheet.ChartObjects.Add(100, 100, 200, 200)
    ' Use the UsedRange property to select the range to chart.
    chrtobj.Chart.ChartWizard ActiveSheet.UsedRange
End Sub
```

Tip

The Chart method of ChartObject is the key to using charting methods and properties such as Chart-Wizard. The Chart method returns the underlying Chart object for the embedded object.

Drawing and Form objects represent graphic objects on a worksheet. The following Worksheet methods control the drawing and form objects on a worksheet:

Arcs	Lines
Buttons	ListBoxes
CheckBoxes	Ovals
DrawingObjects	Pictures
Drawings	Rectangles
DropDowns	ScrollBars
GroupBoxes	Spinners
GroupObjects	TextBoxes
Labels	

To insert a drawing object, use the Add method on the object's collection. The following code adds a line to the worksheet:

```
ActiveSheet.Lines.Add 40, 40, 200, 200
```

The DrawingObjects method returns all of the drawing objects on a worksheet. This is useful for grouping, moving, or deleting multiple drawing objects. The following code groups all of the drawing objects on a worksheet, then moves them as a block to the upper left corner of the worksheet:

```
Sub GroupObjects()
    ' Group all the drawing objects.
    ActiveSheet.DrawingObjects.Group
    ' Move the group to the top.
    ActiveSheet.GroupObjects(1).Top = 0
    ActiveSheet.GroupObjects(1).Left = 0
    ' Ungroup the objects.
    ActiveSheet.GroupObjects(1).Ungroup
End Sub
```

> **Note**
>
> All drawing and form objects are included in the DrawingObjects collection. Excel considers form objects to be drawing objects, even though you don't really "draw" with them.

Inserting OLE Objects

To insert an OLE object in a worksheet, use the Add method in the worksheet's OLEObjects collection, as in the following code:

```
ActiveSheet.OLEObjects.Add ("Word.Document.6")
```

To edit the object, you must activate it. For example:

```
ActiveSheet.OLEObjects(1).Activate
```

Preventing Changes

To prevent changes to a worksheet, use the Protect method. The protection properties return information about a worksheet's current protection status. These properties cannot be used to turn protection on or off.

The following code checks whether a worksheet is protected. If it is not protected, the code prompts the user for a password and sets protection:

```
Sub ProtectSheet()
    Dim sPass As String
    ' Check if sheet is protected.
    If ActiveSheet.ProtectContents = False Then
        ' If not, get a password.
        sPass = InputBox("Enter a password for this sheet")
        ' If user doesn't enter a password, don't set protection.
        If sPass <> "" Then
            ' Protect worksheet.
            ActiveSheet.Protect sPass
        End if
    End If
End Sub
```

Creating Pivot Tables

A *pivot table* is an interactive worksheet table you use to summarize and analyze data from an existing list or table. To add a pivot table to a worksheet, use the worksheet's PivotTablesWizard method. Unlike other collections, there is no Add method for the PivotTables collection.

To create a pivot table using the PivotTableWizard method, you must add fields to the pivot table using the table's AddFields method. The following example was recorded in Excel.

```
Sub Macro1()
    ActiveSheet.PivotTableWizard SourceType:=xlDatabase, _
    SourceData:= _
        "Products!R1C1:R59C7", TableDestination:="", _
        TableName:= _
        "PivotTable2"
    ActiveSheet.PivotTables("PivotTable2").AddFields RowFields:= _
        "Salesperson", ColumnFields:="Product", _
        PageFields:=Array( _
        "Region", "Year")
    ActiveSheet.PivotTables("PivotTable2").PivotFields("Sales"). _
    Orientation _
        = xlDataField
End Sub
```

The Worksheet object and Worksheets collection have specific properties and methods, listed in Table 8.2. Those shown in **bold** are described in the reference section that follows this table. Nonbold items are common to most objects and are described in Chapter 4, "Using Objects."

Table 8.2 Worksheet and Worksheets properties and methods

Activate	FillAcrossSheets[1]
Add[1]	**FilterMode**
Application[2]	**GroupBoxes**
Arcs	**GroupObjects**
AutoFilterMode	Index
Buttons	Item[1]
Calculate	**Labels**
Cells	**Lines**
ChartObjects	**ListBoxes**
CheckBoxes	Move[2]
CheckSpelling	Name
CircularReference	**Next**
ClearArrows	**OLEObjects**
Columns	**OnCalculate**
ConsolidationFunction	**OnData**
ConsolidationOptions	**OnDoubleClick**
ConsolidationSources	**OnEntry**
Copy[2]	**OnSheetActivate**
Count[1]	**OnSheetDeactivate**
Creator[2]	**OptionButtons**
Delete[2]	**Outline**
DisplayAutomaticPageBreaks	**Ovals**
DrawingObjects	**PageSetup**
Drawings	Parent[2]
DropDowns	**Paste**

(continues)

II

Programmer's Reference

Table 8.2 Continued	
PasteSpecial	Scenarios
Pictures	ScrollBars
PivotTables	Select[2]
PivotTableWizard	ShowAllData
Previous	ShowDataForm
PrintOut	Spinners
PrintPreview[2]	StandardHeight
Protect	StandardWidth
ProtectContents	TextBoxes
ProtectDrawingObjects	TransitionExpEval
ProtectScenarios	TransitionFormEntry
Range	Type
Rectangles	Unprotect
Rows	UsedRange
SaveAs	Visible[2]

[1] *Applies to the Worksheets collection.*

[2] *Applies to the Worksheets collection and the Worksheet object.*

worksheet.Arcs

worksheet.Arcs ([Index])

Returns an Arc or collection of Arc objects on a worksheet. The following line of code adds an arc to the current worksheet:

```
ActiveSheet.Arcs.Add 70, 30, 40, 100
```

worksheet.AutoFilterMode

worksheet.AutoFilterMode [= False]

Returns True if a data column on the worksheet has an automatic filter; False if automatic filters are off. If AutoFilterMode is True, you can turn them off by setting this property to False. However, you can't set this property to True directly. Instead, use the AutoFilter method on the Range object to set AutoFilterMode to True.

*worksheet.*Buttons

*worksheet.*Buttons (*[Index]*)

Returns the Buttons object on a worksheet. The following code adds a button to the current worksheet:

```
ActiveSheet.Buttons.Add 20, 20, 60, 40
```

*worksheet.*Calculate( )

Calculates the specified worksheet. The following code calculates the current worksheet:

```
ActiveSheet.Calculate
```

*worksheet.*Cells

*worksheet.*Cells (*[RowIndex]*, *[ColumnIndex]*)

Returns a range object containing a single cell, a row of cells, a column of cells, or all of the cells in a worksheet.

Argument	Description
RowIndex	The number of the row of cells to return.
ColumnIndex	The number of the column of cells to return. For example, column D is column number 4.

If *RowIndex* and *ColumnIndex* are omitted, Cells returns the collection of all cells in the workbook.

The following line of code selects cell D6 on the active worksheet:

```
ActiveSheet.Cells(6,4).Select
```

*worksheet.*ChartObjects

*worksheet.*ChartObjects (*[Index]*)

Returns the chart objects embedded on a worksheet. The following code adds an embedded chart to the current worksheet and then charts the currently selected columns of cells:

```
Sub AddEmbeddedChart( )
    Dim chrtobj As ChartObject, rngColumn As Range
    Set chrtobj = ActiveSheet.ChartObjects.Add(100, 100, 200, 200)
    ' Assumption: user has selected a range of cells.
```

II

Programmer's Reference

```
        For Each rngColumn In Selection.Columns
                chrtobj.Chart.SeriesCollection.Add rngColumn
        Next rngColumn
    End Sub
```

*worksheet.***CheckBoxes**

*worksheet.***CheckBoxes ([*Index*])**

Returns the check boxes on a worksheet. The following line of code adds a check box to the current worksheet:

```
ActiveSheet.CheckBoxes.Add 10, 20, 80, 10
```

*worksheet.***CircularReference()**

Returns a range containing the first circular reference on a worksheet. If no circular references are found, returns a reference to Nothing.

> **Note**
>
> When a formula refers to its own cell, this is called *circular reference*. The reference can be direct or indirect.

The following code clears all of the circular references on the active worksheet:

```
Sub DeleteCircularReferences()
    Dim vCirc As Variant
    Do
        Set vCirc = ActiveSheet.CircularReference
        If TypeName(vCirc) <> "Nothing" Then
                vCirc.Clear
        Else
            Exit Do
        End If
    Loop
End Sub
```

*worksheet.***ClearArrows()**

Clears the arrows used when auditing a worksheet. Figure 8.3 illustrates audit arrows. The following line of code clears the arrows on the active worksheet:

```
ActiveSheet.ClearArrows
```

> **Note**
>
> The Auditing features of Excel allow you to isolate problems within a worksheet.

	A	B	C	D	E	F	G	H
13		Payment no.	Payment dates	Beginning balance	Interest	Principal	Ending balance	Cumulative interest
14		1	9/30/93	$0.00	$0.00	$0.00	$0.00	$0.00
15		2	10/30/93	$0.00	$0.00	$0.00	$0.00	$0.00
16		3	11/30/93	$0.00	$0.00	$0.00	$0.00	$0.00
17		4	12/30/93	$0.00	$0.00	$0.00	$0.00	$0.00
18								
19								
20								
21								
22	CALCULATIONS							
23		Use payme	494.17			Beginning bal	0.00	
24		1st paymen	1			Cumulative in	0.00	
25								

Fig. 8.3
Audit arrows.

Audit arrow

worksheet.**Columns**

worksheet.**Columns ([*Index*])**

Returns the column specified by *Index*. If *Index* is omitted, returns all the columns in a worksheet. The following line of code selects column C in the active worksheet:

```
ActiveSheet.Columns(3).Select
```

worksheet.**ConsolidationFunction**

worksheet.**ConsolidationFunction [= setting]**

Sets or returns the type of calculation used in the following consolidations: xlAverage, xlCount, xlCountNums, xlMax, xlMin, xlProduct, xlStDev, xlStdDevP, xlSum, xlVar, or xlVarP. The default is xlSum.

These settings correspond to the function list in the Consolidate dialog box (see fig. 8.4), accessed by choosing Data, Consolidate.

Consolidation function

Consolidation sources

Consolidation options

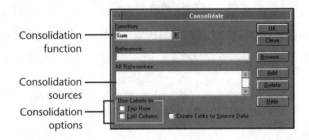

Fig. 8.4
The Consolidate dialog box.

worksheet.**ConsolidationOptions**

Returns a three-element array that corresponds to the Consolidate dialog box check boxes. Choose Data, Consolidate to view the Consolidate dialog box.

Array element	Description
worksheet.ConsolidationOptions	True uses labels from the top row of the source data. The default is False.
worksheet.ConsolidationOptions	True uses labels from the left column of the source data. The default is False.
worksheet.ConsolidationOptions	True creates a link to the source data for each cell in the consolidation. The default is False.

Labels options are useful only when consolidating data by category. Multiple data sources must be organized and labeled identically for these options to work.

worksheet.**ConsolidationSources**

Returns an array listing the consolidation sources for a worksheet. The elements in this array correspond to lines in the All References list box of the Consolidate dialog box. Returns Empty if there are no consolidations on the worksheet.

worksheet.**DisplayAutomaticPageBreaks**
worksheet.**DisplayAutomaticPageBreaks=[True|False]**

True displays the automatic page breaks on a worksheet; False does not display them. The default is False.

> **Caution**
>
> The DisplayAutomaticPageBreaks property can only be set. Trying to query the property for a value causes an error. This appears to be a bug in Excel and might change with new minor releases.

worksheet.**DrawingObjects**

worksheet.**DrawingObjects ([*Index*])**

Index indicates the drawing object to return. If *Index* is omitted, returns all the drawing objects on a worksheet. Drawing objects are those objects shown on the Drawing and Forms toolbars, and include shapes, buttons, drop-down lists, and other controls available from these toolbars.

worksheet.**Drawings**

worksheet.**Drawings ([*Index*])**

Index indicates the drawing to return. If *Index* is omitted, returns all the drawings on a worksheet. Drawings are user-created drawing objects created using the Freehand, Freeform, and Filled Freeform tools on the Drawing toolbar.

worksheet.**DropDowns**

worksheet.**DropDowns ([*Index*])**

Index indicates the drop-down list to return. If *Index* is omitted, returns all the drop-down lists on a worksheet. Drop-down lists are a type of drawing object.

worksheet.**FilterMode**

Returns True if any ranges on a worksheet are currently using a data filter; False otherwise. Data filters are set by choosing Data, Filter. The default is False.

worksheet.**GroupBoxes**

worksheet.**GroupBoxes ([*Index*])**

Index indicates the group box to return. If *Index* is omitted, returns all the group boxes on a worksheet. Group boxes are a type of frame created from the Forms toolbar. The following line of code creates a group box on the active sheet:

```
ActiveSheet.Groupboxes.Add 10, 20, 200, 200
```

worksheet.GroupObjects

worksheet.GroupObjects ([*Index*])

Index indicates the group of drawing objects to return. If *Index* is omitted, returns all the groups on a worksheet. Groups are created by selecting a number of drawing objects on a worksheet, then clicking the Group tool on the Drawing toolbar.

The following code groups all of the drawing objects on a sheet, moves the group to the origin of the sheet, and then ungroups the objects:

```
Sub GroupObjects()
    ActiveSheet.DrawingObjects.Group
    ActiveSheet.GroupObjects(1).Top = 0
    ActiveSheet.GroupObjects(1).Left = 0
    ActiveSheet.GroupObjects(1).Ungroup
End Sub
```

worksheet.Labels

worksheet.Labels ([*Index*])

Index indicates the label to return. If *Index* is omitted, returns all the labels on a worksheet. In Excel, labels are created by clicking the Label button on the Forms toolbar. The following code creates a label on the active sheet:

```
ActiveSheet.Labels.Add 40, 60, 200, 20
```

worksheet.Lines

worksheet.Lines ([*Index*])

Index indicates the line to return. If *Index* is omitted, returns all the lines on a worksheet. In Excel, lines are created by clicking the Line tool on the Drawing toolbar. The following code creates a line on the active sheet:

```
ActiveSheet.Lines.Add 40, 40, 200, 200
```

worksheet.ListBoxes

worksheet.ListBoxes ([*Index*])

Index indicates the list box to return. If *Index* is omitted, returns all the list boxes on a worksheet. In Excel, list boxes are created by clicking the List Box tool on the Forms toolbar. The following code fills a list box on the active sheet:

```
Application.ActiveSheet.Listboxes(1).List =
    Array("Objects", "Properties", "Methods")
```

worksheet.**Next**

Returns the next sheet as indicated by the sheet tabs at the bottom of the window. The following code displays the name of the next sheet:

```
MsgBox ActiveSheet.Next.Name
```

worksheet.**OLEObjects**

worksheet.**OLEObjects ([*Index*])**

Index indicates the OLE or DDE object to return. If *Index* is omitted, returns all the OLE and DDE objects on a worksheet. The following code creates a new OLE object on the active sheet and activates the object for editing:

```
ActiveSheet.OLEObjects.Add ("Word.Document.6").Activate
```

worksheet.**OnCalculate**

worksheet.**OnCalculate [= *procedure*]**

Sets or returns the name of a procedure to run when the worksheet calculates. *Procedure* is not run if another Visual Basic procedure triggers the calculation. Setting the property to " " removes this macro.

worksheet.**OnData**

worksheet.**OnData [= *procedure*]**

Sets or returns the name of a procedure to run when the worksheet updates OLE or DDE links. *Procedure* is not run if another Visual Basic procedure updates the links.

worksheet.**OnDoubleClick**

worksheet.**OnDoubleClick [= *procedure*]**

Sets or returns the name of a procedure to run when the user double-clicks the worksheet. *Procedure* is not run if Visual Basic triggers the double-click, as with `Application.DoubleClick`.

worksheet.**OnEntry**

worksheet.**OnEntry [= *procedure*]**

Sets or returns the name of a procedure to run when the user presses Enter after typing in a cell or on the formula bar. *Procedure* is not run if Visual Basic triggers the entry.

*worksheet.***OnSheetActivate**

*worksheet.***OnSheetActivate** [= *procedure*]

Sets or returns the name of a procedure to run when the user activates the sheet. *Procedure* is not run if Visual Basic activates the sheet.

*worksheet.***OnSheetDeactivate**

*worksheet.***OnSheetDeactivate** [= *procedure*]

Sets or returns the name of a procedure to run when the user deactivates the sheet by switching to another sheet. *Procedure* is not run if Visual Basic deactivates the sheet.

*worksheet.***OptionButtons**

*worksheet.***OptionButtons** ([*Index*])

Index indicates the option button to return. If *Index* is omitted, returns all the option buttons on a worksheet. In Excel, option buttons are created by clicking the Option button on the Forms toolbar. The following line of code creates an option button on the active sheet:

```
ActiveSheet.OptionButtons.Add 80, 80, 100, 10
```

*worksheet.***Outline**

Returns an outline object for the worksheet. The following code turns on automatic outlining for a worksheet, and then displays the top-level view:

```
Sub Outlining( )
    ActiveSheet.Cells(1, 1).AutoOutline
    ActiveSheet.Outline.ShowLevels 1, 1
End Sub
```

*worksheet.***Ovals**

*worksheet.***Ovals** ([*Index*])

Index indicates the oval to return. If *Index* is omitted, returns all the ovals on a worksheet. In Excel, ovals are created by clicking the Oval tool on the Drawing toolbar. The following code creates an oval on the active sheet:

```
ActiveSheet.Ovals.Add 40, 40, 200, 200
```

worksheet.PageSetup

Returns the `PageSetup` object for the worksheet. Use the returned `PageSetup` object to control the printing and layout attributes of the worksheet.

The following line of code sets the center header to print with the active sheet:

```
ActiveSheet.PageSetup.CenterHeader = ActiveWorkbook.FullName
```

worksheet.Paste

worksheet.Paste ([*Destination*], [*Link*])

Pastes the contents of the Clipboard to a range in a worksheet.

Argument	Description
Destination	The range to which the Clipboard contents is pasted. The default is to the current selection.
Link	True to link the pasted data to its source. The default is False.

You can't specify both `Destination` and `Link`. The following line pastes to cell A1 on the current sheet:

```
ActiveSheet.Paste Cells(1,1)
```

Note

Excel displays a warning if the size of the destination range doesn't match the size of the range to paste.

worksheet.PasteSpecial

worksheet.PasteSpecial ([*Format*], [*Link*], [*DisplayAsIcon*], [*IconFileName*], [*IconIndex*], [*IconLabel*])

Pastes data, including fonts and formats, from a selected range or other applications to a selected range. One or more cells must be selected before using `PasteSpecial`.

Argument	Description
Format	The format of the data to paste, as specified in the As list box of the Paste Special dialog box. The default is the first item in the As list. See the on-line help for a complete listing of format options.
Link	True to create a link between the pasted data and its source. The default is False.
DisplayAsIcon	True to display an icon rather than the actual data; False to display data. The default is determined by the source application.
IconFileName	The name of the file containing the icon to display.
IconIndex	The numeric index of the icon within IconFileName.
IconLabel	The label to display under the icon.

Note

The *Format* argument *does not* correspond to the xlClipboardFormat constants returned by Application.ClipboardFormats.

worksheet.**Pictures**

worksheet.**Pictures ([*Index*])**

Index indicates the picture to return. If *Index* is omitted, returns all the pictures on the worksheet. In Excel, pictures are created by choosing Insert, Picture. The following line inserts a picture named "FISH.BMP" on the active sheet:

```
ActiveSheet.Pictures.Insert("FISH.BMP")
```

worksheet.**PivotTables**

worksheet.**PivotTables ([*Index*])**

Index indicates the pivot table to return. If *Index* is omitted, returns all the pivot tables on a worksheet. In Excel, pivot tables are created by choosing the PivotTable Wizard button on the Query and Pivot toolbar. The following code changes the orientation of a pivot field in the pivot table named "Books." Refer to on-line Help to see a complete list of orientation constants.

```
ActiveSheet.PivotTables("Books").PivotFields("Year Published") _
.Orientation = xlDataField
```

worksheet.PivotTableWizard

worksheet.**PivotTableWizard** ([*SourceType*], [*SourceData*], [*TableDestination*], [*TableName*], [*RowGrand*], [*ColumnGrand*], [*SaveData*], [*HasAutoFormat*], [*AutoPage*])

Creates a pivot table on the worksheet. Pivot tables let you view different relationships between rows and columns of data from other worksheets or remote data sources, such as databases. After creating a pivot table, you must add pivot fields and data fields to display useful data.

Argument	Description
SourceType	xlConsolidation if source is multiple consolidation ranges; xlDatabase if source is an Excel list or database; xlExternal if source is another application; xlPivotTable if source is another pivot table. The default is xlDatabase.
SourceData	A range, array of ranges, or two-element array containing an ODBC database source and SQL query string.
TableDestination	A range indicating where to place the pivot table. The default is the active cell.
TableName	The name of the table to be created. The default is "PivotTable*n*."
RowGrand	True to display grand totals for each row; False to omit row totals. The default is True.
ColumnGrand	True to display grand totals for each column; False to omit column totals. The default is True.
SaveData	True to save data in the pivot table; False to rebuild the table from its source each time the workbook is reopened. The default is True.
HasAutoFormat	True automatically reformats the pivot table when fields are moved or refreshed; False does not. The default is True.
AutoPage	If *SourceType* is xlConsolidation, True to create a page field for the consolidation; False to create page fields manually. Ignored for other *SourceTypes*. The default is True.

The following code creates a pivot table from the Access database
BIBLIO.MDB shipped with Visual Basic, version 3.0:

```
Sub BooksPivotTable( )
    ActiveSheet.PivotTableWizard SourceType:=xlExternal, _
        SourceData:=Array("DSN=MS Access
Databases;DBQ=c:\vb3\biblio.mdb;FIL=RedISAM;", _
        "SELECT * FROM AUTHORS, PUBLISHERS, TITLES WHERE _
        TITLES.Au_ID = AUTHORS.Au_ID " & _
        " AND TITLES.PubID = PUBLISHERS.PubID"), _
        TableName:="Books", RowGrand:=False, ColumnGrand:=False
    ActiveSheet.PivotTables("Books").AddFields _
    RowFields:=Array("Author", _
        "Title"), PageFields:="Name"
    ActiveSheet.PivotTables("Books").PivotFields _
    ("Year Published"). _
        Orientation = xlDataField
End Sub
```

worksheet.**Protect**

worksheet.**Protect ([*Password*], [*DrawingObjects*], [*Contents*], [*Scenarios*])**

Prevents changes to various features of a worksheet.

Argument	Description
Password	The password required to unprotect the worksheet. The default is None.
DrawingObjects	True to prevent changes to drawing objects; False to allow changes. The default is True.
Contents	True to prevent changes to the contents of cells; False to allow changes. The default is True.
Scenarios	True to prevent changes to the scenarios; False to allow changes. The default is True.

worksheet.**ProtectContents**

Returns True if cells are protected from changes; False otherwise.

worksheet.**ProtectDrawingObjects**

Returns True if drawing objects are protected from changes; False otherwise.

worksheet.**ProtectScenarios**

The ProtectScenarios property returns True if scenarios are protected from changes; False otherwise. This property is Read-Only.

worksheet.**Range**

worksheet.**Range ([*Cell1*], [*Cell2*])**

Returns a range of cells.

Argument	Description
Cell1	The upper left cell of the range.
Cell2	The lower right cell of the range.

Excel has three forms of the Range method: cell references, strings, and square brackets. Each of the following lines of code selects the same range of cells:

```
ActiveSheet.Range(Cells(1, 1), Cells(4, 4)).Select
ActiveSheet.Range ("A1:D4").Select
[a1:d4].Select
```

worksheet.**Rectangles**

worksheet.**Rectangles ([*Index*])**

Index indicates the rectangle to return. If *Index* is omitted, returns all the rectangles on a worksheet. In Excel, rectangles are created by clicking the Rectangle tool or Filled Rectangle tool on the Drawing toolbar. The following code creates a rectangle on the active sheet:

```
ActiveSheet.Rectangles.Add 100, 100, 200, 200
```

worksheet.**Rows**

worksheet.**Rows ([*Index*])**

Index indicates the number of the row to return. If *Index* is omitted, returns all the rows on a worksheet. The following code selects the fourth row on the current worksheet:

```
ActiveSheet.Rows(4).Select
```

II

Programmer's Reference

*worksheet.*Scenarios

*worksheet.*Scenarios ([*Index*])

A *scenario* is a set of input values that can be applied to a worksheet model. Scenarios are useful for what-if comparisons using different input values.

Index indicates the scenario to return. If *Index* is omitted, returns all the scenarios in a worksheet. In Excel, you create scenarios by choosing Tools, Scenarios. The following code adds a scenario to the current worksheet based on the currently selected cells:

```
ActiveSheet.Scenarios.Add "New Scenario", Selection
```

*worksheet.*ScrollBars

*worksheet.*ScrollBars ([*Index*])

Index indicates the scroll bar form object to return. If *Index* is omitted, returns all the scroll bars on a worksheet. In Excel, scroll bars are created by clicking the Scroll Bar button on the Forms toolbar. The following line of code adds a scroll bar to the current worksheet:

```
ActiveSheet.ScrollBars.Add 10, 10, 100, 10
```

*worksheet.*ShowAllData()

Sets data filters on a worksheet to Show All. Data filters are set by choosing Data, Filter. Data filters temporarily hide rows that do not match the filter criteria. Unlike sorting, filtering does not rearrange a list.

*worksheet.*ShowDataForm()

Displays the data entry dialog box for the worksheet. In Excel, you display this dialog box by choosing Data, Form. By default, this form uses column headings for the data entry fields.

*worksheet.*Spinners

*worksheet.*Spinners ([*Index*])

A *spinner* is a small scroll bar. There is no slider control, only the directional arrows. Spinners are most commonly used next to edit boxes to allow the users to select a valid range of numbers to enter into the edit box.

Index indicates the spinner object to return. If *Index* is omitted, returns all the spinners on a worksheet. In Excel, spinners are created by clicking the Spinner button on the Forms toolbar. The following line of code adds a spinner to the current worksheet:

```
ActiveSheet.Spinners.Add 10, 10, 10, 10
```

worksheet.StandardHeight

Returns the default height of rows in a worksheet, measured in points.

worksheet.StandardWidth

Returns the default width of columns in a worksheet, measured in characters of the zero (0) character in normal font.

worksheet.TextBoxes

worksheet.TextBoxes ([*Index*])

Index indicates the text box to return. If *Index* is omitted, returns all the text boxes on a worksheet. In Excel, text boxes are created by clicking the Text Box button on the Standard toolbar. The following line of code adds a text box to the current worksheet:

```
ActiveSheet.TextBoxes.Add 40, 40, 100, 100
```

worksheet.TransitionExpEval

worksheet.TransitionExpEval [= True | False]

True uses Lotus 1-2-3 rules to evaluate expressions; False uses Excel's standard rules. The default is False.

worksheet.TransitionFormEntry

worksheet.TransitionFormEntry [= True | False]

True uses Lotus 1-2-3 formula syntax; False uses Excel's standard formulas. The default is False.

worksheet.Type

Returns xlWorksheet.

worksheet.Unprotect

worksheet.Unprotect ([*Password*])

Allows changes to a previously protected worksheet.

worksheet.UsedRange

Returns the range of cells that have data entered in them. The following line of code displays the cell address of the used range:

```
MsgBox ActiveSheet.UsedRange.Address
```

Manipulating Visual Basic Modules

A *module* is a sheet that can contain Visual Basic code. Modules don't support most of the property and methods that worksheets do. You can't select or modify specific lines of code. However, you can use modules to archive Visual Basic code as text files and reload those files using Visual Basic.

The ability to save and retrieve Visual Basic files is important if you are working on a large project that requires *source control*. Source control is important if more than one person is writing an application, or if you must keep track of changes. By saving modules as text periodically, you can compare differences between files using a variety of code maintenance tools.

Saving Modules as Text

Use the SaveAs method to save a module as text. The following code saves each module in a workbook as a text file. As a bonus, the sMakeName function converts the module name to a valid MS-DOS file name (you don't need to worry about this if you are working on the Macintosh).

```
Sub Module( )
    Dim sFileName As String
    For Each modNext In Modules
        sFileName = sMakeName(modNext.Name)
        ' If there is there is a filename, save module.
        If sFileName <> "" Then
            modNext.SaveAs sFileName, xlText
        End If
    Next modNext
End Sub
```

```
' Converts a module name to a file name.
Function sMakeName(vText As Variant) As String
    ' If the argument doesn't contain a string, prompt for a name.
    If TypeName(vText) <> "String" Then
        sMakeName = Application.GetSaveAsFilename
        Exit Function
    End If
    ' Otherwise, convert the argument to a valid name.
    Dim iPos As Integer
    ' Name may include spaces, so replace with underscore.
    iPos = InStr(vText, " ")
    Do While iPos <> 0 And iPos < 9
        If iPos <> 0 And iPos < 9 Then
            Mid(vText, iPos, 1) = "_"
        End If
        iPos = InStr(vText, " ")
    Loop
    ' Keep filename to 8 characters.
    vText = Mid(vText, 1, 8)
    ' Add a .BAS extension.
    sMakeName = vText & ".BAS"
End Function
```

Importing Text Files

Use the Insert method to import a text file into a module. Insert won't re-place existing procedures with new ones from the text file—it simply copies in the new file.

The following code demonstrates how to insert text into a module:

```
Sub InsertFile()
    Dim sFileName As String
    ' Prompt for file name to insert.
    sFileName = Application.GetOpenFilename _
    ("Basic modules (*.BAS), *.BAS")
    ' GetOpenFilename returns False (not "") _
      if user presses cancel.
    If sFileName <> "False" Then
        ' Insert the file, merging any declarations.
        ActiveSheet.InsertFile sFileName, True
    End If
End Sub
```

The Module object and Modules collection have specific properties and meth-ods, which are listed in Table 8.3. Properties and methods shown in **bold** are described in the reference section that follows this table. Nonbold items are common to most objects and are described in Chapter 4, "Using Objects."

II

Programmer's Reference

Table 8.3 Module and Modules properties and methods

Activate	OnDoubleClick
Add[1]	OnSheetActivate
Application[2]	OnSheetDeactivate
Copy[2]	**PageSetup**
Count[1]	Parent[2]
Creator[2]	Previous
Delete[2]	PrintOut[2]
Index	Protect
InsertFile	ProtectContents
Item[1]	**SaveAs**
Move[2]	Select[2]
Name	Unprotect
Next	Visible[2]

[1] *Applies to the* Modules *collection.*

[2] *Applies to the* Modules *collection and the* Module *object.*

*module.*InsertFile

*module.*InsertFile (*Filename*, [*Merge*])

Inserts a text file into a module.

Argument	Description
Filename	The name of the file to insert.
Merge	True to place declarations at the beginning of the current module; False to insert all text beginning at the current insertion point. The default is False.

The following line of code inserts the file "C:\TEMP.TXT" at the current insertion point in a module:

```
ActiveSheet.InsertFile "C:\TEMP.TXT"
```

*module.*PageSetup

Returns the PageSetup object for the module. Use the returned PageSetup object to control the printing and layout attributes of the module sheet.

The following line of code sets the center header to print with the active sheet:

```
ActiveSheet.PageSetup.CenterHeader = ActiveWorkbook.FullName
```

module.SaveAs *Filename, FileFormat*

Saves a module as a text file.

Argument	Description
Filename	The name of the file to save the module as. If the file already exists, Excel displays a warning.
FileFormat	Must be xlText for modules.

The following line of code saves the current module as TEMP.TXT:

```
ActiveSheet.SaveAs "C:\TEMP.TXT", xlText
```

Viewing the Worksheet

The Outline object for a worksheet lets you summarize and expand the level of detail in your worksheet. Figures 8.5 and 8.6 show different outline views. Each workbook can have one outline. Outlines can be created automatically if the data on the worksheet is laid out so calculations flow from left to right and top to bottom.

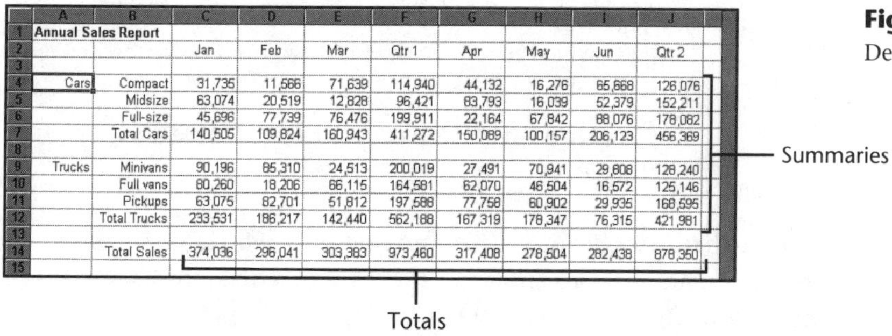

Fig. 8.5
Detail view.

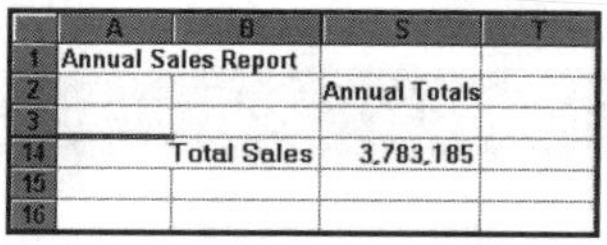

Summaries

Totals

Fig. 8.6
Summary view.

The following code creates an automatic outline for a worksheet, then displays the summary level:

```
' Create an outline for the whole worksheet using automatic styles,
' then show top level.
Sub ShowSummary( )
    ActiveSheet.UsedRange.AutoOutline
    ActiveSheet.Outline.AutomaticStyles = True
    ActiveSheet.Outline.ShowLevels 1, 1
End Sub
```

The following code displays all levels of detail for an outline. Outlines may have up to eight levels.

```
' Show all levels of detail.
Sub ShowDetail( )
    ActiveSheet.Outline.ShowLevels 8, 8
End Sub
```

The following code changes how Excel interprets total and summary layout. It does not change the layout of the worksheet; it merely changes how Excel assigns levels when creating the automatic outline.

```
' Switches outline summary settings back and forth.
Sub ChangeSummaryLayout( )
    If ActiveSheet.Outline.SummaryColumn = xlRight Then
        ActiveSheet.Outline.SummaryColumn = xlLeft
    Else
        ActiveSheet.Outline.SummaryColumn = xlRight
    End If
    If ActiveSheet.Outline.SummaryRow = xlBelow Then
        ActiveSheet.Outline.SummaryRow = xlAbove
    Else
        ActiveSheet.Outline.SummaryRow = xlBelow
    End If
End Sub
```

Outlines have specific properties and methods, which are shown in Table 8.4. Properties and methods shown in **bold** are described in the reference section that follows this table. Nonbold items are common to most objects and are described in Chapter 4, "Using Objects."

Table 8.4 Outline properties and methods

Application
AutomaticStyles
Creator
Parent
ShowLevels
SummaryColumn
SummaryRow

Outline.AutomaticStyles

Outline.AutomaticStyles [= True | False]

True applies automatic styles to the outline; False turns off automatic styles.

Outline.ShowLevels

Outline.ShowLevels ([*RowLevels*], [*ColumnLevels*])

Shows or hides outline levels.

Argument	Description
RowLevels	The number of outline levels to show for rows. Must be between 0 and 8. The default is 0 (no change).
ColumnLevels	The number of outline levels to show for columns. Must be between 0 and 8. The default is 0 (no change).

This line of code shows the top level of an outline, hiding all the detail levels:

```
ActiveSheet.Outline.Showlevels 1,1
```

Outline.SummaryColumn

Outline.SummaryColumn [= xlLeft | xlRight]

xlLeft indicates column summaries are to the left of detail data; xlRight indicates they are to the right. Use with automatic outlining if summary column is not on the left, as Excel expects. The default is xlLeft.

Outline.SummaryRow

Outline.SummaryRow [= xlAbove | xlBelow]

xlAbove indicates row summaries are above detail data; xlBelow indicates they are below (accounting style). Use with automatic outlining if totals are not below data, as Excel expects. The default is xlBelow.

Doing What-If Analysis

A scenario is a named range of data that is used as the basis for calculations. Use scenarios to set up what-if projections where the data changes, but the calculations remain the same. Use the Scenarios collection to add scenarios to a worksheet. Use the Scenario object to change the data or cells within a particular scenario.

Use the Add method to add a scenario to a worksheet. The following line of code creates a new scenario and inserts some data in the scenario's cells:

```
ActiveSheet.Scenarios.Add "New1 Scenario", Selection, _
Array(1,2,3,4,5,6,7,8,9)
```

Use the ChangeScenario method to change the data or cells a scenario contains. The worksheet does not display the changes until you call the Show method. Here is an example:

```
Sub ChangeScenario( )
    With ActiveSheet.Scenarios("New Scenario")
        ' Change values (notice the ChangingCells is required
here)
        .ChangeScenario ChangingCells:=.ChangingCells, _
        Values:=Array(10, 20, 15, 67, 21)
        ' Update display.
        .Show
    End With
End Sub
```

You can report on the scenarios in a worksheet using the CreateSummary method. The following code creates a new worksheet containing a report on the scenarios in the current worksheet. The report is in outline form and you can view summary or details.

```
Sub CreateSummary( )
    ActiveSheet.Scenarios.CreateSummary
End Sub
```

The Scenario object and Scenarios collection have specific properties and methods, which are shown in Table 8.5. Properties and methods shown in **bold** are described in the reference section that follows this table. Nonbold items are common to most objects and are described in Chapter 4, "Using Objects."

Table 8.5 Scenario and scenarios properties and methods	
Add[1]	**Hidden**
Application[2]	Index
ChangeScenario	Item[1]
ChangingCells	Locked
Comment	**Merge**[1]
Count[1]	Name
CreateSummary[1]	Parent[2]
Creator[2]	**Show**
Delete	Values

[1] *Applies to the Scenarios collection.*

[2] *Applies to the Scenarios collection and the Scenario object.*

Scenarios.Add

Scenarios.Add (*Name*, *ChangingCells*, [*Values*], [*Comment*], [*Locked*], [*Hidden*])

Creates a new scenario and adds it to a worksheet.

Argument	Description
Name	The name of the scenario to create. No two scenarios can have the same name.
ChangingCells	A range of cells containing variable data for the scenario.
Values	An array of data used to initialize the values of *ChangingCells*. The default is to use current values of *ChangingCells*.
Comment	A comment to display for the scenario in the Scenario Manager dialog box. The default is the name of the creator and date.
Locked	True to prevent other users from changing the scenario; False to allow other users to change the scenario. The default is True.
Hidden	True to hide the scenario on the worksheet; False to display the scenario. The default is False.

The following line of code adds a scenario based on the currently selected cells:

```
ActiveSheet.Scenarios.Add "New Scenario", Selection
```

scenario.ChangeScenario

scenario.ChangeScenario (*ChangingCells*, [*Values*])

Changes the range and/or cell values for a scenario. You must use the Show method to display changes on the worksheet.

Argument	Description
ChangingCells	The new range of cells to assign to the scenario. The default is no change.
Values	An array containing the new values for the changing cells in the scenario. You must specify *ChangingCells* to use this argument.

The following code changes the scenario New Scenario to refer to the current selection:

```
ActiveSheet.Scenarios("New Scenario").ChangeScenario Selection
```

*scenario.*ChangingCells

Returns the range of cells to which a scenario refers. The following code selects the range of cells for New Scenario:

```
ActiveSheet.Scenarios("New Scenario").ChangingCells.Select
```

Scenarios.CreateSummary

Scenarios.CreateSummary ([*ReportType*], [*ResultCells*])

Creates a new worksheet that summarizes an existing worksheet's scenarios.

Argument	Description
ReportType	xlStandardSummary to create the standard, outlined report; xlPivotTable to create the report as a pivot table. The default is xlStandardSummary.
ResultCells	The range of cells that use the scenarios in their formulas. You must specify *ResultCells* if *ReportType* is xlPivotTable. The default is None.

The following code creates a summary of the scenarios on the current worksheet:

```
ActiveSheet.Scenarios.CreateSummary
```

*scenario.*Hidden

*scenario.*Hidden [= True | False]

True prevents other users from seeing the scenario's name in the Scenario Manager dialog box; False displays the name. The default is False.

*scenario.*Locked

*scenario.*Locked [= True | False]

True prevents other users from changing the scenario; False allows changes to the scenario. The default is True.

Scenarios.Merge

Scenarios.Merge (Source)

Copies the scenarios from *Source* worksheet to another worksheet. Scenerios with the same name are replaced. The following code copies the scenarios from Sheet 1 of BOOK1.XLS to the currently active worksheet:

```
ActiveSheet.Scenarios.Merge ("[BOOK1.XLS]Sheet1")
```

scenario.Show

Displays changes to the scenario. The following code changes the values of cells in a scenario, then displays those changes:

```
With ActiveSheet.Scenarios("New Scenario")
    ' Change values (notice the ChangingCells is required here)
    .ChangeScenario ChangingCells:=.ChangingCells, _
    Values:=Array(10, 20, 15, 67, 21)
    ' Update display.
    .Show
End With
```

Chapter 9

Working with Ranges of Cells

Worksheets contain *cells*—the fundamental unit in Excel. In Visual Basic, you access cells by using the Range object. A Range object may contain one or many cells (see fig. 9.1).

Fig. 9.1
A range of cells.

Range("B13:H17")—
Range containing many cells

Range("F24")—
Range containing
only one cell

This chapter covers the Range and Name objects and the Areas and Characters collections.

In this chapter, you learn how to do the following:

- Access ranges of cells using the different Range methods.

- Access and set the values of cells.

- Search and replace text in worksheets.

- Work with discontiguous ranges of cells.

- Refer to cells by name.

- Format and modify text in cells.

Using Ranges

You use ranges to do most tasks in Excel that involve getting or manipulating worksheet data. For this reason, Range is the most used object in Excel. Because you can get a Range object in so many different ways, Range also can be the most confusing Excel object. Table 9.1 shows the different ways to return a Range object.

Table 9.1 Ways to return a Range object

Type of expression	Description	Examples

Range method	Returns a range based on the address, name, or position of the cells in a worksheet.	`' Select range A1:B2 (two ways).`
		`[a1:b2].Select`
		`Range("A1:B2").Select`

	To select multiple ranges, separate the addresses by commas.	`Select two ranges (two ways).`
		`[a1:b2, b3:c4].Select`
		`Range("A1:B2, B3:C4").Select`
		`' Select a range by name.`
		`Range("NamedRange")`
		`' Select by cell position.`
		`Range(Cells(1, 1), Cells (2, 2))`

Cells method	Returns all the cells in a worksheet or one cell in a worksheet.	`' Select all cells`
		`Cells.Select`
		`'Select cell at A1`
		`Cells(1,1).Select`

Columns method	Returns all the cells in one column.	`' Select column C (two ways).`
		`Columns(3).Select`
		`Columns("C").Select`

Type of expression	Description	Examples
Offset method	Returns a range of cells based on its position relative to another range.	' Selects cell C2. [a1].Offset(1, 2).Select ' Selects cell C4. [d9].Offset(-5, -1).Select
Rows method	Returns all the cells in one row.	' Select row 6. Rows(6).Select
Union method	Joins one or more ranges into a single range.	' Join three ranges into one. Set rng = Union([a1], [b6], [d9])
UsedRange property	Returns a rectangular range that contains all the cells in a worksheet that have ever contained data or formulas.	' Select the used range. ActiveSheet.UsedRange.Select

Another common way to get a range is based on the current selection. Selections don't always include a range of cells, however. Any object that can be selected becomes part of the current selection. This can include charts, figures, text boxes, or any object that can be drawn on a sheet. When using the Selection method, always test to see if the selection is a range before acting on it. The following code displays the address of a selection:

```
Sub TestSelection()
    ' Only Range has an Address property, so test selection.
    If TypeName(Selection) = "Range" Then
        Msgbox Selection.Address
    End If
End Sub
```

Why are there so many different ways to get a range? The different forms of the Range method are provided for convenience. Typing [A1], for example, is easier than typing Range("A1"). In practice, however, the Cells form of Range is really the most useful because it enables you to use variables in the expression. The following code uses the Cells method to create a sales tax table:

```
Sub TaxTable()
    Const TAXRATE = 0.0825
    Dim cAmount As Currency, cTax As Currency
    Dim iColumn As Integer, iRow As Integer, iCashCol As Integer
    iCashCol = 1
    ' Create two major columns.
    For iColumn = 1 To 2
```

II

Programmer's Reference

```
        If iColumn <> 1 Then iCashCol = 3
        ' Create 200 rows.
        For iRow = 1 To 200
            ' Calculate tax for every 25 cents.
            cAmount = cAmount + 0.25
            cTax = cAmount * TAXRATE
            ' Display cash/tax amounts.
            Cells(iRow, iCashCol).Value = cAmount
            Cells(iRow, iCashCol + 1).Value = cTax
        Next iRow
    Next iColumn
End Sub
```

In addition to the many ways of getting a range, Excel also has many ways of referring to the addresses of cells. The "A1-style" references are the most common, but you sometimes encounter other styles. The following table shows the different forms of addresses.

	Using A1 style	Using R1C1 style
Absolute address	$A$1:$B$2	R1C1:R2C2
Relative address	A1:B2	RC:R[1]C[1]
External address	[SYNTAX.XLS]Sheet1!$A$1:$B$2 [SYNTAX.XLS]Sheet1!R1C1:R2C2	

Setting and Returning Values from Cells

To set the value of a cell, use its Value property. Value is the default property for a Range, so you can omit it in code:

```
[a1] = "90210"
```

Similarly, you can set a range of cells to a single value:

```
[a1:d1] = 90210
```

To set the values of a range to more than one value, use an array:

```
[a1:d1] = Array(1, 2, 3, 4)
```

Excel lays out cells in row-major order. To set the values of a column of cells, use the first dimension of a two-dimension array:

```
[a1:a4] = Array(Array(1, 1), Array(2, 1), Array(3, 1), _
    Array(4, 1), Array(5, 1))
```

The second dimension indicates the column number in the range.

Returning values works the same way. If a range contains more than one cell, the returned value is an array; if the range contains more than one column, the array has two dimensions. Use the UBound function to find the number of rows and columns in the returned array.

The following code lines add up the values in a selection:

```
Sub DisplaySum()
    Dim vRange As Variant, vTotal As Variant
    Dim iRowCount As Integer, iRow As Integer, iColumnCount As _
    Integer, iColumn As Integer
    vRange = Selection
    ' If the selection is a single cell, vRange is not an array.
    If IsArray(vRange) = False Then
        vTotal = vRange
    Else
        ' Get the number of rows and columns in the selection.
        iRowCount = UBound(vRange, 1)
        iColumnCount = UBound(vRange, 2)
        ' For each row and column, add up the values.
        For iRow = 1 To iRowCount
            For iColumn = 1 To iColumnCount
                vTotal = vRange(iRow, iColumn) + vTotal
            Next iColumn
        Next iRow
    End If
    ' Display the result.
    MsgBox "The total is: " & vTotal
End Sub
```

Note

All arrays returned by Excel begin at 1. Most programmers are accustomed to arrays starting at 0—the default starting point for arrays in Visual Basic. You can change the default starting point for the arrays you create in Visual Basic by using the Option Base statement. You can't change the starting point for arrays returned by Excel, however.

You can only set and return values from ranges made up of a single block of cells. If a range is a union of ranges or discontiguous (as with a multiple selection), the returned value is that of the first cell in the range. Use the Areas method of the Range object to break unions and multiple selections into single blocks of cells.

Finding and Replacing Text in Cells

The Find and Replace methods act on the text in the cells of a single sheet. If you are accustomed to finding and replacing text using word processing software, Excel's behavior may seem confusing. Here are some points to remember when using these methods:

- Find and Replace are limited to a single sheet at a time.

- Find never reaches the "end" of a range, it simply restarts its search at the top or bottom of the range. See the "Finding All Occurrences of Text" section that follows for an example of how to work around this.

- If the text is not found, Find returns Nothing, which causes an error if you try to activate the returned value. You must always test the result of Find before doing anything with the result.

- Replace replaces all instances in a range; you can't selectively search and replace text using Replace.

With these limitations in mind, using Find and Replace in a sheet is quite simple. For example, the following code fragment finds the text Wombat in the active worksheet:

```
Cells.Find "Wombat"
```

Similarly, this code line replaces all occurrences of Wombat with Wallaby:

```
Cells.Replace "Wombat", "Wallaby"
```

In both cases, nothing happens if Wombat is not found.

Finding All Occurrences of Text

Using the Find method to find multiple occurrences is extremely difficult because it re-finds the first occurrence no matter what you tell it to look "after" or "before." You have to keep track of the first occurrence and compare the results of each FindNext to know when you have found all occurrences of the text.

The following code shows how to find all occurrences of SearchItem in the active workbook:

```
Sub SelectItems(SearchItem)
    For Each ws In ActiveWorkbook.Worksheets
        ' If the worksheet contains SearchItem, then get the _
          addresses.
        If TypeName(ws.Cells.Find(SearchItem)) = "Range" Then
            ' Since SearchItem was found, it is safe to get _
              its address.
```

```
                Set rngFound = ws.Cells.FindNext
                sAddress = rngFound.Address
                ' Repeat until you get back to the first occurrence.
                Do
                    ' Get next occurrence.
                    Set rngFound = ws.Cells.FindNext(after:=rngFound)
                    ' Exit loop if you get back to the first address.
                    If InStr(sAddress, rngFound.Address) Then Exit Do
                    ' Build range address string for selection.
                    sAddress = sAddress & "," & rngFound.Address
                Loop
                ' Activate the worksheet.
                ws.Activate
                ' Select the range.
                Range(sAddress).Select
            End If
        Next ws
    End Sub
```

Selectively Replacing Text

To selectively find and replace text, you must combine the Find and Replace methods in code. The following lines of code demonstrate a find-and-replace operation that enables the user to choose whether or not the text is replaced:

```
    Sub SelectiveReplace(SearchItem, ReplaceItem)
        Do
            ' Check if text is found on worksheet.
            If TypeName(Cells.Find(SearchItem)) = "Range" Then
                ' If text was found, then activate the cell.
                Cells.Find(SearchItem, After:=ActiveCell).Activate
            Else
                ' If text was not found, then display a message _
                    and exit.
                MsgBox "Text not found.", vbOK, "Search and Replace"
                Exit Do
            End If
            ' Find out if user wants to replace the text.
            iAction = MsgBox("Replace text?", vbYesNoCancel, _
            "Search and Replace")
            Select Case iAction
                Case vbYes
                    ' If user chose Yes, then replace the item _
                        and loop again.
                    ActiveCell.Replace SearchItem, ReplaceItem
                Case vbNo
                    ' If user chose No, then skip replace and _
                        loop again.
                Case vbCancel
                    ' If user chose Cancel, end the search.
                    Exit Do
            End Select
        Loop
    End Sub
```

The Range object has specific properties and methods, which are listed in Table 9.2. Properties and methods shown in **bold** are described in the reference section that follows this table. Nonbold items are common to most objects and are described in Chapter 4, "Using Objects."

Table 9.2 Range properties and methods	
Activate	**CurrentArray**
AddIndent	**CurrentRegion**
Address	**Cut**
AddressLocal	**DataSeries**
AdvancedFilter	**Delete**
Application	**Dependents**
ApplyNames	**DialogBox**
ApplyOutlineStyles	**DirectDependents**
Areas	**DirectPrecedents**
AutoFill	**End**
AutoFilter	**EntireColumn**
AutoFit	**EntireRow**
AutoFormat	**FillDown**
AutoOutline	**FillLeft**
BorderAround	**FillRight**
Borders	**FillUp**
Calculate	**Find**
Cells	**FindNext**
Characters	**FindPrevious**
CheckSpelling	**Font**
Clear	**Formula**
ClearContents	**FormulaArray**
ClearFormats	**FormulaHidden**
ClearNotes	**FormulaLocal**
ClearOutline	**FormulaR1C1**
Column	**FormulaR1C1Local**
ColumnDifferences	**FunctionWizard**
Columns	**GoalSeek**
ColumnWidth	**Group**
Consolidate	**HasArray**
Copy	**HasFormula**
CopyPicture	Height
Count	**Hidden**
CreateNames	**HorizontalAlignment**
CreatePublisher	**Insert**
Creator	**Interior**

Item	Row
Justify	RowDifferences
Left	RowHeight
ListNames	Rows
LocationInTable	Run
Locked	Select
Name	Show
NavigateArrow	ShowDependents
Next	ShowDetail
NoteText	ShowErrors
NumberFormat	ShowPrecedents
NumberFormatLocal	Sort
Offset	SortSpecial
Orientation	SoundNote
OutlineLevel	SpecialCells
PageBreak	Style
Parent	SubscribeTo
Parse	Subtotal
PasteSpecial	Summary
PivotField	Table
PivotItem	Text
PivotTable	TextToColumns
Precedents	Top
PrefixCharacter	Ungroup
Previous	UseStandardHeight
PrintOut	UseStandardWidth
PrintPreview	Value
Range	VerticalAlignment
RemoveSubtotal	Width
Replace	Worksheet
Resize	WrapText

range.Activate( )

Makes the first cell in a range the active cell (returned by the ActiveCell property). The worksheet containing a cell must be active before you can activate a range.

range.AddIndent
range.AddIndent [= True | False]

True automatically adds an indent to text formatted using the distributed text alignment style; False does not indent when using the distributed text alignment style. The default is False.

*range.*Address

range.Address ([*RowAbsolute*], [*ColumnAbsolute*], [*ReferenceStyle*], [*External*], [*RelativeTo*])

Returns the address of the range.

Argument	Description
RowAbsolute	True returns the row address in absolute coordinates; False returns the relative row address. The default is True.
ColumnAbsolute	True returns the column address in absolute coordinates; False returns the relative column address. The default is True.
ReferenceStyle	xlA1 returns the address in A1 form; xlR1C1 returns the address in row/column (R1C1) form. The default is xlA1.
External	True includes the workbook and sheet names in the address; False omits these. The default is False.
RelativeTo	The Range object to which the returned address is relative. If the range includes more than one cell, Excel makes the address relative to the upper left cell in the range. Ignored if returning an absolute address. The default is the upper left cell in the specified Range object.

*range.*AddressLocal

range.AddressLocal ([*RowAbsolute*], [*ColumnAbsolute*], [*ReferenceStyle*], [*External*], [*RelativeTo*])

Returns the address of the range in the user's language, as determined by the user's system settings.

Argument	Description
RowAbsolute	True returns the row address in absolute coordinates; False returns the relative row address. The default is True.
ColumnAbsolute	True returns the column address in absolute coordinates; False returns the relative column address. The default is True.
ReferenceStyle	xlA1 returns the address in A1 form; xlR1C1 returns the address in row/column (R1C1) form. The default is xlA1.
External	True includes the workbook and sheet names in the address; False omits these. The default is False.
RelativeTo	The Range object to which the returned address is relative. Ignored if returning an absolute address. The default is the upper left cell in the specified Range object.

range.AdvancedFilter

range.AdvancedFilter (*Action*, [*CriteriaRange*], [*CopyToRange*], [*Unique*])

Filters a list or creates a copy of the cells that result from a filter operation.

Argument	Description
Action	xlFilterInPlace filters the range, hiding all cells that don't match *CriteriaRange*; xlFilterCopy leaves the selected range intact and creates a new copy of all the cells that match *CriteriaRange*.
CriteriaRange	A range of cells whose contents define the criteria for the cells to display or copy. The first row of the range must contain the list headings from which to select.
CopyToRange	For xlFilterCopy, the first cell of the destination to which the filter cells are copied.
Unique	True displays or copies only one instance of rows that match the criteria; False displays or copies all of the rows that match the criteria.

This method corresponds to the Advanced Filter dialog box (see fig. 9.2). To display this dialog box in Excel, choose Data, Filter; then choose the Advanced Filter sub-item. Figure 9.3 shows the result of the filter operation defined in figure 9.2.

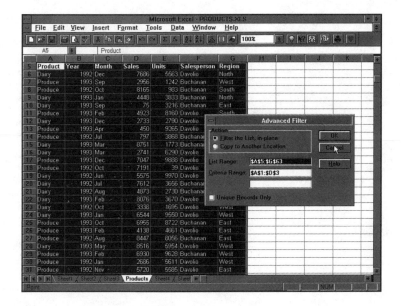

Fig. 9.2
The Advanced Filter dialog box.

II

Programmer's Reference

Fig. 9.3
Result of the filter
operation.

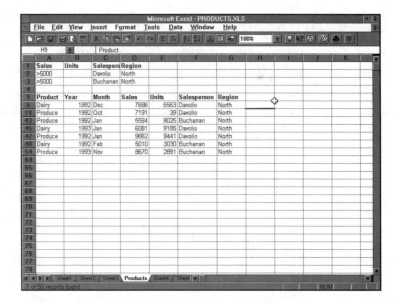

range.ApplyNames

**range.ApplyNames ([Names],
[IgnoreRelativeAbsolute], [UseRowColumnNames],
[OmitColumn], [OmitRow], [Order], [AppendLast])**

Searches formulas in the specified range and replaces references with the
names defined for them.

Argument	Description
Names	An array of strings containing the name to apply to the range. The default is all the names on the sheet.
IgnoreRelativeAbsolute	True replaces all references inside the specified range with names; False replaces relative references with relative names, absolute references with absolute names, and mixed references with mixed names. The default is True.
UseRowColumnNames	True replaces references to cells with column or row names, if an exact cell name can't be found; False does not replace these references. The default is True.
OmitColumn	True omits the column name if the reference is in the same column as the referenced column; False includes the column name. The default is True.

Argument	Description
OmitRow	True omits the row name if the reference is in the same row as the referenced row; False includes the row name. The default is True.
Order	xlRowThenColumn places row names before column names; xlColumnThenRow places column names before row names. The default is xlRowThenColumn.
AppendLast	True replaces all the names in *Names* and all the names already defined for the worksheet; False replaces only the names in *Names*.

This method corresponds to the Apply Names dialog box (see fig. 9.4). In Excel, you display the Apply Names dialog box by choosing Insert, Names; then choosing the Apply Names sub-item.

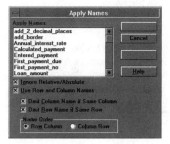

Fig. 9.4
The Apply Names dialog box.

The following line of code applies all the defined names in a worksheet to cell references in all the cells in that worksheet:

```
ActiveSheet.Cells.ApplyNames
```

range.ApplyOutlineStyles()

Applies outlining styles to the specified range.

range.Areas

range.Areas ([*Index*])

Returns all or one of the ranges within a range. Areas is useful for getting the ranges within a discontiguous range, as in a multiple selection. The following lines of code display the addresses of each range in a multiple selection:

```
Sub ShowRanges()
    For each rng In Selection.Areas
        MsgBox rng.Address
    Next rng
End Sub
```

range.AutoFill

range.AutoFill (*Destination,* [*Type*])

Fills the cells in a range with values, formulas, formats, or items from the source Range object. The source range is specified by the *range* object in the preceding syntax. The arguments for AutoFill are listed in the following table:

Argument	Description
Destination	The range of cells to fill.
Type	xlFillDefault lets Excel choose the fill to perform based on any patterns or lists it detects in the items in the source range; xlFillSeries is apparently identical to xlFillDefault; xlFillCopy copies the cell source range to create the fill; xlFillFormats copies the formats from the source range to the destination range; xlFillValues omits the formats in the destination range; xlFillDays fills the destination with days of the month; xlFillWeekdays fills the destination with the names of the days of the week; xlFillMonths fills the destination with the names of the months; xlFillYears fills the destination with years; xlLinearTrend fills the destination by incrementing each value in the source range by one; xlGrowthTrend fills the destination by multiplying the values in the source range by one; xlFillDefault is the default.

This method corresponds to the Series dialog box (see fig. 9.5). To display the Series dialog box in Excel, choose Edit, Fill; then choose the Series sub-item.

Fig. 9.5
The Series dialog box.

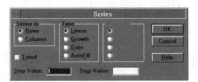

Type constants may be combined using And. The following line of code fills range A1:A15 by incrementing the values in A1:A2 by one, and copies the formats of the source range to the destination:

```
Range("A1:A2").AutoFill ActiveCell.Range("a1:a15"), xlFillFormats _
And xlFillSeries
```

range.AutoFilter

range.AutoFilter ([*Field*], [*Criteria1*], [*Operator*], [*Criteria2*])

Applies a filter to the columns included in *range*. If all arguments are omitted, the AutoFilter method switches the filter on or off for the columns.

Argument	Description
Field	Indicates the column within the range to which the filter criteria are to be applied. 1 is the first column, 2 is the second, and so on.
Criteria1	The first criterion to apply. Rows that meet this criterion are displayed; others are hidden. The default is All.
Operator	xlAnd displays rows that match both *Criteria1* and *Criteria2*; xlOr displays rows that match either criterion. The default is xlAnd.
Criteria2	The second criterion to apply. Rows that meet this criterion are displayed; others are hidden. The default is All.

Criteria are specified by a string containing a value to match or by two special codes:

Criteria code	Matches
"="	Blank fields
"<>"	Nonblank fields

The following code applies a filter to the first column of a worksheet, then switches the filter off. The filter applies only to the used range of the worksheet; blank rows after the last row with data are not filtered (they remain blank). Filters always apply to the entire column, excluding blank cells.

```
Sub DemoAutoFilter()
    ' Create filter for column 1.
    [a1].AutoFilter
    ' Display all non-blank rows.
    [a1].AutoFilter 1, "<>"
    ' Pause.
    MsgBox "Click OK to display blank rows again."
    ' Display all records again.
    [a1].AutoFilter 1, "All"
    ' Turn off auto filter.
    [a1].AutoFilter
End Sub
```

Tip

This example uses the [] range notation. Using [] rather than the Range method is useful shorthand when creating quick demonstrations or testing out features such as this example.

range.AutoFit( )

Sizes the width of the columns and height of the rows in the range so they fit the data contained in the cells of the range.

range.AutoFormat

range.AutoFormat ([*Format*], [*Number*], [*Font*], [*Alignment*], [*Border*], [*Pattern*], [*Width*])

Applies a predefined format to the range.

Argument	Description
Format	A constant that specifies the format to apply. Format constants correspond to the names of formats in the AutoFormat dialog box: xlClassic1; xlClassic2; xlClassic3; xlAccounting1; xlAccounting2; xlAccounting3; xlAccounting4; xlColor1; xlColor2; xlColor3; xlList1; xlList3; xl3DEffects1; xl3dEffects2; xlSimple; xlNone. The default is xlClassic1.
Number	True applies formats to numbers; False omits formatting of numbers. The default is True.
Font	True applies new fonts to the range; False does not change fonts. The default is True.
Alignment	True sets the alignment of cells in the range; False does not. The default is True.
Border	True applies borders to the range; False does not. The default is True.
Pattern	True applies shading patterns to the range; False does not. The default is True.
Width	True adjusts the height and width of cells for best fit; False does not. The default is True.

This method corresponds to the AutoFormat dialog box (see fig. 9.6). To display the AutoFormat dialog box in Excel, choose Format, AutoFormat.

Fig. 9.6

The AutoFormat dialog box.

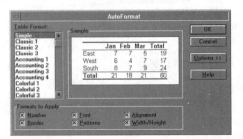

*range.***AutoOutline( )**

Creates an outline for the range. If *range* is a single cell, creates an outline for the entire worksheet. Excel can create an outline automatically if calculations are laid out from top to bottom and right to left. Otherwise, this method causes error 1004.

*range.***BorderAround**

*range.***BorderAround ([*LineStyle*], [*Weight*], [*ColorIndex*], [*Color*])**

Creates a border around a range of cells.

Argument	Description
LineStyle	xlContinuous creates a single continuous line border; xlDash creates a dashed line; xlDot creates a dotted line; xlDouble creates a double line. The default is xlContinous.
Weight	xlHairline creates a hairline (the thinnest); xlThin creates a 1-point line; xlMedium creates a 2-point line; xlThick creates a 4-point line. The default is xlThin.
ColorIndex	A number from 1 to 56 indicating the index of the color in the current color palette. The default is xlAutomatic (the default text color).
Color	An RGB color value. The default is None (determined by ColorIndex).

*range.***Borders**

*range.***Borders ([*Index*])**

Returns one or all borders in a range. If a range does not have a border, the returned Border object has Linestyle xlNone.

*range.***Calculate( )**

Calculates the range of cells.

[*range.*]Cells

[*range.*]Cells ([*RowIndex*], [*ColumnIndex*])

Returns a range of cells within another range. If *range* is omitted, returns a range of cells within the active worksheet using *RowIndex* and *ColumnIndex*, as described on the following page.

Argument	Description
RowIndex	The row number of the cells to return. The default is all rows.
ColumnIndex	The column number of the cells to return. The default is all columns.

The Cell method is often used in For...Next loops to get single cells from within a range.

range.Characters

range.Characters ([Start], [Length])

Returns a Characters collection from within a cell. If the range contains more than one cell, this method causes error 440.

Argument	Description
Start	The position of the first character to return. The default is 1.
Length	The position of the last character to return. The default is the length of the text.

Use the Text property of the Characters collection to get the text contained in the cell. The Characters collection is described later in this chapter. This line of code displays the text in cell A1:

```
MsgBox [A1].Characters.Text
```

range.CheckSpelling

range.CheckSpelling ([CustomDictionary], [IgnoreUppercase], [AlwaysSuggest])

Checks the spelling of the words in a range.

Argument	Description
CustomDictionary	A string indicating the file name of the custom dictionary to be examined if the word is not found in the main dictionary. If omitted, the currently specified dictionary is used. The default is None.

Argument	Description
IgnoreUppercase	True ignores the spelling of words in all uppercase characters; False checks the spelling of all words. The default is False.
AlwaysSuggest	True displays a list of suggested alternate spellings when an incorrect spelling is found; False prompts user for correct spelling. The default is False.

The following code checks the spelling of all the cells on a sheet:

```
Activesheet.Cells.CheckSpelling
```

range.**Clear( )**

Clears the formulas, values, and formatting in a range of cells.

range.**ClearContents( )**

Clears the formulas and values in a range of cells. Preserves formatting.

range.**ClearFormats( )**

Clears the formatting in a range of cells. Preserves formulas and values.

range.**ClearNotes( )**

Clears notes and sound notes from a range of cells.

range.**ClearOutline( )**

Clears the groups created for outlining a range of cells.

range.**Column**

Returns a number indicating the first column in the range. The Column property does not return a range of cells, as does the Columns method.

range.**ColumnDifferences**

range.**ColumnDifferences (*Comparison*)**

Compares the values of cells in each column with the value found in the row indicated by *Comparison* and returns the range of cells that don't match. The returned range does not include cells that contain formulas.

Comparision is a range containing a single cell. The `ColumnDifferences` method uses the row portion of *Comparison* to locate the row of values within the range used in the comparison. The comparision is done column by column. For example, column A is checked for values that are different from the specified row in column A; column B is checked against the row value in column B, and so on. The following line of code compares the values in row 1 to each column in the worksheet and selects the cells that are different from those values:

```
Cells.ColumnDifferences(Range("B1")).Select
```

range.**Columns**

range.**Columns** (*[Index]*)

Returns a range containing one or all of the columns of cells in the source range. The following code selects the first column in a selected range:

```
Selection.Columns(1).Select
```

range.**ColumnWidth**

range.**ColumnWidth** [= *width*]

Sets or returns the column width of a range. The width is specified in points. The default is 8.43.

range.**Consolidate**

range.**Consolidate** (*[Sources]*, *[Function]*, *[TopRow]*, *[LeftColumn]*, *[CreateLinks]*)

Consolidates data from multiple ranges to a single range, specified by the Range object.

Argument	Description
Sources	An array containing the addresses of the ranges to consolidate.
Function	xlAverage averages the values in each cell across the consolidated ranges; xlCount counts the values; xlCountNums counts the numeric values; xlMax uses the largest value found across all ranges; xlMin uses the smallest value; xlProduct multiplies values; xlStDev calculates the standard deviation; xlStDevP calculates the standard deviation and assumes the data represents the entire population; xlSum adds the values; xlVar calculates the variance; xlVarP calculates the variance and assumes the data represents the entire population. The default is xlSum.
TopRow	True consolidates data based on the titles in the top row; False consolidates data by position in each consolidated range. The default is False.

Argument	Description
LeftColumn	True consolidates data based on the titles in the left column; False consolidates data by position in each consolidated range. The default is False.
CreateLinks	Links the consolidation to the source ranges. The default is False.

This method corresponds to the Consolidate dialog box (see fig. 9.7). To display the Consolidate dialog box in Excel, choose Data, Consolidate.

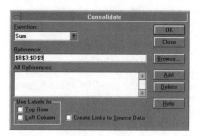

Fig. 9.7
The Consolidate dialog box.

range.Copy

range.Copy ([*Destination*])

Copies a source range to the Destination range. If Destination is a single cell, Excel uses that cell as the upper left corner for the new copy. If Destination is larger than the copied range, Excel autofills Destination based on the source range. If Destination is larger than one cell, but smaller than the source range, the Copy method causes error 1004.

range.CopyPicture

range.CopyPicture ([*Appearance*], [*Format*])

Copies a range to the Clipboard as a picture.

Argument	Description
Appearance	xlScreen copies the range as it appears on-screen; xlPrinter copies the range as it would appear if printed using the current printer setup. The default is xlScreen.
Format	xlPicture creates the copy in PICT format; xlBitmap creates the copy as a bitmap. The default is xlPicture.

The `Application` object's `ClipboardFormats` method returns `xlClipboardFormatPICT` for PICT format data and `xlClipboardFormatBitmap` for bitmaps.

range.CreateNames

range.CreateNames ([*Top*], [*Left*], [*Bottom*], [*Right*])

Creates names for cells in a range based on column or row headings.

Argument	Description
Top	True uses column headings at the tops of rows for names; False does not. The default is True.
Left	True uses row headings from the left column for names; False does not. The default is False.
Bottom	True uses column headings at the bottoms of rows for names; False does not. The default is False.
Right	True uses row headings from the right column for names; False does not. The default is False.

This method corresponds to the Create Names dialog box (see fig. 9.8). To display the Create Names dialog box in Excel, choose Insert, Names; then choose the Create Names sub-item.

Fig. 9.8
The Create Names
dialog box.

range.CreatePublisher

range.CreatePublisher ([*Edition*], [*Appearance*], [*ContainsPICT*], [*ContainsBIFF*], [*ContainsRTF*], [*ContainsVALU*])

Macintosh System 7 or later only. Creates a publisher for a range.

Argument	Description
Edition	The file name of the edition to create. The default is based on the current document name.
Appearance	`xlPrinter` creates the edition at printer resolution; `xlScreen` creates the edition at screen resolution. The default is `xlPrinter`.

Argument	Description
ContainsPICT	True includes PICT format data. The default is True.
ContainsBIFF	True includes BIFF format data. The default is True.
ContainsRTF	True includes RTF format data. The default is True.
ContainsVALU	True includes VALU format data. The default is True.

range.CurrentArray()

Returns the entire range object containing the array formula for the source range. If the range is not part of an array formula, CurrentArray causes error 1004.

Use the HasArray property to test if a range is part of an array formula.

In Excel, you create array formulas by selecting a range, entering a formula, then pressing CTRL+SHIFT+ENTER (Windows) or Command+Shift+Return (Macintosh).

range.CurrentRegion()

Returns a range containing the entire region in which the source range resides. A *region* is a block of cells bounded by blank rows and columns.

range.Cut

range.Cut ([*Destination*])

Cuts a range of cells to the Clipboard and pastes the range to a *Destination* range. If *Destination* is omitted, the cells are not pasted. The source range must be contiguous; multiple selections can't be cut. If *Destination* is a single cell, Excel uses that cell as the upper left corner of the paste location. If *Destination* is larger than the source range, Excel autofills the remaining cells. If *Destination* is more than one cell but smaller than the source range, Cut causes error 1004.

range.DataSeries

range.DataSeries ([*Rowcol*], [*Type*], [*Date*], [*Step*], [*Stop*], [*Trend*])

Creates a data series in the range. This method is very similar to the AutoFill method.

Argument	Description
Rowcol	xlRows creates the series horizontally in rows; xlColumns creates the series vertically in columns. The default is determined by the shape of the range.
Type	xlLinear increments each cell by *Step*; xlGrowth multiplies each cell by *Step*; xlChronological increments each cell by *Step* based on *Date*; xlAutoFill copies the source range to fill the data series. The default is xlLinear.
Date	xlDay to increment by days of the month; xlWeekday to increment by days of the week; xlMonth to increment by month; xlYear to increment by year. Ignored if *Type* is not xlChronological. The default is xlDay.
Step	The number of units to increment for each cell in the series.
Stop	The stop value for the series. The default fills to the end of the range.
Trend	True creates a trend for *Types* xlLinear and xlGrowth. Ignored for other types. The default is False.

The following code creates a sales tax table using DataSeries:

```
Sub TaxTableSeries()
    ' Set initial cell values/formulas for tax table.
    Cells(1, 1).Value = 0.25
    Cells(1, 2).Formula = "=a1*.0825"
    ' Create a series for purchase amount: every 25 cents up to $50.
    Columns(1).DataSeries xlColumns, xlLinear, , 0.25, 50#
    ' Create matching formulas for tax amount.
    ActiveSheet.UsedRange.Columns(2).DataSeries xlColumns, _
    xlAutoFill
End Sub
```

range.Delete

range.Delete ([*Shift*])

Deletes a range of cells. If *Shift* is xlToLeft, remaining cells are shifted to the left; if it is xlUp, cells are shifted up. The default shifts cells based on the shape of the deleted range.

range.Dependents()

Returns a range containing the cells whose values depend directly or indirectly on cells in source range. Direct dependents use the range directly in their formulas. Indirect dependents use other cells in their formulas which, in turn, depend on the original range. If the source range has no dependents, Dependents causes error 1004.

The following line of code selects the dependents of the currently selected cells:

```
Selection.Dependents.Select
```

range.**DialogBox( )**

Displays a dialog box defined by a dialog-box definition table from an Excel 4.0 macro sheet. Returns the value from the dialog box if the user chooses OK; returns False if the user chooses Cancel on that dialog box.

range.**DirectDependents( )**

Returns a range containing the cells that use the source range directly in their formulas. If the source range has no direct dependents, `DirectDependents` causes error 1004.

The following code selects the dependents of the currently selected cells:

```
Selection.DirectDependents.Select
```

range.**DirectPrecedents( )**

Returns a range containing the cells that are used in the formulas of the source range. If the source range has no direct precedents, `DirectPrecedents` causes error 1004.

The following code selects the dependents of the currently selected cells:

```
Selection.DirectPrecedents.Select
```

range.**End**

range.**End (*Direction*)**

Returns the cell marking the extreme boundary of a region of cells. A region is a block of cells surrounded by a row or column of blanks. `Direction` determines the direction in which to search: `xlToLeft`, `xlToRight`, `xlUp`, or `xlDown`. The default is the lower right corner of the region.

range.**EntireColumn( )**

Returns the column or columns in which the range resides.

range.**EntireRow( )**

Returns the row or rows in which the range resides.

range.**FillDown()**

Autofills a range using the top row as the source of the fill.

range.**FillLeft()**

Autofills a range using the far left column as the source of the fill.

range.**FillRight()**

Autofills a range using the far right column as the source of the fill.

range.**FillUp()**

Autofills a range using the bottom row as the source of the fill.

range.**Find**

range.**Find (*What*, [*After*], [*LookIn*], [*LookAt*], [*SearchOrder*], [*SearchDirection*], [*MatchCase*])**

Searches a range for an item and returns the first cell that matches. Find returns a range containing a single cell. Find does not activate or select the cell it finds. If the item was not found, Find returns Nothing.

Argument	Description
What	The item to find. *What* can be a string, a number, or an object.
After	A Range object indicating the cell to search after. The default is the beginning of the range.
LookIn	xlFormulas searches for *What* within the formulas of cells; xlValues searches values; xlNotes searches notes. The default is xlFormulas.
LookAt	xlWhole compares whole cells to *What*; xlPart searches within the contents of cell for *What*. The default is xlPart.
SearchOrder	xlByRows searches one row at a time; xlByColumns searches one column at a time. The default is xlByRows.
SearchDirection	xlNext searches down and to the right of *After*; xlPrevious searches up and to the left of *After*. The default is xlNext.
MatchCase	True performs a case-sensitive search; False ignores case. The default is False.

This method corresponds to the Find dialog box (see fig. 9.9). To display the Find dialog box in Excel, choose Edit, Find.

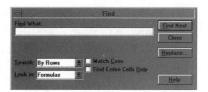

Fig. 9.9
The Find dialog box.

The following code finds cells that contain the phrase "Completely Unique" on the active worksheet and selects the cell that it finds:

```
If TypeName(Cells.Find ("Completely Unique")) = "Range" Then
    Cells.Find ("Completely Unique").Select
End If
```

Notice that this code uses TypeName to determine whether Find returned a range. Checking the return value of Find is very important (and a major head-ache) in Excel—if Find didn't find "Completely Unique" it would return Nothing and the Select method would then cause error 1004. In general, you must call Find twice for every find operation you want to perform: once to test for success, and once to take whatever action you need to take.

To repeat a find operation, use the FindNext or FindPrevious methods.

Note

When Find, FindNext, or FindPrevious finds the last occurrence in the direction of their search, they start over at the top or bottom of the worksheet. This search design can lead to an infinite loop. See the "Finding and Replacing Text in Cells" section earlier in this chapter for a sample of how to work around this limitation.

range.FindNext

range.FindNext ([*After*])

Repeats the last find operation. Returns a range containing a single cell or Nothing, if the item was not found in the range. *After* is a range specifying the starting point for the search; the default is to start from the first cell. If FindNext reaches the last cell of a range, it continues searching at the beginning.

The following code finds the next occurrence of a find operation:

```
Cells.FindNext(ActiveCell).Select
```

range.FindPrevious

range.FindPrevious ([*After*])

Repeats the last find operation. Returns a range containing a single cell or Nothing, if the item was not found in the range. *After* is a range specifying the starting point for the search; the default is to start from the first cell. If FindPrevious reaches the first cell of a range, it continues searching at the end.

The following code finds the previous occurrence of a find operation:

```
Cells.FindPrevious(ActiveCell).Select
```

range.Font

Returns the Font object for a range. If a range contains different font attributes, the Font properties for those attributes return Null. The following code makes the currently selected cells bold:

```
Selection.Font.Bold = True
```

range.Formula

range.Formula [= *a1formula*]

Sets or returns the formula for a range using A1-style addresses. To set a single formula for a range of cells, use a string:

```
Selection.Formula = "=A1*B2"
```

To assign multiple formulas to a range of cells, use an array of strings:

```
[a1:d1].Formula = Array("=1", "=$a$1 + 1", "=$a$1 + 2", "=$a$1 + 3")
```

range.FormulaArray

range.FormulaArray [= *rcformula*]

Sets or returns a formula array for a range using R1C1-style addresses. A *formula array* is a single formula that applies to multiple cells. In Excel, you enter a formula array by pressing Ctrl+Shift+Enter (Windows) or Command+Shift+Return (Macintosh) after typing the formula in the formula bar.

The following code creates an array out of the selected range and assigns it a formula:

```
Selection.FormulaArray = "=R1C1+1"
```

To assign multiple formulas to a range of cells, use an array of strings:

```
[a1:d1].Formula = Array("=1", "=R1C1 + 1", "=R1C2  + 2", "=R3C1 + 3")
```

range.**FormulaHidden**

range.**FormulaHidden [= True | False]**

True hides the formula when the worksheet or workbook is protected; False does not hide the formula. The default is False.

range.**FormulaLocal**

range.**FormulaLocal [= *a1formula*]**

Same as the Formula property, but uses the user's national language for cell references as determined by the current system settings.

range.**FormulaR1C1**

range.**FormulaR1C1 [= *a1formula*]**

Same as the Formula property, but uses R1C1-style cell addresses.

range.**FormulaR1C1Local**

Same as the Formula property, but uses R1C1-style addresses in the user's national language as determined by the current system settings.

range.**FunctionWizard( )**

Runs the Function Wizard for the cell in the upper left corner of the range. Returns True if the user completes the task; False if the user chooses Cancel. If the cell is part of a formula array, the rest of the elements of the array are set to match the formula created by the Function Wizard.

The following code runs the Function Wizard for the first cell in the selected range:

```
Selection.FunctionWizard
```

range.**GoalSeek**

range.**GoalSeek (*Goal, ChangingCell*)**

Adjusts the value *ChangingCell* until the formula of the first cell in *range* evaluates to *Goal*. Returns True if the operation was successful; False if not.

Argument	Description
Goal	The value to reach.
ChangingCell	A Range object containing the cell to change.

This method corresponds to the Goal Seek dialog box (see fig. 9.10). To display the Goal Seek dialog box in Excel, choose Tools, Goal Seek.

Fig. 9.10
The Goal Seek
dialog box.

The following code calculates the principal of a loan based on a monthly payment of $750 and places the result in cell A1.

```
Sub TargetPayment()
    ' Enter the interest rate
    [a2] = .07
    ' Enter the number of years for loan.
    [a3] = 30
    ' Estimate monthly escrow amount (about 2% of principal).
    [a4] = "=($a$1 * .02)/ 12"
    ' Enter formula for figuring the payment + interest + _
      escrow on a house loan.
    [a5] = "=(PPMT($a$2/12, 1, $a$3 * 12, $a$1, 0) + IPMT _
    ($a$2/12, 1, $a$3 * 12, $a$1, 0) * -1) + $a$4"
    ' Figure the principal based on a monthly payment of $750. _
      Place result in A1.
    [a5].GoalSeek 750, [a1]
End Sub
```

*range.*Group

*range.*Group ([xlRows | xlColumns])

Groups a range for outlining. xlRows groups the rows in the range; xlColumns groups the columns in the range. The default is to group by columns. The following code groups the rows of the selected range:

```
Selection.Range xlRows
```

*range.*Group

*range.*Group ([*Start*], [*End*], [*By*], [*Periods*])

Groups the data in the pivot field specified by *range*.

Argument	Description
Start	True groups the first value in the pivot field; a data value groups fields less than or equal to the value. The default is True.
End	True groups the value to the end of the pivot field; a data value groups fields greater than or equal to the value. The default is True.
By	For numeric fields, the size of the groups to create; for date fields grouped by days, the number of days to group. Ignored for other field types. The default is all records.
Periods	For date fields, a seven-element array of Boolean values specifying the period to group:

Index	True groups fields by
1	Seconds
2	Minutes
3	Hours
4	Days
5	Months
6	Quarters
7	Years

The following code groups a selected pivot field by day for the year 1993:

```
ActiveCell.Group start:="1/1/1993", end:="12/31/1993", by:=10, _
periods:=Array(False, False, False, True, False, False, False)
```

range.HasArray

Returns True if *range* is part of a formula array; False if it is not part of an array; Null if *range* contains a mix of array and non-array cells. The following code tests a worksheet to see if it contains any arrays:

```
If Cells.HasArray <> False Then MsgBox "Sheet contains array."
```

range.HasFormula

Returns True if *range* contains formulas and not just fixed values; False if *range* does not contain formulas; Null if *range* contains a mix of values and formulas. The following code tests a worksheet to see if it contains any formulas:

```
If Cells.HasFormula<> False Then MsgBox "Sheet contains formulas."
```

range.Hidden [= True | False]

True hides the row or column of cells; False displays the row or column. The Hidden property only works on entire rows or columns. This code hides the row containing the active cell:

```
Rows(ActiveCell.Row).Hidden = True
```

range.HorizontalAlignment

range.HorizontalAlignment [= *setting*]

xlGeneral left-aligns text and right-aligns numbers; xlLeft left-aligns values; xlRight right-aligns values; xlCenter centers values within each cell of a range; xlCenterAcrossSelection centers values horizontally across the range; both xlJustify and xlDistributed justify wrapped text within cells; xlFill repeats values to fill each cell. The default is xlGeneral.

range.Insert

range.Insert ([*Shift*])

Inserts the current cut or copied range into *range*. If *range* is one cell, Excel shifts the surrounding cells down if *Shift* is xlDown, to the right if *Shift* is xlToRight. If *Shift* is omitted, the surrounding cells shift to the right or left, depending on the shape of the pasted range. If *range* is a multiple of the size of the cut or copied cells, Excel autofills the remaining cells. If *range* is larger than one cell and not a multiple of the size of the cut or copied cells, Insert causes error 1004.

The following code inserts a cut or copy selection at the currently active cell, or inserts a new blank cell if there is no cut or copy selection:

```
ActiveCell.Insert
```

range.Interior

Tip
The Visual Basic RGB function returns an RGB color number using red, green, and blue color values. Each color value is one byte long (0 to 255).

Returns the Interior object for a range. Use the Interior object to change the color or pattern of the background of a range. The following line of code changes the selection's background color to aqua:

```
Selection.Interior.Color = RGB(0, 255, 255)
```

range.Item

range.Item (*RowIndex*, [*ColumnIndex*])

Returns a single row, column, or cell from within a range.

Argument	Description
RowIndex	The number of the row to return, relative to the first cell of the range.
ColumnIndex	The number of the column to return, relative to the first cell of the range. The default is 1.

The following line of code selects the first cell of the selected range:

```
Selection.Item(1,1)
```

These lines of code step through each cell in a selected range, creating a multiplication table:

```
Sub MultiplicationTable()
    iRows = Selection.Rows.Count
    iColumns = Selection.Columns.Count
    For iR = 1 To iRows
        For iC = 1 To iColumns
            Selection.Item(iR, iC).Value = iR * iC
        Next iC
    Next iR
End Sub
```

range.**Justify( )**

Justifies multiline text within cells in a range. Excel displays a warning if text extends below the visible range of a cell. To turn off this warning, set the DisplayAlerts property to False. The Justify method is identical to setting the HorizontalAlignment property to xlJustify.

range.**ListNames( )**

Displays the names and addresses of names for the entire workbook in a range of cells. The first column contains the names, the second column contains the address that each name refers to. The following code displays the list of defined names:

```
[A1].ListNames
```

range.**LocationInTable**

Returns a constant that identifies the part of the pivot table in the first cell of *range*: xlRowHeader, xlColumnHeader, xlPageHeader, xlDataHeader, xlRowItem, xlColumnItem, xlPageItem, xlDataItem, or xlTableBody. Causes error 1006 if the cell is not in a pivot table.

Use `LocationInTable` to determine the type of operations you can perform with the current selection.

*range.*Locked

*range.*Locked [= True | False]

True prevents changes to the cells in *range* when the worksheet is protected; False enables changes to cells in *range* when the worksheet is protected. You can change this property only before protecting a worksheet. The default is True.

*range.*NavigateArrow

*range.*NavigateArrow ([*TowardPrecedent*], [*ArrowNumber*], [*LinkNumber*])

Activates the cell indicated by one of the auditing arrows used to trace dependents, precedents, or errors.

Argument	Description
TowardPrecedent	True activates a precedent; False activates a dependent. Omit when tracing errors.
ArrowNumber	The index of the cell within the formula to activate. In "=a1 + a2," a1 is 1 and a2 is 2. Omit when tracing errors.
LinkNumber	The index of the external link to activate. Omit when tracing errors.

Excel's audit arrows are used to locate logical errors and omissions in a worksheet. By tracing precedents you can walk backwards through the logic used to arrive at a result. By tracing errors, you can find the source of an error in a worksheet.

The following code activates the first precedent in the selected cell's formula:

```
Sub TraceBack()
    ActiveSheet.ClearArrows
    Selection.ShowPrecedents
    Selection.NavigateArrow True, 1
End Sub
```

*range.*Next

Returns a range containing the next cell. If *range* contains more than one cell, Next uses the first cell in the range as the starting point.

range.**NoteText**

range.**NoteText** ([*Text*], [*Start*], [*Length*])

Sets or returns notes for the first cell in *range*.

Argument	Description
Text	The text of the note to set.
Start	The position of the first character within the note to set or return. The default is 1.
Length	The position of the last character within the note to set or return. The default is the length of the note (up to 255).

The following code sets a note for the currently active cell:

```
ActiveCell.NoteText "My notes"
```

This code displays the note for the currently active cell:

```
MsgBox ActiveCell.NoteText
```

range.**NumberFormat**

Sets or returns the number formatting code for a range as a string. If the range contains a mix of formats, returns Null.

Tip
Decimal, thousand, and date separators are all determined by the locale settings of your system.

Table 9.3 Number format symbols	
Symbol	**Description**
General	Displays the number in General format.
#	Digit placeholder. If the number has more digits to the right of the decimal point than there are #'s to the right in the format, Excel rounds the number to as many decimal places as there are #'s to the right. If the number has more digits to the left of the decimal point than there are #'s to the left in the format, Excel displays the extra digits.
0	Digit placeholder. Follows the same rules as the # placeholder, except that if the number has fewer digits than there are zeros in the format, Excel displays the extra zeros. For example, if you want the number 8.9 to appear as 8.90, type #.00 for the format.

(continues)

Table 9.3 Continued	
Symbol	**Description**
?	Digit placeholder. Follows the same rules as the preceding for 0, except that Excel places a space for insignificant zeros on either side of the decimal point so that decimal points align. You also can use this symbol for fractions that have varying numbers of digits.
.	Decimal point. This symbol determines how many digits (0's or #'s) Excel displays to the right and left of the decimal point. If the format contains only #'s to the left of this symbol, Excel begins numbers less than 1 with a decimal point. To avoid this, use 0 as the first digit placeholder to the left of the decimal point instead of #. You also can use the decimal point to create time formats that display fractions of a second.
%	Percentage. Excel multiplies by 100 and adds the % character.
,	Thousands separator. Excel separates thousands by commas if the format contains a comma surrounded by #'s or 0's. A comma following a placeholder scales the number by a thousand. For example, the format #, would scale the number by a thousand and the format #,, would scale the number by a million. The format 0.0,, would display the number 12,200,000 as 12.2.
E- E+ e- e+	Scientific format. If a format contains a 0 or # to the right of an E-, E+, e-, or e+, Excel displays the number in scientific format and inserts an E or e. The number of 0's or #'s to the right determines the exponent's number of digits. E- or e- places a minus sign by negative exponents. E+ or e+ places a minus sign by negative exponents and a plus sign by positive exponents.
$ - + / ( ) : space	Displays these characters. To display a character other than one of these, precede the character with a backslash (\) or enclose the character in double quotation marks (" "). You also can use the slash (/) character for fraction formats.
\	Displays the next character in the format. Excel does not display the backslash. Using this character is the same as enclosing the next character in double quotation marks. If you enter any of the following symbols, Excel provides the backslash for you: ! ^ & ' (left single quotation mark) ' (right single quotation mark) ~ { } = < >
*	Repeats the next character in the format enough times to fill the column width. You cannot have more than one asterisk in one section of a format.
_	Skips the width of the next character. For example, in a format section for positive numbers, you could type _) at the end of a format section for positive numbers to have Excel skip the width of the parenthesis character, so positive numbers align with negative numbers that contain parentheses.

Symbol	Description
"text"	Displays whatever text is inside the double quotation marks.
@	Text placeholder. If there is text entered in the cell, the text from the cell is placed in the format where the @ character appears.
m	Displays the month as a number without leading zeros (1-12). If you use m immediately after the h or hh symbol, Excel displays the minute rather than the month.
mm	Displays the month as a number with leading zeros (01-12). If you use mm immediately after the h or hh symbol, Excel displays the minute rather than the month.
mmm	Displays the month as an abbreviation (Jan-Dec).
mmmm	Displays the month as a full name (January-December).
d	Displays the day as a number without leading zeros (1-31).
dd	Displays the day as a number with leading zeros (01-31).
ddd	Displays the day as an abbreviation (Sun-Sat).
dddd	Displays the day as a full name (Sunday-Saturday).
yy or yyyy	Displays the year as a two-digit number (00-99), or as a four-digit number (1900-2078).
h or hh	Displays the hour as a number without leading zeros (0-23), or as a number with leading zeros (00-23). If the format contains an AM or PM, the hour is based on the 12-hour clock. Otherwise, the hour is based on the 24-hour clock.
m or mm	Displays the minute as a number without leading zeros (0-59), or as a number with leading zeros (00-59). The m or mm must appear immediately after the h or hh symbol, or Excel displays the month rather than the minute.
s or ss	Displays the second as a number without leading zeros (0-59), or as a number with leading zeros (00-59).
[]	Displays hours greater than 24, or minutes or seconds greater than 60. Place the brackets around the leftmost part of the time code; for example, the time code [h]:mm:ss would allow the display of hours greater than 24.
AM/am/A/a/PM/pm/P/p	Displays the hour using a 12-hour clock. Excel displays AM, am, A, or a for times from midnight until noon; and PM, pm, P, or p for times from noon until midnight. If no AM/PM indicator is used, the hour is based on the 24-hour clock.

(continues)

II

Programmer's Reference

Table 9.3 Continued	
Symbol	**Description**
[BLACK]	Displays the characters in the cell in black.
[BLUE]	Displays the characters in the cell in blue.
[CYAN]	Displays the characters in the cell in cyan.
[GREEN]	Displays the characters in the cell in green.
[MAGENTA]	Displays the characters in the cell in magenta.
[RED]	Displays the characters in the cell in red.
[WHITE]	Displays the characters in the cell in white.
[YELLOW]	Displays the characters in the cell in yellow.
[COLOR n]	Displays the corresponding color in the color palette, where n is a number from 0 to 56.
[condition value]	Where condition can be <, >, =, >=, <=, <>, and value can be any number. With the [condition value] symbol, you can set your own criteria for each section of a number format.

range.NumberFormatLocal

Same as NumberFormat, but uses codes based on the user's national language as determined by the current system settings.

range.Offset

range.Offset ([*RowOffset*], [*ColumnOffset*])

Returns a range of cells offset from *range* by a number of rows or columns. If the offset address would be off the worksheet, causes error 1004.

Argument	**Description**
RowOffset	The number of rows to shift down (positive) or up (negative). The default is 0.
ColumnOffset	The number of columns to shift to the right (positive) or left (negative). The default is 0.

The following code selects a range one column left and one row up from the current selection:

```
Selection.Offset(-1,-1)
```

range.**Orientation**

range.**Orientation** [= *setting*]

Sets or returns the orientation of values displayed in a range: xlHorizontal, xlVertical, xlUpward, or xlDownward. The default is xlHorizontal.

range.**OutlineLevel**

range.**OutlineLevel** [= *setting*]

Sets or returns the outline level of rows or columns. If *range* is not a complete row or column, causes error 1004. The following code demotes the selected row one level:

```
Rows(Selection.Row).OutlineLevel = Rows(Selection.Row).OutlineLevel + 1
```

range.**PageBreak**

range.**PageBreak** [= *setting*]

Sets or returns the location of a page break. If *range* is not an entire row or column, PageBreak causes error 1004. xlNone indicates no page break; xlAutomatic indicates automatic page breaks; xlManual sets a page break location. The default is xlNone.

The following code sets a page break at row 20:

```
Rows(20).PageBreak = xlManual
```

This line of code clears all the manual page breaks in a worksheet:

```
Cells.PageBreaks = xlNone
```

The following code selects the first-column page break:

```
Sub FindFirstColPageBreak()
    For Each Column In Columns
        If Column.PageBreak = xlAutomatic Then
            Column.Select
            Exit For
        End If
    Next Column
End Sub
```

range.**Parse**

range.**Parse** ([*ParseLine*], [*Destination*])

Separates the values in a single column into multiple columns. If *range* contains more than one column, causes error 1004.

Argument	Description
ParseLine	A string that indicates where to separate values. For example, "[xxxx][xx]" breaks a column between the fourth and fifth digit or character. "[" begins a field and "]" ends one. If *ParseLine* is longer or shorter than the values in *range*, the line is not parsed. *ParseLine* may also be a range of cells indicating how to parse the column. If omitted, Excel parses the column based on spaces in the values.
Destination	A range indicating the first cell to copy the parsed columns to. The default is the first cell in *range*.

range.PasteSpecial

range.PasteSpecial ([*Paste*], [*Operation*], [*SkipBlanks*], [*Transpose*])

Pastes data from the Clipboard to *range*.

Argument	Description
Paste	xlAll pastes all cell values and attributes; xlFormulas pastes only formulas; xlValues pastes only values; xlFormats pastes only formatting; xlNotes pastes only notes. The default is xlAll.
Operation	xlNone replaces the contents of *range*; xlAdd adds the pasted values to the values in *range*; xlSubtract subtracts the pasted values from the current ones; xlMultiply multiplies values; xlDivide divides the current values by the pasted ones. The default is xlNone.
SkipBlanks	True ignores blank cells on the Clipboard and does not replace those cells in *range* with blanks; False pastes blanks on the Clipboard to *range*. The default is False.
Transpose	True transposes rows and columns on the Clipboard before pasting; False does not. The default is False.

range.PivotField

Returns the PivotField object in the first cell of *range*. If the first cell does not contain a pivot field, causes error 1004.

range.PivotItem

Returns the PivotItem object in the first cell of *range*. If the first cell is not part of a pivot item, causes error 1004.

range.**PivotTable**

Returns the `PivotTable` object in the first cell of *range*. If the first cell is not part of a pivot table, causes error 1004.

range.**Precedents( )**

Returns a range containing the cells whose values are used directly or indirectly to calculate the value of the source range. If the source range has no precedents, `Precedents` causes error 1004.

The following line of code selects the precedents of the currently selected cells:

```
Selection.Precedents.Select
```

range.**PrefixCharacter**

Returns the prefix character for a range containing a label. If the `TransitionNavigKeys` property is True, returns "'" for a left-justified label, "^" for a centered label, """ for a right-justified label, or "\" for a repeated label. The default is "'" for labels and "" for other cells.

range.**Previous**

Returns a range containing the previous cell. If *range* contains more than one cell, `Previous` uses the first cell in the range as the starting point.

range.**PrintOut**

range.**PrintOut ([*From*], [*To*], [*Copies*], [*Preview*])**

Prints the range.

Argument	Description
From	The number of the first page to print. The default is 1.
To	The number of the last page to print. The default is All.
Copies	The number of copies to print. The default is 1.
Preview	True previews the output on screen before printing; False prints without previewing. The default is False.

The following code prints the selected range of cells:

```
Selection.PrintOut
```

range.**PrintPreview( )**

Previews the print output for a range on-screen.

range.**PrintOut**

range.**PrintOut ([*Cell1*], [*Cell2*])**

Returns a range of cells relative to another range.

Argument	Description
Cell1	A string or Range object indicating the first cell of the relative range.
Cell2	A string or Range object indicating the last cell of the relative range.

The following line of code selects cell E5:

```
Range("d4").Range("b2").Select
```

> **Caution**
>
> Not all combinations of range and cell syntaxes are compatible. For example, Range("d4").Range(Cells(1,1)) fails, but Range("d4").Range(Cells(1,1),Cells(1,1)) works fine.

range.**RemoveSubtotal( )**

Removes all the subtotals from a range. See the Subtotal method for information on creating subtotals for a range.

range.**Replace**

range.**Replace (*What, Replacement*, [*LookAt*], [*SearchOrder*], [*MatchCase*])**

Replaces text within the cells in a range. Returns True whether or not the text was found.

Argument	Description
What	The text to find.
Replacement	The replacement text.

Argument	Description
LookAt	xlWhole to search for the entire contents of a cell; xlPart to search within cells. The default is xlPart.
SearchOrder	xlByRows to search down one row at a time; xlByColumns to search to the left one column at a time. The default is xlByRows.
MatchCase	True to perform a case-sensitive search/replace; False to ignore case. The default is False.

The Replace method replaces all the occurrences it finds in the range. The following line of code replaces Wombat with Wallaby in the active worksheet:

```
Cells.Replace "Wombat", "Wallaby"
```

range.Resize

range.Resize ([*RowSize*], [*ColumnSize*])

Changes the number of rows and columns in a range.

Argument	Description
RowSize	The new number of rows in the range. Must be 1 or greater. The default is no change.
ColumnSize	The new number of columns in the range. Must be 1 or greater. The default is no change.

The following code makes a selection one row and one column smaller:

```
Selection.Resize(Selection.Rows.Count - 1, Selection.Columns. _
Count - 1).Select
```

range.Row

Returns the row number of the first cell in a range.

range.RowDifferences

range.RowDifferences (*Comparison*)

Compares the values in *range* to those in *Comparison* and returns the range of cells that do not have the same values in like positions. RowDifferences ignores values in the same column as *Comparison*, even if they are included in the selection. The following code selects all the cells in a worksheet that are different from the active cell (ignoring the column of the active cell):

```
Cells.RowDifferences (ActiveCell).Select
```

range.RowHeight

range.RowHeight [= *setting*]

Sets or returns the height of rows in a range measured in points. Returns Null if the height of the rows varies within the range.

range.Rows

range.Rows ([*Index*])

Returns a collection of one or all the rows included in a range. *Index* is the index of a row in the range, counting from the top. The following line of code selects the first row in a range:

```
Range("A1:D9").Rows(1)
```

The Rows and Columns methods are very useful when formatting a worksheet and when creating outlines. Many methods require an entire row or column, as is returned by these methods.

range.Run

range.Run ([*Arguments*])

Runs an Excel 4.0 macro that begins in the first cell of *range*. *Arguments* is one or more arguments used by the Excel 4.0 macro.

range.Select ([*Replace*])

Selects a range of cells on a sheet. Select is the equivalent of clicking on the object. If *Replace* is False, Select extends the current selection, rather than deselecting previous selections. The default is True.

range.Show( )

Scrolls the worksheet to show *range*. The following line of code scrolls the active worksheet to display cell Z200:

```
[Z200].Show
```

*range.***ShowDependents**

*range.***ShowDependents ([*Remove*])**

Shows or removes the auditing arrows between a range and its dependents. If *Remove* is True, the arrows are removed; if *Remove* is False, they are displayed. The default is False.

*range.***ShowDetail**

*range.***ShowDetail [= True | False]**

True displays rows or columns that are part of an outline; False hides rows or columns that are part of an outline. The *range* must be an entire row or column, otherwise ShowDetail causes error 1004.

*range.***ShowErrors()**

Shows or removes the auditing arrows between a range and cells in its formula that contain error values.

*range.***ShowPrecedents**

*range.***ShowPrecedents ([*Remove*])**

Shows or removes the auditing arrows between a range and its precedents. If *Remove* is True, the arrows are removed; if *Remove* is False, they are displayed. The default is False.

*range.***Sort**

*range.***Sort ([*Key1*], [*Order1*], [*Key2*], [*Type*], [*Order2*], [*Key3*], [*Order3*], [*Header*], [*OrderCustom*], [*MatchCase*], [*Orientation*])**

Sorts a range of cells or the current region if *range* contains one cell. A region is a block of cells surrounded by blank rows or columns.

Argument	Description
Key1	The first row or column to sort. *Key1* may be a single cell or a column/row heading.
Order1	xlAscending sorts *Key1* in ascending order; xlDescending sorts *Key1* in descending order. The default is xlAscending.

(continues)

Argument	Description
Key2	The second row or column to sort. *Key2* may be a single cell or a column/row heading.
Type	This argument is ignored for the Range object.
Order2	xlAscending sorts *Key2* in ascending order; xlDescending sorts *Key2* in descending order. The default is xlAscending.
Key3	The third row or column to sort. *Key3* may be a single cell or a column/row heading.
Order3	xlAscending sorts *Key3* in ascending order; xlDescending sorts *Key3* in descending order. The default is xlAscending.
Header	xlYes does not sort the first column or row in the range; xlNo sorts the first column or row; xlGuess chooses the type of sorting based on the contents of the first row or column. The default is xlGuess.
OrderCustom	The index of a custom sort order from the Sort Options dialog box. The default is 1 (Normal).
MatchCase	True performs case-sensitive sort; False ignores case. The default is False.
Orientation	xlTopToBottom sorts rows; xlLeftToRight sorts columns. The default is xlTopToBottom.

This method corresponds to the Sort and Sort Options dialog boxes (see fig. 9.11). To display the Sort dialog box in Excel, choose Data, Sort.

Fig. 9.11
The Sort and Sort
Options dialog
boxes.

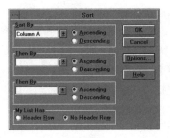

The following line of code sorts a selected range by rows:

```
Selection.Sort ActiveCell
```

*range.***SortSpecial**

*range.***SortSpecial ([*SortMethod*], [*Key1*], [*Order1*], [*Type*], [*Key2*], [*Order2*], [*Key3*], [*Order3*], [*Header*], [*OrderCustom*], [*MatchCase*], [*Orientation*])**

Sorts a range using special Far East options. SortSpecial is identical to Sort with one additional argument, as shown in the following table:

Argument	Description
SortMethod	xlSyllabary sorts phonetically; xlCodePage sorts according to the order of symbols in the code page. The default is xlSyllabary.

*range.***SoundNote**

Returns the SoundNote object in the first cell of the range. Use this method to play and record sound notes. The following code displays the Record dialog box to record a note for the active cell:

```
ActiveCell.SoundNote.Record
```

This line of code plays a sound note:

```
ActiveCell.SoundNote.Play
```

*range.***SpecialCells**

*range.***SpecialCells (*Type*, [*Value*])**

Returns a range containing cells of a specific type.

Argument	Description
Type	xlNotes returns cells with notes; xlConstants returns cells containing constant values; xlFormulas returns cells containing formulas; xlBlanks returns blank cells; xlLastCell returns the last cell of the range; xlVisible returns the cells that are visible in the current window.
Value	Valid if *Type* is xlConstants or xlFormulas. xlNumbers returns cells containing numbers, xlTextValues returns cells containing text; xlLogical returns cells containing logical values; xlErrors returns cells containing error values. The default is All.

II

Programmer's Reference

*range.*Style

Returns the Style object for a range. Returns Null if the range contains a mix of styles. Use the Style object to set or return the style of a range. The following line of code styles the selected cells as Heading 1:

```
Selection.Style = "Heading 1"
```

*range.*SubscribeTo

*range.*SubscribeTo (*Edition*, [*Format*])

Macintosh System 7 only. Subscribes to a published edition.

Argument	Description
Edition	The name of the edition to subscribe to.
Format	xlPicture subscribes to a picture of the edition; xlText subscribes to the text of the edition.

*range.*Subtotal

*range.*Subtotal (*GroupBy, Function, TotalList*, [*Replace*], [*PageBreaks*], [*SummaryBelowData*])

Adds subtotals to the columns in a range of cells.

Argument	Description
GroupBy	The number of the column within the range that contains the groups for which to create subtotals.
Function	xlAverage averages values; xlCount counts nonblank cells; xlCountNums counts cells containing numbers; xlMax lists the maximum cell value; xlMin lists the minimum cell value; xlProduct multiplies all cell values; xlStDev calculates the standard deviation; xlStDevP calculates the standard deviation assuming the data represents the entire population; xlSum adds the cell values; xlVar calculates the variance; xlVarP calculates the variance assuming the data represents the entire population. The default is xlSum.
TotalList	An array containing the numbers of the columns for which totals are to be created.
Replace	True replaces existing subtotals; False does not. The default is False.

Argument	Description
PageBreaks	True adds a page break after each group; False does not. The default is False.
SummaryBelowData	xlBelow displays totals at the bottom of columns; xlAbove displays totals at the top. The default is xlBelow.

This method corresponds to the Subtotal dialog box (see fig. 9.12). To display the Subtotal dialog box in Excel, choose Data, Subtotals.

Fig. 9.12
The Subtotal
dialog box.

The following code creates subtotals for the third column of the selection, grouping them by changes in the first column:

```
Selection.Subtotal 1, xlSum, Array(3)
```

range.Summary

Returns True if a column or row has outline levels below it; False if the column or row shows detail. If *range* is not an entire row or column, causes error 1006. The following code displays True if the selection contains a summary level of an outline:

```
MsgBox Rows(Selection.Row).Summary
```

range.Table

range.Table ([*RowInput*], [*ColumnInput*])

Creates a data table for what-if analysis. A *data table* is a range of cells whose values are calculated based on a row or a column value. The values displayed in the data table can't be changed directly.

Argument	Description
RowInput	A range containing a single cell on which to base the row values of the data table.
ColumnInput	A range containing a single cell on which to base the column values of the data table.

This method corresponds to the Table dialog box (see fig. 9.13). To display the Table dialog box in Excel, choose Data, Table.

Fig. 9.13
The Table dialog
box.

*range.*Text

Returns the value of cells in a range as text. If the cells contain a mix of values, returns Null.

*range.*TextToColumns

*range.*TextToColumns ([*Destination*], [*DataType*], [*TextQualifier*], [*ConsecutiveDelimiter*], [*Tab*], [*Semicolon*], [*Comma*], [*Space*], [*Other*], [*OtherChar*], [*FieldInfo*])

Parses a column containing text into several columns.

Argument	Description
Destination	A range in which to place the parsed columns. Excel uses the first cell in *Destination* to determine where the new columns start, ignoring other cells in the range. The default is the first cell in the source range.
DataType	xlDelimited if the text is delimited by special characters, such as Tabs; xlFixed if the fields in the text are all the same width. The default is xlDelimited.
TextQualifier	xlDoubleQuote interprets items surrounded by double quotes as text; xlSingleQuote uses single quotes as text; xlNone evaluates fields to see if they are text or numbers. The default is xlDoubleQuote.

Argument	Description
ConsecutiveDelimiter	True interprets consecutive delimiters as a single delimiter; False does not. The default is False.
Tab	True uses tabs as the delimiter; False does not. The default is True.
Semicolon	True uses semicolons as the delimiter; False does not. The default is False.
Comma	True uses commas as the delimiter; False does not. The default is False.
Space	True uses spaces as the delimiter; False does not. The default is False.
Other	True uses OtherChar as the delimiter; False does not. The default is False.
OtherChar	The character to use as the delimiter.
FieldInfo	An array that describes the data types of fields in the text. See the Workbook object's OpenText method for a full description.

Note

Delimiters identify where a column of data starts or stops. Only one type of delimiter may be specified.

range.Ungroup()

Ungroups a row or a column from an outline. This "promotes" the row or column one level in the outline. If *range* is not an entire row or column, causes error 1006.

range.UseStandardHeight

Returns True if the cells in the range are the standard height; False if not; and Null if the range has a mix of standard height and other cells.

range.UseStandardWidth

Returns True if the cells in the range are the standard width; False if not; and Null if the range has a mix of standard width and other cells.

range[.Value]

If *range* contains a single cell, returns the value of the cell. If *range* contains more than one cell, returns an array of values. The first dimension of the returned array corresponds to the rows in the range, and the second dimension corresponds to the columns.

The following line of code creates array X from the values in the range A1:D9:

```
X = [A1:D9]     ' X has the dimensions X(1 To 9, 1 To 4)
```

range.VerticalAlignment

range.VerticalAlignment [= *setting*]

Sets or returns the vertical alignment of a range: xlBottom, xlCenter, xlDistributed, xlJustify, or xlTop.

range.Worksheet()

Returns the Worksheet object that contains the range. A worksheet must be active before you can activate any of its cells.

range.WrapText

range.WrapText [= True | False]

True wraps text in cells within the range; False does not. The default is False.

Accessing Areas within a Multiple Selection

An area is a contiguous block of cells; a range can contain one or more areas. The following range has three areas:

```
rngMulti = Union([a1:d4], [e2:f3], [g1])
```

Use the Areas method of the Range object to access each of the areas within a range. This code selects the range A1:D4:

```
rngMulti.Areas(1).Select
```

Many methods require a range to be contiguous, so it is often necessary to use the Areas collection.

Areas have specific properties and methods, which are listed in Table 9.4.

Table 9.4 Areas properties and methods

Application	Creator
Item	Parent
Count	

Referring to Ranges with Names

You can refer to ranges by name rather than address. Names make formulas easier to read, understand, and maintain. Each workbook contains a collection of Name objects. Use this collection to create new names and to find and change existing names.

The following code creates a name for a range and then uses the name to select the range's cells:

```
Sub CreateName()
    ' Add the name to the workbook.
    Names.Add "MyName", "=Sheet2!$A$1:$B$4"
    ' Activate the sheet and select the named range.
    Application.Goto "MyName"
End Sub
```

To display a list of defined names for a workbook, use the ListNames method of the Range object. The following code displays a list of all the names in a workbook, starting with cell A1:

```
[A1].ListNames
```

Some names have predefined meanings. For example, Auto_Load identifies a procedure to run when Excel first starts up. For more information on these predefined names, see Chapter 5, "Controlling the Excel Application."

The Name object and Names collection properties and methods are listed in Table 9.5. Properties and methods shown in **bold** are described in the reference section that follows this table. Nonbold items are common to most objects and are described in Chapter 4, "Using Objects."

Tip
Use the Application object's GoTo method to select a named range. The Range method can't accept a name as an argument.

II

Programmer's Reference

Table 9.5 Name and Names properties and methods

Add[1]	Creator[2]
Application[2]	**Delete**
Category	Index
CategoryLocal	**Item**[1]
Count[1]	**MacroType**

(continues)

Table 9.5 Continued	
Name	RefersToR1C1
NameLocal	RefersToR1C1Local
Parent[2]	ShortcutKey
RefersTo	Value
RefersToLocal	Visible

[1] *Applies to the* Names *collection.*

[2] *Applies to the* Names *collection and the* Name *object.*

Names.Add

Names.Add ([*Name*], [*RefersTo*], [*Visible*], [*MacroType*], [*ShortcutKey*], [*Category*], [*NameLocal*], [*RefersToLocal*], [*CategoryLocal*], [*RefersToR1C1*], [*RefersToR1C1Local*])

Creates a new name and adds it to the workbook's collection of Name objects. Add can set all the Name properties through its arguments.

Argument	Description
Name	The name to create.
RefersTo	The item to which the name refers. This is usually a formula that refers to a range of cells, for example, "=$A$1:$C$3." If a name refers to a procedure, as with Auto_Activate, this formula has the form "=*workbookname*!*modulename*.*procedurename*".
Visible	True displays the name in Excel's name lists; False hides the name. The default is True.
MacroType	xlNone if the name does not refer to an Excel 4.0 macro or command; xlMacro if it refers to an Excel 4.0 macro; xlFunction if it refers to an Excel 4.0 function. The default is xlNone.
ShortcutKey	If the name refers to an Excel 4.0 command, specifies the shortcut key for the command.
Category	If the name refers to an Excel 4.0 function, specifies the category name for the function. The default is user-defined.
NameLocal	The name to use in the language of the user.
RefersToLocal	The item to which the name refers, expressed in the user's national language. The default is *RefersTo*.

Argument	Description
CategoryLocal	If the name refers to an Excel 4.0 function, specifies the category name for the function in the user's national language. The default is *Category*.
RefersToR1C1	The item to which the name refers, expressed in R1C1-address style.
RefersToR1C1Local	The item to which the name refers, expressed in R1C1-address style using the user's national language. The default is *RefersToR1C1*.

The Add method corresponds to the Define Name dialog box (see fig. 9.14). To display the Define Name dialog box in Excel, choose Insert, Names; then choose the sub-item Define. Excel displays one of two different Names dialog boxes, depending on whether your current sheet is a worksheet or a macro sheet.

Fig. 9.14
The Define Name dialog box for worksheets.

The following line of code adds the name "Interest" to the workbook:

```
Names.Add "Interest", "=Sheet1!$B$2"
```

If a name includes blank spaces, surround it with brackets ([]) as shown here:

```
Names.Add "'[Interest Payment]'", "=Sheet1!$a$1"
```

The following line adds an Auto_Activate name to Sheet1. The Auto_Activate name is a predefined name that runs the specified procedure whenever the user activates the worksheet.

```
Names.Add "Sheet1!Auto_Activate", "=BOOK3.XLS! _
[Module 1].Sheet1OnActivate'"
```

name.**Category**

name.**Category** [= *category*]

If the name refers to a custom function or command, sets or returns the category for this name as a string translated to the macro programmer's language.

name.CategoryLocal

name.CategoryLocal [= *setting*]

If the name refers to a custom function or command, sets or returns the category for this name as a string in the language of the user.

name.Delete( )

Deletes a name from the Names collection.

Names[.Item]

Names[.Item] ([*Index*] | [*IndexLocal*] | [*RefersTo*])

Returns a name from the workbook's collection of names.

Argument	Description
Index	The number or name of the name to return.
IndexLocal	The name to return in the user's language.
RefersTo	The item to which the name refers.

The following line of code displays the first name defined in a workbook:

```
MsgBox Names(1).Name
```

This line of code changes the range that the name "Interest" refers to:

```
Names("Interest").RefersTo = "=" & ActiveCell.Address
```

This line of code changes the range that the name "ShuLust" refers to:

```
Names(LdexLocal:="ShuLust").RefersTo = "=" & ActiveCell.Address
```

name.MacroType

name.MacroType [= *setting*]

xlNone if the name does not refer to an Excel 4.0 macro or command; xlMacro if the name refers to an Excel 4.0 macro; xlFunction if the name refers to an Excel 4.0 function. The default is xlNone.

Use MacroType to determine what type of Excel 4.0 macro a name refers to. This property does not return useful information about named ranges or Visual Basic procedure names.

name.Name

name.Name [= *name*]

Sets or returns the name of the Name object. If it is one of the built-in names, it is translated to the language of the programmer.

name.NameLocal

name.NameLocal [= *name*]

Sets or returns the name of the Name object. If it is one of the built-in names, it is translated to the language of the user.

name.RefersTo

name.RefersTo [= *formula*]

Sets or returns the formula that the name refers to, in A1-style notation, in the language of the programmer. If a name refers to a procedure, as with `Auto_Activate` and other predefined names, this formula has the form `"=workbookname!modulename.procedurename"`.

name.RefersToLocal

name.RefersToLocal [= *formula*]

Sets or returns the formula that the name refers to in A1 notation, in the language of the user.

name.RefersToR1C1

name.RefersToR1C1 [= *formula*]

Sets or returns the formula that the name refers to in R1C1-style notation, in the language of the programmer.

name.RefersToR1C1Local

name.RefersToR1C1Local [= *formula*]

Sets or returns the formula that the name refers to in R1C1-style notation, in the language of the user.

II

Programmer's Reference

name.ShortcutKey

name.ShortcutKey [= *keyname*]

Sets or returns the shortcut key for a name that refers to a custom Excel version 4.0 macro command.

> **Note**
>
> See the "Using Ranges" section at the beginning of this chapter for a discussion of A1 and R1C1 notation.

Formatting and Changing Text within Cells

Use the Font property to format all of the text displayed in a cell. The following code changes the font of the selected range to Times:

```
Selection.Font.Name = "Times"
```

Use the Characters collection to format parts of the text in a cell. The following code changes the font of the first character of the active cell to Times:

```
ActiveCell.Characters(1,1).Font.Name = "Times"
```

The following objects have methods that return the Characters collection:

AxisTitle	EditBox
Button	GroupBox
ChartTitle	Label
CheckBox	Labels
DataLabel	OptionButton
DialogFrame	Range
DrawingObjects	TextBox
DropDown	

The method that returns the Characters collection has two arguments:

Argument	Description
Start	The position of the first character to return. The default is 1.
Length	The position of the last character to return. The default is the length of the text.

When working with the Characters collection, remember these points:

- You can only return a Characters collection from a single object, such as a single cell or a single text box.

- The source object must contain text. If a range contains numeric data, the Characters method causes error 1004.

Characters properties and methods are listed in Table 9.6. Properties and methods shown in **bold** are described in the reference section that follows this table. Nonbold items are common to most objects and are described in Chapter 4, "Using Objects."

Table 9.6 Characters properties and methods

Application	**Font**
Caption	**Insert**
Count	Parent
Creator	**Text**
Delete	

*characters.*Caption

This property is identical to Text.

*characters.*Count

Returns the number of characters in the collection.

*characters.*Delete( )

Deletes the text in the Characters collection. The following code deletes the first three characters in cell A1:

```
[A1].Characters(1,3).Delete
```

*characters.*Font

Returns the Font object for the characters. Use the returned Font object to change the appearance of the characters in the Characters collection.

*characters.*Insert

*characters.*Insert (*String*)

Inserts a string before the characters in the Characters collection. The following code inserts a line of text at the end of the current text in cell A1:

```
[A1].Characters.([A1].Characters.Count, 1).Insert("This is _
inserted at the end.")
```

*characters.*Text

Use the Text property of the Characters collection to get the text contained in the cell. The following line of code displays the first three characters in cell A1:

```
MsgBox [A1].Characters(1,3).Text
```

Chapter 10

Linking and Embedding

Linking is the insertion of a reference into an object. *Embedding* is the insertion of an object into a document. A copy of the object becomes part of the document. If the object changes, it is updated in both the document and at the object's origin. Excel enables you to link and embed information, or *objects,* created with other applications. This is called *Object Linking and Embedding* (OLE).

This chapter covers the OLEObject, Picture, TextBox, and SoundNote objects.

In this chapter, you learn how to do the following:

- Link and embed objects in a workbook using OLE, pictures, and text boxes.

- Use the Picture object and Pictures collection.

- Use the TextBox object and TextBoxes collection.

- Attach sounds to a cell.

Adding Links and Pictures

Excel lets you take "pictures" of ranges and display them in charts, dialog sheets, or other worksheets. These pictures are links to the original cells and change when the source cells change, but the picture can't be edited directly.

Use the Add method to insert a picture from the Clipboard. The following lines of code copy a range of cells and then create a picture from them.

```
Sub CreatePicture()
    [a1:b4].Copy
    ActiveSheet.Pictures.Add 1, 1, 100, 100
End Sub
```

Use the `Insert` method to insert a picture from a file. The file must be a graphics file. The following code inserts a bitmap in a sheet:

```
ActiveSheet.Pictures.Insert "IMAGE.BMP"
```

Once you've inserted a picture in a worksheet, chart, or dialog sheet, it becomes part of that object's `Pictures` collection. The following code deletes all the pictures in a sheet:

```
ActiveSheet.Pictures.Delete
```

The `Picture` object and `Pictures` collection have specific properties and methods, which are listed in Table 10.1. Properties and methods shown in **bold** are described in the reference section that follows this table. Nonbold items are common to most objects and are described in Chapter 4, "Using Objects."

Table 10.1 Picture and pictures properties and methods	
Add[1]	**Interior**[2]
Application[2]	Item[1]
Border[2]	Left[2]
BottomRightCell	**Locked**[2]
BringToFront[2]	Name
Copy[2]	**OnAction**[2]
CopyPicture[2]	Parent[2]
Count[1]	**Paste**[1]
Creator[2]	**Placement**[2]
Cut[2]	**PrintObject**[2]
Delete[2]	**Select**[2]
Duplicate[2]	SendToBack[2]
Enabled[2]	**Shadow**[2]
Formula[2]	Top[2]
Group[1]	**TopLeftCell**
Height[2]	Visible[2]
Index	Width[2]
Insert[1]	ZOrder[2]

[1] *Applies to the Pictures collection.*

[2] *Applies to the Pictures collection and the Picture object.*

Pictures.Add

Pictures.Add (*Left, Top, Width, Height*)

Creates a link from data on the Clipboard and embeds the link in a sheet as a `Picture` object. Causes error 1004 if there is no linkable data currently on the Clipboard. To add a picture to a sheet from a file, use the `Insert` method.

Argument	Description
Left	The distance between the left edge of the sheet and the right edge of the picture in points.
Top	The distance between the top edge of the sheet and the top edge of the picture in points.
Width	The width of the picture in points.
Height	The height of the picture in points.

The following code adds a picture if the Clipboard contains valid data:

```
Sub AddPicture()
    FormatsArray = Application.ClipboardFormats
    For Each iFormat In FormatsArray
        If iFormat = xlClipboardFormatLink Then
            ActiveSheet.Pictures.Add 1, 1, 100, 100
            Exit For
        End If
    Next iFormat
End Sub
```

picture.Border

Returns the `Border` object for a picture or all pictures on a sheet. Use this property to change the border of a picture. The following code changes the borders of all pictures on a sheet to medium weight:

```
ActiveSheet.Pictures.Border.Weight = xlMedium
```

picture.BottomRightCell

Returns the cell under the bottom right corner of the picture.

II

Programmer's Reference

*picture.*Copy

*picture.*Copy [(*index*)]

Copies one or all pictures on the sheet to the Clipboard. If *index* is used, only that picture is copied, otherwise all pictures on a worksheet are copied. The following code copies the first picture on a sheet to the Clipboard:

```
ActiveSheet.Pictures(1).Copy
```

This code copies all the pictures on a sheet:

```
ActiveSheet.Pictures.Copy
```

*picture.*CopyPicture

*picture.*CopyPicture ([*Appearance*], [*Format*])

Copies one or all pictures in a sheet to the Clipboard using a specific format.

Argument	Description
Appearance	xlScreen copies the range as it appears on-screen; xlPrinter copies the range as it would appear if printed using the current printer setup. The default is xlScreen.
Format	xlPicture creates the copy in PICT format; xlBitmap creates the copy as a bitmap. The default is xlPicture.

*picture.*Cut

*picture.*Cut [(*index*)]

Cuts one or all pictures on the sheet to the Clipboard. If *index* is used, only that picture is cut, otherwise all pictures on a worksheet are cut. The following code cuts the first picture on a sheet to the Clipboard:

```
ActiveSheet.Pictures(1).Cut
```

This code cuts all the pictures on a sheet:

```
ActiveSheet.Pictures.Cut
```

*picture.*Delete

*picture.*Delete [(*index*)]

Deletes one or all pictures on the sheet. Does not change the contents of the Clipboard. If *index* is used, only that picture is deleted, otherwise all pictures on a worksheet are deleted. The following code deletes the first picture on a sheet to the Clipboard:

```
ActiveSheet.Pictures(1).Delete
```

This code deletes all the pictures on a sheet:

```
ActiveSheet.Pictures.Delete
```

picture.Duplicate

picture.Duplicate [(*index*)]

Makes a copy of one or all pictures on a sheet and returns the object (or collection) that was created. If *index* is used, only that picture is duplicated, otherwise all pictures on a worksheet are duplicated. The following code duplicates the first picture on a sheet and moves it up 10 points:

```
ActiveSheet.Pictures(1).Duplicate.Top = Pictures(1).Top -10
```

picture.Enabled

picture.Enabled [= True | False]

True enables one or all pictures on the sheet to respond to click events; False disables click events. A picture responds to click events if its OnAction property is set to a procedure name. The default is True.

picture.Formula

Returns the formula of a picture. A picture has a formula if it is a link, for example, "=WordDocument¦'C:\BOOKQUE\01CH07.DOC'!'!DDE_LINK3'".

Picture.Group( )

Groups a collection of pictures so that they can be selected, moved, copied, or deleted as a single object. The following code groups all the objects on a sheet:

```
ActiveSheet.Pictures.Group
```

Pictures.Insert

Pictures.Insert (*Filename*, [*Converter*])

Inserts a picture into a sheet from a file and adds it to the Pictures collection. Returns the Picture object that was inserted.

Argument	Description
Filename	The name of the file to insert.
Converter	Identifies the file converter to use when loading the file: xlBMP, xlWMF, xlPLT, xlCGM, xlHGL, xlPIC, xlEPS, xlDRW, xlTIF, xlWPG, xlDXF, xlPCX, or xlPCT. Using the Insert method causes error 1004 if *Converter* doesn't match the format of the file. The default selects *Converter* based on the contents of the file.

The following line of code inserts balloon.bmp on the sheet and sets its Top property:

```
ActiveSheet.Pictures.Insert ("balloon.bmp").Top = 1
```

*picture.*Interior

Returns the Interior object for one or all of the pictures on a sheet. Use the Interior object properties to set the shading and color of the interior of a picture. The following code shades the interior of all the picture objects on a sheet:

```
ActiveSheet.Pictures.Interior.Pattern = xlGray16
```

*picture.*Locked

*picture.*Locked [= True | False]

True prevents changes to one or all the pictures on a sheet while the sheet is protected; False allows changes. The default is True.

*picture.*OnAction

*picture.*OnAction [= *procedure*]

Sets or returns the name of a procedure to run when one or all pictures on the sheet are clicked. The following code causes the procedure Foo() to run when the user clicks the picture FooPic:

```
ActiveSheet.Pictures("FooPic").OnAction = "Foo"
```

Pictures.Paste

Pictures.Paste ([*Link*])

Pastes the contents of the Clipboard to a sheet and adds it to the sheet's Pictures collection. If *Link* is True, the Paste method creates a link to the source data; False embeds the object. The default is False. Causes error 1004 if there is no linkable data currently on the Clipboard.

The following lines of code paste a link to a sheet if the data is linkable:

```
Sub PasteLink()
    FormatsArray = Application.ClipboardFormats
    For Each iFormat In FormatsArray
        If iFormat = xlClipboardFormatLink Then
            ActiveSheet.Pictures.Paste True
            Exit For
        End If
    Next iFormat
End Sub
```

picture.**Placement**

picture.**Placement [= xlMoveAndSize | xlMove | xlFreeFloating]**

Sets or returns how the picture is attached to the cells below it. The default is `xlFreeFloating`.

picture.**PrintObject**

picture.**PrintObject [= True | False]**

True prints the picture with the worksheet; False does not. The default is True. The following code turns off printing for all the pictures on a sheet:

```
ActiveSheet.Pictures.PrintObject = False
```

picture.**Select**

picture.**Select ([*Replace*])**

Selects one or all of the pictures on a sheet. `Select` is the equivalent of clicking the object. If *Replace* is False, `Select` extends the current selection, rather than deselecting previous selections. The default is True.

picture.**Shadow**

picture.**Shadow [= True | False]**

True creates a background shadow for one or all the pictures on the sheet; False removes the shadow. The default is False.

picture.**TopLeftCell**

Returns the cell that lies under the top-left part of the picture.

Linking and Embedding with OLE

Object Linking and Embedding (OLE) is a technology Microsoft developed to bring data from different applications into a single document. In theory, the concept of an "application" starts to fall away as documents include spreadsheets, word processing text, charts, and drawings. OLE manages the connections between applications; in fact, Visual Basic uses OLE facilities to communicate with applications outside of Excel.

In Visual Basic, you can use OLE to:

- Add links to documents created by other applications.

- Embed objects created by other applications.

- Automate tasks in other applications.

OLE is a relatively new technology and many software companies are still struggling to incorporate it into their applications—even those that have incorporated OLE offer different levels of support. Microsoft Word version 6.0, and Microsoft Excel version 5.0, support OLE completely. You can get a good idea of the potential of OLE by using these applications together.

Caution

OLE is still cutting edge and can tax older, slower machines because it requires both source and container applications to run at the same time. OLE can also crash occasionally—though it is difficult to trace which application is at fault. Use these features with caution.

Adding Linked Objects

Use the Add method to create links to documents from other applications. Linked documents are stored separately from the workbook so they can be maintained at a central source, such as a network location.

The following code adds a link to an existing Word document DOC2.DOC:

```
ActiveSheet.OLEObjects.Add , "DOC2.DOC", True
```

To edit the document, activate it:

```
ActiveSheet.OLEObjects(1).Activate
```

Linked objects are not edited "in place"—that is, they start the source application in a new window.

To update a link from its source, use the Update method. For example:

```
ActiveSheet.OLEObjects(1).Update
```

Adding Embedded Objects

Use the Add method to embed documents from other applications in a workbook. Embedded documents are stored inside the workbook.

The following code adds a new embedded Word document:

```
ActiveSheet.OLEObjects.Add "Word.Document.6"
```

To edit the document, activate it:

```
ActiveSheet.OLEObjects(1).Activate
```

Embedded objects are edited "in place"—that is, you edit directly in the object on the workbook.

Automating Tasks in Other Applications

Some applications give access to their macro language from their linked and embedded objects. Currently there are three applications (Windows only) that support this: Excel, Word, and Shapeware Visio (a drawing tool).

The OLEObject object and OLEObjects collection have specific properties and methods, which are listed in Table 10.2. Properties and methods shown in **bold** are described in the reference section that follows this table. Nonbold items are common to most objects and are described in Chapter 4, "Using Objects."

Table 10.2 OLEObject and OLEObjects properties and methods	
Activate	**Cut**[2]
Add[1]	**Delete**[2]
Application[2]	**Duplicate**[2]
AutoUpdate	**Enabled**[2]
Border[2]	**Group**[1]
BottomRightCell	Height[2]
BringToFront[2]	Index
Copy[2]	**Interior**[2]
CopyPicture[2]	Item[1]
Count[1]	Left
Creator[2]	**Locked**[2]

(continues)

Programmer's Reference

II

Table 10.2 Continued

Name	SendToBack[2]
Object	Shadow[2]
OLEType	Top[2]
OnAction[2]	TopLeftCell
Parent[2]	Update
Paste	Verb
Placement[2]	Visible[2]
PrintObject[2]	Width[2]
Select[2]	ZOrder[2]

[1] *Applies to the* OLEObjects *collection.*

[2] *Applies to the* OLEObjects *collection and the* OLEObject *object.*

oleobject.Activate( )

Activates the OLE object for editing. Activating an OLE object for editing may take a little while, depending on the source application.

OLEObjects.Add

OLEObjects.Add ([*ClassType*], [*Filename*], [*Link*], [*DisplayAsIcon*], [*IconFileName*], [*IconIndex*], [*IconLabel*])

Inserts an OLE object in a sheet and adds it to the sheet's OLEObjects collection.

Argument	Description
ClassType	The class name of the OLE object to add. *ClassType* is ignored if *Filename* is specified and *Link* is True. See the comments after this table for some examples and a more complete explanation.
Filename	The file to use from which to create the OLE object. If omitted, Add creates a new empty document of *ClassType*.
Link	True creates a link to *Filename*; False embeds the document (changes to the source file are not reflected in the OLE object). The default is False.
DisplayAsIcon	True displays the source application's icon rather than the document; False displays the document in the worksheet. Many applications don't support False for this argument— in those cases, the application's icon is displayed regardless of this argument. The default is False.

Argument	Description
IconFileName	The name of an icon file to use as the source for the displayed icon (rather than using the application's default icon). The default is None.
IconIndex	The index of the icon within *IconFileName* to display. The default is 1.
IconLabel	The text to display under the icon. The default is None.

The Add method corresponds to the Object dialog box (see fig. 10.1). To display the Object dialog box in Excel, choose Insert, Object.

Each of the applications listed in the Object Type list box has a class type. The following table lists some common applications and class types.

Application	Class type
Microsoft Equation Editor	Equation
Microsoft Equation Draw	MSDraw
Microsoft Word Document (any version)	WordDocument
Microsoft Word Document (any version)	Word.Document
Microsoft Word 2.0 Document	Word.Document.2
Microsoft Word 6.0 Document	Word.Document.6
Microsoft Word Picture (version 6.0)	Word.Picture.6
MS Note-It	Note-It
MS WordArt	WordArt
Package (a file of any format)	Package
Microsoft PaintBrush	PBrush
Microsoft Quick Recorder	SoundRec
Microsoft Excel Chart	Excel.Chart
Microsoft Excel Worksheet	Excel.Sheet
Microsoft Excel Worksheet (version 5.0)	Excel.Sheet.5
Microsoft Excel Worksheet (version 5.0)	Excel.Chart.5
Shapeware Visio Drawing (version 2.0)	ShapewareVISIO20

Fig. 10.1
The Object dialog
box.

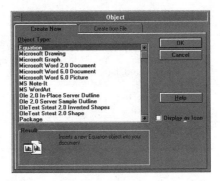

The easiest way to find out the class type of an object not in this list is to
record inserting the object in Excel. The following code was recorded from
my system to help build the previous table.

```
' Macro5 Macro
' Macro recorded 3/4/94 by jeffwe
Sub Macro5()
    ActiveSheet.OLEObjects.Add("Equation", , False, False).Activate
    ActiveSheet.OLEObjects.Add("MSDraw", , False, False).Activate
    ActiveSheet.OLEObjects.Add("WordDocument", , False, _
    False).Activate
    ActiveSheet.OLEObjects.Add("Word.Picture.6", , False, _
    False).Activate
    ActiveSheet.OLEObjects.Add("Note-It", , False, False).Activate
    ActiveSheet.OLEObjects.Add("WordArt", , False, False).Activate
    ActiveSheet.OLEObjects.Add("Package", , False, False).Activate
    ActiveSheet.OLEObjects.Add("PBrush", , False, False).Activate
    ActiveSheet.OLEObjects.Add("SoundRec", , False, False).Activate
End Sub
```

oleobject.AutoUpdate

oleobject.AutoUpdate [= True | False]

True updates the OLE object automatically when the source changes; False
requires manual updates. Valid only if the object's OLEType property is
xlOLELink. The default is True.

oleobject.Border

Returns the Border object for one or all OLE objects on a sheet. Use this property to change the border of an object.

oleobject.BottomRightCell

Returns the cell under the bottom-right corner of the OLE object.

oleobject.Copy

Copies one or all OLE objects on the sheet to the Clipboard. The following code copies the first OLE object on a sheet to the Clipboard:

```
ActiveSheet.OLEObjects(1).Copy
```

The following code copies all the pictures on a sheet:

```
ActiveSheet.OLEObjects.Copy
```

oleobject.CopyPicture
oleobject.CopyPicture ([*Appearance*], [*Format*])

Copies one or all OLE objects in a sheet to the Clipboard using a specific format.

Argument	Description
Appearance	xlScreen copies the object as it appears on-screen; xlPrinter copies the object as it would appear if printed using the current printer setup. The default is xlScreen.
Format	xlPicture creates the copy in PICT format; xlBitmap creates the copy as a bitmap. The default is xlPicture.

oleobjects.Cut
oleobjects.Cut [(*index*)]

Cuts one or all OLE objects on the sheet to the Clipboard. If *index* is used, only that OLE object is cut, otherwise all OLE objects on a worksheet are cut. The following code cuts the first OLE objects on a sheet to the Clipboard:

```
ActiveSheet.OLEObjects(1).Cut
```

This code cuts all the OLE objects on a sheet:

```
ActiveSheet.OLEObjects.Cut
```

oleobjects.Delete
oleobjects.Delete [(*index*)]

Deletes one or all OLE objects on the sheet. Does not change the contents of the Clipboard. If *index* is used, only that OLE object is deleted, otherwise all OLE objects on a worksheet are deleted. The following code deletes the first OLE objects on a sheet to the Clipboard.

II

Programmer's Reference

```
ActiveSheet.OLEObjects(1).Delete
```

This code deletes all the OLE objects on a sheet:

```
ActiveSheet.OLEObjects.Delete
```

*oleobjects.***Duplicate**

*oleobjects.***Duplicate [(*index*)]**

Makes a copy of one or all OLE objects on a sheet, and returns the object (or collection) that was created. If *index* is used, only that OLE object is duplicated, otherwise all OLE objects on a worksheet are duplicated. The following code duplicates the first OLE object on a sheet and moves it down slightly:

```
ActiveSheet.OLEObjects(1).Duplicate.Top = Pictures(1).Top -10
```

*oleobject.***Enabled**

*oleobject.***Enabled [= True | False]**

True enables one or all OLE objects on the sheet to respond to click events; False disables responses to click events. The default is True.

*oleobjects.***Group( )**

Groups a collection of OLE objects so they can be selected, moved, copied, or deleted as a single object. The following code groups all the objects on a sheet:

```
ActiveSheet.OLEObjects.Group
```

*oleobject.***Interior**

Returns the Interior object for one or all of the OLE objects on a sheet. Use the Interior object properties to set the shading and color of the interior of an OLE object. The following code shades the interior of all the OLE objects on a sheet:

```
ActiveSheet.OLEObjects.Interior.Pattern = xlGray16
```

*oleobject.***Locked**

*oleobject.***Locked [= True | False]**

True prevents changes to one or all the OLE objects on a sheet while the sheet is protected; False allows changes. The default is True.

oleobject.Object

Returns the OLE Automation object for an active OLE object that supports OLE Automation. This lets you manipulate the embedded object using its properties and methods. If the object is not active or does not support OLE Automation, attempting to access the Object property causes error 1004.

Currently there are three applications that support OLE Automation:

- Microsoft Excel, version 5.0

- Microsoft Word for Windows, version 6.0

- Shapeware Visio for Windows, version 2.0

The next version of Microsoft Project, once it is released, is also supposed to support OLE Automation.

Using the returned object is less than straightforward, however. To return the OLE Automation object from an embedded Word document, use the form *oleobject*.Object.Application.WordBasic.

The following code shows how to use the OLE Automation object from a Word document to insert some text using WordBasic commands from Excel:

```
Sub AutomateWord()
    ' Add an OLE object to the sheet.
    Set WordEmbedding = _
    ActiveSheet.OLEObjects.Add("Word.Document.6")
    ' Activate the object for editing.
    WordEmbedding.Activate
    ' Get the underlying OLE object.
    With WordEmbedding.Object.Application.WordBasic
            ' WordBasic language commands
            .Insert "these" & Chr$(13)
            .Bold True
            .Insert "words" & Chr$(13)
            .Bold False
            .Insert "come" & Chr$(13)
            .Bold True
            .Insert "from" & Chr$(13)
            .Bold False
            .Insert "Excel"
    End With
    ' Activate a cell (deactivates OLE object)
    ActiveCell.Activate
End Sub
```

*oleobject.*OLEType

Returns xlOLELink if the object is linked; xlOLEEmbed if the object is embedded. Linked objects are stored in separate files in the source application's native format. Embedded files are stored within an Excel workbook using the OLE storage structure.

*oleobject.*OnAction

*oleobject.*OnAction [= *procedure*]

Sets or returns the name of a procedure to run when one or all OLE objects on the sheet are clicked. The following code causes the procedure UpdateAll() to run when the user clicks the OLE object Picture1:

```
ActiveSheet.Pictures("Picture1").OnAction = "UpdateAll"
```

*oleobjects.*Paste

*oleobjects.*Paste ([*Link*])

Pastes the contents of the Clipboard to a sheet and adds it to the sheet's OLEObjects collection. If *Link* is True, this method creates a link to the source data; False embeds the object. The default is False. Attempting to use the Paste method causes error 1004 if there is no linkable data currently on the Clipboard.

The following code pastes a link to a sheet if the data is linkable:

```
Sub PasteLink()
    FormatsArray = Application.ClipboardFormats
    For Each iFormat In FormatsArray
        If iFormat = xlClipboardFormatLink Then
            ActiveSheet.OLEObjects.Paste True
            Exit For
        End If
    Next iFormat
End Sub
```

*oleobject.*Placement

*oleobject.*Placement [= xlMoveAndSize | xlMove | xlFreeFloating]

Sets or returns how the OLE object is attached to the cells below it. The default is xlFreeFloating.

oleobject.**PrintObject**

oleobject.**PrintObject [= True | False]**

True prints the OLE object with the worksheet; False does not. The default is True. The following code turns off printing for all the OLE objects on a sheet:

```
ActiveSheet.OLEObjects.PrintObject = False
```

oleobject.**Select**

oleobject.**Select ([*Replace*])**

Selects one or all of the OLE objects on a sheet. Select is the equivalent of clicking the object. If *Replace* is False, Select extends the current selection, rather than deselecting previous selections. The default is True.

oleobject.**Shadow**

oleobject.**Shadow [= True | False]**

True creates a background shadow for one or all the OLE objects on the sheet; False removes the shadow. The default is False.

oleobject.**TopLeftCell**

Returns the cell that lies under the top left of the OLE object.

oleobject.**Update( )**

Updates a linked OLE object from its source document.

oleobject.**Verb**

oleobject.**Verb ([*Verb*])**

Sends a verb to the OLE object's source application. Two commonly supported verbs are xlOpen and xlPrimary. xlOpen opens the object in its source application; xlPrimary opens the object for editing in place within the worksheet, if possible.

An object may support other verbs, but it is almost impossible to find out what they are. One way is to run an application called REGEDIT which is shipped with Windows. Use this command line:

```
REGEDIT /V
```

In REGEDIT, search for "Verbs" in the OLE application to obtain the verbs supported by the application. The OLE Registration Info Editor is shown in figure 10.2.

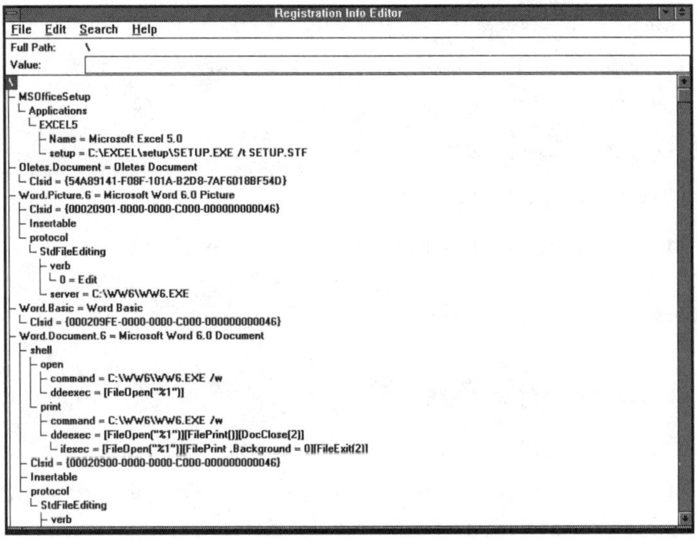

Fig. 10.2
The OLE Registration Info Editor.

Embedding Text as a Text Box

A text box displays multiple lines of text on a worksheet, chart, or dialog sheet. Use the `TextBoxes` collection to create and retrieve text boxes. Use the `TextBox` object to add and manipulate text in a text box.

The following code adds a text box to a worksheet:

```
ActiveSheet.TextBoxes.Add 1, 1, 100, 100
```

This code adds text to the text box:

```
ActiveSheet.TextBoxes(1).Text = "This is some text to add."
```

> **Note**
>
> Text boxes are a simple way to display text in a worksheet. Although they don't support full word-processing features, they require much less memory than an embedded OLE document.

You can format portions of text within a text box by using the `Characters` method. The following code makes the first 20 characters in a text box bold:

```
ActiveSheet.TextBoxes(1).Characters(1,20).Font.Bold = True
```

The TextBox object and TextBoxes collection have specific properties and methods, which are listed in Table 10.3. Properties and methods shown in **bold** are described in the reference section that follows this table. Nonbold items are common to most objects and are described in Chapter 4, "Using Objects."

Table 10.3 TextBox and TextBoxes properties and methods

Add[1]	Index
AddIndent[2]	**Interior**[2]
Application[2]	Item[1]
AutoSize[2]	Left[2]
Border[2]	**Locked**[2]
BottomRightCell	**LockedText**[2]
BringToFront[2]	Name
Caption[2]	**OnAction**[2]
Characters[2]	**Orientation**[2]
CheckSpelling[2]	Parent[2]
Copy[2]	**Placement**[2]
CopyPicture[2]	**PrintObject**[2]
Count[1]	**RoundedCorners**[2]
Creator[2]	**Select**[2]
Cut[2]	SendToBack[2]
Delete[2]	**Shadow**[2]
Duplicate[2]	**Text**[2]
Enabled[2]	Top[2]
Font[2]	**TopLeftCell**
Formula[2]	**VerticalAlignment**[2]
Group[1]	Visible[2]
Height[2]	Width[2]
HorizontalAlignment[2]	ZOrder[2]

[1] *Applies to the TextBoxes collection.*

[2] *Applies to the TextBoxes collection and the TextBox object.*

II

Programmer's Reference

TextBoxes.Add

TextBoxes.Add (*Left, Top, Width, Height*)

Creates an empty text box on the sheet and adds it to the sheet's TextBoxes collection. Returns the TextBox object that was created.

Argument	Description
Left	The distance between the left edge of the sheet and the right edge of the text box in points.
Top	The distance between the top edge of the sheet and the top edge of the text box in points.
Width	The width of the text box in points.
Height	The height of the text box in points.

The following code adds a text box to a sheet and displays some text in it:

```
ActiveSheet.TextBoxes.Add (1, 1, 100, 100).Text = "Vigorous _
writing is concise."
```

textbox.AddIndent

textbox.AddIndent [= True | False]

Applies to the Far East version of Excel only. True adds extra space at the beginning and end of each line if the text is displayed vertically and its alignment is distributed; False does not add space. The default is False.

textbox.AutoSize

textbox.AutoSize [= True | False]

True automatically resizes one or all text boxes to fit the text it contains; False preserves the text box size. The default is False.

textbox.Border

Returns the Border object for one or all text boxes on a sheet. Use this property to change the border of a picture. The following code changes the borders of all pictures on a sheet to medium weight:

```
ActiveSheet.Pictures.Border.Weight = xlMedium
```

textbox.BottomRightCell

Returns the cell under the bottom right corner of the text box.

textbox.Caption

textbox.Caption [= *text*]

Sets or returns the text in the text box. This property is identical to the Text property.

textbox.Characters

textbox.Characters ([*Start*], [*Length*])

Returns a Characters object representing the text or a portion of the text from a text box. Use the returned Characters object to format all or part of the text in a text box.

Argument	Description
Start	The position of the first character to return. The default is 1.
Length	The number of characters to return. The default is the number of characters between *Start* and the end of the text in the text box.

The following code makes the first five characters in a text box bold:

```
ActiveSheet.TextBoxes(1).Characters(1, 5).Font.Bold = True
```

textbox.CheckSpelling

textbox.CheckSpelling ([*CustomDictionary*], [*IgnoreUppercase*], [*AlwaysSuggest*])

Checks the spelling of the words in one or all text boxes on a sheet.

Argument	Description
CustomDictionary	A string indicating the file name of the custom dictionary to examine if the word is not found in the main dictionary. If omitted, the currently specified dictionary is used. The default is None.
IgnoreUppercase	True ignores the spelling of words in all uppercase characters; False checks the spelling of all words. The default is False.
AlwaysSuggest	True displays a list of suggested alternate spellings when an incorrect spelling is found; False prompts the user for correct spelling. The default is False.

II

Programmer's Reference

The following code checks the spelling of all the text boxes on a sheet:

```
Activesheet.TextBoxes.CheckSpelling
```

textboxes.Copy

textboxes.Copy [(*index*)]

Copies one or all text boxes on the sheet to the Clipboard. If *index* is used, only that text box is copied, otherwise all text boxes on a worksheet are copied. The following code copies the first text box on a sheet to the Clipboard:

```
ActiveSheet.TextBoxes(1).Copy
```

This code copies all the text boxes on a sheet:

```
ActiveSheet.TextBoxes.Copy
```

textboxes.CopyPicture

textboxes.CopyPicture ([*Appearance*], [*Format*])

Copies one or all text boxes on a sheet to the Clipboard using a bitmap or picture format.

Argument	Description
Appearance	xlScreen, the default, copies the text box as it appears on-screen; xlPrinter copies the text box as it would appear if printed using the current printer setup.
Format	xlPicture, the default, creates the copy in PICT format; xlBitmap creates the copy as a bitmap.

textboxes.Cut

textboxes.Cut [(*index*)]

Cuts one or all text boxes on the sheet to the Clipboard. If *index* is used, only that text box is cut, otherwise all text boxes on a worksheet are cut. The following code cuts the first text box on a sheet to the Clipboard:

```
ActiveSheet.TextBoxes(1).Cut
```

This code cuts all the text boxes on a sheet:

```
ActiveSheet.TextBoxes.Cut
```

textboxes.**Delete**

textboxes.**Delete [(*index*)]**

Deletes one or all text boxes on the sheet. Does not change the contents of the Clipboard. If *index* is used, only that text box is deleted, otherwise all text boxes on a worksheet are deleted. The following code deletes the first text box on a sheet to the Clipboard:

```
ActiveSheet.TextBoxes(1).Delete
```

This code deletes all the text boxes on a sheet:

```
ActiveSheet.TextBoxes.Delete
```

textboxes.**Duplicate**

textboxes.**Duplicate [(*index*)]**

Makes a copy of one or all text boxes on a sheet, and returns the object (or collection) that was created. If *index* is used, only that text box is duplicated, otherwise all text boxes on a worksheet are duplicated. The following code duplicates the first text box on a sheet and moves it up slightly:

```
ActiveSheet.TextBoxes(1).Duplicate.Top = TextBoxes(1).Top -10
```

textbox.**Enabled**

textbox.**Enabled [= True | False]**

True enables one or all text boxes on the sheet to respond to click events; False disables the response to click events. If a text box is disabled, the user can't select it or enter text in it. The default is True.

textbox.**Font**

Returns the Font object for one or all text boxes on a sheet. Use the returned Font object to set the font attributes for *all* of the text in the text box. To format *portions* of text within a text box, use the Characters method.

The following code makes all of the text bold in all the text boxes on a sheet:

```
ActiveSheet.TextBoxes.Font.Bold = True
```

textbox.Formula

textbox.Formula [= *formula*]

Sets or returns the formula for one or all text boxes on a sheet. The following line of code displays the value of cell B2 in a text box:

```
ActiveSheet.TextBoxes("Text 1").Formula = "B2"
```

TextBoxes.Group()

Groups a collection of text boxes so that they can be selected, moved, copied, or deleted as a single object. The following code groups all the text boxes on a sheet:

```
ActiveSheet.TextBoxes.Group
```

textbox.HorizontalAlignment

textbox.HorizontalAlignment [= *setting*]

Available values for *setting* are xlLeft, xlRight and xlCenter. xlLeft left-aligns text; xlRight right-aligns text; xlCenter centers values within each cell of a range; xlJustify justifies wrapped text in the text box. The default is xlLeft.

textbox.Interior

Returns the Interior object for one or all of the text boxes on a sheet. Use the Interior object properties to set the shading and color of the interior of a text box. The following code shades the interior of all the text box objects on a sheet:

```
ActiveSheet.TextBoxes.Interior.Pattern = xlGray16
```

textbox.Locked

textbox.Locked [= True | False]

True prevents changes to the contents and position of one or all the text boxes on a sheet while the sheet is protected; False allows changes. The default is True.

textbox.**LockedText**

textbox.**LockedText [= True | False]**

True prevents changes to the contents of one or all the text boxes on a sheet while the sheet is protected; False allows changes. The default is True.

textbox.**OnAction**

textbox.**OnAction [= *procedure*]**

Sets or returns the name of a procedure to run when one or any of the text boxes on the sheet are clicked. The following code causes the procedure Validate() to run when the user clicks the text box ValidText:

```
ActiveSheet.TextBoxes("ValidText").OnAction = "Validate"
```

textbox.**Orientation**

textbox.**Orientation [= *setting*]**

Sets or returns the orientation of text displayed in one or all text boxes: xlHorizontal, xlVertical, xlUpward, or xlDownward. The default is xlHorizontal.

textbox.**Placement**

textbox.**Placement [= xlMoveAndSize | xlMove | xlFreeFloating]**

Sets or returns how one or all text boxes on a sheet are attached to the cells below them. If the placement of a text box is xlMoveAndSize, the text box moves and resizes with the cells it is attached to; xlMove causes the text box to move, but not be resized; and xlFreeFloating means there is no cell attachment and the text box stays where it is drawn. The default is xlFreeFloating.

textbox.**PrintObject**

textbox.**PrintObject [= True | False]**

True prints one or all text boxes with the sheet; False does not. The default is True. The following code turns off printing for all the text boxes on a sheet:

```
ActiveSheet.TextBoxes.PrintObject = False
```

textbox.**RoundedCorners**

textbox.**RoundedCorners [= True | False]**

True rounds the corners of one or all text boxes; False displays square corners. The default is False.

textbox.**Select**

textbox.**Select ([*Replace*])**

Selects one or all of the text boxes on a sheet. `Select` is the equivalent of clicking the object. If `Replace` is False, `Select` extends the current selection, rather than deselecting previous selections. The default is True.

textbox.**Shadow**

textbox.**Shadow [= True | False]**

True creates a background shadow for one or all the text boxes on the sheet; False removes the shadow. The default is False.

textbox.**Text**

textbox.**Text [= *text*]**

Sets or returns the text in one or all the text boxes on a sheet. This property is the same as the `Caption` property for this object. Use the `Characters` method to format text within a text box. The following code returns the text in the first text box on a sheet:

```
sText = ActiveSheet.TextBoxes(1).Text
```

The following code clears all of the text boxes on a sheet by setting their text property to " ":

```
ActiveSheet.TextBoxes.Text = ""
```

textbox.**TopLeftCell**

Returns the cell that lies under the top-left corner of the text box.

textbox.VerticalAlignment

textbox.VerticalAlignment [= *setting*]

Sets or returns the vertical alignment of one or all the text boxes on a sheet. Valid settings are xlBottom, xlCenter, xlDistributed, xlJustify, or xlTop. The default is xlTop.

Recording and Playing Sounds

A sound note attaches recorded sounds and comments to a range. The SoundNote method of the Range object is used to create a SoundNote object. Use the methods of the returned SoundNote object to record and play sounds.

The following code records a sound note for a cell:

```
ActiveCell.SoundNote.Record
```

This code plays the sound note:

```
ActiveCell.SoundNote.Play
```

Note

Recording and playing sounds generally requires special hardware, usually an add-on sound board.

The SoundNote object has specific properties and methods, which are listed in Table 10.4. Properties and methods shown in **bold** are described in the reference section that follows this table. Nonbold items are common to most objects and are described in Chapter 4, "Using Objects."

Table 10.4 SoundNote properties and methods

Application	Parent
Creator	**Play**
Delete	**Record**
Import	

II

Programmer's Reference

*soundnote.*Delete( )

Deletes a sound note. If a cell does not have a sound note, this method does not cause an error. The following code deletes a sound note from a cell:

```
ActiveCell.SoundNote.Delete
```

*soundnote.*Import

*soundnote.*Import (*Filename*)

Creates a sound note from a file. Generates an error if the file does not exist. The following code inserts the sound BOING.WAV in the currently active cell and then plays the sound:

```
ActiveCell.SoundNote.Import ("BOING.WAV").Play
```

*soundnote.*Play( )

Plays the sound note in the first cell of a range. If the cell does not have a sound note, Play does not cause an error. The following code plays the sound note in the currently active cell:

```
ActiveCell.SoundNote.Play
```

The following lines of code play all of the sound notes in a selected range:

```
Sub PlayAll()
    For Each rng In ActiveSheet.Selection
        rng.SoundNote.Play
    Next rng
End Sub
```

*soundnote.*Record( )

Creates a sound note by starting the Microsoft Quick Recorder. The following code records a sound note for the currently active cell:

```
ActiveCell.SoundNote.Record
```

Chapter 11

Printing and Displaying Results

Excel controls the appearance of objects using Style, Border, and Font objects. Most visible objects in Excel have methods that return these objects. For example, the Range object has a Borders method. The following line of code uses the Color property of the returned Borders object to change the border color to red:

```
Range("A1").Borders.Color = RGB(255, 0, 0)
```

This chapter covers the Style, Border, Font, and PageSetup objects.

In this chapter, you learn how to do the following:

- Print and preview objects.

- Apply automatic formatting.

- Create and apply styles.

- Change the borders and fonts of objects.

- Control page layout.

Printing and Previewing

Use the PrintOut method of an object to print it. Use the PrintPreview method of an object to preview before actually printing. The following objects have print and print preview methods:

- Chart, Charts

- DialogSheet, DialogSheets

- ■ Range

- ■ Sheets

- ■ Window

- ■ Workbook

- ■ Worksheet, Worksheets

The `Module` and `Modules` objects have the `PrintOut` method, but do not have `PrintPreview`.

The following code prints the current selection:

```
Selection.PrintOut
```

For more information, see descriptions of the `PrintOut` and `PrintPreview` methods in the sections of this book covering the specified objects.

Applying Automatic Formats

The `AutoFormat` method lets you apply predefined formats to a `Chart` or `Range` object. Refer to the on-line documentation for a complete listing of the automatic formats. Use the `AutoFormat` method to get good-looking results fast.

The following code applies the `Classic1` automatic formats to the active worksheet:

```
ActiveSheet.AutoFormat xlClassic1
```

Similarly, this code automatically reformats a chart:

```
ActiveChart.AutoFormat Gallery:=xlColumn, Format:=9
```

Controlling Styles

The `Styles` collection and `Style` object control the styles in a workbook. The `Style` object contains all style attributes, font, number format, alignment, and so on, as properties.

To add a style, use the `Add` method. To apply a style to a `Range`, set the range's `Style` property.

The following code adds a style to a workbook and sets the style's appearance:

```
Sub AddStyle()
    With ActiveWorkbook.Styles.Add ("NewStyle")
```

```
            .Font.Name = "Times"
            .Font.Bold = True
            .Borders.LineStyle = xlThin
        End With
    End Sub
```

The following code applies the new style to a selected range:

```
    Selection.Style = "NewStyle"
```

The `Style` object corresponds to the Style dialog box. To display the Style dialog box in Excel (see fig. 11.1), choose Format, Style.

Fig. 11.1
The Style
dialog box.

The `Style` object and `Styles` collection have specific properties and methods, which are listed in Table 11.1. Properties and methods shown in **bold** are described in the reference section that follows this table. Nonbold items are common to most objects and are described in Chapter 4, "Using Objects."

Table 11.1 Style and Styles properties and methods

Add[1]	**IncludeProtection**
AddIndent	**Interior**
Application[2]	Item[1]
Borders	**Locked**
Count[1]	**Merge**
Creator[2]	**Name**
Delete	**NameLocal**
Font	**NumberFormat**
FormulaHidden	**NumberFormatLocal**
HorizontalAlignment	**Orientation**
IncludeAlignment	Parent[2]
IncludeBorder	**Value**
IncludeFont	**VerticalAlignment**
IncludeNumber	**WrapText**
IncludePatterns	

[1] Applies to the `Styles` collection.

[2] Applies to the `Styles` collection and the `Style` object.

Styles.Add

Styles.Add (*Name*, [*BasedOn*])

Creates a new style and adds it to the workbooks `Styles` collection. Returns the `Style` object that is created.

Argument	Description
Name	The name of the style to create. If the workbook already has a style with this name, Add causes error 1004.
BasedOn	A range object containing a single cell that has the formatting on which to base the new style. The default is to base the new style on the Normal style.

The following code adds a style to a workbook, then sets the style's font attributes:

```
Sub AddStyle()
    With ActiveWorkbook.Styles.Add("Text")
        .Font.Italic = True
        .Font.Name = "Courier"
    End With
End Sub
```

style.AddIndent

style.AddIndent [= True | False]

True adds space at the beginning and end of each line of text with the distributed text alignment style; False does not add space. The default is False.

style.Delete( )

Deletes a style from a workbook. The following code deletes the style named `"Text"`:

```
ActiveWorkbook.Styles("Text").Delete
```

style.Font

Returns the `Font` object for the style. Use the `Font` object to set or return the font attributes of a style. The following code specifies underline for the font of the Normal style:

```
ActiveWorkbook.Styles("Normal").Font.Underline = xlSingle
```

style.**FormulaHidden**

style.**FormulaHidden [= True | False]**

True hides the formula of cells formatted with this style when the worksheet is protected; False does not. The default is False.

style.**HorizontalAlignment**

style.**HorizontalAlignment [= *setting*]**

xlGeneral left-aligns text and right-aligns numbers; xlLeft left-aligns values; xlRight right-aligns values; xlCenter centers values within each cell of a range; xlCenterAcrossSelection centers values horizontally across the range; xlJustify and xlDistributed both justify wrapped text within cells; xlFill repeats values to fill each cell. The default is xlGeneral.

style.**IncludeAlignment**

style.**IncludeAlignment [= True | False]**

True includes the HorizontalAlignment, VerticalAlignment, WrapText, and Orientation properties in the style; False omits these properties. (The properties may be set, but they have no effect when the style is applied. A selection's exsisting alignment is unaffected if the style in question is applied to the selection.) The default is True.

style.**IncludeBorder**

style.**IncludeBorder [= True | False]**

True includes the Borders properties in the style; False omits these properties. (The properties may be set, but they have no effect when the style is applied.) The default is True.

style.**IncludeFont**

style.**IncludeFont [= True | False]**

True includes the Font property in the style; False omits the Font property. (The property may be set, but it has no effect when the style is applied.) The default is True.

style.IncludeNumber

style.IncludeNumber [= True | False]

True includes the NumberFormat property in the style; False omits the NumberFormat property. (The property may be set, but it has no effect when the style is applied.) The default is True.

style.IncludePatterns

style.IncludePatterns [= True | False]

True includes the Interior properties in the style; False omits these properties. (The properties may be set, but they have no effect when the style is applied.) The default is True.

Note

Cells and graphics have an interior property that defines items such as Color, ColorIndex, and Pattern (crisscross, checker, and so on) among others.

style.IncludeProtection

style.IncludeProtection [= True | False]

True includes the FormulaHidden and Locked properties in the style; False omits these properties. (The properties may be set, but they have no effect when the style is applied.) The default is True.

style.Interior

Returns the Interior object for a style. Use the Interior object to change the color or pattern of the background of a style. The following code changes the Text style's background color to aqua:

```
ActiveWorkbook.Styles("Text").Interior.Color = RGB(0, 255, 255)
```

Note

RGB is a function that takes three parameters representing Red, Green, and Blue, respectively. Valid values for the parameters are from 0-255 and represent the mixture of the three colors required to create another color.

style.Locked

style.Locked [= True | False]

True prevents changes to the cells with this style when the worksheet is protected; False allows changes to cells when the worksheet is protected. The default is True.

Styles.Merge

Styles.Merge (*Workbook*)

Copies the styles from one workbook into another, replacing any duplicate styles in the target workbook. The following code copies the styles in BOOK1.XLS to the active workbook:

```
ActiveWorkbook.Styles.Merge "BOOK1.XLS"
```

style.Name

Returns the name of a style. If the name is one of the built-in names, it is returned in the national language used by the programmer to create the procedure.

The following code checks if a style name already exists in a workbook (names must be unique for the Add method to work):

```
' Checks if a new style name has already been used.
Function bCheckName(sNewStyle, Optional bRefresh) As Boolean
    ' Optimization: keep a copy of the style list.
    Static sStyleNames As String
    ' If bRefresh is not omitted and it's True, clear the style list.
    If TypeName(bRefresh) = "Boolean" Then
        If bRefresh = True Then sStyleNames = ""
    End If
    ' If style list is "" rebuild it.
    If Len(sStyleNames) = 0 Then
        For Each sty In ActiveWorkbook.Styles
            ' Use comma to tell where each style name ends.
            sStyleNames = sty.Name & "," & sStyleNames
        Next sty
    End If
    ' Check if style name is already defined (this is very fast).
    If InStr(sStyleNames, sNewStyle & ",") = 0 Then
        ' Return true if name is not already defined.
        bCheckName = True
    Else
        ' Return False if name is defined.
        bCheckName = False
    End If
End Function
```

style.NameLocal

Returns the name of a style. If the name is one of the built-in names, it is returned in the national language used by the current user.

style.NumberFormat

style.NumberFormat [= *format*]

Sets or returns the format code for numbers with this style. The following code adds the style `"NewNumber"` and sets its number format:

```
ActiveWorkbook.Styles.Add("NewNumber").NumberFormat = _
"$#,##0_);[Red]($#,##0)"
```

style.NumberFormatLocal

Same as `NumberFormat`, but uses codes based on the user's national language as determined by the current system settings.

style.Orientation

style.Orientation [= *setting*]

Sets or returns the orientation of values displayed in a cell formatted with this style: `xlHorizontal`, `xlVertical`, `xlUpward`, or `xlDownward`. The default is `xlHorizontal`.

style.Value

Returns the name of a style. The following code displays the name of the first style defined in a workbook:

```
MsgBox ActiveWorkbook.Style(1).Value
```

style.VerticalAlignment

style.VerticalAlignment [= *setting*]

Sets or returns the vertical alignment of cells with `xlBottom`, `xlCenter`, `xlDistributed`, `xlJustify`, or `xlTop`.

*style.*WrapText

*style.*WrapText [= True | False]

True wraps text in cells with the style; False does not. The default is False.

Controlling Borders

The Borders collection and Border object control the border attributes for most visible objects.

The Range and Style objects both have a Borders method that returns a collection. The Borders collection contains four elements identified by these constants: xlTop, xlBottom, xlRight, and xlLeft. You can set the properties for these elements individually or all at once.

The following code applies a border to a range:

```
ActiveCell.Borders.LineStyle = xlDouble
```

Objects that have a Border method which returns a Border object are listed below:

Arc	ErrorBars
Arcs	Floor
Axis	Gridlines
AxisTitle	GroupObject
ChartArea	GroupObjects
ChartObject	HiLoLines
ChartObjects	Legend
ChartTitle	LegendKey
CheckBox	Line
CheckBoxes	Lines
DataLabel	OLEObject
DataLabels	OLEObjects
DownBars	OptionButton
Drawing	OptionButtons
DrawingObjects	Oval
Drawings	Ovals
DropLines	Picture

Pictures	SeriesLines
PlotArea	TextBox
Point	Trendline
Rectangle	UpBars
Rectangles	Walls
Series	

The following code applies a border to a text box:

```
ActiveSheet.TextBoxes(1).Border.LineStyle = xlDouble
```

The `Border` object corresponds to the settings in the Border tab of the Format Cells dialog box. To display the Border format options in Excel (see fig. 11.2), choose Format, Cells; then select the Border tab.

Fig. 11.2
The border options in the Format Cells dialog box.

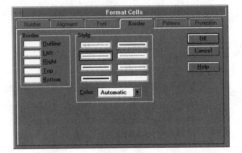

The `Border` and `Borders` collection have specific properties and methods, which are listed in Table 11.2. Properties and methods shown in **bold** are described in the reference section that follows this table. Nonbold items are common to most objects and are described in Chapter 4, "Using Objects."

Table 11.2 Border and Borders properties and methods

Application[2]
Color[2]
ColorIndex[2]
Creator[2]
Item[1]
LineStyle[2]
Parent[2]
Value
Weight[2]

[1] *Applies to the Borders collection.*

[2] *Applies to the Borders collection and the Border object.*

*border.*Color

*border.*Color [= *rgbcolor*]

Sets or returns the color of one or all borders for a `Style` or `Range` object. The color is a long integer, created with the RGB function.

The following code sets all four borders of the active cell to red:

```
ActiveCell.Borders.Color = RGB(255, 0 , 0)
```

The following code sets the top border of the active cell to blue:

```
ActiveCell.Borders(xlTop).Color = RGB(0, 0 , 255)
```

*border.*ColorIndex

*border.*ColorIndex [= *colorindex*]

Sets or returns the color of one or all borders for a `Style` or `Range` object. The *colorindex* is an integer indicating the position of the color in the current color palette. The default is `xlAutomatic`.

*border.*LineStyle

*border.*LineStyle [= *setting*]

Sets or returns the line style of one border or all four borders of a `Style` or `Range` object. Can be `xlContinuous`, `xlDash`, `xlDot`, `xlDashDot`, `xlDashDotDot`, `xlGray50`, `xlGray75`, `xlGray25`, `xlDouble`, `xlNone`, or `xlAutomatic`. The default is `xlContinuous`.

*border.*Value

*border.*Value [= *setting*]

Same as the `LineStyle` property.

*border.*Weight

Sets or returns the weight of one border or all four borders of a `Style` or `Range` object. Can be `xlHairline`, `xlThin`, `xlMedium`, or `xlThick`. The default is `xlThin`.

Controlling Fonts

The Font object controls the font attributes for these objects:

AxisTitle	GroupObjects
Button	Legend
Buttons	LegendEntry
Characters	PlotArea
ChartArea	Range
ChartTitle	Style
DataLabel	TextBox
DataLabels	TextBoxes
DrawingObjects	TickLabels
GroupObject	

Each of these objects has a Font method that returns its Font object. The following code sets the font of a range to the Times Roman typeface:

```
[A1:B12].Font.Name = "Times Roman"
```

Note

You can't determine what fonts are installed on the system directly from within Visual Basic. Setting the font name to a font that does not exist does not cause an error, and no change is made to the existing font.

The Font object properties correspond to the settings in the Font tab of the Format Cells dialog box. To display the Font options in Excel (see fig. 11.3), choose Format, Cells; then select the Font tab.

Fig. 11.3
The font options in the Format Cells dialog box.

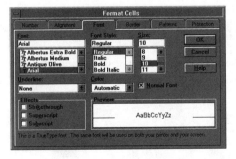

The font object and fonts collection have specific properties and methods, which are listed in Table 11.3. Properties and methods shown in **bold** are described in the reference section that follows this table. Nonbold items are common to most objects and are described in Chapter 4, "Using Objects."

Table 11.3 Font and Fonts properties and methods

Application	**OutlineFont**
Background	Parent
Bold	**Shadow**
Color	**Size**
ColorIndex	**Strikethrough**
Creator	**Subscript**
FontStyle	**Superscript**
Italic	**Underline**
Name	

font.Background

font.Background [= setting]

Sets or returns the appearance of the font's background: xlAutomatic, xlOpaque, or xlTransparent. This property is only valid for text on charts.

font.Bold

font.Bold [= True | False]

True makes the font bold; False displays the font in normal weight. The default is False.

font.Color

font.Color [= *rgbcolor*]

Sets or returns the color of the font. The color is a long integer, created with the RGB function. The following code sets the font of the active cell to red:

```
ActiveCell.Font.Color = RGB(255, 0 , 0)
```

font.ColorIndex

font.ColorIndex [= *colorindex*]

Sets or returns the color of one or all borders for a Style or Range object. The *colorindex* is an integer indicating the position of the color in the current color palette. The default is xlAutomatic.

font.FontStyle

font.FontStyle [= *setting*]

Sets or returns the font weight as a string. In English, valid settings are: `"Bold"`, `"Italic"`, `"Bold Italic"`, and `"Regular"`. The language of these settings is determined by the system settings of the user's machine.

It is simpler to use the `Bold` and `Italic` properties when setting font weight. `FontStyle` is useful when displaying font information for the user.

font.Italic

font.Italic [= True | False]

True makes the font italic; False displays the font in normal weight. The default is False.

font.Name

font.Name [= *fontname*]

Sets or returns the name of the font. If *fontname* does not correspond to one of the fonts installed on the system, no error is returned. You can't determine what fonts are installed directly from within Visual Basic.

The following line of code sets the font of the active cell to Times Roman:

```
ActiveCell.Font.Name = "Times Roman"
```

font.OutlineFont

font.OutlineFont [= True | False]

True displays the font as an outline on the Apple Macintosh. This property has no effect in Microsoft Windows. The default is False.

font.Shadow

font.Shadow [= True | False]

True displays a shadow for the font on the Apple Macintosh; False omits the shadow. This property has no effect in Microsoft Windows. The default is False.

*font.*Size

*font.*Size [= *size*]

Sets or returns the size of the font in points. *size* must be between 1 and 409 points.

*font.*Strikethrough

*font.*Strikethrough [= **True** | **False**]

True draws a line through the center of characters in the font; False does not. The default is False.

*font.*Subscript

*font.*Subscript [= **True** | **False**]

True makes the font subscript by shifting characters down three points; False does not. The default is False.

*font.*Superscript

*font.*Superscript [= **True** | **False**]

True makes the font superscript by shifting characters up three points; False does not. The default is False.

*font.*Underline

*font.*Underline [= *setting*]

Sets or returns the underlining of a font: xlNone, xlSingle, xlDouble, xlSingleAccounting, or xlDoubleAccounting. The default is xlNone.

Controlling the Page Setup

The PageSetup object controls the printing and layout attributes for the Worksheet, DialogSheet, Module, Chart, and Window objects.

To print an object, use the object's PrintOut method.

The PageSetup object corresponds to the settings in the Page Setup dialog box. To display the Page Setup dialog box in Excel (see fig. 11.4), choose File, Page Setup.

The PageSetup object has specific properties and methods, which are listed in Table 11.4. Properties and methods shown in **bold** are described in the reference section that follows this table. Nonbold items are common to most objects and are described in Chapter 4, "Using Objects."

Fig. 11.4
The Page Setup dialog box.

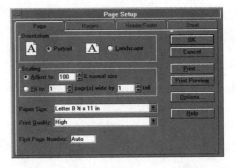

Table 11.4 PageSetup properties and methods

Application	LeftMargin
BlackAndWhite	**Order**
BottomMargin	**Orientation**
CenterFooter	**PaperSize**
CenterHeader	Parent
CenterHorizontally	**PrintArea**
CenterVertically	**PrintGridlines**
ChartSize	**PrintHeadings**
Creator	**PrintNotes**
Draft	**PrintQuality**
FirstPageNumber	**PrintTitleColumns**
FitToPagesTall	**PrintTitleRows**
FitToPagesWide	**RightFooter**
FooterMargin	**RightHeader**
HeaderMargin	**RightMargin**
LeftFooter	**TopMargin**
LeftHeader	**Zoom**

pagesetup.BlackAndWhite

pagesetup.BlackAndWhite [= True | False]

True prints in black and white; False prints in color, if available. The default is False.

pagesetup.**BottomMargin**

pagesetup.**BottomMargin** [= *margin*]

Sets or returns the bottom margin in points. The default is 72 points (1 inch).

pagesetup.**CenterFooter**

pagesetup.**CenterFooter** [= *footer*]

Sets or returns the text to print as the center footer. The default is Page &P.

Table 11.5 lists the codes used to display special information in headers and footers.

Table 11.5 Header and footer codes	
Type of information to display	**Code**
Page number	&P
Total number of pages	&N
Current date	&D
Current time	&T
Name of file	&F
Sheet tab name	&A

pagesetup.**CenterHeader**

pagesetup.**CenterHeader** [= *header*]

Sets or returns the text to print in the center header. The default is &A.

pagesetup.**CenterHorizontally**

pagesetup.**CenterHorizontally** [= **True** | **False**]

True centers the object horizontally on the page; False left-aligns the object. The default is False.

pagesetup.CenterVertically

pagesetup.CenterVertically [= True | False]

True centers the object vertically on the page; False top-aligns the object. The default is False.

pagesetup.ChartSize

pagesetup.ChartSize [= *setting*]

Valid only for the PageSetup of Chart objects that appear as stand-alone sheets. Sets or returns the scaling method used when printing charts: xlFitToPage, xlScreenSize, or xlFullPage. The default is xlFullPage.

pagesetup.Draft

pagesetup.Draft [= True | False]

True omits graphics when printing; False includes graphics. The default is False.

pagesetup.FirstPageNumber

pagesetup.FirstPageNumber [= *pagenumber*]

Sets or returns the number from which to begin printing. The default is xlAutomatic.

pagesetup.FitToPagesTall

pagesetup.FitToPagesTall [= *number*]

Valid only for the PageSetup of the Worksheet object. Scales the printed output vertically to fit the indicated *number* of pages. Ignored if Zoom is not False.

pagesetup.FitToPagesWide

pagesetup.FitToPagesWide [= *number*]

Valid only for the PageSetup of the Worksheet object. Scales the printed output horizontally to fit the indicated *number* of pages. Ignored if Zoom is not False.

pagesetup.FooterMargin

pagesetup.FooterMargin [= *margin*]

Sets or returns the distance between the footer and the bottom of the page in points. The default is 36 points (1/2 inch).

pagesetup.**HeaderMargin**

pagesetup.**HeaderMargin** [= *margin*]

Sets or returns the distance between the header and the top of the page in points. The default is 36 points (1/2 inch).

pagesetup.**LeftFooter**

pagesetup.**LeftFooter** [= *footer*]

Sets or returns the text to print as the left footer. The default is " ".

pagesetup.**LeftHeader**

pagesetup.**LeftHeader** [= *header*]

Sets or returns the text to print as the left header. The default is " ".

pagesetup.**LeftMargin**

pagesetup.**LeftMargin** [= *margin*]

Sets or returns the left page margin in points. The default is 54 points (3/4 inch).

pagesetup.**Order**

pagesetup.**Order** [= xlDownThenOver | xlOverThenDown]

Valid only for the PageSetup of the Worksheet object. Sets or returns the print order of pages on a sheet: xlDownThenOver or xlOverThenDown. The default is xlDownThenOver (see fig. 11.5).

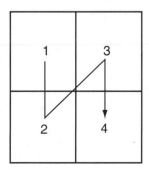 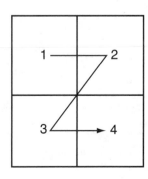

Fig. 11.5
The PageSetup printing order.

pagesetup.Orientation

pagesetup.Orientation [= xlPortrait | xlLandscape]

xlPortrait prints a page in a portrait, or vertical, orientation; xlLandscape prints a page in a landscape, or horizontal, orientation. The default is xlPortrait.

pagesetup.PaperSize

pagesetup.PaperSize [= *setting*]

Sets or returns a constant indicating the size of the paper on which to print. The default in the U.S. is xlPaperLetter.

Constant	Meaning
xlPaperLetter	Letter (8 1/2X11 in.)
xlPaperLetterSmall	Letter Small (8 1/2X11 in.)
xlPaperTabloid	Tabloid (11X17 in.)
xlPaperLedger	Ledger (17X11 in.)
xlPaperLegal	Legal (8 1/2X14 in.)
xlPaperStatement	Statement (5 1/2X8 1/2 in.)
xlPaperExecutive	Executive (7 1/2X10 1/2 in.)
xlPaperA3	A3 (297X420 mm)
xlPaperA4	A4 (210X297 mm)
xlPaperA4Small	A4 Small (210X297 mm)
xlPaperA5	A5 (148X210 mm)
xlPaperB4	B4 (250X354 mm)
xlPaperB5	B5 (182X257 mm)
xlPaperFolio	Folio (8 1/2X13 in.)
xlPaperQuarto	Quarto (215X275 mm)
xlPaper10x14	10X14 in.
xlPaper11x17	11X17 in.

Constant	Meaning
xlPaperNote	Note (8 1/2X11 in.)
xlPaperEnvelope9	Envelope #9 (3 7/8X8 7/8 in.)
xlPaperEnvelope10	Envelope #10 (4 1/8X9 1/2 in.)
xlPaperEnvelope11	Envelope #11 (4 1/2X10 3/8 in.)
xlPaperEnvelope12	Envelope #12 (4 1/2X11 in.)
xlPaperEnvelope14	Envelope #14 (5X11 1/2 in.)
xlPaperCsheet	C-size sheet
xlPaperDsheet	D-size sheet
xlPaperEsheet	E-size sheet
xlPaperEnvelopeDL	Envelope DL (110X220 mm)
xlPaperEnvelopeC3	Envelope C3 (324X458 mm)
xlPaperEnvelopeC4	Envelope C4 (229X324 mm)
xlPaperEnvelopeC5	Envelope C5 (162X229 mm)
xlPaperEnvelopeC6	Envelope C6 (114X162 mm)
xlPaperEnvelopeC65	Envelope C65 (114X229 mm)
xlPaperEnvelopeB4	Envelope B4 (250X353 mm)
xlPaperEnvelopeB5	Envelope B5 (176X250 mm)
xlPaperEnvelopeB6	Envelope B6 (176X125 mm)
xlPaperEnvelopeItaly	Envelope (110X230 mm)
xlPaperEnvelopeMonarch	Envelope Monarch (3 7/8X7 1/2 in.)
xlPaperEnvelopePersonal	Envelope (3 5/8X6 1/2 in.)
xlPaperFanfoldUS	U.S. Standard Fanfold (14 7/8X11 in.)
xlPaperFanfoldStdGerman	German Standard Fanfold (8 1/2X12 in.)
xlPaperFanfoldLegalGerman	German Legal Fanfold (8 1/2X13 in.)
xlPaperUser	User defined

pagesetup.PrintArea

pagesetup.PrintArea [= *rangestring*]

Valid only for the PageSetup of the Worksheet object. Sets or returns the address of a range to print. The default is " " to print all. The following line of code sets a worksheet to print only the current selection:

```
ActiveSheet.PageSetup.PrintArea = Selection.Address
```

pagesetup.PrintGridlines

pagesetup.PrintGridlines [= True | False]

Valid only for the PageSetup of the Worksheet object. True prints grid lines; False does not. The default is True.

pagesetup.PrintHeadings

pagesetup.PrintHeadings [= True | False]

Valid only for the PageSetup of the Worksheet object. True prints column and row headings on each page; False does not. The default is False.

pagesetup.PrintNotes

pagesetup.PrintNotes [= True | False]

Valid only for the PageSetup of the Worksheet object. True prints notes attached to cells; False does not. The default is False.

pagesetup.PrintQuality

pagesetup.PrintQuality [= *array*]

Sets or returns a two-element array that indicates the horizontal and vertical print quality. Valid settings are –1 (lowest quality) to –4 (highest quality). Return values are 65535 (lowest quality) to 65532 (highest quality). (Many printers don't support vertical print quality.)

The following code sets print quality for the worksheet to low:

```
ActiveSheet.PageSetup.PrintQuality = Array(-1, -1)
```

pagesetup.**PrintTitleColumns**

pagesetup.**PrintTitleColumns** [= *columnaddress*]

Valid only for the PageSetup of the Worksheet object. Sets or returns the address of columns to repeat on the left side of each page. If you specify only part of a column or columns, PrintTitleColumns expands the range to full columns. The default is " " (don't repeat columns).

The following code repeats column A on each printed page of the worksheet:

```
ActiveSheet.PageSetup.PrintTitleColumns = "$A$1"
```

pagesetup.**PrintTitleRows**

pagesetup.**PrintTitleRows** [= *rowaddress*]

Valid only for the PageSetup of the Worksheet object. Sets or returns the address of rows to repeat on the left side of each page. If you specify only part of a row or rows, PrintTitleColumns expands the range to full rows. The default is " " (don't repeat rows).

The following code repeats row 1 on each printed page of the worksheet:

```
ActiveSheet.PageSetup.PrintTitleRows = "$A$1"
```

pagesetup.**RightFooter**

pagesetup.**RightFooter** [= *footer*]

Sets or returns the text to print as the right footer. The default is " ".

pagesetup.**RightHeader**

pagesetup.**RightHeader** [= *header*]

Sets or returns the text to print as the right header. The default is " ".

pagesetup.**RightMargin**

pagesetup.**RightMargin** [= *margin*]

Sets or returns the right page margin in points. The default is 54 points (3/4 inch).

pagesetup.TopMargin

pagesetup.TopMargin [= *margin*]

Sets or returns the top margin in points. The default is 72 points (1 inch).

pagesetup.Zoom

pagesetup.Zoom [= *percentage*]

Valid only for the PageSetup of the Worksheet object. Sets or returns the percentage by which to scale printed output. Must be between 10 and 400, or False. The default is 100.

When this property is False, scaling is determined by the FitToPagesWide and FitToPagesTall properties.

Chapter 12

Getting and Manipulating Stored Data

Excel provides two tools for accessing data stored in worksheets and external databases:

- Pivot tables enable you to gather data from many sources and view the relationships between items.

- The XLODBC add-in retrieves data directly from an Object Database Connectivity (ODBC) database and places the data in a worksheet or in a file.

Both tools provide read-only access to data. You cannot modify data in Excel and pass it back to the data source using pivot tables or XLODBC.

In this chapter, you learn how to do the following:

- View data with pivot tables.

- Create pivot tables from data stored in Excel.

- Create pivot tables from data stored in an external database.

- Use pivot tables to view different relationships between data.

- Use Visual Basic to create and manipulate pivot tables.

- Access data in ODBC databases with XLODBC.XLA.

This chapter covers the `PivotTable`, `PivotField`, and `PivotItem` objects. It also covers the XLODBC.XLA add-in functions.

Viewing Data with Pivot Tables

Pivot tables enable you to manipulate the relationships between columns in a table of data. You can use pivot tables to analyze different relationships, summarize data, and chart results.

Each field in a pivot table represents a column of data in a table. The table may come from an Excel sheet, an external database, or another pivot table. A pivot table has four different types of fields, as shown in figure 12.1.

Fig. 12.1
The anatomy of a pivot table.

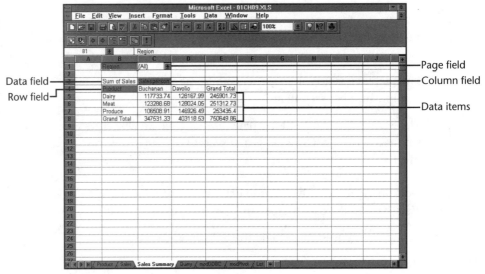

You can change a pivot table by dragging fields to different positions. For example, you might drag the Region page field to the pivot table's row fields and drag Salesperson to the page field (see fig. 12.2).

When you move pivot table fields, you see a different relationship between items. You can't easily get this view by looking directly at the source data, because the data has 72 dimensions.

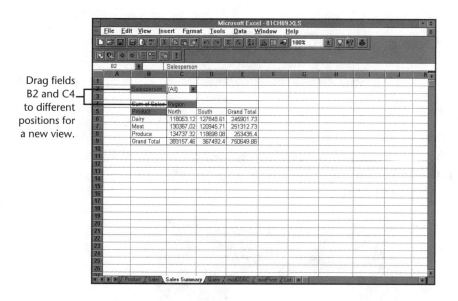

Drag fields
B2 and C4
to different
positions for
a new view.

Fig. 12.2
Moving fields in
a pivot table.

Creating Pivot Tables

Use the PivotTable Wizard to create a pivot table in a worksheet.

To run the PivotTable Wizard, follow these steps:

1. Choose **D**ata, **P**ivotTable. Excel displays the first step of the PivotTable
   Wizard (see fig. 12.3).

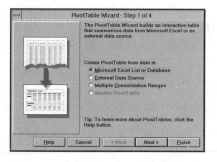

Fig. 12.3
The PivotTable
Wizard dialog
box, step 1.

2. Choose which type of data to use as a source by clicking one of the
   option buttons; then click **F**inish. The PivotTable Wizard displays different dialog boxes, depending on your choice. If you click the first
   option button, for example, the PivotTable Wizard creates a pivot table
   from an Excel list or database (a worksheet). When you click Next, Excel
   displays the next PivotTable Wizard dialog box, as shown in figure 12.4.

Fig. 12.4
The PivotTable
Wizard dialog
box, step 2.

3. Select the range to use as the source data. (You can use the mouse to select the sheet and range from the worksheet behind this dialog box.) Then click Next. Excel displays the next PivotTable Wizard dialog box, as shown in figure 12.5. Notice that this dialog box presents several fields, each corresponding to a column in the range that you specified.

Fig. 12.5
The PivotTable
Wizard dialog
box, step 3.

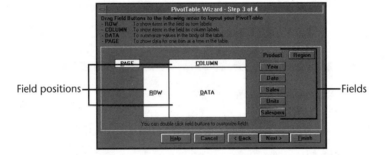

Field positions —

— Fields

4. Drag fields to **C**olumn, **R**ow, **D**ata, and **P**age field positions. You can place more than one field in a position. You must place at least one field in the data position.

5. Double-click a field to change the data displayed in the field. When you double-click a field, Excel displays the PivotTable Field dialog box, shown in figure 12.6.

6. When you finish setting up the pivot fields, click **F**inish. Excel displays the final step in the PivotTable Wizard dialog box (see fig. 12.7).

7. Select pivot-table options by clicking the check boxes. By default, Excel includes totals for rows and columns, and automatically formats the table. You should use these default settings; you can always change them later. Click **F**inish to create the pivot table.

> **Note**
>
> You should create pivot tables in separate empty worksheets. Pivot tables can change shape and size as you rearrange their fields, so you might overwrite adjacent cells if the worksheet doesn't have enough room.

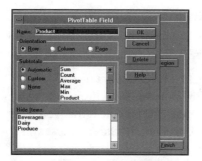

Fig. 12.6
The PivotTable
Field dialog box.

Fig. 12.7
The PivotTable
Wizard dialog
box, step 4.

Modifying Pivot Tables

When you create a pivot table in a worksheet, Excel displays the Query and
Pivot toolbar, shown in figure 12.8. Use this toolbar to make changes to an
existing pivot table.

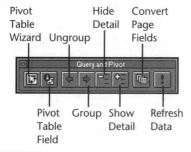

Fig. 12.8
The Query and
Pivot toolbar.

To add or remove fields from a pivot table, click the PivotTable Wizard button. Excel displays the dialog box for step 3 of the PivotTable Wizard.

To modify a field, select a field and click the PivotTable Field button. Excel
displays the PivotTable Field dialog box.

II

Programmer's Reference

Viewing and Hiding Detail

Tip

Double-clicking
a label or data
item in a pivot
table also
displays detail.

To view additional information about an item in a pivot table, select the item
and click the Show Detail button in the Query and Pivot toolbar.

If the item is a data field, Excel creates a new sheet with the detail from the
source data. If the item is a label, Excel displays the Show Detail dialog box,
shown in figure 12.9. Excel adds the field that you select in the Show Detail
dialog box to the row or column of the label that you select.

Fig. 12.9

The Show Detail
dialog box.

To hide detail, use the Show Detail dialog box to select the label, and then
click the Hide Detail toolbar button.

Using Data from External Databases

Pivot tables are a useful tool for importing data from external databases. To
use a pivot table to get data from an external database, you must use a database that supports the Object Database Connectivity (ODBC) standard, you
must have drivers (DLLs) for that database correctly installed on your system,
and you must have access privileges to the database. All these things differ
from database to database and from site to site, so ask your local database
expert if you have any questions about your installation, drivers, or access
privileges.

To use a pivot table to import data from an external database, follow these
steps:

1. Choose **D**ata, **P**ivotTable. Excel displays step 1 of the PivotTable
   Wizard.

2. Select the **E**xternal Data Source option and click Next. Excel displays
   step 2 of the PivotTable Wizard for an external data source, as shown
   in figure 12.10.

Fig. 12.10

Step 2 of the
PivotTable Wizard
for an external
data source.

3. Choose **G**et Data. Excel starts Microsoft Query and displays the Select Data Source dialog box (see fig. 12.11). This dialog box displays the types of databases that are available to your system. If you don't see the type of database that you are trying to access, it isn't correctly installed on your system.

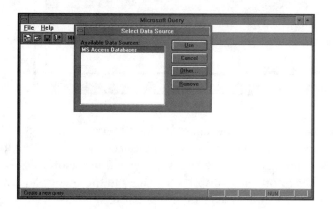

Fig. 12.11
Microsoft Query's Select Data Source dialog box.

4. Select the database type by double-clicking its name. Microsoft Query displays the Select Database dialog box (see fig. 12.12).

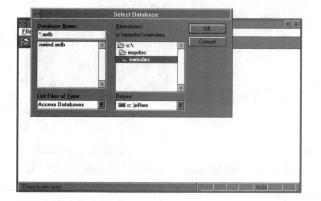

Fig. 12.12
Microsoft Query's Select Database dialog box.

5. Select the file name of the database to open. Microsoft Query displays the Add Tables dialog box (see fig. 12.13).

Fig. 12.13
Microsoft Query's
Add Tables dialog
box.

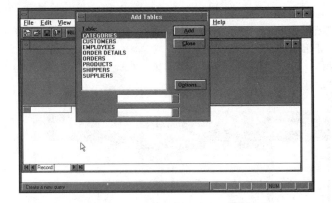

6. Double-click each of the tables you want to use in the pivot table. A table is the equivalent of an Excel worksheet and contains multiple fields (columns) of related data. When you finish adding tables, click **C**lose. Microsoft Query displays the tables in the Query window (see fig. 12.14). A line shows the relationships between related fields in each table. Not all tables in a database have related fields, so not all tables are connected by a line.

Fig. 12.14
Tables loaded in
Microsoft Query.

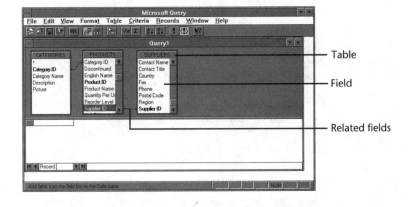

7. Double-click each of the fields to retrieve for the pivot table. Fields can be from any table, but only tables with related fields make much sense in a single pivot table.

8. When you finish selecting fields, choose **F**ile, Return Data to Excel. Microsoft Query performs the query and returns to step 2 of the PivotTable Wizard.

9. Click Next and proceed through the remaining steps of the PivotTable Wizard, as described in the "Creating Pivot Tables" section earlier in this chapter.

Microsoft Query can combine data from multiple databases, perform complicated SQL queries, and much more. To learn more about using Microsoft Query with external databases, see Microsoft Query's on-line Help or Excel's documentation.

Using Pivot Tables in Code

Creating a pivot table in Visual Basic is a two-step process:

1. Use the `PivotTableWizard` method to create a pivot table.

2. Use the `AddFields` method to add fields to the pivot table and display data.

The following code lines create a new pivot table and then add fields to the pivot table:

```
' Creates a pivot table from the Sales sheet of PRODUCTS.XLS
' in the Excel CBT directory.
Sub CreatePivot()
     ' Create a new, blank worksheet.
     Worksheets.Add
     ' Add Pivot table.
     ActiveSheet.PivotTableWizard SourceType:=xlDatabase, _
          SourceData:= Sheets("Sales").UsedRange, _
          TableDestination:=ActiveCell, TableName:= _
          "pvtSalesSummary", SaveData:=False
     ' Using the pivot table that was just created.
     With ActiveSheet.PivotTables("pvtSalesSummary")
          ' Add row, column, and page fields to the pivot table.
          .AddFields RowFields:="Product", _
               ColumnFields:="Salesperson", PageFields:="Region"
          ' Add data field.
          .PivotFields("Sales").Orientation = xlDataField
          ' Show totals of sales, rather than count (default).
          .PivotFields("Count of Sales").Function = xlSum
     End With
End Sub
```

Changing Views

You can control the display of pivot table fields by setting their `Orientation` property. The following code lines swap the Product and Salesperson pivot fields in the `pvtSalesSummary` pivot table that you created earlier:

II

Programmer's Reference

```
' "Pivots" the column and row fields.
Sub PivotRowColumn()
    With ActiveSheet.PivotTables("pvtSalesSummary")
        .PivotFields("Product").Orientation = xlColumnField
        .PivotFields("Salesperson").Orientation = xlRowField
    End With
End Sub
```

The following code lines swap the `Region` and `Salesperson` pivot fields in the `pvtSalesSummary` pivot table that you created earlier:

```
' "Pivots" the row and page fields.
Sub PivotPageRow()
    With ActiveSheet.PivotTables("pvtSalesSummary")
        .PivotFields("Region").Orientation = xlRowField
        .PivotFields("Salesperson").Orientation = xlPageField
    End With
End Sub
```

Showing and Hiding Detail

When you view or hide detail for pivot-field labels, use the `InnerDetail` property to set the detail field. Use the `PivotItem` object's `ShowDetail` property to show or hide the detail. The following code lines show the monthly details for a salesperson named Buchanan:

```
Sub ShowSalesDetail()
    With Sheets("Sales Summary").PivotTables("pvtSalesSummary")
        ' InnerDetail controls the field to use for the details.
        .InnerDetail = "Month"
        ' Setting ShowDetail to True displays the detail.
        .PivotFields("Salesperson").PivotItems("Buchanan") _
            .ShowDetail = True
    End With
End Sub
```

Using `ShowDetails` on a pivot item that is part of a data field creates a new worksheet that contains the detail rows from the source data instead of changing the pivot table. The following code line creates a new worksheet that contains the details for the first item in the data field of a pivot table:

```
Sheets("Sales Summary").PivotTables("pvtSalesSummary") _
    .DataBodyRange.ShowDetail = True
```

To see the detail for other cells in the data field, use the `Offset` method with the range returned by `DataBodyRange`. The following lines create a new worksheet with the details of a cell that is two cells down and to the left of the origin of the data range in a pivot table:

```
Sub ShowDataItemDetail()
    ' Activate the sheet containing the pivot table
```

```
            ' (required to Activate cell)
            Sheets("Sales Summary").Activate
            ' Using the range that contains the data field items...
            With ActiveSheet.PivotTables("pvtSalesSummary") _
                .DataBodyRange
                ' Activate the cell to display detail for.
                .Offset(2, 2).Activate
                ' Show the detail.
                ActiveCell.ShowDetail = True
            End With
      End Sub
```

The `PivotTable` object and `PivotTables` collection have specific properties and methods, which are listed in Table 12.1. Properties and methods shown in **bold** are described in the reference section that follows this table. Nonbold items are common to most objects and are described in Chapter 4, "Using Objects."

Table 12.1 PivotTable and PivotTables properties and methods

AddFields	**PageRange**
Application[2]	Parent[2]
ColumnFields	**PivotFields**
ColumnGrand	**RefreshDate**
ColumnRange	**RefreshName**
Count[1]	**RefreshTable**
Creator[2]	**RowFields**
DataBodyRange	**RowGrand**
DataFields	**RowRange**
DataLabelRange	**SaveData**
HasAutoFormat	**ShowPages**
HiddenFields	**SourceData**
InnerDetail	**TableRange**[1]
Item[1]	**TableRange**[2]
Name	Value
PageFields	**VisibleFields**

[1] *Applies to the `PivotTables` collection.*

[2] *Applies to the `PivotTables` collection and the `PivotTable` object.*

*pivottable.*AddFields

*pivottable.*AddFields ([*RowFields*], [*ColumnFields*], [*PageFields*], [*AddToTable*])

Adds row, column, and page fields to the pivot table.

Argument	Description
RowFields	A pivot field or array of pivot fields to add as rows to the pivot table.
ColumnFields	A pivot field or array of pivot fields to add as columns to the pivot table.
PageFields	A pivot field or array of pivot fields to add as pages to the pivot table.
AddToTable	True appends the new fields to existing row, column, or page fields; False replaces existing fields.

You must specify one or more of the `RowFields`, `ColumnFields`, or `PageFields` arguments.

*pivottable.*ColumnFields

Returns column pivot fields in the pivot table.

*pivottable.*ColumnGrand

*pivottable.*ColumnGrand [= True | False]

True displays grand totals for column fields; False does not. The default is True.

*pivottable.*ColumnRange

Returns the range that contains the column pivot fields of the pivot table. Use this method to control the appearance of the column fields in a pivot table.

The following code line highlights a pivot table's `ColumnRange` by changing its interior color to red:

```
ActiveSheet.PivotTables("pvtSalesSummary") _
    .ColumnRange.Interior.Color = RGB(255, 0, 0)
```

pivottable.**DataBodyRange**

Returns the range that contains the data items and totals in the pivot table. Use this method to control the appearance of the data items in a pivot table.

The following code line highlights a pivot table's `DataBodyRange` by changing its interior color to aqua:

```
ActiveSheet.PivotTables("pvtSalesSummary") _
    .DataBodyRange.Interior.Color = RGB(0, 255, 255)
```

pivottable.**DataFields**

Returns the pivot fields that are the data items in the pivot table.

pivottable.**DataLabelRange**

Returns the range that contains the labels for the pivot table's data items. Use this method to control the appearance of the data label in a pivot table.

This range begins in the upper left corner of the pivot table. The following code line highlights a pivot table's `DataLabelRange` by changing its interior color to yellow:

```
ActiveSheet.PivotTables("pvtSalesSummary") _
    .DataLabelRange.Interior.Color = RGB(255, 255, 0)
```

pivottable.**HasAutoFormat**

pivottable.**HasAutoFormat [= True | False]**

True automatically reformats the pivot table when the fields are moved or the data is refreshed; False does not reformat the table automatically. The default is True.

pivottable.**HiddenFields**

Returns from the source data the fields that are not currently included in the pivot table.

The following code displays the hidden columns of data as row fields in a pivot table:

```
Sub AddRemainingRows()
    For each pvtfld In ActiveSheet.PivotTables("pvtSalesSummary") _
        .HiddenFields
    pvtfld.orientation = xlRowField
    Next pvtfld
End Sub
```

II

Programmer's Reference

pivottable.**InnerDetail**

pivottable.**InnerDetail [=** *fieldname*]

Sets or returns the name of the field used for detail when the pivot table generates a detail sheet. Pivot tables create a detail sheet when the user double-clicks a cell in the DataBodyRange or when a pivot item's ShowDetail property is set to True.

The following code shows sales by month when the user double-clicks a pivot item in the pvtSaleSummary pivot table:

```
ActiveSheet.PivotTables("pvtSalesSummary").InnerDetail = "Month"
```

pivottable.**PageFields**

Returns one or all of the page fields in the pivot table.

pivottable.**PageRange**

Returns the range that contains the page fields in the pivot table. Use this method to control the appearance of the page pivot fields in a pivot table.

The following code line highlights a pivot table's PageRange by changing its interior color to blue:

```
ActiveSheet.PivotTables("pvtSalesSummary") _
    .PageRange.Interior.Color = RGB(0, 0, 255)
```

pivottable.**PivotFields**

pivottable.**PivotFields ([*index*])**

Returns one or all of the PivotField objects in a pivot table. Use this method to control the placement and display of fields in a pivot table.

The following code line makes a pivot field a page field:

```
ActiveSheet.PivotTables("pvtSalesSummary") _
    .PivotFields("Salesperson").Orientation = xlPageField
```

pivottable.**RefreshDate**

Returns the date and time when the pivot table was last refreshed.

The following Auto_Open() procedure refreshes a pivot table if it hasn't already been refreshed today:

```
Sub Auto_Open()
    dtRefresh = Sheets("Sales Summary") _
        .PivotTables("pvtSalesSummary").RefreshDate
    If DateValue(Now) > DateValue(dtRefresh) Then
        Sheets("Sales Summary").PivotTables("pvtSalesSummary") _
            .RefreshTable
    End If
End Sub
```

pivottable.RefreshName

Returns the name of the person who last refreshed the pivot table.

pivottable.RefreshTable( )

For pivot tables that contain copies of their underlying data, this method refreshes the pivot table from the data source. For pivot tables that do not contain copies of their underlying data, this method creates an in-memory copy of the data and refreshes the pivot table from the data source.

When you open a workbook that contains a pivot table that does not contain a copy of its underlying data, you must refresh that table before you can make changes to it. This is true regardless of where the source data resides—even if it's in another sheet in the same workbook.

This method returns True if the data is refreshed successfully. The following code refreshes a PivotTable:

```
Sheets("Sales Summary").PivotTable("pvtSalesSummary").RefreshTable
```

pivottable.RowFields

Returns the row pivot fields in the pivot table.

pivottable.RowGrand

pivottable.RowGrand [= True | False]

True displays grand totals for column fields; False does not. The default is True.

pivottable.RowRange

Returns the range that contains the row fields in the pivot table. Use this method to control the appearance of the row pivot fields in a pivot table.

The following code line highlights a pivot table's RowRange by changing its interior color to green:

```
ActiveSheet.PivotTables("pvtSalesSummary").RowRange. _
    Interior.Color = RGB(0, 255, 0)
```

*pivottable.*SaveData

*pivottable.*SaveData [= True | False]

True saves the pivot table's underlying data with the table definition in the workbook; False saves only the pivot table's definition. The default is True.

Caution

Saving the data with the pivot table can make a workbook very large. The data is stored twice—in its source and in the pivot table. This is true even if the data source is the workbook that contains the pivot table.

---

*pivottable.*ShowPages

*pivottable.*ShowPages ([*PageField*])

Makes one copy of the pivot table for each entry in the page field. Each new pivot table is placed in a new worksheet, which is named according to the entry in the page field.

The following code line creates a new pivot table for each region entry in the page field:

```
Sheets("Sales Summary").PivotTables("pvtSalesSummary") _
    .ShowPages("Region")
```

Note

The new pivot tables are identical to the original pivot table, except that each of the new tables has a different page-field entry selected.

*pivottable.*SourceData

Returns information that indicates the source of the data for the pivot table. The type of information returned depends on the type of source for the pivot table, as indicated in the following table:

Source	Return value
An Excel list or database	The address of the source data.
An external database	An array containing the ODBC connection string and the SQL string used to retrieve the data.
Multiple consolidation ranges	A two-dimensional array that contains the references and associated page field items.
Another pivot table	One of the preceding values, depending on the source of the original pivot table.

Note

Because SQL command strings can be very long, each SQL string is broken into 200-character segments and placed in a separate array element.

*pivottable.*TableRange1

Returns the range that contains the entire pivot table, *excluding* the page fields. Use this method to control the appearance of the pivot table.

*pivottable.*TableRange2

Returns the range that contains the entire pivot table, *including* the page fields. Use this method to control the appearance of the pivot table.

*pivottable.*VisibleFields

Returns the pivot fields that are currently displayed in the pivot table as a field or an array of fields.

The following code hides all the visible fields in a pivot table:

```
Sub RemoveFields()
    For Each pvtfld In Sheets("Sales Summary") _
        .PivotTables("pvtSalesSummary").VisibleFields
        pvtfld.Orientation = xlHidden
    Next pvtfld
End Sub
```

Using Pivot Fields in Code

Use the PivotTable object's PivotFields method to get any of the pivot fields in a table. PivotTable also has the following methods, which get specific types of pivot fields from the pivot table:

PivotTable method	Returns
ColumnFields	All the PivotField objects that are column fields.
DataFields	All the PivotField objects that are data fields.
HiddenFields	All the PivotField objects that are not currently displayed in the pivot table but that appear in step 3 of the PivotTable Wizard.
PageFields	All the PivotField objects that are page fields.
RowFields	All the PivotField objects that are row fields.
VisibleFields	All the PivotField objects that are visible in the pivot table.

As mentioned in the "Changing Views" section earlier in this chapter, the Orientation property controls the placement of a field in a pivot table. Pivot fields have five possible Orientation settings:

Orientation setting	Description
xlColumnField	Displays the pivot field as a column in the pivot table.
xlDataField	Displays the pivot field as a data field in the pivot table.
xlHidden	Removes the pivot field from the pivot table.
xlPageField	Displays the pivot field as a page field in the pivot table.
xlRowField	Displays the pivot field as a row in the pivot table.

Setting Orientation to xlHidden removes the field from the pivot table. To add the hidden field back to the table, set Orientation to one of the other values.

The PivotField object and PivotFields collection have specific properties and methods, which are listed in Table 12.2. Properties and methods shown in **bold** are described in the reference section that follows this table. Nonbold items are common to most objects and are described in Chapter 4, "Using Objects."

Table 12.2 PivotField and PivotFields properties and methods	
Application[2]	LabelRange
BaseField	Name
BaseItem	**NumberFormat**
Calculation	**Orientation**
ChildField	Parent[2]
ChildItems	**ParentField**
Count[1]	**ParentItems**
Creator[2]	**PivotItems**
CurrentPage	**Position**
DataRange	**SourceName**
DataType	**Subtotals**
Function	**TotalLevels**
GroupLevel	Value
HiddenItems	**VisibleItems**
Item[1]	

[1] *Applies to the* PivotFields *collection.*

[2] *Applies to the* PivotFields *collection and the* PivotField *object.*

pivotfield.BaseField

Returns or sets the base field for the custom calculation. This property is valid for data fields only.

pivotfield.BaseItem

Returns or sets the item in the base field for the custom calculation. This property is valid for data fields only.

pivotfield.Calculation

pivotfield.Calculation [= *setting*]

For pivot fields that are data items in a pivot table, this property sets or returns the type of calculation done by the pivot field: xlDifferenceFrom, xlIndex, xlNormal, xlPercentDifferenceFrom, xlPercentOf, xlPercentOfColumn, xlPercentOfRow, xlPercentOfTotal, or xlRunningTotal. The default is xlNormal (which displays the value of the field).

For pivot fields that are row, column, page, or hidden fields, this property causes error 1004.

pivotfield.ChildField

For grouped pivot fields, this property returns the subordinate (child) field. For pivot fields that are not grouped, this property causes error 1006.

pivotfield.ChildItems

For grouped items, this method returns the collection of PivotItem objects that belong to the subordinate field. For pivot fields that are not grouped, this property returns an empty PivotItems collection.

pivotfield.CurrentPage

pivotfield.CurrentPage [= pivotItemName]

For pivot fields that are page fields, this property sets or returns the pivot item that is currently selected for the page. You set the CurrentPage value with a string, but it returns a PivotItem object.

The following code gets the name of the region currently displayed in the Region page field:

```
sRegion = Sheets("Sales Summary").PivotTables("pvtSalesSummary") _
    .PivotFields("Region").CurrentPage.Name
```

This code changes a page field to display the North region:

```
Sheets("Sales Summary").PivotTables("pvtSalesSummary") _
    .PivotFields("Region").CurrentPage = "North"
```

pivotfield.DataRange

Returns the range of cells that contains the data displayed for the pivot field.

pivotfield.DataType

Returns one of the following constants, each of which identifies the type of data in a pivot field: xlText, xlNumber, or xlDate.

pivotfield.Function

pivotfield.Function [= *setting*]

For pivot fields that are data items, this property sets or returns the function used to calculate the values displayed. These functions are xlAverage, xlCount, xlCountNums, xlMax, xlMin, xlProduct, xlStDev, xlStDevP, xlSum, xlVar, or xlVarP. The default is xlCount. For other types of pivot fields, this property causes error 1006.

The following code changes the count of sales to the sum of sales in a pivot table:

```
Sheets("Sales Summary").PivotTables("pvtSalesSummary") _
    .PivotFields("Count of Sales").Function = xlSum
```

Caution

If you change the function of a data item, you also change the data item's name. After you make the change shown in this example, "Count of Sales" becomes "Sum of Sales."

---

pivotfield.GroupLevel

For grouped fields, this property returns the placement of the field within the group of fields. The highest-level parent field (the leftmost parent field) is 1, its child is 2, and so on.

For fields that are not part of a group, this method returns 1.

pivotfield.HiddenItems

Returns in the pivot field the pivot items that are not currently displayed.

pivotfield.LabelRange

Returns the range that contains the label for the pivot field. Use this method to control the appearance of pivot-field labels.

The following code line sets a pivot-field label in a boldface font:

```
Sheets("Sales Summary").PivotTables("pvtSalesSummary") _
    .PivotFields("Product").LabelRange.Font.Bold = True
```

pivotfield.**NumberFormat**

pivotfield.**NumberFormat [=** *formatcode***]**

Sets or returns the number format for the pivot field.

pivotfield.**Orientation**

pivotfield.**Orientation [=** *setting***]**

Sets or returns a constant that indicates the location of a pivot field in a pivot table. The constants are xlHidden, xlRowField, xlColumnField, xlPageField, and xlDataField.

Use this property to add or remove fields from a pivot table and to change the view of data in a pivot table.

The following code line adds the Year field to a pivot table as a row:

```
Sheets("Sales Summary").PivotTables("pvtSalesSummary") _
    .PivotFields("Year").Orientation - xlRowField
```

pivotfield.**ParentField**

For grouped pivot fields, this property returns the superior (parent) field. For pivot fields that are not grouped, this method causes error 1006.

pivotfield.**ParentItems**

For grouped items, this method returns the collection of PivotItem objects that belong to the superior field. For pivot fields that are not grouped, this method returns an empty PivotItems collection.

pivotfield.**PivotItems**

pivotfield.**PivotItems ([***Index***])**

Returns one or all of the PivotItem objects in a pivot field. Use this method to control the display of items in a pivot field.

pivotfield.**Position**

pivotfield.**Position [=** *index***]**

Sets or returns the index of a pivot field among other pivot fields with the same orientation. If there are three row pivot fields, for example, the topmost field is Position 1, the middle field is 2, and the bottom field is 3.

Use this property to change the ordering of column, row, and page fields. The following code sets the active pivot field to position 5:

```
ActiveCell.PivotField.Position = 5
```

*pivotfield.*SourceName

Returns the name of the field as it appears in the data source. This name may differ from the label that appears in the pivot table. The following example returns the name of the active item:

```
ItemText = ActiveCell.PivotItem.SourceName
```

*pivotfield.*Subtotals

*pivotfield.*Subtotals [= *array*]

Sets or returns an array of Boolean values that indicate the types of subtotals to include for a pivot field. The array has the following elements:

Element	Type of subtotal
1	Automatic (default)
2	Sum
3	Count
4	Average
5	Max
6	Min
7	Product
8	Count of numbers
9	Standard deviation (StdDev)
10	Standard deviation, global population (StdDevp)
11	Variance (Var)
12	Variance, global population (Varp)

II

Programmer's Reference

*pivotfield.***TotalLevels**

For grouped fields, this returns the number of levels in the entire group. This number is the same for all pivot fields in the group.

For fields that are not part of a group, this method returns 1.

*pivotfield.***VisibleItems**

Returns a collection of `PivotItem` objects in the pivot field that are currently visible.

Using Pivot Items in Code

Use the `PivotField` object's `PivotItems` method to get any of the pivot items in a field. The `PivotItem` object is useful primarily for controlling the level of detail displayed in a pivot table:

- Use the `ShowDetail` property to create summaries and display details.

- Use the `Visible` method to hide and display items.

The `PivotItem` object and `PivotItems` collection have specific properties and methods, which are listed in Table 12.3. Properties and methods shown in **bold** are described in the reference section that follows this table. Nonbold items are common to most objects and are described in Chapter 4, "Using Objects."

Table 12.3 PivotItem and PivotItems properties and methods	
Application[2]	Parent[2]
ChildItems	**ParentItem**
Count[1]	**ParentShowDetail**
Creator[2]	**Position**
DataRange	**ShowDetail**
Item[1]	**SourceName**
LabelRange	Value
Name	Visible

[1] *Applies to the* `PivotItems` *collection.*

[2] *Applies to the* `PivotItems` *collection and the* `PivotItem` *object.*

*pivotitem.***ChildItems**

For grouped items, this property returns the collection of `PivotItem` objects that belong to the subordinate item. For pivot items that are not grouped, this property returns an empty `PivotItems` collection.

*pivotitem.***DataRange**

Returns the range of cells that contains the data displayed for the pivot item.

*pivotitem.***LabelRange**

Returns the range that contains the label for the pivot item. Use this method to control the appearance of pivot-item labels.

The following code line sets a pivot-item label in boldface:

```
Sub PivotLabel()
    With Sheets("Sales Summary").PivotTables("pvtSalesSummary") _
        .PivotFields("Month")
        .PivotItems(1).LabelRange.Font.Bold = True
    End With
End Sub
```

*pivotitem.***ParentItem**

For grouped items, returns the collection of `PivotItem` objects that belong to the superior field. For pivot items that are not grouped, returns an empty `PivotItems` collection.

*pivotitem.***ParentShowDetail**

For grouped pivot items, this property returns True if the item is visible (because the parent item is showing detail) or False if the item is not showing (because the parent item is hiding detail).

For pivot items that are not grouped, this property returns an error.

Caution

You cannot trap the error that `ParentShowDetail` returns. Instead, returning the property returns a variable of type error and attempting to set the property causes a type mismatch (error 13).

---

pivotitem.Position

pivotitem.Position [= *index*]

Sets or returns the index of a pivot item in the pivot field. For example, if a pivot field contains three items, the first item is Position 1, the middle item is 2, and the last item is 3.

Use this property to change the ordering of pivot items in a field.

The following code moves the pivot item for the month of January to the end of the last position in the pivot field:

```
Sub ChangeItemOrder()
    With Sheets("Sales Summary") _
            .PivotTables("pvtSalesSummary").PivotFields("Month")
            .PivotItems("Jan").Position = 12
        End With
End Sub
```

pivotitem.ShowDetail

pivotitem.ShowDetail [= True | False]

True displays the detail for the pivot item; False hides the detail. You must set the pivot table's InnerDetail property before setting the pivot item's ShowDetail property to True.

The following code shows the Salesperson details for the month of January:

```
Sub ShowItemDetail()
    With Sheets("Sales Summary").PivotTables("pvtSalesSummary")
        .InnerDetail = "Salesperson"
        .PivotFields("Month").PivotItems("Jan").ShowDetail = True
    End With
End Sub
```

pivotitem.SourceName

Returns the name of the item as it appears in the data source. This name may differ from the label that appears in the pivot table.

Retrieving Data with XLODBC.XLA

The Excel ODBC add-in (XLODBC.XLA) enables you to access ODBC databases such as Microsoft Access, Microsoft SQL, ORACLE, Rdb/VMS, and DB2. To use XLODBC.XLA, you need these components:

- XLODBC.XLA and XLODBC.DLL installed in your Windows system directory. You may have to move these files from where Excel installs them to the Windows system directory on your machine.

- An ODBC-compliant database. This chapter uses Microsoft Access as an example, but any compliant database will do.

- The ODBC Administrator (ODBCADM.EXE).

- The proper ODBC drivers (DLLs) and documentation for the database you are using. These may be hard to come by—particularly the documentation. Try to get help from a database expert in your organization.

To load the XLODBC.XLA add-in, follow these steps:

1. Choose Tools, Add-Ins. Excel displays the Add-Ins dialog box.

2. If XLODBC is listed in the **A**dd-Ins Available list box, click the check box beside its name to load the add-in.

3. If XLODBC is not listed in the list box, choose **B**rowse. Excel displays the Browse dialog box. Use this dialog box to locate the XLODBC.XLA file.

4. Double-click the XLODBC.XLA file name. Excel adds the add-in to the **A**dd-Ins Available list box and loads the add-in.

After you load XLODBC, you can use it to retrieve data and perform actions on ODBC databases. Using the XLODBC functions involves four fundamental steps:

1. Opening the database

2. Performing actions with SQL statements

3. Retrieving the results of the SQL statements

4. Closing the database

Connecting to ODBC Databases

To open an ODBC database, you use the SQLOpen() function. This function uses an ODBC connection string to identify the database to open. ODBC connection strings differ for different types of databases. Following are the forms for three types of databases:

II

Programmer's Reference

Database	Connection string syntax
Microsoft Access	DSN=*registeredname*;DBQ=*filename*; UID=*user*;PWD=*passwrd*; [LoginTimeOut=*seconds*]
Microsoft SQL	ODBC;UID=*user*;PWD=*passwrd*; DATABASE=*dbname*; [LoginTimeOut=*seconds*]
ORACLE	ODBC;DSN=*dbname*;DBQ=*server*;UID=*user*; PWD=*passwrd*

The easiest way to get the appropriate connection string is to connect to the database, using the Drivers dialog box, and retrieve the connection string.

The following code lines display the Drivers dialog box and return the connection string in cell A1 of the active sheet:

```
Sub GetConnectString()
    ' Create a blank worksheet.
    Worksheets.Add
    ' Connect to a database using the Drivers dialog box.
    vConnectID = SQLOpen("",ActiveSheet.Range("A1"))
    ' Close the database.
    vConnectID = SQLClose(vConnectID)
End Sub
```

The following code line is an example of a connection string for a Microsoft Access database:

```
"DSN=MS Access Databases;DBQ=c:\excel\nwind.mdb;FIL=RedISAM;"
```

Querying ODBC Databases

To execute a SQL statement, you use the SQLExecQuery() function. This function uses the connection ID that SQLOpen() returns.

The following code lines open a database and perform a query:

```
Sub DoQuery()
    vConnect= SQLOpen("DSN=MS Access _
        Databases;DBQ=c:\excel\nwind.mdb;FIL=RedISAM;")
    vResult =SQLExecQuery(vConnect, "SELECT CATEGORIES." _
        "Category Name"", PRODUCTS.""English Name""," & _
        " PRODUCTS.""Units In Stock"", PRODUCTS." _
        "Unit Price"" FROM CATEGORIES" & " CATEGORIES, _
        PRODUCTS PRODUCTS WHERE PRODUCTS.""Category ID"" =" & _
        " CATEGORIES.""Category ID""ORDER BY CATEGORIES." _
        "Category Name""")
End Sub
```

XLODBC functions do not accept string arguments that exceed 255 characters. You can avoid this limitation by placing longer queries in an array.

The following code lines convert a long SQL string to an array that you can pass to `SQLExecQuery()`:

```
' Create array of 250-character strings from one long string.
Function QuerytoArray(strQuery As String) As Variant
    Dim intSize, intCount As Integer
    intSize = (Len(strQuery) + 250) \ 250
    ' XLODBC statements require the array to be column-major,
    ' hence the two-dimensional array tmpArray(intSize, 1).
    ReDim tmpArray(intSize, 1) As String
    For intCount = 1 To intSize
        tmpArray(intCount, 1) = Mid$(strQuery, (intCount - 1) _
            * 251,250)
    Next intCount
    QuerytoArray = tmpArray
End Function
```

SQL is a language unto itself, so SQL statements can be quite complicated. Fortunately, there are many books about SQL, including the following:

- Date, C. J., *A Guide to the SQL Standard* (Addison-Wesley, 1989).

- Emerson, Sandra L., Marcy Darnovsky, and Judith S. Bowman, *The Practical SQL Handbook* (Addison-Wesley, 1989).

- Groff, James R., and Paul N. Weinberg, *Using SQL* (Osborne McGraw-Hill, 1990).

- Gruber, Martin, *Understanding SQL* (Sybex, 1990).

- Hursch, Jack L., and Carolyn J. Hursch, *SQL, the Structured Query Language* (TAB Books, 1988).

- Pascal, Fabian, *SQL and Relational Basics* (M & T Books, 1990).

- Trimble, J. Harvey, Jr., and David Chappell, *A Visual Introduction to SQL* (Wiley, 1989).

- Van der Lans, Rick F., *Introduction to SQL* (Addison-Wesley, 1988).

- Vang, Soren, *SQL and Relational Databases* (Microtrend Books, 1990).

- Viescas, John, *Quick Reference Guide to SQL* (Microsoft Press, 1989).

Retrieving Results

After you query a database, use `SQLRetrieve()` or `SQLRetrieveToFile()` to get the results. The following code line displays the result of a query in the active worksheet:

```
vResult = SQLRetrieve(vConnect, ActiveSheet.Cells(1, 1), , , True)
```

II

Programmer's Reference

Closing an ODBC Database

After you finish working with a database, make sure that you close it. Leaving the database open consumes resources on the database server. To close a database, use the `SQLClose()` function.

The following code closes an open database:

```
vResult = SQLClose(vConnect)
```

> **Caution**
>
> Failure to close a remote database prior to exiting Excel can cause unpredictable results, both in Excel and the remote database. The system may hang, or data corruption could occur, or both.

Evaluating Errors

Unlike Excel properties and methods, XLODBC functions do not ordinarily cause trappable errors; instead, these functions return an error value that is determined by the target database. You can test this error value to determine whether the function succeeded or failed. If the function failed, use `SQLError()` to get detailed information about the nature of the error.

The following code tests the results from an `SQLOpen()` function:

```
Sub TestError()
    vConnect= SQLOpen("DSN=MS Access Databases; _
        DBQ=c:\excel\nwind.mdb;FIL=RedISAM;")
    If IsError(vConnect) Then
        vError = SQLError()
    End If
    If IsArray(vError) Then
        Msgbox vError(1) & ", " & vError(2) & ", " & vError(3)
    Else
        MsgBox "No additional information is available"
    End If
End Sub
```

Using XLODBC.XLA Functions

After you load the XLODBC.XLA file, the following functions are available:

Function	Description
SQLBind()	Specifies a worksheet column or reference in which to place the results from the SQL query.
SQLClose()	Closes the connection to the database.

Function	Description
SQLError()	Returns the SQL error number of any data-access error that occurs from any of the other ODBC add-in functions.
SQLExecQuery()	Executes the SQL statement.
SQLGetSchema()	Returns information about the open database.
SQLOpen()	Connects to a database by using the ODBC functions.
SQLRequest()	Requests a connection and executes an SQL query.
SQLRetrieve()	Retrieves the results from SQLExecQuery() and places them in a worksheet.
SQLRetrieveToFile()	Retrieves the results from SQLExecQuery() and places them in a file.

The following reference section describes these XLODBC.XLA functions in more detail.

SQLBind

SQLBind (*ConnectionNum*, *[Column]*, *[Reference]*)

Specifies where results are placed when the SQLRetrieve() function retrieves them.

Argument	Description
ConnectionNum	The unique connection ID of the data source, returned by SQLOpen(), for which you want to define storage.
Column	The number of the result set that you want bound. Columns in the result set are numbered from left to right, starting with 1. If you omit this argument, all bindings for the connection are removed. Column number 0 contains row numbers for the result set. If column number 0 is bound, SQLRetrieve() returns row numbers in the bound location.
Reference	A Range object that indicates the location of a single cell in a worksheet where you want to bind the results. If you omit this argument, binding is removed for the column.

SQLBind() returns an array that lists (by column number) the bound columns for the current connection. If SQLBind() cannot bind the column to the cell indicated in the *Reference* argument, it returns the error value xlErrNA

(2042). If the connection is not valid or if you try to bind a cell that is not available, `SQLBind()` returns the error value `xlErrValue` (2015). If the *Reference* argument refers to more than one cell, `SQLBind()` returns the error value `xlErrRef` (2023). If `SQLRetrieve()` does not have a destination parameter, `SQLBind()` places the result set in the location indicated by the *Reference* argument.

`SQLBind()` tells the ODBC Administrator where to place results that the `SQLRetrieve()` function retrieves. The results are placed in the reference cell and in the cells immediately below it. Use `SQLBind()` if you want to place the results from different columns in disjointed worksheet locations. Call `SQLBind()` for each column in the result set. A binding remains valid as long as the connection is open. Calls to `SQLBind()` do not affect results that have already been retrieved.

SQLClose

SQLClose (*ConnectionNum*)

Closes a connection to an external database. The *ConnectionNum* argument specifies the connection ID of the database to close.

If the connection is successfully closed, `SQLClose()` returns 0. If the connection is not valid, the function returns the error value `xlErrValue` (2015). If `SQLClose()` cannot disconnect from the data source, it returns the error value `xlErrRef` (2023).

The following code closes a database previously opened with `SQLOpen()`:

```
vResult = SQLClose(vConnect)
```

SQLError()

When called after one of the other XLODBC functions fails due to an ODBC error, this function returns an array that contains detailed error information. When called after no ODBC error has occurred, `SQLError()` uses the error value `xlErrNA` (2042) to return an array that contains one element.

If the function succeeds, the returned array has three elements:

Element	Description
1	A string that contains a number indicating the ODBC error class and subclass.

Element	Description
2	A numeric value indicating the database native error code (0 if no error).
3	A text message that describes the source and nature of the error.

The following code displays a detailed error message after an ODBC error occurs:

```
Sub DisplayODBCError()
    Dim vErrSQL As Variant, iErr As Integer
    vErrSQL = SQLError()
    ' If the returned array has only 1 element,
    ' then no ODBC error occurred.
    If UBound(vErrSQL) = 1 Then
        MsgBox "No ODBC error occurred."
    Else
        ' Display the error's three elements.
        MsgBox vErrSQL(1) & ", " & vErrSQL(2) & ", " & vErrSQL(3)
    End If
End Sub
```

Note

If more than one ODBC error occurs, the returned array has two dimensions rather than one. Each row contains the preceding three elements for each error that occurs.

SQLExecQuery

SQLExecQuery (*ConnectionNum, QueryText*)

Sends a SQL statement to an open database. `SQLExecQuery()` executes the SQL statement only. Use `SQLRetrieve()` or `SQLRetrieveToFile()` to get the results.

Argument	Description
ConnectionNum	The connection ID returned by `SQLOpen()` that identifies the database.
QueryText	The SQL statement to execute. The query must follow the SQL syntax guidelines for the specific driver. This argument cannot exceed 255 characters. If an SQL statement is longer than that, break the string into smaller pieces and pass them as elements in an array.

The value that `SQLExecQuery()` returns depends on the type of SQL statement executed:

SQL statement	Return value
SELECT	The number of columns in the result set.
UPDATE, INSERT, or DELETE	The number of rows affected by the statement.
Any other valid SQL statement	0

If `SQLExecQuery()` cannot execute the query on the specified data source, it returns the error value `xlErrNA` (2042). If the connection is not valid, the function returns the error value `xlErrValue` (2015).

When you call `SQLExecQuery()`, the new results replace any pending results on that connection.

The following code performs a query on an open database:

```
vResult =SQLExecQuery(intConnect, "SELECT CATEGORIES.""Category Name"", _
    PRODUCTS.""English Name""," & " PRODUCTS.""Units In Stock"", _
    PRODUCTS.""Unit Price"" FROM CATEGORIES" & " CATEGORIES, _
    PRODUCTS PRODUCTS WHERE PRODUCTS.""Category ID"" =" & _
    " CATEGORIES.""Category ID""ORDER BY CATEGORIES.""Category Name""")
```

SQLGetSchema

SQLGetSchema (*ConnectionNum*, *TypeNum*, [*QualifierText*])

Returns information about the structure of the database.

Argument	Description
ConnectionNum	The unique connection ID of the data source to which `SQLOpen()` has connected you and for which you want information.
TypeNum	Specifies the type of information to return, as shown in the following table.
QualifierText	A string that qualifies a search; included for *TypeNum* 3, 4, and 5 only.

The *TypeNum* argument has these possible values:

TypeNum value	Description	*QualifierText* meaning
1	A list of available data sources.	Not used.
2	A list of databases on the current connection.	Not used.
3	A list of owners in a database on the current connection.	The name of the database.
4	A list of tables for a given owner and database on the current connection.	The database name, followed by the owner's name, with a period separating the two.
5	A list of columns in a particular table and their ODBC SQL data types in a two-dimensional array. The first field contains the name, the second field is the ODBC SQL data type of the column.	The name of the table from which to retrieve the column and information.
6	The user ID of the current user.	Not used.
7	The name of the current database.	Not used.
8	The name of the database defined during setup or by using the ODBC Administrator.	Not used.
9	The name of the database management system that the database uses (ORACLE or SQL Server, for example).	Not used.
10	The server name for the database.	Not used.
11	The term that the database uses to refer to the owners (for example, "owner", "Authorization ID", or "Schema").	Not used.
12	The term that the database uses to refer to a table (for example, "TABLE" or "file").	Not used.
13	The term that the database uses to refer to a qualifier (for example, "database" or "directory").	Not used.
14	The term that the database uses to refer to a procedure (for example, "database procedure", "stored procedure", or "procedure").	Not used.

If `SQLGetSchema()` cannot find the requested information, it returns the error value `xlErrNA` (2042). If the connection is not valid, this function returns the error value `xlErrValue` (2015).

SQLOpen

SQLOpen (*ConnectionStr*, [*OutputRef*], [*DriverPrompt*])

Connects to a database and returns the *ConnectionNum* used by other XLODBC statements.

Argument	Description
ConnectionStr	The ODBC connection string that the database uses. This string is often referred to as the Data Source Name (DSN).
OutputRef	A Range object containing a single cell that identifies the location in which to place the completed connection string.
DriverPrompt	1 always displays the driver dialog box; 2 displays the driver dialog box if the information provided by the connection string and the data source specification is not sufficient to complete the connection; 3 displays the same dialog box as 2, except that options that are not required are dimmed and unavailable; 4 does not display the driver dialog box. The default is 2.

If successful, `SQLOpen()` returns a connection ID. This number can be used with the other ODBC functions. If `SQLOpen()` cannot connect to the database, it returns the error value `xlErrNA` (2042).

ConnectionStr is different for different types of ODBC databases. The best way to get this information is to use *OutputRef* to return the string. The following code lines display the Drivers dialog box and return the connection string in cell A1 of the active sheet:

```
Sub GetConnectString()
    ' Create a blank worksheet.
    Worksheets.Add
    ' Connect to a database using the Drivers dialog box.
    vConnectID = SQLOpen("",ActiveSheet.Range("A1"))
    ' Close the database.
    vConnectID = SQLClose(vConnectID)
End Sub
```

Following is an example of a connection string for a Microsoft Access database:

```
"DSN=MS Access Databases;DBQ=c:\excel\nwind.mdb;FIL=RedISAM;"
```

SQLRequest

SQLRequest (*ConnectionStr, QueryText, [OutputRef], [DriverPrompt], [ColNamesLogical]*)

Connects to an external data source and runs a query. SQLRequest() combines the tasks performed by SQLOpen(), SQLExecQuery(), SQLRetrieve(), and SQLClose().

Argument	Description
ConnectionStr	The ODBC connection string that the database uses. This string is often referred to as the Data Source Name (DSN).
QueryText	The SQL statement to execute. The query must follow the SQL syntax guidelines for the specific driver. The *QueryText* argument cannot exceed 255 characters. If the SQL statement is longer than that, break the string into smaller pieces and pass them as elements in an array.
OutputRef	A Range object that contains a single cell that identifies the location in which to place the completed connection string.
DriverPrompt	1 always displays the driver dialog box; 2 displays the driver dialog box if the information provided by the connection string and the data source specification is not sufficient to complete the connection; 3 displays the same dialog box as 2, except that options that are not required are dimmed and unavailable; 4 does not display the driver dialog box. The default is 2.
ColNamesLogical	True includes the column names as the first row of the result; False omits the names. The default is False.

If SQLRequest() succeeds, it returns an array of query results or the number of rows affected by the query. If the function cannot complete all its actions, it returns an error value. If SQLRequest() cannot access the data source by using the connection string specified in the *ConnectionStr* argument, it returns the error value xlErrNA (2042).

The following code lines use SQLRequest() to perform a quick query and display the results in the active sheet:

```
Sub QuickQuery()
    Dim vResult As Variant, strConnect As String, strQuery As String
    ' Build connect string and SQL Query.
    strConnect = "DSN=MS Access _
        Databases;DBQ=c:\mspdoc\nwindms\nwind.mdb;FIL=RedISAM;"
    strQuery = "SELECT CATEGORIES.""Category Name"", _
        PRODUCTS.""English Name""," & " PRODUCTS.""Units In Stock"", _
```

```
                    PRODUCTS.""Unit Price"" FROM CATEGORIES" & _
                    " CATEGORIES, PRODUCTS PRODUCTS WHERE PRODUCTS.""Category ID"" _
                    =" & " CATEGORIES.""Category ID""ORDER BY CATEGORIES." _
                    "Category Name"""
            ' Connect to database and execute query.
            vResult = SQLRequest(strConnect, strQuery)
            ' If SQLRequest worked, it returns an array.
            If IsArray(vResult) Then
                ' Assign the array to a range on the active worksheet.
                ActiveSheet.Range(Cells(1, 1), Cells(UBound(vResult, 1), _
                    UBound(vResult, 2))) = vResult
            Else
                MsgBox "Could not retrieve data."
            End If
        End Sub
```

SQLRetrieve

SQLRetrieve (*ConnectionNum*, [*DestinationRef*], [*MaxColumns*], [*MaxRows*], [*ColNamesLogical*], [*RowNumsLogical*], [*NamedRngLogical*], [*FetchFirstLogical*])

Retrieves all or part of the results from a query executed by SQLExecQuery().

Argument	Description
ConnectionNum	The connection ID returned by SQLOpen().
DestinationRef	A Range object that specifies where the results should be placed. If destination refers to a single cell, SQLRetrieve() returns all the pending results in that cell and in the cells to the right and below it. If you omit this argument, SQLRetrieve() uses the bindings established by SQLBind().
MaxColumns	The maximum number of columns returned to the worksheet, starting at *DestinationRef*. If *MaxColumns* specifies fewer columns than are available in the result, SQLRetrieve() discards the remaining columns. If you omit the *MaxColumns* argument, all the columns are returned.
MaxRows	The maximum number of rows returned to the worksheet. If *MaxRows* specifies fewer rows than are available in the results, SQLRetrieve() discards the remaining rows. If you omit this argument, all the rows are returned. If a query returns *MaxRows*, the query is complete.
ColNamesLogical	True returns the column names as the first row of results; False omits column names. The default is False.
RowNumsLogical	If *DestinationRef* is specified, True uses the first column in the result set as row numbers; False omits row numbers. The default is False.

Argument	Description
NamedRngLogical	True creates a named range for each column of the results; False does not create names. The default is False.
FetchFirstLogical	True retrieves results from the beginning of the result set; False retrieves results in chunks, the size of which are determined by *MaxRows*. When no more rows are in the result set, SQLRequest() returns 0. The default is True.

SQLRetrieve() returns the number of rows in the result set. If SQLRetrieve() cannot retrieve the results, it returns the error value xlErrNA (2042). If no data is found, SQLRetrieve() returns 0.

The following code lines connect to a database, perform a query, and display the results in a new worksheet:

```
Sub ODBCGetData()
    Dim strSQLConnect As String, strSQLQuery As String
    Dim vConnect As Variant, vResult As Variant

    strSQLConnect = "DSN=MS Access _
        Databases;DBQ=c:\mspdoc\nwindms\nwind.mdb;FIL=RedISAM;"

    ' This string is limited to 255 characters.
    strSQLQuery = "SELECT CATEGORIES.""Category Name"", _
        PRODUCTS.""English Name""," & " PRODUCTS.""Units In Stock"", _
        PRODUCTS.""Unit Price"" FROM CATEGORIES" & " CATEGORIES, _
        PRODUCTS PRODUCTS WHERE PRODUCTS.""Category ID"" =" & _
        " CATEGORIES.""Category ID""ORDER BY CATEGORIES." _
        "Category Name"""

    'Connect to the database.
    vConnect = SQLOpen(strSQLConnect, , 2)

    ' Perform query.
    vResult = SQLExecQuery(vConnect, strSQLQuery)

    ' Create a new worksheet.
    With Worksheets.Add
        ' Display results with column headings in the worksheet.
        vResult = SQLRetrieve(vConnect, .Cells(1, 1), , , True)
        ' Format the columns so that they are readable.
        .Columns.AutoFit
    End With

    ' Close database.
    vResult = SQLClose(vConnect)
End Sub
```

SQLRetrieveToFile

SQLRetrieveToFile (*ConnectionNum, Destination, ColNamesLogical, ColumnDelimiter*)

Retrieves all the results from a query executed by `SQLExecQuery()` and places them in a file.

Caution

`SQLRetrieveToFile()` does not work correctly on all machines. In many cases, the function creates a 0-byte file and returns `xlErrNA`. (Microsoft is aware of this problem and may fix it if there is a maintenance release of Excel.)

Argument	Description
ConnectionNum	The connection ID returned by `SQLOpen()`.
Destination	The path and name of the file in which to place the results. If the file exists, `SQLRetrieveToFile()` over-writes it. If the file doesn't exist, the function creates it.
ColNamesLogical	True returns the column names as the first row of results; False omits column names. The default is False.
ColumnDelimiter	Specifies the character used to separate the elements in each row. The default is the Tab character (`Chr$(9)`).

`SQLRetrieveToFile()` creates a file in CSV format and returns the number of rows retrieved. If `SQLRetrieveToFile()` cannot retrieve the results or cannot create the file, it returns the error value `xlErrNA` (2042).

The following code lines open a database, perform a query, and write the results to a file:

```
Sub QueryToFile()
    ' Create connect and query strings.
    strSQLConnect = "DSN=MS Access _
        Databases;DBQ=c:\mspdoc\nwindms\nwind.mdb;FIL=RedISAM;"
    ' This string is limited to 255 characters.
    strSQLQuery = "SELECT CATEGORIES.""Category Name""", _
        PRODUCTS.""English Name""," & " PRODUCTS.""Units In Stock""", _
        PRODUCTS.""Unit Price"" FROM CATEGORIES" & " CATEGORIES, _
        PRODUCTS PRODUCTS WHERE PRODUCTS.""Category ID"" =" & _
        " CATEGORIES.""Category ID""ORDER BY CATEGORIES." _
        "Category Name"""
    'Connect to the database.
    vConnect = SQLOpen(strSQLConnect, , 2)
```

```
        ' Perform query.
        vResult = SQLExecQuery(vConnect, strSQLQuery)
        ' Write the results to a file.
        vResult = SQLRetrieveToFile(vConnect, "C:\EXCEL\RESULTS.CSV")

        ' Close database.
        vResult = SQLClose(vConnect)
End Sub
```

Chapter 13

Creating Charts

Excel can create many styles of high-quality charts and graphs from data on a worksheet (see fig. 13.1). Visual Basic enables you to create all these charts and control all chart attributes.

Fig. 13.1
Types of charts.

In this chapter, you learn how to do the following:

- Create charts using the Chart Wizard.

- Embed charts in a worksheet.

- Create stand-alone chart sheets.

- Change and combine chart types.

This chapter covers the following objects:

    Chart

    ChartArea

```
ChartGroup

ChartGroups

ChartObject

ChartObjects

Charts

ChartTitle
```

Using the Chart Wizard

The `ChartWizard` method enables you to chart data quickly using predefined chart formats. It is a way to get good-looking charts fast, without worrying about chart format details.

Using the Chart Wizard is a two-step process. First, you must create a chart; then call the `ChartWizard` method on the `Chart` object. You can combine these steps into a single line. The following code, for example, charts the selected range:

```
Charts.Add.ChartWizard Selection
```

`Charts.Add` creates a new (blank) chart sheet. `ChartWizard Selection` charts the selected range, filling in the chart.

Similarly, you can create an embedded chart using the `ChartObject` object:

```
ChartObjects.Add(1, 1, 100, 100).Chart.ChartWizard Selection
```

An embedded chart is one that is on a worksheet. With embedded charts, you have to provide the location and size of the object, `(1 , 1, 100, 100)`, and you have to use the object's `Chart` method to get at the contained chart.

`ChartWizard` does a "best guess" for the arguments you omit. By default, the Chart Wizard creates a simple column chart. You can get more involved by specifying a chart type and format. The following code line creates a wireframe 3-D surface chart from the selected data:

```
Charts.Add.ChartWizard Selection, xl3DSurface, 2
```

The Chart Wizard also can modify existing charts. The following code line sets a title for the active chart:

```
ActiveChart.ChartWizard Title:="1994 Health-Care Spending Projections"
```

Embedding Charts in Sheets

The `ChartObjects` collection and `ChartObject` object create and control charts that are embedded in worksheets, chart sheets, or dialog sheets. You use the `ChartObjects` method of the appropriate sheet object to add embedded charts (see fig. 13.2).

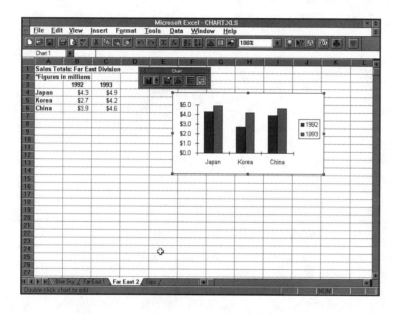

Fig. 13.2
An embedded chart and charting tools.

The `ChartObject` object is similar to drawing objects, such as the `Picture` object. In fact, it shares many of the same methods and properties.

Adding an embedded chart object does not automatically plot the selected data. To display a graph within the embedded chart, you must use the `ChartWizard` or `SeriesCollection` method of the embedded object's `Chart` object, as in the following code:

```
Sub QuickChart( )
    Dim chrtobj As ChartObject
    ' Add a chart object to the worksheet.
    Set chrtobj = ActiveSheet.ChartObjects.Add(100, 100, 200, 200)
    ' Use the UsedRange property to select the range to chart.
    chrtobj.Chart.ChartWizard ActiveSheet.UsedRange
End Sub
```

The `Chart` object and `ChartObjects` collection have specific properties and methods, which are listed in Table 13.1. Properties and methods shown in **bold** are described in the reference section that follows this table. Nonbold items are common to most objects and are described in Chapter 4, "Using Objects."

Tip
Using the `ChartWizard` method to plot and set chart properties is faster than setting the individual properties because this method combines many actions into a single screen update.

II

Programmer's Reference

Tip
The Chart method of ChartObject is the key to using the charting methods and properties, such as ChartWizard. The Chart method returns the contained Chart object for the embedded object.

Table 13.1 ChartObject and ChartObjects properties and methods

Activate	**Interior**[2]
Add[1]	Item[1]
Application[2]	**Left**[2]
Border[2]	**Locked**[2]
BottomRightCell	Name
BringToFront[2]	**OnAction**[2]
Chart	Parent[2]
Copy[2]	**Placement**[2]
CopyPicture[2]	**PrintObject**[2]
Count[1]	**RoundedCorners**[2]
Creator[2]	**Select**[2]
Cut[2]	SendToBack[2]
Delete[2]	Shadow[2]
Duplic**ate**[2]	Top[2]
Enabled[2]	**TopLeftCell**
Group[1]	Visible[2]
Height[2]	Width[2]
Index	ZOrder[2]

[1] *Applies to the ChartObjects collection.*

[2] *Applies to the ChartObjects collection and the ChartObjects object.*

chartobject.Activate()

Activates the Chart object for editing. The following code activates the first embedded chart on a sheet and displays the Chart toolbar:

```
ActiveSheet.ChartObjects(1).Activate
```

chartobjects.Add

chartobjects.Add (*Left, Top, Width, Height*)

Creates a blank Chart object on a sheet and adds it to the worksheet's ChartObjects collection.

Argument	Description
Left	The distance between the left edge of the sheet and the right edge of the Chart object in points.
Top	The distance between the top edge of the sheet and the top edge of the Chart object in points.

Argument	Description
Width	The width of the Chart object in points.
Height	The height of the Chart object in points.

This method does not plot data within the Chart object. To do so, you use the ChartWizard or SeriesCollection method of the object's Chart object. The following code lines add a Chart object and plot the data in the cells A1:C6:

```
Sub QuickChart()
    Dim chrtobj As ChartObject
    ' Add a chart object to the worksheet.
    Set chrtobj = ActiveSheet.ChartObjects.Add(100, 100, 200, 200)
    ' Chart the range A1:C6
    chrtobj.Chart.ChartWizard ActiveSheet.Range("A1:C6")
End Sub
```

chartobject.Border

Returns the Border object for one or all Chart objects on a sheet. Use this property to change the border of an embedded chart. The following code changes the borders of all embedded charts on a sheet to medium weight:

```
ActiveSheet.ChartObjects.Border.Weight = xlMedium
```

chartobject.BottomRightCell

Returns the cell under the bottom right corner of the embedded chart.

chartobject.Chart

Returns the embedded Chart object's contained chart. This method is critical to plotting data and controlling the display of the chart.

The following code lines use the returned Chart object from an embedded chart to plot three series of data and set some of the chart display properties:

```
Sub CreateChart()
    Dim chrtobj As ChartObject
    ' Add a chart object to the worksheet.
    Set chrtobj = ActiveSheet.ChartObjects.Add(100, 100, 200, 200)
    ' Use the Chart method to return the underlying Chart.
    With chrtobj.Chart
        ' Create a data series from a range.
        .SeriesCollection.Add ActiveSheet.Range("A1:C4")
        ' Change the chart type to line chart.
        .Type = xlLine
```

```
                    ' HasTitle creates a default title: "Title".
                    .HasTitle = True
                    ' Change title text.
                    .ChartTitle.Text = "Return on Investment"
                    ' Set the series titles displayed in the legend key.
                    .SeriesCollection(1).Name = "Mutual Funds"
                    .SeriesCollection(2).Name = "Stocks"
                    .SeriesCollection(3).Name = "Bonds"
            End With
    End Sub
```

*chartobject.*Copy( )

Copies one or all chart objects on the sheet to the Clipboard. The following code copies the first Chart object on a sheet to the Clipboard:

```
    ActiveSheet.ChartObjects(1).Copy
```

The following code copies all the Chart objects on a sheet:

```
    ActiveSheet.ChartObjects.Copy
```

*chartobject.*CopyPicture

*chartobject.*CopyPicture ([*Appearance*], [*Format*])

Copies one or all Chart objects on a sheet to the Clipboard using a specific format.

Argument	Description
Appearance	xlScreen copies the chart as it appears on-screen; xlPrinter copies the chart as it would appear if printed using the current printer setup. The default is xlScreen.
Format	xlPicture creates the copy in PICT format; xlBitmap creates the copy as a bitmap. The default is xlPicture.

*chartobject.*Cut( )

Cuts one or all Chart objects on the sheet to the Clipboard. The following code cuts the first Chart object on a sheet to the Clipboard:

```
    ActiveSheet.ChartObject(1).Cut
```

The following code cuts all the Chart objects on a sheet:

```
    ActiveSheet.ChartObjects.Cut
```

chartobject.**Delete( )**

Deletes one or all Chart objects on the sheet. Does not change the contents of the Clipboard. The following code deletes the first Chart object on a sheet to the Clipboard:

```
ActiveSheet.ChartObjects(1).Delete
```

The following code deletes all the Chart objects on a sheet:

```
ActiveSheet.ChartObjects.Delete
```

chartobject.**Duplicate( )**

Makes a copy of one or all Chart objects on a sheet and returns the object (or collection) that was created. The following code duplicates the first Chart object on a sheet and moves it down slightly:

```
ActiveSheet.ChartObjects(1).Duplicate.Top = ChartObjects(1).Top -10
```

chartobject.**Enabled**

Groups a collection of pictures so that you can select, move, copy, or delete them as a single object. The following code groups the first three Chart objects on a sheet:

```
ActiveSheet.ChartObjects(1).Group
ActiveSheet.ChartObjects(2).Group
ActiveSheet.ChartObjects(3).Group
```

chartobjects.**Group**

Groups a collection of embedded charts so that you can select, move, copy, or delete them as a single object. The following code groups all the embedded charts on a sheet:

```
ActiveSheet.ChartObjects.Group
```

chartobject.**Interior**

Returns the Interior object for one or all of the Chart objects on a sheet. Use the Interior object properties to set the shading and color of the interior of Chart objects. The following code shades the interior of all the Chart objects on a sheet:

```
ActiveSheet.ChartObjects.Interior.Pattern = xlGray16
```

*chartobject.*Locked

*chartobject.*Locked [= **True** | **False**]

True prevents changes to one or all the chart on a sheet while the sheet is protected; False allows changes. The default is True.

*chartobject.*OnAction

*chartobject.*OnAction [= *procedure*]

Sets or returns the name of a procedure to run when one or all charts on the sheet are clicked. The following code causes the procedure UpdateChart( ) to run when the user clicks the chart named Inventory:

```
ActiveSheet.ChartObjects("Inventory").OnAction = "UpdateChart"
```

*chartobject.*Placement

*chartobject.*Placement [= **xlMoveAndSize** | **xlMove** | **xlFreeFloating**]

Sets or returns how one or all Chart objects on a sheet are attached to the cells below it. The default is xlFreeFloating.

*chartobject.*PrintObject

*chartobject.*PrintObject [= **True** | **False**]

True prints one or all embedded charts with the worksheet; False does not. The default is True. The following code turns off printing for all the charts on a sheet:

```
ActiveSheet.ChartObjects.PrintObject = False
```

*chartobject.*RoundedCorners

*chartobject.*RoundedCorners [= **True** | **False**]

True rounds the corners of one or all Chart objects; False displays square corners. The default is False.

*chartobject.***Select**

*chartobject.***Select ([*Replace*])**

Selects one or all of the Chart objects on a sheet. Select is the equivalent of clicking on the object. If *Replace* is False, Select extends the current selection rather than deselects previous selections. The default is True.

The following code selects the chart named Inventory and adds it to the list of currently selected items:

```
ActiveSheet.ChartObjects("Inventory").Select False
```

*chartobject.***Shadow**

*chartobject.***Shadow [= True | False]**

True creates a background shadow for one or all the chars on the sheet; False removes the shadow. The default is False.

*chartobject.***TopLeftCell**

Returns the cell that lies under the top-left part of the chart.

Creating and Manipulating Charts

The Charts collection and Chart object create and control chart sheets in a workbook. You use the Charts method of the Workbook object to add chart sheets to a workbook. You use the Chart object to control the data, appearance, and format of the chart (see fig. 13.3).

The Charts collection does not include embedded charts; it includes only stand-alone chart sheets. Embedded charts do have a Chart method, however, which returns their contained Chart object.

The Chart object and Charts collection have specific properties and methods, which are listed in Table 13.2. Properties and methods shown in **bold** are described in the reference section that follows this table. Nonbold items are common to most objects and are described in Chapter 4, "Using Objects."

Fig. 13.3
A chart with its major parts labeled.

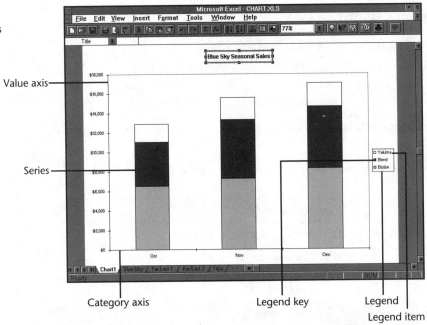

Value axis

Series

Category axis

Legend key

Legend

Legend item

Table 13.2 Chart and Charts properties and methods

Activate	ColumnGroups
Add[1]	Copy[2]
Application[2]	CopyPicture
ApplyDataLabels	Corners
Arcs	Count[1]
Area3DGroup	CreatePublisher
AreaGroups	Creator[2]
AutoFormat	Delete[2]
AutoScaling	DepthPercent
Axes	Deselect
Bar3DGroup	DisplayBlanksAs
BarGroups	DoughnutGroups
Buttons	DrawingObjects
ChartArea	Drawings
ChartGroups	DropDowns
ChartObjects	Elevation
ChartTitle	Evaluate
ChartWizard	Floor
CheckBoxes	GapDepth
CheckSpelling	GroupBoxes
Column3DGroup	GroupObjects

HasAxis	PlotArea
HasLegend	PlotVisibleOnly
HasTitle	Previous
HeightPercent	PrintOut[2]
Index	PrintPreview[2]
Item[1]	Protect
Labels	ProtectContents
Legend	ProtectDrawingObjects
Line3DGroup	RadarGroups
LineGroups	Rectangles
Lines	RightAngleAxes
ListBoxes	Rotation
Move[2]	SaveAs
Name	ScrollBars
Next	Select[2]
OLEObjects	SeriesCollection
OnDoubleClick	SizeWithWindow
OnSheetActivate	Spinners
OnSheetDeactivate	SubType
OptionButtons	SurfaceGroup
Ovals	TextBoxes
PageSetup	Type
Parent[2]	Unprotect
Paste	Visible[2]
Perspective	Walls
Pictures	WallsAndGridlines2D
Pie3DGroup	XYGroups
PieGroups	

[1] *Applies to the* Charts *collection.*

[2] *Applies to the* Charts *collection and the* Chart *object.*

charts.Add

charts.Add ([*Before*], [*After*], [*Count*])

Creates a new chart sheet and adds it to the Charts and Sheets collections.

Argument	Description
Before	The sheet object to insert the new sheet before. For example, Sheets("Sheet1").

(continues)

Argument	Description
After	The sheet object to insert the new sheet after. Don't specify both *Before* and *After*.
Count	The number of sheets to add. The default is 1.

The following code adds a chart sheet to the current workbook:

```
Charts.Add
```

chart.ApplyDataLabels

chart.ApplyDataLabels ([*Type*], [*LegendKey*])

Applies data labels to all series on a chart.

Argument	Description
Type	xlNone does not display data labels; xlShowValue displays each point value as its data label; xlShowLabel displays the category for the point; xlShowPercent displays the percentage of the total (pie and doughnut charts only); xlShowLabelAndPercent displays both the percentage of the total and category for the point (pie and doughnut charts only). The default is xlShowValue.
LegendKey	True shows the legend key next to the point; False omits this symbol. The legend key is the symbol that appears next to the series title in the legend box. The default is False.

The following code displays categories (row or column headings) as labels for the points in the currently active chart:

```
ActiveChart.ApplyDataLabels xlShowLabel
```

chart.Arcs

chart.Arcs ([*Index*])

Returns the arc objects on a chart. The following code adds an arc to the current sheet:

```
ActiveChart.Arcs.Add 70, 30, 40, 100
```

chart.**Area3DGroup**

Returns the `ChartGroup` object for a chart that has a `Type` property setting of `xl3DArea`. A `ChartGroup` object is a section of a chart, such as the bar representing a month. If any series on the chart is set to `xl3DArea`, all of the series are displayed as 3-D area. `Area3DGroup` returns Nothing if the chart is not a 3-D area chart.

> **Note**
>
> Because you can't combine 3-D charts with 2-D charts, all 3-D charts are in only one chart group.

The following code creates a line chart and then changes one of the series to 3-D area (thus changing the entire chart). At the end, the code uses the `Area3DGroup` method to set the subtype of the area chart group.

```
Sub Add3DAreaGroup()
    With Charts.Add
        .Type = xlLine
        ' Create a data series for the chart.
        .SeriesCollection.Add Sheets("Sheet2").Range("A1:C4")
        ' Change all data series to 3DArea:
        .SeriesCollection(3).Type = xl3dArea
        ' Change the area group's subtype
        .Area3DGroup.SubType = 2
        ' Previous line equivalent to the following:
        ' .ChartGroups(1).SubType = 2
    End With
End Sub
```

chart.**AreaGroups**

chart.**AreaGroups** (*[Index]*)

Returns a `ChartGroups` collection containing the `ChartGroup` object for the series on a chart that has a `Type` property setting of `xlArea`. `AreaGroups` returns Nothing if the chart is not an area chart.

> **Note**
>
> The collection returned by the `AreaGroups` method never contains more than one element.

The following code creates a line chart and then charts the same data again using an area chart. At the end, the code uses the `AreaGroups` method to set the subtype of the area chart group.

```
Sub AddAreaGroup( )
    With Charts.Add
        .Type = xlLine
        ' Create a data series for the chart.
        .SeriesCollection.Add Sheets("Sheet2").Range("A1:C4")
        ' Create a new data series for the chart using the same data
        .SeriesCollection.Add Sheets("Sheet2").Range("A1:C4")
        ' Add a chart group for the new data series.
        .SeriesCollection(4).Type = xlArea
        .SeriesCollection(5).Type = xlArea
        .SeriesCollection(6).Type = xlArea
        ' Change the area group's sub-type
        .AreaGroups(1).SubType = 2
        ' Previous line equivalent to the following:
        ' .ChartGroups(2).SubType = 2
    End With
End Sub
```

chart.AutoFormat

chart.AutoFormat (*Gallery*, [*Format*])

Applies a built-in or custom autoformat to a chart.

Argument	Description
Gallery	The type of chart to format built-in types are xl3DArea, xl3DBar, xl3DColumn, xl3DLine, xl3DPie, xl3DSurface, xlArea, xlBar, xlColumn, xlCombination, xlDefaultAutoFormat, xlDoughnut, xlLine, xlPie, xlRadar, and xlXYScatter. Use xlCustom if the format is a custom format.
Format	The index of the format option from the built-in format list or the name of the custom format if *Gallery* is xlAutoformat.

This method corresponds to the AutoFormat dialog box for charts. To display the AutoFormat dialog box in Excel, select a chart and choose Autoformat from the Format menu (see fig. 13.4).

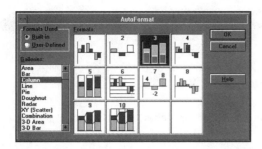

Fig. 13.4
The Chart
AutoFormat
dialog box.

chart.AutoScaling

chart.AutoScaling [= True | False]

True scales a 3-D chart so that it is closer in size to the equivalent 2-D chart;
False does not scale. Valid only if the RightAngleAxes property is True. The
default is True.

chart.Axes

chart.Axes ([*Type*], [*AxisGroup*])

Returns one or all the axes on a chart.

Argument	Description
Type	For 2-D charts: xlValue or xlCategory. For 3-D charts: xlSeries. The default returns all the axes on the chart.
AxisGroup	For 2-D charts: xlPrimary or xlSecondary. For 3-D charts: xlPrimary only. The default returns primary axes.

The following code selects the value axis on a chart:

```
ActiveChart.Axes(xlValue).Select
```

chart.Bar3DGroup

Returns the ChartGroup object for a chart that has a Type property setting of
xl3DBar. If any series on the chart is set to xl3DBar, all of the series are displayed as 3-D bar. Bar3DGroup returns Nothing if the chart is not a 3-D bar
chart.

> **Note**
>
> Because you can't combine 3-D charts with 2-D charts, all 3-D charts are in only one chart group.

The following code creates a line chart and then changes one of the series to 3-D bar (thus changing the entire chart). At the end, the code uses the `Bar3DGroup` method to set the subtype of the bar chart group.

```
Sub Add3DBarGroup( )
    With Charts.Add
        .Type = xlLine
        ' Create a data series for the chart.
        .SeriesCollection.Add Sheets("Sheet2").Range("A1:C4")
        ' Change all data series to 3DBar:
        .SeriesCollection(3).Type = xl3dBar
        ' Change the bar group's sub-type
        .Bar3DGroup.SubType = 2
        ' Previous line equivalent to the following:
        ' .ChartGroups(1).SubType = 2
    End With
End Sub
```

chart.BarGroups

chart.BarGroups ([*Index*])

Returns a `ChartGroups` collection containing the `ChartGroup` object for the series on a chart that has a `Type` property setting of `xlBar`. `BarGroups` returns Nothing if the chart is not a bar chart.

> **Note**
>
> The collection returned by the `BarGroups` method never contains more than one element.

The following lines of code create a line chart and then chart the same data again using a bar chart. At the end, the code uses the `BarGroups` method to set the subtype of the area chart group.

```
Sub AddAreaGroup( )
    With Charts.Add
        .Type = xlLine
        ' Create a data series for the chart.
        .SeriesCollection.Add Sheets("Sheet2").Range("A1:C4")
        ' Create a new data series for the chart using the same data.
        .SeriesCollection.Add Sheets("Sheet2").Range("A1:C4")
        ' Add a chart group for the new data series.
```

```
              .SeriesCollection(4).Type = xlBar
              .SeriesCollection(5).Type = xlBar
              .SeriesCollection(6).Type = xlBar
              ' Change the area group's subtype
              .BarGroups(1).SubType = 2
              ' Previous line equivalent to the following:
              ' .ChartGroups(2).SubType = 2
      End With
End Sub
```

chart.**Buttons**

chart.**Buttons ([*Index*])**

Returns the Buttons object on a chart. The following line of code adds a button to the current chart:

```
ActiveChart.Buttons.Add 20, 20, 60, 40
```

chart.**ChartArea**

Returns the ChartArea object for the chart. You use the ChartArea object to control the appearance of the background area of the chart. The following code changes the background of a chart to red:

```
ActiveChart.ChartArea.Interior.Color = RGB(255, 0, 0)
```

chart.**ChartGroups**

chart.**ChartGroups ([*Index*])**

Returns one or all of the ChartGroup objects in a chart. You create chart groups by setting the chart type of a series to a new type. Use the ChartGroup object to control the appearance of all the series of a specific chart type.

chart.**ChartObjects**

chart.**ChartObjects ([*Index*])**

Returns the chart objects embedded on a chart. The following lines of code add an embedded chart to the current worksheet and then chart the currently selected columns of cells:

```
Sub AddEmbeddedChart()
    Dim chrtobj As ChartObject, rngColumn As Range
    ActiveChart.ChartObjects.Add(100, 100, 200, 200)
    ' Plot some data in the embedded chart
    ActiveChart.ChartObjects(1).SeriesCollection.Add
Sheets("Sheet1").Range("A1:C4")
End Sub
```

*chart.***ChartTitle**

Returns the `ChartTitle` object for a chart. If the chart does not have a title, it returns Nothing. To create a chart title object, set the chart's `HasTitle` property to True. Use the returned `ChartTitle` object to control the text and appearance of the title.

The following code lines create a title on a chart and set the text of the title:

```
Sub AddTitle( )
    ' Create the chart title object.
    ActiveChart.HasTitle = True
    ' Change title text.
    ActiveChart.ChartTitle.Text = "Return on Investment"
End sub
```

*chart.***ChartWizard**

*chart.***ChartWizard ([*Source*], [*Gallery*], [*Format*], [*PlotBy*], [*CategoryLabels*], [*SeriesLabels*], [*HasLegend*], [*Title*], [*CategoryTitle*], [*ValueTitle*], [*ExtraTitle*])**

Controls the most commonly used aspects of a chart. `ChartWizard` does a "best guess" for the arguments you omit.

Tip
Using the `ChartWizard` method to plot and set chart properties is faster than setting the individual properties because it combines many actions into a single screen update.

Argument	Description
Source	A range object indicating the data to chart.
Gallery	Indicates the type of chart to create: xlArea, xlBar, xlColumn, xlLine, xlPie, xlRadar, xlXYScatter, xlCombination, xl3DArea, xl3DBar, xl3DColumn, xl3DLine, xl3DPie, xl3DSurface, or xlDoughnut. The default is based on the type of data in *Source*.
Format	The index of the built-in automatic format from the chart Autoformats dialog box. The default is based on the type of data in *Source*.
PlotBy	xlRows plots data series by rows; xlColumns plots data series by columns. The default is xlColumns.
CategoryLabels	If *Source* contains category labels, the number of rows or columns in *Source* that the labels occupy.
SeriesLabels	If *Source* contains series labels, the number of rows or columns in *Source* that the labels occupy.
HasLegend	True includes a legend in the chart; False omits it. The default is True.

Argument	Description
Title	The title of the chart. The default is no title.
CategoryTitle	The title of the category axis. The default is no title.
ValueTitle	The title of the value axis. The default is no title.
ExtraTitle	For 2-D charts, the second title for the value axis. For 3-D charts, the title of the series axis. The default is no title.

The following code line sets the title but does not change other aspects of the active chart:

```
ActiveChart.ChartWizard title:="New Title"
```

chart.**CheckBoxes**

chart.**CheckBoxes ([*Index*])**

Returns the check boxes on a chart. The following code adds a check box to the current chart:

```
ActiveChart.CheckBoxes.Add 10, 20, 80, 10
```

chart.**CheckSpelling**

chart.**CheckSpelling ([*CustomDictionary*], [*IgnoreUppercase*], [*AlwaysSuggest*])**

Checks the spelling of the words in a chart.

Argument	Description
CustomDictionary	A string indicating the file name of the custom dictionary to examine if the word is not found in the main dictionary. If omitted, the currently specified dictionary is used. The default is None.
IgnoreUppercase	True ignores the spelling of words in all uppercase characters; False checks the spelling of all words. The default is False.
AlwaysSuggest	True displays a list of suggested alternate spellings when an incorrect spelling is found; False prompts the user for the correct spelling. The default is False.

The following code checks the spelling of all the text on the active chart:

```
ActiveChart.CheckSpelling
```

*chart.*Column3DGroup

Returns the `ChartGroup` object for a chart that has a `Type` property setting of `xl3DColumn`. If any series on the chart is set to `xl3DColumn`, all of the series are displayed as 3-D columns. `Column3DGroup` returns Nothing if the chart is not a 3-D column chart.

The following lines of code create a line chart and then change one of the series to a 3-D column (thus changing the entire chart). At the end, the code uses the `Column3DGroup` method to set the subtype of the column chart group.

```
Sub Add3DBarGroup( )
    With Charts.Add
        .Type = xlLine
        ' Create a data series for the chart.
        .SeriesCollection.Add Sheets("Sheet2").Range("A1:C4")
        ' Change all data series to 3DColumn:
        .SeriesCollection(3).Type = 3DColumn
        ' Change the column group's subtype
        .Column3DGroup.SubType = 2
        ' Previous line equivalent to the following:
        ' .ChartGroups(1).SubType = 2
    End With
End Sub
```

*chart.*ColumnGroups

*chart.*ColumnGroups ([*Index*])

Returns a `ChartGroups` collection containing the `ChartGroup` object for the series on a chart that has a `Type` property setting of `xlColumn`. `ColumnGroups` returns Nothing if the chart is not a column chart.

The following code lines create a line chart and then chart the same data again using a column chart. At the end, the code uses the `ColumnGroups` method to set the subtype of the column chart group.

```
Sub AddAreaGroup( )
    With Charts.Add
        .Type = xlLine
        ' Create a data series for the chart.
        .SeriesCollection.Add Sheets("Sheet2").Range("A1:C4")
        ' Create a new data series for the chart using the same data.
        .SeriesCollection.Add Sheets("Sheet2").Range("A1:C4")
        ' Add a chart group for the new data series.
```

```
            .SeriesCollection(4).Type = xlColumn
            .SeriesCollection(5).Type = xlColumn
            .SeriesCollection(6).Type = xlColumn
            ' Change the column group's subtype
            .ColumnGroups(1).SubType = 2
            ' Previous line equivalent to the following:
            ' .ChartGroups(2).SubType = 2
        End With
    End Sub
```

chart.Copy

chart.Copy ([*Before*], [*After*])

Copies one or all of the chart sheets to a new location in a workbook.

Argument	Description
Before	The sheet object to insert the new sheets before; for example, Sheets("Sheet1").
After	The sheet object to insert the new sheets after. Don't specify both *Before* and *After*.

If both *Before* and *After* are omitted, Copy creates a new workbook to contain the sheets. The following line creates a new workbook containing a copy of all the charts in the current workbook:

```
    Charts.Copy
```

To copy an individual chart sheet, use a single Chart object. The following code line creates a copy of the active chart and adds it to the Charts collection:

```
    ActiveChart.Copy Before:=ActiveChart
```

chart.CopyPicture

chart.CopyPicture ([*Appearance*], [*Format*], [*Size*])

Copies a chart to the Clipboard using a bit-map or picture format.

Argument	Description
Appearance	xlScreen copies the chart as it appears on-screen; xlPrinter copies the chart as it would appear if printed using the current printer setup. The default is xlPrinter.

(continues)

Argument	Description
Format	xlPicture creates the copy in PICT format; xlBitmap creates the copy as a bitmap. The default is xlPicture.
Size	xlScreen sizes the picture to match the size displayed on-screen; xlPrinter sizes the picture to match the printed size. The default is xlPrinter.

*chart.*Corners

Returns the Corners object of a 3-D chart. If the chart is not 3-D, it causes error 1004. Use the Corners object to select the corners of a 3-D chart so that the user can rotate the chart. The following code line selects the corners of a 3-D chart, which is the only thing you can do with the Corners object:

```
ActiveChart.Corners.Select
```

*chart.*CreatePublisher

*chart.*CreatePublisher ([*Edition*], [*Appearance*], [*Size*], [*ContainsPICT*], [*ContainsBIFF*], [*ContainsRTF*], [*ContainsVALU*])

Macintosh System 7.0 or later only. Creates a publisher for a chart.

Argument	Description
Edition	The file name of the edition to create. The default is based on the current document name.
Appearance	xlPrinter creates the edition at printer resolution; xlScreen creates the edition at screen resolution. The default is xlPrinter.
ContainsPICT	True includes PICT format data. The default is True.
ContainsBIFF	True includes BIFF format data. The default is True.
ContainsRTF	True includes RTF format data. The default is True.
ContainsVALU	True includes VALU format data. The default is True.

chart.**Delete( )**

Deletes one or all of the chart sheets in a workbook. The following code deletes the chart named `Inventory`:

```
Charts("Inventory").Delete
```

chart.**DepthPercent**

chart.**DepthPercent [= *percentage*]**

Sets or returns the depth of a 3-D chart as a percentage of the chart width. Must be between 20 and 2000. The default is 200.

chart.**Deselect( )**

Cancels the selection of a chart.

chart.**DisplayBlanksAs**

chart.**DisplayBlanksAs [= *setting*]**

`xlNotPlotted` omits blank cells from plotted series; `xlInterpolated` interpolates the values of blank cells based on the other values in the series; or `xlZero` plots blank cells as zero values. The default is `xlNotPlotted`.

chart.**DoughnutGroups**

chart.**DoughnutGroups ([*Index*])**

Returns a `ChartGroups` collection containing the `ChartGroup` object for the series on a chart that has a `Type` property setting of `xlDoughnut`. `DoughnutGroups` returns Nothing if the chart is not a doughnut chart.

The following code lines create a line chart and then chart the same data again using a doughnut chart:

```
Sub AddAreaGroup()
    With Charts.Add
        .Type = xlLine
        ' Create a data series for the chart.
        .SeriesCollection.Add Sheets("Sheet2").Range("A1:C4")
        ' Create a new data series for the chart using the same data.
        .SeriesCollection.Add Sheets("Sheet2").Range("A1:C4")
        ' Add a chart group for the new data series.
        .SeriesCollection(4).Type = xlColumn
        .SeriesCollection(5).Type = xlColumn
        .SeriesCollection(6).Type = xlColumn
    End With
End Sub
```

chart.**DrawingObjects**

chart.**DrawingObjects ([*Index*])**

Returns one or all of the drawing objects on a chart. *Drawing objects* are those objects shown on the Drawing toolbar. Besides shapes, they also include buttons and drop-down lists. The following code selects all the drawing objects on a chart:

```
ActiveChart.DrawingObjects.Select
```

The following code line selects a drawing object named Text1 on the chart:

```
ActiveChart.DrawingObjects("Text1").Select
```

chart.**Drawings**

chart.**Drawings ([*Index*])**

Returns one or all of the freehand drawing objects on a chart. The following code selects all the drawing objects on a chart:

```
ActiveChart.Drawings .Select
```

The following code line selects the first drawing object on the chart:

```
ActiveChart.Drawings(1).Select
```

chart.**DropDowns**

chart.**DropDowns ([*Index*])**

Returns one or all of the DropDown objects on a chart. The following code selects all the drawing objects on a chart:

```
ActiveChart.Drawings .Select
```

The following code line selects the first freehand drawing on the chart:

```
ActiveChart.Drawings(1).Select
```

chart.**Elevation**

chart.**Elevation [= *degrees*]**

Sets or returns the angle at which you view a 3-D chart. If the chart is not a 3-D chart, setting this property causes error 1005. Must be between –90 and 90 for most types; between 0 and 44 for 3-D bar charts. The default is 15.

chart.**Floor**

Returns the `Floor` object of a 3-D chart. If the chart is not 3-D, this method still returns a `Floor` object, but you can't set its properties. You use the `Floor` object to control the display of the floor of a 3-D chart.

The following code line makes the floor of a 3-D chart red:

```
ActiveChart.Floor.Interior.Color = RGB(255,0,0)
```

chart.**GapDepth**

chart.**GapDepth** [= *percentage*]

Sets or returns the distance between the data series in a 3-D chart as a percentage of the marker width. Ignored for 2-D charts. Must be between 0 and 500. The default is 50.

chart.**GroupBoxes**

chart.**GroupBoxes** ([*Index*])

Returns one or all of the freehand `GroupBox` objects on a chart. The following code selects all the `GroupBox` objects on a chart:

```
ActiveChart.GroupBoxes.Select
```

The following code line selects the first `GroupBox` object on the chart:

```
ActiveChart.GroupBoxes(1).Select
```

chart.**GroupObjects**

chart.**GroupObjects** ([*Index*])

Returns one or all of the grouped drawing objects on a chart. The following code adds some random drawing objects, groups the objects, and then moves them down slightly:

```
Sub GroupObjects()
    ActiveChart.Lines.Add 10, 10, 29, 49
    ActiveChart.Rectangles.Add 10, 10, 29, 49
    ActiveChart.Ovals.Add 10, 10, 29, 49
    ActiveChart.DrawingObjects.Group
    MsgBox ActiveChart.GroupObjects(1).Top = _
    ActiveChart.GroupObjects(1).Top + 20
End Sub
```

chart.**HasAxis**

chart.**HasAxis [=** *array*]

Sets or returns a two-dimensional array of Boolean values that indicate which axes exist on a chart. The first dimension of *array* indicates the axis: xlCategory, xlValue, or xlSeries. The second *array* dimension indicates the axis group: xlPrimary or xlSecondary. Series axes apply only to 3-D charts, and 3-D charts have only one set of axes.

The following code lines display two axes for the value axis and none for the categories axis:

```
Sub SetAxes( )
    With ActiveChart
        .HasAxis(xlValue, xlPrimary) = True
        .HasAxis(xlValue, xlSecondary) = True
        .HasAxis(xlCategory, xlPrimary) = False
    End With
End Sub
```

Axes may be deleted or created if you change the chart type or AxisGroup property.

chart.**HasLegend**

chart.**HasLegend [= True | False]**

True creates a Legend object for the chart; False removes the object. The default is True.

chart.**HasTitle**

chart.**HasTitle [= True | False]**

True creates a ChartTitle object for the chart; False removes the object. The default is False.

The following code lines create a title for a chart and set the text in a chart:

```
Sub ChartTitle( )
    ActiveChart.HasTitle = True
    ActiveChart.ChartTitle.Text = "Current Inventory"
End Sub
```

chart.**HeightPercent**

Sets or returns the height of a 3-D chart as a percentage of the chart width. Ignored for 2-D charts. The default is 100.

chart.**Index**

Returns the position of the chart sheet in the tab order.

chart.**Labels**

chart.**Labels ([*Index*])**

Returns one or all of the `Label` objects on a chart. The following code selects all the `Label` objects on a chart:

```
ActiveChart.Label.Select
```

The following code line selects the first `Label` object on the chart:

```
ActiveChart.Label(1).Select
```

chart.**Legend**

Returns the `Legend` object for a chart. Returns Nothing if the chart does not have a legend. Use the `HasLegend` property to create a legend for a chart. You use the `Legend` object to control the display of a chart's legend.

The following code moves a chart's legend to the top of the chart:

```
ActiveChart.Legend.Top = 1
```

chart.**Line3DGroup**

Returns the `ChartGroup` object for a chart that has a `Type` property setting of `xl3DLine`. If any series on the chart is set to `xl3DLine`, all of the series are displayed as 3-D column. `Line3DGroup` returns Nothing if the chart is not a 3-D line chart.

The following lines of code create a line chart and then change one of the series to 3-D line (thus changing the entire chart). At the end, the code uses the `Line3DGroup` method to set the subtype of the column chart group.

```
Sub Add3DLineGroup()
    With Charts.Add
        .Type = xlLine
        ' Create a data series for the chart.
        .SeriesCollection.Add Sheets("Sheet2").Range("A1:C4")
        ' Change all data series to xl3DLine:
        .SeriesCollection(3).Type = xl3DLine
        ' Change the column group's subtype
        .Line3DGroup.SubType = 2
        ' Previous line equivalent to the following:
        ' .ChartGroups(1).SubType = 2
    End With
End Sub
```

chart.**LineGroups**

chart.**LineGroups** ([*Index*])

Returns a ChartGroups collection containing the ChartGroup object for the series on a chart that has a Type property setting of xlLine. LineGroups returns Nothing if the chart does not contain a line chart series.

The following code creates a bar chart and then charts the same data again using a line chart. At the end, the code uses the LineGroups method to set the subtype of the line chart group.

```
Sub AddLineGroup( )
    With Charts.Add
        .Type = xlBar
        ' Create a data series for the chart.
        .SeriesCollection.Add Sheets("Sheet2").Range("A1:C4")
        ' Create a new data series for the chart using the same data.
        .SeriesCollection.Add Sheets("Sheet2").Range("A1:C4")
        ' Add a chart group for the new data series.
        .SeriesCollection(4).Type = xlLine
        .SeriesCollection(5).Type = xlLine
        .SeriesCollection(6).Type = xlLine
        ' Change the column group's subtype
        .LineGroups(1).SubType = 2
        ' Previous line equivalent to the following:
        ' .ChartGroups(2).SubType = 2
    End With
End Sub
```

chart.**Lines**

chart.**Lines** ([*Index*])

Returns one or all of the Line objects on a chart. The following code selects all the Line objects on a chart:

```
ActiveChart.Lines.Select
```

The following code line selects the first Line object on the chart:

```
ActiveChart.Lines(1).Select
```

chart.**ListBoxes**

chart.**ListBoxes** ([*Index*])

Returns one or all of the ListBox objects on a chart. The following code selects all the ListBox objects on a chart:

```
ActiveChart.ListBoxes.Select
```

The following code line selects the first `Drawing` object on the chart:

```
ActiveChart.ListBoxes(1).Select
```

chart.Move

chart.Move ([*Before*], [*After*])

Changes the order of sheets in a workbook.

Argument	Description
Before	The sheet object to move the chart sheet before. For example, Sheets("Sheet1").
After	The sheet object to move the chart sheet after.

You must specify either *Before* or *After*, but not both. The following code moves the Inventory chart after sheet 4:

```
Charts("Inventory").Move After:=Sheets("Sheet4")
```

chart.Next

Returns the next chart sheet. The following code line selects the next chart sheet in a workbook:

```
ActiveChart.Next.Select
```

chart.OLEObjects

chart.OLEObjects ([*Index*])

Returns one or all of the `OLEObject` objects on a chart. The following code adds an embedded Word version 6.0 document to a chart and activates it for editing:

```
ActiveChart.OLEObjects.Add("Word.Document.6", , False, _
    False).Activate
```

chart.OnDoubleClick

chart.OnDoubleClick [= *procedure*]

Sets or returns the name of a procedure to run when the user double-clicks the chart. *procedure* is not run if Visual Basic activates the chart.

chart.**OnSheetActivate**

chart.**OnSheetActivate** [= *procedure*]

Sets or returns the name of a procedure to run when the user activates the chart. *procedure* is not run if Visual Basic activates the chart.

chart.**OnSheetDeactivate**

chart.**OnSheetDeactivate** [= *procedure*]

Sets or returns the name of a procedure to run when the user deactivates the chart by switching to another sheet or object. *procedure* is not run if Visual Basic deactivates the chart.

chart.**OptionButtons**

chart.**OptionButtons** ([*Index*])

Returns one or all of the OptionButton objects on a chart. The following code selects all the OptionButton objects on a chart:

```
ActiveChart.OptionButtons.Select
```

The following code line selects the first OptionButton object on the chart:

```
ActiveChart.OptionButtons(1).Select
```

chart.**Ovals**

chart.**Ovals** ([*Index*])

Returns one or all of the Oval objects on a chart. The following code selects all the Oval objects on a chart:

```
ActiveChart.Ovals.Select
```

The following line of code selects the first Oval object on the chart:

```
ActiveChart.Ovals(1).Select
```

chart.**PageSetup**

Returns the PageSetup object for the chart. You use the returned PageSetup object to control the printing and layout attributes of the chart.

The following code sets the scaling method you use when printing a chart sheet:

```
ActiveSheet.PageSetup.ChartSize = xlScreenSize
```

chart.Paste

chart.Paste ([*Type*])

Pastes a chart from the Clipboard to the specified chart. *Type* specifies the type of information to paste from the chart to the Clipboard: xlFormats, xlFormulas, xlAll. The default is xlAll.

chart.Perspective

chart.Perspective [= *angle*]

Sets or returns the perspective for the 3-D chart view. Must be between 0 and 100. This property is ignored if the RightAngleAxes property is True or if the chart is 2-D. The default is 30.

chart.Pictures

chart.Pictures ([*Index*])

Returns one or all of the Picture objects on a chart. The following code selects all the Picture objects on a chart:

```
ActiveChart.Pictures.Select
```

The following code line selects the first Picture object on the chart:

```
ActiveChart.Pictures(1).Select
```

chart.Pie3DGroup

Returns the ChartGroup object for a chart that has a Type property setting of xl3DPie. If any series on the chart is set to xl3DPie, all of the series are displayed as 3-D pie. Pie3DGroup returns Nothing if the chart is not a 3-D pie chart.

The following code lines create a line chart and then change one of the series to 3-D pie (thus changing the entire chart). At the end, the code uses the Pie3DGroup method to set the subtype of the pie chart group.

```
Sub Add3DLineGroup( )
    With Charts.Add
        .Type = xlLine
        ' Create a data series for the chart.
        .SeriesCollection.Add Sheets("Sheet2").Range("A1:C4")
        ' Change all data series to xl3DPie:
        .SeriesCollection(3).Type = xl3DPie
        ' Change the column group's subtype
        .Pie3DGroup.SubType = 2
```

```
                         ' Previous line equivalent to the following:
                         ' .ChartGroups(1).SubType = 2
                End With
        End Sub
```

chart.**PieGroups**

chart.**PieGroups ([*Index*])**

Returns a ChartGroups collection containing the ChartGroup object for the series on a chart that has a Type property setting of xlPie. PieGroups returns Nothing if the chart does not contain a pie chart series.

The following code creates a bar chart and then charts the same data again using a pie chart. At the end, the code uses the PieGroups method to set the subtype of the pie chart group.

```
        Sub AddLineGroup( )
                With Charts.Add
                        .Type = xlBar
                        ' Create a data series for the chart.
                        .SeriesCollection.Add Sheets("Sheet2").Range("A1:C4")
                        ' Create a new data series for the chart using the same data.
                        .SeriesCollection.Add Sheets("Sheet2").Range("A1:C4")
                        ' Add a chart group for the new data series.
                        .SeriesCollection(4).Type = xlPie
                        .SeriesCollection(5).Type = xlPie
                        .SeriesCollection(6).Type = xlPie
                        ' Change the column group's subtype
                        .PieGroups(1).SubType = 2
                        ' Previous line equivalent to the following:
                        ' .ChartGroups(2).SubType = 2
                End With
        End Sub
```

chart.**PlotArea**

Returns the PlotArea object for the chart. You use the PlotArea object to control the background immediately behind the plotted series. The following code changes the color of the plot area to green:

```
        ActiveChart.PlotArea.Interior.Color = RGB(0, 255, 0)
```

The following line of code restores the default formatting for the plot area:

```
        ActiveChart.PlotArea.ClearFormats
```

chart.**PlotVisibleOnly**

chart.**PlotVisibleOnly [= True | False]**

True plots only visible cells; False plots visible and hidden cells. The default is True.

chart.**Previous**

Returns the previous chart sheet in the sheets tab order. The following code selects the previous chart sheet:

```
ActiveSheet.Previous.Select
```

chart.**PrintOut**

chart.**PrintOut ([*From*], [*To*], [*Copies*], [*Preview*])**

Prints one or all charts in a workbook.

Argument	Description
From	The number of the first page to print. The default is 1.
To	The number of the last page to print. The default is All.
Copies	The number of copies to print. The default is 1.
Preview	True previews the output on-screen before printing; False prints without previewing. The default is False.

The following code line prints all the charts in a workbook:

```
Charts.PrintOut
```

The following code prints only the active chart:

```
ActiveChart.PrintOut
```

chart.**PrintPreview( )**

Previews the print output of one or all charts on-screen. The following code previews all the charts in a workbook:

```
Charts.PrintPreview
```

The following code line previews only the active chart:

```
ActiveChart.PrintPreview
```

chart.**Protect**

chart.**Protect ([*Password*], [*DrawingObjects*], [*Contents*], [*Scenarios*])**

Prevents changes to various features of a chart.

Argument	Description
Password	The password required to unprotect the chart. The default is None.
DrawingObjects	True prevents changes to drawing objects; False allows changes. The default is True.
Contents	True prevents changes to the contents of the chart; False allows changes. The default is True.
Scenarios	Ignored for charts.

chart.**ProtectContents**

Returns True if the chart contents are protected from changes; otherwise, returns False.

chart.**ProtectDrawingObjects**

Returns True if drawing objects are protected from changes; otherwise, returns False.

chart.**RadarGroups**

chart.**RadarGroups ([*Index*])**

Returns a ChartGroups collection containing the ChartGroup object for the series on a chart that has a Type property setting of xlRadar. RadarGroups returns Nothing if the chart does not contain a radar chart series.

The following lines of code create a bar chart and then chart the same data again using a radar chart. At the end, the code uses the RadarGroups method to set the subtype of the radar chart group.

```
Sub AddLineGroup( )
    With Charts.Add
        .Type = xlBar
```

```
          ' Create a data series for the chart.
          .SeriesCollection.Add Sheets("Sheet2").Range("A1:C4")
          ' Create a new data series for the chart using the same data.
          .SeriesCollection.Add Sheets("Sheet2").Range("A1:C4")
          ' Add a chart group for the new data series.
          .SeriesCollection(4).Type = xlRadar
          .SeriesCollection(5).Type = xlRadar
          .SeriesCollection(6).Type = xlRadar
          ' Change the radar group's subtype
          .RadarGroups(1).SubType = 2
          ' Previous line equivalent to the following:
          ' .ChartGroups(2).SubType = 2
     End With
End Sub
```

chart.**Rectangles**

chart.**Rectangles ([*Index*])**

Returns one or all of the Rectangle objects on a chart. The following code selects all the Rectangle objects on a chart:

```
ActiveChart.Rectangles.Select
```

The following code selects the first Rectangle object on the chart:

```
ActiveChart.Rectangles(1).Select
```

chart.**RightAngleAxes**

chart.**RightAngleAxes [= True | False]**

True displays chart axes at right angles, independent of chart rotation or elevation. Applies only to 3-D line, column, and bar charts; ignored for all other chart types. The default is False.

If RightAngleAxes is True, the Perspective property is ignored.

chart.**Rotation**

chart.**Rotation [= *degrees*]**

Sets or returns the rotation of the 3-D chart view in degrees. Must be between 0 and 360, except for 3-D bar charts, where the value must be between 0 and 44. Ignored for 2-D charts. The default is 20.

II

Programmer's Reference

*chart.*SaveAs

*chart.*SaveAs (*Filename, [FileFormat], [Password], [WriteResPassword], [ReadOnlyRecommended], [CreateBackup]*)

Saves a chart to disk.

Argument	Description
Filename	The name of the file used to save the chart. The default is to the current sheet name.
FileFormat	A constant that determines the format of the file to save. See the Workbook object's FileFormat property for a list of these constants. The default is xlNormal.
Password	A password the user must enter to open the file. The default is None.
WriteResPassword	A password the user must enter to open the file for write access. The default is None.
ReadOnlyRecommended	True causes Excel to display a message recommending read-only access when the file is opened for write access; False causes Excel to not display the message. The default is False.
CreateBackup	True saves the previous version of the file using the BAK extension; False saves only the current version. The default is False.

*chart.*ScrollBars

*chart.*ScrollBars (*[Index]*)

Returns one or all of the ScrollBar objects on a chart. The following code selects all the ScrollBar objects on a chart:

```
ActiveChart.ScrollBars.Select
```

The following code selects the first ScrollBar object on the chart:

```
ActiveChart.ScrollBars(1).Select
```

*chart.*Select

*chart.*Select (*[Replace]*)

Selects one or all chart sheets in a workbook. If *Replace* is True, the chart is added to the current selection list; if False, other selections are cancelled. The default is False.

The following code selects the chart sheet named Inventory:

```
Charts("Inventory").Select
```

The following code selects all chart sheets in the workbook (it does not select embedded charts):

```
Charts.Select
```

chart.SeriesCollection
chart.SeriesCollection ([*Index*])

Returns one or all Series objects from a chart. A *series* is a set of points plotted for a single category of data. On a line chart, the SeriesCollection method corresponds to all the points on a single line. You use the Series and SeriesCollection objects to plot data on a chart.

The following code adds a single series (a single column of data) to a chart:

```
ActiveChart.SeriesCollection.Add Sheets("Sheet1").Range("A1:A4")
```

The following code adds four series (four columns of data) to a chart:

```
ActiveChart.SeriesCollection.Add Sheets("Sheet1").Range("A1:D4")
```

You can change the chart type of a series to display multiple types of charts (ChartGroups) on a single chart. The following line of code displays a series as a pie chart:

```
ActiveChart.SeriesCollection(1).Type = xlPie
```

chart.SizeWithWindow
chart.SizeWithWindow [= True | False]

True resizes the chart to match the size of the chart sheet window; False does not. Ignored for embedded charts. The default is False.

chart.Spinners
chart.Spinners ([*Index*])

Returns one or all of the Spinner objects on a chart. The following code selects all the Spinner objects on a chart:

```
ActiveChart.Spinners.Select
```

The following code selects the first Spinner object on the chart:

```
ActiveChart.Spinners(1).Select
```

chart.SubType

chart.SubType [= *index*]

Sets or returns the subtype for all chart groups in the chart. `index` corresponds to the index of the subtype in the Chart Types options dialog box. Each chart type has a different number of subtypes. To see the possible subtypes in Excel, select a chart and choose Chart Types from the Format menu; then choose Options. Use the `SubType` property of the `ChartGroup` object to change the subtype of a single chart group.

chart.SurfaceGroup

Returns the `ChartGroup` object for a chart that has a `Type` property setting of `xl3DSurface`. If any series on the chart is set to `xl3DSurface`, all of the series are displayed as surface charts. `SurfaceGroup` returns Nothing if the chart is not a surface chart.

The following lines of code create a line chart and then change one of the series to `xl3DSurface` (thus changing the entire chart). At the end, the code uses the `SurfaceGroup` method to set the subtype of the surface chart group.

```
Sub Add3DLineGroup( )
    With Charts.Add
        .Type = xlLine
        ' Create a data series for the chart.
        .SeriesCollection.Add Sheets("Sheet2").Range("A1:C4")
        ' Change all data series to xl3DSurface:
        .SeriesCollection(3).Type = xl3DSurface
        ' Change the surface group's subtype
        .SurfaceGroup.SubType = 2
        ' Previous line equivalent to the following:
        ' .ChartGroups(1).SubType = 2
    End With
End Sub
```

chart.TextBoxes

chart.TextBoxes ([*Index*])

Returns one or all of the `TextBox` objects on a chart. The following code selects all the `TextBox` objects on a chart:

```
ActiveChart.TextBoxes.Select
```

The following line of code selects the first `TextBox` object on the chart:

```
ActiveChart.TextBoxes(1).Select
```

chart.Type

chart.Type [= *setting*]

Sets or returns the type for all chart groups in the chart: xlArea, xlBar, xlColumn, xlLine, xlPie, xlRadar, xlXYScatter, xlCombination, xl3DArea, xl3DBar, xl3DColumn, xl3DLine, xl3DPie, xl3DSurface, or xlDoughnut. The default is xlColumn.

The following code changes the active chart to a 3-D bar chart:

```
ActiveChart.Type = xl3DBar
```

To change the type of a single chart group, use the ChartGroup object.

chart.Unprotect

chart.Unprotect ([*Password*])

Changes a protected chart sheet to unprotected (changes allowed). *Password* is required if the protection was set using a password.

chart.Walls

Returns the Walls object of a 3-D chart. For 2-D charts, returns Nothing. You use the Walls object to control the display of the area immediately behind and below plotted 3-D data.

The following code sets the color of the walls on a 3-D chart to red:

```
ActiveChart.Walls.Interior.Color = RGB(255, 0, 0)
```

chart.WallsAndGridlines2D

chart.WallsAndGridlines2D [= True | False]

True draws grid lines in 2-D on a 3-D chart; False draws them in 3-D. Ignored for 2-D charts. The default is False.

chart.XYGroups

chart.XYGroups ([*Index*])

Returns a ChartGroups collection containing the ChartGroup object for the series on a chart that has a Type property setting of xlXYScatter. XYGroups returns Nothing if the chart does not contain a scatter chart series.

The following code creates a bar chart and then charts the same data again using a scatter chart. At the end, the code uses the XYGroups method to set the subtype of the scatter chart group.

```
Sub AddLineGroup( )
    With Charts.Add
        .Type = xlBar
        ' Create a data series for the chart.
        .SeriesCollection.Add Sheets("Sheet2").Range("A1:C4")
        ' Create a new data series for the chart using the same data.
        .SeriesCollection.Add Sheets("Sheet2").Range("A1:C4")
        ' Add a chart group for the new data series.
        .SeriesCollection(4).Type = xlXYScatter
        .SeriesCollection(5).Type = xlXYScatter
        .SeriesCollection(6).Type = xlXYScatter
        ' Change the scatter group's subtype
        .XYGroups(1).SubType = 2
        ' Previous line equivalent to the following:
        ' .ChartGroups(2).SubType = 2
    End With
End Sub
```

Creating a Chart Title

The ChartTitle object controls the text and appearance of the title on a chart. You use the HasTitle property of the Chart object to create a title on a chart. Use the ChartTitle method of the Chart object to get the ChartTitle object for a chart.

The following lines of code add a title to a chart and set its text:

```
Sub SetChartTitle( )
    ActiveChart.HasTitle = True
    ActiveChart.ChartTitle.Text = "Sales Projections"
End Sub
```

The ChartTitle object has specific properties and methods, which are listed in Table 13.3. Properties and methods shown in **bold** are described in the reference section that follows this table. Nonbold items are common to most objects and are described in Chapter 4, "Using Objects."

Table 13.3 ChartTitle properties and methods

Application	**Delete**
Border	**Font**
Caption	**HorizontalAlignment**
Characters	**Interior**
Creator	**Left**

Name	Shadow
Orientation	Text
Parent	Top
Select	VerticalAlignment

*charttitle.*Border

Returns the Border object for the chart title. If a chart does not have a border, the returned Border object has Linestyle xlNone.

*charttitle.*Caption

*charttitle.*Caption [= text]

Same as the Text property.

*charttitle.*Characters

*charttitle.*Characters ([*Start*], [*Length*])

Returns a Characters object representing the text or a portion of the text from the title. Use the returned Characters object to format all or part of the text in a chart title.

Argument	Description
Start	The position of the first character to return. The default is 1.
Length	The number of characters to return. The default is the number of characters between *Start* and the end of the text in the title.

The following code makes the first five characters in a title bold:

```
ActiveChart.ChartTitle.Characters(1, 5).Font.Bold = True
```

*charttitle.*Delete( )

Removes the title from a chart.

*charttitle.*Font

Returns the Font object for the chart title. The following code line makes the title italic:

```
ActiveChart.ChartTitle.Font.Italic = True
```

*charttitle.*HorizontalAlignment

*charttitle.*HorizontalAlignment [= *setting*]

xlLeft left aligns text; xlRight right aligns text; xlCenter centers text. The default is xlLeft.

*charttitle.*Interior

Returns the Interior object for the chart title. Use the Interior object properties to set the shading and color of the interior of the title. The following code shades the interior of the entire title:

```
ActiveChart.ChartTitle.Interior.Pattern = xlGray16
```

*charttitle.*Orientation

*charttitle.*Orientation [= *setting*]

Sets or returns the orientation of text displayed in the title: xlHorizontal, xlVertical, xlUpward, or xlDownward. The default is xlHorizontal.

*charttitle.*Select( )

Selects the title of a chart.

*charttitle.*Shadow

*charttitle.*Shadow [= **True** | **False**]

True creates a background shadow for the title; False removes the shadow. The default is False.

*charttitle.*Text

*charttitle.*Text [= *text*]

Sets or returns the text displayed in the chart title. The default is Title.

charttitle.**VerticalAlignment**

charttitle.**VerticalAlignment [= *setting*]**

Sets or returns the vertical alignment of the title: xlBottom, xlCenter, xlDistributed, xlJustify, or xlTop. The default is xlTop.

Working with Multiple Chart Groups

The ChartGroups collection and ChartGroup object can be a series that is charted as a specific chart type. You set the Type property of a Series to create a ChartGroup, and you use the ChartObjects method of the Chart object to get a ChartGroup object.

The following lines of code create a chart and add a new chart group (see fig. 13.5):

```
Sub CreateChartGroup()
    ' Create a bar chart.
    Charts.Add.ChartWizard Sheets("Sheet1").Range("A1:D4"), xlBar
    'Change one of the series to a pie chart (creates a new _
     chart group)
    ActiveChart.SeriesCollection(4).Type = xlPie
End Sub
```

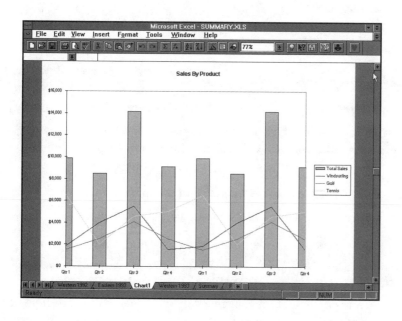

Fig. 13.5
A chart with multiple chart groups.

Programmer's Reference

II

The `ChartGroup` object and `ChartGroups` collection have specific properties and methods, which are listed in Table 13.4. Properties and methods shown in **bold** are described in the reference section that follows this table. Nonbold items are common to most objects and are described in Chapter 4, "Using Objects."

Table 13.4 ChartGroup and ChartGroups properties and methods

Application[2]	HasUpDownBars
AxisGroup	**HiLoLines**
Count[1]	Item[1]
Creator[2]	**Overlap**
DoughnutHoleSize	Parent[2]
DownBars	**RadarAxisLabels**
DropLines	**SeriesCollection**
FirstSliceAngle	**SeriesLines**
GapWidth	**SubType**
HasDropLines	**Type**
HasHiLoLines	**UpBars**
HasRadarAxisLabels	**VaryByCategories**
HasSeriesLines	

[1] *Applies to the `ChartGroups` collection.*

[2] *Applies to the `ChartGroups` collection and the `ChartGroup` object.*

chartgroup.AxisGroup

chartgroup.AxisGroup [= xlPrimary | xlSecondary]

Sets or returns the axis type for the chart group. For 3-D charts, only `xlPrimary` is valid. You use `AxisGroup` to change the primary axis from one chart group to another when displaying multiple types of charts.

The following code makes the second chart group the primary axis:

```
ActiveChart.ChartGroups(2).AxisGroup = xlPrimary
```

chartgroup.DoughnutHoleSize

chartgroup.DoughnutHoleSize [= *percentage*]

Sets or returns the size of the hole in a doughnut chart group. The hole size is expressed as a percentage of the chart size from 10 to 90 percent. The default is 50.

chartgroup.**DownBars**

Returns the DownBars object for the chart group. You use the DownBars object properties to control the appearance of the down bar. The following code selects the down bars on a chart:

```
ActiveChart.ChartGroups(1).DownBars.Select
```

chartgroup.**DropLines**

Returns the DropLines object for the chart group. You use the DropLines object properties to control the appearance of the drop lines. The following code selects the drop lines on a chart:

```
ActiveChart.ChartGroups(1).DropLines.Select
```

chartgroup.**FirstSliceAngle**

chartgroup.**FirstSliceAngle [= *degrees*]**

Sets or returns the angle of the first pie or doughnut slice for a pie, 3-D pie, or doughnut chart group, in degrees clockwise from vertical. Ignored for other chart types. The default is 0.

chartgroup.**GapWidth**

chartgroup.**GapWidth [= *percentage*]**

Sets or returns the space between bar or column clusters as a percentage of the width of a bar or column. Must be between 0 and 500. The default is 150.

chartgroup.**HasDropLines**

chartgroup.**HasDropLines [= True | False]**

True displays drop lines on a line or area chart. Ignored for other chart types. The default is False.

chartgroup.**HasHiLoLines**

chartgroup.**HasHiLoLines [= True | False]**

True displays high-low lines on a line chart. Ignored for other chart types. The default is False.

chartgroup.**HasRadarAxisLabels**

chartgroup.**HasRadarAxisLabels [= True | False]**

True displays data labels on the axis on a radar chart. Ignored for other chart types. The default is False.

chartgroup.**HasSeriesLines**

chartgroup.**HasSeriesLines [= True | False]**

True displays series lines on a column or bar chart. Ignored for other chart types. The default is False.

chartgroup.**HasUpDownBars**

chartgroup.**HasUpDownBars [= True | False]**

True displays up and down bars on a line chart. Ignored for other chart types. The default is False.

chartgroup.**HiLoLines**

Returns the HiLoLines object for a line chart. Returns Nothing for other chart types. The following code line selects the high-low lines on a chart:

```
ActiveChart.ChartGroups(1).HiLoLines.Select
```

chartgroup.**Overlap**

chartgroup.**Overlap [= *percentage*]**

Sets or returns the amount of overlap between items on a bar or column chart as a percentage of the bar/column width. Must be between –100 (single-width spacing) and 100 (completely overlapping). The default is 0 (no spacing).

chartgroup.**RadarAxisLabels**

Returns the radar axis labels for a radar chart as a TickLabels collection. Returns Nothing for other chart types.

chartgroup.**SeriesCollection**

chartgroup.**SeriesCollection ([*Index*])**

Returns one or all `Series` objects from a chart group. The following code adds a single series (a single column of data) to a chart group:

```
ActiveChart.ChartGroups(1).SeriesCollection.Add _
Sheets("Sheet1").Range("A1:A4")
```

The following code adds four series (four columns of data) to a chart group:

```
ActiveChart.ChartGroups(1).SeriesCollection.Add _
Sheets("Sheet1").Range("A1:D4")
```

You can change the chart type of a series to create additional chart groups. The following line of code displays a series as a pie chart:

```
ActiveChart.ChartGroups(1).SeriesCollection(1).Type = xlPie
```

chartgroup.**SeriesLines**

Returns the `SeriesLines` object for a stacked bar or column chart. Returns Nothing for other chart types. The following code selects the series lines on a chart:

```
ActiveChart.ChartGroups(1).SeriesLines.Select
```

chartgroup.**SubType**

chartgroup.**SubType [= *index*]**

Sets or returns the subtype for a chart group. `index` corresponds to the index of the subtype in the Chart Types options dialog box. Each chart type has a different number of subtypes. To see the possible subtypes in Excel, select a chart and choose Chart Types from the Format menu; then choose Options.

chartgroup.**Type**

chartgroup.**Type [= *setting*]**

Sets or returns the chart type of all the series in the chart group: `xlArea`, `xlBar`, `xlColumn`, `xlLine`, `xlPie`, `xlRadar`, `xlXYScatter`, `xlCombination`, `xl3DArea`, `xl3DBar`, `xl3DColumn`, `xl3DLine`, `xl3DPie`, `xl3DSurface`, or `xlDoughnut`. The default is `xlColumn`.

The following code changes a chart group to a bar chart series:

```
ActiveChart.ChartGroups(1).Type = xlBar
```

Tip
Setting the type of a chart group to any 3-D chart changes the entire chart to that type.

II

Programmer's Reference

chartgroup.UpBars

Returns the UpBars object for the chart group. Use the UpBars object properties to control the appearance of the up bars. The following code line selects the up bars on a chart:

```
ActiveChart.ChartGroups(1).UpBars.Select
```

chartgroup.VaryByCategories

If the chart group has only one series, True assigns a different color or pattern to each data marker; False displays the series in a single color. Ignored if more than one series exists. The default is False.

Chapter 14

Controlling Charts

In Chapter 13 you learned how to create a chart and embed it into a worksheet. Now that you have a chart on your worksheet, how do you manipulate it? In this chapter you learn to alter the visible aspects of the charts you create.

In this chapter, you learn how to do the following:

- Plot series on a chart.

- Control data labels and tick labels.

- Control axes, titles, and legends.

- Control the formatting aspects of charts.

This chapter covers the following objects:

Axis	LegendEntry
AxisTitle	LegendKey
ChartArea	PlotArea
Corners	Point
DataLabel	Series
DownBars	SeriesCollection
DropLines	SeriesLines
ErrorBars	TickLabels
Floor	Trendline
Gridlines	UpBars
HiLoLines	Wall
Legend	

Plotting Series on a Chart

The `SeriesCollection` and `Series` object create and control data series in a chart. You use the `SeriesCollection` method of the `Chart` object to add data series to a chart and manipulate those series.

A *series* is a single row or column of data that belongs to a category of data. On a line chart, a series is plotted as a single line (see fig. 14.1).

Fig. 14.1
Series on a chart.

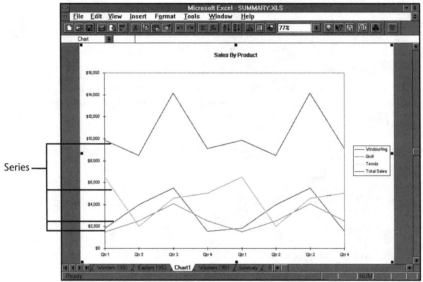

The `Series` object and `SeriesCollection` collection have specific properties and methods, which are listed in Table 14.1. Properties and methods shown in **bold** are described in the reference section that follows this table. Nonbold items are common to most objects and are described in Chapter 4, "Using Objects."

Table 14.1 Series and SeriesCollection properties and methods	
Add[1]	Creator[2]
Application[2]	**DataLabels**
ApplyDataLabels	**Delete**
AxisGroup	**ErrorBar**
Border	**ErrorBars**
ClearFormats	**Explosion**
Copy	**Extend**
Count[1]	**Formula**

FormulaLocal	Name
FormulaR1C1	Parent[2]
FormulaR1C1Local	Paste[2]
HasDataLabels	PictureType
HasErrorBars	PictureUnit
Interior	PlotOrder
InvertIfNegative	Points
Item[1]	Select
MarkerBackgroundColor	Smooth
MarkerBackgroundColorIndex	Trendlines
MarkerForegroundColor	Type
MarkerForegroundColorIndex	Values
MarkerStyle	XValues

[1] *Applies to the SeriesCollection collection.*

[2] *Applies to the SeriesCollection collection and the Series object.*

SeriesCollection.Add

SeriesCollection.Add (*Source*, [*Rowcol*], [*SeriesLabels*], [*CategoryLabels*], [*Replace*])

Adds one or more series of data to a chart.

Argument	Description
Source	A range or array of Point objects specifying the data in a chart. If the range contains multiple categories, Add creates a series for each of those categories.
Rowcol	xlRows creates a series for each row in *Source*; xlColumns creates a series for each column in *Source*. The default is xlColumns.
SeriesLabels	True uses the first row or column in *Source* as labels for values; False does not. Ignored if *Source* is an array. If omitted, Excel uses the type of data in the first row or column to determine whether value labels are displayed.
CategoryLabels	True uses the first row or column in *Source* as labels for categories; False does not. Ignored if *Source* is an array. If omitted, Excel uses the type of data in the first row or column to determine whether category labels are displayed.
Replace	True replaces the values for existing categories with the values for categories from *Source*. Ignored if *Source* does not contain category labels.

The following lines of code create a chart and plot the currently selected data on a worksheet:

```
Sub ChartSelection()
    Set chrtobj = ActiveSheet.ChartObjects.Add(100, 100, 200, 200)
    ' ASSUMES: user has selected a range of cells.
    chrtobj.Chart.SeriesCollection.Add Selection
End Sub
```

series.**ApplyDataLabels**

series.**ApplyDataLabels ([*Type*], [*LegendKey*])**

Applies data labels to the series.

Argument	Description
Type	xlNone does not display data labels; xlShowValue displays each point value as its data label; xlShowLabel displays the category for the point; xlShowPercent displays the percentage of the total (pie and doughnut chart groups only); xlShowLabelAndPercent displays both the percentage of the total and the category for the point (pie and doughnut chart groups only). The default is xlShowValue.
LegendKey	True shows the legend key next to the point; False omits this symbol. The legend key is the symbol that appears next to the series title in the legend box. The default is False.

The following code displays categories as labels for the points in the first series of the currently active chart:

```
ActiveChart.SeriesCollection(1).ApplyDataLabels xlShowLabel
```

series.**AxisGroup**

series.**AxisGroup [= xlPrimary | xlSecondary]**

Sets or returns the axis type for the series. For 3-D charts, only xlPrimary is valid. Use AxisGroup to change the primary axis from one chart group to another when displaying multiple types of charts.

The following code makes the chart group containing the sixth series the primary axis:

```
ActiveChart.SeriesCollection(6).AxisGroup = xlPrimary
```

series.**Border**

Returns one or all the Border objects for a series. If a series does not have a border, the returned Border object has Linestyle xlNone.

The following code line highlights a series by applying a double line border:

```
ActiveChart.SeriesCollection(1).Border.LineStyle = xlDouble
```

series.**ClearFormats( )**

Restores the default formatting for a series. The following lines of code clear the formats for all series on a chart:

```
Sub ClearSeriesFormats()
    Dim srs As Series
    For Each srs In ActiveChart.SeriesCollection
        srs.ClearFormats
    Next srs
End Sub
```

series.**Copy( )**

Copies a series to the Clipboard.

series.**DataLabels**

series.**DataLabels ([*Index*])**

Returns one or all of the DataLabel objects in a series. Data labels appear next to the points plotted in a chart. Use the returned DataLabel object to set the text and control the appearance of these labels.

The following line of code sets the text for the first point in a series:

```
ActiveChart.SeriesCollection(1).DataLabels(1).Text = "Starting Point"
```

series.**Delete( )**

Deletes a series from a chart. It does not place the deleted series on the Clipboard, as does Cut.

*series.*ErrorBar

*series.*ErrorBar (*Direction, Include, Type, [Amount], [MinusValues]*)

Adds error bars to a series. Causes error 1004 if used with a series in a 3-D chart.

Argument	Description
Direction	x1X displays error bars along the chart's X-axis; x1Y displays bars along the Y-axis.
Include	The type of error bar to display: x1PlusValues, x1MinusValues, x1None, or x1Both.
Type	The calculation method for sizing the error bars: x1FixedValue, x1Percent, x1StDev, x1StError, or x1Custom.
Amount	The positive error amount to display. Used only when Type = x1Custom.
MinusValues	The negative error amount to display. Used only when Type = x1Custom.

This method corresponds to the Error Bars dialog box. To display the Error Bars dialog box in Excel, select a series and choose Insert, Error Bars (see fig. 14.2).

Fig. 14.2
The Error Bars dialog box.

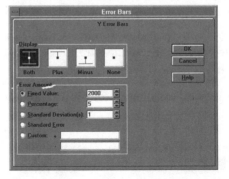

*series.*ErrorBars

Returns the ErrorBars object for the series. You use the returned ErrorBars object to control the display of error bars. The following code selects the error bars on a series:

```
ActiveChart.SeriesCollection(1).ErrorBars.Select
```

series.Explosion

series.Explosion [= *percentage*]

Sets or returns the percentage of pie-chart or doughnut-chart slice explosion. The default is 0 (no explosion).

SeriesCollection.Extend

SeriesCollection.Extend (*Source*, [*Rowcol*], [*CategoryLabels*])

Adds data values to existing series (instead of creating new series, as with Add).

Argument	Description
Source	A range or array of Point objects specifying the data to chart.
Rowcol	xlRows creates a series for each row in *Source*; xlColumns creates a series for each column in *Source*. The default is xlColumns.
CategoryLabels	True uses the first row or column in *Source* as labels for categories; False does not. Ignored if *Source* is an array. If omitted, Excel uses the type of data in the first row or column to determine whether category labels are displayed.

The following code line adds data points in the range A1:C4 to the existing data series on a chart:

```
ActiveChart.SeriesCollect.Extend Sheets("Sheet1").Range("A1:C4")
```

series.Formula

series.Formula [= *A1formula*]

Sets or returns the formula for a series. The formula for a series uses the SERIES worksheet function. The following code sets the data to which a series refers, using the Formula property:

```
ActiveChart.SeriesCollection(1).Formula = _
"=SERIES(,,Sheet2!$A$1:$A$4,2)"
```

series.FormulaLocal

series.FormulaLocal [= *A1formula*]

Sets or returns the formula for a series using the language of the user.

series.**FormulaR1C1**

series.**FormulaR1C1 [=** *R1C1formula*]

Sets or returns the formula for a series using R1C1-style cell references.

series.**FormulaR1C1Local**

series.**FormulaR1C1Local [=** *R1C1formula*]

Sets or returns the formula for a series using R1C1-style cell references in the language of the user.

series.**HasDataLabels**

series.**HasDataLabels [= True | False]**

True displays data labels for the series; False removes data labels. The default is False.

series.**HasErrorBars**

series.**HasErrorBars [= True | False]**

True displays error bars for the series; False removes error bars. The default is False.

series.**Interior**

Returns the Interior object for the series. You use the returned Interior object to change the interior of the series, such as the color of the bars on a bar chart. The following code changes the interior of one of the series on a chart:

```
ActiveChart.SeriesCollection(1).Interior.Color = RGB(255,0,0)
```

series.**InvertIfNegative**

series.**InvertIfNegative [= True | False]**

True inverts the pattern in the item for negative values; False uses the same pattern as positive values. The default is False.

series.**MarkerBackgroundColor**

series.**MarkerBackgroundColor [=** *rgbcolor*]

For line, scatter, and radar charts, sets or returns the marker background color as an RGB value. Ignored for other chart types.

series.**MarkerBackgroundColorIndex**

series.**MarkerBackgroundColorIndex** [= *colorindex*]

For line, scatter, and radar charts, sets or returns the marker background color as an index into the current color palette. Ignored for other chart types.

series.**MarkerForegroundColor**

series.**MarkerForegroundColor** [= *rgbcolor*]

For line, scatter, and radar charts, sets or returns the marker foreground color as an RGB value. Ignored for other chart types.

series.**MarkerForegroundColorIndex**

series.**MarkerForegroundColorIndex** [= *colorindex*]

For line, scatter, and radar charts, sets or returns the marker foreground color as an index into the current color palette. Ignored for other chart types.

series.**MarkerStyle**

series.**MarkerStyle** [= *setting*]

For line, scatter, and radar charts, sets or returns the style of the point marker for a series: xlSquare, xlDiamond, xlTriangle, xlX, xlStar, xlDot, xlDash, xlCircle, xlPlus, or xlPicture.

series.**Paste( )**

Pastes a series from the Clipboard to the chart.

SeriesCollection.Paste

SeriesCollection.Paste ([*Rowcol*], [*SeriesLabels*], [*CategoryLabels*], [*Replace*], [*NewSeries*])

Pastes a range or a collection of series from the Clipboard into the series collection of a chart.

Argument	Description
Rowcol	xlRows creates a series for each row on the Clipboard; xlColumns creates a series for each column on the Clipboard. The default is xlColumns.
SeriesLabels	True uses the first row or column on the Clipboard as labels for values; False does not. If omitted, Excel uses the type of data in the first row or column to determine whether value labels are displayed.
CategoryLabels	True uses the first row or column on the Clipboard as labels for categories; False does not. If omitted, Excel uses the type of data in the first row or column to determine whether category labels are displayed.
Replace	True replaces the values for existing categories with the values for categories from the Clipboard. Ignored if the Clipboard does not contain category labels.
NewSeries	True pastes the values as new series; False replaces the values for existing categories with the values for categories from the Clipboard. Ignored if the Clipboard does not contain category labels. The default is True.

The following code pastes a range on the Clipboard into a chart, creating a new data series for the data:

```
ActiveChart.SeriesCollection.Paste
```

series.**PictureType**

series.**PictureType** [= *setting*]

For column and bar picture charts, sets or returns a constant indicating how pictures are displayed: xlStretch, xlStack, or xlScale. Causes error 1006 for other chart types. The default is xlStretch.

series.**PictureUnit**

series.**PictureUnit** [= *value*]

Tip

To create a picture chart, paste a picture to a data series in a chart.

For column and bar picture charts with PictureType xlScale, sets or returns the unit value of each picture. Ignored for other chart types. The default is 1.

series.**PlotOrder**

series.**PlotOrder** [= *index*]

Sets or returns the order of the series on a chart. In a bar chart, for example, the first (leftmost) bar has a PlotOrder of 1. You can change only the plot order for Chart objects containing a single chart type, and for the ChartGroups object (multiple chart types). PlotOrder reorders the indexes in the SeriesCollection object.

The following line of code plots the third series first and changes its index in the series collection to 1:

```
ActiveChart.SeriesCollection(3).PlotOrder = 1
```

series.Points

series.Points ([*Index*])

Returns one or all Point objects in a series. You use the returned Point objects to control the display of data points. The following code adds a data label to one point in a series:

```
ActiveSheet.SeriesCollection(1).Points(1).DataLabel = "Starting Point"
```

series.Select()

Selects a data series.

series.Smooth

series.Smooth [= True | False]

For line and scatter charts, True smoothes curves; False does not. Ignored for other chart types. The default is False.

series.Trendlines

series.Trendlines ([*Index*])

Returns one or all of the Trendline objects for a series. Use Trendlines to add trendlines to a chart and control their display. The following code adds a trendline to a series:

```
ActiveChart.SeriesCollection(1).Trendlines.Add
```

series.Type

series.Type [= *setting*]

Sets or returns the chart type of the series: xlArea, xlBar, xlColumn, xlLine, xlPie, xlRadar, xlXYScatter, xlCombination, xl3DArea, xl3DBar, xl3DColumn, xl3DLine, xl3DPie, xl3DSurface, or xlDoughnut. The default is xlColumn.

II

Programmer's Reference

Tip
Setting the type of
a series to any 3-D
chart changes the
entire chart to that
type.

The following code changes a series to a bar chart series:

```
ActiveChart.SeriesCollection.Type = xlBar
```

To change the type of an entire chart, use the `Chart` object. To change the type of a chart group, use the `ChartGroup` object.

series.Values

series.Values [= *array*]

Sets or returns an array of values for the points in the data series. The following code sets the values for a data series using an array:

```
ActiveChart.SeriesCollection(1).Values = _
    Array(Array(5,1), Array(10,1), Array(7,1), Array(3,1))
```

series.XValues

series.XValues [= *array*]

For scatter charts, sets or returns an array of the X values of the series. Ignored for other chart types. The following code sets the X values for a data series using an array:

```
ActiveChart.SeriesCollection(1).XValues = _
    Array(Array(5,1), Array(10,1), Array(7,1), Array(3,1))
```

Controlling Axes

Most 2-D charts have two axes: a *value* (x) axis and a *category* (y) axis. In contrast, 3-D charts have one axis, called a *series* axis (see fig. 14.3). Excel creates an `Axes` collection for each chart. The elements of this collection correspond to the value and category or series axes on the chart.

To get one of these axes from a chart, use the chart's `Axes` method and a constant. You use the following code, for example, to select the chart's category axis:

```
ActiveChart.Axes(xlCategory).Select
```

Two-dimensional charts can also include primary and secondary axes. To create a secondary axis, use the `AxisGroup` property of a `Series` object. You can use the following code to create a secondary axis for the second series on a chart:

```
ActiveChart.SeriesCollection(2).AxisGroup = xlSecondary
```

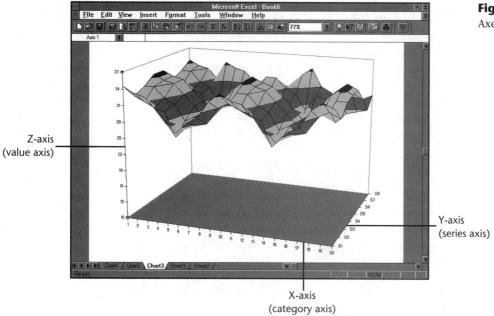

Z-axis
(value axis)

Y-axis
(series axis)

X-axis
(category axis)

Fig. 14.3
Axes on a chart.

After you create a secondary axis, the Axes collection has two dimensions.
The second dimension specifies the primary or secondary axis. Then you can
use the following code to select the secondary value axis:

```
ActiveChart.Axes(xlValue, xlSecondary).Select
```

To add a title to an axis, you use the HasTitle and AxisTitle properties. The
following lines of code add a title to the category axis:

```
Sub CreateAxisTitle ()
    ActiveChart.Axes(xlCategory).HasTitle = True
    ActiveChart.Axes(xlCategory).AxisTitle.Text = "Category Axis"
End Sub
```

Tip
Creating a second-
ary axis for a series
creates a new chart
group for that
series.

The Axis object and Axes collection have specific properties and methods,
which are listed in Table 14.2. Properties and methods shown in **bold** are
described in the reference section that follows this table. Nonbold items are
common to most objects and are described in Chapter 4, "Using Objects."

II

Programmer's Reference

Table 14.2 Axis and Axes properties and methods

Application[2]	MajorUnitIsAuto
AxisBetweenCategories	MaximumScale
AxisGroup	MaximumScaleIsAuto
AxisTitle	MinimumScale
Border	MinimumScaleIsAuto
CategoryNames	MinorGridlines
Count[1]	MinorTickMark
Creator[2]	MinorUnit
Crosses	MinorUnitIsAuto
CrossesAt	Parent[2]
Delete	ReversePlotOrder
HasMajorGridlines	ScaleType
HasMinorGridlines	Select
HasTitle	TickLabelPosition
Item[1]	TickLabels
MajorGridlines	TickLabelSpacing
MajorTickMark	TickMarkSpacing
MajorUnit	Type

[1] *Applies to the Axes collection.*

[2] *Applies to the Axes collection and the Axis object.*

*axis.*AxisBetweenCategories

*axis.*AxisBetweenCategories [= True | False]

For the category axis, True indicates that the value axis crosses the category axis between categories. For other axes, causes error 1004. The default is True.

*axis.*AxisGroup

Returns xlPrimary if the axis is the primary axis; returns xlSecondary if it is the secondary axis.

*axis.*AxisTitle

Returns the AxisTitle object for the axis. The following code lines create a title and set its text:

```
Sub AxisTitle()
    ActiveChart.Axes(xlCategory).HasTitle = True
    ActiveChart.Axes(xlCategory).AxisTitle.Text = "Category Axis"
End Sub
```

axis.**Border**

Returns the Border object for the axis. If an axis does not have a border, the returned border object has Linestyle xlNone.

axis.**CategoryNames**

axis.**CategoryNames** [= *array*]

Sets or returns all the category names for the axis. *array* may be an array of strings or a range of cells containing the category names.

axis.**Crosses**

axis.**Crosses** [= *setting*]

For 2-D charts, sets or returns where the axis crosses the other axis: xlAutomatic, xlMinimum, xlMaximum, or xlCustom. If xlCustom, the axis crosses as the value in the CrossesAt property. Ignored for 3-D and radar charts. The default is xlAutomatic.

axis.**CrossesAt**

axis.**CrossesAt** [= *setting*]

If Crosses is xlCustom, sets or returns the point on the value axis where the category axis crosses. Otherwise, it is ignored.

axis.**Delete( )**

Deletes an axis.

axis.**HasMajorGridlines**

axis.**HasMajorGridlines** [= **True | False**]

For the primary axis, True displays major grid lines; False hides major grid lines. The default is False.

axis.**HasMinorGridlines**

axis.**HasMinorGridlines** [= **True | False**]

For the primary axis, True displays minor grid lines; False hides minor grid lines. The default is False.

axis.HasTitle

axis.HasTitle [= True | False]

True displays a title for the axis; False removes the title. The default is False.

Axes.Item

Axes.Item (*Type*, [*AxisGroup*])

Returns a single Axis from the chart's Axes collection.

Argument	Description
Type	For 2-D charts, xlValue returns the value axis; xlCategory returns the category axis. For 3-D charts, xlSeries returns the axis (only one axis exists).
AxisGroup	xlPrimary returns the primary axis; xlSecondary returns the secondary axis. 3-D charts have only a primary axis. The default is xlPrimary.

This method is the default for the Axes collection, which means that you can omit the word Item. For example, the following lines are equivalent:

```
Charts(1).Axes.Item(xlValue).Select
Charts(1).Axes(xlValue).Select
```

axis.MajorGridlines

Returns the major Gridlines object for the axis. The following lines of code create a major grid line and select it:

```
Sub AxisMajorGridlines()
    ActiveChart.Axes(xlCategory).HasMajorGridlines = True
    ActiveChart.Axes(xlCategory).MajorGridlines.Select
End Sub
```

axis.MajorTickMark

axis.MajorTickMark [= *setting*]

Sets or returns the type of major tick mark for the specified: xlNone, xlInside, xlOutside, or xlCross. The default is xlOutside.

axis.MajorUnit

axis.MajorUnit [= *value*]

For the value axis, sets or returns the major units. Setting this property sets the MajorUnitIsAuto property to False. For other axes, causes error 1006. Use the TickMarkSpacing property to set tick mark spacing on the category axis.

axis.MajorUnitIsAuto

axis.MajorUnitIsAuto [= True | False]

For the value axis, True calculates major units for the value axis automatically; False uses the value from MajorUnit. For other axes, causes error 1006. The default is True.

axis.MaximumScale

axis.MaximumScale [= *maximum*]

For the value axis, sets or returns the maximum value. Applies only to the value axis. For other axes, causes error 1006. Setting this property sets the MaximumScaleIsAuto property to False.

axis.MaximumScaleIsAuto

For the value axis, True calculates the maximum value for the value axis automatically; False uses the value from MaximumScale. For other axes, causes error 1006. The default is True.

axis.MinimumScale

For the value axis, sets or returns the minimum value on the value axis. For other axes, causes error 1006. Setting this property sets the MinimumScaleIsAuto property to False.

axis.MinimumScaleIsAuto

For the value axis, True calculates the minimum value for the value axis automatically; False uses the value from MinimumScale. For other axes, causes error 1006. The default is True.

II

Programmer's Reference

axis.**MinorGridlines**

Returns the minor `Gridlines` object for the axis. The following code lines create a minor grid line and select it:

```
Sub AxisMinorGridlines()
    ActiveChart.Axes(xlCategory).HasMinorGridlines = True
    ActiveChart.Axes(xlCategory).MinorGridlines.Select
End Sub
```

axis.**MinorTickMark**

axis.**MinorTickMark [= *setting*]**

Sets or returns the type of minor tick mark for the axis: xlNone, xlInside, xlOutside, or xlCross. The default is xlNone.

axis.**MinorUnit**

axis.**MinorUnit [= *value*]**

For the value axis, sets or returns the minor units. Setting this property sets the MinorUnitIsAuto property to False. For other axes, causes error 1006. Use the TickMarkSpacing property to set tick mark spacing on the category axis.

axis.**MinorUnitIsAuto**

axis.**MinorUnitIsAuto [= True | False]**

For the value axis, True calculates minor units for the value axis automatically; False uses the value from MinorUnit. For other axes, causes error 1006. The default is True.

axis.**ReversePlotOrder**

axis.**ReversePlotOrder [= True | False]**

True plots points from last to first; False plots in normal order. Causes error 1006 for radar charts. The default is False.

axis.**ScaleType**

axis.**ScaleType [= xlLinear | xlLogarithmic]**

For the value axis, xlLinear uses a linear scale, and xlLogarithmic uses a base-10 logarithmic scale. For other axes, causes error 1006. The default is xlLinear.

axis.Select( )

Selects an axis.

axis.TickLabelPosition

axis.TickLabelPosition [= *setting*]

Sets or returns the position of tick labels on the axis: xlNone, xlLow, xlHigh, or xlNextToAxis. The default is xlNextToAxis.

axis.TickLabels

Returns the TickLabels object for the axis. You use the TickLabels object to control the orientation and font of the tick labels on an axis.

axis.TickLabelSpacing

axis.TickLabelSpacing [= *number*]

For category and series axes, sets or returns the number of categories or series between tick labels. Label spacing on the value axis is always calculated automatically. The default is 1.

axis.TickMarkSpacing

axis.TickMarkSpacing [= *number*]

For category and series axes, sets or returns the number of categories or series between tick labels. You use the MajorUnit and MinorUnit properties to set tick mark spacing on the value axis. The default is 1.

axis.Type

Returns the type of the axis: xlCategory, xlValue, or xlSeries (only 3-D charts have xlSeries).

Creating Axis Titles

Each axis on a chart can have a title. To create an axis title, use the HasTitle property of the Axis object. To set the text of the title, you use the Text property of the AxisTitle object.

II

Programmer's Reference

To create an axis title and set its text, use the following lines of code:

```
Sub CreateAxisTitle ()
    ActiveChart.Axes(xlCategory).HasTitle = True
    ActiveChart.Axes(xlCategory).AxisTitle.Text = "Category Axis"
End Sub
```

The AxisTitle object has specific properties and methods, which are listed in Table 14.3. Properties and methods shown in **bold** are described in the reference section that follows this table. Nonbold items are common to most objects and are described in Chapter 4, "Using Objects."

Table 14.3 AxisTitle properties and methods	
Application	Left
Border	Name
Caption	**Orientation**
Characters	Parent
Creator	**Select**
Delete	**Shadow**
Font	**Text**
HorizontalAlignment	Top
Interior	**VerticalAlignment**

*axistitle.*Border

Returns the Border object for the axis title. If an axis title does not have a border, the returned Border object has Linestyle xlNone.

The following code adds a border to an axis title:

```
Charts("chart1").Axes(xlCategory).AxisTitle.Border.LineStyle = _
    xlDouble
```

*axistitle.*Caption

*axistitle.*Caption [= *text*]

Same as the Text property.

*axistitle.*Characters

*axistitle.*Characters ([*Start*], [*Length*])

Returns a Characters object representing the text or a portion of the text from the title. You use the returned Characters object to format all or part of the text in an axis title.

Argument	Description
Start	The position of the first character to return. The default is 1.
Length	The number of characters to return. The default is the number of characters between *Start* and the end of the text in the title.

The following code makes the first five characters in an axis title bold:

```
ActiveChart.Axes(xlCategory).AxisTitle.Characters(1, 5).Font. Bold = True
```

axistitle.Delete( )

Deletes an axis title.

axistitle.Font

Returns the Font object for the axis title. The following code makes the title italic:

```
ActiveChart.Axes(xlCategory).AxisTitle.Font.Italic = True
```

axistitle.HorizontalAlignment
axistitle.HorizontalAlignment [= *setting*]

xlLeft left-aligns text; xlRight right-aligns text; and xlCenter centers text. The default is xlLeft.

axistitle.Interior

Returns the Interior object for the axis title. Use the Interior object properties to set the shading and color of the interior of the title. The following code shades the interior of the title:

```
ActiveChart.Axes(xlCategory).AxisTitle.Interior.Pattern = xlGray16
```

axistitle.Orientation
axistitle.Orientation [= *setting*]

Sets or returns the orientation of text displayed in the title: xlHorizontal, xlVertical, xlUpward, or xlDownward. The default is xlHorizontal.

*axistitle.***Select()**

Selects the title of an axis.

*axistitle.***Shadow**

*axistitle.***Shadow [= True | False]**

True creates a background shadow for the title; False removes the shadow. The default is False.

*axistitle.***Text**

*axistitle.***Text [= *text*]**

Sets or returns the text displayed in the title.

*axistitle.***VerticalAlignment**

*axistitle.***VerticalAlignment [= *setting*]**

Sets or returns the vertical alignment of the title: xlBottom, xlCenter, xlDistributed, xlJustify, or xlTop. The default is xlTop.

Controlling Data Labels

Excel labels the data points on a chart if the Series object's HasLabels property is True. You can control the appearance and display of these labels by using the DataLabel object.

To get data labels from a Series, use the DataLabels method. The following code lines, for example, create data labels for a series and then select the labels:

```
Sub CreateDataLabels ()
    ActiveChart.SeriesCollection(1).HasLabels = True
    ActiveChart.SeriesCollection(1).DataLabels.Select
End Sub
```

To get a data label from a Point or a Trendline object, use the DataLabel method. You use the following code to select a data label on a point:

```
ActiveChart.SeriesCollection(1).Points(3).DataLabel.Select
```

The DataLabel object and DataLabels collection have specific properties and methods, which are listed in Table 14.4. Properties and methods shown in **bold** are described in the reference section that follows this table. Nonbold items are common to most objects and are described in Chapter 4, "Using Objects."

Table 14.4 DataLabel and DataLabels properties and methods	
Application[2]	Name[2]
AutoText[2]	NumberFormat[2]
Border[2]	NumberFormatLinked[2]
Caption[2]	Orientation[2]
Characters	Parent[2]
Count[1]	Select[2]
Creator[2]	Shadow[2]
Delete[2]	ShowLegendKey[2]
Font[2]	Text[2]
HorizontalAlignment[2]	Top[2]
Interior[2]	Type[2]
Item[1]	VerticalAlignment[2]
Left[2]	

[1] *Applies to the* DataLabels *collection.*

[2] *Applies to the* DataLabels *collection and the* DataLabel *object.*

datalabel.AutoText

datalabel.AutoText [= True | False]

True generates appropriate text based on context; False requires the text to be set using the Text property.

datalabel.Border

Returns the Border object for one or all the labels. If a label does not have a border, the returned Border object has Linestyle xlNone.

datalabel.Caption

datalabel.Caption [= *text*]

Same as the Text property.

datalabel.Characters

datalabel.Characters ([*Start*], [*Length*])

Returns a Characters object representing the text or a portion of the text from the label. You use the returned Characters object to format all or part of the text in a label.

Argument	Description
Start	The position of the first character to return. The default is 1.
Length	The number of characters to return. The default is the number of characters between Start and the end of the text in the label.

datalabel.Delete( )

Deletes one or all data labels.

datalabel.Font

Returns the Font object for one or all data labels.

datalabel.HorizontalAlignment

datalabel.HorizontalAlignment [= *setting*]

xlLeft left-aligns text; xlRight right-aligns text; and xlCenter centers text. The default is xlLeft.

datalabel.Interior

Returns the Interior object for one or all data labels.

datalabel.NumberFormat

datalabel.NumberFormat [= *format*]

Sets or returns the number formatting code for one or all data labels as a string. If the data labels contain a mix of formats, returns Null.

datalabel.NumberFormatLinked

datalabel.NumberFormatLinked [= True | False]

True links the number format to the cells so that the number format changes in the labels when it changes in the cells. The default is True.

datalabel.**Orientation**

datalabel.**Orientation [=** *setting***]**

Sets or returns the orientation of text displayed in the label: `xlHorizontal`, `xlVertical`, `xlUpward`, or `xlDownward`. The default is `xlHorizontal`.

datalabel.**Select( )**

Selects one or all data labels.

datalabel.**Shadow**

datalabel.**Shadow [= True | False]**

True creates a background shadow for the label; False removes the shadow. The default is False.

datalabel.**ShowLegendKey**

datalabel.**ShowLegendKey [= True | False]**

True displays a data label legend key; False hides the key. The default is False.

datalabel.**Text**

datalabel.**Text [=** *text***]**

Sets or returns the text displayed in one or all data labels.

datalabel.**Type**

datalabel.**Type [=** *setting***]**

Sets or returns the type of data labels to display: `xlNone`, `xlShowValue`, `xlShowLabel`, `xlShowPercent`, or `xlShowLabelAndPercent`.

datalabel.**VerticalAlignment**

datalabel.**VerticalAlignment [=** *setting***]**

Sets or returns the vertical alignment of the label: `xlBottom`, `xlCenter`, `xlDistributed`, `xlJustify`, or `xlTop`. The default is `xlTop`.

Controlling Tick Labels on an Axis

Excel labels the tick marks on an axis if the `Axis` object's `TickLabelPosition` property is a value other than `xlNone`. You can control the appearance and display of these labels by using the `TickLabel` object.

To get labels from an `Axis` object, use the `TickLabels` method. You can use the following code to select the labels of the value axis of a chart:

```
ActiveChart.Axes(xlValue).TickLabels.Select
```

The `TickLabel` object has specific properties and methods, which are listed in Table 14.5. Properties and methods shown in **bold** are described in the reference section that follows this table. Nonbold items are common to most objects and are described in Chapter 4, "Using Objects."

Table 14.5 TickLabel properties and methods	
Application	**NumberFormat**
Creator	**NumberFormatLinked**
Delete	**Orientation**
Font	Parent
Name	**Select**

ticklabels.Delete( )

Deletes the tick labels.

ticklabels.Font

Returns the `Font` object for the tick labels.

ticklabels.NumberFormat

ticklabels.NumberFormat [= *format*]

Sets or returns the number formatting code for one or all tick labels as a string. If the tick labels contain a mix of formats, returns Null.

ticklabels.NumberFormatLinked

ticklabels.NumberFormatLinked [= True | False]

True links the number format to the cells so that the number format changes in the labels when it changes in the cells. The default is True.

ticklabel.**Orientation**

ticklabel.**Orientation** [= *setting*]

Sets or returns the orientation of text displayed in the label: xlHorizontal, xlVertical, xlUpward, or xlDownward. The default is xlHorizontal.

ticklabels.**Select( )**

Selects the tick labels.

Getting Individual Points in a Series

Each data point on a series corresponds to a Point object. You use the Point object to delete, copy, or change the appearance of individual points on a chart.

To get a point from a Series object, you use the Points method. Use the following code to select a point from within a series:

```
ActiveChart.SeriesCollection(1).Points(1).Select
```

The Point object and Points collection have specific properties and methods, which are listed in Table 14.6. Properties and methods shown in **bold** are described in the reference section that follows this table. Nonbold items are common to most objects and are described in Chapter 4, "Using Objects."

Table 14.6 Point and Points properties and methods

Application[2]	**InvertIfNegative**
ApplyDataLabels	Item[1]
Border	**MarkerBackgroundColor**
ClearFormats	**MarkerBackgroundColorIndex**
Copy	**MarkerForegroundColor**
Count[1]	**MarkerForegroundColorIndex**
Creator[2]	**MarkerStyle**
DataLabel	Parent[2]
Delete	**Paste**
Explosion	**PictureType**
HasDataLabel	**PictureUnit**
Interior	**Select**

[1] *Applies to the Points collection.*

[2] *Applies to the Points collection and the Point object.*

point.ApplyDataLabels

point.ApplyDataLabels ([*Type*], [*LegendKey*])

Applies data labels to a point in a series.

Argument	Description
Type	xlNone does not display data labels; xlShowValue displays each point value as its data label; xlShowLabel displays the category for the point; xlShowPercent displays the percentage of the total (pie and doughnut chart groups only); xlShowLabelAndPercent displays both the percentage of the total and the category for the point (pie and doughnut chart groups only). The default is xlShowValue.
LegendKey	True shows the legend key next to the point; False omits this symbol. The legend key is the symbol that appears next to the series title in the legend box. The default is False.

The following code displays categories as labels for the first point in the first series of the currently active chart:

```
ActiveChart.SeriesCollection(1).Points(1)ApplyDataLabels _
    xlShowLabel
```

point.Border

Returns the Border object for the point. If a point does not have a border, the returned Border object has Linestyle xlNone.

point.ClearFormats( )

Restores the default formatting for a point.

point.Copy( )

Copies a point.

point.DataLabel

Returns the DataLabel object for a point.

point.Delete( )

Deletes a point.

point.Explosion

point.Explosion [= *percentage*]

Sets or returns the percentage of pie-chart or doughnut-chart slice explosion for the point. Ignored for other chart types. The default is 0, or no explosion. (No explosion indicates the tip of the pie slice is in the center of the pie.)

point.HasDataLabel

point.HasDataLabel [= True | False]

True displays data labels for the point; False removes data labels. The default is False.

point.Interior

Returns the Interior object for the point.

point.InvertIfNegative

point.InvertIfNegative [= True | False]

True inverts the pattern in the item for negative values; False uses the same pattern as positive values. The default is False.

point.MarkerBackgroundColor

point.MarkerBackgroundColor [= *rgbcolor*]

For line, scatter, and radar charts, sets or returns the marker background color as an RGB value. Ignored for other chart types.

point.MarkerBackgroundColorIndex

point.MarkerBackgroundColorIndex [= *colorindex*]

For line, scatter, and radar charts, sets or returns the marker background color as an index into the current color palette. Ignored for other chart types.

point.MarkerForegroundColor

point.MarkerForegroundColor [= *rgbcolor*]

For line, scatter, and radar charts, sets or returns the marker foreground color as an RGB value. Ignored for other chart types.

point.**MarkerForegroundColorIndex**

point.**MarkerForegroundColorIndex** [= *colorindex*]

For line, scatter, and radar charts, sets or returns the marker foreground color as an index into the current color palette. Ignored for other chart types.

point.**MarkerStyle**

point.**MarkerStyle** [= *setting*]

For line, scatter, and radar charts, sets or returns the style of the point marker for a series: xlSquare, xlDiamond, xlTriangle, xlX, xlStar, xlDot, xlDash, xlCircle, xlPlus, or xlPicture.

point.**Paste( )**

Pastes a point from the Clipboard into the currently active series.

point.**PictureType**

point.**PictureType** [= *setting*]

For column and bar picture charts, sets or returns a constant indicating how pictures are displayed: xlStretch, xlStack, or xlScale. Causes error 1006 for other chart types. The default is xlStretch.

point.**PictureUnit**

point.**PictureUnit** [= *value*]

Tip
To create a picture chart, paste a picture to a data series in a chart.

For column and bar picture charts with PictureType xlScale, sets or returns the unit value of each picture. Ignored for other chart types. The default is 1.

point.**Select( )**

Selects the point.

Controlling the Chart Area

The *chart area* is the region containing the entire chart, legends, and other objects. You use the ChartArea object to change the display attributes of the entire chart and to clear the entire chart quickly.

To get the `ChartArea` object, you use the `ChartArea` method of the `Chart` object. You can use the following code, for example, to select the chart area:

```
ActiveChart.ChartArea.Select
```

To clear the chart area, you use the `Clear` method. The following code erases the active chart but does not delete the chart sheet:

```
ActiveChart.ChartArea.Clear
```

The `ChartArea` object has specific properties and methods, which are listed in Table 14.7. Properties and methods shown in **bold** are described in the reference section that follows this table. Nonbold items are common to most objects and are described in Chapter 4, "Using Objects."

Table 14.7 ChartArea properties and methods

Application	**Interior**
Border	Left
Clear	Name
ClearContents	Parent
ClearFormats	**Select**
Copy	**Shadow**
Creator	Top
Font	Width
Height	

chartarea.Border

Returns the `Border` object for the chart area. If the plot area does not have a border, the returned `Border` object has `Linestyle xlNone`.

chartarea.Clear( )

Clears the entire chart without removing the chart sheet, which erases the chart contents and formatting. The following code clears a chart:

```
ActiveChart.ChartArea.Clear
```

chartarea.ClearContents()

Clears the contents of the chart but does not clear its formats. The following code removes all the series from a chart:

```
ActiveChart.ChartArea.ClearContents
```

II

Programmer's Reference

*chartarea.*ClearFormats( )

Restores the default formatting for the entire chart. The following line of code restores the default formatting for a chart:

```
ActiveChart.ChartArea.ClearFormats
```

*chartarea.*Copy( )

Copies the contents and formats of a chart (but not the chart sheet) to the Clipboard.

*chartarea.*Font

Returns the Font object for the entire chart. Returns Null for font properties that are mixed. The following code makes all the text in a chart italic:

```
Charts("chart1").ChartArea.Font.Italic = True
```

*chartarea.*Interior

Returns the Interior object for the chart area.

*chartarea.*Select( )

Selects the chart area.

*chartarea.*Shadow

Returns True if the ChartArea object has a shadow, False otherwise. The following code sets the Shadow property of a ChartArea to True:

```
Charts("chart1").ChartArea.Shadow = True
```

Controlling the Plot Area

The *plot area* is the region immediately behind the plotted data. Use the PlotArea object to change the display attributes of the plotted data.

To get the PlotArea object, use the PlotArea method of the Chart object. You can use the following code, for example, to change the background color of the plot area:

```
ActiveChart.PlotArea.Interior.Color = RGB(0,0,255)
```

The `PlotArea` object has specific properties and methods, which are listed in Table 14.8. Properties and methods shown in **bold** are described in the reference section that follows this table. Nonbold items are common to most objects and are described in Chapter 4, "Using Objects."

Table 14.8 PlotArea properties and methods

Application	Left
Border	Name
ClearFormats	Parent
Creator	**Select**
Font	Top
Height	Width
Interior	

plotarea.Border

Returns the `Border` object for the plot area. If the plot area does not have a border, the returned `Border` object has `Linestyle xlNone`.

plotarea.ClearFormats( )

Restores the default formatting for the plot area.

plotarea.Interior

Returns the `Interior` object for the plot area.

plotarea.Select( )

Selects the plot area.

Controlling the Chart's Legend

You control the legend on a chart by using the `Legend` object. To add a legend to a chart, you use the `Chart` object's `HasLegend` property (see fig. 14.4).

The following code adds a legend to a chart that does not already have a legend (charts can have only one legend):

```
ActiveChart.HasLegend = True
```

Fig. 14.4
The chart legend.

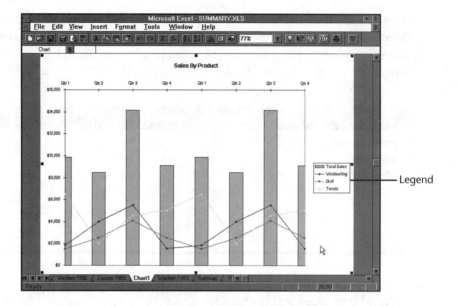

Legend

To get a legend from a Chart object, you use the Legend method. You can use the following code, for example, to add a drop shadow to a chart's legend:

```
ActiveChart.Legend.Shadow = True
```

The Legend object has specific properties and methods, which are listed in Table 14.9. Properties and methods shown in **bold** are described in the reference section that follows this table. Nonbold items are common to most objects and are described in Chapter 4, "Using Objects."

Table 14.9 Legend properties and methods

Application	**LegendEntries**
Border	Name
Creator	Parent
Delete	**Position**
Font	**Select**
Height	**Shadow**
Interior	Top
Left	Width

legend.Border

Returns the Border object for the legend. If a legend does not have a border, the returned Border object has Linestyle xlNone.

legend.Delete( )

Deletes the legend.

legend.Font

Returns the Font object for the legend.

legend.Interior

Returns the Interior object for the legend.

legend.LegendEntries

legend.LegendEntries ([*Index*])

Returns one or all of the LegendEntry objects in the legend. You use the returned LegendEntry objects to format the legend. The following line of code makes the first legend entry italic:

```
Charts("chart1").Legend.LegendEntries(1).Font.Italic = True
```

legend.Position

legend.Position [= *setting*]

Sets or returns the position of the legend: xlBottom, xlCorner, xlTop, xlRight, or xlLeft. The default is xlLeft.

legend.Select( )

Selects the legend.

legend.Shadow

legend.Shadow [= True | False]

True creates a background shadow for the legend; False removes the shadow. The default is False.

Changing the Text in a Legend

The name displayed in the chart's legend comes from the series name. To change this text, you set the Name property of the Series object, as follows:

```
ActiveChart.SeriesCollection(1).Name = "New Legend Entry Name"
```

You control the *appearance* of the text in a legend's `LegendEntry` object. The following code bolds the text in the first legend entry:

```
ActiveChart.Legend.LegendEntries(1).Font.Bold = True
```

The `LegendEntry` object and `LegendEntries` collection have specific properties and methods, which are listed in Table 14.10. Properties and methods shown in **bold** are described in the reference section that follows this table. Nonbold items are common to most objects and are described in Chapter 4, "Using Objects."

Table 14.10 LegendEntry and LegendEntries properties and methods

Application[2]	Index
Count[1]	Item[1]
Creator[2]	**LegendKey**
Delete	Parent[2]
Font	Select

[1] *Applies to the* `LegendEntries` *collection.*

[2] *Applies to the* `LegendEntries` *collection and the* `LegendEntry` *object.*

*legendentry.*Delete( )

Deletes the entry from the legend.

*legendentry.*Font

Returns the `Font` object for the legend. The following code line makes the first legend entry italic:

```
Charts("chart1").Legend.LegendEntries(1).Font.Italic = True
```

*legendentry.*LegendKey

Returns the `LegendKey` object for the legend entry.

*legendentry.*Select( )

Selects the legend entry.

Changing the Legend Key

The *legend key* is the symbol that marks the data points for a series. You control the appearance of this symbol by using the LegendKey object.

To get a legend key from a Legend object, use the LegendKey method. You can use the following code, for example, to set the marker style for a legend key (see fig. 14.5):

```
ActiveChart.Legend.LegendKey.MarkerStyle = xlCircle
```

The LegendKey object has specific properties and methods, which are listed in Table 14.11. Properties and methods shown in **bold** are described in the reference section that follows this table. Nonbold items are common to most objects and are described in Chapter 4, "Using Objects."

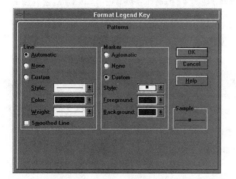

Fig. 14.5
The Format Legend Key dialog box.

Table 14.11 LegendKey properties and methods

Application	**MarkerBackgroundColorIndex**
Border	**MarkerForegroundColor**
ClearFormats	**MarkerForegroundColorIndex**
Creator	**MarkerStyle**
Delete	Parent
Interior	**Select**
InvertIfNegative	**Smooth**
MarkerBackgroundColor	

legendkey.Border

Returns the Border object for the legend key. If a legend does not have a border, the returned Border object has Linestyle xlNone.

*legendkey.*ClearFormats( )

Restores the default formatting for a legend key.

*legendkey.*Delete( )

Deletes the legend key.

*legendkey.*Interior

Returns the Interior object for the legend key.

*legendkey.*InvertIfNegative

*legendkey.*InvertIfNegative [= True | False]

True inverts the pattern in the item for negative values; False uses the same pattern as positive values. The default is False.

*legendkey.*MarkerBackgroundColor

*legendkey.*MarkerBackgroundColor [= *rgbcolor*]

For line, scatter, and radar charts, sets or returns the marker background color as an RGB value. Ignored for other chart types.

*legendkey.*MarkerBackgroundColorIndex

*legendkey.*MarkerBackgroundColorIndex [= *colorindex*]

For line, scatter, and radar charts, sets or returns the marker background color as an index into the current color palette. Ignored for other chart types.

*legendkey.*MarkerForegroundColor

*legendkey.*MarkerForegroundColor [= *rgbcolor*]

For line, scatter, and radar charts, sets or returns the marker foreground color as an RGB value. Ignored for other chart types.

*legendkey.*MarkerForegroundColorIndex

*legendkey.*MarkerForegroundColorIndex
[= *colorindex*]

For line, scatter, and radar charts, sets or returns the marker foreground color as an index into the current color palette. Ignored for other chart types.

*legendkey.*MarkerStyle

*legendkey.*MarkerStyle [= *setting*]

For line, scatter, and radar charts, sets or returns the style of the point marker for a series: xlSquare, xlDiamond, xlTriangle, xlX, xlStar, xlDot, xlDash, xlCircle, xlPlus, or xlPicture.

*legendkey.*Select()

Selects a legend key.

*legendkey.*Smooth

*legendkey.*Smooth [= True | False]

For line and scatter charts, True smoothes curves; False does not. Ignored for other chart types. The default is False.

Creating Trendlines

The Trendline object controls the appearance of trendlines on a chart. You use the Trendlines method of the Series object to create a trendline on a chart (see fig. 14.6).

The following code adds a trendline to a series:

```
ActiveChart.SeriesCollection(1).Trendlines.Add
```

The Trendline object and Trendlines collection have specific properties and methods, which are listed in Table 14.12. Properties and methods shown in **bold** are described in the reference section that follows this table. Nonbold items are common to most objects and are described in Chapter 4, "Using Objects."

Fig. 14.6
A trendline
on a chart.

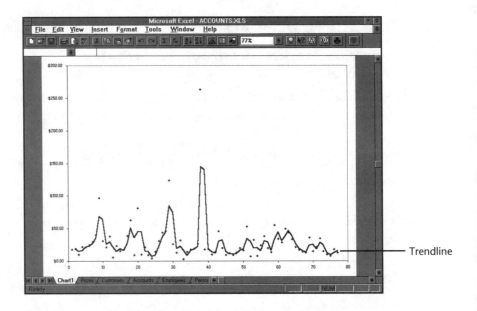

Trendline

Table 14.12 Trendline and Trendlines properties and methods

Add[1]	Index
Application[2]	**Intercept**
Backward	**InterceptIsAuto**
Border	Item[1]
ClearFormats	Name
Count[1]	**NameIsAuto**
Creator[2]	**Order**
DataLabel	Parent[2]
Delete	**Period**
DisplayEquation	**Select**
DisplayRSquared	**Type**
Forward	

---

[1] *Applies to the* Trendlines *collection.*

[2] *Applies to the* Trendlines *collection and the* Trendline *object.*

trendlines.Add

trendlines.Add ([Type], [Order], [Period], [Forward], [Backward], [Intercept], [DisplayEquation], [DisplayRSquared], [Name])

Creates a trendline and applies it to a series.

Argument	Description
Type	The type of the trendline to add: xlLinear, xlLogarithmic, xlExponential, xlPolynomial, xlMovingAvg, or xlPower. The default is xlLinear.
Order	If the type is xlPolynomial, specifies the trendline order, a number from two to six.
Period	If the type is xlMovingAvg, specifies the trendline period. Must be between one and the number of data points in the series.
Forward	The number of periods or units that the trendline extends forward.
Backward	The number of periods or units that the trendline extends backward.
Intercept	Sets the trendline intercept. The default is to determine the intercept by regression.
DisplayEquation	True displays the equation of the trendline on the chart.
DisplayRSquared	True displays the R-squared value of the trendline on the chart.
Name	The name of the trendline.

The following code line adds a trendline to a series on a chart:

```
Charts("chart1").SeriesCollection(1).Trendlines.Add
```

trendline.Backward

trendline.Backward [= *periods*]

Sets or returns the number of periods that the trendline extends backward. Must be between 0 and 0.5. The default is 0. The following code extends a trendline one-half period back:

```
Charts("chart1").SeriesCollection(1).Trendlines(1).Backward = 0.5
```

Note

A moving average trendline is calculated based on a sequence of averages computed from data within a chart. To create a moving average trendline, specify the periods on which the average is based. A typical period is one day.

*trendline.*Border

Returns the Border object for the trendline. If a trendline does not have a border, the returned Border object has Linestyle xlNone.

*trendline.*ClearFormats( )

Restores the default formatting for a trendline.

*trendline.*DataLabel

Returns the DataLabel object for a trendline.

*trendline.*Delete( )

Deletes the trendline.

*trendline.*DisplayEquation

*trendline.*DisplayEquation [= True | False]

True displays the equation for the trendline as a data label. Setting this property to True creates a data label for the trendline. False removes the equation from the data label. The default is False.

*trendline.*DisplayRSquared

*trendline.*DisplayRSquared [= True | False]

True displays the R-squared value for the trendline as a data label. Setting this property to True creates a data label for the trendline. False removes the R-squared value from the data label. The default is False.

*trendline.*Forward

*trendline.*Forward [= *periods*]

Sets or returns the number of periods that the trendline extends forward. Must be between 0 and 0.5. The default is 0. The following code extends a trendline one-half period forward:

```
Charts("chart1").SeriesCollection(1).Trendlines(1).Forward = 0.5
```

*trendline.*Intercept

*trendline.*Intercept [= *value*]

Sets or returns the point where the trendline crosses the value axis. Setting this property changes the InterceptIsAuto property to False.

*trendline.*InterceptIsAuto

*trendline.*InterceptIsAuto [= True | False]

True calculates the point where the trendline crosses the value axis using regression; False uses the Intercept property setting. The default is True.

*trendline.*NameIsAuto

*trendline.*NameIsAuto [= True | False]

True names the trendline automatically; False uses the Name property to set the name. The default is True.

*trendline.*Order

*trendline.*Order [= *index*]

If the trendline type is xlPolynomial, sets or returns the index of the trendline in the Trendlines collection. Ignored for other types.

*trendline.*Period

*trendline.*Period [= *period*]

If the trendline type is xlMovingAvg, sets or returns the period of the trendline. Ignored for other types.

*trendline.*Select( )

Selects the trendline.

*trendline.*Type

*trendline.*Type [= *setting*]

Sets or returns the type of the trendline: xlLinear, xlLogarithmic, xlExponential, xlPolynomial, xlMovingAvg, or xlPower.

II

Programmer's Reference

Adding Series Lines to a Stacked Bar or Column Chart

Stacked bar and column charts can connect data points using *series lines* (see fig. 14.7). To add series lines to a chart, you use the HasSeriesLines property of the ChartGroup object.

Fig. 14.7
Series lines
connect data
points.

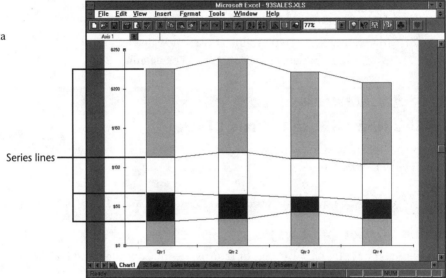

You can use the following code to add series lines to a stacked column chart (notice that it uses the ColumnGroups method to return the column chart group):

```
ActiveChart.ColumnGroups(1).HasSeriesLines = True
```

To get a SeriesLines object, you use the SeriesLines method of the chart group. The following code selects the series lines on a chart:

```
ActiveChart.ColumnGroups(1).SeriesLines.Select
```

The SeriesLines object has specific properties and methods, which are listed in Table 14.13. Properties and methods shown in **bold** are described in the reference section that follows this table. Nonbold items are common to most objects and are described in Chapter 4, "Using Objects."

Table 14.13 SeriesLines properties and methods	
Application	Name
Border	Parent
Creator	**Select**
Delete	

*serieslines.*Border

Returns the Border object for the series lines. If lines do not have a border, the returned Border object has Linestyle xlNone.

*serieslines.*Delete()

Deletes the series lines.

*serieslines.*Select()

Selects the series lines.

Adding High-Low Lines to a Line Chart

Line charts can connect high and low points by using a high-low line (see fig. 14.8). To add a high-low line to a chart, you use the HasHiLoLines property of the ChartGroup object.

The following code adds high-low lines to a stacked column chart (notice that it uses the LineGroups method to return the column chart group):

```
ActiveChart.LineGroups(1).HasHiLoLines = True
```

To get a HiLoLines object, you use the HiLoLines method of the chart group. You can use the following code to select the series lines on a chart:

```
ActiveChart.LineGroups(1).HiLoLines.Select
```

The HiLoLines object has specific properties and methods, which are listed in Table 14.14. Properties and methods shown in **bold** are described in the reference section that follows this table. Nonbold items are common to most objects and are described in Chapter 4, "Using Objects."

Fig. 14.8
High-low lines
connect high and
low points.

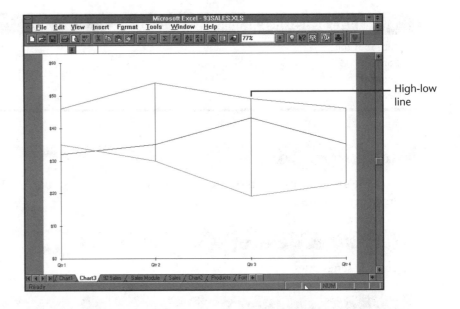

High-low
line

Table 14.14 HiLoLines properties and methods

Application	Name
Border	Parent
Creator	**Select**
Delete	

*hilolines.***Border**

Returns the Border object for the lines. If the lines do not have a border, the returned Border object has Linestyle xlNone.

*hilolines.***Delete( )**

Deletes the high-low lines.

*hilolines.***Select( )**

Selects the lines.

Adding Grid Lines to an Axis

Axes can display major and minor grid lines (see fig. 14.9). To add major grid lines to an axis, you use the HasMajorGridLines property of the Axis object.

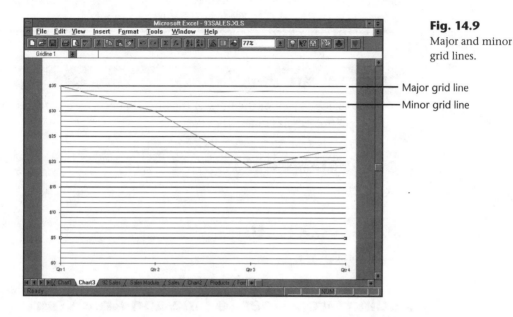

Fig. 14.9
Major and minor grid lines.

— Major grid line
— Minor grid line

You can use the following code, for example, to add major grid lines to the value axis:

```
ActiveChart.Axes(xlValue).HasMajorGridLines = True
```

To add minor grid lines to an axis, use the HasMinorGridLines property of the Axis object. The following code adds minor grid lines to the category axis:

```
ActiveChart.Axes(xlCategory).HasMinorGridLines = True
```

To get a Gridlines object, you use the MajorGridlines or MinorGridlines method of the Axis object. The following code selects the major grid lines on the value axis:

```
ActiveChart.Axes(xlValue).MajorGridLines.Select
```

The Gridlines object has specific properties and methods, which are listed in Table 14.15. Properties and methods shown in **bold** are described in the reference section that follows this table. Nonbold items are common to most objects and are described in Chapter 4, "Using Objects."

Table 14.15 Gridlines properties and methods	
Application	Name
Border	Parent
Creator	**Select**
Delete	

*gridlines.***Border**

Returns the Border object for the lines. If the lines do not have a border, the returned Border object has Linestyle xlNone.

*gridlines.***Delete( )**

Deletes the lines.

*gridlines.***Select( )**

Selects the lines.

Adding Drop Lines to Line and Area Charts

Line and area charts can display the distance between their data points and the category axis by using drop lines (see fig. 14.10). To add a drop line to a chart, you use the HasDropLines property of the ChartGroup object.

The following code adds drop lines to a line chart (notice that it uses the LineGroups method to return the column chart group):

```
ActiveChart.LineGroups(1).HasDroplines = True
```

To get a DropLines object, you use the DropLines method of the chart group. You can use the following code, for example, to select the drop lines on a chart:

```
ActiveChart.LineGroups(1).Droplines.Select
```

The DropLines object has specific properties and methods, which are listed in Table 14.16. Properties and methods shown in **bold** are described in the reference section that follows this table. Nonbold items are common to most objects and are described in Chapter 4, "Using Objects."

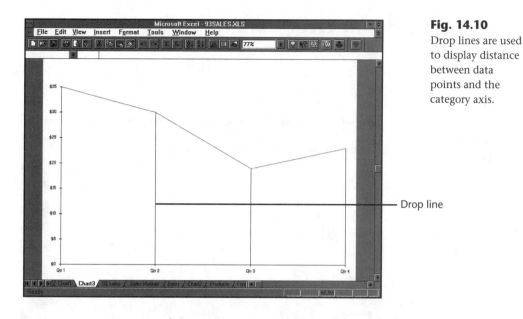

Fig. 14.10
Drop lines are used
to display distance
between data
points and the
category axis.

Table 14.16 DropLines properties and methods	
Application	Name
Border	Parent
Creator	**Select**
Delete	

droplines.**Border**

Returns the Border object for the lines. If the lines do not have a border, the returned Border object has Linestyle xlNone.

droplines.**Delete( )**

Deletes the lines.

droplines.**Select( )**

Selects the lines.

Adding Error Bars to a Series

With error bars, 2-D charts can display various error ranges for data points (see fig. 14.11). To add error bars to a series, you use the `ErrorBars` method of the `Series` object.

Fig. 14.11
Error bars display
error ranges for
data points.

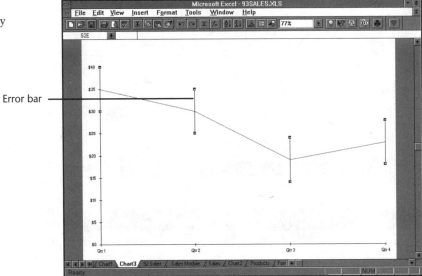

Error bar

You can use the following code, for example, to add error bars to a series:

```
ActiveChart.SeriesCollection(1).ErrorBar xlY, xlBoth, xlStDev, 1
```

To get an `ErrorBars` object, you use the `ErrorBars` method of the `Series` object. The following code removes the "caps" from the ends of error bars:

```
ActiveChart.SeriesCollection(1).ErrorBars.EndStyle = xlNoCap
```

The `ErrorBars` object has specific properties and methods, which are listed in Table 14.17. Properties and methods shown in **bold** are described in the reference section that follows this table. Nonbold items are common to most objects and are described in Chapter 4, "Using Objects."

Table 14.17 ErrorBars properties and methods

Application	**EndStyle**
Border	Name
ClearFormats	Parent
Creator	**Select**
Delete	

*errorbars.***Border**

Returns the Border object for the error bars. If the error bars do not have a border, the returned Border object has Linestyle xlNone.

*errorbars.***ClearFormats( )**

Restores the default formatting for the error bars.

*errorbars.***Delete( )**

Deletes the error bars.

*errorbars.***EndStyle**

*errorbars.***EndStyle [= xlCap | xlNoCap]**

xlCap adds short perpendicular lines to the ends of error bars; xlNoCap removes these lines. This property always returns True, but this result may be a bug, so don't rely on it staying this way in the future.

*errorbars.***Select( )**

Selects the error bars.

Creating Open/High/Low/Close Line Charts

Open/high/low/close line charts are useful for showing stock price fluctuations and other changes in data (see fig. 14.12). You create these charts by adding up bars and down bars to a chart.

To add an up or down bar to a chart, you use the HasUpDownBars property of the ChartGroup object. You can use the following code, for example, to add up and down bars to a line chart:

```
ActiveChart.LineGroups(1).HasUpDownBars = True
```

To get an UpBars object, you use the UpBars method of the chart group. The following code selects the up bars on a chart:

```
ActiveChart.LineGroups(1).UpBars.Select
```

To get a DownBars object, you use the DownBars method of the chart group. The following code selects the down bars on a chart:

```
ActiveChart.LineGroups(1).DownBars.Select
```

Fig. 14.12
Open/High/Low/
Close line chart.

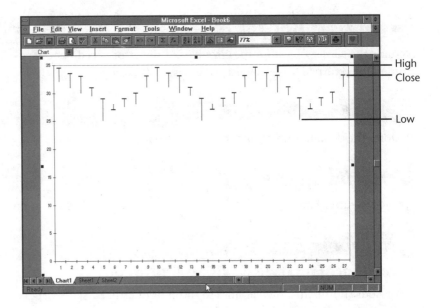

The UpBars and DownBars objects have specific properties and methods, which are listed in Table 14.18. Properties and methods shown in **bold** are described in the reference section that follows this table. Nonbold items are common to most objects and are described in Chapter 4, "Using Objects."

Table 14.18 UpBars and DownBars properties and methods

Application	**Interior**
Border	Name
Creator	Parent
Delete	**Select**

upbars.Border

Returns the Border object for the bars. If the bars do not have a border, the returned Border object has Linestyle xlNone.

upbars.Delete( )

Deletes the bars.

upbars.Interior

Returns the Interior object for the bars.

upbars.Select( )

Selects the bars.

Controlling the Display of 3-D Charts

In figure 14.13, you can see that 3-D charts have three display attributes not available with 2-D charts: the floor, walls, and corners.

You use the Chart object's Floor, Wall, and Corner methods to get these respective objects. The Floor and Wall objects are used to change the appearance of the 3-D plot area. The Corners object is used only to select the chart corners so that the user can rotate the 3-D chart.

The Floor and Wall objects have specific properties and methods, which are listed in Table 14.19. Properties and methods shown in **bold** are described in the reference section that follows this table. Nonbold items are common to most objects and are described in Chapter 4, "Using Objects."

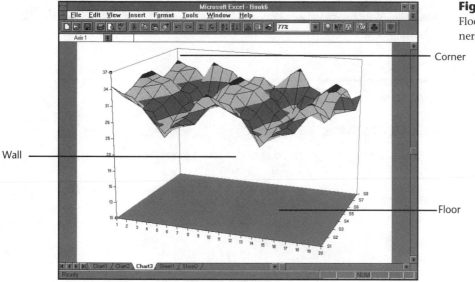

Fig. 14.13
Floor, walls, and corners on a 3-D chart.

Corner

Wall

Floor

II

Programmer's Reference

Table 14.19 Floor and Wall properties and methods	
Application	**Interior**
Border	Name
ClearFormats	Parent
Creator	**Select**

*floor.*Border

Returns the Border object for the floor or wall. If the floor or wall does not have a border, the returned Border object has Linestyle xlNone.

*floor.*Interior

Returns the Interior object for the floor or wall.

*floor.*Select( )

Selects the floor or wall.

The properties and methods for the Corners object are listed in Table 14.20.

Table 14.20 Corners properties and methods	
Application	Parent
Creator	**Select**
Name	

*corners.*Select( )

Selects the corners of a chart so that the user can rotate them.

Chapter 15

Creating Graphics

In addition to using Excel's charting and formatting tools, you can also add graphic shapes to worksheets, charts, and dialog sheets. You can draw these shapes by hand or create them using Visual Basic. Figure 15.1 shows some of the objects that you can draw.

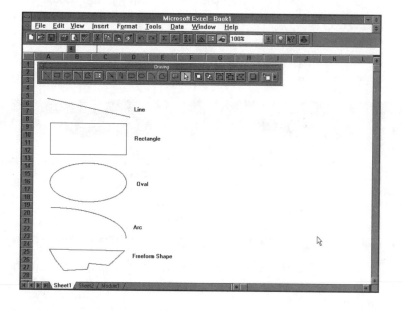

Fig. 15.1
Drawing objects
on a worksheet.

In this chapter, you learn how to do the following:

- Draw graphics with Excel's drawing tools.

- Manipulate and group drawing objects using Visual Basic.

- Draw several types of shapes using Visual Basic.

- Insert pictures from files using Visual Basic.

This chapter covers the `DrawingObject`, `GroupObject`, `Arc`, `Line`, `Oval`, `Picture`, and `Rectangle` objects.

> **Note**
>
> Excel considers any object that can be "drawn" a drawing object. By this definition, buttons, labels, charts, and OLE objects are all drawing objects. This chapter discusses only the graphic shapes among those drawing objects.

Using Excel's Drawing Tools

Using Excel's drawing tools, you can graphically enhance worksheets, charts, and custom dialog boxes. To draw on a sheet, follow these steps:

1. Display the Drawing toolbar (see fig. 15.2). If it is not already showing, choose **V**iew, **T**oolbars, and then select Drawing in the Toolbars list box. Then click the OK button to display the Drawing toolbar.

Fig. 15.2
The Drawing toolbar.

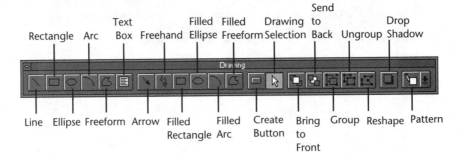

2. Click the toolbar button of the type of shape that you want to draw.

3. On the sheet, click the start point for the shape and then drag to the end point of the shape. For freeform shapes, you must double-click to stop drawing.

To change the appearance of a drawing on a sheet, follow these steps:

1. Right-click the edge of the object. Excel displays a pop-up menu.

2. Choose Format Object from the menu. Excel displays the Format Object dialog box (see fig. 15.3).

3. Change the Patterns, Protection, and Properties attributes of the object as appropriate, then click OK.

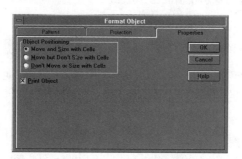

Fig. 15.3
The Format Object dialog box.

Working with Drawing Objects

Worksheets, charts, and dialog sheets have `DrawingObjects` collections that contain all the objects that you can draw on the sheet. The following are drawing objects:

Arc	Line
Button	ListBox
ChartObject	OLEObject
CheckBox	OptionButton
Drawing	Oval
DropDown	Picture
EditBox	Rectangle
GroupBox	ScrollBar
GroupObject	Spinner
Label	TextBox

`EditBox` is available only on dialog sheets.

Use the `DrawingObjects` collection to perform block operations on all the drawing objects on a sheet. Typical operations include grouping, deleting, and initializing the objects.

The following code line selects all the drawing objects so that you can move or copy them as a unit:

```
ActiveSheet.DrawingObjects.Select
```

This line deletes all the drawing objects on a sheet:

```
ActiveSheet.DrawingObjects.Delete
```

You can get individual objects from the `DrawingObjects` collection by using the object's name. The following code line sets the `Text` property of a Comments text box:

```
ActiveSheet.DrawingObjects("txtComments").Text = "Some comments..."
```

If a sheet contains only one type of drawing object, you can set the `DrawingObjects` properties. For example, if a sheet contains only `Line` objects, you can use the following code line to add arrows to all the lines:

```
ActiveSheet.DrawingObjects.ArrowHeadStyle = xlClosed
```

However, if the sheet contains a mix of drawing objects, the preceding code line does nothing. You cannot set the `ArrowHeadStyle` property of the `DrawingObjects` collection if it contains a mix of object types.

Tip

DrawingObject is a *metaobject;* that is, it exists only as a container of other drawing objects.

To set object-specific properties in the `DrawingObjects` collection, use a `For Each` loop with a conditional statement that checks the `TypeName` of the object. The following code lines perform various tasks on the objects in the `DrawingObjects` collection:

```
Sub ModifyDrawingObjects()
    ' Get each drawing object on the sheet.
    For Each drwObj In ActiveSheet.DrawingObjects
        ' Perform an appropriate action for each type of object.
        Select Case TypeName(drwObj)
```

```
                    Case "Arc", "Oval", "Rectangle"
                        drwObj.Interior.Color = RGB(255, 0, 0)
                    Case "Button", "GroupBox"
                        drwObj.Accelerator = Mid(drwObj.Caption, 1, 1)
                    Case "ChartObject"
                        drwObj.Chart.Type = xlLine
                    Case "CheckBox", "OptionButton"
                        drwObj.Value = True
                    Case "Drawing"
                        drwObj.Reshape 2, False
                    Case "DropDown", "ListBox"
                        drwObj.AddItem "New entry"
                    Case "EditBox", "TextBox"
                        drwObj.Text = "Your comments here."
                    Case "GroupObject"
                        drwObj.Ungroup
                    Case "Label"
                        drwObj.Caption = "A label"
                    Case "Line"
                        drwObj.ArrowHeadStyle = xlOpen
                    Case "OLEObject"
                        drwObj.Activate
                    Case "Picture"
                        drwObj.Border.Weight = xlMedium
                    Case "ScrollBar", "Spinner"
                        drwObj.Value = drwObj.Min
                End Select
            Next drwObj
    End Sub
```

Table 15.1 lists the properties and methods that apply to the `DrawingObjects` collection and shows the objects that use each property or method. **Bold** entries indicate properties and methods that you can use on the `DrawingObjects` collection, as well as on individual objects in the collection. These properties and methods affect the appropriate objects (as indicated by the table) when you use them with the `DrawingObjects` collection.

The behavior of many of these properties and methods varies from object to object. Refer to the reference sections in chapters 5-20 for the property or method description of individual objects. Property and method descriptions for drawing objects are found primarily in this chapter and in Chapter 13, "Creating Charts."

Tip
Use the `DrawingObjects` collection to pass all of a sheet's drawing objects to procedures for evaluation or initialization.

II

Programmer's Reference

Table 15.1 DrawingObjects properties and methods

Property/method	Arcs	Buttons	ChartObject	CheckBox	Drawing	DropDown	GroupBox	GroupObject	Label	Line	ListBox	OLEObject	OptionButton	Oval	Picture	Rectangle	ScrollBar	Spinner	TextBox	EditBox
Accelerator		✔		✔			✔		✔				✔							
AddIndent		✔																	✔	
AddItem						✔	✔				✔									
Application	✔	✔	✔	✔	✔	✔	✔	✔	✔	✔	✔	✔	✔	✔	✔	✔	✔	✔	✔	✔
ArrowHeadLength										✔										
ArrowHeadStyle										✔										
ArrowHeadWidth										✔										
AutoSize		✔																	✔	
Border	✔		✔	✔	✔				✔		✔	✔	✔	✔	✔	✔			✔	
BringToFront	✔	✔	✔	✔	✔	✔	✔	✔	✔	✔	✔	✔	✔	✔	✔	✔	✔	✔	✔	✔
CancelButton		✔																		
Caption		✔		✔			✔		✔				✔						✔	✔
Characters		✔		✔			✔		✔				✔						✔	✔
CheckSpelling		✔		✔			✔	✔	✔				✔						✔	
Copy	✔	✔	✔	✔	✔	✔	✔	✔	✔	✔	✔	✔	✔	✔	✔	✔	✔	✔	✔	✔
CopyPicture	✔	✔	✔	✔	✔	✔	✔	✔	✔	✔	✔	✔	✔	✔	✔	✔	✔	✔	✔	✔
Creator	✔	✔	✔	✔	✔	✔	✔	✔	✔	✔	✔	✔	✔	✔	✔	✔	✔	✔	✔	✔
Cut	✔	✔	✔	✔	✔	✔	✔	✔	✔	✔	✔	✔	✔	✔	✔	✔	✔	✔	✔	✔
DefaultButton		✔																		
Delete	✔	✔	✔	✔	✔	✔	✔			✔	✔	✔	✔	✔	✔	✔	✔	✔	✔	✔
DismissButton		✔																		
Display3DShading				✔		✔	✔				✔		✔				✔	✔		

Property/ method	Objects																			
	Arc	Button	ChartObject	CheckBox	Drawing	DropDown	GroupBox	GroupObject	Label	Line	ListBox	OLEObject	OptionButton	Oval	Picture	Rectangle	ScrollBar	Spinner	TextBox	EditBox
DisplayVertical Scrollbar																				✔
DropDownLines	✔	✔	✔	✔	✔	✔	✔		✔	✔	✔	✔	✔	✔	✔	✔	✔	✔	✔	
Duplicate	✔	✔	✔	✔	✔	✔	✔	✔	✔	✔	✔	✔	✔	✔	✔	✔	✔	✔	✔	✔
Enabled	✔	✔	✔	✔	✔	✔	✔	✔	✔	✔	✔	✔	✔	✔	✔	✔	✔	✔	✔	✔
Font		✔							✔										✔	
Height	✔	✔	✔	✔	✔	✔	✔	✔	✔	✔	✔	✔	✔	✔	✔	✔	✔	✔	✔	✔
HelpButton		✔																		
HorizontalAlignment	✔																		✔	
InputType																				✔
Interior	✔		✔	✔	✔		✔				✔	✔	✔	✔	✔				✔	
LargeChange																	✔			
Left	✔	✔	✔	✔	✔	✔	✔	✔	✔	✔	✔	✔	✔	✔	✔	✔	✔	✔	✔	✔
LinkCombo																				
LinkedCell				✔		✔					✔		✔				✔	✔		
List						✔					✔									
ListFillRange						✔					✔									
ListIndex						✔					✔									
Locked	✔	✔	✔	✔	✔	✔	✔	✔	✔	✔	✔	✔	✔	✔	✔	✔	✔	✔	✔	✔
LockedText		✔																	✔	
Max																	✔	✔		
Min																	✔	✔		
MultiLine																				✔
MultiSelect											✔									

(continues)

Table 15.1 Continued

Property/ method	Arc	Button	ChartObject	CheckBox	Drawing	DropDown	GroupBox	GroupObject	Label	Line	ListBox	OLEObject	OptionButton	Oval	Picture	Rectangle	ScrollBar	Spinner	TextBox	EditBox
OnAction	✔	✔	✔	✔	✔	✔	✔	✔	✔	✔	✔	✔	✔	✔	✔	✔	✔	✔	✔	✔
Orientation		✔																	✔	
Parent	✔	✔	✔	✔	✔	✔	✔		✔	✔	✔	✔	✔	✔	✔	✔	✔	✔	✔	
PhoneticAccelerator	✔		✔			✔		✔				✔								
Placement	✔	✔	✔	✔	✔	✔	✔	✔	✔	✔	✔	✔	✔	✔	✔	✔	✔	✔	✔	
PrintObject	✔	✔	✔	✔	✔	✔	✔	✔	✔	✔	✔	✔	✔	✔	✔	✔	✔	✔	✔	
RemoveAllItems						✔					✔									
RemoveItem						✔					✔									
RoundedCorners			✔													✔			✔	
Select	✔	✔	✔	✔	✔	✔	✔	✔	✔	✔	✔	✔	✔	✔	✔	✔	✔	✔	✔	✔
SendToBack	✔	✔	✔	✔	✔	✔	✔		✔	✔	✔	✔	✔	✔	✔	✔	✔	✔	✔	
Shadow			✔		✔		✔					✔		✔	✔	✔			✔	
SmallChange																	✔	✔		
Text		✔		✔		✔			✔				✔						✔	✔
Top	✔	✔	✔	✔	✔	✔	✔	✔	✔	✔	✔	✔	✔	✔	✔	✔	✔	✔	✔	✔
Ungroup								✔												
Value				✔		✔					✔		✔				✔	✔		
VerticalAlignment		✔																	✔	
Vertices					✔															
Visible	✔	✔	✔	✔	✔	✔	✔		✔	✔	✔	✔	✔	✔	✔	✔	✔	✔	✔	✔
Width	✔	✔	✔	✔	✔	✔	✔		✔	✔	✔	✔	✔	✔	✔	✔	✔	✔	✔	✔
ZOrder	✔	✔	✔	✔	✔	✔	✔		✔	✔	✔	✔	✔	✔	✔	✔	✔	✔	✔	✔

Grouping Objects as a Single Unit

You can link drawing objects together as a group. Grouped objects can be selected, moved, and deleted as a single unit.

To group objects in Excel, follow these steps:

1. Select the objects to group by clicking the objects while holding down the Shift key.

2. Click the Group button on the Drawing toolbar (see fig. 15.4).

Drawing Selections

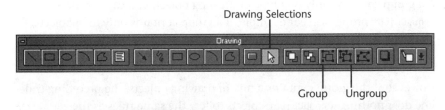

Fig. 15.4
The Drawing Selection, Group, and Ungroup buttons.

Group   Ungroup

> **Note**
>
> On worksheets and charts, you must click the Drawing Selection button (see fig. 15.4) before you can select drawing objects.

You cannot select the individual objects in a group unless you first ungroup the objects. To ungroup objects, follow these steps:

1. Select the group by clicking one of the objects in the group.

2. Click the Ungroup button on the Drawing toolbar (see fig. 15.4).

To group drawing objects using Visual Basic, you use the `Group` method. The following code line groups all the freeform shape objects on a sheet:

```
ActiveSheet.Drawings.Group
```

`Group` operates on collections of objects. When you use the `Selection` method, you can create collections that consist of a single type of object (`Drawings`, `Buttons`, `TextBoxes`, and so on) or of different types. The following code lines select three objects of different types and create a group:

```
Sub CreateGroup()
    ' Using the drawing objects on the active sheet,
    With ActiveSheet.DrawingObjects
        ' Select drawing object by name, replace current selection.
        .Item("edtComments").Select True
        ' Select two more, extending the selection.
```

Programmer's Reference

```
                        .Item("butOK").Select False
                        .Item("lblStatus").Select False
                End With
                ' Group the selection.
                Selection.Group
        End Sub
```

The `Group` method creates a `GroupObject` object. You access these objects with the `GroupObjects` or `DrawingObjects` collection. The following code line ungroups the group named `Group 6`:

```
        ActiveSheet.GroupObjects("Group 6").Ungroup
```

If a group contains only one type of drawing object, you can set the `GroupObject` properties. For example, if a group contains only `Line` objects, you can use the following code line to add arrows to all the lines:

```
        ActiveSheet.GroupObject("linGroup").ArrowHeadStyle = xlClosed
```

However, if the group contains a mix of drawing objects, the preceding code line does nothing. `GroupObject` objects follow the same rules as the `DrawingObjects` collection.

Tip

`GroupObject` is a *metaobject*; that is, it exists only as a container of other drawing objects.

Table 15.2 lists the `GroupObject` properties and methods. These properties and methods affect the drawing objects in the group. The behavior of many of these properties and methods varies from object to object. Refer to the reference sections in chapters 5-20 for the property or method description of the individual objects. Property and method descriptions for drawing objects are found primarily in this chapter and in Chapter 13, "Creating Charts."

Table 15.2 GroupObject and GroupObjects properties and methods

AddIndent[2]	Delete[2]
Application[2]	Duplicate[2]
ArrowHeadLength[2]	Enabled[2]
ArrowHeadStyle[2]	Font[2]
ArrowHeadWidth[2]	Group[1]
AutoSize[2]	Height[2]
Border[2]	HorizontalAlignment[2]
BottomRightCell	Index
BringToFront[2]	Interior[2]
CheckSpelling[2]	Item[1]
Copy[2]	Left[2]
CopyPicture[2]	Locked[2]
Count[1]	Name
Creator[2]	OnAction[2]
Cut[2]	Orientation[2]

Parent[2]	Top[2]
Placement[2]	TopLeftCell
PrintObject[2]	Ungroup[2]
RoundedCorners[2]	VerticalAlignment[2]
Select[2]	Visible[2]
SendToBack[2]	Width[2]
Shadow[2]	ZOrder[2]

[1] *Applies to the* GroupObjects *collection.*

[2] *Applies to the* GroupObjects *collection and the* GroupObject *object.*

Changing Interior Colors and Patterns

Most visible objects have an Interior object that controls the color and pattern displayed inside the object. Each of the objects in the following list has a Interior method that returns an Interior object:

CheckBox	Picture
DataLabel	Pictures
DownBars	PlotArea
Drawing	Point
DrawingObjects	Range
Floor	Rectangle
GroupObject	Series
Legend	Style
LegendKey	TextBox
OLEObject	UpBars
OptionButton	Walls
Oval	

To change the interior of one of these objects, set the interior properties. The following code line changes the interior color of a rectangle to green:

```
ActiveSheet.Rectangles(1).Interior.Color = RGB(0, 255, 0)
```

Table 15.3 lists the properties and methods of the Interior object. Those shown in **bold** are described in the reference section that follows this table. Nonbold items are common to most objects and are described in Chapter 4, "Using Objects."

Table 15.3 Interior properties and methods
Application
Color
ColorIndex
Creator
Parent
Pattern
PatternColor
PatternColorIndex

*interior.*Color

*interior.*Color [= *rgbcolor*]

Sets or returns the color of the interior of an object. The color is a long integer, created with the RGB function.

The following code line sets the interior of a selection to red:

```
Selection.Interior.Color = RGB(255, 0 , 0)
```

*interior.*ColorIndex

*interior.*ColorIndex [= *colorindex*]

Sets or returns the color of the interior of an object. The *colorindex* is an integer that indicates the position of the color in the current color palette. Set this property to xlAutomatic to use the automatic fill style.

*interior.*Pattern

*interior.*Pattern [= *setting*]

Sets or returns a constant that indicates the fill pattern of an object's interior. The constant can be any one of the following:

xlAutomatic	xlGray50
xlChecker	xlGray75
xlCrissCross	xlGray8
xlDown	xlGrid
xlGray16	xlHorizontal
xlGray25	xlLightDown

xlLightHorizontal	xlSemiGray75
xlLightUp	xlSolid
xlLightVertical	xlUp
xlNone	xlVertical

The default is xlAutomatic. The following code line sets the interior fill pattern of a selection to xlCrissCross:

```
Selection.Interior.Pattern = xlCrissCross
```

interior.PatternColor

interior.PatternColor [= *rgbcolor*]

Sets or returns the color of the fill pattern for the interior of an object. The color is a long integer, created with the RGB function.

The following code line sets the interior fill pattern of a selection to blue:

```
Selection.Interior.PatternColor = RGB(0, 0 , 255)
```

interior.PatternColorIndex

interior.PatternColorIndex [= *colorindex*]

Sets or returns the color of the fill pattern of an object. The *colorindex* is an integer that indicates the position of the color in the current color palette. The default is xlAutomatic.

Drawing Arcs

Arcs can be filled or empty (see fig. 15.5). You can combine arcs with other shapes to draw many types of figures. Use the Add method of the Arcs collection to draw an arc on a sheet.

The following code line draws an arc on a sheet:

```
ActiveSheet.Arcs.Add 1, 1, 100, 100
```

Use the arc's Border object to change the outline of an arc. The following code line changes the weight of the arc's outline:

```
ActiveSheet.Arcs(1).Border.Weight = xlMedium
```

Use the arc's Interior object to fill the arc with a color or pattern. The following code line shades the interior of an arc:

```
ActiveSheet.Arcs(1).Interior.Pattern = xlGray75
```

The Arc object and Arcs collection have specific properties and methods, which are listed in Table 15.4. Properties and methods shown in **bold** are described in the reference section that follows this table. Nonbold items are common to most objects and are described in Chapter 4, "Using Objects."

Fig. 15.5
Types of arcs.

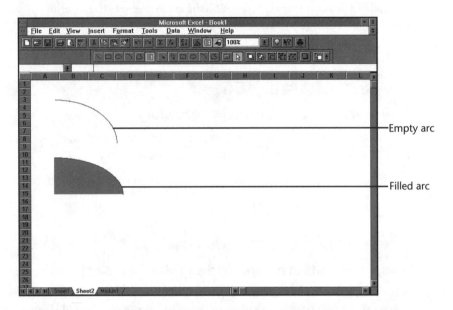

Empty arc

Filled arc

Table 15.4 Arc and Arcs properties and methods

Add[1]	**Interior**[2]
Application[2]	**Item**[1]
Border[2]	Left[2]
BottomRightCell	**Locked**[2]
BringToFront[2]	Name
Copy[2]	**OnAction**[2]
CopyPicture[2]	Parent[2]
Count[1]	**Placement**[2]
Creator[2]	**PrintObject**[2]
Cut[2]	**Select**[2]
Delete[2]	SendToBack[2]
Duplicate[2]	Top[2]
Enabled[2]	**TopLeftCell**[2]
Group[1]	Visible[2]
Height[2]	Width[2]
Index	ZOrder[2]

[1] *Applies to the Arcs collection.*

[2] *Applies to the Arcs collection and the Arc object.*

Arcs.Add

Arcs.Add (*X1, Y1, X2, Y2*)

Draws an arc on a sheet.

Argument	Description
X1	The distance, in points, between the left edge of the sheet and the starting point of the arc.
Y1	The distance, in points, between the top edge of the sheet and the starting point of the arc.
X2	The distance, in points, between the left edge of the sheet and the end point of the arc.
Y2	The distance, in points, between the top edge of the sheet and the end point of the arc.

The following code line draws an arc on the active sheet:

```
ActiveSheet.Arcs.Add 10, 20, 110,120
```

arc.Border

Returns the Border object for one or all arcs on a sheet. Use this property to change the border of an object. The following code line changes the borders of all arcs on a sheet to medium weight:

```
ActiveSheet.Arcs.Border.Weight = xlMedium
```

arc.BottomRightCell

Returns the cell under the bottom right corner of the arc.

arc.Copy( )

Copies one or all arcs on the sheet to the Clipboard.

The following code line copies the first arc on a sheet to the Clipboard:

```
ActiveSheet.Arcs(1).Copy
```

The next code line copies all the arcs on a sheet:

```
ActiveSheet.Arcs.Copy
```

arc.**CopyPicture**

arc.**CopyPicture** (*[Appearance]*, *[Format]*)

Copies one or all arcs on a sheet to the Clipboard, using a specific format.

Argument	Description
Appearance	xlScreen copies the object as it appears on-screen; xlPrinter copies the object as it would appear if printed using the current printer setup. The default is xlScreen.
Format	xlPicture creates the copy in PICT format; xlBitmap creates the copy as a bitmap. The default is xlPicture.

arc.**Cut( )**

Cuts one or all arcs on the sheet to the Clipboard.

The following code line cuts the first arc on a sheet to the Clipboard:

```
ActiveSheet.Arcs(1).Cut
```

This line cuts all the arcs on a sheet:

```
ActiveSheet.Arcs.Cut
```

arc.**Delete( )**

Deletes one or all arcs on the sheet. This method does not change the contents of the Clipboard.

The following code line deletes the first arc on a sheet to the Clipboard:

```
ActiveSheet.Arcs(1).Delete
```

This line deletes all the arcs on a sheet:

```
ActiveSheet.Arcs.Delete
```

arc.**Duplicate( )**

Makes a copy of one or all arcs on a sheet and returns the object (or collection) that was created.

The following code line duplicates the first arc on a sheet and moves it up slightly:

```
ActiveSheet.Arcs(1).Duplicate.Top = ActiveSheet.Arcs(1).Top -10
```

arc.Enabled

arc.Enabled [= True | False]

True enables one or all arcs on the sheet to respond to click events; False disables them. An arc responds to click events if its `OnAction` property is set to a procedure name. The default is True.

Arcs.Group( )

Groups a collection of arcs so that they can be selected, moved, copied, or deleted as a single object.

The following code line groups all the arcs on a sheet:

```
ActiveSheet.Arcs.Group
```

Arcs.Index

The `Index` property returns the index number of an arc within an `Arcs` collection.

arc.Interior

Returns the `Interior` object for one or all of the arcs on a sheet. Use the `Interior` object properties to set the shading and color of the interior of an object.

The following code line shades the interior of all the arc objects on a sheet:

```
ActiveSheet.Arcs.Interior.Pattern = xlGray16
```

Arcs.Item

Arcs.Item (*Index*)

The `Item` method returns a single arc when `Index` is specified, or a collection of arcs when no `Index` is specified.

arc.Locked

arc.Locked [= True | False]

True prevents changes to one or all the arcs on a sheet while the sheet is protected; False allows changes. The default is True.

*arc.*OnAction

*arc.*OnAction [= *procedure*]

Sets or returns the name of a procedure to run when one or all arcs on the sheet are clicked.

The following code line causes the procedure Foo() to run when the user clicks the object arcImedies:

```
ActiveSheet.Arc("arcImedies").OnAction = "Foo"
```

*arc.*Placement

*arc.*Placement [= xlMoveAndSize | xlMove | xlFreeFloating]

Sets or returns the way the arc is attached to the cells below it. The value can be xlMoveAndSize, xlMove or xlFreeFloating. The default is xlFreeFloating.

*arc.*PrintObject

*arc.*PrintObject [= True | False]

True prints the arc with the worksheet; False does not. The default is True.

The following code line turns off printing for all the arcs on a sheet:

```
ActiveSheet.Arcs.PrintObject = False
```

*arc.*Select

*arc.*Select ([*Replace*])

Selects one or all of the arcs on a sheet. Select is the equivalent of clicking the object. If *Replace* is False, Select extends the current selection, instead of deselecting previous selections. The default is True.

*arc.*TopLeftCell

Returns the cell that lies under the top-left part of the arc.

Drawing Freeform Shapes

To create freeform shapes, you use the Freeform or Freehand drawing tools on the Drawing toolbar. Freeform shapes may be open, closed, filled, or empty (see fig. 15.6). Use the Add method of the Drawings collection to create a freeform shape on a sheet.

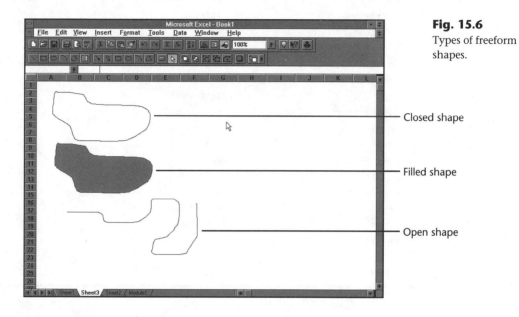

Fig. 15.6
Types of freeform shapes.

The following code line adds a closed shape to a sheet:

```
ActiveSheet.Drawings.Add 10, 20, 110,120, True
          ' Use True for closed shapes, False for open.
```

Because the shape is created with only a start and end point, the result is a straight line. To create more complex shapes and add vertices, use AddVertex.

The following code line adds a vertex to a shape:

```
ActiveSheet.Drawings(1).AddVertex 50, 70
```

Use the shape's Interior object to fill the shape with a color or pattern. The following code line shades the interior of a shape:

```
ActiveSheet.Drawings(1).Interior.Pattern = xlGray75
```

The Drawing object and Drawings collection have specific properties and methods, which are listed in Table 15.5. Properties and methods shown in **bold** are described in the reference section that follows this table. Nonbold items are common to most objects and are described in Chapter 4, "Using Objects."

Tip

Don't confuse the Drawings collection with the DrawingObjects collection, which contains all the different types of drawing objects on a sheet.

Table 15.5 Drawing and Drawings properties and methods

Add[1]	Item[1]
AddVertex	Left[2]
Application[2]	**Locked**[2]
Border[2]	Name
BottomRightCell	**OnAction**[2]
BringToFront[2]	Parent[2]
Copy[2]	**Placement**[2]
CopyPicture[2]	**PrintObject**[2]
Count[1]	**Reshape**[2]
Creator[2]	**Select**[2]
Cut[2]	SendToBack[2]
Delete[2]	**Shadow**[2]
Duplicate[2]	Top[2]
Enabled[2]	**TopLeftCell**
Group[1]	**Vertices**
Height[2]	Visible[2]
Index	Width[2]
Interior[2]	ZOrder[2]

[1] *Applies to the Drawings collection.*

[2] *Applies to the Drawings collection and the Drawing object.*

Drawings.Add

Drawings.Add (*X1, Y1, X2, Y2, Closed*)

Draws a freeform shape on a sheet. Because you can create the freeform shape with only a start and end point, the result is a straight line. To create more complex shapes and vertices use AddVertex.

Argument	Description
X1	The distance, in points, between the left edge of the sheet and the starting point of the drawing.
Y1	The distance, in points, between the top edge of the sheet and the starting point of the drawing.
X2	The distance, in points, between the left edge of the sheet and the end point of the drawing.
Y2	The distance, in points, between the top edge of the sheet and the end point of the drawing.

Argument	Description
Closed	True closes the figure by drawing a line between the starting and end point; False leaves the figure open. The difference between these two settings is apparent only after you add a vertex to the drawing.

The following code line draws a freeform shape on the active sheet:

```
ActiveSheet.Drawings.Add 10, 20, 110,120, True
```

drawing.AddVertex

drawing.AddVertex (*Left*, *Top*)

Adds a point to a freeform shape.

Argument	Description
Left	The distance, in points, between the left edge of the sheet and the point to add.
Top	The distance, in points, between the top edge of the sheet and the point to add.

The following code lines draw a random polygon on a sheet:

```
Sub DrawRandomPolygon()
    MaxX = ActiveWindow.UsableWidth
    MaxY = ActiveWindow.UsableHeight
    With ActiveSheet.Drawings.Add(1, 1, MaxX, MaxY, True)
        For i = 1 To 5
            .AddVertex Int(MaxX * Rnd) + 1, Int(MaxY * Rnd) + 1
        Next
    End With
End Sub
```

drawing.Border

Returns the Border object for one or all drawings on a sheet. Use this property to change the border of an object.

The following code line changes the borders of all freeform shapes on a sheet to medium weight:

```
ActiveSheet.Drawings.Border.Weight = xlMedium
```

II

Programmer's Reference

drawing.BottomRightCell

Returns the cell under the bottom-right corner of the drawing.

drawing.Copy( )

Makes a copy of one or all drawings on a sheet and returns the object (or collection) that was created.

The following code line duplicates the first drawing on a sheet and moves it up slightly:

```
ActiveSheet.Drawings(1).Duplicate.Top = _ _
    ActiveSheet.Drawings(1).Top -10
```

drawing.CopyPicture

drawing.CopyPicture ([*Appearance*], [*Format*])

Copies to the Clipboard one or all drawings in a sheet, using a specific format.

Argument	Description
Appearance	xlScreen copies the object as it appears on-screen; xlPrinter copies the object as it would appear if printed using the current printer setup. The default is xlScreen.
Format	xlPicture creates the copy in PICT format; xlBitmap creates the copy as a bitmap. The default is xlPicture.

drawing.Cut( )

Cuts one or all drawings on the sheet to the Clipboard.

The following code line cuts the first drawing on a sheet to the Clipboard:

```
ActiveSheet.Drawings(1).Cut
```

This line cuts all the drawings on a sheet:

```
ActiveSheet.Drawings.Cut
```

drawing.Delete( )

Deletes one or all drawings on the sheet. This method does not change the contents of the Clipboard.

The following code line deletes the first drawing on a sheet to the Clipboard:

```
ActiveSheet.Drawings(1).Delete
```

drawing.Duplicate( )

Makes a copy of one or all drawings on a sheet and returns the object (or collection) created.

The following code line duplicates the first drawing on a sheet and moves it down slightly:

```
ActiveSheet.Drawings(1).Duplicate.Top = _
    ActiveSheet.Drawings(1).Top -10
```

drawing.Enabled

drawing.Enabled [= True | False]

True enables one or all drawings on the sheet to respond to click events; False disables them from responding. A drawing responds to click events if its OnAction property is set to a procedure name. The default is True.

Drawings.Group( )

Groups a collection of drawings so they can be selected, moved, copied, or deleted as a single object.

The following code line groups all the drawings on a sheet:

```
ActiveSheet.Drawings.Group
```

drawing.Interior

Returns the Interior object for one or all of the drawings on a sheet. Use the Interior object properties to set the shading and color of the interior of an object.

The following code line shades the interior of all the drawing objects on a sheet:

```
ActiveSheet.Drawings.Interior.Pattern = xlGray16
```

drawing.Locked

drawing.Locked [= True | False]

True prevents changes to one or all the drawings on a sheet while the sheet is protected; False allows changes. The default is True.

*drawing.*OnAction

*drawing.*OnAction [= *procedure*]

Sets or returns the name of a procedure to run when one or all drawings on the sheet are clicked.

*drawing.*Placement

*drawing.*Placement [= xlMoveAndSize | xlMove | xlFreeFloating]

Sets or returns the way that the drawing is attached to the cells below it. The value can be xlMoveAndSize, xlMove, or xlFreeForm. The default is xlFreeFloating.

*drawing.*PrintObject

*drawing.*PrintObject [= True | False]

True prints the drawing with the worksheet; False does not. The default is True.

The following code line turns off printing for all the drawings on a sheet:

```
ActiveSheet.Drawings.PrintObject = False
```

*drawing.*Reshape

*drawing.*Reshape (*Vertex*, *Insert*, [*Left*], [*Top*])

Inserts or moves a point in a drawing.

Argument	Description
Vertex	The index of the point before which to move or insert the new point.
Insert	True inserts a new point; False moves an existing point.
Left	The distance, in points, between the left edge of the sheet and the point to add or move.
Top	The distance, in points, between the top edge of the sheet and the point to add or move.

The following code line moves the second point in a drawing:

```
ActiveSheet.Drawings(1).Reshape 2, False, 42, 100
```

drawing.Select

drawing.Select ([*Replace*])

Selects one or all of the drawings on a sheet. Select is the equivalent of clicking the object. If *Replace* is False, Select extends the current selection, instead of deselecting previous selections. The default is True.

drawing.Shadow

drawing.Shadow [= True | False]

True adds a drop-shadow to the object; False removes the shadow. The default is False.

drawing.TopLeftCell

Returns the cell that lies under the top-left part of the drawing.

drawing.Vertices

Returns a two-dimensional array that contains the x- and y-coordinates of the points in the drawing. The UBound of the returned array is the number of points in the drawing.

Drawing Lines and Arrows

Lines can be plain or end with a variety of arrowheads (see fig. 15.7). To draw a line or arrow on a sheet, use the Add method of the Lines collection.

The following code line draws a line on a sheet:

```
ActiveSheet.Lines.Add 1, 1, 100, 100
```

To add an arrowhead to a line, use the line's `ArrowHeadStyle` property. The following code line turns a line into an arrow:

```
ActiveSheet.Lines(1).ArrowHeadStyle = xlClosed
```

The following code changes an arrow back into a line:

```
ActiveSheet.Lines(1).ArrowHeadStyle = xlNone
```

Use the arc's `Border` object to change the color of a line or arrow. This line changes a line's color to red:

```
ActiveSheet.Arcs(1).Border.Color = RGB(255, 0, 0)
```

You can also use the `Border` object to change the line style of a line or arrow. The following code line draws a broken line:

```
ActiveSheet.Lines(1).Border.LineStyle = xlDash
```

The `Line` object and `Lines` collection have specific properties and methods, which are listed in Table 15.6. Properties and methods shown in **bold** are described in the reference section that follows this table. Nonbold items are common to most objects and are described in Chapter 4, "Using Objects."

Fig. 15.7
Types of lines.

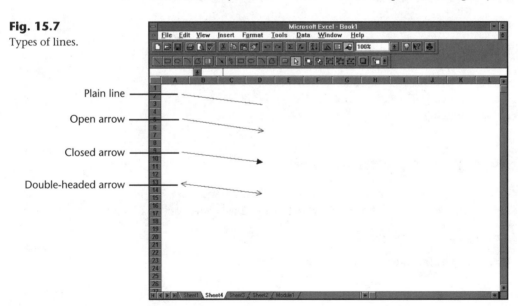

Table 15.6 Line and Lines properties and methods

Add[1]	Height[2]
Application[2]	Index
ArrowHeadLength[2]	**Item**[1]
ArrowHeadStyle[2]	Left[2]
ArrowHeadWidth[2]	**Locked**[2]
Border[2]	Name
BottomRightCell	**OnAction**[2]
BringToFront[2]	Parent[2]
Copy[2]	**Placement**[2]
CopyPicture[2]	**PrintObject**[2]
Count[1]	**Select**[2]
Creator[2]	SendToBack[2]
Cut[2]	Top[2]
Delete[2]	**TopLeftCell**
Duplicate[2]	Visible[2]
Enabled[2]	Width[2]
Group	ZOrder[2]

[1] *Applies to the Lines collection.*

[2] *Applies to the Lines collection and the Line object.*

Lines.Add

Lines.Add (*X1, Y1, X2, Y2*)

Draws a line on a sheet.

Argument	Description
X1	The distance, in points, between the left edge of the sheet and the starting point of the line.
Y1	The distance, in points, between the top edge of the sheet and the starting point of the line.
X2	The distance, in points, between the left edge of the sheet and the end point of the line.
Y2	The distance, in points, between the top edge of the sheet and the end point of the line.

The following code line draws a line on the active sheet:

```
ActiveSheet.Lines.Add 10, 20, 110,120
```

*line.*ArrowHeadLength

*line.*ArrowHeadLength [= xlShort | xlMedium | xlLong]

Sets or returns the length of the arrowhead on a line. The default is xlMedium.

*line.*ArrowHeadStyle

*line.*ArrowHeadStyle [= *setting*]

Sets or returns the style of the arrowhead on a line: xlNone, xlOpen, xlClosed, xlDoubleOpen, or xlDoubleClosed. The default is xlNone.

The following code line adds an arrowhead to a line:

```
ActiveSheet.Lines(1).ArrowHeadStyle = xlOpen
```

*line.*ArrowHeadWidth

*line.*ArrowHeadWidth [= xlNarrow | xlMedium | xlWide]

Sets or returns the width of the arrowhead on a line. The default is xlMedium.

*line.*Border

Returns the Border object for one or all lines on a sheet. Use this property to change the border of an object.

The following code line changes the borders of all lines on a sheet to medium weight:

```
ActiveSheet.Lines.Border.Weight = xlMedium
```

*line.*BottomRightCell

Returns the cell under the bottom-right corner of the line.

*line.*Copy( )

Makes a copy of one or all lines on a sheet and returns the object (or collection) created.

line.**CopyPicture**

line.**CopyPicture ([*Appearance*], [*Format*])**

Copies one or all lines in a sheet to the Clipboard, using a specific format.

Argument	Description
Appearance	xlScreen copies the object as it appears on-screen; xlPrinter copies the object as it would appear if printed using the current printer setup. The default is xlScreen.
Format	xlPicture creates the copy in PICT format; xlBitmap creates the copy as a bitmap. The default is xlPicture.

line.**Cut( )**

Cuts one or all lines on the sheet to the Clipboard.

The following code line cuts the first line on a sheet to the Clipboard:

```
ActiveSheet.Lines(1).Cut
```

line.**Delete( )**

Deletes one or all lines on the sheet. This method does not change the contents of the Clipboard.

The following code line deletes the first line on a sheet to the Clipboard:

```
ActiveSheet.Lines(1).Delete
```

line.**Duplicate( )**

Makes a copy of one or all lines on a sheet and returns the object (or collection) created.

line.**Enabled**

line.**Enabled [= True | False]**

True enables one or all lines on the sheet to respond to click events; False disables them from responding. A line responds to click events if its OnAction property is set to a procedure name. The default is True.

Lines.Group( )

Groups a collection of lines so they can be selected, moved, copied, or deleted as a single object.

The following code line groups all the lines on a sheet:

```
ActiveSheet.Lines.Group
```

line.Locked

line.Locked [= True | False]

True prevents changes to one or all the lines on a sheet while the sheet is protected; False allows changes. The default is True.

line.OnAction

line.OnAction [= *procedure*]

Sets or returns the name of a procedure to run when one or all lines on the sheet are clicked.

line.Placement

line.Placement [= xlMoveAndSize | xlMove | xlFreeFloating]

Sets or returns the way that the line is attached to the cells below it. The default is `xlFreeFloating`.

line.PrintObject

line.PrintObject [= True | False]

True prints the lines with the worksheet; False does not. The default is True.

The following code line turns off printing for all the lines on a sheet:

```
ActiveSheet.Lines.PrintObject = False
```

line.Select

line.Select ([*Replace*])

Selects one or all of the lines on a sheet. `Select` is the equivalent of clicking the object. If *Replace* is False, `Select` extends the current selection, instead of deselecting previous selections. The default is True.

line.TopLeftCell

Returns the cell that lies under the top-left part of the line.

Drawing Circles and Ovals

Use the Add method of the Ovals collection to draw a circle or oval on a sheet.
Figure 15.8 shows some of the ovals that you can draw.

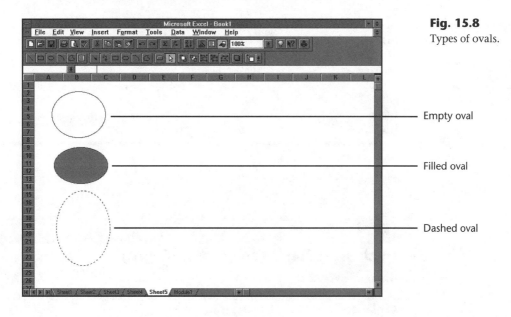

Fig. 15.8
Types of ovals.

Empty oval

Filled oval

Dashed oval

II

Programmer's Reference

The following code line draws a circle on a sheet:

```
ActiveSheet.Ovals.Add 1, 1, 100, 100
```

Use the oval's Interior object to change the fill color or pattern of an oval.
The following code line colors a circle red:

```
ActiveSheet.Ovals(1).Interior.Color = RGB(255, 0, 0)
```

Use the oval's Border object to change the line style of an oval. The following
code line draws the border of an oval as a broken line:

```
ActiveSheet.Ovals(1).Border.LineStyle = xlDash
```

The Oval object and Ovals collection have specific properties and methods,
which are listed in Table 15.7. Properties and methods shown in **bold** are
described in the reference section that follows this table. Nonbold items are
common to most objects and are described in Chapter 4, "Using Objects."

Table 15.7 Oval and Ovals properties and methods

Add[1]	Item[1]
Application[2]	Left[2]
Border[2]	**Locked**[2]
BottomRightCell	Name
BringToFront[2]	**OnAction**[2]
Copy[2]	Parent[2]
CopyPicture[2]	**Placement**[2]
Count[1]	**PrintObject**[2]
Creator[2]	**Select**[2]
Cut[1]	SendToBack[2]
Delete[2]	**Shadow**[2]
Duplicate[2]	Top[2]
Enabled[2]	**TopLeftCell**
Group[1]	Visible[2]
Height[2]	Width[2]
Index	ZOrder[2]
Interior[2]	

[1] *Applies to the Ovals collection.*

[2] *Applies to the Ovals collection and the Oval object.*

Ovals.Add

Ovals.Add (*Left, Top, Width, Height*)

Draws an oval on a sheet.

Argument	Description
X1	The distance, in points, between the left edge of the sheet and the right edge of the oval.
Y1	The distance, in points, between the top edge of the sheet and the top of the oval.
X2	The distance, in points, between the left edge of the sheet and the left edge of the oval.
Y2	The distance, in points, between the top edge of the sheet and the bottom edge of the oval.

The following code line draws an oval on the active sheet:

```
ActiveSheet.Ovals.Add 10, 20, 110,120
```

oval.Border

Returns the Border object for one or all ovals on a sheet. Use this property to change the border of an object.

oval.BottomRightCell

Returns the cell under the bottom-right part of the oval.

oval.Copy( )

Copies to the Clipboard one or all ovals on the sheet.

The following code line copies the first oval on a sheet to the Clipboard:

```
ActiveSheet.Ovals(1).Copy
```

oval.CopyPicture

oval.CopyPicture ([*Appearance*], [*Format*])

Copies to the Clipboard one or all ovals on a sheet, using a specific format.

Argument	Description
Appearance	xlScreen copies the object as it appears on-screen; xlPrinter copies the object as it would appear if printed using the current printer setup. The default is xlScreen.
Format	xlPicture creates the copy in PICT format; xlBitmap creates the copy as a bitmap. The default is xlPicture.

oval.Cut( )

Cuts one or all ovals on the sheet to the Clipboard.

The following code line cuts the first oval on a sheet to the Clipboard:

```
ActiveSheet.Ovals(1).Cut
```

oval.Delete( )

Deletes one or all ovals on the sheet. This method does not change the contents of the Clipboard.

oval.Duplicate( )

Makes a copy of one or all ovals on a sheet and returns the object (or collection) created.

oval.Enabled

oval.Enabled [= True | False]

True enables one or all ovals on the sheet to respond to click events; False disables them from responding. An oval responds to click events if its OnAction property is set to a procedure name. The default is True.

Ovals.Group( )

Groups a collection of ovals so they can be selected, moved, copied, or deleted as a single object.

The following code line groups all the ovals on a sheet:

```
ActiveSheet.Ovals.Group
```

oval.Interior

Returns the Interior object for one or all of the ovals on a sheet. Use the Interior object properties to set the shading and color of an object's interior.

oval.Locked

oval.Locked [= True | False]

True prevents changes to one or all the ovals on a sheet while the sheet is protected; False allows changes. The default is True.

oval.OnAction

oval.OnAction [= *procedure*]

Sets or returns the name of a procedure to run when one or all ovals on the sheet are clicked.

oval.Placement

oval.Placement [= xlMoveAndSize | xlMove | xlFreeFloating]

Sets or returns the way that the oval is attached to the cells below it. The default is xlFreeFloating.

oval.PrintObject

oval.PrintObject [= True | False]

True prints the ovals with the worksheet; False does not. The default is True.

The following code line turns off printing for all the ovals on a sheet:

```
ActiveSheet.Ovals.PrintObject = False
```

oval.Select

oval.Select ([*Replace*])

Selects one or all of the ovals on a sheet. Select is the equivalent of clicking the object. If *Replace* is False, Select extends the current selection, instead of deselecting previous selections. The default is True.

oval.Shadow

oval.Shadow [= True | False]

True adds a drop shadow to the object; False removes the shadow. The default is False.

oval.TopLeftCell

Returns the cell that lies under the top-left part of the oval.

Inserting Pictures

Use the Insert method of the Pictures collection to insert a picture from a file. The file must be a graphics file, such as a bit-map or PICT file.

The following code line inserts a bitmap in a sheet:

```
ActiveSheet.Pictures.Insert "IMAGE.BMP"
```

Use the Paste method to insert a picture from the Clipboard. Before you insert a picture from the Clipboard, you must check whether the Clipboard contains valid data.

The following code pastes a picture if the Clipboard contains valid data:

```
Sub PastePicture()
    FormatsArray = Application.ClipboardFormats
    For Each iFormat In FormatsArray
        Select Case iFormat
            Case xlClipboardFormatBIFF, xlClipboardFormatBIFF2,
```

```
            xlClipboardFormatBIFF3, _
                        xlClipboardFormatBIFF4, _
                        xlClipboardFormatBitmap, xlClipboardFormatCGM, _
                        xlClipboardFormatCSV, xlClipboardFormatPICT, _
                        xlClipboardFormatPrintPICT, _
                        xlClipboardFormatScreenPICT, _
                        xlClipboardFormatToolFace, _
                        xlClipboardFormatToolFacePICT
                        ActiveSheet.Pictures.Paste
                        Exit For
                End Select
            Next iFormat
        End Sub
```

Tip

Excel can take "pictures" of ranges, charts, and other linkable data. These pictures display data that the user cannot edit.

After you insert a picture in a worksheet, chart, or dialog sheet, it becomes part of that object's `Pictures` collection. The following code line deletes all the pictures in a sheet:

```
ActiveSheet.Pictures.Delete
```

Drawing Rectangles

Use the `Add` method of the `Rectangles` collection to draw a rectangle on a sheet. Figure 15.9 shows some of the types of rectangles that you can draw.

Fig. 15.9

Types of rectangles.

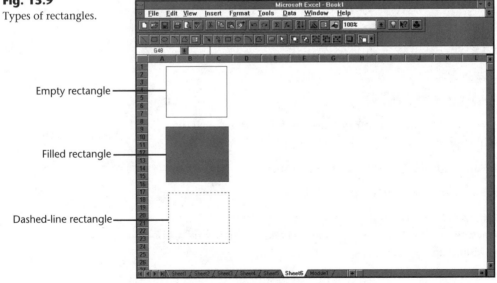

Empty rectangle

Filled rectangle

Dashed-line rectangle

The following code line draws a rectangle on a sheet:

```
ActiveSheet.Rectangles.Add 1, 1, 100, 100
```

Use the rectangle's `Interior` object to change the fill color or pattern of a rectangle. The following code line colors a rectangle blue:

```
ActiveSheet.Rectangles(1).Interior.Color = RGB(0, 0, 255)
```

Use the rectangle's `Border` object to change the line style of a rectangle. This line draws the border of a rectangle as a dashed line:

```
ActiveSheet.Rectangles(1).Border.LineStyle = xlDash
```

The `Rectangle` object and `Rectangles` collection have specific properties and methods, which are listed in Table 15.8. Properties and methods shown in **bold** are described in the reference section that follows this table. Nonbold items are common to most objects and are described in Chapter 4, "Using Objects."

Table 15.8 Rectangle and Rectangles properties and methods	
Add[1]	Item[1]
Application[2]	Left[2]
Border[2]	**Locked**[2]
BottomRightCell	Name
BringToFront[2]	**OnAction**[2]
Copy[2]	Parent[2]
CopyPicture[2]	**Placement**[2]
Count[1]	**PrintObject**[2]
Creator[2]	**RoundedCorners**[2]
Cut[2]	**Select**[2]
Delete[2]	SendToBack[2]
Duplicate[2]	**Shadow**[2]
Enabled[2]	Top[2]
Group[1]	**TopLeftCell**
Height[2]	Visible[2]
Index	Width[2]
Interior[2]	ZOrder[2]

[1] *Applies to the* `Rectangles` *collection.*

[2] *Applies to the* `Rectangles` *collection and the* `Rectangle` *object.*

II

Programmer's Reference

Rectangles.Add

Rectangles.Add (*Left, Top, Width, Height*)

Draws a rectangle on a sheet.

Argument	Description
Left	The distance, in points, between the left edge of the sheet and the right edge of the rectangle.
Top	The distance, in points, between the top edge of the sheet and the top of the rectangle.
Width	The width, in points, of the rectangle.
Height	The height, in points, of the rectangle.

The following code line draws a rectangle on the active sheet:

```
ActiveSheet.Rectangles.Add 10, 20, 40,10
```

rectangle.Border

Returns or sets the border of the rectangle. The following code sets the ColorIndex of a rectangle on the active sheet to 10:

```
ActiveSheet.Rectangles(1).Border.ColorIndex = 10
```

rectangle.BottomRightCell

Returns the cell under the bottom-right corner of the rectangle. The following code displays a message box with the reference for the cell under the bottom-right corner of the rectangle:

```
MsgBox "The bottom right corner is " & _
ActiveSheet.Rectangle(1).BottomRightCell.Address
```

rectangle.Copy( )

Copies to the Clipboard one or all rectangles on the sheet.

The following code line copies to the Clipboard the first rectangle on a sheet:

```
ActiveSheet.Rectangles(1).Copy
```

*rectangle.*CopyPicture
*rectangle.*CopyPicture ([*Appearance*], [*Format*])

Copies to the Clipboard one or all rectangles on a sheet, using a specific format.

Argument	Description
Appearance	xlScreen copies the object as it appears on-screen; xlPrinter copies the object as it would appear if printed using the current printer setup. The default is xlScreen.
Format	xlPicture creates the copy in PICT format; xlBitmap creates the copy as a bitmap. The default is xlPicture.

*rectangle.*Cut( )

Cuts one or all rectangles on the sheet to the Clipboard.

The following code line cuts the first rectangle on a sheet to the Clipboard:

```
ActiveSheet.Rectangles(1).Cut
```

*rectangle.*Delete( )

Deletes one or all rectangles on the sheet. This method does not change the contents of the Clipboard.

*rectangle.*Duplicate( )

Makes a copy of one or all rectangles on a sheet and returns the object (or collection) created.

*rectangle.*Enabled
*rectangle.*Enabled [= True | False]

True enables one or all rectangles on the sheet to respond to click events; False disables them from responding. A rectangle responds to click events if its OnAction property is set to a procedure name. The default is True.

Rectangle.Group( )

Groups a collection of rectangles so they can be selected, moved, copied, or deleted as a single object.

The following code line groups all the rectangles on a sheet:

```
ActiveSheet.Rectangles.Group
```

II

Programmer's Reference

*rectangle.*Interior

Returns the Interior object for one or all of the rectangles on a sheet. Use the Interior object properties to set the shading and color of the object's interior.

*rectangle.*Locked

*rectangle.*Locked [= True | False]

True prevents changes to one or all the rectangles on a sheet while the sheet is protected; False allows changes. The default is True.

*rectangle.*OnAction

*rectangle.*OnAction [= *procedure]*

Sets or returns the name of a procedure to run when one or any rectangles on the sheet are clicked.

*rectangle.*Placement

*rectangle.*Placement [= xlMoveAndSize | xlMove | xlFreeFloating]

Sets or returns the way that the rectangle is attached to the cells below it. The default is xlFreeFloating.

*rectangle.*PrintObject

*rectangle.*PrintObject [= True | False]

True prints the rectangles with the worksheet; False does not. The default is True.

The following code line turns off printing for all the rectangles on a sheet:

```
ActiveSheet.Rectangles.PrintObject = False
```

*rectangle.*RoundedCorners

*rectangle.*RoundedCorners [= True | False]

True rounds the corners of a rectangle; False displays square corners. The default is False.

rectangle.Select

rectangle.Select ([Replace])

Selects one or all of the rectangles on a sheet. `Select` is the equivalent of clicking the object. If `Replace` is False, `Select` extends the current selection, instead of deselecting previous selections. The default is True.

rectangle.Shadow

rectangle.Shadow [= True | False]

True adds a drop shadow to the object; False removes the shadow. The default is False.

rectangle.TopLeftCell

Returns the cell that lies under the top-left corner of the rectangle.

Chapter 16

Customizing Menus and Toolbars

You can customize Excel's workspace by changing the menus and toolbars that Excel displays and by adding new menus and toolbars to Excel. In fact, you can make Excel appear to be a completely customized application. This customization is useful when programming vertical applications and enterprise information systems (EIS).

In this chapter, you learn how to do the following:

- Create and modify menus.

- Assign procedures to run when a menu item is clicked.

- Distribute menus to other users.

- Add and remove menu bars, menus, and menu items dynamically.

- Create and modify toolbars.

- Assign procedures to run when a toolbar button is clicked.

- Add and remove toolbar and buttons dynamically.

This chapter covers the MenuBar, Menu, MenuItem, Toolbar, and ToolbarButton objects.

Editing Menus

Use Excel's Menu Editor to modify the menus that Excel displays. To start the menu editor, follow these steps:

1. Select or add a module sheet.

2. Choose **T**ools, Men**u** Editor. Excel displays the Menu Editor only when a module sheet is active (see fig. 16.1).

Fig. 16.1
The Menu Editor.

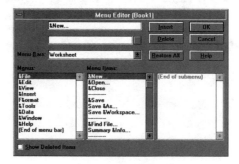

Excel menus have four parts, as shown in figure 16.2.

Fig. 16.2
Parts of a menu (menu objects).

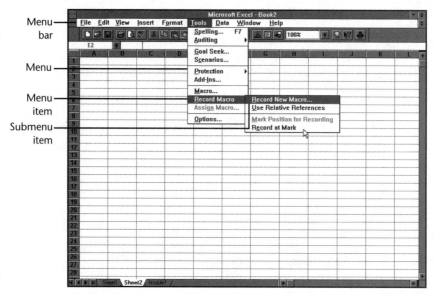

Menu bars change to reflect Excel's current context. While a worksheet is active, the Worksheet menu bar is displayed. When you switch to a module, the Visual Basic Module menu bar replaces the Worksheet menu bar, and so on.

Menu bars contain menus. In Excel, *menus* organize related tasks. These tasks are indicated by *menu items*. Each menu item performs a specific action when selected. The action may be a task, such as sorting, or a step toward a task, such as displaying a dialog box.

Submenu items subordinate a task one more level. For example, Record Macro gives you the submenu choices of recording a new macro, using relative references, or recording at a mark. Submenu items are used whenever displaying a dialog box would be obtrusive to a task.

Attaching Procedures to Menu Items

You can assign Visual Basic procedures to run when a user clicks a certain menu item. You can assign procedures only to menu items and submenu items that you have added; you can't attach procedures to menus or to built-in menu items.

To attach a procedure to a custom menu item, follow these steps:

1. From the Menu Editor, select the menu item by clicking its name in the Menu Items or Submenu Items list box.

2. In the Macro list box, type the name of the procedure to attach. Click OK.

Saving and Distributing Menus

Menu changes are saved with files. The changes last while the file is open. When a menu is saved with a workbook, it is *local* to that workbook—that is, it disappears as soon as you close the workbook. To make the changes available to all workbooks, save the changes to a workbook template.

A workbook template is a special type of Excel file (*.XLT) that provides a layout for new files. Excel defines two types of templates: the default template is named BOOK.XLT; custom templates may have any base name (other than CHART) and end with .XLT. Templates must be saved in Excel's startup directory (\EXCEL\XLSTART) if they are to be available automatically.

To create a template, follow these steps:

1. From the **F**ile menu, choose **N**ew.

2. Enter data, formats, and menu changes as appropriate.

3. Choose **F**ile, Save **A**s. Select Template from the Save File as Type list box and select Excel's start-up directory from the directories list box (usually \EXCEL\XLSTARTUP).

4. Type the base name of the file in the File Name text box. The base name is used as the default name for new files created from this template. For example, use BOOK for the default template—default names are BOOK1.XLS, BOOK2.XLS, and so on.

5. Click OK to save the file.

The new template is not automatically available until you restart Excel. After you restart Excel, Excel displays the New dialog box, shown in figure 16.3, and lists the template types if you have multiple template files in the start-up directory.

Fig. 16.3
The New dialog box. Sales is an added template.

To distribute a template to other users, simply copy the template file to their startup directory and restart Excel on their machine.

Creating and Displaying Menu Bars Dynamically

Excel changes menu bars when you activate various types of sheets and windows. The MenuBars collection contains all of these built-in menu bars. Use the constants in Table 16.1 to get at a specific menu. (Shortcut menus use strings rather than constants.)

Table 16.1 Built-in menu bar constants	
Constant	**Returns this menu bar**
xlWorksheet	Worksheet, macro sheet, and dialog sheet
xlChart	Chart
xlModule	Visual Basic module

Constant	Returns this menu bar
`xlNoDocuments`	No documents open
`xlInfo`	Info Window
`"Shortcut Menus 1"`	General worksheet, module, and toolbar shortcut menus
`"Shortcut Menus 2"`	Drawing object and dialog sheet shortcut menus
`"Shortcut Menus 3"`	Charting shortcut menus
`xlWorksheet4`	Excel version 4.0 worksheet menu bar
`xlChart4`	Excel version 4.0 chart menu bar
`xlWorksheetShort`	Excel version 3.0 short worksheet menu
`xlChartShort`	Excel version 3.0 short chart menu

The following code returns a reference to the worksheet menu bar:

```
Set mnubrWorksheet = MenuBars(xlWorksheet)
```

When you have a reference to a menu bar, you can get the menus it contains or add new menus to it. For instructions on adding menus to a menu bar, see the section "Creating and Displaying Menus Dynamically" later in this chapter.

Excel also enables you to create your own menu bars. The following code creates a new menu bar:

```
MenuBars.Add("New Menu Bar")
```

To display a menu bar, use the `Activate` method. This code displays the new menu bar:

```
MenuBars("New Menu Bar").Activate
```

If you ran the preceding line without looking ahead, you may have been surprised that you just wiped out the menu bar. The new menu bar is blank and it replaced the built-in menu bar when you activated it.

Note

While the Debug window is displayed, you won't see changes you make to the menu bar. You can't modify the Debug menu bar.

II

Programmer's Reference

To restore the built-in menu bar, activate it. The following code activates the module menu bar:

```
MenuBars(xlModule).Activate
```

> **Note**
>
> You can't activate a built-in menu bar if it conflicts with the current context. For example, you can't activate the worksheet menu bar while a module sheet is active.

The MenuBar object and MenuBars collection have specific properties and methods, which are listed in Table 16.2. Properties and methods shown in **bold** are described in the reference section that follows this table. Nonbold items are common to most objects and are described in Chapter 4, "Using Objects."

Table 16.2 MenuBar and MenuBars properties and methods

Activate

Add[1]

Application[2]

BuiltIn

Caption

Count[1]

Creator

Delete

Index

Item[1]

Menus

Parent[2]

Reset

[1] *Applies to the MenuBars collection.*

[2] *Applies to the MenuBars collection and the MenuBar object.*

menubar.Activate( )

Displays a menu bar. Causes error 1004 if you attempt to activate a built-in menu bar that conflicts with the current context—for example, if you try to activate the module menu while a worksheet is active.

MenuBars.Add

MenuBars.Add ([*Name*])

Adds a new, custom menu bar. *Name* is displayed in the Excel menu bar list and is used to identify the menu bar. The following code adds a new empty menu bar:

```
Menus.Add "New Menu"
```

*menubar.*BuiltIn

Returns True if the menu bar is a built-in menu bar; False if it is a custom menu. The following lines of code check to determine if the current menu bar is built in. If the menu bar is custom, the code replaces it with the appropriate built-in menu bar.

```
Sub DisplayBuiltinMenuBar()
    If Application.ActiveMenuBar.BuiltIn = False Then
        ' Important: Ignore errors for this next step.
        On Error Resume Next
            ' Set activate each of the built-in menus
            ' Only the one in the right context works,
            ' others all cause errors, but the error is ignored.
            MenuBars(xlWorksheet).Activate
            MenuBars(xlModule).Activate
            MenuBars(xlChart).Activate
            MenuBars(xlNoDocuments).Activate
            MenuBars(xlInfo).Activate
        ' Turn off error trapping (don't ignore errors).
        On Error GoTo 0
    End If
End Sub
```

*menubar.*Caption

Returns the name of the menu bar. This is the same as the Name property for the menu bar.

*menubar.*Delete()

Deletes a menu bar.

*menubar.*Menus

*menubar.*Menus ([*Index*])

Returns one or all of the Menu objects for a menu bar. Use the returned Menu objects to add new menus and modify existing menus on a menu bar.

*menubar.*Reset()

For built-in menu bars, restores the default settings and removes any custom menus or menu items that were added. Causes error 1004 for custom menu bars.

Creating and Displaying Menus Dynamically

You can use Visual Basic to create menus dynamically at runtime. This is useful when installing and removing add-in components and when creating systems that make menus available at the appropriate times within a workbook.

Use the Add method to add menus to a menu bar. The following code adds a Procedures menu to the Worksheet menu bar:

```
MenuBars(xlWorksheet).Menus.Add "&Procedures", "&Window"
```

Use the Delete method to remove menus from a menu bar. The following code deletes the Help menu:

```
MenuBars(xlWorksheet).Menus("Help").Delete
```

Use the Reset method to restore the default settings of a built-in menu. The following code restores the Help menu, previously deleted from the menu bar:

```
MenuBars(xlWorksheet).Reset
```

The Menu object and Menus collection have specific properties and methods, which are listed in Table 16.3. Properties and methods shown in **bold** are described in the reference section that follows this table. Nonbold items are common to most objects and are described in Chapter 4, "Using Objects."

Table 16.3 Menu and Menus properties and methods

Add[1]
Application[2]
Caption
Count[1]
Creator[2]
Delete
Enabled
Index

```
Item¹
MenuItems
Parent²
```

¹ *Applies to the Menus collection.*

² *Applies to the Menus collection and the Menu object.*

Menus.Add

Menus.Add (*Caption*, [*Before*], [*Restore*])

Adds a new custom menu to a menu bar or restores a previously deleted built-in menu.

Argument	Description
Caption	The name of the menu. Use the ampersand to specify the accelerator key; for example, &File.
Before	The index or the name of the menu before which to insert the new menu. The default is the Help menu.
Restore	True restores a previously deleted built-in menu; False adds a new custom menu. The default is False.

The following code adds a new menu to the worksheet menu bar:

```
MenuBars(xlWorksheet).Menus.Add "&Procedures", "&Window"
```

The following code restores the Help menu after it has been deleted:

```
MenuBars(xlWorksheet).Menus.Add "&Help", Restor:=True
```

> **Note**
>
> By default, menus are added before the Help menu. If you delete the Help menu, the default is to add menus as the last menu. To add menus after Help, delete the Help menu and then restore it at the desired location.

menu.Caption

menu.Caption [= *name*]

Sets or returns the name of a menu. The name appears on the menu bar. Use the ampersand to specify the accelerator key. For example, &File.

Programmer's Reference

menu.Delete( )

Deletes a custom or built-in menu from a menu bar. Use the Add method to restore a built-in menu.

The following code deletes the Procedures custom menu:

```
MenuBars(xlWorksheet).Menus("&Procedures").Delete
```

menu.Enabled

menu.Enabled [= True | False]

True enables a menu so it responds to user events, such as clicking; False disables the menu so it does not respond to user events. Disabled menus are grayed on the menu bar.

menu.Item

menu.Item (*Index*)

Returns a Menu object from the Menus collection. This is the default method for Menus, so Item may be omitted. *Index* may be the name of the menu or its index on the menu bar. If you use a name, the case and ampersand in *Index* are ignored. The Menus collection is indexed from 1 to Menus.Count.

The following code returns the File menu from the worksheet menu bar:

```
Set mnuFile = MenuBars(xlWorksheet).Menus("File")
```

menu.MenuItems

menu.MenuItems ([*Index*])

Returns one or all MenuItem objects from a menu. Use the returned MenuItem object to add or modify menu items on a menu.

The following code adds a menu item to the Tools menu:

```
MenuBars(xlWorksheet).Menus("Tools").MenuItems.Add "&Get Quotes"
```

Adding Items to Menus

You can use Visual Basic to create menu items dynamically at runtime. This approach is useful when updating lists on a menu. Excel's Window list is an example of a use for dynamic menu items.

Use the Add method to add menu items to a menu. The following code adds an item to the Window menu:

```
MenuBars(xlWorksheet).Menus("Window").MenuItems.Add "&Locator Map"
```

Use the Add method with a hyphen to add a separator bar to a menu. A *separator bar* is a horizontal line drawn between two menu items. This code adds a separator bar to the Window menu:

```
MenuBars(xlWorksheet).Menus("Window").MenuItems.Add "-"
```

Use the Delete method to remove items from a menu. This code deletes the menu item added above:

```
MenuBars(xlWorksheet).Menus("Window").MenuItems("Locator Map").Delete
```

Use the Reset method to restore the default settings of a built-in menu. This code restores the Window menu:

```
MenuBars(xlWorksheet).Menus("Window").Reset
```

The MenuItem object and MenuItems collection have specific properties and methods, which are listed in Table 16.4. Properties and methods shown in **bold** are described in the reference section that follows this table. Nonbold items are common to most objects and are described in Chapter 4, "Using Objects."

Table 16.4 MenuItem and MenuItems properties and methods

Add[1]
AddMenu
Application[2]
Caption
Checked
Count[1]
Creator[2]
Delete
Enabled
Index
Item[1]
Parent[2]

---

[1] *Applies to the MenuItems collection.*

[2] *Applies to the MenuItems collection and the MenuItem object.*

MenuItems.Add

MenuItems.Add (*Caption*, [*OnAction*], [*ShortcutKey*], [*Before*], [*Restore*])

Adds a custom menu item to a menu and restores previously deleted built-in menu items.

Argument	Description
Caption	The name of the menu item. Use an ampersand to specify the accelerator key; for example, &Delete. Use a hyphen to add a separator bar to the menu.
Before	The index or the name of the menu item before which to insert the new item. The default is to add the item as the last item on the menu.
OnAction	The name of a procedure to run when the menu item is clicked.
ShortcutKey	Macintosh only. Sets the shortcut key for the menu item.
Before	The index or the name of the menu item before which to insert the new item. The default is to add the item as the last item on the menu.
Restore	True restores a previously deleted built-in menu item; False adds a new custom menu item. The default is False.

The following code adds a new menu to the worksheet menu bar:

```
MenuBars(xlWorksheet).Menus.Add "&Procedures", "&Window"
```

The following code restores the Help menu after it has been deleted:

```
MenuBars(xlWorksheet).Menus.Add "&Help", Restore:=True
```

MenuItems.AddMenu

MenuItems.AddMenu (*Caption*, [*Before*], [*Restore*])

Adds a submenu to a menu or restores a previously deleted built-in submenu.

Argument	Description
Caption	The name of the submenu. Use an ampersand to specify the accelerator key; for example, &Advanced.
Before	The index or the name of the menu item to insert the new menu before. The default is to insert the submenu as the last item in the menu.

Argument	Description
Restore	True restores a previously deleted built-in submenu; False adds a new custom submenu. The default is False.

The following code adds a new submenu to the Tools menu:

```
MenuBars(xlWorksheet).Menus("Tools").MenuItems.AddMenu "&Procedures"
```

This code restores the Help menu after it has been deleted:

```
MenuBars(xlWorksheet).Menus("Tools").MenuItems.AddMenu _
"&Protection", Restore:=True
```

menuitem.Caption

menuitem.Caption [= *name*]

Sets or returns the name of a menu item. The name appears on the menu bar. Use an ampersand to specify the accelerator key; for example, &Sort.

menuitem.Checked

menuitem.Checked [= True | False]

True places a check mark beside the menu item; False removes the check mark. The default is False.

menuitem.Delete()

Deletes a custom or built-in menu item from a menu. Use the Add method to restore a built-in menu item.

The following code deletes the Procedures item menu from the Tools menu:

```
MenuBars(xlWorksheet).Menus("Tools").MenuItems("Procedures").Delete
```

menuitem.Enabled

menuitem.Enabled [= True | False]

True enables a menu item so it responds to user events, such as clicking; False disables the item so it does not respond to user events. Disabled items are grayed on the menu.

Tip
Using an ellipsis (...) to indicate menu items that display dialog boxes is standard programming practice cited in Windows and Macintosh user interface guidelines.

II

Programmer's Reference

MenuItems.Item

MenuItems.Item (*Index*)

Returns a `MenuItem` object from the `MenuItems` collection. This is the default method for `MenuItems`, so the word "Item" may be omitted. *Index* may be the name of the item or its index on the menu. If you use a name, the case and ampersand in *Index* are ignored.

The following code returns the Save item from the File menu:

```
Set mnuitFile =
MenuBars(xlWorksheet).Menus("File").MenuItems("Save")
```

Creating and Editing Toolbars

You can customize your workspace by creating new toolbars and by changing existing, built-in toolbars. Changes are saved with your system and remain in effect until you delete or reset the toolbars. A typical toolbar is shown in figure 16.4.

Fig. 16.4
A toolbar in Excel.

From within Excel you can do the following toolbar-related activities:

■ Create new toolbars.

■ Add buttons to new and existing toolbars.

■ Change the image displayed on a button.

■ Change the procedure assigned to a button.

■ Distribute custom toolbars to others.

The following sections describe how to perform these tasks manually from within Excel. To learn how to perform these tasks using the Visual Basic programming language, see the sections "Creating and Displaying Toolbars Dynamically" and "Adding Buttons to Toolbars Dynamically," later in this chapter.

Creating New Toolbars

To create a new toolbar in Excel:

1. Choose **V**iew, **T**oolbars. Excel displays the Toolbars dialog box (see fig. 16.5).

Fig. 16.5
The Toolbars dialog box.

2. Type the name of the toolbar to create in the Toolbar Name text box.

3. Click **N**ew. Excel displays the Customize dialog box (see fig. 16.6).

Fig. 16.6
The Customize dialog box.

Adding Buttons to Toolbars

To add a button to a toolbar, do the following:

1. Drag a button from the Buttons list on the Customize dialog box onto the destination toolbar.

2. If the button is from the Custom category, Excel displays the Assign Macro dialog box (see fig. 16.7).

3. In the Macro Name text box, type the name of a procedure to run when the button is clicked. Click OK.

Programmer's Reference

II

Fig. 16.7
The Assign Macro
dialog box.

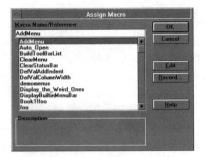

Changing the Procedure Assigned to a Button

To change the assigned procedure name:

1. Display the Customize dialog box.

2. Choose **T**ools, Assig**n** Macro. (The Tools and shortcut menus display Assign Macro only while the Customize dialog box is displayed.) Excel displays the Assign Macro dialog box.

3. Type the new procedure name in the Macro Name text box and click OK.

Changing a Button Image

To edit a button image:

1. Display the Customize dialog box.

2. Left mouse click on the button to edit. Excel displays a shortcut menu.

3. Choose **E**dit Button Image. (The shortcut menu only displays Edit Button Image while the Customize dialog box is on-screen.) Excel displays the Button Editor (see fig. 16.8).

Fig. 16.8
The Button Editor.

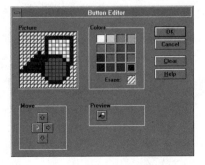

4. Edit the image and click OK.

Distributing Toolbars with Files

You can distribute custom toolbars to other users by attaching them to a workbook, add-in, or template file. When other users open the file, the toolbar is installed on their system. The user opens the file only once to install the toolbar.

To attach a toolbar to a file:

1. Open or create the file to which you want to attach the toolbar.

2. Display a Module sheet.

3. Choose **T**ools, Attach **T**oolbar. Excel displays the Attach Toolbars dialog box (see fig. 16.9).

4. Select a toolbar and click **C**opy. You can attach as many toolbars as you like to a file.

5. Click OK and save the file. Excel defines the XLB file extension for toolbars, though you can use a file extension of your choice.

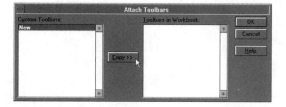

Fig. 16.9
The Attach Toolbars dialog box.

II

Programmer's Reference

Creating and Displaying Toolbars Dynamically

You can use Visual Basic to create toolbars dynamically at runtime. This procedure is useful when installing and removing add-in components and when creating systems that make tools available at the appropriate times (just as Excel alters its menus as you switch between contexts).

Use the Add method of the Toolbars collection to add toolbars dynamically. The following code adds a new custom toolbar:

```
Toolbars.Add "Budget Tools"
```

Tip
If the buttons on the toolbar run Visual Basic procedures, make sure the file containing those procedures is on the user's path or in Excel's library directory (\EXCEL\LIBRARY by default).

Adding a toolbar automatically displays it. You can hide the toolbar using its `Visible` property. The following code adds a toolbar, but does not display it:

```
Toolbars.Add ("Invoicing Tools").Visible = False
```

Toolbar position is controlled by the `Position`, `Top`, and `Left` properties. `Position` determines whether the toolbar floats or is attached to the edge of the window. The following code makes the Standard toolbar a floating toolbar:

```
Toolbars("Standard").Position = xlFloatingToolbar
```

You remove a custom toolbar using the `Delete` method. You can't delete built-in toolbars, but you can restore their default setting using the `Reset` method.

Following are the names of the built-in toolbars Excel provides:

Auditing

Chart

Drawing

Formatting

Forms

Full Screen

Microsoft

Query and Pivot

Standard

Stop Recording

TipWizard

Visual Basic

WorkGroup

The `Toolbar` object and `Toolbars` collection have specific properties and methods, which are listed in Table 16.5. Properties and methods shown in **bold** are described in the reference section that follows this table. Nonbold items are common to most objects and are described in Chapter 4, "Using Objects."

Table 16.5 Toolbar and toolbars properties and methods

Add[1]
Application[2]
BuiltIn
Count[1]
Creator[2]
Delete
Height
Item[1]
Left
Name
Parent[2]
Position
Reset
ToolbarButtons
Top
Visible
Width

[1] *Applies to the* Toolbars *collection.*

[2] *Applies to the* Toolbars *collection and the* Toolbars *object.*

Toolbars.Add

Toolbars.Add ([*Name*])

Adds a new custom toolbar. Name is the name that appears on Excel's toolbar list and on the title bar of the toolbar. The default is Toolbar *n*.

The following code adds the Custom Tools toolbar:

```
ToolBars.Add "Custom Tools"
```

toolbar.BuiltIn

Returns True if the toolbar is built-in, False if it is a custom toolbar.

toolbar.Delete( )

Deletes a custom toolbar. You cannot delete built-in toolbars, although attempting to delete a built-in toolbar does not cause an error. The following code deletes the Custom Tools toolbar:

```
ToolBars.Delete "Custom Tools"
```

*toolbar.*Position

*toolbar.*Position [= *setting*]

Sets or returns the position of a toolbar: xlTop, xlLeft, xlRight, xlBottom, or xlFloating. Use the Visible property to display a toolbar.

The following code displays a floating toolbar:

```
Sub DisplayToolBar()
     Toolbars("Custom Tools").Visible = True
     Toolbars("Custom Tools").Position = xlFloatingtoolbar
End Sub
```

*toolbar.*Reset()

Restores the default settings of a built-in toolbar, removing any custom buttons that may have been added. The following code restores the defaults settings for the Standard toolbar:

```
Toolbars("Standard").Reset
```

*toolbar.*ToolbarButtons

*toolbar.*ToolbarButtons ([*Index*])

Returns one or all ToolbarButton objects from a toolbar. Use the returned ToolbarButton object to add or modify buttons on a toolbar.

The following code adds a button to the Standard toolbar:

```
Toolbars("Standard").ToolbarButtons.Add 27, _
OnAction:="Display_Chart"
```

Adding Buttons to Toolbars Dynamically

You can add buttons to toolbars dynamically at runtime. This is useful when installing and removing add-in components and to make tools available at the appropriate times.

Use the Add method of the ToolbarButtons collection to add buttons dynamically. The following code adds the Sorting button to the Standard toolbar:

```
Toolbars("Standard").Toolbarbuttons.Add 134
```

The preceding line uses button ID 134. This is the built-in button for sorting in ascending order. By default, this button retains its built-in function; you can redefine it, however, by specifying a procedure to run. The following code adds the same button, but reassigns it to run CustomSort() when clicked:

```
Toolbars("Standard").Toolbarbuttons.Add 134, OnAction:="CustomSort"
```

Changing the Appearance of Buttons

You can choose from over 200 buttons in Excel. These buttons are listed in Table 16.7, later in this chapter. You're not limited to those buttons, however. You can change the appearance of a button by editing it directly or by pasting in a new bitmap.

Use the Edit method to edit a button. The following code displays Excel's Button Editor for a toolbar button:

```
Toolbars("Standard").Toolbarbuttons(1).Edit
```

Use the PasteFace method to paste a bitmap onto a button. The following code pastes a bitmap from the Clipboard to a button:

```
Toolbars("Standard").Toolbarbuttons(1).PasteFace
```

You can't change the appearance of these buttons, because they all display drop-down lists:

Button ID	Name
68	Font name
69	Font size
70	Style
166	Scenarios
178	TipWizard
189	Zoom control
198	Borders
232	Pattern
233	Color
234	Chart type
235	Shape
236	Font color

Tip

Excel's buttons are 15 pixels high by 16 pixels wide. Larger images are scaled accordingly, but don't look very good.

II

Programmer's Reference

Adding Spaces Between Buttons

Excel uses the button ID 0 to add spaces between buttons. Spaces between buttons are about one-quarter the width of a button. These lines of code add a space and then a button:

```
Sub AddButtonSpace()
    Toolbars("Standard").ToolbarButtons.Add 0
    Toolbars("Standard").ToolbarButtons.Add 27
End Sub
```

The `ToolbarButton` object and `ToolbarButtons` collection have specific properties and methods, which are listed in Table 16.6. Properties and methods shown in **bold** are described in the reference section that follows this table. Nonbold items are common to most objects and are described in Chapter 4, "Using Objects."

Table 16.6 ToolbarButton and ToolbarButtons properties and methods	
Add[1]	**Id**
Application[2]	**IsGap**
BuiltIn	Item
BuiltInFace	**Move**
Copy	Name
CopyFace	**OnAction**
Count[1]	Parent[2]
Creator[2]	**PasteFace**
Delete	**Pushed**
Edit	**Reset**
Enabled	Width

[1] *Applies to the* `ToolbarButtons` *collection.*

[2] *Applies to the* `ToolbarButtons` *collection and the* `ToolbarButton` *object.*

ToolbarButtons.Add

ToolbarButtons.Add ([*Button*], [*Before*], [*OnAction*], [*Pushed*], [*Enabled*])

Adds a button to a custom or built-in toolbar.

Argument	Description
Button	A number indicating the button to display. See Table 16.7 for a list of the button IDs.
Before	The index of the button before which to insert the new button. The default is to add the button as the last button on the toolbar.
OnAction	The name of a procedure to run when the button item is clicked.
Pushed	True makes the button appear pressed on the toolbar; False displays the normal appearance (unpressed). The default is False.
Enabled	True enables a button, so it can respond to user events such as clicking; False disables the button so it does not respond to user events. Disabled buttons are grayed on the toolbar.

The following code adds a button to the standard toolbar:

```
Toolbars("Standard").ToolbarButtons.Add 27, , "PlaySoundNotes"
```

*toolbarbutton.***BuiltIn**

Returns True if the button is built-in; False if it is a custom button.

*toolbarbutton.***BuiltInFace**

*toolbarbutton.***BuiltInFace [= True]**

Returns True if the button's appearance comes from one of the built-in button IDs; False if it is a button face. Set to True to replace a custom face with a built-in one. You can set BuiltInFace to False.

*toolbarbutton.***Copy**

*toolbarbutton.***Copy (*Toolbar, Before*)**

Copies a button to another location.

Argument	Description
Toolbar	The Toolbar object to which to copy the button.
Before	The index of the destination toolbar button before which you want to place the copied button.

The following code makes a copy of a button on the Custom Tools toolbar:

```
Toolbars("Custom Tools").ToolbarButtons(1).Copy Toolbars _
("Custom Tools"), 1
```

toolbarbutton.**CopyFace()**

Copies the bitmap of the button's appearance to the Clipboard.

toolbarbutton.**Delete()**

Deletes a button from a toolbar. Use the Reset method to restore built-in buttons that you delete.

toolbarbutton.**Edit()**

Edits the button using the Button Editor.

toolbarbutton.**Enabled**

toolbarbutton.**Enabled [= True | False]**

True enables a button so it responds to user events, such as clicking; False disables the button so it does not respond to user events. Disabled buttons are grayed on the toolbar.

toolbarbutton.**Id**

Returns the ID that determines the button's appearance. See Table 16.7 for a list of button IDs.

toolbarbutton.**IsGap**

Returns True if the button is a gap, rather than an actual button.

toolbarbutton.**Move**

toolbarbutton.**Move (*Toolbar*, *Before*)**

Moves a button to another location on the current toolbar or another toolbar.

Argument	Description
Toolbar	The Toolbar object to which to move the button.
Before	The index of the destination toolbar button before which you want the moved button located.

The following code moves a button from one location to another on the Custom Tool toolbar:

```
Toolbars("Custom Tools").ToolbarButtons(1).Move Toolbars _
("Custom Tools"), 2
```

toolbarbutton.OnAction

toolbarbutton.OnAction [= *procedure*]

Sets or returns a procedure to run when the button is pressed.

toolbarbutton.PasteFace( )

Pastes a bitmap from the Clipboard to the button.

toolbarbutton.Pushed

toolbarbutton.Pushed [= True | False]

True displays the button pushed in; False displays the normal appearance (unpressed). The default is determined by Add.

toolbarbutton.Reset( )

Restores a built-in button's default settings on a built-in toolbar. The following code restores the standard settings of the first button on the Standard toolbar:

```
Toolbars("Standard").ToolbarButtons(1).Reset
```

Table 16.7 shows the toolbar buttons that Excel provides. Use the button ID with the Add method when adding buttons to a toolbar.

Table 16.7 Toolbar button IDs

Button ID	Appears as	Description
0	Blank space	Separates groups of toolbar buttons
1		Open
2		Save
3		Print
4		Print Preview
5		Set Print Area
6		Insert MS Excel 4.0 Macro
7		Insert Worksheet
8		Insert Chart Sheet
9		New Workbook
10		Undo
11		Repeat
12		Cut
13		Copy
14		Paste
15		Clear Contents
16		Clear Formats
17		Paste Formats

Button ID	Appears as	Description
18		Paste Values
19		Delete
20		Delete Row
21		Delete Column
22		Insert
23		Insert Row
24		Insert Column
25		Fill Right
26		Fill Down
27		Equal Sign
28		Plus Sign
29		Minus Sign
30		Multiplication Sign
31		Division Sign
32		Exponentiation Sign
33		Left Parenthesis
34		Right Parenthesis
35		Colon

(continues)

II

Programmer's Reference

Table 16.7 Continued

Button ID	Appears as	Description
36		Comma
37		Percent Sign
38		Dollar Sign
39		AutoSum
40		Function Wizard
41		Paste Names
42		Constrain Numeric
43		Outline Border
44		Left Border
45		Right Border
46		Top Border
47		Bottom Border
48		Bottom Double Border
49		Dark Shading
50		Light Shading
51		Drop Shadow
52		AutoFormat
53		Currency Style

Button ID	Appears as	Description
54		Percent Style
55		Comma Style
56		Increase Decimal
57		Decrease Decimal
58		Bold
59		Italic
60		Underline
61		Strikethrough
62		Cycle Font Color
63		Align Left
64		Center
65		Align Right
66		Justify Align
67		Center Across Columns
68	Font name	Font
69	Font size	Font Size
70	Style	Style
71		Increase Font Size

(continues)

Table 16.7 Continued		
Button ID	**Appears as**	**Description**
72		Decrease Font Size
73		Vertical Text
74		Rotate Text Up
75		Rotate Text Down
76		Line
77		Arrow
78		Freehand
79		Text Box
80		Create Button
81		Selection
82		Reshape
83		Rectangle
84		Ellipse
85		Arc
86		Polygon
87		Freeform
88		Filled Rectangle
89		Filled Ellipse

Button ID	Appears as	Description
90		Filled Arc
91		Filled Polygon
92		Filled Freeform
93		Group Objects
94		Ungroup Objects
95		Bring To Front
96		Send To Back
97		Custom
98		Record Macro
99		Stop Macro
100		Run Macro
101		Step Macro
102		Resume Macro
103		Area Chart AutoFormat
104		Bar Chart AutoFormat
105		Column Chart AutoFormat
106		Stacked Column Chart AutoFormat
107		Line Chart AutoFormat

(continues)

Table 16.7 Continued

Button ID	Appears as	Description
108		Pie Chart AutoFormat
109		3-D Area Chart AutoFormat
110		3-D Bar Chart AutoFormat
111		3-D Column Chart AutoFormat
112		3-D Perspective Column Chart AutoFormat
113		3-D Line Chart AutoFormat
114		3-D Pie Chart AutoFormat
115		XY (Scatter) Chart AutoFormat
116		3-D Surface Chart AutoFormat
117		Radar Chart AutoFormat
118		Line/Column Chart AutoFormat
119		Volume/High-Low-Close Chart AutoFormat
120		Default Chart
121		ChartWizard
122		Horizontal Gridlines
123		Vertical Gridlines
124		Legend
125		Camera

Button ID	Appears as	Description
126		Calculate Now
127		Spelling
128		Help
129		Ungroup
130		Group
131		Show Outline Symbols
132		Select Visible Cells
133		Select Current Region
134		Sort Ascending
135		Sort Descending
136		Lock Cell
137		Freeze Panes
138		Zoom In
139		Zoom Out
140		Check Box
141		Option Button
142		Edit Box
143		Scroll Bar

(continues)

Table 16.7 Continued		
Button ID	**Appears as**	**Description**
144		List Box
145		Doughnut Chart AutoFormat
146	N/A	Can't be used
147		Remove Dependent Arrows
148		Trace Dependents
149		Remove Precedent Arrows
150	N/A	Can't be used
151	N/A	Can't be used
152	N/A	Can't be used
153		Remove All Arrows
154		Attach Note
155	N/A	Can't be used
156	N/A	Can't be used
157	N/A	Can't be used
158	N/A	Can't be used
159	N/A	Can't be used
160		Microsoft FoxPro
161	N/A	Can't be used

Button ID	Appears as	Description
162		Routing Slip
163		Send Mail
164		Update File
165		Toggle Read Only
166	Scenarios	Scenarios
167		PivotTable Wizard
168		AutoFilter
169	N/A	Can't be used
170		Refresh Data
171		PivotTable Field
172		Show Pages
173		Show Detail
174		Trace Error
175		Hide Detail
176		Double Underline
177		Find File
178	TipWizard	TipWizard Box
179		TipWizard

(continues)

Table 16.7 Continued

Button ID	Appears as	Description
180		Tip Help
181		Group Box
182		Drop-Down
183		Spinner
184		Drawing Selection
185		Format Painter
186		Tab Order
187		Run Dialog
188		Combination List-Edit
189	Zoom control	Zoom Control
190		Insert Module
191		Object Browser
192		Menu Editor
193		Toggle Breakpoint
194		Instant Watch
195		Step Into
196		Step Over
197		Combination Drop-Down Edit

Button ID	Appears as	Description
198	Borders	Borders
199		Label
200		Custom
201		Custom
202		Microsoft Word
203		Microsoft Mail
204		Microsoft PowerPoint
205		Microsoft Project
206		Custom
207		Custom
208		Custom
209		Custom
210		Custom
211		Custom
212		Custom
213		Custom
214		Custom
215		Custom
216		Microsoft Access

(continues)

Table 16.7 Continued

Button ID	Appears as	Description
217		Custom
218		Custom
219		Custom
220		Custom
221		Custom
222		Custom
223		Custom
224		Custom
225		Custom
226		Custom
227		Microsoft Schedule+
228		Custom
229		Custom
230		Custom
231		Custom
232	Pattern	Pattern
233	Color	Color
234	Chart type	Chart Type

Button ID	Appears as	Description
235	Shape	Shape
236	Font color	Font Color
237		Custom
238		Control Properties
239		Toggle Grid
240		Drawing
241		Full Screen
242		Trace Precedents
243		Show Info Window
244		Edit Code
245		Insert Dialog

Chapter 17

Creating and Displaying Dialog Boxes

When creating programs, you often may need to query the user for information. Dialog boxes are used to have this conversation with the user. You can interact with users by displaying built-in or custom dialog boxes. Dialog boxes structure information and respond to user events such as clicking an OK button.

In this chapter, you learn how to do the following:

- Display Excel's built-in dialog boxes.

- Create and display custom dialog boxes.

- Get information from the user by using dialog boxes.

- Display information to the user by using dialog boxes.

- Run procedures from dialog boxes.

This chapter covers the following objects:

```
Dialog
DialogSheet
DialogFrame
Button
Label
```

Using Built-In Dialog Boxes

You can display the following three types of built-in dialog boxes with Visual Basic in Excel:

- MsgBox and InputBox display simple input and message dialog boxes.

- The GetFileSaveAs and GetFileOpen methods display the Excel File Open and File Save dialog boxes.

- The Show method displays any of the other Excel dialog boxes. Show also performs the task associated with the dialog box.

Simple Message and Input Boxes

The MsgBox function is ideal for displaying errors and warnings to users. MsgBox has the following form:

MsgBox

MsgBox (*prompt*, [*buttons*], [*title*], [*helpfile, context*])

Argument	Description
prompt	The text to display in the body of the message box.
buttons	One or more constant values that indicate the number and type of buttons that appear in the message box. See Table 17.1 for a list of these constants.
title	The text for the title bar of the message box.
helpfile	The help file that contains information about this message.
context	The context ID of the topic in *helpfile* that explains this message.

Table 17.1 MsgBox button constants

Category	Constant	Description
Button	vbOKOnly	OK button
	vbOKCancel	OK and Cancel buttons
	vbAbortRetryIgnore	Abort, Retry, and Ignore buttons
	vbYesNoCancel	Yes, No, and Cancel buttons
	vbYesNo	Yes and No buttons
	vbRetryCancel	Retry and Cancel buttons

Category	Constant	Description
Icon	vbCritical vbQuestion vbExclamation vbInformation	Critical Message icon Warning Query icon Warning Message icon Information Message icon
Default button	vbDefaultButton1 vbDefaultButton2 vbDefaultButton3	First button Second button Third button
Modality	vbApplicationModal	Application modal; the user must respond to the message box before continuing work in the current application
	vbSystemModal	System modal; all applications are suspended until the user responds

II

Programmer's Reference

The following line of code displays the message box shown in figure 17.1:

```
iAnswer = MsgBox ("Reached end of worksheet. Continue on?", _
vbOKCancel, "Search and Replace")
```

Fig. 17.1
A user-generated message box.

Use And to combine button values. The following line of code displays a message box with Retry and Cancel buttons. Cancel is the default. The dialog box halts other applications until the user makes a choice:

```
iAnswer = MsgBox("Disk not ready.", vbRetryCancel And
vbDefaultButton2 And vbSystemModal)
```

Caution

When specifying values for a MsgBox, do not combine more than one value from the same category. Choose only one button constant, one icon, one default button, and one modality constant. Include only the categories you want. Combining more than one value from the same category can cause unpredictable results.

When the user clicks a button, the message box closes, and MsgBox returns a value indicating which button was clicked. These return values are shown in Table 17.2. Use the return value to determine a course of action, as in the following example:

```
If iAnswer = vbCancel Then Exit Sub
```

Table 17.2 MsgBox return values	
User clicks	**Value returned**
OK	vbOK
Cancel	vbCancel
Abort	vbAbort
Retry	vbRetry
Ignore	vbIgnore
Yes	vbYes
No	vbNo

The InputBox function is ideal for simple data-entry tasks, such as getting a single value or cell address from the user. InputBox has the following form:

InputBox

InputBox (*prompt*, [*title*], [*default*], [*left*], [*top*], [*helpfile, context*])

Argument	Description
prompt	The text to display in the body of the message box.
title	The text for the title bar of the message box.
default	The default value to fill in.
left	The distance (in points) between the left edge of the sheet and the right edge of the input box.
top	The distance (in points) between the top edge of the sheet and the top edge of the input box.
helpfile	The help file that contains information about this input box.
context	The context ID of the topic in *helpfile* that explains this input box.

The following line of code displays an InputBox to get some data from the user (see fig. 17.2):

```
vAnswer = InputBox("Enter a value to multiply cells by", "Multiply")
```

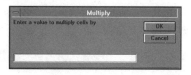

Fig. 17.2
Input box
requesting
user data.

Excel also provides an InputBox method with the Application object. This method is exactly the same as the InputBox statement, except that it takes an additional *type* argument. *type* indicates the type of data to enter. See Table 17.3 for these codes.

Table 17.3 InputBox method type codes	
Type	**Data accepted**
0	Formula
1	Number
2	Text
4	Boolean (True/False)
8	Array of data from a range of cells or reference to cells
16	Error value
64	Array of data from a range of cells

If the user enters data that can't be interpreted as the specified type, Excel displays a message box and lets the user try again. The default *type* is 2 (Text). The following line of code uses the InputBox method to prompt for a cell reference:

```
vSource = Application.Inputbox("Enter the range to chart", _
    "Charting", type:=8)
```

If the user doesn't enter a cell reference, Excel displays a Reference is not valid message (see fig. 17.3). The user can then try again.

Fig. 17.3
Error box resulting
from invalid input.

Use the `InputBox` method when you want to screen input without writing your own validation code.

> **Note**
>
> Both the `InputBox` function and method return False if the user clicks Cancel and True if the user clicks OK.

Open File and File Save Dialog Boxes

A common task in programming user interaction is getting file and path specifications. Creating these dialog boxes on your own is difficult because it requires querying the operating system and displaying the returned information graphically. Excel solves this problem by providing the `GetOpenFilename` and `GetSaveAsFilename` methods with the `Application` object.

Both methods provide very simple one-line ways to get valid file specifications. The following line of code displays Excel's File Open dialog box (see fig. 17.4):

```
sFilename = Application.GetOpenFilename("Text files (*.TXT),*.txt")
```

Fig. 17.4

The `GetOpen-Filename` method produces the File Open dialog box.

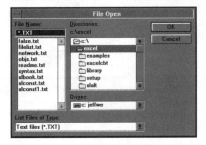

The following line of code displays Excel's File Save As dialog box (see fig. 17.5):

```
sFilename = Application.GetSaveAsFilename _
("Excel files (*.XL*),*.XL*")
```

Fig. 17.5

The `GetSaveAs-Filename` method produces the File Save As dialog box.

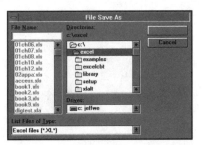

Both methods return file names but don't actually open or save the files. Because you can change the title and button text of the dialog boxes, these dialog boxes are useful for just about any file operation you need to perform.

The following lines of code show how to use GetOpenFilename and GetSaveAsFilename to import and export a text file from Visual Basic modules:

```
Sub ImportFile()
    vFilename = Application.GetOpenFilename("Basic files (*.BAS),
*.bas", , "Import Module")
    If vFilename <> False Then
        Modules.Add.InsertFile vFilename
    End If
End Sub

Sub ExportFile()
    If TypeName(ActiveSheet) = "Module" Then
        vDefaultFilename = Left(ActiveSheet.Name, 8) & ".BAS"
        vFilename = Application.GetSaveAsFilename _
            (vDefaultFilename, "Basic files _
            (*.BAS), *.bas", , "Export Module")
        ActiveSheet.SaveAs vFilename, xlText
    End If
End Sub
```

Excel Dialog Boxes

The Dialogs collection contains all the built-in Excel dialog boxes. Each dialog box in the collection is identified by a constant listed in Table 17.4. Use the Show method to display any of these dialog boxes.

The following line of code displays the dialog box for formatting borders:

```
Application.Dialogs.Show(xlDialogBorder).Show
```

Excel's dialog boxes are context-sensitive—that is, they may look different depending on the current selection or on what type of sheet is active. In the case of the preceding line of code, Show displays the Format Cells dialog box (see fig. 17.6) if a range of cells is selected.

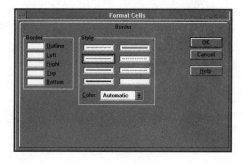

Fig. 17.6
The Format Cells dialog box.

Unlike the GetOpenFilename and GetSaveAsFilename methods, Show actually performs the task associated with the dialog box. If the user selects a border and clicks OK, the selected cells are formatted accordingly. You can't intercept these actions, modify the dialog box's behavior, or get the dialog box's settings.

> **Note**
>
> Show returns True if the user clicks OK or False if the user clicks Cancel.

You need to be careful when using Show with Excel's built-in dialog boxes. Not all dialog boxes are valid in certain contexts. For example, you can't display the Menu Editor when a worksheet or chart is active. Trying to display a dialog box in the wrong context causes error 1004.

Table 17.4 lists the constants that identify Excel's dialog boxes in the Dialogs collection and shows the conditions under which you can display the dialog box. Some of the constants change the cursor state rather than display a dialog box (for example, xlDialogSize).

> **Caution**
>
> Excel may crash if you attempt to display a dialog box in the wrong context, trap the error, and attempt to show another dialog box. Avoid displaying dialog boxes in the wrong context.

Table 17.4 Dialog box constants by context

Dialog constant	Work-sheet	Chart	Dialog	Module	Current selection/comments
xlDialogActivate	✔	✔	✔	✔	
xlDialogActiveCellFont	✔				Range
xlDialogAddChartAutoformat		✔			
xlDialogAddinManager	✔	✔	✔	✔	
xlDialogAlignment	✔				
xlDialogApplyNames	✔				
xlDialogApplyStyle	✔				

Dialog constant	Work-sheet	Chart	Dialog	Module	Current selection/ comments
xlDialogAppMove	✔	✔	✔	✔	Application must be windowed
xlDialogAppSize	✔	✔	✔	✔	Application must be windowed
xlDialogArrangeAll	✔	✔	✔	✔	
xlDialogAssignToObject	✔	✔	✔		Any object with OnAction property
xlDialogAssignToTool					Can't access from code
xlDialogAttachText		✔			
xlDialogAttachToolbars	✔	✔	✔	✔	
xlDialogAttributes	✔	✔	✔		
xlDialogAxes		✔			
xlDialogBorder	✔				
xlDialogCalculation	✔		✔	✔	
xlDialogCellProtection	✔				
xlDialogChangeLink	✔				Linked object
xlDialogChartAddData		✔			
xlDialogChartTrend		✔			Series
xlDialogChartWizard		✔			
xlDialogCheckboxProperties	✔	✔	✔		Check box
xlDialogClear	✔	✔			
xlDialogColorPalette	✔	✔	✔		
xlDialogColumnWidth	✔				
xlDialogCombination		✔			
xlDialogConsolidate	✔				

II

Programmer's Reference

(continues)

Table 17.4 Continued

Dialog constant	Work-sheet	Chart	Dialog	Module	Current selection/comments
xlDialogCopyChart		✔			
xlDialogCopyPicture	✔	✔	✔		
xlDialogCreateNames	✔				
xlDialogCreatePublisher					Macintosh only
xlDialogCustomizeToolbar	✔	✔	✔	✔	
xlDialogDataDelete	✔				Range
xlDialogDataLabel		✔			Series or point
xlDialogDataSeries	✔				
xlDialogDefineName	✔	✔	✔	✔	
xlDialogDefineStyle	✔				
xlDialogDeleteFormat	✔			✔	
xlDialogDeleteName	✔	✔	✔	✔	
xlDialogDemote	✔				
xlDialogDisplay	✔		✔	✔	
xlDialogEditboxProperties			✔		Edit box
xlDialogEditColor					Can't access from code
xlDialogEditDelete	✔				
xlDialogEditionOptions					Macintosh only
xlDialogEditSeries		✔			Series
xlDialogErrorbarX		✔			Series
xlDialogErrorbarY		✔			Series
xlDialogExtract	✔				Range
xlDialogFileDelete	✔	✔	✔	✔	

Dialog constant	Work-sheet	Chart	Dialog	Module	Current selection/ comments
xlDialogFillGroup	✔				Range
xlDialogFillWorkgroup	✔				
xlDialogFilterAdvanced	✔				Range
xlDialogFindFile	✔	✔	✔	✔	
xlDialogFont	✔				
xlDialogFontProperties	✔				Range
xlDialogFormatAuto	✔				Range
xlDialogFormatChart		✔			Series
xlDialogFormatCharttype	✔	✔			
xlDialogFormatFont	✔				
xlDialogFormatLegend		✔			Legend
xlDialogFormatMain		✔			
xlDialogFormatMove	✔				
xlDialogFormatNumber	✔				
xlDialogFormatOverlay		✔			Chart overlay
xlDialogFormatSize	✔				
xlDialogFormatText	✔				Range containing text
xlDialogFormulaFind	✔			✔	
xlDialogFormulaGoto	✔	✔	✔	✔	
xlDialogFormulaReplace	✔				
xlDialogFunctionWizard	✔				
xlDialogGalleryArea		✔			
xlDialogGalleryBar		✔			
xlDialogGalleryColumn		✔			
xlDialogGalleryCustom		✔			

(continues)

II

Programmer's Reference

Table 17.4 Continued

Dialog constant	Work-sheet	Chart	Dialog	Module	Current selection/comments
xlDialogGalleryDoughnut		✔			
xlDialogGalleryLine		✔			
xlDialogGalleryPie		✔			
xlDialogGalleryRadar		✔			
xlDialogGalleryScatter		✔			
xlDialogGallery3dArea		✔			
xlDialogGallery3dBar		✔			
xlDialogGallery3dColumn		✔			
xlDialogGallery3dLine		✔			
xlDialogGallery3dPie		✔			
xlDialogGallery3dSurface		✔			
xlDialogGoalSeek	✔				
xlDialogGridlines		✔			
xlDialogInsert	✔				
xlDialogInsertObject	✔		✔		
xlDialogInsertPicture	✔	✔			
xlDialogInsertTitle		✔			
xlDialogLabelProperties	✔	✔	✔		Label
xlDialogListboxProperties	✔	✔	✔		List box
xlDialogMacroOptions			✔	✔	
xlDialogMailLogon	✔	✔	✔	✔	
xlDialogMailNextLetter	✔	✔	✔	✔	Mail system must be installed
xlDialogMainChart		✔			
xlDialogMainChartType		✔			
xlDialogMenuEditor	✔	✔	✔	✔	

Dialog constant	Work-sheet	Chart	Dialog	Module	Current selection/comments
xlDialogMove			✔		Dialog frame
xlDialogNew	✔	✔	✔	✔	
xlDialogNote	✔				
xlDialogObjectProperties	✔	✔	✔		OLE object
xlDialogObjectProtection	✔	✔	✔		OLE object
xlDialogOpen	✔	✔	✔	✔	
xlDialogOpenLinks	✔	✔			Workbook must contain links
xlDialogOpenMail	✔				Mail system must be installed
xlDialogOpenText					Can't access from code
xlDialogOptionsCalculation	✔	✔	✔	✔	
xlDialogOptionsChart		✔			
xlDialogOptionsEdit	✔	✔	✔	✔	
xlDialogOptionsGeneral	✔	✔	✔	✔	
xlDialogOptionsListsAdd	✔	✔	✔	✔	
xlDialogOptionsTransition	✔	✔	✔	✔	
xlDialogOptionsView	✔	✔	✔	✔	
xlDialogOutline	✔				
xlDialogOverlay		✔			
xlDialogOverlayChartType		✔			
xlDialogPageSetup	✔	✔	✔	✔	
xlDialogParse	✔				Range containing text

(continues)

Programmer's Reference

II

Table 17.4 Continued

Dialog constant	Work-sheet	Chart	Dialog	Module	Current selection/ comments
xlDialogPasteSpecial	✔	✔	✔		Clipboard must contain linkable data
xlDialogPatterns	✔	✔			
xlDialogPivotFieldGroup	✔				Pivot field
xlDialogPivotFieldProperties	✔				Pivot field
xlDialogPivotFieldUngroup	✔				Pivot field
xlDialogPivotShowPages	✔				Pivot table
xlDialogPivotTableWizard	✔				Range or pivot table
xlDialogPlacement			✔		Dialog frame
xlDialogPrint	✔	✔	✔	✔	
xlDialogPrinterSetup	✔	✔	✔	✔	
xlDialogPrintPreview	✔	✔	✔		
xlDialogPromote	✔				Outline row or column
xlDialogProtectDocument	✔	✔	✔	✔	
xlDialogPushbuttonProperties	✔	✔	✔		Button
xlDialogReplaceFont	✔				
xlDialogRoutingSlip	✔	✔			
xlDialogRowHeight	✔				
xlDialogRun	✔	✔	✔	✔	
xlDialogSaveAs	✔	✔	✔	✔	
xlDialogSaveCopyAs	✔	✔	✔		OLE object
xlDialogSaveNewObject	✔	✔			
xlDialogSaveWorkbook	✔	✔	✔		

Dialog constant	Work-sheet	Chart	Dialog	Module	Current selection/comments
xlDialogSaveWorkspace	✔	✔	✔	✔	
xlDialogScale		✔			
xlDialogScenarioAdd	✔				Scenario
xlDialogScenarioCells	✔				
xlDialogScenarioEdit	✔				Scenario
xlDialogScenarioMerge	✔				
xlDialogScenarioSummary	✔				Scenario
xlDialogScrollbarProperties	✔	✔	✔		Scroll bar
xlDialogSelectSpecial	✔				
xlDialogSendMail	✔				Mail system must be installed
xlDialogSeriesAxes		✔			Series
xlDialogSeriesOrder		✔			Series
xlDialogSeriesX		✔			Series
xlDialogSeriesY		✔			Series
xlDialogSetControlValue	✔				
xlDialogSetPrintTitles	✔				
xlDialogSetUpdateStatus	✔				Linked
xlDialogShowDetail	✔				Outline row or column
xlDialogShowToolbar	✔	✔	✔	✔	
xlDialogSize			✔		Dialog frame
xlDialogSort	✔				
xlDialogSortSpecial	✔				

(continues)

Table 17.4 Continued

Dialog constant	Work-sheet	Chart	Dialog	Module	Current selection/comments
`xlDialogSplit`	✔		✔		
`xlDialogStandardFont`	✔				
`xlDialogStandardWidth`	✔				
`xlDialogStyle`	✔				
`xlDialogSubscribeTo`					Macintosh only
`xlDialogSubtotalCreate`	✔				Range
`xlDialogSummaryInfo`	✔	✔	✔	✔	
`xlDialogTable`	✔				
`xlDialogTabOrder`			✔		
`xlDialogTextToColumns`	✔				Range
`xlDialogUnhide`	✔	✔	✔	✔	
`xlDialogUpdateLink`	✔				Linked object
`xlDialogVbaInsertFile`					Can't access from code
`xlDialogVbaMakeAddin`	✔		✔	✔	
`xlDialogVbaProcedureDefinition`				✔	Procedure name
`xlDialogView3d`		✔			
`xlDialogWindowMove`	✔	✔	✔	✔	Window
`xlDialogWindowSize`	✔	✔	✔	✔	Window
`xlDialogWorkbookAdd`	✔	✔	✔	✔	
`xlDialogWorkbookCopy`	✔	✔	✔	✔	
`xlDialogWorkbookInsert`	✔	✔	✔	✔	
`xlDialogWorkbookMove`	✔	✔	✔	✔	
`xlDialogWorkbookName`	✔	✔	✔	✔	

Dialog constant	Work-sheet	Chart	Dialog	Module	Current selection/comments
xlDialogWorkbookNew	✔	✔	✔	✔	
xlDialogWorkbookOptions	✔	✔	✔	✔	
xlDialogWorkbookProtect	✔	✔	✔	✔	
xlDialogWorkbookTabSplit	✔	✔	✔	✔	
xlDialogWorkbookUnhide	✔	✔	✔	✔	
xlDialogWorkgroup	✔	✔	✔	✔	
xlDialogWorkspace	✔	✔	✔	✔	
xlDialogZoom	✔	✔			

The `Dialog` object and `Dialogs` collection have specific properties and methods, which are listed in Table 17.5. The method shown in **bold** is described in the reference section that follows this table. Nonbold items are common to most objects and are described in Chapter 4, "Using Objects."

Table 17.5 Dialog object properties and methods

Application[2]
Count[1]
Creator[2]
Item[1]
Parent[2]
Show

---

[1] *Applies to the `Dialogs` collection.*

[2] *Applies to the `Dialogs` collection and the `Dialog` object.*

dialog.Show

dialog.Show ([*Arg1*, …, *ArgN*])

Displays a built-in dialog box. *Arg1* to *ArgN* specify the initial settings for built-in dialog box controls. If omitted, controls display Excel's built-in defaults.

The following line of code displays the Find dialog box with the word Wombat in the Find What text box:

```
Application.Dialogs(xlDialogFormulaFind).Show "Wombat"
```

Use the Show method of the DialogSheet object to show a custom dialog box. The following line of code displays a custom dialog box named dlgGetAccountInfo:

```
DialogSheets("dlgGetAccountInfo").Show
```

Creating Custom Dialog Boxes

You create your own custom dialog boxes by adding dialog sheets to a work-book. To create a dialog sheet, follow these steps:

1. Right-click a sheet tab.

2. Choose Insert from the pop-up menu.

3. Choose Dialog in the Insert dialog box.

You create controls in the dialog box with the tools in the Forms toolbar, which is displayed by default when you create a dialog sheet (see fig. 17.7).

Fig. 17.7
A dialog sheet.

Forms toolbar

Dialog frame

Dialog sheet tab

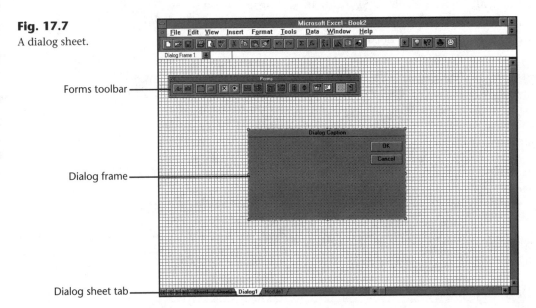

To draw a control, simply click the control's button in the Forms toolbar and position the cursor approximately where the upper right corner of the control should start. Then hold down the left mouse button and drag to size the con-trol on the dialog box. Figure 17.8 shows examples of common Excel controls.

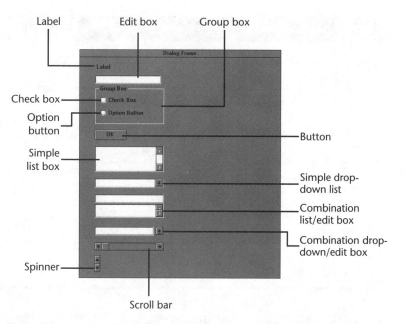

Fig. 17.8
Samples of various
Excel controls.

Each control is suited for a different category of task, although there is some
overlap. Table 17.6 lists the Excel controls and descriptions of each control.

Tip
Make sure that you
draw your controls
within the bound-
aries of the dialog
frame; otherwise,
they will not be
visible when you
run the dialog box.

Table 17.6 Excel controls

Control	Description
Label	Displays text that the user can't change. (This is called *static text* on the Mac.)
Edit box	Displays text that the user can input and/or modify. Edit boxes can scroll text.
Group box	Visually and functionally groups controls.
Button	Performs an action when clicked.
Check box	Displays a True/False/Mixed option. Multiple check boxes can be checked in any one group.
Option button	Displays a True/False/Mixed option. Only one option button can be selected in any one group. (This is called the *Radio button* on the Mac.)
List box	Displays a scrollable list of items. The user can select one or more of the items.

(continues)

Programmer's Reference

Table 17.6 Continued	
Control	**Description**
Combination list/edit box	Combines an edit box with a list box. The user can type entries in the list box but must write code to add those entries to the list box.
Drop-down list	Displays a scrollable list that "drops down" when the down arrow is clicked. The user can select one item from the list.
Combination drop-down/ edit list	The same as the drop-down list, except that the user can type entries in the list. You must write code to add those entries to the list.
Scroll bar	Enables users to "scroll" through a range of numeric values, using the mouse.
Spinner	A shorter version of a scroll bar, limited to positive integer values.

Note

If you are used to the Visual Basic Standard edition, you'll miss the capability to load custom controls in Visual Basic for Applications. Microsoft is still working on providing some form of custom controls for applications. It is difficult to predict when these will be available.

In addition to the control in the Forms toolbar, you can include OLE objects and drawings in a dialog box. To include these objects in a dialog sheet, follow the same procedures you would for any sheet.

Running a Dialog Box

To see how a custom dialog box looks at runtime, click the Run Dialog button in the Forms toolbar. A running custom dialog box is shown in figure 17.9.

To close the dialog box, click OK or Cancel, or double-click the window control box.

To run a custom dialog from code, use the Show method on the DialogSheet object. The following line of code runs the dialog sheet named Dialog1:

```
DialogSheets("Dialog1").Show
```

If you run a dialog from within a procedure, the lines after the Show method don't execute until the user closes the dialog box. To run code while a dialog box is active, attach a procedure to a control.

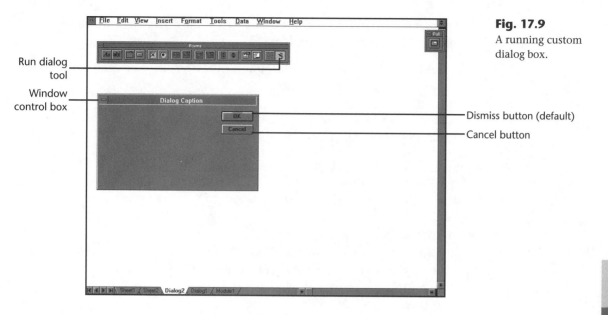

Run dialog tool

Window control box

Dismiss button (default)

Cancel button

Fig. 17.9
A running custom dialog box.

Setting Control Properties

The OK and Cancel buttons are created automatically for each new dialog sheet. You can delete or change these buttons, but you should be aware of both buttons' properties.

To view or change a control's properties, follow these steps:

1. Select the control.

2. Click the Control Properties button in the Forms toolbar. Excel displays the Format Object dialog box (see fig. 17.10).

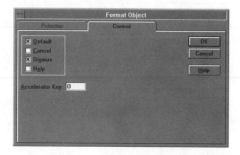

Fig. 17.10
The Format Object dialog box.

The properties listed in the Format Object dialog box are different for each type of control. For buttons, the following three properties are very important:

■ Default. If checked, the button gets clicked if the user presses Enter without first tabbing to a different command button.

- `Cancel`. If checked, clicking the button closes the dialog box and sets the return value of `Show` to False.

- `Dismiss`. If checked, clicking the button closes the dialog box and sets the return value of `Show` to True.

`Cancel` and `Dismiss` are opposites, so they can't both be checked. Any button can be the default button, however.

Another important property is the Accelerator key. This is the letter in the control's caption that appears underlined. The user can press this key rather than using the mouse to click the control.

Naming Controls

If you plan to create more than one dialog box, using descriptive names for the controls you create is a good idea. Excel automatically names and numbers the controls you create, but these names don't tell you much about what the control does.

Descriptive names make it easy to identify and keep track of control objects in code. The following table shows some descriptive names for various control and object types:

Control	Sample names
Dialog sheet	dlgEmployeeStatus dlgGetAccountInfo dlgPostResults
Dialog frame	dlgfEmployeeStatus dlgfGetAccountInfo dlgfPostResults
Label	lblStatusMsg
Edit box	edtComments edtFilename edtAccountName
Button	butOK butCancel butEdit butSendNow
Check box	chkBold chkAttachment
Option button	optReadOnly optReadWrite
Scroll bar	scrListedRange scrEmployees

To name a control, follow these steps:

1. Select the control.

2. In the upper left corner of the screen, double-click the default control name (see fig. 17.11).

Name box ──▶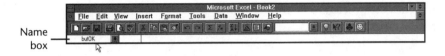

Fig. 17.11
The Name box is located at the left end of the formula bar.

3. Type the new name and press Enter.

Attaching Procedures to Controls

Each control responds to a specific user event. You can perform tasks when these events occur by attaching event procedures to controls. Table 17.7 lists the event that each control or object detects. The events are described in terms of mouse clicks, but equivalent keyboard actions also trigger the events.

Table 17.7 User events to which the controls respond	
Control or object	**Event detected**
Dialog frame	Excel displays the dialog.
Label	None in dialog sheet; click in worksheet or chart.
Edit box	Change (any user typing).
Group box	None in dialog sheet; click in worksheet or chart.
Button	Click.
Check box	Click.
Option button	Click.
List box	Double-click (selects item).
Combination list/edit box	Double-click in list or typing in the edit portion.
Drop-down list	Double-click (selects item).
Combination drop-down/edit list	Double-click (selects item).
Scroll bar	Scroll bar movement.
Spinner	Click the up or down arrow.

II

Programmer's Reference

To create a new event procedure for a control, follow these steps:

1. Select the control.

2. Click the Edit Code button in the Forms toolbar. Excel creates a new event procedure for the control.

Excel names the procedures it creates, using the control's name as shown in the following example:

```
'
' Button1_Click Macro
'
'
Sub Button1_Click()
End Sub
```

If you change the name of the procedure, Excel cannot find the procedure to run for the control and displays an error when an event occurs for the control. To fix this, you must reattach the procedure to the control.

> **Caution**
>
> If you change the name of the control, Excel does not change the names of existing event procedures. It's a good idea to name controls correctly before creating event procedures for them. If you don't, the code still works, but it is difficult to see the correspondence between controls and their event procedures.

To attach an existing procedure to a control, follow these steps:

1. Right-click the control.

2. From the pop-up menu, choose Assign Macro. Excel displays the Assign Macro dialog box (see fig. 17.12).

Fig. 17.12
The Assign Macro dialog box.

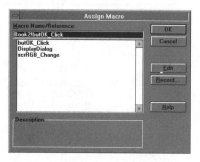

3. Select the name of the procedure to assign to the control, and click OK.

Adding and Removing Items from Lists

The combination list/edit box and combination drop-down/edit box controls do not provide a built-in way to add items to their lists. If you run a dialog with one of these controls, you can type in the edit box; but when you press Enter, nothing happens.

To add items to these lists, you must create a default button in the form and write some code in the button's event procedure.

Figure 17.13 shows a combination list/edit box control and an associated default button.

Edit box ⟶   Default button; runs
butAdd_Click()

Fig. 17.13
Adding items
to a list box.

The following lines of code are in the Add button's event procedure:

```
' OnAction event procedure for the default button on the form.
Sub butAdd_Click()
     ' Using the edit box associated with the list box.
     With ActiveDialog.Evaluate("edtNames")
          ' If the edit box contains text, add the item.
          If .Caption <> "" Then
               ' Add the item to the list box.
               ActiveDialog.Evaluate("lstNames").AddItem .Caption
               ' Clear the edit box.
               .Caption = ""
               ' Focus switches to button if you press Enter, so
               ' return focus to the edit-box list.
               ActiveDialog.Focus = .Name
          End If
     End With
End Sub
```

The procedure is a little different for combination drop-down/edit box controls because they do not have a separate edit box. Following is the default button code to use when you add items to a drop-down/edit box control:

```
' OnAction event procedure for the default button on a form.
Sub butAdd_Click()
     With ActiveDialog.Evaluate("drpCombo")
          If .Caption <> "" Then
               .AddItem .Caption
               .Caption = ""
               ' Focus switches to button if you press Enter, so
               ' return focus to the drop-down list.
```

```
                    ActiveDialog.Focus = .Name
                End If
            End With
        End Sub
```

Controlling Tab Order

The *tab order* among controls is the order in which focus moves from control to control as the user presses the Tab key. The first control usually is an edit box (for data entry) or a command button (to accept default settings). After that, the tab order usually moves from left to right and down.

The default tab order of controls is the order in which they are drawn in a sheet. Because you usually change the layout of a dialog box at least once before finishing it (an optimistic estimate), you probably will end up with some controls in the wrong tab order.

To change the tab order of controls, follow these steps:

1. Right-click any blank area of the dialog sheet (not a control). Excel displays a pop-up menu.

2. Choose Tab Order from the menu. Excel displays the Tab Order dialog box (see fig. 17.14).

Fig. 17.14

The Tab Order dialog box.

3. Select a control from the list box, and click the up arrow or down arrow to move the control up or down in the tab order. Click OK when done.

The tab order corresponds to the ZOrder property of controls. ZOrder returns a number indicating the tab order of the control. The DialogFrame is always 1, the first control on the form is 2, and so on. You cannot change the ZOrder property in code. Instead, use the BringToFront and SendToBack methods.

The following line of code makes an edit box the first control in the tab order:

```
DialogSheets("dlgWord").EditBoxes("edtFilename").SendToBack
```

The following line of code makes a button the last control in the tab order:

```
DialogSheets("dlgWord").Buttons("butCancel").BringToFront
```

You cannot change the tab order of controls while a dialog box is running, so it is generally more useful to set tab order by using the Tab Order dialog box.

Using Dialog Boxes in Code

Custom dialog boxes are created in dialog sheets. In Visual Basic, these sheets are `DialogSheet` objects and part of the workbook's `DialogSheets` collection.

Use the `DialogSheet` object to do the following:

- Display and close the custom dialog box.

- Get and set values from controls in the dialog box.

- Modify the dialog box at run time.

Running a Custom Dialog Box in Code

Use the `Show` method to run a custom dialog box in code. The following line of code runs a dialog box with the sheet named `dlgGetAccountInfo`:

```
DialogSheets("dlgGetAccountInfo").Show
```

Note

Naming dialog sheets descriptively is a good idea. A sheet named `Dialog1`, for example, doesn't say much about its purpose—a sheet named `InputAddress` is much clearer. Remember that someone else may have to modify or maintain your code, and using descriptive names for all aspects of a project makes that job easier.

The current Visual Basic procedure is suspended while the dialog box is displayed. Execution continues only when the user closes the dialog box. Add code to event procedures for the control in the dialog box to run Visual Basic code while the dialog box is visible.

Getting Values from Controls

When the user enters data in a custom dialog box, the values that he or she entered in the controls are stored in the dialog sheet. To get the values from these controls, use the `Value` property of the control.

The following line of code gets the setting from the Bold option button in a dialog sheet:

```
bBold = DialogSheets("dlgFonts").OptionButtons("optBold").Value
```

The `EditBox` object doesn't have a `Value` property; use the `Text` or `Caption` property instead. The following line of code enters the data in the User Name edit box:

```
sUser = DialogSheets("dlgLogon").EditBoxes("edtUserName").Text
```

Setting and Resetting Values of Controls

The values entered by a user are stored in the dialog sheet and are visible the next time the dialog box is displayed. Sometimes, this is the behavior you want; more often, it isn't.

To reset controls, create a `DialogFrame` event procedure that reinitializes the values of the controls. Use the `Value` properties of the collection objects to reset values quickly. For example:

```
' General procedure to reset dialog values to 0 or "".
Sub dlgfGeneral_Show()
    With ActiveDialog
        ' Clear all edit boxes.
        .EditBoxes.Text = ""
        ' Clear all check boxes.
        .CheckBoxes.Value = False
    End With
End Sub
```

The event procedure for the dialog frame runs just before the dialog box is displayed.

Closing a Custom Dialog Box in Code

Clicking the Dismiss or Cancel button closes a dialog box. To close a dialog box in code, use the `Hide` method in an event procedure, as in the following example:

```
ActiveDialog.Hide
```

If you use `Hide` outside an event procedure, it hides the dialog sheet in the workbook.

Changing a Custom Dialog Box in Code

When you run a custom dialog box, it becomes active. While a dialog box is *inactive*, you can change any of its properties or controls in code. While the dialog box is *active*, you can change only a few aspects.

Changes to the active dialog box aren't displayed until the dialog box is closed and displayed again. For example, you can add a button to an active dialog box with the following line of code, but the button will not be visible until the next time the dialog box is displayed.

```
ActiveDialog.Buttons.Add 20, 20, 20, 20
```

You can't redisplay the active dialog box from within an event procedure.

When adding controls to a dialog box in code, use the `Top` and `Left` properties of the sheet's `DialogFrame` object to make sure that the control is within the boundaries of the area displayed when you `Show` the dialog box.

The following lines of code add a scroll bar to the right edge of a dialog box:

```
Sub AddScrollBar()
    With ActiveSheet.DialogFrame
        ActiveSheet.ScrollBars.Add .Left + .Width - 10, .Top, 10,
.Height
    End With
End Sub
```

The `DialogSheet` object and `DialogSheets` collection have specific properties and methods, which are listed in Table 17.8. Properties and methods shown in **bold** are described in the reference section that follows this table. Nonbold items are common to most objects and are described in Chapter 4, "Using Objects."

Table 17.8 DialogSheet and DialogSheets properties and methods

Activate	**Move**[2]
Add[1]	Name
Application[2]	**Next**
Arcs	**OLEObjects**
Buttons	**OnDoubleClick**
ChartObjects	**OnSheetActivate**
CheckBoxes	**OnSheetDeactivate**
CheckSpelling	**OptionButtons**
Copy[2]	**Ovals**
Count[1]	**PageSetup**
Creator[2]	Parent[2]
DefaultButton	**Paste**
Delete[2]	**PasteSpecial**
DialogFrame	**Pictures**
DisplayAutomaticPageBreaks	**Previous**
DrawingObjects	PrintOut[2]
Drawings	PrintPreview[2]
DropDowns	**Protect**
EditBoxes	**ProtectContents**
Evaluate	**ProtectDrawingObjects**
Focus	**Rectangles**
GroupBoxes	**SaveAs**
GroupObjects	**ScrollBars**
Hide	Select[2]
Index	**Show**
Item[1]	**Spinners**
Labels	**TextBoxes**
Lines	**Unprotect**
ListBoxes	Visible[2]

[1] *Applies to the* `DialogSheets` *collection.*

[2] *Applies to the* `DialogSheets` *collection and the* `DialogSheet` *object.*

II

Programmer's Reference

dialogsheet.Activate( )

Activates a dialog sheet in a workbook. Use the Show method to display a custom dialog as a dialog box.

DialogSheets.Add

DialogSheets.Add ([Before], [After], [Count])

Creates a new dialog sheet and adds it to the workbook's DialogSheets collection.

Argument	Description
Before	The sheet object to insert the new sheet before—for example: Sheets("Sheet1").
After	The sheet object to insert the new sheet after. Don't specify both *Before* and *After*.
Count	The number of dialog sheets to add. The default is 1.

The following line of code adds a dialog sheet to the current workbook:

```
DialogSheets.Add
```

dialogsheet.Arcs

dialogsheet.Arcs *([Index])*

Returns one or all Arc objects in a dialog sheet.

Note

When drawing objects in a dialog sheet, use the Top and Left properties of the sheet's DialogFrame object to make sure that the drawing is within the boundaries of the area displayed when you Show the dialog box.

The following lines of code add an arc to a dialog box:

```
Sub DrawDialogGraphics()
    With DialogSheets("dlgGraphics")
        ' Get the origins of the dialog box using the returned _
          DialogFrame object.
        iXOffset = .DialogFrame.Top
        iYOffset = .DialogFrame.Left
        ' Draw an arc within the dialog box's frame.
```

```
            .Arcs.Add iXOffset , iYOffset , iXOffset + 60, iYOffset + 40
            ' Display the dialog box.
            .Show
        End With
    End Sub
```

dialogsheet.Buttons

dialogsheet.Buttons ([*Index*])

Returns one or all Button objects in a dialog sheet. Use the returned object to add buttons or to get and set button properties in a custom dialog box.

The following line of code disables a button in a custom dialog box:

```
DialogSheets("dlgGetAccountInfo").Buttons("butOK").Enabled = False
```

dialogsheet.ChartObjects

dialogsheet.ChartObjects ([*Index*])

Returns one or all embedded ChartObjects in a dialog sheet. Use the returned object to add buttons or to get and set button properties in a custom dialog box.

The following lines of code add an embedded chart to a dialog box and then display the dialog:

```
Sub ChartInDialogBox()
    With DialogSheets("dlgShowInventory")
        ' Create chart (skip this step if chart was already added _
            to dialog sheet)
        .ChartObjects.Add(.DialogFrame.Left, .DialogFrame.Top, _
.DialogFrame.Width, .DialogFrame.Height)
        ' ASSUMPTION: User has selected a range of cells to chart.
        ChartObjects(1).Chart.SeriesCollection.Add Selection
        ' Display dialog box.
        .Show
    End With
End Sub
```

dialogsheet.CheckBoxes

dialogsheet.CheckBoxes ([*Index*])

Returns one or all CheckBox objects in a dialog sheet. Use the returned object to add check boxes or to get and set check-box properties in a custom dialog box.

II

Programmer's Reference

The following line of code selects (checks) a check box in a custom dialog box:

```
DialogSheets("dlgGetAccountInfo").CheckBoxes("chkPreferred") _
. Value = xlOn
```

dialogsheet. CheckSpelling

dialogsheet. CheckSpelling ([*CustomDictionary*], [*IgnoreUppercase*], [*AlwaysSuggest*])

Checks the spelling of the words in a dialog sheet.

Argument	Description
CustomDictionary	A string indicating the file name of the custom dictionary to examine if the word is not found in the main dictionary. If omitted, the currently specified dictionary is used. The default is None.
IgnoreUppercase	True ignores the spelling of words in uppercase characters; False checks the spelling of all words. The default is False.
AlwaysSuggest	True displays a list of suggested alternate spellings when an incorrect spelling is found; False prompts user for correct spelling. The default is False.

You can't use CheckSpelling while a dialog box is active. To work around this, check the spelling of objects in a custom dialog box before or after the box is displayed.

The following lines of code check the spelling of all the objects in a dialog box after the user closes the dialog:

```
Sub CheckDialogBoxSpelling()
    With DialogSheets("dlgGetAccountInfo)
        ' Display the dialog box.
        .Show
        ' After user closes the dialog box, check spelling.
        .CheckSpelling
    End With
End Sub
```

Because you can't display a custom dialog box while checking its spelling, there is no way to give the user a clear idea of what changes are being made.

Caution

Using the CheckSpelling method while a custom dialog box is active can crash Excel.

---

*dialogsheet.*Copy

*dialogsheet.*Copy ([*Before*], [*After*])

Creates a copy of one or all dialog sheets in a workbook.

Argument	Description
Before	The sheet object to insert the copied dialog sheets before—for example: Sheets("Sheet1").
After	The sheet object to insert the copied dialog sheets after. Don't specify both *Before* and *After*.

If both *Before* and *After* are omitted, Copy creates a new workbook to contain the dialog sheets. The following line of code creates a copy of all the dialog sheets in the current workbook:

```
DialogSheets.Copy
```

To copy an individual sheet, use a single dialog-sheet object. The following line of code creates a copy of the active dialog sheet and adds it to the Sheets collection:

```
ActiveSheet.Copy Before:=ActiveSheet
```

*dialogsheet.*DefaultButton

*dialogsheet.*DefaultButton [= *buttonname*]

Sets or returns the name of the button in the dialog to be selected by default. You can't set or return this property unless the dialog is displayed. This means that the property can be used only from within an event procedure of an object in the dialog box.

The following line of code sets a dialog box's default button to a button named butOK:

```
ActiveDialog.DefaultButton = "butOK"
```

*dialogsheet.*Delete( )

Deletes one or all dialog sheets in a workbook.

*dialogsheet.*DialogFrame( )

Returns the DialogFrame object for a dialog box. The dialog frame is the region displayed when the dialog box is active. Use DialogFrame object properties to set or return the caption, position, and size of a dialog box.

II

Programmer's Reference

The following line of code changes the caption of a dialog box:

```
DialogSheets("dlgGetAccountInfo").DialogFrame.Caption = "New Account"
```

Because the positions of objects in a dialog sheet are measured from the upper left corner of the sheet (rather than the display area of the dialog box), it often is necessary to use the Top and Left properties of DialogFrame to position controls in a dialog box.

dialogsheet.**DisplayAutomaticPageBreaks**

dialogsheet.**DisplayAutomaticPageBreaks [= True | False]**

True displays the automatic page breaks in a dialog; False does not. The default is False.

Caution

This property can only be set. Trying to return a value causes an error. This appears to be a bug in Excel and could change with new minor releases.

---

dialogsheet.**DrawingObjects**

dialogsheet.**DrawingObjects ([*Index*])**

Returns one or all drawing objects in a dialog. *Drawing objects* are those objects shown in the Forms and Drawing toolbars. The following line of code deletes all the drawing objects in a dialog:

```
ActiveDialog.DrawingObjects.Delete
```

The following line of code places the user's name in an edit box named edtName:

```
ActiveDialog.DrawingObjects("edtName").Text = Application.UserName
```

dialogsheet.**Drawings**

dialogsheet.**Drawings ([*Index*])**

Returns one or all freehand Drawing objects in a dialog. The following line of code deletes all of the freehand Drawing objects in a chart:

```
ActiveChart.Drawings.Delete
```

The following line of code hides the first freehand `Drawing` objects in the chart:

```
ActiveChart.Drawings(1).Delete
```

> **Note**
>
> Changing the tab order of objects in an active dialog sheet doesn't update the display. You must close the dialog box and use Show to display it again. There is no easy way to do this directly in Visual Basic.

dialogsheet.**DropDowns**

dialogsheet.**DropDowns ([*Index*])**

Returns one or all `DropDown` objects in a dialog. The following lines of code add a list of the sheet names in the active workbook to a list box:

```
Sub AddItems()
    For Each sht In Sheets
        ActiveDialog.DropDowns("drpEmployee").AddItem sht.Name
    Next sht
End Sub
```

dialogsheet.**EditBoxes**

dialogsheet.**EditBoxes ([*Index*])**

Returns one or all `EditBox` objects in a dialog. The following lines of code display a text file in an edit box:

```
Sub LoadFile()
    Dim strBuffer As String, sFileName As String
    ' Get a file name to view.
    sFileName = Application.GetOpenFilename("Text files (*.TXT), _
    *.TXT")
    ' Open the file for binary access -- buffer length equals _
      length of file.
    Open sFileName For Binary As #1 Len = FileLen(sFileName)
    ' Reserve the correct amount of space in a variable.
    strBuffer = Space$(FileLen(sFileName))
    ' Load the contents of the file into the variable.
    Get #1, 1, strBuffer
    ' Display the contents of the file in the edit box _
      edtFileView.
    ' ASSUMPTION: This is called from a custom dialog.
    ActiveDialog.EditBoxes("edtFileView").Text = strBuffer
    ' Close the file.
    Close #1
End Sub
```

II

Programmer's Reference

*dialogsheet.***Evaluate**

*dialogsheet.***Evaluate (*Name*)**

Converts an object name to an object reference. In a dialog sheet, you can use Evaluate rather than the drawing-object methods (EditBoxes, GroupBoxes, and so on) to return those objects.

The following example sets the properties of some objects in a custom dialog box:

```
Sub SetInitialValues()
    With DialogSheet("dlgGetAccountInfo")
        .Evaluate("edtFileView").Text = ""
        .Evaluate("drpAccounts").Enabled = False
        .Evaluate("butOK").Enabled = False
    End With
End Sub
```

*dialogsheet.***Focus**

*dialogsheet.***Focus [= *objectname*]**

Sets or returns the name of an object in the active dialog box that has focus. The dialog box must be active to set or return this property.

The following line sets the focus to the edit box edtFileView in the active dialog box:

```
ActiveDialog.Focus = "edtFileView"
```

*dialogsheet.***GroupBoxes**

*dialogsheet.***GroupBoxes ([*Index*])**

Returns one or all GroupBox objects in a dialog box. The following line of code hides all the GroupBox objects in a dialog box:

```
ActiveChart.GroupBoxes.Visible = False
```

The following line of code displays a hidden GroupBox:

```
ActiveChart.GroupBoxes("grpFileOption").Visible = True
```

*dialogsheet.***GroupObjects**

*dialogsheet.***GroupObjects ([*Index*])**

Returns one or all GroupObject objects in a dialog sheet. Use the properties and methods of the returned GroupObject to select and move multiple drawing objects as a unit. Use the Group method to create a group; use the Ungroup method to remove items from a group.

The following lines of code group the option buttons in a dialog sheet so that they can be moved as a unit:

```
Sub SelectOptionButtons()
    ' Ungroup all objects.
    Activesheet.DrawingObjects.Ungroup
    ' Group option buttons.
    ActiveSheet.OptionButtons.Group
    ' Select the group.
    ActiveSheet.GroupObject(1).Select
End Sub
```

dialogsheet.Hide

dialogsheet.Hide ([*Cancel*])

Closes the active dialog box. If `Cancel` is False, the edit-box contents are validated; if True, no validation occurs. The default is False. The dialog box must be active.

The following line of code closes the active dialog box:

```
ActiveDialog.Hide
```

dialogsheet.Labels

dialogsheet.Labels ([*Index*])

Returns one or all `Label` objects in a dialog box. The following line of code selects all the `Label` objects in a dialog sheet:

```
ActiveSheet.Labels.Select
```

The following line of code sets the caption for a label in the active dialog box:

```
ActiveDialog.Labels(1).Caption = "New Text"
```

dialogsheet.Lines

dialogsheet.Lines ([*Index*])

Returns one or all `Line` objects in a dialog sheet.

> **Note**
>
> When drawing objects in a dialog sheet, use the `Top` and `Left` properties of the sheet's `DialogFrame` object to make sure that the drawing is within the area displayed when you show the dialog box.

The following lines of code add a line to a dialog box:

```
Sub DrawDialogGraphics()
    With DialogSheets("dlgGraphics")
        ' Get the origins of the dialog box using the returned _
          DialogFrame object.
        iXOffset = .DialogFrame.Top
        iYOffset = .DialogFrame.Left
        ' Draw a line within the dialog box's frame.
        .Lines.Add iXOffset , iYOffset , iXOffset + 60, iYOffset + 40
        ' Display the dialog box.
        .Show
    End With
End Sub
```

dialogsheet.ListBoxes

dialogsheet.ListBoxes ([*Index*])

Returns one or all ListBox objects in a dialog. The following line of code adds an item to a list box named lstUser in the active dialog:

```
ActiveDialog.ListBoxes("lstUser").AddItem "List Text"
```

dialogsheet.Move

dialogsheet.Move ([*Before*], [*After*])

Changes the order of sheets in a workbook.

Argument	Description
Before	The sheet object to move the new sheet before— for example: Sheets("Sheet1").
After	The sheet object to move the sheet after.

You must specify either *Before* or *After*, but not both. The following line moves the active dialog sheet to the end of the list of sheets in the workbook:

```
ActiveSheet.Move After:=Sheets(Sheets.Count)
```

dialogsheet.Next

Returns the next sheet as indicated by the sheet tabs at the bottom of the window. The following line of code displays the name of the next sheet:

```
MsgBox ActiveSheet.Next.Name
```

dialogsheet.OLEObjects

dialogsheet.OLEObjects ([*Index*])

Returns one or all OLEObject objects in a dialog. The following lines of code add an embedded Word 6.0 document to a dialog box and activate it for editing:

```
Sub AddWordObject()
    With DialogSheets("dlgWord").OLEObjects.Add("Word.Document.6", _
    , False, False)
        .Top = DialogSheets("dlgWord").DialogFrame.Top
        .Left = DialogSheets("dlgWord").DialogFrame.Left
        .Width = DialogSheets("dlgWord").DialogFrame.Width
        .Height = DialogSheets("dlgWord").DialogFrame.Height
        .Activate
        DialogSheets("dlgWord").Show
    End With
End Sub
```

dialogsheet.OnDoubleClick

dialogsheet.OnDoubleClick [= *procedure*]

Sets or returns the name of a procedure to run when the user double-clicks the edge of the dialog frame or a graphic object (such as a picture or rectangle) in a dialog sheet. This event is not detected when the dialog box is active.

dialogsheet.OnSheetActivate

dialogsheet.OnSheetActivate [= *procedure*]

Sets or returns the name of a procedure to run when a dialog sheet receives focus. This event does not occur when the dialog box receives focus, such as when it is closed or hidden.

dialogsheet.OnSheetDeactivate

dialogsheet.OnSheetDeactivate [= *procedure*]

Sets or returns the name of a procedure to run when a dialog sheet loses focus. This event does not occur when the dialog box loses focus, such as when it is closed or hidden.

dialogsheet.OptionButtons

dialogsheet.OptionButtons ([*Index*])

Returns one or all OptionButton objects in a dialog. The following line checks the option button named optUser in the active dialog:

```
ActiveDialog.OptionButtons("optUser").Value = xlOn
```

dialogsheet.Ovals

dialogsheet.Ovals ([*Index*])

Returns one or all `Oval` objects in a dialog sheet. The following lines of code add an oval to a dialog box:

```
Sub DrawDialogGraphics()
    With DialogSheets("dlgGraphics")
        ' Get the origins of the dialog box using the returned _
          DialogFrame object.
        iXOffset = .DialogFrame.Top
        iYOffset = .DialogFrame.Left
        ' Draw an ovalwithin the dialog box's frame.
        .Ovals.Add iXOffset , iYOffset , iXOffset + 60, iYOffset + 40
        ' Display the dialog box.
        .Show
    End With
End Sub
```

dialogsheet.PageSetup

Returns the `PageSetup` object for the dialog sheet. Use the returned `PageSetup` object to control the printing and layout attributes of the dialog sheet.

dialogsheet.Paste

dialogsheet.Paste ([*Destination*], [*Link*])

Pastes the contents of the Clipboard into a dialog sheet.

Argument	Description
Destination	Ignored for dialog sheets.
Link	True to link the pasted data to its source. The default is False.

The following line of code pastes a copied range to the dialog sheet as a picture:

```
ActiveSheet.Paste
```

dialogsheet.PasteSpecial

dialogsheet.PasteSpecial ([*Format*], [*Link*], [*DisplayAsIcon*], [*IconFileName*], [*IconIndex*], [*IconLabel*])

Pastes data from other applications to a dialog sheet.

Argument	Description
Format	The format of the data to paste, as specified in the As list box of the Paste Special dialog box. The default is the first item in the As list.
Link	True to create a link between the pasted data and its source. The default is False.
DisplayAsIcon	True to display an icon rather than the actual data; False to display data. The default is determined by the source application.
IconFileName	The name of the file containing the icon to display.
IconIndex	The numeric index of the icon within *IconFileName*.
IconLabel	The label to display below the icon.

Note

The *Format* argument *does not* correspond to the xlClipboardFormat constants returned by Application.ClipboardFormats.

*dialogsheet.*Pictures
*dialogsheet.*Pictures ([*Index*])

Returns one or all Picture objects in an active dialog sheet. The following line of code selects all the Picture objects in an active dialog sheet:

```
ActiveSheet.Pictures.Select
```

The following line selects the first Picture object in a dialog sheet:

```
ActiveSheet.Pictures(1).Select
```

*dialogsheet.*Previous

Returns the preceding sheet in the sheets' tab order. The following line of code selects the preceding dialog sheet:

```
ActiveSheet.Previous.Select
```

*dialogsheet.*PrintOut
*dialogsheet.*PrintOut ([*From*], [*To*], [*Copies*], [*Preview*])

Prints one or all dialog sheets in a workbook.

Argument	Description
From	The number of the first page to print. The default is 1.
To	The number of the last page to print. The default is All.
Copies	The number of copies to print. The default is 1.
Preview	True previews the output on-screen before printing; False prints without previewing. The default is False.

The following line of code prints all the dialog sheets in a workbook:

```
DialogSheets.PrintOut
```

The following line of code prints only the dialog sheet named dlgWord:

```
DialogSheets("dlgWord").PrintOut
```

Note

You can't print or print-preview a dialog sheet while a custom dialog is active.

dialogsheet.PrintPreview( )

Previews the print output of one or all dialog sheets. The following line of code previews all the dialog sheets in a workbook:

```
DialogSheets.PrintPreview
```

The following line of code previews only the active dialog sheet:

```
ActiveSheet.PrintPreview
```

dialogsheet.Protect

dialogsheet.Protect ([*Password*], [*DrawingObjects*], [*Contents*], [*Scenarios*])

Prevents changes to various features of a dialog sheet.

Argument	Description
Password	The password required to unprotect the sheet. The default is None.
DrawingObjects	True prevents changes to Drawing objects; False allows changes. The default is True.

Argument	Description
Contents	True prevents changes to the contents of the chart; False allows changes. The default is True.
Scenarios	Ignored for dialog sheets.

dialogsheet.**ProtectContents**

Returns True if the dialog sheet is protected from changes; False otherwise.

dialogsheet.**ProtectDrawingObjects**

Returns True if Drawing objects are protected from changes; False otherwise.

dialogsheet.**Rectangles**

dialogsheet.**Rectangles ([*Index*])**

Returns one or all Rectangle objects in a dialog. The following line of code selects all the Rectangle objects in a dialog:

```
ActiveSheet.Rectangles.Select
```

The following line of code selects the first Rectangle object in the dialog:

```
ActiveSheet.Rectangles(1).Select
```

dialogsheet.**SaveAs**

dialogsheet.**SaveAs (*Filename*, [*FileFormat*], [*Password*], [*WriteResPassword*], [*ReadOnlyRecommended*], [*CreateBackup*])**

Saves a dialog sheet to disk.

Argument	Description
Filename	The name of the file to save the chart as. The default is the current sheet name.
FileFormat	A constant that determines the format of the file to save. See the Workbook object's FileFormat property for a list of these constants. The default is xlNormal.
Password	A password the user must enter to open the file. The default is None.

(continues)

Argument	Description
WriteResPassword	A password the user must enter to open the file for write access. The default is None.
ReadOnlyRecommended	True causes Excel to display a message recommending read-only access when the file is opened for write access; False does not display the message. The default is False.
CreateBackup	True saves the preceding version of the file, using the BAK extension; False saves only the current version. The default is False.

dialogsheet.ScrollBars

dialogsheet.ScrollBars ([*Index*])

Returns one or all ScrollBar objects in a dialog. The following line of code selects all the ScrollBar objects in a dialog sheet:

```
ActiveSheet.ScrollBars.Select
```

The following line of code selects the first ScrollBar object in the dialog sheet:

```
ActiveSheet.ScrollBars(1).Select
```

dialogsheet.Select

dialogsheet.Select ([*Replace*])

Selects one or all dialog sheets in a workbook. If *Replace* is True, the dialog sheet is added to the current selection list; if False, other selections are canceled. The default is False.

The following line of code selects the dialog sheet named dlgWord:

```
DialogSheets("dlgWord").Select
```

The following line of code selects all dialog sheets in the workbook:

```
DialogSheets.Select
```

dialogsheet.Show( )

Displays a custom dialog box. Use the Hide method to close a custom dialog box. You must first close a dialog box before you can show it again.

The following line of code shows a custom dialog box named dlgWord:

```
DialogSheets("dlgWord").Show
```

*dialogsheet.*Spinners

*dialogsheet.*Spinners ([*Index*])

Returns one or all Spinner objects in a dialog. The following line of code selects all the Spinner objects in a dialog sheet:

```
ActiveSheet.Spinners.Select
```

The following line of code selects the first Spinner object in the dialog sheet:

```
ActiveSheet.Spinners(1).Select
```

*dialogsheet.*TextBoxes

*dialogsheet.*TextBoxes ([*Index*])

Returns one or all the TextBox objects in a dialog. The following line of code selects all the TextBox objects in a dialog sheet:

```
ActiveSheet.TextBoxes.Select
```

The following line of code selects the first TextBox object in the dialog sheet:

```
ActiveSheet.TextBoxes(1).Select
```

Tip
Text boxes can't accept input while a dialog box is active. Use an edit box to accept user input.

*dialogsheet.*Unprotect

*dialogsheet.*Unprotect ([*Password*])

Changes a protected dialog sheet to unprotected (changes allowed). Password is required if the protection was set using a password.

*dialogsheet.*Visible

*dialogsheet.*Visible [= True | False]

True displays the dialog sheet; False hides the dialog sheet. Does not affect the dialog box that may be displayed from the sheet. Use Show and Hide to display and hide a custom dialog box.

Using the *DialogFrame*

Each custom dialog box has one DialogFrame object. DialogFrame determines the size and position of the dialog box when it is shown. It also controls the text in the dialog box's title bar and can execute an event procedure when the dialog box is displayed.

II

Programmer's Reference

To change the text in a dialog box's title bar, set the `DialogFrame`'s `Caption` property. The following line of code displays new text in the title bar:

```
ActiveDialog.DialogFrame.Caption = "New Text"
```

To position a dialog box, use the `Left` and `Top` properties. The following lines of code move the dialog to the upper left corner of the current sheet:

```
Sub MoveDialog()
    ActiveDialog.DialogFrame.Top = 1
    ActiveDialog.DialogFrame.Left = 1
End Sub
```

To size a dialog box, use the `Width` and `Height` properties. The following lines of code display the dialog at the full size of the active window:

```
Sub MaximizeDialog()
    ActiveDialog.DialogFrame.Width = ActiveWindow.Width
    ActiveDialog.DialogFrame.Height = ActiveWindow.Height
End Sub
```

To run a procedure when the dialog box is displayed, use the `OnAction` property. The following line runs the procedure `Initialize()` when the dialog box is displayed:

```
DialogSheets("dlgWord").DialogFrame.OnAction = "Initialize"
```

The `DialogFrame` object has specific properties and methods, which are listed in Table 17.9. Properties and methods shown in **bold** are described in the reference section that follows this table. Nonbold items are common to most objects and are described in Chapter 4, "Using Objects."

Table 17.9 DialogFrame properties and methods

Application	LockedText
Caption	Name
Characters	**OnAction**
CheckSpelling	Parent
CopyPicture	**Select**
Creator	**Text**
Height	Top
Left	Width
Locked	

*dialogframe.*Caption

*dialogframe.*Caption [= *titlebartext*]

Sets or returns the text displayed in the title bar of the dialog box.

dialogframe.Characters

dialogframe.Characters ([*Start*], [*Length*])

Returns a Characters collection object representing the text in the title bar. Unlike other Characters collections, you can't set the font or formatting properties of characters in a title bar.

dialogframe.CheckSpelling

dialogframe.CheckSpelling ([*CustomDictionary*], [*IgnoreUppercase*], [*AlwaysSuggest*])

Checks the spelling of the words in the title bar.

> **Caution**
>
> Do not use the CheckSpelling method when a dialog box is displayed. Doing this causes a fatal error to the program that is running.

dialogframe.CopyPicture

dialogframe.CopyPicture ([*Appearance*], [*Format*])

Copies the dialog frame to the Clipboard, using a bit-map or picture format.

Argument	Description
Appearance	xlScreen copies the dialog frame as it appears on-screen; xlPrinter copies the button as it would appear if printed using the current printer setup. The default is xlScreen.
Format	xlPicture creates the copy in PICT format; xlBitmap creates the copy as a bitmap. The default is xlPicture.

dialogframe.Locked

dialogframe.Locked [= True | False]

True prevents changes to the contents and position of the dialog frame while the dialog sheet is protected; False allows changes. The default is True.

dialogframe.LockedText

dialogframe.LockedText [= True | False]

True prevents changes to the contents of the title bar while the dialog sheet is protected; False allows changes. The default is True.

*dialogframe.***OnAction**

*dialogframe.***OnAction** [= *procedure*]

Sets or returns a procedure to run when the dialog box is displayed. The following line of code assigns the InitializeSetting() to run when the dialog box named wrdDialog is displayed:

```
Dialogsheets("wrdDialog").DialogFrame.OnAction =
"InitializeSettings"
```

*dialogframe.***Select**

*dialogframe.***Select** ([*Replace*])

Selects the dialog frame. (Selecting is the equivalent of clicking the object.) If Replace is False, Select extends the current selection, rather than deselecting previous selections. The default is True.

*dialogframe.***Text**

*dialogframe.***Text** [= *titlebartext*]

Same as the Caption property.

Running Procedures Using Buttons

Buttons run Visual Basic procedures when clicked. Buttons can be in dialog sheets, charts, or worksheets. Use the sheet's Buttons collection to access Button objects.

Use the Add method to add buttons to a sheet. The following line of code adds a button to the active sheet:

```
ActiveSheet.Buttons. Add 20,20, 20,10
```

Use the OnAction property to set the procedure to run when the button is clicked. The following line of code runs the procedure PrintAll() when the user clicks the button named butPrint:

```
ActiveSheet.Buttons("butPrint").OnAction = "PrintAll"
```

Buttons in dialog sheets have four special properties:

- Dismiss is True if the button closes the dialog box and returns True to the Show method.

- Cancel is True if the button closes the dialog box and returns False to the Show method.

■ Default is True if the button is the default action for the dialog box. The default button is clicked if the user presses Enter without clicking another button.

■ Help is True if the button displays on-line Help for the dialog box. The Help button is clicked if the user presses F1.

The Button object and Buttons collection have specific properties and methods, which are listed in Table 17.10. Properties and methods shown in **bold** are described in the reference section that follows this table. Nonbold items are common to most objects and are described in Chapter 4, "Using Objects."

Table 17.10 Button and Buttons properties and methods

Accelerator[2]	**HelpButton**[2]
Add[1]	Height[2]
AddIndent[2]	**HorizontalAlignment**[2]
Application[2]	Index
AutoSize[2]	**Item**[1]
BottomRightCell	Left[2]
BringToFront[2]	**Locked**[2]
CancelButton[2]	**LockedText**[2]
Caption[2]	Name
Characters[2]	**OnAction**[2]
CheckSpelling[2]	**Orientation**[2]
Copy[2]	Parent[2]
CopyPicture[2]	**PhoneticAccelerator**[2]
Count[1]	**Placement**[2]
Creator[2]	**PrintObject**[2]
Cut[2]	**Select**[2]
DefaultButton[2]	SendToBack[2]
Delete[2]	**Text**[2]
DismissButton[2]	Top[2]
Duplicate[2]	**TopLeftCell**
Enabled[2]	**VerticalAlignment**[2]
Font[2]	Visible[2]
Formula[2]	Width[2]
Group[1]	ZOrder[2]
Height[2]	

[1] Applies to the Buttons collection.

[2] Applies to the Buttons collection and the Button object.

*button.*Accelerator

*button.*Accelerator [= *character*]

Sets or returns the accelerator key for one or all buttons in a sheet. character is a single letter that matches one of the letters in the caption of the button. Excel underlines the accelerator key displayed in the caption.

The following lines of code set the caption and accelerator key for the OK button in a custom dialog box:

```
Sub CommandButton()
      With DialogSheets("dlgGetAccountInfo")
          .Buttons("butOK").Caption = "OK"
          .Buttons("butOK").Accelerator = "O"
          .Show
      End With
End Sub
```

Buttons.Add

Buttons.Add (*Left, Top, Width, Height*)

Adds a button to a sheet.

Argument	Description
Left	The distance (in points) between the left edge of the sheet and the left edge of the button.
Top	The distance (in points) between the top edge of the sheet and the top edge of the button.
Width	The width (in points) of the button.
Height	The height (in points) of the button.

Note

In dialog sheets, Left and Top are measured from the upper left corner of the sheet, not the upper left corner of the dialog box. Offset Left and Top are measured from the Left and Top properties of the DialogFrame object to keep buttons in the visible portion of the dialog box.

The following line of code adds a button to a custom dialog box:

```
DialogSheets("dlgGetAccountInfo").Buttons. Add 20,20, 20,10
```

button.AddIndent

button.AddIndent [= True | False]

(Far East version only) True automatically adds an indent to text formatted with the distributed text alignment style; False omits the indent. The default is False.

button.AutoSize

button.AutoSize [= True | False]

True automatically resizes one or all buttons in a dialog sheet to fit the caption text; False uses the `Height` and `Width` property settings. The default is False.

button.BottomRightCell

For buttons in worksheets, returns the cell underneath the bottom right corner of the button. Causes error 1004 for buttons in dialog sheets and charts.

button.CancelButton

button.CancelButton [= True | False]

True makes the button the Cancel button in a dialog sheet. (This property is ignored for buttons in other types of sheets.) The Cancel button closes the custom dialog box and sets the return value of the `Show` method to False.

The following line of code makes the button named `butCancel` the Cancel button in a dialog sheet:

```
DialogSheets("dlgWord").Buttons("butCancel").Cancel = True
```

button.Caption

button.Caption [= *text*]

Sets or returns the text to display in one or all buttons in a sheet.

button.Characters

button.Characters ([*Start*], [*Length*])

Returns a `Characters` collection object representing the text in the button. Unlike other `Characters` collections, you can't set the font or formatting properties of `Characters` object in a button. Use the `Font` property to change the font attributes of a button's caption.

button.**CheckSpelling**

button.**CheckSpelling ([*CustomDictionary*], [*IgnoreUppercase*], [*AlwaysSuggest*])**

Checks the spelling of the words in one or all buttons in a sheet. You can't use CheckSpelling when a dialog box is displayed.

button.**Copy( )**

Copies one or all buttons to the Clipboard.

button.**CopyPicture**

button.**CopyPicture ([*Appearance*], [*Format*])**

Copies one or all buttons to the Clipboard, using a bit-map or picture format.

Argument	Description
Appearance	xlScreen copies the button as it appears on-screen; xlPrinter copies the button as it would appear if printed using the current printer setup. The default is xlScreen.
Format	xlPicture creates the copy in PICT format; xlBitmap creates the copy as a bitmap. The default is xlPicture.

button.**Cut( )**

Cuts one or all buttons from the current sheet and places them in the Clipboard.

button.**DefaultButton**

button.**DefaultButton [= True | False]**

True makes the button the default button in a dialog sheet. (This property is ignored for buttons in other types of sheets.) The default button is the button clicked if the user presses Enter without first selecting any other object in the dialog box.

The following line of code makes the button named butOK the default button in a dialog sheet:

```
DialogSheets("dlgWord").Buttons("butOK").Default = True
```

button.Delete( )

Removes one or all buttons from a sheet without placing them in the Clipboard.

button.DismissButton

button.DismissButton [= True | False]

True makes the button the Dismiss button in a dialog sheet. (This property is ignored for buttons in other types of sheets.) The Dismiss button closes the dialog box and sets the return value of Show to True. For example, you set the Save button to be a Dismiss button when opening a dialog box, and only after the user has entered data, change the button to its normal state to save the changes. This prevents executing the code for the save until the user has actually entered data.

The following line of code makes the button named butOK the Close button in a dialog sheet:

```
DialogSheets("dlgWord").Buttons("butOK").Dismiss = True
```

Note

You cannot have more than one of each of these types of buttons in a custom dialog box: Default, Cancel, and Dismiss. A single button can combine compatible attributes, however. For example, a button can be the Default and Dismiss button at the same time.

button.Duplicate( )

Makes a copy of one or all buttons in a sheet and returns the object (or collection) that was created. The following line of code duplicates the first button object in a sheet and moves it down slightly:

```
ActiveSheet.Buttons(1).Duplicate.Top = ActiveSheet.Buttons(1).Top-10
```

button.Enabled

button.Enabled [= True | False]

True enables one or all buttons in the sheet to respond to click events; False disables. A button responds to click events if its OnAction property is set to a procedure name. The default is True.

button.Font

Returns the Font object for one or all buttons in a sheet. Use the returned Font object to set the font-attributes caption of the button.

The following line of code underlines the caption of all the buttons in a sheet:

```
ActiveSheet.Buttons.Font.Underline = xlSingle
```

button.Formula

button.Formula [= *formula*]

Sets or returns the formula for the caption of one or all buttons in a sheet. The following line of code displays the value of cell B2 in a button caption:

```
ActiveSheet.Buttons("butOK").Formula = "=Sheet2!$B$8"
```

buttons.Group( )

Groups a collection of buttons so they can be selected, moved, copied, or deleted as a single object. The following line of code groups all the buttons in a sheet:

```
ActiveSheet.Buttons.Group
```

button.HelpButton

button.HelpButton [= True | False]

True makes the button the Help button in a dialog sheet. (This property is ignored for buttons in other types of sheets.) When the user presses F1, the Help button is clicked, and any OnAction procedure for the button is run.

The following line of code makes the button named butHelp the Help button in a dialog sheet:

```
DialogSheets("dlgWord").Buttons("butHelp").Help = True
```

button.HorizontalAlignment

button.HorizontalAlignment [= *setting*]

Causes error 1006 for buttons in dialog sheets. For buttons in other sheets, xlLeft left-aligns caption, xlRight right-aligns caption, xlCenter centers caption in the button, and xlJustify justifies wrapped text within the button's caption. The default is xlCenter.

button.**Locked**

button.**Locked [= True | False]**

True prevents changes to the contents and position of one or all buttons in a sheet while the sheet is protected; False allows changes. The default is True.

button.**LockedText**

button.**LockedText [= True | False]**

True prevents changes to the contents of one or all buttons in a sheet while the sheet is protected; False allows changes. The default is True.

button.**OnAction**

button.**OnAction [= *procedure*]**

Sets or returns the name of a procedure to run when one or any of the buttons in the sheet are clicked. The following line causes the procedure `Validate()` to run when the user clicks the `butValidText` button:

```
ActiveSheet.Button("butValidText").OnAction = "Validate"
```

button.**Orientation**

button.**Orientation [= *setting*]**

For buttons in dialog sheets, causes error 1006. For buttons in other types of sheets, sets or returns the orientation of the caption of one or all buttons: `xlHorizontal`, `xlVertical`, `xlUpward`, or `xlDownward`. The default is `xlHorizontal`.

button.**PhoneticAccelerator**

button.**PhoneticAccelerator [= *setting*]**

(Far East version only) Sets or returns the phonetic keyboard accelerator key character for one or all buttons in a sheet. The phonetic accelerator is used when the system accelerator mode is switched to phonetic characters (as opposed to Roman characters, which use the `Accelerator` property).

*button.*Placement

*button.*Placement [= xlMoveAndSize | xlMove | xlFreeFloating]

Causes error 1006 for buttons in dialog sheets and charts. For buttons in other types of sheets, sets or returns how one or all buttons in a sheet are attached to the cells below them. The default is xlFreeFloating.

*button.*PrintObject

*button.*PrintObject [= True | False]

True prints one or all buttons with the sheet; False does not. The default is True. The following line of code turns off printing for all the buttons in a sheet:

```
ActiveSheet.Buttons.PrintObject = False
```

button.Select

*button.*Select ([*Replace*])

Selects one or all buttons in a sheet. (Selecting is the equivalent of clicking the object.) If Replace is False, Select extends the current selection, rather than deselecting previous selections. The default is True.

*button.*Text

Same as the Caption property.

*button.*TopLeftCell

For buttons in worksheets, returns the cell underneath the upper left corner of the button. Causes error 1004 for buttons in dialog sheets and charts.

*button.*VerticalAlignment

*button.*VerticalAlignment [= *setting*]

For buttons in dialog sheets, causes error 1006. For buttons in other types of sheets, sets or returns the vertical alignment of one or all buttons in a sheet. Valid settings are xlBottom, xlCenter, xlDistributed, xlJustify, and xlTop. The default is xlTop.

Displaying Noneditable Data with Labels

Labels display text or data that can't be edited. Labels can be in dialog sheets, charts, or worksheets. Use the sheet's `Labels` collection to access `Label` objects.

Use the `Add` method to add labels to a sheet. The following line of code adds a label to the active sheet:

```
ActiveSheet.Labels.Add 20,20, 20,10
```

Use the `Caption` property to display data in a label. The following line of code displays a status message in a dialog box:

```
ActiveDialog.Labels("lblStatus").Caption = "Connecting to data
source..."
```

Labels often identify noncaptioned controls in sheets. They also enable you to add accelerator keys for noncaptioned controls. The following lines of code set the caption and accelerator keys for the File Name label in a custom dialog box:

```
Sub Label()
    With DialogSheets("dlgFormat")
        .Evaluate("lblFileName").Caption = "File Name"
        .Evaluate("lblFileName").Accelerator = "N"
        .Show
    End With
End Sub
```

When a user presses the accelerator key for a label, focus moves to the next control in the tab order—in this case, the File Name edit box.

Labels in worksheets and charts can respond to click events through the `OnAction` property. Labels in dialog sheets do not allow `OnAction` to be set.

The `Label` object and `Labels` collection have specific properties and methods, which are listed in Table 17.11. Properties and methods shown in **bold** are described in the reference section that follows this table. Nonbold items are common to most objects and are described in Chapter 4, "Using Objects."

II

Programmer's Reference

Table 17.11 Label and Labels properties and methods

Accelerator[2]	Item[1]
Add	Left[2]
Application[2]	**Locked**[2]
BottomRightCell	**LockedText**[2]
BringToFront[2]	Name
Caption[2]	**OnAction**[2]
Characters[2]	Parent[2]
CheckSpelling[2]	**PhoneticAccelerator**[2]
Copy[2]	**Placement**[2]
CopyPicture[2]	**PrintObject**[2]
Count[1]	**Select**[2]
Creator[2]	SendToBack[2]
Cut[2]	**Text**[2]
Delete[2]	Top[2]
Duplicate[2]	**TopLeftCell**
Enabled[2]	Visible[2]
Group[1]	Width[2]
Height[2]	ZOrder[2]
Index	

[1] *Applies to the Labels collection.*

[2] *Applies to the Labels collection and the Label object.*

label.Accelerator

label.Accelerator [= *character*]

Sets or returns the accelerator key for one or all labels in a sheet. *character* is a single letter that matches one of the letters in the label. Excel underlines the accelerator key displayed in the label.

Use labels to assign accelerator keys to controls that don't have accelerator-key properties, such as list and edit boxes.

Labels.Add

Labels.Add (*Left, Top, Width, Height*)

Adds a label to a sheet.

Argument	Description
Left	The distance (in points) between the left edge of the sheet and the left edge of the object.
Top	The distance (in points) between the top edge of the sheet and the top edge of the object.

Argument	Description
Width	The width (in points) of the object.
Height	The height (in points) of the object.

> **Note**
>
> In dialog sheets, Left and Top are measured from the upper left corner of the sheet, not the upper left corner of the dialog box. Offset Left and Top are measured from the Left and Top properties of the DialogFrame object to keep the object in the visible portion of the dialog box.

The following line of code adds a label to a custom dialog box:

```
DialogSheets("dlgGetAccountInfo").Labels.Add 20,20, 20,10
```

label.BottomRightCell

For labels in worksheets, returns the cell underneath the bottom right corner of the group box. For labels in dialog sheets and charts, causes error 1006.

label.Caption

label.Caption [= *text*]

Sets or returns the text that appears in one or all labels in a sheet. This property is identical to the Text property.

label.Characters

label.Characters ([*Start*], [*Length*])

Returns a Characters collection object representing the caption. Unlike other Characters collections, you can't set the font or formatting properties of a Characters object in a label.

label.CheckSpelling

label.CheckSpelling ([*CustomDictionary*], [*IgnoreUppercase*], [*AlwaysSuggest*])

Checks the spelling of the words in one or all labels in a sheet. You can't use CheckSpelling when a dialog box is displayed.

label.Copy( )

Copies one or all labels in a sheet to the Clipboard.

label.CopyPicture

label.CopyPicture ([*Appearance*], [*Format*])

Copies one or all labels in a sheet to the Clipboard, using a bit-map or picture format.

Argument	Description
Appearance	xlScreen copies the object as it appears on-screen; xlPrinter copies the object as it would appear if printed using the current printer setup. The default is xlScreen.
Format	xlPicture creates the copy in PICT format; xlBitmap creates the copy as a bitmap. The default is xlPicture.

label.Cut( )

Cuts one or all labels from the current sheet and places them in the Clipboard.

label.Delete( )

Removes one or all labels from a sheet without placing them in the Clipboard.

label.Duplicate( )

Makes a copy of one or all labels in a sheet and returns the object (or collection) that was created.

label.Enabled

label.Enabled [= True | False]

True enables one or all labels in the sheet to respond to user events; False disables. A label responds to click events if it appears in a worksheet or chart and its OnAction property is set to a procedure name. Labels in dialog sheets do not respond to user events. The default is True. Disabling a label also disables its accelerator key.

labels.Group( )

Groups a collection of labels so they can be selected, moved, copied, or deleted as a single object. The following line of code groups all the labels in a sheet:

```
ActiveSheet.Labels.Group
```

label.Locked

label.Locked [= True | False]

True prevents changes to the contents and position of one or all the labels in a sheet while the sheet is protected; False allows changes. The default is True.

label.LockedText

label.LockedText [= True | False]

True prevents changes to the contents of one or all the labels in a sheet while the sheet is protected; False allows changes. The default is True.

label.OnAction

label.OnAction [= *procedure*]

For labels in charts and worksheets, sets or returns the name of a procedure to run when one or any of the labels in the sheet are clicked. Labels in dialog sheets do not respond to click events.

label.PhoneticAccelerator

label.PhoneticAccelerator [= *setting*]

(Far East version only) Sets or returns the phonetic keyboard accelerator key character for one or all labels in a sheet. The phonetic accelerator is used when the system accelerator mode is switched to phonetic characters (as opposed to Roman characters, which use the Accelerator property).

label.Placement

label.Placement [= xlMoveAndSize | xlMove | xlFreeFloating]

For labels in dialog sheets and charts, causes error 1006. For labels in worksheets, sets or returns how one or all labels on a sheet are attached to the cells below them. The default is xlFreeFloating.

label.PrintObject

label.PrintObject [= True | False]

True prints one or all labels with the sheet; False does not. The default is True. The following line of code turns off printing for all the labels in a sheet:

```
ActiveSheet.Labels.PrintObject = False
```

label.Select

label.Select ([*Replace*])

Selects one or all labels in a sheet. (Selecting is the equivalent of clicking the object.) If *Replace* is False, Select extends the current selection, rather than deselecting previous selections. The default is True.

label.Text

Same as the Caption property.

label.TopLeftCell

For labels in worksheets, returns the cell underneath the upper left corner of the label. Causes error 1004 for labels in dialog sheets and charts.

Chapter 18

Using Additional Display Controls

Excel provides you with a variety of controls that allow you to interact with the users of your applications. These controls include edit boxes for obtaining data, check boxes and option buttons for yes/no queries, different styles of lists that present choices, scroll bars to easily position data, and spinners to quickly spin through a list.

This chapter explains each of these controls, their associated methods and properties, and how to utilize them within your applications.

In this chapter, you learn how to do the following:

- Use edit boxes to retrieve and display data.
- Use check boxes and option buttons and add them to applications.
- Group controls.
- Display lists with drop-down list boxes and list boxes.
- Use scroll bars.
- Use spinners.

This chapter covers the following objects:

EditBox	DropDown
CheckBox	ListBox
OptionButton	ScrollBar
GroupBox	Spinner

Getting and Displaying Data with Edit Boxes

Edit boxes get and display data that can be edited. The data may be text or numbers. Edit boxes can only exist on dialog sheets. Use the sheet's `EditBoxes` collection to access `EditBox` objects.

Use the `Add` method to add edit boxes to a sheet. The following line adds an edit box to a dialog sheet:

```
DialogSheets("dlgGetAccountInfo").EditBox.Add 20,20, 20,10
```

Use the `InputType` property to validate the type of data a user enters. The following line requires that a zip code be entered as an integer; other types of data will re-prompt the user before the dialog box is closed:

```
ActiveDialog.EditBoxes("edtZipCode").InputType = xlInteger
```

Use the `Text` property to get or set the data displayed in an edit box. The following line gets the data from an edit box:

```
sUser = ActiveDialog.EditBoxes("edtUserName").Text
```

The data in an edit box is truncated after 255 characters, so it is not well suited for displaying large amounts of text.

Edit boxes are similar to text boxes on other types of sheets. Unlike text boxes, however, you can't control the font characteristics of text in an edit box. Text boxes displayed on custom dialog boxes can't be edited, so this is a limitation you must live with.

The `EditBox` object and `EditBoxes` collection have specific properties and methods, which are listed in Table 18.1. Properties and methods shown in **bold** are described in the reference section that follows this table. Nonbold items are common to most objects and are described in Chapter 4, "Using Objects."

Table 18.1 EditBox and EditBoxes properties and methods

Add[1]	**Caption**[2]
Application[2]	**Characters**[2]
BottomRightCell	**Copy**[2]
BringToFront[2]	**CopyPicture**[2]

Count[1]	**LockedText**
Creator[2]	**MultiLine**[2]
Cut[2]	Name
Delete[2]	**OnAction**[2]
DisplayVerticalScrollBar[2]	Parent[2]
Duplicate[2]	**Placement**[2]
Enabled[2]	**PrintObject**[2]
Group[1]	Select[2]
Height[2]	SendToBack[2]
Index	**Text**[2]
InputType[2]	Top[2]
Item[1]	**TopLeftCell**
Left[2]	Visible[2]
LinkedObject	Width[2]
Locked[2]	ZOrder[2]

[1] *Applies to the EditBoxes collection.*

[2] *Applies to the EditBoxes collection and the EditBox object.*

EditBoxes.Add

EditBoxes.Add (*Left, Top, Width, Height*)

Adds an edit box to a sheet.

Argument	Description
Left	The distance between the left edge of the sheet and the left edge of the object in points.
Top	The distance between the top edge of the sheet and the top edge of the object in points.
Width	The width of the object in points.
Height	The height of the object in points.

> **Note**
>
> *Left* and *Top* of dialog sheets are measured from the upper left corner of the sheet, not the upper left corner of the dialog box. Offset *Left* and *Top* from the Left and Top properties of the DialogFrame object to keep the object on the visible portion of the dialog box.

The following line adds an edit box to a custom dialog box:

```
DialogSheets("dlgGetAccountInfo").EditBoxes.Add 20,20, 20,10
```

editbox.**BottomRightCell**

Because edit boxes can't be placed on a worksheet, setting or returning this property causes error 1006.

editbox.**Caption**

editbox.**Caption [= *text*]**

Sets or returns the text that appears next to one or all edit boxes on a sheet. This property is identical to the Text property. For EditBoxes collection, this property can only be set.

editbox.**Characters**

editbox.**Characters ([*Start*], [*Length*])**

Returns a Characters collection object representing the caption. Unlike other Characters collections, you can't set the font or formatting properties of a Characters object in an edit box.

editbox.**Copy()**

Copies one or all edit boxes on a sheet to the Clipboard.

editbox.**CopyPicture**

editbox.**CopyPicture ([*Appearance*], [*Format*])**

Copies one or all edit boxes on a sheet to the Clipboard using a bit-map or picture format.

Argument	Description
Appearance	xlScreen copies the object as it appears on-screen; xlPrinter copies the object as it would appear if printed using the current printer setup. The default is xlScreen.
Format	xlPicture creates the copy in PICT format; xlBitmap creates the copy as a bitmap. The default is xlPicture.

editbox.Cut()

Cuts one or all edit boxes from the current sheet and places them onto the Clipboard.

editbox.Delete()

Removes one or all edit boxes from a sheet, without placing them on the Clipboard.

editbox.DisplayVerticalScrollBar

editbox.DisplayVerticalScrollBar [= True | False]

True displays a vertical scroll bar on one or all edit boxes on a sheet; False does not display a scroll bar.

editbox.Duplicate()

Makes a copy of one or all edit boxes on a sheet and returns the object (or collection) that was created.

editbox.Enabled

editbox.Enabled [= True | False]

True enables one or all edit boxes on the sheet to respond to user events; False disables. An edit box responds to user events if its OnAction property is set to a procedure name. The default is True.

editbox.Group( )

Groups a collection of edit boxes so that they can be selected, moved, copied, or deleted as a single object. The following line groups all the edit boxes on a sheet:

```
ActiveSheet.EditBoxes.Group
```

editbox.InputType

editbox.InputType [= *setting*]

Sets or returns the type of input accepted in one or all edit boxes on the sheet: xlFormula, xlInteger, xlNumber, xlReference, or xlText. Entries are validated when the user closes the dialog box by pressing the Dismiss button. Entries are not validated if the user closes a type dialog box by pressing Cancel.

The following line sets the input type of an edit box to xlInteger (text entries are not accepted):

```
ActiveDialog.Evaluate("edtZipCode").InputType = xlInteger
```

editbox.LinkedObject

Returns the name of a list box linked to the edit box as a combination list, edit box. The following line links an edit box and a list box:

```
ActiveSheet.DrawingObjects(Array("edtZip", "lstZip")).LinkCombo
True
```

The following line displays the name of the list box linked to the edit box:

```
MsgBox ActiveSheet.Evaluate("edtZip").LinkedObject
```

editbox.Locked

editbox.Locked [= True | False]

True prevents changes to the contents and position of one or all edit boxes on a sheet while the sheet is protected; False allows changes. The default is True.

editbox.LockedText

editbox.LockedText [= True | False]

True prevents changes to the contents of one or all edit boxes on a sheet while the sheet is protected; False allows changes. The default is True.

editbox.MultiLine

editbox.MultiLine [= True | False]

True displays multiple lines in an edit box; False displays text as one long line. Multiline edit boxes display carriage returns as vertical space.

The following line makes all the edit boxes on a sheet multiline:

```
ActiveSheet.EditBoxes.Multiline = True
```

editbox.OnAction

editbox.OnAction [= *procedure*]

Sets or returns the name of a procedure to run when the user types in the edit box.

The following lines show how to create a simple password entry edit box. The first edit box, edtPass, is placed outside the dialog frame so that it cannot be seen.

```
' Sets the OnAction properties for the two edit boxes.
Sub SetOnAction()
    ' The entry and display edit boxes use the same OnAction _
      procedure.
    ActiveDialog.Evaluate("edtPass").OnAction = "edtPass_Change"
    ActiveDialog.Evaluate("edtPassDisplay").OnAction = _
    "edtPass_Change"
End Sub

' Displays asterisks on the visible edit box, while the off-screen _
  edit box receives input.
Sub edtPass_Change()
    With ActiveDialog
    ' When the user enters the edtPassDisplay edit box, _
      switch focus to the other edit box.
    If .Focus <> "edtPass" Then .Focus = "edtPass"
    ' Display asterisks (*) instead of characters in the _
      display box.
        .Evaluate("edtPassDisplay").Caption =
String$(Len(.Evaluate("edtPass").Caption), "*")
    End With
End Sub
```

editbox.Placement

The Placement property sets or returns how an object is attached to the cells below it. Because edit boxes can't be placed on a worksheet, setting or returning this property causes error 1006.

editbox.**PrintObject**

True prints one or all edit boxes with the sheet; False does not. The default is True. The following line turns off printing for all edit boxes on a sheet:

```
ActiveSheet.EditBoxes.PrintObject = False
```

editbox.**Text**

editbox.**Text** [= *text*]

Same as the `Caption` property.

editbox.**TopLeftCell**

The `TopLeftCell` property returns the cell under the top left corner of an object. Because edit boxes can't be placed on a worksheet, setting or returning this property causes error 1006.

Getting True/False Values with Check Boxes

Check boxes indicate a True/False option. Check boxes aren't exclusive—that is, you can have multiple check boxes marked True at the same time. Check boxes can be on dialog sheets, charts, or worksheets. Use the sheet's `CheckBoxes` collection to access `CheckBox` objects.

Use the `Add` method to add check boxes to a sheet. The following line adds a check box to the active sheet:

```
ActiveSheet.CheckBoxes.Add 20,20, 20,10
```

Use the `Value` property to determine whether a check box is checked. The following line formats the a range of cells as bold if the Bold check box is checked:

```
Range("A1:A5").Font.Bold = ActiveDialog.CheckBoxes("chkBold").Value
```

The `CheckBox` object and `CheckBoxes` collection have specific properties and methods, which are listed in Table 18.2. Properties and methods shown in **bold** are described in the reference section that follows this table. Nonbold items are common to most objects and are described in Chapter 4, "Using Objects."

Table 18.2 CheckBox and CheckBoxes properties and methods

Accelerator[2]	**Interior**[2]
Add[1]	Item[1]
Application[2]	Left[2]
Border[2]	**LinkedCell**[2]
BottomRightCell	**Locked**[2]
BringToFront[2]	**LockedText**[2]
Caption[2]	Name
Characters[2]	**OnAction**[2]
CheckSpelling[2]	Parent[2]
Copy[2]	**PhoneticAccelerator**[2]
CopyPicture[2]	**Placement**[2]
Count[1]	**PrintObject**[2]
Creator[2]	**Select**[2]
Cut[2]	SendToBack[2]
Delete[2]	Text[2]
Display3DShading[2]	Top[2]
Duplicate[2]	**TopLeftCell**
Enabled[2]	**Value**[2]
Group[1]	Visible[2]
Height[2]	Width[2]
Index	ZOrder[2]

[1] *Applies to the CheckBoxes collection.*

[2] *Applies to the CheckBoxes collection and the CheckBox object.*

checkbox.Accelerator

checkbox.Accelerator [= *character*]

Sets or returns the accelerator key for one or all check boxes on a sheet.
character is a single letter that matches one of the letters in the caption on
the check box. Excel underlines the accelerator key displayed in the caption.

The following lines set the caption and accelerator key for the Bold check box
on a custom dialog box.

```
Sub CheckBox()
    With DialogSheets("dlgFormat")
        .Evaluate("chkBold").Caption = "Bold"
        .Evaluate("chkBold").Accelerator = "B"
        .Show
    End With
End Sub
```

CheckBoxes.Add

CheckBoxes.Add (*Left, Top, Width, Height*)

Adds a check box to a sheet.

Argument	Description
Left	The distance between the left edge of the sheet and the left edge of the object in points.
Top	The distance between the top edge of the sheet and the top edge of the object in points.
Width	The width of the object in points.
Height	The height of the object in points.

Note

Left and *Top* of dialog sheets are measured from the upper left corner of the sheet, not the upper left corner of the dialog box. Offset *Left* and *Top* from the Left and Top properties of the DialogFrame object to keep the object on the visible portion of the dialog box.

The following line adds a check box to a custom dialog box:

```
DialogSheets("dlgGetAccountInfo").CheckBoxes.Add 20,20, 20,10
```

checkbox.Border

Returns the Border object for one or all check boxes on a sheet. For check boxes on worksheets and charts, use the returned Border object properties to change the border of a check box. You can't get or set Border properties of check boxes on dialog sheets. The following line changes the borders of all check boxes on a worksheet to medium weight:

```
Worksheets(1).CheckBoxes.Border.Weight = xlMedium
```

checkbox.**BottomRightCell**

For check boxes on worksheets, returns the cell under the bottom right corner of the check box. For check boxes on dialog sheets and charts, causes error 1006.

checkbox.**Caption**

checkbox.**Caption** [= *text*]

Sets or returns the text that appears next to one or all check boxes on a sheet. This property is identical to the Text property.

checkbox.**Characters**

checkbox.**Characters** ([*Start*], [*Length*])

Returns a Characters collection object representing the caption. Unlike other Characters collections, you can't set the font or formatting properties of a Characters object in a check box.

checkbox.**CheckSpelling**

checkbox.**CheckSpelling** ([*CustomDictionary*], [*IgnoreUppercase*], [*AlwaysSuggest*])

Checks the spelling of the words in one or all check boxes on a sheet. You can't use CheckSpelling when a dialog box is displayed.

checkbox.**Copy( )**

Copies one or all check boxes on a sheet to the Clipboard.

checkbox.**CopyPicture**

checkbox.**CopyPicture** ([*Appearance*], [*Format*])

Copies one or all check boxes on a sheet to the Clipboard using a bit-map or picture format.

Argument	Description
Appearance	xlScreen copies the object as it appears on-screen; xlPrinter copies the object as it would appear if printed using the current printer setup. The default is xlScreen.
Format	xlPicture creates the copy in PICT format; xlBitmap creates the copy as a bitmap. The default is xlPicture.

*checkbox.*Cut( )

Cuts one or all check boxes from the current sheet and places them onto the Clipboard.

*checkbox.*Delete( )

Removes one or all check boxes from a sheet, without placing them on the Clipboard.

*checkbox.*Display3DShading

*checkbox.*Display3DShading [= True | False]

For check boxes on worksheets and charts, True displays 3-D visual effects. You can't get or set this property for check boxes on dialog sheets.

*checkbox.*Duplicate( )

Makes a copy of one or all check boxes on a sheet and returns the object (or collection) that was created. The following line duplicates the first check box on a sheet and moves it up slightly:

```
ActiveSheet.CheckBoxes(1).Duplicate.Top = _
ActiveSheet.CheckBoxes(1).Top -10
```

*checkbox.*Enabled

*checkbox.*Enabled [= True | False]

True enables one or all check boxes on the sheet to respond to user events; False disables. A check box responds to click events if its OnAction property is set to a procedure name. The default is True.

*checkboxes.*Group( )

Groups a collection of check boxes so that they can be selected, moved, copied, or deleted as a single object. The following line groups all the check boxes on a sheet:

```
ActiveSheet.CheckBoxes.Group
```

*checkbox.*Interior

Returns the Interior object for one or all check boxes on a sheet. For check boxes on worksheets and charts, use the Interior object properties to set the shading and color of the interior of a check box. You can't get or set `Interior` properties for check boxes on dialog sheets.

checkbox.**LinkedCell**

checkbox.**LinkedCell [= *address*]**

Sets or returns the address of a one or more cells linked to the check box's value. When a value is placed in the cell, the check box takes this value. Likewise, if the value of the check box changes, that value also is placed in the cell.

The following line links a check box to a cell on a sheet:

```
ActiveSheet.CheckBoxes(1).LinkedCell = "Sheet2!$A$1"
```

checkbox.**Locked**

checkbox.**Locked [= True | False]**

True prevents changes to the contents and position of one or all check boxes on a sheet while the sheet is protected; False allows changes. The default is True.

checkbox.**LockedText**

checkbox.**LockedText [= True | False]**

True prevents changes to the contents of one or all check boxes on a sheet while the sheet is protected; False allows changes. The default is True.

checkbox.**OnAction**

checkbox.**OnAction [= *procedure*]**

Sets or returns the name of a procedure to run when one or any of the check boxes on the sheet is clicked. The following line causes the procedure `Validate()` to run when the user clicks the check box `chkValidText`:

```
ActiveSheet.Evaluate("chkValidText").OnAction = "Validate"
```

checkbox.**PhoneticAccelerator**

checkbox.**PhoneticAccelerator [= *setting*]**

(Far East version only) Sets or returns the phonetic keyboard accelerator key character for one or all check boxes on a sheet. The phonetic accelerator is used when the system accelerator mode is switched to phonetic characters (as opposed to Roman characters, which use the Accelerator property).

*checkbox.*Placement

*checkbox.*Placement [= xlMoveAndSize | xlMove | xlFreeFloating]

For check boxes on dialog sheets and charts, causes error 1006. For check boxes on worksheets, sets or returns how one or all check boxes on a sheet is attached to the cells below them. The default is xlFreeFloating.

*checkbox.*PrintObject

*checkbox.*PrintObject [= True | False]

True prints one or all check boxes with the sheet; False does not. The default is True. The following line turns off printing for all the check boxes on a sheet:

```
ActiveSheet.CheckBoxes.PrintObject = False
```

*checkbox.*Select

*checkbox.*Select ([*Replace*])

Selects one or all check boxes on a sheet. Select is the equivalent of clicking on the object. If *Replace* is False, Select extends the current selection, rather than deselecting previous selections. The default is True.

*checkbox.*Text

Same as the Caption property.

*checkbox.*TopLeftCell

For check boxes on worksheets, returns the cell under the top left corner of the button. Causes error 1004 for check boxes on dialog sheets and charts.

*checkbox.*Value

*checkbox.*Value [= xlOn | xlOff | xlMixed]

Sets or returns the value of one or all check boxes on a sheet. xlOn means the check box is marked with an X; xlOff means the check box is unmarked;

`xlMixed` means that the check box contains a gray square (reflects a mix of values). Setting `Value` to True is equivalent to `xlOn`, and False is equivalent to `xlOff`, though the values are not equal.

The following line checks a check box:

```
ActiveDialog.CheckBoxes("chkBold") = xlOn
```

Getting True/False Values with Option Buttons

Option buttons indicate a True/False option. Option buttons are exclusive—that is, you can have only one option button marked True in any one group. Option buttons can be on dialog sheets, charts, or worksheets. Use the sheet's `OptionButtons` collection to access `OptionButton` objects.

Use the `Add` method to add option buttons to a sheet. The following line adds an option button to the active sheet:

```
ActiveSheet.OptionButtons.Add 20,20, 20,10
```

Use the `Value` property to determine whether an option button is checked. The following line superscripts a range of cells if the `Superscript` option button is checked:

```
Range("A1:A5").Font.Superscript =
ActiveDialog.OptionButtons("optSuperscript").Value
```

To create multiple groups of option buttons, place them in a group box. Option buttons within a group box are exclusive within the group. That is, you can select only one button in the group as True, but multiple groups can be on the sheet.

The `OptionButton` object and `OptionButtons` collection have specific properties and methods, which are listed in Table 18.3. Properties and methods shown in **bold** are described in the reference section that follows this table. Nonbold items are common to most objects and are described in Chapter 4, "Using Objects."

Table 18.3 OptionButton and OptionButtons properties and methods	
Accelerator[2]	**Border**[2]
Add[1]	**BottomRightCell**
Application[2]	BringToFront[2]

(continues)

Table 18.3 Continued

Caption[2]	LinkedCell[2]
Characters[2]	Locked[2]
CheckSpelling[2]	LockedText[2]
Copy[2]	Name
CopyPicture[2]	OnAction[2]
Count[1]	Parent[2]
Creator[2]	PhoneticAccelerator[2]
Cut[2]	Placement[2]
Delete[2]	PrintObject[2]
Display3DShading[2]	Select[2]
Duplicate[2]	SendToBack[2]
Enabled[2]	Text[2]
Group[1]	Top[2]
Height[2]	TopLeftCell
Index	Value[2]
Interior[2]	Visible[2]
Item[1]	Width[2]
Left[2]	ZOrder[2]

---

[1] *Applies to the* OptionButtons *collection.*

[2] *Applies to the* OptionButtons *collection and the* OptionButton *object.*

optionbutton.Accelerator

optionbutton.Accelerator [= character]

Sets or returns the accelerator key for one or all option buttons on a sheet. *character* is a single letter that matches one of the letters in the caption on the option button. Excel underlines the accelerator key displayed in the caption.

The following lines set the caption and accelerator key for the Bold option button on a custom dialog box.

```
Sub CommandButton()
    With DialogSheets("dlgWord")
        .Evaluate("optBold").Caption = "Bold"
        .Evaluate("optBold").Accelerator = "B"
        .Show
    End With
End Sub
```

OptionButtons.Add

OptionButtons.Add (*Left, Top, Width, Height*)

Adds an option button to a sheet.

Argument	Description
Left	The distance between the left edge of the sheet and the left edge of the button in points.
Top	The distance between the top edge of the sheet and the top edge of the button in points.
Width	The width of the button in points.
Height	The height of the button in points.

Note

Left and *Top* of dialog sheets are measured from the upper left corner of the sheet, not the upper left corner of the dialog box. Offset *Left* and *Top* from the Left and Top properties of the DialogFrame object to keep buttons on the visible portion of the dialog box.

The following line adds an option button to a custom dialog box:

```
DialogSheets("dlgGetAccountInfo").OptionButtons. Add 20,20, 20,10
```

optionbutton.Border

Returns the Border object for one or all option buttons on a sheet. For objects on worksheets and charts, use the returned Border object properties to change the border of an object. You can't get or set Border properties of objects on dialog sheets.

optionbutton.BottomRightCell

For option buttons on worksheets, returns the cell under the bottom right corner of the option button. Causes error 1004 for option buttons on dialog sheets and charts.

optionbutton.Caption

optionbutton.Caption [= *text*]

Sets or returns the text to display in one or all option buttons on a sheet.

*optionbutton.*Characters

*optionbutton.*Characters ([*Start*], [*Length*])

Returns a Characters collection object representing the caption of the option button. Unlike other Characters collections, you can't set the font or formatting properties of a Characters object in an option button.

*optionbutton.*CheckSpelling

*optionbutton.*CheckSpelling ([*CustomDictionary*], [*IgnoreUppercase*], [*AlwaysSuggest*])

Checks the spelling of the words in one or all option buttons on a sheet. You can't use CheckSpelling when a dialog box is displayed.

optionbutton.Copy( )

Copies one or all option buttons to the Clipboard.

*optionbutton.*CopyPicture

*optionbutton.*CopyPicture ([*Appearance*], [*Format*])

Copies one or all option buttons to the Clipboard using a bit-map or picture format.

Argument	Description
Appearance	xlScreen copies the button as it appears on-screen; xlPrinter copies the button as it would appear if printed using the current printer setup. The default is xlScreen.
Format	xlPicture creates the copy in PICT format; xlBitmap creates the copy as a bitmap. The default is xlPicture.

*optionbutton.*Cut( )

Cuts one or all option buttons from the current sheet and places them onto the Clipboard.

*optionbutton.*Delete( )

Removes one or all option buttons from a sheet, without placing them on the Clipboard.

optionbutton.Display3DShading

optionbutton.Display3DShading [= True | False]

For option buttons on worksheets and charts, True displays 3-D visual effects. You can't get or set this property for objects on dialog sheets.

optionbutton.Duplicate( )

Makes a copy of one or all option buttons on a sheet and returns the object (or collection) created.

optionbutton.Enabled

optionbutton.Enabled [= True | False]

True enables one or all option buttons on the sheet to respond to click events; False disables. An option button responds to click events if its OnAction property is set to a procedure name. The default is True.

Disabling an option button prevents its value from changing—users can't select or deselect the button.

optionbuttons.Group( )

Groups a collection of option buttons so that they can be selected, moved, copied, or deleted as a single object. The following line groups all the option buttons on a sheet:

```
ActiveSheet.OptionButtons.Group
```

optionbutton.Interior

Returns the Interior object for one or all option buttons on a sheet. For objects on worksheets and charts, use the Interior object properties to set the shading and color of the interior of a drop-down list. You can't get or set Interior properties for objects on dialog sheets.

optionbutton.LinkedCell

optionbutton.LinkedCell [= *address*]

Sets or returns the address of a cell linked to the option button's value. When a value is placed in the cell, the object takes this value. Likewise, if the value of the object changes, that value is also placed in the cell.

II

Programmer's Reference

The following line links an option button to a cell on a sheet:

```
ActiveSheet.Evaluate("optBold").LinkedCell = "Sheet2!A2"
```

optionbutton.**Locked**

optionbutton.**Locked [= True | False]**

True prevents changes to the contents and position of one or all the option buttons on a sheet while the sheet is protected; False allows changes. The default is True.

optionbutton.**LockedText**

optionbutton.**LockedText [= True | False]**

True prevents changes to the contents of one or all option buttons on a sheet while the sheet is protected; False allows changes. The default is True.

optionbutton.**OnAction**

optionbutton.**OnAction [= *procedure*]**

Sets or returns the name of a procedure to run when one or any option buttons on the sheet is clicked.

optionbutton.**PhoneticAccelerator**

optionbutton.**PhoneticAccelerator [= setting]**

(Far East version only) Sets or returns the phonetic keyboard accelerator key character for one or all option buttons on a sheet. The phonetic accelerator is used when the system accelerator mode is switched to phonetic characters (as opposed to Roman characters, which use the `Accelerator` property).

optionbutton.**Placement**

optionbutton.**Placement [= xlMoveAndSize | xlMove | xlFreeFloating]**

For option buttons on dialog sheets and charts, causes error 1006. For option buttons on other types of sheets, sets or returns how one or all buttons on a sheet is attached to the cells below them. The default is `xlFreeFloating`.

optionbutton.PrintObject

optionbutton.PrintObject [= True | False]

True prints one or all option buttons with the sheet; False does not. The default is True. The following line turns off printing for all the option buttons on a sheet:

```
ActiveSheet.OptionButtons.PrintObject = False
```

optionbutton.Select

optionbutton.Select ([*Replace*])

Selects one or all option buttons on a sheet. Select is the equivalent of clicking on the object. If *Replace* is False, Select extends the current selection rather than deselecting previous selections. The default is True.

optionbutton.Text

Same as the Caption property.

optionbutton.TopLeftCell

For option buttons on worksheets, returns the cell under the top left corner of the button. Causes error 1004 for option buttons on dialog sheets and charts.

optionbutton.Value

optionbutton.Value [= xlOn | xlOff | xlMixed]

Sets or returns the value of one or all option buttons on a sheet. xlOn means that the option button is selected; xlOff means that the option button is deselected; xlMixed means that the option button contains a gray dot. Setting Value to True is equivalent to xlOn, and False is equivalent to xlOff, although the values are not equal.

The following line selects an option button:

```
ActiveDialog.Evaluate("optBold") = xlOn
```

Grouping Controls with Group Boxes

Group boxes create a visual frame around a group of controls. This frame is also functional, in that option buttons within the frame are exclusive within the group. Group boxes can exist on dialog sheets, worksheets, and charts. Use the sheet's GroupBoxes collection to access GroupBox objects.

II

Programmer's Reference

Use the Add method to add a group box to a sheet. The following line adds a group box to the active sheet:

```
ActiveSheet.GroupBoxes.Add 20,20, 20,10
```

To create multiple groups of option buttons, place them in a group box. Option buttons within a group box are exclusive within the group. You can select only one button in the group as True, but multiple groups can be on the sheet.

The GroupBox object and GroupBoxes collection have specific properties and methods, which are listed in Table 18.4. Properties and methods shown in **bold** are described in the reference section that follows this table. Nonbold items are common to most objects and are described in Chapter 4, "Using Objects."

Table 18.4 GroupBox and GroupBoxes properties and methods

Accelerator[2]	Index
Add[1]	Item
Application[2]	Left[2]
BottomRightCell	**Locked**[2]
BringToFront[2]	**LockedText**[2]
Caption[2]	Name
Characters[2]	**OnAction**[2]
CheckSpelling[2]	Parent[2]
Copy[2]	**PhoneticAccelerator**[2]
CopyPicture[2]	**Placement**[2]
Count[1]	**PrintObject**[2]
Creator[2]	**Select**[2]
Cut[2]	SendToBack[2]
Delete[2]	**Text**[2]
Display3DShading[2]	Top[2]
Duplicate[2]	**TopLeftCell**[2]
Enabled[2]	Visible[2]
Group[1]	Width[2]
Height[2]	ZOrder[2]

[1] *Applies to the GroupBoxes collection.*

[2] *Applies to the GroupBoxes collection and the GroupBox object.*

groupbox.Accelerator

groupbox.Accelerator [= *character*]

Sets or returns the accelerator key for one or all group boxes on a sheet. *character* is a single letter that matches one of the letters in the caption on the group box. Excel underlines the accelerator key displayed in the caption.

The following lines set the caption and accelerator key for the File Option group box on a custom dialog box.

```
Sub GroupBox()
    With DialogSheets("dlgFormat")
        .Evaluate("grpFileOptions").Caption = "File Options"
        .Evaluate("grpFileOptions").Accelerator = "F"
        .Show
    End With
End Sub
```

When a user presses the accelerator key for a group box, focus moves to the first control in the group box. The "first" control is the control in the group box with the lowest ZOrder property.

GroupBoxes.Add

GroupBoxes.Add (*Left, Top, Width, Height*)

Adds a group box to a sheet.

Argument	Description
Left	The distance between the left edge of the sheet and the left edge of the object in points.
Top	The distance between the top edge of the sheet and the top edge of the object in points.
Width	The width of the object in points.
Height	The height of the object in points.

The following line adds a group box to a custom dialog box:

```
DialogSheets("dlgGetAccountInfo").GroupBoxes.Add 20,20, 20,10
```

> **Note**
>
> *Left* and *Top* of dialog sheets are measured from the upper left corner of the sheet, not the upper left corner of the dialog box. Offset *Left* and *Top* from the Left and Top properties of the DialogFrame object to keep the object on the visible portion of the dialog box.

groupbox.**BottomRightCell**

For group boxes on worksheets, returns the cell under the bottom right corner of the group box. For group boxes on dialog sheets and charts, causes error 1006.

groupbox.**Caption**

groupbox.**Caption** [= *text*]

Sets or returns the text that appears at the top of a group box. This property is identical to the Text property.

groupbox.**Characters**

groupbox.**Characters** ([*Start*], [*Length*])

Returns a Characters collection object representing the caption. Unlike other Characters collections, you can't set the font or formatting properties of a Characters object in a group box.

groupbox.**CheckSpelling**

groupbox.**CheckSpelling** ([*CustomDictionary*], [*IgnoreUppercase*], [*AlwaysSuggest*])

Checks the spelling of the words in one or all group boxes on a sheet. You can't use CheckSpelling when a dialog box is displayed.

groupbox.**Copy( )**

Copies one or all group boxes on a sheet to the Clipboard.

groupboxes.**CopyPicture**

groupboxes.**CopyPicture** ([*Appearance*], [*Format*])

Copies one or all group boxes on a sheet to the Clipboard using a bit-map or picture format.

Argument	Description
Appearance	xlScreen copies the object as it appears on-screen; xlPrinter copies the object as it would appear if printed using the current printer setup. The default is xlScreen.
Format	xlPicture creates the copy in PICT format; xlBitmap creates the copy as a bitmap. The default is xlPicture.

*groupbox.***Cut( )**

Cuts one or all group boxes from the current sheet and places them onto the Clipboard.

*groupbox.***Delete( )**

Removes one or all group boxes from a sheet, without placing them on the Clipboard.

*groupbox.***Display3DShading**

*groupbox.***Display3DShading [= True | False]**

For group boxes on worksheets and charts, True displays 3-D visual effects. You can't get or set this property for group boxes on dialog sheets.

*groupbox.***Duplicate( )**

Makes a copy of one or all group boxes on a sheet and returns the object (or collection) created.

*groupbox.***Enabled**

*groupbox.***Enabled [= True | False]**

True enables one or all group boxes on the sheet to respond to user events; False disables. A group box responds to click events if it appears on a worksheet or chart and its OnAction property is set to a procedure name. Group boxes on dialog sheets do not respond to user events. The default is True. Disabling a group box also disables its accelerator key.

*groupboxes.***Group( )**

Groups a collection of group boxes so that they can be selected, moved, copied, or deleted as a single object. The following line groups all the group boxes on a sheet:

```
ActiveSheet.GroupBoxes.Group
```

*groupbox.***Locked**

*groupbox.***Locked [= True | False]**

True prevents changes to the contents and position of one or all the group boxes on a sheet while the sheet is protected; False allows changes. The default is True.

groupbox.**LockedText**

groupbox.**LockedText [= True | False]**

True prevents changes to the contents of one or all group boxes on a sheet while the sheet is protected; False allows changes. The default is True.

groupbox.**OnAction**

groupbox.**OnAction [= *procedure*]**

For group boxes on charts and worksheets, sets or returns the name of a procedure to run when the border of one or any group boxes on the sheet is clicked. Group boxes on dialog sheets do not respond to click events.

groupbox.**PhoneticAccelerator**

groupbox.**PhoneticAccelerator [= *setting*]**

(Far East version only) Sets or returns the phonetic keyboard accelerator key character for one or all group boxes on a sheet. The phonetic accelerator is used when the system accelerator mode is switched to phonetic characters (as opposed to Roman characters, which use the Accelerator property).

groupbox.**Placement**

groupbox.**Placement [= xlMoveAndSize | xlMove | xlFreeFloating]**

For group boxes on dialog sheets and charts, causes error 1006. For group boxes on worksheets, sets or returns how one or all group boxes on a sheet is attached to the cells below them. The default is xlFreeFloating.

groupbox.**PrintObject**

groupbox.**PrintObject [= True | False]**

True prints one or all group boxes with the sheet; False does not. The default is True. The following line turns off printing for all the group boxes on a sheet:

```
ActiveSheet.GroupBoxes.PrintObject = False
```

groupbox.**Select**

groupbox.**Select ([*Replace*])**

Selects one or all labels boxes on a sheet. Select is the equivalent of clicking on the object. If Replace is False, Select extends the current selection rather than deselecting previous selections. The default is True.

groupbox.Text

groupbox.Text [= *text*]

Same as the `Caption` property.

groupbox.TopLeftCell

For group boxes on worksheets, returns the cell under the top left corner of the group box. Causes error 1004 for group boxes on dialog sheets and charts.

Displaying Lists with Drop-Down List Boxes

Drop-down lists enable users to choose one item from a number of text choices. Drop-down lists conserve space because the list "drops down" when the user clicks the down arrow at the right of the control. Drop-down lists can be on dialog sheets, charts, or worksheets. Use the sheet's `DropDowns` collection to access `DropDown` objects.

Use the `Add` method to add drop-down lists to a sheet. The following line adds a drop-down list to the active sheet:

```
ActiveSheet.DropDowns.Add 20,20, 20,10
```

Use the `AddItem` method to add a single entry to a drop-down list. The following line adds the word `Wombat` to the Marsupials drop-down list:

```
ActiveSheet.DropDowns("drpMarsupials").AddItem "Wombat"
```

Use the `ListFillRange` property to add entries from a range of cells. The following line adds the data in the range A1:A5 to the Marsupials drop-down list:

```
ActiveSheet.DropDowns("drpMarsupials").ListFillRange _
="Sheet2!$A$1:$A$5"
```

Use the `List` and `ListItem` properties to return the currently selected item. The following code displays a message containing the selected text in the Marsupials drop-down list:

```
Sub ShowFavorite()
    With ActiveSheet.DropDowns("drpMarsupials")
        MsgBox .List(.ListItem)
    End With
End Sub
```

> **Note**
>
> The `Value` property is the same as the `ListItem` property for the `DropDown` object.

Dialog sheets also have a special type of drop-down list called a *combination drop-down/edit list*. Unlike simple drop-downs, these objects have a space the user can type in. Combination drop-down, edit lists have the following three properties not found in simple drop-downs:

- Text

- Caption

- Characters

These three properties all return the text typed in the drop-down list's edit box. The drop-down list doesn't have built-in capability to add items to its own list, however. To do this, you must add code to the event procedure of another object.

The `DropDown` object and `DropDowns` collection have specific properties and methods, which are listed in Table 18.5. Properties and methods shown in **bold** are described in the reference section that follows this table. Nonbold items are common to most objects and are described in Chapter 4, "Using Objects."

Table 18.5 DropDown and DropDowns properties and methods

Add[1]	**Delete**[2]
AddItem[2]	**Display3DShading**[2]
Application[2]	**DropDownLines**[2]
BottomRightCell	**Duplicate**[2]
BringToFront[2]	**Enabled**[2]
Caption[2]	**Group**[1]
Characters[2]	Height[2]
Copy[2]	Index
CopyPicture[2]	Item[1]
Count[1]	Left[2]
Creator[2]	**LinkedCell**[2]
Cut[2]	**LinkedObject**

List[2]	RemoveItem[2]
ListCount	Select[2]
ListFillRange[2]	Selected[2]
ListIndex[2]	SendToBack[2]
Locked[2]	Text[2]
Name	Top[2]
OnAction[2]	TopLeftCell
Parent[2]	Value[2]
PhoeneticAccelerator[1]	Visible[2]
Placement[2]	Width[2]
PrintObject[2]	ZOrder[2]
RemoveAllItems[2]	

[1] *Applies to the DropDowns collection.*

[2] *Applies to the DropDowns collection and the DropDown object.*

DropDowns.Add

DropDowns.Add (*Left, Top, Width, Height, [Editable]*)

Adds a DropDown object to a sheet.

Argument	Description
Left	The distance between the left edge of the sheet and the left edge of the object in points.
Top	The distance between the top edge of the sheet and the top edge of the object in points.
Width	The width of the object in points.
Height	The height of the object in points.
Editable	True adds a combination drop-down, edit box; False adds a simple drop-down list. The default is False.

Note

Left and *Top* of dialog sheets are measured from the upper left corner of the sheet, not the upper left corner of the dialog box. Offset *Left* and *Top* from the Left and Top properties of the DialogFrame object to keep the object on the visible portion of the dialog box.

The following line adds a drop-down list to a custom dialog box:

```
DialogSheets("dlgGetAccountInfo").DropDowns. Add (20,20, 20,10)
```

*dropdown.***AddItem**

*dropdown.***AddItem (*Text*, [*Index*])**

Adds an entry to one or all drop-down lists on a sheet.

Argument	Description
Text	The text of the entry to add.
Index	The index of the new entry in the drop-down list.

Using AddItem clears the ListFillRange property. The following line adds an entry to a drop-down list box:

```
ActiveDialog.DropDowns("drpStates").AddItem "FL"
```

*dropdown.***BottomRightCell**

For drop-down lists on worksheets, returns the cell under the bottom right corner of the object. For drop-down lists on dialog sheets and charts, causes error 1006.

*dropdown.***Caption**

*dropdown.***Caption [= *text*]**

For combination drop-down edit boxes, sets or returns the text in the edit box. For plain drop-down lists causes error 1006.

*dropdown.***Characters**

*dropdown.***Characters ([*Start*], [*Length*])**

For combination drop-down edit boxes, sets or returns the Characters object representing the text in the edit box. For plain drop-down lists causes error 1006.

*dropdown.***Copy( )**

Copies one or all drop-down lists on a sheet to the Clipboard.

*dropdown.*CopyPicture

*dropdown.*CopyPicture ([*Appearance*], [*Format*])

Copies one or all drop-down lists on a sheet to the Clipboard using a bit-map or picture format.

Argument	Description
Appearance	xlScreen copies the object as it appears on-screen; xlPrinter copies the object as it would appear if printed using the current printer setup. The default is xlScreen.
Format	xlPicture creates the copy in PICT format; xlBitmap creates the copy as a bitmap. The default is xlPicture.

*dropdown.*Cut( )

Cuts one or all drop-down lists from the current sheet and places them onto the Clipboard.

*dropdown.*Delete( )

Removes one or all drop-down lists from a sheet, without placing them on the Clipboard.

*dropdown.*Display3DShading

*dropdown.*Display3DShading [= True | False]

For drop-down lists on worksheets and charts, True displays 3-D visual effects. You can't get or set this property for objects on dialog sheets.

*dropdown.*DropDownLines

*dropdown.*DropDownLines [= number]

Sets or returns the number of lines displayed when a list is dropped down. The following lines set the number of lines displayed equal to the number of items in the list—trimming off blank lines:

```
Sub TrimList()
    With ActiveSheet.DropDowns(1)
        .DropDownLines = .ListCount
    End With
End Sub
```

dropdown.Duplicate( )

Makes a copy of one or all drop-down lists on a sheet and returns the object (or collection) created. The following line duplicates the first object on a sheet and moves it down slightly:

```
ActiveSheet.DropDowns(1).Duplicate.Top = DropDowns(1).Top -10
```

dropdown.Enabled

dropdown.Enabled [= True | False]

True enables one or all drop-down lists on the sheet to respond to user events; False disables. An object responds to click events if its OnAction property is set to a procedure name. The default is True.

dropdown.Group ( )

Groups a collection of drop-down lists so that they can be selected, moved, copied, or deleted as a single object. The following line groups all the drop-down lists on a sheet:

```
ActiveSheet.DropDowns.Group
```

dropdown.LinkedCell

dropdown.LinkedCell [= *address*]

Sets or returns the address of a one or more cells linked to the drop-down list's value. When a value is placed in the cell, the object takes this value. Likewise, if the value of the object changes, that value also is placed in the cell.

> **Note**
>
> For drop-down lists, the value linked to the cell is the index of the item in the list, not the text of the list item.

The following line links a drop-down list to a cell on a sheet:

```
ActiveSheet.DropDowns(1).LinkedCell = "Sheet2!A1"
```

dropdown.**LinkedObject**

For combination drop-down edit boxes, returns the name of the drop-down list object. For simple drop-down lists returns " ". This method is more useful when working with list, edit box combinations.

dropdown.**List**

dropdown.**List** (*[Index]*) [= *entries*]

Sets or returns the entries from a drop-down list. *Index* is the index of the item to set or return. If omitted, sets or returns an array.

The following line assigns three entries to a drop-down list:

```
ActiveDialog.Evaluate("drpCombo").List = Array("Russ", "jon", "jose")
```

The preceding line replaces all pre-existing items in the list. Use the AddItem method to add items to an existing list.

dropdown.**ListCount**

Returns the number of items in a drop-down list. The following lines set the number of lines displayed equal to the number of items in the list, trimming off blank lines:

```
Sub TrimList()
    With ActiveSheet.DropDowns(1)
        .DropDownLines = .ListCount
    End With
End Sub
```

dropdown.**ListFillRange**

dropdown.**ListFillRange** [= *address*]

Sets or returns the address of a column of cells used to fill the items of a drop-down list. If *address* contains more than one column of cells, only the first column is used.

The following line displays the values from the range A1:A5 in a drop-down list named drpRange:

```
ActiveDialog.Evaluate("drpRange").ListFillRange _
"Sheet2!$A$1:$A$5"
```

dropdown.ListIndex

dropdown.ListIndex [= *index*]

Sets or returns the index of the selected item in a drop-down list.

dropdown.Locked

dropdown.Locked [= True | False]

True prevents changes to the contents and position of one or all drop-down lists on a sheet while the sheet is protected; False allows changes. The default is True.

dropdown.OnAction

dropdown.OnAction [= *procedure*]

Sets or returns the name of a procedure to run when the user selects an item from a drop-down list.

For combination drop-down lists, the OnAction procedure also runs when the user types in the attached edit box. The OnAction procedure is not run when the user presses Enter. To detect when the Enter key is pressed, add a default button to the dialog box and add an event procedure for that button.

```
' OnAction event procedure for the default button on a form.
Sub butAdd_Click()
    With ActiveDialog.Evaluate("drpCombo")
        If .Caption <> "" Then
            .AddItem .Caption
            .Caption = ""
            ' Focus switches to button if you press Enter, so
            ' return focus to the drop-down list.
            ActiveDialog.Focus = .Name
        End If
    End With
End Sub
```

dropdown.PhoneticAccelerator

dropdown.PhoneticAccelerator [= *setting*]

(Far East version only) Sets or returns the phonetic keyboard accelerator key character for one or all drop-down lists on a sheet. The phonetic accelerator is used when the system accelerator mode is switched to phonetic characters (as opposed to Roman characters, which use the Accelerator property).

dropdown.**Placement**

dropdown.**Placement [= xlMoveAndSize | xlMove | xlFreeFloating]**

For drop-down lists on dialog sheets and charts, causes error 1006. For drop-down lists on worksheets, sets or returns how one or all objects on a sheet is attached to the cells below them. The default is xlFreeFloating.

dropdown.**PrintObject**

dropdown.**PrintObject [= True | False]**

True prints one or all drop-down lists with the sheet; False does not. The default is True. The following line turns off printing for all the drop-down lists on a sheet:

```
ActiveSheet.DropDownLists.PrintObject = False
```

dropdown.**RemoveAllItems( )**

Deletes all the list items from one or all drop-down lists on a sheet. The following line deletes the list items from a drop-down list:

```
ActiveDialog.Evaluate("drpCombo").RemoveAllItems
```

dropdown.**RemoveItem**

dropdown.**RemoveItem (*Index*, [*Count*])**

Deletes one or more list items from one or all drop-down lists on a sheet.

Argument	Description
Index	The index of the first item to delete.
Count	The number of items to delete. The default is 1.

The following lines delete the currently selected item from a drop-down list:

```
ActiveDialog.Evaluate("drpCombo").RemoveItem
ActiveDialog.Evaluate("drpCombo").ListIndex
```

*dropdown.*Select

*dropdown.*Select ([*Replace*])

Selects one or all drop-down lists on a sheet. Select is the equivalent of clicking on the object. If *Replace* is False, Select extends the current selection rather than deselecting previous selections. The default is True.

*dropdown.*Selected

*dropdown.*Selected = *index*

Selects the item with the specified index. This is the same as the ListIndex property, although Selected can't return a value for a DropDown object.

*dropdown.*Text

*dropdown.*Text [= *text*]

For combination drop-down edit boxes, sets or returns the text in the edit box. For simple drop-down lists, causes error 1006. Identical to the Caption property.

*dropdown.*TopLeftCell

For drop-down lists on worksheets, returns the cell under the top left corner of the object. Causes error 1004 for drop-down lists on dialog sheets and charts.

*dropdown.*Value

*dropdown.*Value [= *index*]

Sets or returns the index of the currently selected item of one or all drop-down lists on a sheet. This is the same as the ListIndex property. For the DropDowns collection, this property can be set but not returned.

Displaying Lists with List Boxes

List boxes enable users to choose one or more items from a number of text choices. List boxes can be on dialog sheets, charts, or worksheets. Use the sheet's ListBoxes collection to access ListBox objects.

Use the Add method to add list boxes to a sheet. The following line adds a list box to the active sheet:

```
ActiveSheet.ListBoxes.Add 20,20, 20,10
```

Use the `AddItem` method to add a single entry to a list box. The following line adds the word Wombat to the Marsupials list box:

```
ActiveSheet.ListBoxes("lstMarsupials").AddItem "Wombat"
```

Use the `ListFillRange` property to add entries from a range of cells. The following line adds the data in the range A1:A5 to the Marsupials list box:

```
ActiveSheet.ListBoxes("lstMarsupials").ListFillRange = _
"Sheet2!$A$1:$A$5"
```

Use the `List` and `ListItem` properties to return the currently selected item. The following line displays a message containing the selected text in the Marsupials list box:

```
Sub ShowFavorite()
    With ActiveSheet.ListBoxes("lstMarsupials")
        MsgBox .List(.ListItem)
    End With
End Sub
```

> **Note**
>
> The `Value` property is the same as the `ListItem` property for the `ListBox` object.

Dialog sheets also have a special type of list box called a *combination list/edit box*. Unlike simple list boxes, these objects have an edit box linked to them. Combination list, edit boxes use the `LinkedObject` property to link the list box to the edit box.

The `ListBox` object and `ListBoxes` collection have specific properties and methods, which are listed in Table 18.6. Properties and methods shown in **bold** are described in the reference section that follows this table. Nonbold items are common to most objects and are described in Chapter 4, "Using Objects."

Table 18.6 ListBox and ListBoxes properties and methods

Add[1]	**CopyPicture**[2]
AddItem[2]	Count[1]
Application[2]	Creator[2]
BottomRightCell	**Cut**[2]
BringToFront[2]	**Delete**[2]
Copy[2]	**Display3DShading**[2]

(continues)

II

Programmer's Reference

Table 18.6 Continued

Duplicate[2]	OnAction[2]
Enabled[2]	Parent[2]
Group[1]	Placement[2]
Height[2]	PrintObject[2]
Index	RemoveAllItems[2]
Item[1]	RemoveItem[2]
Left[2]	Select[2]
LinkedCell[2]	Selected[2]
LinkedObject	SendToBack[2]
List[2]	Top[2]
ListCount	TopLeftCell
ListFillRange[2]	Value[2]
ListIndex[2]	Visible[2]
Locked[2]	Width[2]
MultiSelect[2]	ZOrder[2]
Name	

[1] *Applies to the ListBoxes collection.*

[2] *Applies to the ListBoxes collection and the ListBox object.*

ListBoxes.Add

ListBoxes.Add (*Left, Top, Width, Height*)

Adds a list box to a sheet.

Argument	Description
Left	The distance between the left edge of the sheet and the left edge of the list box in points.
Top	The distance between the top edge of the sheet and the top edge of the button in points.
Width	The width of the button in points.
Height	The height of the button in points.

> **Note**
>
> *Left* and *Top* of dialog sheets are measured from the upper left corner of the sheet, not the upper left corner of the dialog box. Offset *Left* and *Top* from the Left and Top properties of the DialogFrame object to keep buttons on the visible portion of the dialog box.

The following line adds a list box to a custom dialog box:

```
DialogSheets("dlgGetAccountInfo").ListBoxes. Add 20,20, 20,10
```

*listbox.*AddItem
*listbox.*AddItem (*Text*, [*Index*])

Adds an entry to one or all list boxes on a sheet.

Argument	Description
Text	The text of the entry to add.
Index	The index of the new entry in the list box.

Using AddItem clears the ListFillRange property. The following line adds an entry to a list box:

```
ActiveDialog.ListBoxes("lstStates").AddItem "FL"
```

*listbox.*BottomRightCell

For list boxes on worksheets, returns the cell under the bottom right corner of the object. For list boxes on dialog sheets and charts, causes error 1006.

*listbox.*Copy( )

Copies one or all list boxes on a sheet to the Clipboard.

*listbox.*CopyPicture
*listbox.*CopyPicture ([*Appearance*], [*Format*])

Copies one or all list boxes on a sheet to the Clipboard using a bit-map or picture format.

Argument	Description
Appearance	xlScreen copies the object as it appears on-screen; xlPrinter copies the object as it would appear if printed using the current printer setup. The default is xlScreen.
Format	xlPicture creates the copy in PICT format; xlBitmap creates the copy as a bitmap. The default is xlPicture.

listbox.Cut( )

Cuts one or all list boxes from the current sheet and places them onto the Clipboard.

listbox.Delete( )

Removes one or all list boxes from a sheet, without placing them on the Clipboard.

listbox.Display3DShading

listbox.Display3DShading [= True | False]

For list boxes on worksheets and charts, True displays 3-D visual effects. You can't get or set this property for objects on dialog sheets.

listbox.Duplicate( )

Makes a copy of one or all list boxes on a sheet and returns the object (or collection) created.

listbox.Enabled

listbox.Enabled [= True | False]

True enables one or all list boxes on the sheet to respond to user events; False disables. An object responds to click events if its OnAction property is set to a procedure name. The default is True.

listboxes.Group( )

Groups a collection of list boxes so that they can be selected, moved, copied, or deleted as a single object. The following line groups all the list boxes on a sheet:

```
ActiveSheet.ListBoxes.Group
```

listbox.**LinkedCell**

listbox.**LinkedCell [=** *address*]

Sets or returns the address of one or more cells linked to the list box's value. When a value is placed in the cell, the object takes this value. Likewise, if the value of the object changes, that value is also placed in the cell.

> **Note**
>
> For list boxes, the value linked to the cell is the index of the item in the list, not the text of the list item.

The following line links a list box to a cell on a sheet:

```
ActiveSheet.ListBoxes("lstState").LinkedCell = "Sheet2!A2"
```

listbox.**LinkedObject**

For combination list edit boxes, returns the name of the edit box linked to the list box. For simple list boxes returns "". The following line links an edit box and a list box:

```
ActiveSheet.DrawingObjects(Array("edtZip", "lstZip")).LinkCombo True
```

The following line displays the name of the edit box linked to the list box:

```
MsgBox ActiveSheet.Evaluate("lstZip").LinkedObject
```

listbox.**List**

listbox.**List ([***Index***]) [=** *entries*]

Sets or returns the entries from a list box. *Index* is the index of the item to set or return. If omitted, sets or returns an array.

The following line assigns three entries to a list box:

```
ActiveDialog.Evaluate("lstNames").List = Array("Russ", "jon", _
"jose")
```

The preceding line replaces all pre-existing items in the list. Use the AddItem method to add items to an existing list.

listbox.**ListCount**

Returns the number of items in a list box. The following lines find an item in a list:

```
Sub FindItem()
    With ActiveSheet.ListBoxes("lstNames")
        For i = 1 To .ListCount
            If Instr(.List(i), "Russ") <> 0 Then
                .ListIndex = i
                Exit For
            End If
        Next i
    End With
End Sub
```

listbox.**ListFillRange**

listbox.**ListFillRange** [= *address*]

Sets or returns the address of a column of cells used to fill the items of a list box. If *address* contains more than one column of cells, only the first column is used.

The following line displays the values from the range A1:A5 in a list named lstRange:

```
ActiveDialog.Evaluate("lstRange").ListFillRange = _
"Sheet2!$A$1:$A$5"
```

listbox.**ListIndex**

listbox.**ListIndex** [= *index*]

Sets or returns the index of the selected item in a list box.

listbox.**Locked**

listbox.**Locked** [= **True** | **False**]

True prevents changes to the contents and position of one or all the list boxes on a sheet while the sheet is protected; False allows changes. The default is True.

listbox.**MultiSelect**

listbox.**MultiSelect** [= **xlNone** | **xlSimple** | **xlExtended**]

xlNone allows selecting only one item at a time; xlSimple allows selecting multiple items, clicking on an item selects/deselects it; xlExtended allows selecting multiple items using the Shift key to extend a selection and the Ctrl key to select additional items.

Use the `Value` or `ListIndex` properties to get and set the selected item in a single-select list box.

Use the `Selected` property to get and set the selected items in a multiselect list box. Multiselect list boxes cannot be linked to cells using the `LinkedCell` property.

listbox.**OnAction**

listbox.**OnAction** [= *procedure*]

Sets or returns the name of a procedure to run when the user selects an item from a drop-down list.

> **Note**
>
> When you create a combination list edit box, both objects are selected. It is easy to accidentally assign an `OnEvent` procedure to both objects instead of just one. Make sure that the correct object is selected by assigning it a procedure through the Excel user interface.

listbox.**Placement**

listbox.**Placement** [= **xlMoveAndSize** | **xlMove** | **xlFreeFloating**]

For list boxes on dialog sheets and charts, causes error 1006. For list boxes on worksheets, sets or returns how one or all objects on a sheet is attached to the cells below them. The default is `xlFreeFloating`.

listbox.**PrintObject**

listbox.**PrintObject** [= **True** | **False**]

True prints one or all list boxes with the sheet; False does not. The default is True. The following line turns off printing for all the list boxes on a sheet:

```
ActiveSheet.ListBoxes.PrintObject = False
```

listbox.**RemoveAllItems( )**

Deletes all list items from one or all list boxes on a sheet. The following line deletes the list items from a list box:

```
ActiveDialog.Evaluate("lstNames").RemoveAllItems
```

*listbox.***RemoveItem**

*listbox.***RemoveItem (***Index,* **[***Count***]) (***Index,* **[***Count***])**

Deletes one or more list items from one or all list boxes on a sheet.

Argument	Description
Index	The index of the first item to delete.
Count	The number of items to delete. The default is 1.

The following lines delete the currently selected item from a list box:

```
ActiveDialog.Evaluate("lstNames").RemoveItem
ActiveDialog.Evaluate("lstNames").ListIndex
```

*listbox.***Select**

*listbox.***Select ([***Replace***])**

Selects one or all list boxes on a sheet. Select is the equivalent of clicking on the object. If *Replace* is False, Select extends the current selection, rather than deselecting previous selections. The default is True.

*listbox.***Selected**

*listbox.***Selected = ***array*

For multiselect list boxes, sets or returns an array of Boolean values indicating which items are selected. For single select list boxes, causes error 1004.

This function returns an array containing the selected items in a multiselect list box:

```
Function vMultiSelect() As Variant
    Dim i As Integer, iNumberSelected As Integer
    ' Create an array to hold the selected items.
    ReDim sSelection(1 To Active Dialog.Evaluate _
    ("lstMulti").ListCount) As String
    ' For each item in the list, add it to sSelected if its item _
      is True.
    For i = 1 To ActiveDialog.Evaluate("lstMulti").ListCount
        If ActiveDialog.Evaluate("lstMulti").Selected(i) = True Then
            ' Keep track of how many items were selected.
            iNumberSelected = iNumberSelected + 1
            ' Add the item to sSelection.
            sSelection(iNumberSelected) = ActiveDialog.Evaluate _
            ("lstMulti").List(i)
        End If
```

```
        Next i
        If iNumberSelected <> 0 Then
            ' Trim off elements not used.
            ReDim Preserve sSelection(1 To iNumberSelected)
            ' Return an array containing the selected items.
            vMultiSelect = sSelection
        Else
            ' Return False if no items were selected.
            vMultiSelect = False
        End If
End Function
```

*listbox.***TopLeftCell**

For list boxes on worksheets, returns the cell under the top left corner of the object. Causes error 1004 for list boxes on dialog sheets and charts.

*listbox.***Value**

*listbox.***Value [=** *index***]**

Sets or returns the index of the currently selected item of one or all list boxes on a sheet. This is the same as the ListIndex property. For the ListBoxes collection, this property can be set but not returned.

Using Scroll Bars

Scroll bars enable users to move quickly through a wide range of numeric values. Scroll bars can be on dialog sheets, charts, or worksheets. Use the sheet's ScrollBars collection to access ScrollBar objects.

Use the Add method to add scroll bars to a sheet. The following line adds a scroll bar to the active sheet:

```
ActiveSheet.ScrollBars.Add 100,100, 20,100
```

Use the Value property to get the position of the slider on the scroll bar. The following code creates a "color mixer" out of three scroll bars on a sheet:

```
' Event procedure for 3 scroll bars controlling Red, Green, and _
Blue mix.
Sub scrRGB_Change()
    ' Using the scroll bars on the sheet.
    With ActiveSheet.ScrollBars
        ' Maximum scroll value.
        .Max = 255
        ' Create an RGB color from the three scroll bar values.
        lColorMix = RGB(.Item("scrRed").Value,
```

```
        .Item("scrGreen").Value, .Item("scrBlue").Value)
            ' Set the selected range to the color.
        Selection.Interior.Color = lColorMix
        End With
    End Sub
```

The `ScrollBar` object and `ScrollBars` collection have specific properties and methods, which are listed in Table 18.7. Properties and methods shown in **bold** are described in the reference section that follows this table. Nonbold items are common to most objects and are described in Chapter 4, "Using Objects."

Table 18.7 ScrollBar and ScrollBars properties and methods

Add[1]	**LinkedCell**[2]
Application[2]	**Locked**[2]
BottomRightCell	**Max**[2]
BringToFront[2]	**Min**[2]
Copy[2]	Name
CopyPicture[2]	**OnAction**[2]
Count[1]	Parent[2]
Creator[2]	**Placement**[2]
Cut[2]	**PrintObject**[2]
Delete[2]	**Select**[2]
Display3DShading[2]	SendToBack[2]
Duplicate[2]	**SmallChange**[2]
Enabled[2]	Top[2]
Group[1]	**TopLeftCell**
Height[2]	**Value**[2]
Index	Visible[2]
Item[1]	Width[2]
LargeChange[2]	ZOrder[2]
Left[2]	

[1] *Applies to the ScrollBars collection.*

[2] *Applies to the ScrollBars collection and the ScrollBar object.*

scrollbars.Add

scrollbars.Add (*Left, Top, Width, Height*)

Adds a scroll bar to a sheet.

Argument	Description
Left	The distance between the left edge of the sheet and the left edge of the scroll bar in points.
Top	The distance between the top edge of the sheet and the top edge of the scroll bar in points.
Width	The width of the scroll bar in points.
Height	The height of the scroll bar in points.

Note

Left and *Top* of dialog sheets are measured from the upper left corner of the sheet, not the upper left corner of the dialog box. Offset *Left* and *Top* from the Left and Top properties of the DialogFrame object to keep buttons on the visible portion of the dialog box.

The following lines add a scroll bar to the right edge of a custom dialog box:

```
Sub AddScrollBar()
    With ActiveSheet.DialogFrame
        ActiveSheet.ScrollBars.Add .Left + .Width - 10, .Top, 10, .Height
    End With
End Sub
```

Note

If you add a scroll bar to an active dialog box, the display is not updated until the dialog box is closed and reopened.

scrollbar.BottomRightCell

For scroll bars on worksheets, returns the cell under the bottom right corner of the scroll bar. Causes error 1004 for scroll bars on dialog sheets and charts.

scrollbar.Copy()

Copies one or all scroll bars to the Clipboard.

*scrollbar.*CopyPicture

*scrollbar.*CopyPicture ([*Appearance*], [*Format*])

Copies one or all scroll bars to the Clipboard using a bit-map or picture format.

Argument	Description
Appearance	xlScreen copies the button as it appears on-screen; xlPrinter copies the button as it would appear if printed using the current printer setup. The default is xlScreen.
Format	xlPicture creates the copy in PICT format; xlBitmap creates the copy as a bitmap. The default is xlPicture.

*scrollbar.*Cut( )

Cuts one or all scroll bars from the current sheet and places them onto the Clipboard.

*scrollbar.*Delete( )

Removes one or all scroll bars from a sheet, without placing them on the Clipboard.

*scrollbar.*Display3DShading

*scrollbar.*Display3DShading [= True | False]

For scroll bars on worksheets and charts, True displays 3-D visual effects. You can't get or set this property for objects on dialog sheets.

*scrollbar.*Duplicate( )

Makes a copy of one or all scroll bars on a sheet and returns the object (or collection) created.

*scrollbar.*Enabled

*scrollbar.*Enabled [= True | False]

True enables one or all scroll bars on the sheet to respond to click events; False disables. A scroll bar responds to click events if its OnAction property is set to a procedure name. The default is True.

Disabling a scroll bar prevents its value from changing—users can't select or deselect the button.

*scrollbars.*Group( )

Groups a collection of scroll bars so that they can be selected, moved, copied, or deleted as a single object. The following line groups all the scroll bars on a sheet:

```
ActiveSheet.ScrollBars.Group
```

*scrollbar.*LargeChange

*scrollbar.*LargeChange [= *value*]

Sets or returns the amount that the scroll bar moves when the user clicks in the scroll bar body region (as opposed to the arrows at the ends of the scroll bar). The default is 10.

*scrollbar.*LinkedCell

*scrollbar.*LinkedCell [= *address*]

Sets or returns the address of a cell linked to the scroll bar's value. When a value is placed in the cell, the object takes this value. Likewise, if the value of the object changes, that value is also placed in the cell.

The following line links a scroll bar to a cell on a sheet:

```
ActiveSheet.Evaluate("scrColor").LinkedCell = "Sheet2!A2"
```

*scrollbar.*Locked

*scrollbar.*Locked [= True | False]

True prevents changes to the contents and position of one or all the scroll bars on a sheet while the sheet is protected; False allows changes. The default is True.

*scrollbar.*Max

*scrollbar.*Max [= *value*]

Sets or returns the maximum value for one or all scroll bars on a sheet. The default is 100.

*scrollbar.*Min

*scrollbar.*Min [= *value*]

Sets or returns the minimum value for one or all scroll bars on a sheet. The default is 0.

*scrollbar.*OnAction

*scrollbar.*OnAction [= *procedure*]

Sets or returns the name of a procedure to run when one or any scroll bars on the sheet is clicked.

*scrollbar.*Placement

*scrollbar.*Placement [= xlMoveAndSize | xlMove | xlFreeFloating]

For scroll bars on dialog sheets and charts, causes error 1006. For scroll bars on other types of sheets, sets or returns how one or all buttons on a sheet is attached to the cells below them. The default is xlFreeFloating.

*scrollbar.*PrintObject

*scrollbar.*PrintObject [= True | False]

True prints one or all scroll bars with the sheet; False does not. The default is True. The following line turns off printing for all the scroll bars on a sheet:

```
ActiveSheet.ScrollBars.PrintObject = False
```

*scrollbar.*Select

*scrollbar.*Select ([*Replace*])

Selects one or all scroll bars on a sheet. Select is the equivalent of clicking on the object. If Replace is False, Select extends the current selection rather than deselecting previous selections. The default is True.

*scrollbar.*SmallChange

*scrollbar.*SmallChange [= *value*]

Sets or returns the amount that the scroll bar moves when the user clicks on the arrows at the ends of the scroll bar. The default is 1.

*scrollbar.*TopLeftCell

For scroll bars on worksheets, returns the cell under the top left corner of the button. Causes error 1004 for scroll bars on dialog sheets and charts.

*scrollbar.*Value

*scrollbar.*Value [= *value*]

Sets or returns the position of the slider in the scroll bar. Must be between `Min` and `Max` properties. The following line displays the value of a scroll bar:

```
MsgBox ActiveDialog.ScrollBars(1).Value
```

You can only set the `Value` property for the `ScrollBars` collection property.

Using Spinners

Spinners enable users to move quickly through a range of integers. Spinners can be on dialog sheets, charts, or worksheets. Use the sheet's `Spinners` collection to access `Spinner` objects.

Use the `Add` method to add spinners to a sheet. The following line adds a spinner to the active sheet:

```
ActiveSheet.Spinners.Add 100,100, 20,20
```

Use the `Value` property to get the value of a spinner. The following line displays a spinner's value in a cell:

```
Range("A1") = ActiveSheet.Spinners("spnCount").Value
```

The `Spinner` object and `Spinners` collection have specific properties and methods, which are listed in Table 18.8. Properties and methods shown in **bold** are described in the reference section that follows this table. Nonbold items are common to most objects and are described in Chapter 4, "Using Objects."

Table 18.8 Spinner and Spinner properties and methods	
Add[1]	Count[1]
Application[2]	Creator[2]
BottomRightCell	**Cut**[2]
BringToFront[2]	**Delete**[2]
Copy[2]	**Display3DShading**[2]
CopyPicture[2]	**Duplicate**[2]

(continues)

Table 18.8 Continued

Enabled[2]	Parent[2]
Group[1]	Placement[2]
Height[2]	PrintObject[2]
Index	Select[2]
Item[1]	SendToBack[2]
Left[2]	SmallChange[2]
LinkedCell[2]	Top[2]
Locked[2]	TopLeftCell
Max[2]	Value[2]
Min[2]	Visible[2]
Name	Width[2]
OnAction[2]	ZOrder[2]

[1] *Applies to the Spinners collection.*

[2] *Applies to the Spinners collection and the Spinner object.*

spinners.Add

spinners.Add (*Left, Top, Width, Height*)

Adds a spinner to a sheet.

Argument	Description
Left	The distance between the left edge of the sheet and the left edge of the spinner in points.
Top	The distance between the top edge of the sheet and the top edge of the spinner in points.
Width	The width of the spinner in points.
Height	The height of the spinner in points.

Note

Left and *Top* of dialog sheets are measured from the upper left corner of the sheet, not the upper left corner of the dialog box. Offset *Left* and *Top* from the Left and Top properties of the DialogFrame object to keep buttons on the visible portion of the dialog box.

The following line adds a spinner to a custom dialog box:

```
DialogSheets("dlgGetAccountInfo").Spinners. Add 20,20, 20,10
```

*spinner.***BottomRightCell**

For spinners on worksheets, returns the cell under the bottom right corner of the option button. Causes error 1004 for spinners on dialog sheets and charts.

*spinner.***Copy( )**

Copies one or all spinners to the Clipboard.

*spinner.***CopyPicture**

*spinner.***CopyPicture ([*Appearance*], [*Format*])**

Copies one or all spinners to the Clipboard using a bit-map or picture format.

Argument	Description
Appearance	xlScreen copies the button as it appears on-screen; xlPrinter copies the button as it would appear if printed using the current printer setup. The default is xlScreen.
Format	xlPicture creates the copy in PICT format; xlBitmap creates the copy as a bitmap. The default is xlPicture.

*spinner.***Cut( )**

Cuts one or all spinners from the current sheet and places them onto the Clipboard.

*spinner.***Delete( )**

Removes one or all spinners from a sheet, without placing them on the Clipboard.

*spinner.***Display3DShading**

*spinner.***Display3DShading [= True I False]**

For spinners on worksheets and charts, True displays 3-D visual effects. You can't get or set this property for objects on dialog sheets.

*spinner.*Duplicate( )

Makes a copy of one or all spinners on a sheet and returns the object (or collection) created.

*spinner.*Enabled

*spinner.*Enabled [= True | False]

True enables one or all spinners on the sheet to respond to click events; False disables. A spinner responds to click events if its OnAction property is set to a procedure name. The default is True.

Disabling a spinner prevents its value from changing.

*spinners.*Group( )

Groups a collection of spinners so that they can be selected, moved, copied, or deleted as a single object. The following line groups all the spinners on a sheet:

```
ActiveSheet.Spinners.Group
```

*spinner.*LinkedCell

*spinner.*LinkedCell [= *address*]

Sets or returns the address of a cell linked to the spinner's value. When a value is placed in the cell, the object takes this value. Likewise, if the value of the object changes, that value also is placed in the cell.

The following line links a spinner to a cell on a sheet:

```
ActiveSheet.Evaluate("spnCount").LinkedCell = "Sheet2!A2"
```

*spinner.*Locked

*spinner.*Locked [= True | False]

True prevents changes to the contents and position of one or all spinners on a sheet while the sheet is protected; False allows changes. The default is True.

*spinner.*Max

*spinner.*Max [= *value*]

Sets or returns the maximum value for a spinner. Must be a positive whole number between the Min property and 30,000. The default is 30,000.

*spinner.*Min

Sets or returns the minimum value for a spinner. Must be a positive whole number between the Max property and 0. The default is 0.

*spinner.*OnAction

*spinner.*OnAction [= *procedure*]

Sets or returns the name of a procedure to run when one or any of the spinners on the sheet is clicked.

*spinner.*Placement

*spinner.*Placement [= xlMoveAndSize | xlMove | xlFreeFloating]

For spinners on dialog sheets and charts, causes error 1006. For spinners on other types of sheets, sets or returns how one or all buttons on a sheet is attached to the cells below them. The default is xlFreeFloating.

*spinner.*PrintObject

*spinner.*PrintObject [= True | False]

True prints one or all spinners with the sheet; False does not. The default is True. The following line turns off printing for all spinners on a sheet:

```
ActiveSheet.Spinners.PrintObject = False
```

*spinner.*Select

*spinner.*Select ([*Replace*])

Selects one or all spinners on a sheet. Select is the equivalent of clicking on the object. If *Replace* is False, Select extends the current selection rather than deselecting previous selections. The default is True.

*spinner.*SmallChange

*spinner.*SmallChange [= *value*]

Sets or returns the increment to add or delete from the spinner's value when the user clicks the spin buttons. Must be a positive whole number between Min and Max properties. The default is 1.

*spinner.*TopLeftCell

For spinners on worksheets, returns the cell under the top left corner of the spinner. Causes error 1004 for spinners on dialog sheets and charts.

*spinner.*Value

*spinner.*Value [= *value*]

Sets or returns the numeric value for the spinner. Must be between Min and Max properties.

Chapter 19

Sending and Receiving Mail

You can use electronic mail to distribute workbooks and other types of files to people who are linked by networks. When you circulate workbooks by electronic mail, you can get feedback quickly from a wide variety of people.

In this chapter, you learn how to do the following:

- Send workbooks through electronic mail as attachments.

- Route workbooks through a list of people one at a time.

- Use electronic mail to distribute other types of files, such as toolbars, templates, and add-ins.

- Use the `RoutingSlip` and `Mailer` objects to route files and workbooks.

Sending Mail from Excel

You can distribute workbooks to other users on a network by sending the workbook as an attachment or by routing the workbook. The guidelines on the following page apply.

II

Programmer's Reference

■ Send the workbook as an attachment when you want to distribute the workbook quickly to one or more users without tracking its status.

■ Route the workbook when you want to send a workbook to individuals one at a time, enabling each user to forward the workbook to the next person on the list, or when you want to track the progress of the workbook as it is received.

Caution

Distributing workbooks across mail gateways, such as those used to link to the Internet, may not work. Before you do so, be sure to test this with your particular gateways.

To send a workbook as an attachment, follow these steps:

1. Open the workbook in Excel.

2. Choose **F**ile, Send. Excel starts your installed mail system and attaches the active workbook to the message. In figure 19.1, the Microsoft mail system is installed and the workbook BOOK1.XLS is active.

Fig. 19.1
The Microsoft mail system.

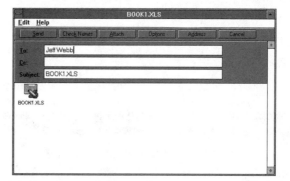

3. Enter the names of the people to receive the workbook, and send the message.

To route a workbook, follow these steps:

1. Open the workbook in Excel.

2. Choose **F**ile, Route. Excel displays the Routing Slip dialog box (see fig. 19.2).

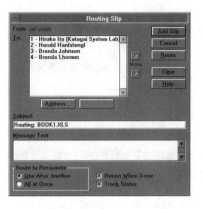

Fig. 19.2
The Routing Slip
dialog box.

3. Click the A**d**dress button and select the names of the people to receive the workbook. Excel displays your mail system's Address dialog box, which should look similar to that shown in figure 19.3.

Fig. 19.3
Microsoft Mail's
Address dialog box.

4. Click OK to close the Address dialog box. Click Route to send the workbook.

Routing Workbooks to the Next Person

After you route a workbook, the people that receive the workbook can open it from within their mail system by double-clicking on the Excel icon or by saving the workbook from their mail system and loading the workbook in Excel. If you send the workbook to one addressee after the other, each can make changes to the workbook and route it to the next person on the list.

To route a workbook on to the next person, follow these steps:

1. Choose **F**ile, Route. Excel displays the Routing Slip dialog box (see fig. 19.4).

Fig. 19.4
The dialog box
used to route a
workbook to the
next person.

2.   Click the first option button (**R**oute document to...) and click OK.

Tracking the Progress of Routed Workbooks

If the Track Status check box of the Routing Slip dialog box (refer to fig. 19.2)
is selected when you route a workbook, you get a message each time that
someone forwards the workbook to the next person.

If the Return When Done check box is selected, the workbook returns to you
when the last person on the list closes the workbook.

Distributing Other Types of Files

Most users send workbooks through electronic mail to get feedback on the
worksheets and charts in a workbook. However, you also can use mail to
install toolbars, templates, or add-ins on users' machines.

Distributing Toolbars Using Mail

You distribute toolbars by attaching them to a workbook and sending the
workbook through the mail.

To attach a toolbar to a workbook, follow these steps:

1.   Open or create the workbook to which you want to attach the toolbar.

2.   Display a module sheet.

3.   Choose **T**ools, Attach **T**oolbar. Excel displays the Attach Toolbars dialog
     box.

4.   Choose the toolbar that you want to attach. Then click the **C**opy but-
     ton. You can attach as many toolbars to a workbook as you want.

5.   Click OK and save the workbook. Excel defines the XLB file extension
     for toolbars, although you can use any file extension you want.

To send a toolbar workbook through the mail, send it as an attachment or
route it as you would any other workbook. When those receiving the workbook open it, the toolbars are installed automatically.

> **Note**
>
> If the buttons on the toolbar run Visual Basic procedures, you must ensure that the workbook containing those procedures is on the user's path.

Distributing Templates Using Mail

Templates control the styles, menus, and sheet layout of new workbooks. They provide a way to structure similar types of workbooks. Excel defines two types of templates: the default template (named BOOK.XLT) and custom templates. To be available automatically, templates must be saved in Excel's startup directory (\EXCEL\XLSTART).

You can distribute template files through the mail just as you would any file, but it is harder to ensure that the template is correctly installed on each machine. One solution is to create a file that installs itself when opened in mail.

To create a template that installs itself when opened from mail, follow these steps:

1. Create a workbook with the layout, menus, formatting, and procedures that you want to include in the template.

2. Add an Auto_Open procedure that installs the file as a template (see the code that follows).

3. Save the workbook. (Auto_Open saves the file in template form, so you can save the source for the template as a regular workbook.)

4. Route the workbook through the mail.

5. When individuals open the routed workbook, Auto_Open installs the file as a template and then routes the file to the next person.

The following code is an example of an Auto_Open procedure that installs a file as a template:

```
' Module: modAutoStart.
' Installs the template when the user opens the file from mail.
Sub Auto_Open()
    ' Check for errors.
    On Error Resume Next
    Dim sTemplateName As String, sFilePath As String
    ' If this file was received in mail, then install the _
    template.
    ' This line prevents the file from reinstalling every time the
    ' file is opened.
```

> **Tip**
>
> In this case, routing a workbook is best, because you are notified when individuals install the file. With this notification, you can track who has current versions of your templates.

```
If ActiveWorkbook.HasRoutingSlip Then
    ' Hide this module.
    Modules("modAutoStart").Visible = False
    ' Set the name of the template to create.
    ' (Place your file name here.)
    sTemplateName = "MAIL.XLT"
    ' Route to the next person (assumes that the file was _
        sent to people one after another).
    ActiveWorkbook.Route
    ' Remove the routing slip from the template.
    ActiveWorkbook.HasRoutingSlip = False
    ' Save the file as a template in the user's
    ' Excel startup directory.
    ActiveWorkbook.SaveAs Application _
        .StartupPath & "\" & sTemplateName, xlTemplate
    ' Display a message if the file is not saved
    ' (user may cancel replacing an existing version).
    If Err Then MsgBox "Template was not installed."
    ' Close this file without saving
    ' (the default is workbook format).
    ActiveWorkbook.Close False
    ' Make sure the template marked as Read/Write.
    SetAttr Application.StartupPath & "\" _
        & sTemplateName, vbNormal
    ' If there are no errors, display a message
    ' indicating success.
    If Err = 0 Then MsgBox _
        "Template was successfully installed."
End If
' Reset error code and turn off error checking.
Err = 0
On Error GoTo 0
End Sub
```

Distributing Add-ins Using Mail

You cannot open or edit add-in (*.XLA) files in Excel, so you cannot send them as you can other files. One solution is to create a file that installs an add-in when the file is opened in mail.

To create a workbook that installs an add-in when opened from mail, follow these steps:

1. Copy the add-in to a disk drive that is shared on the network and then copy the add-in to the default Excel directory (usually C:\EXCEL) on your machine.

2. Create a workbook that contains an Auto_Open procedure that copies the add-in file to the user's machine and creates a template (see the code that follows).

3. In that workbook, create a reference to the add-in in the default Excel directory (usually C:\EXCEL for PCs) on your machine.

To create a reference, choose **T**ools, **R**eferences. Excel displays the References dialog box (see fig. 19.5).

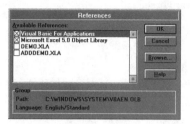

Fig. 19.5
The References
dialog box.

Click **B**rowse and select the add-in's file name from the File Name list.

4. Save the workbook.

5. Route the workbook through the mail.

6. When individuals open the routed workbook, `Auto_Open` copies the add-in, installs it, creates a template with a reference to the add-in, and then routes the file to the next person.

> **Note**
>
> To use the add-in's procedures, a worksheet must have a reference to an add-in. There is no easy way to create this reference. Creating a template with a reference to the add-in is a kludge, but it works.

The following code is an example of an `Auto_Open` procedure that installs an add-in from a network drive:

```
' Installs an add-in when the user opens the file from mail.
Sub nAuto_Open()
    Dim sAddinPath As String, sAddinName As String
    Dim sTemplateName As String, sFilePath As String
    ' Check for errors.
    On Error Resume Next
    ' If this file was received in mail, then install the add-in.
    ' This line prevents the file from reinstalling every time
    ' that the file is opened.
    If ActiveWorkbook.HasRoutingSlip Then
        ' Hide this module.
        Modules("modAutoStart").Visible = False
```

```
                              ' Provide the network path for the file.
                              sAddinPath = "\\public\tools\excel"
                              sAddinName = "estimate.xla"
                              ' Copy file to the directory where EXCEL.EXE is _
                                installed.
                              FileCopy sAddinPath & "\" & sAddinName, _
                                  Application.Path & "\" & sAddinName
                              ' Install the add-in.
                              With Application.AddIns.Add(Application.Path & _
                                  "\" & sAddinName)
                                  ' Install the add-in.
                                  .Installed = True
                              End With
                              ' Set the name of the template to create
                              ' -- creating the default template in this case.
                              sTemplateName = "BOOK.XLT"
                              ' Route to the next person (assumes that the file
                              ' was sent to people one after another).
                              ActiveWorkbook.Route
                              ' Remove the routing slip from this file.
                              ActiveWorkbook.HasRoutingSlip = False
                              ' Save the file as a template in the user's
                              ' Excel startup directory.
                              ActiveWorkbook.SaveAs Application.StartupPath & _
                                  "\" & sTemplateName, xlTemplate
                              ' Close this file without saving.
                              ActiveWorkbook.Close False
                              ' Set the template to Read/Write.
                              SetAttr Application.StartupPath & "\" _
                                  & sTemplateName, vbNormal
                              If Err = 0 Then
                                  MsgBox "Add-in was installed successfully."
                              Else
                                  MsgBox "Add-in was not installed."
                              End If
                          End If
                          ' Turn off error checking and reset the error code.
                          On Error GoTo 0
                          Err = 0
                      End Sub
```

Sending Attached Files from Code

To send files, access the Send File dialog box by choosing File, Send from
the Excel menubar. Use the Send Mail dialog box (fig. 19.6) to send files as
attachments in mail. The following code line starts the mail system and
attaches the active workbook to a message:

```
Application.Dialogs(xlDialogSendMail).Show
```

The Show method returns True if the user sends the message, or False if the
user clicks Cancel.

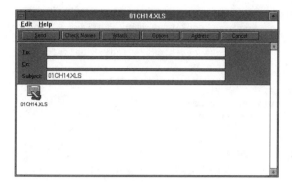

Fig. 19.6
The Send Mail
dialog box with an
attached workbook.

When you send a workbook as an attachment, all the people on the To and
Cc lines receive the message at once. You can't track the progress of a message sent this way.

Using Routing Slips

Use the `RoutingSlip` object to route files through the mail. To add a routing
slip to a workbook, use the `HasRoutingSlip` property.

The following code line adds a routing slip to a workbook:

```
ActiveWorkbook.HasRoutingSlip = True
```

Use the `RoutingSlip` properties to specify who is to receive the workbook and
how the workbook is to be delivered. Use the `Route` method to send the workbook.

The following code lines add a routing slip to a workbook, set the names of
the people to receive the workbook and other routing slip properties, and
then send the workbook through the mail:

```
Sub RouteWorkbook()
    ' Add a routing slip to this workbook.
    ActiveWorkbook.HasRoutingSlip = True
    With ActiveWorkbook.RoutingSlip
        ' Add the names of people to receive the workbook.
        .Recipients = Array("Hiroko Ito (Katagai System Lab)", _
            "Herold Hanfstengl", "Brenda Johnson", _
            "Brenda Lhormer")
        ' Set the text of the Subject and Message lines in mail.
        .Subject = "For your review"
        .Message = "Please send on to next person _
            with your comments."
        ' Deliver the message to recipients one after the other.
```

II

Programmer's Reference

```
                    .Delivery = xlOneAfterAnother
                    ' Send workbook back when the last person has reviewed.
                    .ReturnWhenDone = True
                    ' Send messages back as individuals forward to next _
                      person.
                    .TrackStatus = True
            End With
            ' Route the workbook.
            ActiveWorkbook.Route
        End Sub
```

The RoutingSlip object has specific properties and methods, which are listed in Table 19.1. Properties and methods shown in **bold** are described in the reference section that follows this table. Nonbold items are common to most objects and are described in Chapter 4, "Using Objects."

Table 19.1 RoutingSlip properties and methods

Application
Creator
Delivery
Message
Parent
Recipients
Reset
ReturnWhenDone
Status
Subject
TrackStatus

routingslip.Delivery

routingslip.Delivery [= xlOneAfterAnother | xlAllAtOnce]

xlOneAfterAnother routes the workbook sequentially to each recipient; xlAllAtOnce routes the workbook to all recipients at the same time. You can set this property only before the workbook is routed. The default is xlOneAfterAnother.

routingslip.**Message**

routingslip.**Message [= *text*]**

Sets or returns the text that appears in the body of the message. The default is "The enclosed document has a routing slip. When you are done reviewing this document, choose Send from the Microsoft Excel File menu to return the document to its sender."

routingslip.**Recipients**

routingslip.**Recipients [= *array*]**

Sets or returns an array that contains the list of people to receive the workbook. Your mail system must recognize the names.

The following code line sends a message to three people. The last one is on a CompuServe account reached through a gateway to the Internet.

```
ActiveWorkbook.RoutingSlip.Recipients = Array("Mark Simone", _
    "John Cheever", "netmail!12345,6666@compuserve.com")
```

When you return the value of Recipients, it contains only the names that have not yet received the workbook.

Tip
Mail addresses vary a great deal from location to location. Check with a network expert for information on gateway names.

routingslip.**Reset()**

Clears the RoutingSlip properties of a workbook.

routingslip.**ReturnWhenDone**

routingslip.**ReturnWhenDone [= True | False]**

True returns the workbook to the person who originally sent it after the last person on the To list closes the routed workbook; False does not send the message back. The default is True.

routingslip.**Status**

Returns a constant that indicates the status of a routed workbook: xlNotYetRouted, xlRoutingInProgress, or xlRoutingComplete.

routingslip.**Subject**

routingslip.**Subject [=** *text*]

Sets or returns the Subject line in the message of a routed workbook. The default is Routing:*filename*.

routingslip.**TrackStatus**

routingslip.**TrackStatus [= True | False]**

True returns a message to the person who originally sent the workbook as each person on the To list routes the workbook forward; False does not send a message back. The default is True.

Using Macintosh PowerTalk Mailers

The Macintosh PowerTalk mail system uses a special Mailer object to route workbooks. Mailer is similar to RoutingSlip, but has a few different properties.

To add a Mailer to a workbook, use the HasMailer property. The following code line adds a mailer to the active workbook:

```
ActiveWorkbook.HasMailer = True
```

Use the Mailer properties to specify who will receive the workbook and how the workbook will be delivered. Use the SendMailer method to send the workbook.

The following code lines add a Mailer to a workbook, set the names of the people to receive the workbook, set other Mailer properties, and then send the workbook through PowerTalk mail:

```
Sub MailWorkbook()
    ActiveWorkbook.HasMailer = True
    With ActiveWorkbook.Mailer
        .ToRecipients = Array("John Williams", "Russ Johnson")
        .Subject = "Benefits of converting to Windows."
    End With
End Sub
```

To specify Mailer addresses, use one of the following formats:

■ A record in the Preferred Personal Catalog; for example,
"John Williams" or "Russ Johnson".

■ A full path specifying either a record in a personal catalog (such as
DRIVED:Personal Folder:Mail Catalog:Sal Malone) or a plain record
(such as DRIVED:Folder:Sal).

- A relative path from the current working directory specifying either a personal catalog record (such as `Mail Catalog:Sal Malone`) or a plain record (such as `Sal Malone`).

- A path in a PowerShare catalog tree of the form `CATALOG_NAME:node:RECORD_NAME`, where *node* is a path to a PowerShare catalog. An example of a complete path is `AppleTalk:Building 3 Zone:Mac Attack`.

The `Mailer` object has specific properties and methods, which are listed in Table 19.2. Properties and methods shown in **bold** are described in the reference section that follows this table. Nonbold items are common to most objects and are described in Chapter 4, "Using Objects."

Table 19.2 Mailer properties and methods

```
Application
BCCRecipients
CCRecipients
Creator
Enclosures
Parent
Received
SendDateTime
Sender
Subject
ToRecipients
```

mailer.BCCRecipients

mailer.BCCRecipients [= *array*]

Sets or returns an array of addresses to receive "blind carbon copies" of the workbook. Blind carbon copies are simply copies that don't appear on the Cc line. These copies are useful for general sneakiness.

mailer.CCRecipients

mailer.CCRecipients [= *array*]

Sets or returns an array of addresses to receive regular copies of the workbook.

*mailer.*Enclosures

*mailer.*Enclosures [= *array*]

Sets or returns an array containing the file specifications of files to include as attachments. You can use relative paths, which are assumed to be based on the current directory.

*mailer.*Received

*mailer.*Received [= True | False]

True indicates that the workbook was received through the mail; False indicates that the mailer was created on your machine and not sent through the mail.

*mailer.*SendDateTime

Returns the date and time that the workbook was sent.

*mailer.*Sender

Returns the name of the person who sent the workbook.

*mailer.*Subject

*mailer.*Subject [= *text*]

Sets or returns the Subject line of the message.

*mailer.*ToRecipients

*mailer.*ToRecipients [= *array*]

Sets or returns an array of addresses to receive the workbook.

Chapter 20

Advanced Topics

The following four topics are advanced, because they extend Visual Basic in Excel (and because these topics don't conveniently fit anywhere else in this book):

- On-line Help provides a convenient way to distribute information about applications and procedures created with Visual Basic.

- Add-ins add custom features to Excel, so that the features seem to be built in to the program.

- Version 3.0 of Visual Basic creates stand-alone programs that can use Excel objects.

- Dynamic-link libraries (DLLs) provide low-level functions that control aspects of the operating system and other applications.

In this chapter, you learn how to do the following:

- Create and compile on-line Help topics.

- Display Help for dialog boxes and Visual Basic procedures.

- Load add-in files in Excel.

- Install add-in files on other users' machines.

- Create add-ins from workbook and template files.

- Use Visual Basic Version 3.0 with Excel.

- Declare and call DLL functions.

■ Use the AddIn object's methods and properties.

■ Use the Application object's methods and properties.

Creating On-Line Help

To create on-line Help, you need the following:

■ A word processor that can create rich-text-format (RTF) files

■ The Microsoft Help Compiler, Version 3.0 or later

Most popular word-processing programs can create RTF files, although you may have to install an RTF file converter if you did not choose the appropriate option when you installed your word-processing software.

The Microsoft Help Compiler is available with several Microsoft products, most notably Microsoft Visual Basic, Professional Edition, and Microsoft Visual C/C++, Professional Edition. Each product that provides the Help Compiler contains extensive information about formatting and compiling your files for Help. This chapter doesn't reproduce that information; instead, it summarizes the most important points.

Understanding the Parts of a Help Topic

Help topics use footnotes, underlining, and hidden text to set the various Help-specific attributes of a file. Figure 20.1 shows a typical Help topic.

Fig. 20.1
The parts of a
Help topic.

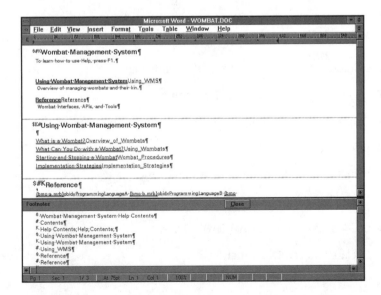

The following footnotes have special meaning in Help topics:

Footnote symbol	Meaning
$	The title of the topic. Titles are displayed in the title bar of the Help window.
#	The context of the topic. *Contexts* are unique identifiers that are used to display a topic. Contexts are mapped to numbers, or *context IDs*, in a section of the Help project file (HPJ). This unique ID is used by applications to zero in on this particular item in the Help file.
K	Search keywords for the topic. These keywords are displayed in the Help Search dialog box and are the equivalent of an index in the Help system.

The following types of formatting have special meaning in Help topics:

Formatting	Meaning
Double underlining	Jump to another topic. Double-underlined text must be followed by hidden text with no intervening spaces.
Single underlining	Pop up a topic. Single-underlined text must be followed by hidden text with no intervening spaces.
Hidden text	The context of the topic to jump to or to pop up.

Note

Jumping to a Help topic causes another help panel to be displayed, based on the context ID chosen. This panel has the same features and abilities (Search, Back, Forward, and so on) as other help panels. Popping up a topic is much more simplistic. A text box with no controls is shown with the desired text. Pressing any key or mouse button removes the text box.

Compiling Topics

The Help Compiler reads a Help project file to locate the files to compile and to map Help contexts to context IDs. A Help project file is a text file that looks like the following:

```
; WOMBAT.HPJ
; Comments are set off by semicolons.
; Help compiler build options
[OPTIONS]
```

```
; Title for main help window
title = Wombat Management System Help
; Button to use for Contents
contents = Contents
; Location of help files
root = c:\wombat\help
bmroot = c:\wombat\help\art
; Topic files to compile.
[FILES]
cont.rtf
procs.rtf
ref.rtf
; Context to Context ID mapping.
[MAP]
Contents 1
FileMenu 100
EditMenu 200
Copy 201
Print 101
PrintSetup 102
ViewMenu 300
FullScreen 306
HelpMenu 600
```

To compile the preceding project, use a DOS command line such as the following:

```
HC31.EXE WOMBAT.HPJ
```

Figure 20.2 shows the Help topic that you generate by compiling the preceding project.

Fig. 20.2

A compiled
Help topic.

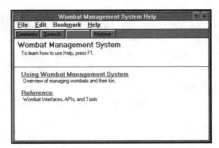

Note

Although Help is a Windows or Macintosh application, the Help Compiler is a DOS-only tool.

Displaying On-Line Help

After you create Help topics, you can display them in a variety of ways from within Excel:

- By using the `Help` method
- By assigning a context ID to a message or input box
- By creating a Help button in a custom dialog box
- By assigning a context ID to a Visual Basic procedure

Using the *Help* Method

Use the `Application` object's `Help` method to display Help from anywhere in code. The following code line displays a topic from the WOMBAT.HLP file created earlier in this chapter:

```
Application.Help "c:\excel\wombat.hlp", 5020
```

When the Help file is displayed, Help has focus, but the Excel procedure continues to execute.

You can use the `Help` method to display topics from any Help file, including MAINXL.HLP and VBA_XL.HLP. You must know the context IDs in those files, however, to display topics other than the "Contents" topic.

The following code line displays the worksheet-functions index from Excel's Visual Basic Help file:

```
Application.Help "vba_xl.hlp", &H18061
```

Displaying Help with *MsgBox* and *InputBox*

The `MsgBox` and `InputBox` functions take arguments that identify the Help file and context ID to display when the user clicks the Help button or presses F1.

The following code lines display a message box that uses the Help file created earlier in this chapter:

```
' Declarations
Dim sHelpFile As String
sHelpFile = "wombat.hlp"
Const HLP_ERR_RANGE = 1001

Sub MsgHelp()
    MsgBox "You must first select a range of cells.", , , _
        sHelpFile, HLP_ERR_RANGE
End Sub
```

Tip

In Windows, you can use an unqualified file name, such as WOMBAT.HLP, if the file is in the Windows directory or in the DOS path.

II

Programmer's Reference

Tip

Use constants to identify context IDs in your code. Constants make it easier to verify that Help is displaying the correct topic.

Adding Help for Custom Dialog Boxes

To add Help to a custom dialog box, you first add a Help button to the dialog box and then create an event procedure to display Help.

To add a Help button to a custom dialog box, follow these steps:

1. Using the Forms toolbar, draw a button in the dialog box.

2. Set the button's Help property to True.

3. Add to the button an event procedure that displays Help.

Figure 20.3 shows a custom dialog box with a Help button added.

Fig. 20.3
A custom dialog box with a Help button.

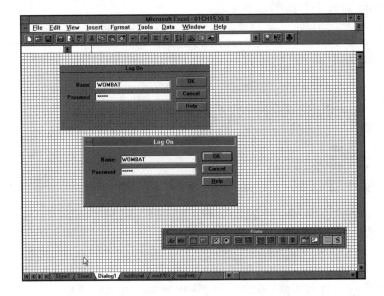

The following code lines show an event procedure for a Help button in a custom dialog box:

```
' Public Declarations
Const HLP_DLG_OPEN = 5050
Public gsHelpFile = "c:\excel\wombat.hlp"

' Event procedure for Help button.
Sub butHelp_Click()
    Application.Help gsHelpFile, HLP_DLG_OPEN
End Sub
```

When the user clicks the Help button in the custom dialog box or presses F1, Excel runs butHelp_Click().

> **Note**
>
> Excel considers pressing F1 the same as clicking on the Help button, and therefore runs the event procedure attached to the Help button when F1 is pressed.

Adding Help for Visual Basic Procedures

Use the `Application` object's `MacroOptions` method to provide Help for procedures that you write in Visual Basic. Help for procedures is visible only from the Object Browser and the Function Wizard; you cannot get help on your procedures in the Code window.

The following code lines set the Help file and context ID for the `getCross()` procedure:

```
Sub SetHelp()
    Application.MacroOptions Macro: _
        ="'01CH15.XLS'!getCross", Description: _
        ="Gets crosstab information", StatusBar: _
        ="Get Crosstab data", HelpContextID: _
        ="1099", HelpFile:="wombat.hlp"
End Sub
```

Using Add-ins

Add-ins extend Excel's capabilities by adding features, menus, and toolbars that work as though they were built in to Excel. An add-in consists of an add-in file (*.XLA) and may use one or more dynamic-link libraries (*.XLL or *.DLL). Excel ships with the add-ins listed in Table 20.1. This applies to Excel for Windows only.

Table 20.1 Add-ins shipped with Excel

Name	File(s)	Description
MS Excel 4.0 Add-In Functions	ADDINFNS.XLA	Provides backward compatibility for Microsoft Excel 4.0 add-in functions.
MS Excel 4.0 Analysis Functions	ANALYSF.XLA	Provides backward compatibility for Microsoft Excel 4.0 analysis functions.
MS Excel 4.0 Analysis Tools	ANALYSIS.XLA	Provides backward compatibility for Microsoft Excel 4.0 analysis tools.

(continues)

Table 20.1 Continued

Name	File(s)	Description
Analysis ToolPak	ANALYSIS.XLL	Adds financial and engineering functions, and provides tools to perform statistical and engineering analysis.
Analysis ToolPak	ATPVBAEN.XLA	Adds Visual Basic for Applications functions for Analysis ToolPak.
AutoSave	AUTOSAVE.XLA	Automatically saves your workbook at a time interval that you specify.
Crosstab sheet function	CROSSFNC XLA	Adds the Excel 4.0 crosstab sheet function.
Q+E Add-In	QE.XLA, QEXLA.DLL	Allows Excel 4.0 macros to use Microsoft Query functions.
Report Manager	REPORTS.XLA	Prints reports that consist of a set sequence of views and scenarios.
Slideshow Template	SLIDES.XLT, SLIDES.XLA, XLSLIDES.DLL	Creates slide shows from worksheets and charts.
Solver Add-In	SOLVER.XLA, SOLVER.DLL	Helps you use a variety of numeric methods for equation solving and optimization.
Update Add-In Links	UPDTLINK.XLA	Updates links to Microsoft Excel 4.0 add-ins to access the new built-in functionality directly.
View Manager	VIEWS.XLA	Creates, stores, and displays different views of a worksheet.
ODBC Add-In	XLODBC.XLA, XLODBC.DLL	Enables you to use ODBC functions to connect to external data sources directly.
Microsoft Query Add-In	XLQUERY.XLA	Retrieves data from tables and external databases using Microsoft Query.

The preceding add-ins may or may not be installed on your system, depending on the options that you chose when installing Excel. Most files are installed in the \EXCEL\LIBRARY subdirectory by default. The Object Database Connectivity (ODBC) files are installed in the Windows system directory. If you can't find the files in those locations, run Excel Setup again and choose the Add-Ins option.

Loading Add-ins

Before you can use the functions that the add-in provides, you must load the add-in in Excel.

To load an add-in, follow these steps:

1. Choose **To**ols, Add-**I**ns. Excel displays the Add-Ins dialog box (see fig. 20.4).

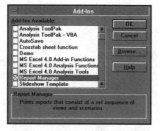

Fig. 20.4
The Add-Ins dialog box.

2. If the add-in is listed in the **A**dd-Ins Available list box, load the add-in by clicking the check box beside the add-in's name. Loaded add-ins are marked with an x.

3. If the add-in is not listed in the list box, click **B**rowse. Excel displays the Browse dialog box (see fig. 20.5).

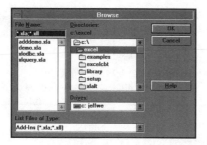

Fig. 20.5
The Browse dialog box.

4. Double-click the file name of the add-in that you want to load. Excel adds the add-in to the **A**dd-Ins Available list box and loads the add-in.

To make an add-in's procedures available to other Visual Basic procedures, you must add a reference to an add-in, as follows:

1. Display a Visual Basic module.

2. Choose **T**ools, Re**f**erences. Excel displays the References dialog box (see fig. 20.6).

Fig. 20.6
The References
dialog box.

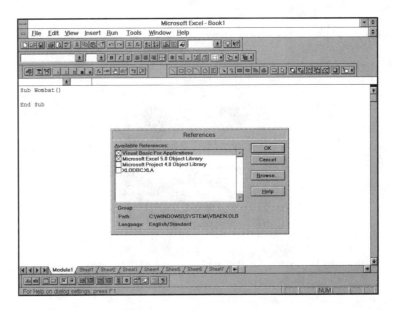

3. Click the check box beside the add-in's name to establish a reference to that add-in; then click OK to close the dialog box.

> **Caution**
>
> Each add-in consumes memory and takes time to load. Loading more than three or four add-ins when you run Excel can cause significant problems, depending on installed memory and other running applications.

Using Add-in Functions in Cells

When you load an add-in, you add its functions to the function lists in the Function Wizard.

To use the Function Wizard to paste a function, follow these steps:

1. Select a cell in a worksheet, and click the Function Wizard button in the Standard toolbar. Excel displays the Function Wizard (see fig. 20.7). Notice that the functions are grouped by category, according to add-in.

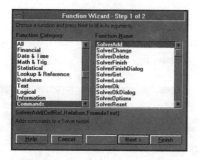

Fig. 20.7
The Function
Wizard, step 1.

2. In the Function **C**ategory list box, click the add-in's name to list its functions in the Function **N**ame list box. Then select the function by double-clicking its name in the Function **N**ame list box. Excel displays the next step of the Function Wizard (see fig. 20.8).

Fig. 20.8
The Function
Wizard, step 2.

3. Enter values for the function's arguments and choose **F**inish when you are done. Functions can accept cell addresses, numbers, or other functions as their arguments.

Using Add-in Functions in Code

If you have established a reference to the add-in, you can call the add-in's procedures directly in code, just as you would any other Visual Basic procedure.

The following code line uses the Analysis ToolPak add-in to convert a binary number to decimal:

```
x = Bin2Dec(100111)
```

To see the procedures that a Visual Basic add-in provides, follow these steps:

1. Display a module sheet.

2. Choose **V**iew, **O**bject Browser or press F2. Excel displays the Object Browser dialog box (see fig. 20.9).

Fig. 20.9

The Object Browser dialog box.

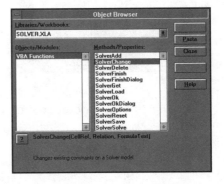

3. Drop down the **L**ibraries/Workbooks list and select the add-in to use.

4. Select the function to use from the **M**ethods/Properties list.

5. Choose **P**aste to paste the function into the Code window.

> **Note**
>
> If you get a Sub or Function not defined error when you try to run your code, make sure that Excel has a reference to the add-in (choose Tools, References).

Of the add-ins that ship with Excel, the following provide procedures that you can call from Visual Basic:

■ Solver (SOLVER.XLA) provides a variety of numeric methods for equation solving and optimization.

■ ODBC (XLODBC.XLA) provides ODBC functions to connect to external databases.

- Microsoft Query (XLQUERY.XLA) retrieves data from tables and external databases.

- Analysis ToolPak (ATPVBAEN.XLA) provides numerical and financial-analysis functions.

- Update Add-In Links (UPDTLINK.XLA) updates links to Microsoft Excel 4.0 add-ins to access new built-in features directly.

Table 20.2 takes a closer look at the procedures that you can access from these add-ins.

Table 20.2 Add-in procedures that can be called from Visual Basic

Add-in	Procedures provided
SOLVER.XLA	SolverAdd(CellRef:=, Relation:=, FormulaText:=)
	SolverChange(CellRef:=, Relation:=, FormulaText:=)
	SolverDelete(CellRef:=, Relation:=, FormulaText:=)
	SolverFinish(KeepFinal:=, ReportArray:=)
	SolverFinishDialog(KeepFinal:=, ReportArray:=)
	SolverGet(TypeNum:=, SheetName:=)
	SolverLoad(LoadArea:=)
	SolverOk(SetCell:=, MaxMinVal:=, ValueOf:=, ByChange:=)
	SolverOkDialog(SetCell:=, MaxMinVal:=, ValueOf:=, ByChange:=)
	SolverOptions(MaxTime:=, Iterations:=, Precision:=, AssumeLinear:=, StepThru:=, Estimates:=, Derivatives:=, SearchOption:=, IntTolerance:=, Scaling:=)
	SolverReset
	SolverSave(SaveArea:=)
	SolverSolve(UserFinish:=, ShowRef:=)
XLODBC.XLA	SQLBind(ConnectionNum:=, Column:=, Reference:=)
	SQLClose(ConnectionNum:=)
	SQLError
	SQLExecQuery(ConnectionNum:=, QueryText:=)
	SQLGetSchema(ConnectionNum:=, TypeNum:=, QualifierText:=)

(continues)

Table 20.2 Continued

Add-in	Procedures provided
	SQLOpen(ConnectionStr:=, OutputRef:=, DriverPrompt:=) SQLRequest(ConnectionStr:=, QueryText:=, OutputRef:=, DriverPrompt:=, ColNamesLogical:=) SQLRetrieve(ConnectionNum:=, DestinationRef:=, MaxColumns:=, MaxRows:=, ColNamesLogical:=, RowNumsLogical:=, NamedRngLogical:=, FetchFirstLogical:=) SQLRetrieveToFile(ConnectionNum:=, Destination:=, ColNamesLogical:=, ColumnDelimiter:=)
XLQUERY.XLA	QueryGetData(ConnectionStr:=, QueryText:=, KeepQueryDef:=, FieldNames:=, RowNumbers:=, Destination:=, Execute:=) QueryGetDataDialog(ConnectionStr:=, QueryText:=, KeepQueryDef:=, FieldNames:=, RowNumbers:=, Destination:=, Execute:=) QueryRefresh(Ref:=)
ATPVBAEN.XLA	Accrint(issue:=, first_interest:=, settlement:=, Rate:=, par:=, Frequency:=, basis:=) Accrintm(issue:=, settlement:=, Rate:=, par:=, basis:=) Amordegrc(cost:=, date_purchased:=, first_period:=, salvage:=, Period:=, Rate:=, year_basis:=) Amorlinc(cost:=, date_purchased:=, first_period:=, salvage:=, Period:=, Rate:=, year_basis:=) Anova1 inprng:=, outrng:=, grouped:=, Labels:=, alpha:= Anova1Q inprng:=, outrng:=, grouped:=, Labels:=, alpha:= Anova2 inprng:=, outrng:=, sample_rows:=, alpha:= Anova2Q inprng:=, outrng:=, sample_rows:=, alpha:= Anova3 inprng:=, outrng:=, Labels:=, alpha:= Anova3Q inprng:=, outrng:=, Labels:=, alpha:= BesselI(x:=, N:=) BesselJ(x:=, N:=) BesselK(x:=, N:=) BesselY(x:=, N:=) Bin2Dec(Number:=) Bin2Hex(Number:=, places:=) Bin2Oct(Number:=, places:=)

Add-in	**Procedures provided**
	Complex(real_num:=, i_num:=, suffix:=)
	Convert(Number:=, from_unit:=, to_unit:=)
	Coupdaybs(settlement:=, maturity:=, Frequency:=, basis:=)
	Coupdays(settlement:=, maturity:=, Frequency:=, basis:=)
	Coupdaysnc(settlement:=, maturity:=, Frequency:=, basis:=)
	Coupncd(settlement:=, maturity:=, Frequency:=, basis:=)
	Coupnum(settlement:=, maturity:=, Frequency:=, basis:=)
	Couppcd(settlement:=, maturity:=, Frequency:=, basis:=)
	Cumipmt(Rate:=, NPer:=, Pv:=, start_period:=, end_period:=, type_payment:=)
	Cumprinc(Rate:=, NPer:=, Pv:=, start_period:=, end_period:=, type_payment:=)
	Dec2Bin(Number:=, places:=)
	Dec2Hex(Number:=, places:=)
	Dec2Oct(Number:=, places:=)
	Delta(number1:=, number2:=)
	Descr inprng:=, outrng:=, grouped:=, Labels:=, Summary:=, ds_large:=, ds_small:=, confid:=
	DescrQ inprng:=, outrng:=, grouped:=, Labels:=, Summary:=, ds_large:=, ds_small:=, confid:=
	Disc(settlement:=, maturity:=, pr:=, redemption:=, basis:=)
	Dollarde(fractional_dollar:=, fraction:=)
	Dollarfr(decimal_dollar:=, fraction:=)
	Duration(settlement:=, maturity:=, coupon:=, yld:=, Frequency:=, basis:=)
	Edate(start_date:=, months:=)
	Effect(nominal_rate:=, npery:=)
	EoMonth(start_date:=, months:=)
	Erf(lower_limit:=, upper_limit:=)
	Erfc(x:=)
	Expon inprng:=, outrng:=, damp:=, stderrs:=, Chart:=, Labels:=
	ExponQ inprng:=, outrng:=, damp:=, stderrs:=, Chart:=, Labels:=

II

Programmer's Reference

(continues)

Table 20.2 Continued	
Add-in	**Procedures provided**
	Factdouble(Number:=)
	Fourier inprng:=, outrng:=, invers:=, Labels:=
	FourierQ inprng:=, outrng:=, invers:=, Labels:=
	Ftestv inprng1:=, inprng2:=, outrng:=, Labels:=, alpha:=
	FtestvQ inprng1:=, inprng2:=, outrng:=, Labels:=, alpha:=
	FvSchedule(principal:=, schedule:=)
	Gcd(number1:=, number2:=, ... inumber$n$:=)
	GeStep(Number:=, step:=)
	Hex2Bin(Number:=, places:=)
	Hex2Dec(Number:=)
	Hex2Oct(Number:=, places:=)
	Histogram inprng:=, outrng:=, binrng:=, pareto:=, chartc:=, Chart:=, Labels:=
	HistogramQ inprng:=, outrng:=, binrng:=, pareto:=, chartc:=, Chart:=, Labels:=
	ImAbs(inumber:=)
	Imaginary(inumber:=)
	ImArgument(inumber:=)
	ImConjugate(inumber:=)
	ImCos(inumber:=)
	ImDiv(inumber1:=, inumber2:=)
	ImExp(inumber:=)
	ImLn(inumber:=)
	ImLog10(inumber:=)
	ImLog2(inumber:=)
	ImPower(inumber:=, Number:=)
	ImProduct(inumber1:=, inumber2:=,... inumber$n$:=)
	ImReal(inumber:=)
	ImSin(inumber:=)
	ImSqrt(inumber:=)
	ImSub(inumber1:=, inumber2:=)
	ImSum(inumber1:=, inumber2:=,... inumber$n$:=)
	Intrate(settlement:=, maturity:=, investment:=, redemption:=, basis:=)

Add-in	Procedures provided
	IsEven(Number:=)
	IsOdd(Number:=)
	Lcm(number1:=, number2:=,... inumber*n*:=)
	Mcorrel inprng:=, outrng:=, grouped:=, Labels:=
	McorrelQ inprng:=, outrng:=, grouped:=, Labels:=
	Mcovar inprng:=, outrng:=, grouped:=, Labels:=
	McovarQ inprng:=, outrng:=, grouped:=, Labels:=
	MDuration(settlement:=, maturity:=, coupon:=, yld:=, Frequency:=, basis:=)
	Moveavg inprng:=, outrng:=, interval:=, stderrs:=, Chart:=, Labels:=
	MoveavgQ inprng:=, outrng:=, interval:=, stderrs:=, Chart:=, Labels:=
	MRound(Number:=, multiple:=)
	Multinomial(number1:=, number2:=,..., number*n*:=)
	Networkdays(start_date:=, end_date:=, holidays:=)
	Nominal(effect_rate:=, npery:=)
	Oct2Bin(Number:=, places:=)
	Oct2Dec(Number:=)
	Oct2Hex(Number:=, places:=)
	OddFPrice(settlement:=, maturity:=, issue:=, first_coupon:=, Rate:=, yld:=, redemption:=, Frequency:=, basis:=)
	OddFYield(settlement:=, maturity:=, issue:=, first_coupon:=, Rate:=, pr:=, redemption:=, Frequency:=, basis:=)
	OddLPrice(settlement:=, maturity:=, last_interest:=, Rate:=, yld:=, redemption:=, Frequency:=, basis:=)
	OddLYield(settlement:=, maturity:=, last_interest:=, Rate:=, pr:=, redemption:=, Frequency:=, basis:=)
	Price(settlement:=, maturity:=, Rate:=, yld:=, redemption:=, Frequency:=, basis:=)
	Pricedisc(settlement:=, maturity:=, discount:=, redemption:=, basis:=)
	Pricemat(settlement:=, maturity:=, issue:=, Rate:=, yld:=, basis:=)
	Pttestm inprng1:=, inprng2:=, outrng:=, Labels:=, alpha:=, difference:=

(continues)

II

Programmer's Reference

Table 20.2 Continued

Add-in	Procedures provided
	PttestmQ inprng1:=, inprng2:=, outrng:=, Labels:=, alpha:=, difference:=
	Pttestv inprng1:=, inprng2:=, outrng:=, Labels:=, alpha:=, difference:=
	PttestvQ inprng1:=, inprng2:=, outrng:=, Labels:=, alpha:=, difference:=
	Quotient(numerator:=, denominator:=)
	Randbetween(bottom:=, Top:=)
	Random outrng:=, variables:=, Points:=, distribution:=, seed:=, randarg1:=, randarg2:=, randarg3:=, randarg4:=, randarg5:=
	RandomQ outrng:=, variables:=, Points:=, distribution:=, seed:=, randarg1:=, randarg2:=, randarg3:=, randarg4:=, randarg5:=
	RankPerc inprng:=, outrng:=, grouped:=, Labels:=
	RankPercQ inprng:=, outrng:=, grouped:=, Labels:=
	Received(settlement:=, maturity:=, investment:=, discount:=, basis:=)
	Regress inpyrng:=, inpxrng:=, constant:=, Labels:=, confid:=, soutrng:=, residuals:=, sresiduals:=, rplots:=,
	1plots:=, routrng:=, nplots:=, poutrng:=
	RegressQ inpyrng:=, inpxrng:=, constant:=, Labels:=, confid:=, soutrng:=, residuals:=, sresiduals:=, rplots:=,
	1plots:=, routrng:=, nplots:=, poutrng:=
	Sample inprng:=, outrng:=, method:=, Rate:=, Labels:=
	SampleQ inprng:=, outrng:=, method:=, Rate:=, Labels:=
	SeriesSum(x:=, N:=, m:=, coefficients:=)
	SqrtPI(Number:=)
	Tbilleq(settlement:=, maturity:=, discount:=)
	Tbillprice(settlement:=, maturity:=, discount:=)
	Tbillyield(settlement:=, maturity:=, pr:=)
	Ttestm inprng1:=, inprng2:=, outrng:=, Labels:=, alpha:=, difference:=
	TtestmQ inprng1:=, inprng2:=, outrng:=, Labels:=, alpha:=, difference:=
	Weeknum(serial_number:=, return_type:=)
	Workday(start_date:=, days:=, holidays:=)
	XIrr(Values:=, dates:=, guess:=)

Add-in	Procedures provided
	XNpv(Rate:=, Values:=, dates:=)
	Yearfrac(start_date:=, end_date:=, basis:=)
	Yield(settlement:=, maturity:=, Rate:=, par:=, redemption:=, Frequency:=, basis:=)
	Yielddisc(settlement:=, maturity:=, pr:=, redemption:=, basis:=)
	Yieldmat(settlement:=, maturity:=, issue:=, Rate:=, pr:=, basis:=)
	zTestm inprng1:=, inprng2:=, outrng:=, Labels:=, alpha:=, difference:=, var1:=, var2:=
	zTestmQ inprng1:=, inprng2:=, outrng:=, Labels:=, alpha:=, difference:=, var1:=, var2:=
UPDTLINK.XLA	AllBooks
	BtnHelp_Click
	DefineStrings
	FindLinks CurBook:=
	Main
	ReLink LinkPath:=, LinkName:=, CurBook:=
	SingleBook

Creating Add-ins

Add-ins created from workbook files (XLS) do not create a new workbook when loaded. Add-ins created from template files (XLT), however, create a new workbook based on the source template when the add-in is loaded. SLIDES.XLT is an example of a template add-in.

To create an add-in from a workbook or template file, follow these steps:

1. Open the file in Excel and display a module.

2. Choose **T**ools, Make **A**dd-In. Excel displays the Make Add-In dialog box (see fig. 20.10).

3. Click OK.

4. Save the file as the source for the add-in. You cannot edit XLA files, so you must keep the XLS or XLT file if you want to be able to modify the add-in later.

Fig. 20.10
The Make Add-In
dialog box.

Distributing Add-in Files

When you distribute add-ins to other users, you must copy the files to those users' machines and load the add-in in Excel. If you are providing functions that will be called from Visual Basic, you also must add a reference to the add-in.

The procedures that you follow to install an add-in differ, depending on whether the add-in consists of a single file or multiple files.

Installing Single-File Add-ins

Single-file add-ins can contain Visual Basic procedures, toolbars, menus, and templates. Such add-ins do not call dynamic-link libraries (*.DLL or *.XLL) or other add-ins.

To install a single-file add-in on a machine, follow these steps:

1. Copy the add-in to the user's machine. The following code line, for example, uses the Add method to copy an add-in to a local machine from a network location:

   ```
   Addins.Add "\\public\tools\excel\addins\demo.xla", True
   ```

   Add copies the add-in file to Excel's \LIBRARY directory and adds the add-in's title to the add-in list.

2. Load the add-in in Excel. The following line of code loads the add-in:

   ```
   Addins("Demo").Installed = True
   ```

3. If the add-in must be available to procedures in Visual Basic, add a reference to the add-in. You cannot do this directly in code. Instead, you must instruct users how to do this manually, or provide a template file with a reference to the add-in.

The following lines of code demonstrate how you install an add-in and install a template with a reference to the add-in. sPath can be a network drive or a floppy drive.

```
' Installs an add-in.
Sub InstallAddin(sPath As String, sAddinName As String)
    ' Copy file to the \EXCEL\LIBRARY directory.
    With Addins.Add(sPath & sAddinName, True)
        ' Load the addin.
        .Installed = True
    End With
End Sub

' Copies a Template file to the user's XLSTART directory.
' The Template file must be created manually and have a reference
' to the add-in.
Sub InstallTemplate(sPath As String, sTemplateName As String)
    ' Copy file to the directory where EXCEL.EXE is installed.
    ' Save the file as a template in the user's
    ' Excel startup directory.
    FileCopy sPath & sTemplateName, Application.StartupPath
    ' Mmake the template Read/Write.
    SetAttr Application.StartupPath & "\" & sTemplateName,
vbNormal
End Sub
```

Using Add-ins That Use Other Files

Add-ins that use DLLs, XLLs, or other files present two problems that you don't encounter with single-file add-ins:

- You must ensure that the add-in can find its dependent files.

- You must check the versions of the dependent files before installing over existing files.

When you compile an add-in, Excel writes the paths of any dependent files in the add-in. When you install your add-in on other machines (or if you move the add-in on your own machine), the add-in must search for any DLLs, templates, or other files that it uses. The search follows this order:

Tip

If an add-in uses a DLL, you should install both the XLL file and the DLL in the user's Windows system directory. This practice ensures that the add-in can find its DLL.

1. The absolute build path. (*Build* refers to the path in which the files were installed when you compiled the add-in.)

2. The relative build path.

3. The current directory.

4. The Windows directory.

5. The Windows system directory.

6. The DOS path.

Because Excel's LIBRARY directory typically is not in the DOS path, you should not rely on the `AddIns` collection's `Add` method to copy multifile add-ins to new systems. Instead, use the `FileCopy` statement.

The following code lines install a multifile add-in in the user's Windows system directory and then load the add-in on the user's machine:

```
' Declarations
Declare Function GetSystemDirectory Lib "KERNEL" _
    (ByVal lpBuffer As String,ByVal nSize As Integer) As Integer
' Demonstrates calling InstallFiles.
Sub CopyDemo()
    ' Copy the files to the Windows system directory.
    InstallFiles "b:\", Array("DEMO.XLA", "DEMO.DLL")
    ' Load the add-in in Excel.
    With Addins.Add "DEMO.XLA"
        .Installed = True
    End With
End Sub


' Copies files to Windows system directory and compares file dates.
Sub InstallFiles(sSourceDirectory As String, vFileInstall As _
Variant)
    Dim sTemp As String * 144
    Dim sSysDirectory As String
    Dim iCopy As Integer
    ' Turn on error checking (for file/drive related errors).
    On Error GoTo errInstallFiles
    ' Get the Windows system directory.
    iWorked = GetSystemDirectory(sTemp, 144)
    ' If the previous API call worked, trim the returned string.
    If iWorked Then

        sSysDirectory = Mid(sTemp, 1, _
            InStr(sTemp, Chr(0))- 1) & "\"

    ' Otherwise, return an error to the user.
    Else
        MsgBox "Couldn't get system directory. Operation _
        canceled."
        End
    End If
    ' For each file in the vFileInstall array.
    For Each sNewFile In vFileInstall
        ' Check whether the file exists.
        If Len(Dir(sSysDirectory & sNewFile)) = 0 Then
            ' If it doesn't, copy the new file.
            FileCopy sSourceDirectory & sNewFile, _
                sSysDirectory & sNewFile
        Else
            ' Otherwise, compare the date stamps on the files.
            dtExisting = FileDateTime(sSysDirectory & sNewFile)
```

```
                    dtNew = FileDateTime(sSourceDirectory & sNewFile)
                    ' If new file is more recent, copy over old file.
                    If dtExisting < dtNew Then
                        FileCopy sSourceDirectory & sNewFile, _
                            sSysDirectory & sNewFile
                    ' Otherwise, ask the user what to do.
                    Else
                        iCopy = MsgBox("A newer version of " & _
                            sNewFile & " exists on your system. _
                            Keep newer version?", vbYesNoCancel)
                        Select Case iCopy
                            Case vbYes
                                ' Don't copy file.
                            Case vbNo
                                ' Copy file anyway.
                                If iCopy Then FileCopy _
                                    sSourceDirectory & sNewFile, _
                                    sSysDirectory & sNewFile
                            Case vbCancel
                                ' End this procedure.
                                MsgBox "Operation canceled, _
                                    installation is not complete."
                                End
                        End Select
                    End If
                End If
            Next sNewFile
    Exit Sub

    ' Error handler.
    errInstallFiles:
        Select Case Err
            ' Disk full.
            Case 61
                MsgBox "Disk full. Free some space and try again."
                End
            ' Disk drive not ready or path not found.
            Case 71, 76
                iCopy = MsgBox("Drive " & _
                    sSourceDirectory & _
                    " is not ready or could not be found. Try again?", _
                    vbOKCancel)
                Select Case iCopy
                    ' The user chose OK, so try again.
                    Case vbOK
                        Err = 0
                        Resume
                    ' The user chose Cancel, so end.
                    Case vbCancel
                        ' End this procedure.
                        MsgBox "Cancelled, install not completed."
                        End
                End Select
```

```
                            ' Unknown error.
                    Case Else
                            MsgBox "Error " & Err & " occurred.  & _
                                    Installation is not complete."
                            End
            End Select
    End Sub
```

Working with the *AddIn* Object

The AddIns collection and the AddIn object enable you to load, unload, and get information about add-ins. You cannot use the AddIn object to create an add-in or establish a reference to an add-in; you can perform those tasks only through Excel's user interface.

To install a new add-in in Excel, use the Add method. The following code line copies an add-in file from drive B to the Excel LIBRARY directory:

```
    Addins.Add "B:\DEMO.XLA", True
```

To load an add-in in Excel, use the Installed property. The following code line loads the add-in installed with the preceding code line:

```
    Addins("DEMO").Installed = True
```

Add-ins are identified by their Title property. The AddIns collection uses the index of the add-in or its Title to return a specific add-in. The following code line installs the Analysis ToolPak, for example:

```
    Addins("Analysis Toolpak").Installed = True
```

> **Note**
>
> Most collections use the object's Name property to identify items. The AddIns collection, however, uses Name to return the file name of the add-in.

The AddIn object and AddIns collection have specific properties and methods, which are listed in Table 20.3. Properties and methods shown in **bold** are described in the reference section that follows this table. Nonbold items are common to most objects and are described in Chapter 4, "Using Objects."

Table 20.3 AddIn and AddIns properties and methods	
Add[1]	Comments
Application[2]	Count[1]
Author	Creator[2]

FullName	Parent[2]
Installed	Path
Item	Subject
Keywords	Title
Name	

[1]*Applies to the AddIns collection.*

[2]*Applies to the AddIns collection and the AddIn object.*

addins.Add

addins.Add (*Filename*, [*CopyFile*])

Adds an add-in to Excel's add-in list and (optionally) copies the add-in file from an external drive to the user's system.

Argument	Description
Filename	The name of the add-in file. If you don't specify a path, Excel searches for the file in the current directory, the Windows and Windows system directories, and the DOS path.
CopyFile	True copies the file from a network or floppy drive to the Excel LIBRARY directory; False does not copy the file.

addin.Author

Returns the name entered in the file's summary information for the add-in's source workbook.

addin.Comments

Returns comments entered in the file's summary information for the add-in's source workbook.

addin.FullName

Returns the file name and path of the add-in file.

addin.Installed

addin.Installed [= True | False]

True loads the add-in in Excel; False unloads the add-in.

addins.Item

addins.Item(*Index*)

Returns a single add-in or a collection of add-ins.

addin.Keywords

Returns the keywords entered in the file's summary information for the add-in's source workbook.

addin.Path

Returns the path of the add-in file.

addin.Subject

Returns the subject entered in the file's summary information for the add-in's source workbook. When the add-in is selected, the subject is displayed at the bottom of the Add-Ins dialog box.

addin.Title

Returns the title entered in the file's summary information for the add-in's source workbook. Use `Title` to select a specific add-in from the `AddIns` collection.

Using Excel from Visual Basic Version 3.0

Visual Basic for Applications (VBA) is a close relative of Visual Basic version 3.0 (VB3). VBA is built in to Excel, but VB3 is a stand-alone programming tool.

VB3 has the following advantages over VBA:

- *Smaller, lighter applications.* VB3 applications tend to be smaller than equivalent VBA applications and require less memory when running.

- *Stand-alone EXEs.* VB3 can create compiled EXE programs that you can run directly from Windows rather than from within another application, such as Excel.

- *Custom controls.* VB3 applications can incorporate several specialized tools called *custom controls*. Custom controls are not available in VBA.

- *Built-in data access.* You can link VB3 controls directly to database tables and fields.

On the other hand, VBA has some advantages over VB3, including the following:

- *Built-in objects.* Excel objects are available automatically in VBA. To use these in VB3, you must take special steps (described in the following section).

- *Faster access to objects.* Accessing object properties and methods is 4 to 10 times faster in VBA than in VB3. However, VB3 partially compensates for this disadvantage by being faster in some nonobject operations.

- *New language constructions.* VBA has some statements, such as For Each and With...End With, that VB3 does not yet have.

Starting Excel from VB3

VB3 isn't built in to Excel, so you must take some special steps to access Excel objects. To get Excel objects from VB3, you use the CreateObject and GetObject functions.

The following code lines start Excel from VB3 and return Excel's Application object:

```
' VB3 Code.
' Declarations.
Global Application As Object
Sub ConnectToExcel()
    ' Start a copy of Excel.
    Set Application = CreateObject("Excel.Application")
    ' Make the copy visible (it starts invisibly otherwise).
    Application.Visible = True
End Sub
```

After you connect to Excel, you can use the Application object to get and use other objects. The following code lines create and save a workbook:

```
' VB3 Code.
Sub CreateWorkbook()
    Dim objWorkbook As Object
    Set objWorkbook = Application.Workbooks.Add
    objWorkbook.SaveAs "VB3WRK.XLS"
End Sub
```

Using VBA Code in VB3

Perhaps the easiest way to learn how to program Excel from VB3 is to look at the changes that you must make to run VBA code in VB3.

To use VBA code in VB3, follow these steps:

1. Save the VBA module as text, and load it in the VB3 project.

2. Declare object variables, and use the CreateObject or GetObject functions to establish references to the application's objects.

3. Modify object references so that they are explicit.

4. Delete the named portion of named arguments.

5. Declare built-in constants (xlNone, xlOn, and so on) in the VB3 project. (For a list of the built-in constants and their values, see Appendix C, "Table of Intrinsic Constants".)

6. Replace With ... End With statements with explicit object references.

The following example shows VBA code that has been modified to run in VB3. **Bold** indicates items that were added to the code. ~~Strikethrough~~ indicates items that were deleted from the VBA code.

```
' VB3 Declare object variables.
Dim Application As Object
Dim chrtObj As Object

Sub AddEmbeddedChart ()
    ' VB3 Get the running copy of Excel
    ' (use CreateObject to start new copy.)
    Set Application = GetObject(, "Excel.Application")
    ' Create a new workbook.
    Application.Workbooks.Add
    ' Add some random values to cells.
    For i = 1 To 10
        Application.ActiveSheet.Cells(i, 1).Value = 20 * Rnd
    Next
    ' Add an embedded chart. VB3 replace With with an object
    ' variable, remove named arguments.
    With Set chrtObj = Application.ActiveSheet. _
        ChartObjects.Add(Left:=100, Top:=100, Width:=200, _
            Height:=200)
    ' Plot some data on the chart. VB3 adds object variables
    ' and removes named arguments.
    chrtObj.Chart.SeriesCollection.Add source:=Application _
        .Range("A1:A10")
    End With
End Sub
```

Moving VBA Code to VB3

Before you move code from VBA to VB3, change all object references to be explicit from the Application object. Then test the code within VBA. VBA knows without being told what the Application object is, you have to tell VB3 that Application is an Excel Application object.

After you load code into VB3, create an object variable named Application that refers to the Excel Application object. Make this a global variable in a module so that it is easy to include in a project.

You may want to do the same thing with other commonly recorded object names, as in the following example:

```
' Commonly used object variables.
Global Application As Object
Global ActiveWorkbook As Object
Global ActiveSheet As Object

' Initialize objects.
Sub Main()
    ' Start Excel running.
    Set Application = CreateObject("Excel.Application")
    ' Make Excel visible.
    Application.Visible = True
    ' Microsoft Excel starts with no loaded workbook, so create _
      one.
    Application.Workbooks.Add
    Set ActiveWorkbook = Application.ActiveWorkbook
    Set ActiveSheet = Application.ActiveSheet
End Sub
```

Calling VBA Procedures from VB3

Procedures written in VB3 can call VBA procedures by using the Application object's Run method, as in the following example:

```
' VB3.
Dim Application As Object
Sub Main()
    Set Application = CreateObject("Excel.Application")
    Application.Workbook.Open "BOOK1.XLS"
    Application.Run "SubWithNoArgs"
End Sub

' VBA BOOK1.XLS
Sub SubWithNoArgs ()
    MsgBox "I been to the desert on a Sub with no args."
End Sub
```

If the VBA procedure uses arguments, place them after the procedure name. Use commas to separate the arguments from each other and from the procedure name. The following code line runs a VBA procedure with two arguments:

```
Application.Run "SubWith2Args", 1234, "String Arg"
```

If the arguments that you pass to a VBA procedure cannot be coerced to match the expected type, Run simply fails without causing an error. You can test whether Run succeeded, however, by checking its return value.

The following code lines run a VBA procedure and test for success:

```
'VB3
Sub TestVBAProc()
    vRet = Application.Run("BOOK1.XLS!SubWith2Args", _
        1234, "String Arg")
    If IsNull(vRet) = False Then MsgBox "Procedure ran OK."
End If
```

Run returns different values, depending on the type of procedure that you call:

Run returns	If
Null	The VBA Sub or Function failed.
True	The VBA Sub succeeded.
The function's return value	The VBA Function succeeded.

Limiting Aspects of VB3

When calling VBA procedures from VB3, you must observe the following restrictions.

- You cannot pass arrays. You can work around this restriction, however, by converting the array to a string and then parsing the string within the called procedure.

- You cannot pass nonOLE objects. VB3 controls and objects are not the same as Excel OLE objects. VB3 uses the Object data type for OLE objects.

- You cannot call back. You cannot call procedures created with VB3 from procedures written in the VBA.

- You cannot pass by reference. Even if a VBA procedure's arguments are declared ByRef, changes to those arguments cannot affect VB3 variables.

Using Dynamic-Link Libraries

Dynamic-link libraries (DLLs) are used throughout Windows. Windows itself consists of several DLLs that contain the procedures that all applications use to perform their activities, such as displaying windows, displaying graphics, and managing memory. Visual Basic provides ways to perform many of these tasks. For example, the Visual Basic `Shell` function is equivalent to the Windows `WinExec` function.

Still, some things are difficult or impossible to do using only Visual Basic. For example, Windows provides functions to get and modify strings in application INI files. Using only Visual Basic to modify EXCEL5.INI requires many lines of code.

DLLs enable you to extend Visual Basic almost indefinitely, but using them has a cost: you must declare and call DLL functions correctly. Any mistake can stop your program or crash the system.

Declaring and Calling Functions

Using a DLL function requires two steps:

1. Declare the function.

2. Call the function.

The following code line declares a DLL function that writes settings to an application's initialization file (*.INI):

```
Declare Function WritePrivateProfileString Lib "KERNEL" _
    (ByVal lpApplicationName As String,lpKeyName As Any, _
    lpString As Any, ByVal lplFileName As String) As Integer
```

The following code line uses `WritePrivateProfileString()` to add a line to Excel's INI file (EXCEL5.INI):

```
iWorked = WritePrivateProfileString("Microsoft Excel", ByVal
"OPEN", _
    ByVal "C:\EXCEL\LIBRARY\DEMO.XLA", "C:\WINDOWS\EXCEL5.INI")
```

The new line loads an add-in when Excel starts.

Most DLL functions return a nonzero value if they succeed or 0 if they fail. When returning a piece of data, such as a string or a handle, a DLL function usually returns the data as an argument that was passed to the function by reference (`ByRef`).

When a function returns a string in an argument, you must allocate enough space for the string, so you must create one that is at least as large as the return value. Using a string that is too small causes a general protection fault—a fatal error.

The `GetWindowsDirectory()` function returns the Windows directory as one of its arguments. You must create a string at least 144 characters long to hold this information. The following code gets the Windows directory and displays it in a message box:

```
' Declarations.
Declare Function GetWindowsDirectory Lib "Kernel" (ByVal lpBuffer _
    As String,ByVal nSize As Integer) As Integer
Sub ShowWindowsDirectory()
    ' Create a string large enough to hold any possible path.
    Dim sWinDir As String * 144
    ' GetWindowsDirectory returns the length of the string,
    ' if successful.
    iLength = GetWindowsDirectory(sWinDir, 144)
    ' If successful, trim the extra space and display the path.
    If iLength <> 0 Then
        MsgBox Mid$(sWinDir, 1, iLength)
    End If
End Sub
```

Converting C Declarations to Visual Basic

The DLL functions are most commonly documented with C-language syntax. To call them correctly from Visual Basic, you must translate them into valid `Declare` statements. Table 20.4 shows how to translate some declarations.

Table 20.4 Equivalent C and Visual Basic declarations

C-language declaration	Equivalent Visual Basic declaration	Call with
Pointer to a string (LPSTR) String ptr (MAC)	ByVal S As String	Any String or Variant variable
Pointer to an integer (LPINT) short* (MAC)	I As Integer	Any Integer or Variant variable
Pointer to a long integer (LPDWORD) long* (MAC)	L As Long	Any Long or Variant variable
Pointer to a structure (for example, LPRECT) Rect* (MAC)	S As Rect	Any variable of that user-defined type

C-language declaration	Equivalent Visual Basic declaration	Call with
Integer (INT, UINT, WORD, and BOOL) short (MAC)	ByVal I As Integer	Any Integer or Variant variable
Handle (hWnd, hDC, hMenu, and so on)	ByVal h As Integer	Any Integer or Variant variable
Long (DWORD and LONG)	ByVal L As Long	Any Long or Variant variable
Pointer to an array	I As Integer	The first element of integers in the array, such as I(0)
Pointer to a void (void *)	As Any	Any variable (use ByVal when passing a string)
Void (function return value) NULL	Sub procedure As Any	Not applicable ByVal 0&

Calling Other DLLs

The Lib *libname* clause in the Declare statement tells Visual Basic where to find the DLL. For the Windows DLLs, *libname* is User, GDI, Kernel, or one of the other system DLLs, such as MMSystem. For other DLLs, *libname* is a file specification that can include a path.

The following code line declares the function Splatter() in the file DEMO.DLL:

```
Declare Function Splatter Lib "c:\windows\demo.dll" _
    (ByVal in, ByVal out)
```

Passing Arguments

By default, Visual Basic passes arguments by reference (a 32-bit far address). Many DLL functions, however, expect an argument to be passed by value. If you pass an argument by reference to a function that expects an argument passed by value, the function gets bad data and doesn't work correctly.

To pass an argument by value, place the ByVal keyword in front of the argument declaration in the Declare statement. This practice ensures that each time you call the function, the argument is passed by value.

Some DLL procedures can accept multiple types of data for the same argument. To pass more than one type of data, declare the argument with As Any to remove type restrictions.

When you use As Any, Visual Basic assumes that the argument is passed by reference. Use ByVal in the actual call to the function to pass arguments by value. When passing strings, you use ByVal to convert a Visual Basic string to a null-terminated string.

Using the *Alias* Keyword

DLL functions can have names that Visual Basic does not allow. For example, some Windows functions begin with an underscore character, but in Visual Basic you cannot begin an identifier with an underscore. To correct this problem, use the Alias keyword.

The following code line declares the _lopen() function and creates an alias, LOpen(), that you can use in Visual Basic:

```
Declare Function LOpen Lib "kernel" Alias "_lopen" _
    (ByVal fn As String,ByVal f As Integer) As Integer
```

Applying Special DLL Considerations

Most DLL functions expect strings that are terminated by the Null character (Chr$(0)). Passing a string ByVal appends a null character to the string. Likewise, you can find the end of returned strings by searching for Chr$(0), using the Visual Basic InStr function.

Usually you can pass numeric arrays only to DLL functions. To pass a numeric array to a DLL function, pass the first element of the array ByRef. Arrays that you pass this way should not exceed 64K.

To pass a null pointer to a DLL function, declare the argument As Any and pass the expression ByVal 0&.

Pass handles (hWnd, hDC, and so on) to DLL functions as ByVal Integer. Arguments that return handles should be declared simply as Integer. *Handles* are used throughout Windows to identify such objects as windows and devices.

You cannot pass Excel objects to DLL functions unless the DLL was written with OLE 2.0 in mind. The OLE 2.0 libraries define ways to get information about Excel objects.

Utilizing Common DLL Function Declarations

The following code lines show some of the Windows DLL functions that are commonly used in Visual Basic. These DLL functions are a small subset of the many functions that Windows provides.

```
' Gets a string from a section in WIN.INI.
Declare Function GetProfileString Lib "Kernel" _
    (ByVal lpAppName As String, lpKeyName As Any,ByVal _
    lpDefault As String, ByVal lpReturnedString As String, _
    ByVal nSize As Integer) As Integer

' Writes a string to a section in WIN.INI.
Declare Function WriteProfileString Lib "Kernel" _
    (ByVal lpApplicationName As String, lpKeyName As Any, _
    lpString As Any) As Integer

' Gets an integer value from an entry in a section of WIN.INI.
Declare Function GetProfileInt Lib "Kernel" _
    (ByVal lpAppName As String, ByVal lpKeyName As String, _
    ByVal nDefault As Integer) As Integer

' Gets an integer value from an entry
' in a section in an application's .INI file.
Declare Function GetPrivateProfileInt Lib "Kernel" _
    (ByVal lpApplicationName As String, ByVal lpKeyName _
    As String, ByVal nDefault As Integer, ByVal lpFileName _
    As String) As Integer

' Gets a string from a section in an application's .INI file.
Declare Function GetPrivateProfileString Lib "Kernel" _
    (ByVal lpApplicationName As String, lpKeyName As Any, _
    ByVal lpDefault As String, ByVal lpReturnedString As String, _
    ByVal nSize As Integer, ByVal lpFileName As String) As Integer

' Writes a string to a section in an application's .INI file.
Declare Function WritePrivateProfileString Lib "Kernel" _
    (ByVal lpApplicationName As String, lpKeyName As Any, _
    lpString As Any, ByVal lplFileName As String) As Integer

' Gets the Windows directory. For example, "\WINDOWS"
Declare Function GetWindowsDirectory Lib "Kernel" _
    (ByVal lpBuffer As String, ByVal nSize As Integer) As Integer

' Gets the Windows system directory. For example, "\WINDOWS\SYSTEM"
Declare Function GetSystemDirectory Lib "Kernel" _
    (ByVal lpBuffer As String, ByVal nSize As Integer) As Integer

' Clears data from the Clipboard.
Declare Function EmptyClipboard Lib "User" () As Integer

' Switches the focus to a specific window.
Declare Function SetFocusAPI Lib "User" Alias "SetFocus" _
    (ByVal hWnd As Integer) As Integer

' Gets the handle of the window that has focus.
Declare Function GetFocus Lib "User" () As Integer

' Gets the handle of the currently active window.
Declare Function GetActiveWindow Lib "User" () As Integer
```

From Here

Programming is a vast field bounded only by the limits of your imagination. From this point in your experience, there may be several directions that, as a seasoned VBA programmer, you may be interested in pursuing:

- Microsoft Visual Basic, Professional Edition. This package is the full-strength version of Visual Basic that includes many custom controls, the Help Compiler, the Windows API Help, and many code samples.

- Microsoft Office Development Kit includes all the Microsoft Office product and programming documentation on CD-ROM, along with many professional-quality samples written in Excel, Visual Basic, and Microsoft Word.

- *Programming Windows,* by Charles Petzold, explains many of the underlying concepts of programming Windows. Although this book is written for C programmers, you can use all the concepts and most of the Windows API calls in Visual Basic.

- *Inside OLE 2.0*, by Kraig Brockschmidt, and *OLE 2 Programmer's Reference*, Volumes 1 and 2, explain how to create and access applications with the OLE libraries. These are the definitive technical books on OLE 2.0.

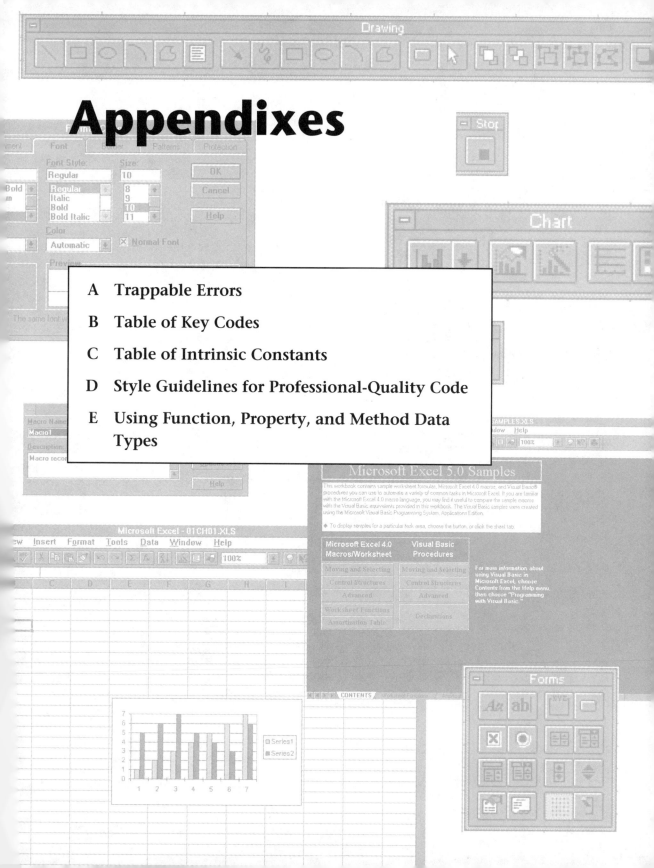

Appendixes

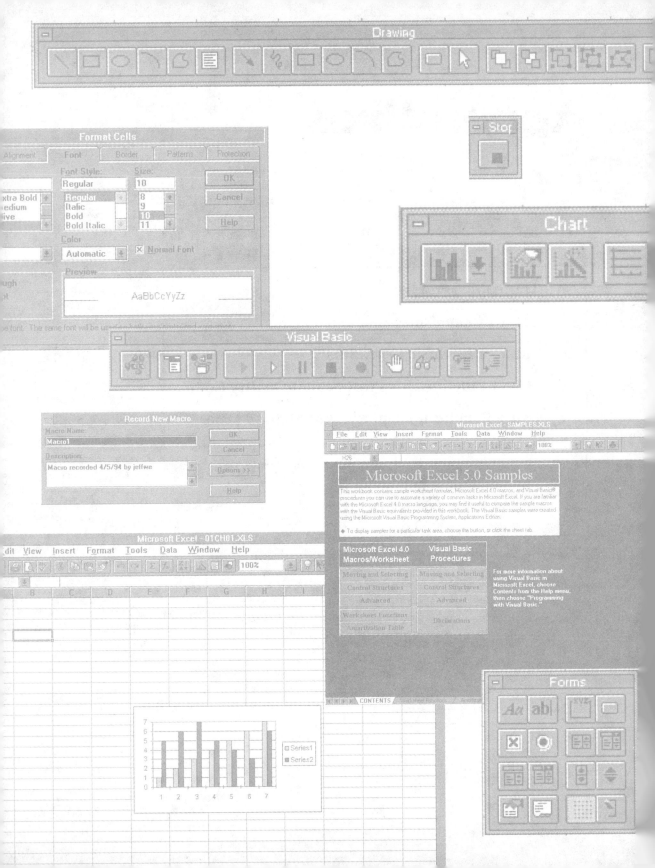

Appendix A

Trappable Errors

This appendix lists the errors that can be trapped in Visual Basic with Excel. The error codes are returned by the Err function; the error messages are returned by the Error function.

Tip
When writing code that handles errors, use the number returned by Err, because the messages may change between versions of Visual Basic.

There are two programming strategies for trapping errors:

- Polling using On Error Resume Next

- Error handlers using On Error Goto

Polling for Errors

The Polling method enables you to check for errors after each statement that may generate an error if unable to successfully complete. The advantage of this method is that you know exactly what line of code caused the error.

Polling is essential when programming with Excel objects. Errors with Excel objects tend to be vague (refer to Table A.2 later in this appendix for a list of these errors). There are seven errors to cover about 1,400 methods and properties, so you usually have to know exactly what line of code failed to handle the situation effectively.

In the following code, the lines numbered (with bold text) within the comments are explained in detail following the example. The following code shows how to poll for errors:

```
Sub PollingDemo()
    ' (1) Start polling for errors.
    On Error Resume Next
    ' (2) This line returns error 1004 if an outline can't be created.
    Selection.AutoOutline
    ' (3) If there was an error...
    If Err Then
```

```
                            ' (4) Alert user of the error.
                            Application.Statusbar = "Can't create outline on this _
                            selection."
                            Beep
                            ' (5) Important! Reset error back to 0.
                            Err = 0
                        End If
                        '(6) Turn off error trapping.
                        On Error GoTo 0
                    End Sub
```

1. The first step is to turn on polling. `On Error Resume Next` prevents errors from halting the program—instead Visual Basic simply assigns the error value to `Err` and continues to the next line of code. `Err` is a system value maintained by Visual Basic to report errors.

2. The `AutoOutline` method does not work on all selections. It is impossible to test the selection to see if it will work *before* you call `AutoOutline`. Your only choice is to test *after* you call `AutoOutline`—possibly causing an error.

3. If there is an error, `Err` is set to a nonzero value (in this case, 1004). This tells you that the method failed, but unless you parse the string returned by `Error`, you can't tell *what* method failed. Parsing error strings is a bad idea, since they may change from version to version of Visual Basic. Your only real solution is to poll for errors after each method you think might fail.

4. Alerting the user is a good idea, especially to errors that could be fatal to the execution of the application, such as failure to open a necessary file. In the preceding code, the user is alerted through a message that appears on the status bar. Using the status bar rather than a message box is less intrusive and doesn't interrupt the user's work. Be sure to clear the status bar on the next user action so the message doesn't remain in view indefinitely.

5. Reset `Err` to 0. Otherwise, subsequent polling will reflect the current error value (1004) even if no error occurs.

6. Turn off polling before exiting the procedure. Polling should only be left on where needed, and turned off when return values are no longer being checked.

Using Error Handlers

Error handlers are blocks of code that handle a general set of errors. One of the nice things about handlers is that they move all the error-handling code to the end of the procedure—out of the main logic of the procedure.

Unlike polling, execution doesn't continue in a straight line from the top of a procedure to the bottom. Instead, execution jumps to the error handler when an error occurs. In the following code the lines numbered (in bold text) within the comments are explained in detail following the example. The following code shows how you might use error trapping by setting up an error handler:

```
' Opens a file for Input. Returns file number if successful, 0 if _
    failure.
Function iOpenFile(sFilename As String) As Integer
    Dim iFilenumber As Integer, iTries As Integer
    ' (1) Turn on error handling.
    On Error GoTo iOpenFileErr
    ' Get a free file number.
    iFilenumber = FreeFile()
    ' (2) Open file. We don't know if the file exists yet, so _
        might cause an error.
    Open sFilename For Input As iFilenumber
    ' (7) Return file number so user can manipulate file.
    iOpenFile = iFilenumber
    ' Important! Turn off error handling.
    On Error GoTo 0
    ' Clear status bar.
    Application.StatusBar = ""
    ' (8) Important! Exit procedure before the error handler.
    Exit Function
    ' (3) Label identifies error handler. This label must be unique _
        to the workbook.
iOpenFileErr:
    ' Classic way to do this: Select Case on the error code, _
    with a Case statement
    ' for each possibility.
    Select Case Err
        Case 52, 53, 75, 76 ' Bad file name or number, file not _
        found, or path error.
            ' (4) Display a status message indicating the error.
            Application.StatusBar = "File not found."
            ' Prompt the user for the file to open.
            sFilename = Application.GetOpenFilename(, , _
            "Choose file to open")
            ' If the user chose Cancel...
            If sFilename = "False" Then
                ' Return 0 to indicate that the function _
                didn't open a file.
```

```
                                iOpenFile = 0
                                ' Turn off error handling and exit.
                                On Error GoTo 0
                                Exit Function
                        End If
                Case 55 ' File already open by VB for an incompatible _
                        read/write access.
                        ' This shouldn't happen, but if it does, return 0 _
                         and exit.
                        iOpenFile = 0
                        On Error GoTo 0
                        Exit Function
                Case 67 ' (5) Too many files are open
                        Application.StatusBar = "Too many files or _
                        applications open."
                        MsgBox "Close one or more files or applications _
                        and try again."
                        iOpenFile = 0
                        On Error GoTo 0
                        Exit Function
                Case 70 ' Permission denied.
                        Application.StatusBar = "Permission denied."
                        MsgBox "You can't open " & sFilename & _
                                ". It requires a password or is in use by _
                                another application."
                        iOpenFile = 0
                        On Error GoTo 0
                        Exit Function
                Case 71 ' Disk not ready.
                        ' Keep track of the number of tries.
                        iTries = iTries + 1
                        ' Let the user try twice, but don't beat them over _
                        the head.
                        If iTries < 3 Then
                                Application.StatusBar = "Can't read from drive."
                                MsgBox "Make sure the disk is inserted and the _
                                drive door is closed."
                        ' Fail after second try -- maybe the user changed _
                        his/her mind.
                        Else
                                iOpenFile = 0
                                On Error GoTo 0
                                Exit Function
                        End If
                Case Else
                        ' Report the error, so you can fix it.
                        MsgBox "An unanticipated error occurred. Please report " & _
                                "the following information to AppBug: " & Chr$(10) & _
                                "Procedure: iOpenFile" & Chr$(10) & _
                                "Error: " & Err & Error()
                                iOpenFile = 0
                                On Error GoTo 0
                        Exit Function
        End Select
```

```
    ' (6) You must tell Visual Basic to return after handling _
    the error.
    Resume
End Function
```

1. The first step is to turn on error handling. `On Error Goto iOpenFileErr` sets up an error handler—in this case `iOpenFileErr`.

2. The Open statement can cause any number of errors. If an error occurs, the code jumps immediately to (3); otherwise it continues straight to (7).

3. The Select Case statement handles all the known problems that might occur while opening a file.

4. The most common problems can be solved by asking the user for the correct file name. If possible, it is a good idea to let users correct problems. The preceding block of code uses Excel's Open File dialog box.

5. In some cases, there is no easy solution, so the function may fail. It is a good idea to pass back 0 or False to indicate failure, rather than simply ending the program. This way, the caller can decide whether to stop or continue.

6. After the error is handled, `Resume` returns execution to line (2) to open the file; `Resume Next` returns execution to line (7).

7. Return values should be meaningful to the caller. In the preceding code, if `iOpenFile` is not 0, then the file handle (or reference number on the Macintosh) is used to access and close the open file.

8. Be sure to exit the procedure before the error handler; otherwise, execution continues at (3), and so on. In the preceding code, the `Case Else` runs if you do not exit the procedure.

Tip

Name error handlers after the procedure in which they reside, using the form `procedurenameErr`. The names will always be unique and you'll avoid naming conflicts.

Error Handling as a Shortcut

Sometimes it's easier to test for an error rather than make sure an action is valid before performing that action. Testing for errors is a common practice in Basic programming—nothing happens faster than an error, so it's also a way to speed up some operations.

The following code replaces `wombat` with `wallaby` on the active sheet. Several errors might occur: the active sheet might not be a worksheet and therefore not have a `UsedRange` property; the active sheet might be protected; or it might be open for read-only access. Rather than testing each case, the code simply tests for an error after the Replace.

Appendixes

```
Sub ShortCuts()
    On Error Resume Next
    ActiveSheet.UsedRange.Replace "wombat", "wallaby"
    If Err Then MsgBox "Couldn't perform change."
    Err = 0
    On Error GoTo 0
End Sub
```

Programmer-Defined Error Codes

I've programmed for a long time and never found a case where I *had* to create a system of programmer-defined errors. I prefer to use the return 0 (False) from functions to indicate failure, as shown in "Using Error Handlers" earlier in this appendix. Still, I can imagine a very large application where developers might want to pass back error codes of their own. This section is for you.

Any error code not assigned by the application can be programmer-defined. (Refer to Table A.1 in the following section for a list of application error codes.) It's a good idea to start these error codes at an arbitrary high number—say 10,000—and increment by five. This ensures that your error codes won't conflict with application error codes and also leaves space for your own future additions.

All of the unassigned error codes have the predefined error message User-defined error. You can't change this string, so you have to maintain a list of your error codes and what they mean internally, perhaps as comments in code.

To trigger the error, use the Error statement. The following code detects the conditions of a programmer-defined error and triggers the error:

```
Sub ProgrammerDefined()
    On Error GoTo ProgrammerDefinedErr
    ' Some complicated code...
    ' Mail system not available error (programmer-defined).
    Error 10500
    ' More complicated code...
    Exit Sub
ProgrammerDefinedErr:
    Select Case Err
        Case 10500   ' Mail system unavailable.
            If MsgBox("Send later?", vbOKCancel) Then _
            gbDelayedMailFlag = True
        Case Else
    End Select
    Err = 0
    Resume Next
End Sub
```

As you can see, the `ProgrammerDefined` procedure is not very "code complete," but it does demonstrate how to trigger and handle a programmer-defined error. Finding an appropriate use for this is up to you!

Trappable Error Codes

Tables A.1 and A.2 list all the error codes you can trap in Visual Basic with Excel. The Excel object-defined errors (`1000` to `1006`) are actually user-defined errors. This means that you can't trigger them using the `Error` statement, the way you can with the general error messages.

Table A.1 General trappable errors

Error code	Error message
3	Return without GoSub
5	Invalid procedure call
6	Overflow
7	Out of memory
9	Subscript out of range
10	Duplicate definition
11	Division by zero
12	Precision lost converting Variant
13	Type mismatch
14	Out of string space
16	String expression too complex
17	Can't perform requested operation
18	User interrupt occurred
20	Resume without error
28	Out of stack space
35	Sub or function not defined
47	Too many DLL application clients

(continues)

Appendixes

Table A.1 Continued	
Error code	**Error message**
48	Error in loading DLL
49	Bad DLL calling convention
51	Internal error
52	Bad file name or number
53	File not found
54	Bad file mode
55	File already open
57	Device I/O error
58	File already exists
59	Bad record length
61	Disk full
62	Input past end of file
63	Bad record number
67	Too many files
68	Device unavailable
70	Permission denied
71	Disk not ready
74	Can't rename with different drive
75	Path/File access error
76	Path not found
91	Object variable not set
92	For loop not initialized
93	Invalid pattern string
94	Invalid use of Null
423	Property or method not found
424	Object required

Error code	Error message
430	Class doesn't support OLE automation
438	Object doesn't support this property or method
440	OLE automation error
445	Object doesn't support this action
446	Object doesn't support named arguments
447	Object doesn't support current locale setting
448	Named argument not found
449	Argument not optional
450	Wrong number of arguments
451	Object not a collection
452	Invalid ordinal
453	Function not defined in specified DLL
454	Code resource not found
455	Code resource lock error

Table A.2 Excel object-defined trappable errors

Error code	Error message
1000	*Classname* does not have *propertyname* property
1001	*Classname* does not have *methodname* method
1002	Missing required argument *argumentname*
1003	Invalid number of arguments
1004	*Methodname* method of *classname* class failed
1005	Unable to set the *propertyname* property of the *classname* class
1006	Unable to get the *propertyname* property of the *classname* class

Appendix B

Table of Key Codes

The SendKeys and OnKey methods use codes to identify the special keys on the keyboard. These codes are listed in Table B.1. Alphanumeric keys are identified by their normal character, for example, "a".

The Chr and Asc functions use numeric codes for characters. Table B.2 lists the numeric codes for characters in the ANSI character set.

Table B.1 Special key codes

Key name	Key code
BACKSPACE	"{BACKSPACE}" or "{BS}"
BREAK	"{BREAK}"
CAPS LOCK	"{CAPSLOCK}"
CLEAR	"{CLEAR}"
DELETE or DEL	"{DELETE}" or "{DEL}"
DOWN arrow	"{DOWN}"
END	"{END}"
ENTER (numeric keypad)	"{ENTER}"
ENTER	"~"
ESC	"{ESCAPE} or {ESC}"
HELP	"{HELP}"
HOME	"{HOME}"
INS	"{INSERT}"
LEFT arrow	"{LEFT}"

Table B.1 Continued	
Key name	**Key code**
NUM LOCK	"{NUMLOCK}"
PAGE DOWN	"{PGDN}"
PAGE UP	"{PGUP}"
RETURN	"{RETURN}"
RIGHT arrow	"{RIGHT}"
SCROLL LOCK	"{SCROLLLOCK}"
TAB	"{TAB}"
UP arrow	"{UP}"
F1	"{F1}"
F2	"{F2}"
F3	"{F3}"
F4	"{F4}"
F5	"{F5}"
F6	"{F6}"
F7	"{F7}"
F8	"{F8}"
F9	"{F9}"
F10	"{F10}"
F11	"{F11}"
F12	"{F12}"
F13	"{F13}"
F14	"{F14}"
F15	"{F15}"
SHIFT	"+"
CTRL	"^"
ALT or OPTION	"%"
COMMAND	"*"

Table B.2 Character codes

Number	Character
1	Not supported
2	Not supported
3	Not supported
4	Not supported
5	Not supported
6	Not supported
7	Not supported
8	Not supported
9	Tab
10	Line feed
11	Not supported
12	Not supported
13	Carriage return
14	Not supported
15	Not supported
16	Not supported
17	Not supported
18	Not supported
19	Not supported
20	Not supported
21	Not supported
22	Not supported
23	Not supported
24	Not supported
25	Not supported

(continues)

Appendixes

Table B.2 Continued

Number	Character
26	Not supported
27	Not supported
28	Not supported
29	Not supported
30	
31	
32	Space
33	!
34	"
35	#
36	$
37	%
38	&
39	'
40	(
41	)
42	*
43	+
44	,
45	—
46	.
47	/
48	0
49	1
50	2
51	3

Number	Character
52	4
53	5
54	6
55	7
56	8
57	9
58	:
59	;
60	<
61	=
62	>
63	?
64	@
65	A
66	B
67	C
68	D
69	E
70	F
71	G
72	H
73	I
74	J
75	K
76	L
77	M

(continues)

Appendixes

Table B.2 Continued

Number	Character
78	N
79	O
80	P
81	Q
82	R
83	S
84	T
85	U
86	V
87	W
88	X
89	Y
90	Z
91	[
92	\
93	]
94	^
95	_
96	'
97	a
98	b
99	c
100	d
101	e
102	f
103	g

Number	Character
104	h
105	i
106	j
107	k
108	l
109	m
110	n
111	o
112	p
113	q
114	r
115	s
116	t
117	u
118	v
119	w
120	x
121	y
122	z
123	{
124		
125	}
126	~
127	Not supported
128	Not supported
129	Not supported

(continues)

Appendixes

Table B.2 Continued

Number	Character
130	,
131	ƒ
132	"
133	…
134	†
135	‡
136	^
137	‰
138	Š
139	<
140	Œ
141	
142	
143	
144	
145	'
146	'
147	"
148	"
149	•
150	–
151	—
152	~
153	™
154	š
155	>

Number	Character
156	œ
157	Not supported
158	Not supported
159	Ÿ
160	
161	¡
162	¢
163	£
164	¤
165	¥
166	¦
167	§
168	¨
169	©
170	ª
171	«
172	¬
173	
174	®
175	¯
176	°
177	±
178	²
179	³
180	´
181	µ

(continues)

Table B.2 Continued

Number	Character
182	¶
183	·
184	,
185	¹
186	°
187	≫
188	¼
189	½
190	¾
191	¿
192	À
193	Á
194	Â
195	Ã
196	Ä
197	Å
198	Æ
199	Ç
200	È
201	É
202	Ê
203	Ë
204	Ì
205	Í
206	Î
207	Ï

Number	Character
208	Đ
209	Ñ
210	Ò
211	Ó
212	Ô
213	Õ
214	Ö
215	×
216	Ø
217	Ù
218	Ú
219	Û
220	Ü
221	Ý
222	Þ
223	ß
224	à
225	á
226	â
227	ã
228	ä
229	å
230	æ
231	ç
232	è
233	é

(continues)

Table B.2 Continued	
Number	**Character**
234	ê
235	ë
236	ì
237	í
238	î
239	ï
240	ð
241	ñ
242	ò
243	ó
244	ô
245	õ
246	ö
247	÷
248	Ø
249	ù
250	ú
251	û
252	ü
253	ý
254	þ
255	ÿ

Appendix C

Table of Intrinsic Constants

Visual Basic in Excel defines almost 800 different constants. These constants are "built in" and used throughout the documentation.

When debugging, it is often important to determine what constant is associated with a return value. For example, if a property returns –4105, it is hard to know that means xlAutomatic unless you look up the value somewhere.

When programming Excel from Visual Basic, version 3.0, it is essential to know the values associated with constants, because Visual Basic 3.0 does not have access to Excel's built-in constants.

Tables C.1 to C.20 group constants by category to make it easier to find possible return values when programming specific tasks.

Table C.1 General constants

Category	Constant	Value
Common values	xlNormal	–4143
	xlAutomatic	–4105
	xlAll	–4104
Boolean values	xlOff	–4146
	xlOn	1
	xlYes	1
	xlMixed	2
	xlNo	2

(continues)

Table C.1 Continued

Category	Constant	Value
Horizontal and vertical alignment	xlTop	−4160
	xlRight	−4152
	xlLeft	−4131
	xlJustify	−4130
	xlDistributed	−4117
	xlCenter	−4108
	xlBottom	−4107
	xlGeneral	1
	xlFill	5
	xlCenterAcrossSelection	7

Table C.2 Application control

Category	Constant	Value
Activating applications	xlMicrosoftWord	1
	xlMicrosoftPowerPoint	2
	xlMicrosoftMail	3
	xlMicrosoftAccess	4
	xlMicrosoftFoxPro	5
	xlMicrosoftProject	6
	xlMicrosoftSchedulePlus	7
Data entry mode	xlOff	−4146
	xlOn	1
	xlStrict	2
Excel built-in dialog boxes	xlDialogOpen	1
	xlDialogOpenLinks	2
	xlDialogSaveAs	5
	xlDialogFileDelete	6
	xlDialogPageSetup	7
	xlDialogPrint	8
	xlDialogPrinterSetup	9
	xlDialogArrangeAll	12
	xlDialogWindowSize	13
	xlDialogWindowMove	14
	xlDialogRun	17
	xlDialogSetPrintTitles	23
	xlDialogFont	26
	xlDialogDisplay	27
	xlDialogProtectDocument	28
	xlDialogCalculation	32
	xlDialogExtract	35
	xlDialogDataDelete	36
	xlDialogSort	39
	xlDialogDataSeries	40
	xlDialogTable	41
	xlDialogFormatNumber	42
	xlDialogAlignment	43
	xlDialogStyle	44
	xlDialogBorder	45

Category	Constant	Value
Excel built-in dialog boxes	xlDialogCellProtection	46
	xlDialogColumnWidth	47
	xlDialogClear	52
	xlDialogPasteSpecial	53
	xlDialogEditDelete	54
	xlDialogInsert	55
	xlDialogDefineName	61
	xlDialogCreateNames	62
	xlDialogFormulaGoto	63
	xlDialogFormulaFind	64
	xlDialogGalleryArea	67
	xlDialogGalleryBar	68
	xlDialogGalleryColumn	69
	xlDialogGalleryLine	70
	xlDialogGalleryPie	71
	xlDialogGalleryScatter	72
	xlDialogCombination	73
	xlDialogGridlines	76
	xlDialogAxes	78
	xlDialogAttachText	80
	xlDialogPatterns	84
	xlDialogMainChart	85
	xlDialogOverlay	86
	xlDialogScale	87
	xlDialogFormatLegend	88
	xlDialogFormatText	89
	xlDialogParse	91
	xlDialogUnhide	94
	xlDialogWorkspace	95
	xlDialogActivate	103
	xlDialogCopyPicture	108
	xlDialogDeleteName	110
	xlDialogDeleteFormat	111
	xlDialogNew	119
	xlDialogRowHeight	127
	xlDialogFormatMove	128
	xlDialogFormatSize	129
	xlDialogFormulaReplace	130
	xlDialogSelectSpecial	132
	xlDialogApplyNames	133
	xlDialogReplaceFont	134
	xlDialogSplit	137
	xlDialogOutline	142
	xlDialogSaveWorkbook	145
	xlDialogCopyChart	147
	xlDialogFormatFont	150
	xlDialogNote	154
	xlDialogSetUpdateStatus	159
	xlDialogColorPalette	161
	xlDialogChangeLink	166
	xlDialogAppMove	170
	xlDialogAppSize	171
	xlDialogMainChartType	185
	xlDialogOverlayChartType	186
	xlDialogOpenMail	188
	xlDialogSendMail	189
	xlDialogStandardFont	190

Appendixes

(continues)

Table C.2 Continued

Category	Constant	Value
Excel built-in dialog boxes	xlDialogConsolidate	191
	xlDialogSortSpecial	192
	xlDialogGallery3dArea	193
	xlDialogGallery3dColumn	194
	xlDialogGallery3dLine	195
	xlDialogGallery3dPie	196
	xlDialogView3d	197
	xlDialogGoalSeek	198
	xlDialogWorkgroup	199
	xlDialogFillGroup	200
	xlDialogUpdateLink	201
	xlDialogPromote	202
	xlDialogDemote	203
	xlDialogShowDetail	204
	xlDialogObjectProperties	207
	xlDialogSaveNewObject	208
	xlDialogApplyStyle	212
	xlDialogAssignToObject	213
	xlDialogObjectProtection	214
	xlDialogCreatePublisher	217
	xlDialogSubscribeTo	218
	xlDialogAttributes	219
	xlDialogShowToolbar	220
	xlDialogPrintPreview	222
	xlDialogEditColor	223
	xlDialogFormatMain	225
	xlDialogFormatOverlay	226
	xlDialogEditSeries	228
	xlDialogDefineStyle	229
	xlDialogGalleryRadar	249
	xlDialogEditionOptions	251
	xlDialogZoom	256
	xlDialogInsertObject	259
	xlDialogSize	261
	xlDialogMove	262
	xlDialogFormatAuto	269
	xlDialogGallery3dBar	272
	xlDialogGallery3dSurface	273
	xlDialogCustomizeToolbar	276
	xlDialogWorkbookAdd	281
	xlDialogWorkbookMove	282
	xlDialogWorkbookCopy	283
	xlDialogWorkbookOptions	284
	xlDialogSaveWorkspace	285
	xlDialogChartWizard	288
	xlDialogAssignToTool	293
	xlDialogPlacement	300
	xlDialogFillWorkgroup	301
	xlDialogWorkbookNew	302
	xlDialogScenarioCells	305
	xlDialogScenarioAdd	307
	xlDialogScenarioEdit	308
	xlDialogScenarioSummary	311
	xlDialogPivotTableWizard	312
	xlDialogPivotFieldProperties	313

Category	Constant	Value
Excel built-in dialog boxes	xlDialogOptionsCalculation	318
	xlDialogOptionsEdit	319
	xlDialogOptionsView	320
	xlDialogAddinManager	321
	xlDialogMenuEditor	322
	xlDialogAttachToolbars	323
	xlDialogOptionsChart	325
	xlDialogVbaInsertFile	328
	xlDialogVbaProcedureDefinition	330
	xlDialogRoutingSlip	336
	xlDialogMailLogon	339
	xlDialogInsertPicture	342
	xlDialogGalleryDoughnut	344
	xlDialogChartTrend	350
	xlDialogWorkbookInsert	354
	xlDialogOptionsTransition	355
	xlDialogOptionsGeneral	356
	xlDialogFilterAdvanced	370
	xlDialogMailNextLetter	378
	xlDialogDataLabel	379
	xlDialogInsertTitle	380
	xlDialogFontProperties	381
	xlDialogMacroOptions	382
	xlDialogWorkbookUnhide	384
	xlDialogWorkbookName	386
	xlDialogGalleryCustom	388
	xlDialogAddChartAutoformat	390
	xlDialogChartAddData	392
	xlDialogTabOrder	394
	xlDialogSubtotalCreate	398
	xlDialogWorkbookTabSplit	415
	xlDialogWorkbookProtect	417
	xlDialogScrollbarProperties	420
	xlDialogPivotShowPages	421
	xlDialogTextToColumns	422
	xlDialogFormatCharttype	423
	xlDialogPivotFieldGroup	433
	xlDialogPivotFieldUngroup	434
	xlDialogCheckboxProperties	435
	xlDialogLabelProperties	436
	xlDialogListboxProperties	437
	xlDialogEditboxProperties	438
	xlDialogOpenText	441
	xlDialogPushbuttonProperties	445
	xlDialogFunctionWizard	450
	xlDialogSetControlValue	455
	xlDialogSaveCopyAs	456
	xlDialogOptionsListsAdd	458
	xlDialogSeriesAxes	460
	xlDialogSeriesX	461
	xlDialogSeriesY	462
	xlDialogErrorbarX	463
	xlDialogErrorbarY	464
	xlDialogFormatChart	465
	xlDialogSeriesOrder	466

(continues)

Table C.2 Continued		
Category	**Constant**	**Value**
Excel built-in dialog boxes	xlDialogStandardWidth	472
	xlDialogScenarioMerge	473
	xlDialogSummaryInfo	474
	xlDialogFindFile	475
	xlDialogActiveCellFont	476
	xlDialogVbaMakeAddin	478
International settings	xlCountryCode	1
	xlCountrySetting	2
	xlDecimalSeparator	3
	xlThousandsSeparator	4
	xlListSeparator	5
	xlUpperCaseRowLetter	6
	xlUpperCaseColumnLetter	7
	xlLowerCaseRowLetter	8
	xlLowerCaseColumnLetter	9
	xlLeftBracket	10
	xlRightBracket	11
	xlLeftBrace	12
	xlRightBrace	13
	xlColumnSeparator	14
	xlRowSeparator	15
	xlAlternateArraySeparator	16
	xlDateSeparator	17
	xlTimeSeparator	18
	xlYearCode	19
	xlMonthCode	20
	xlDayCode	21
	xlHourCode	22
	xlMinuteCode	23
	xlSecondCode	24
	xlCurrencyCode	25
	xlGeneralFormatName	26
	xlCurrencyDigits	27
	xlCurrencyNegative	28
	xlNoncurrencyDigits	29
	xlMonthNameChars	30
	xlWeekdayNameChars	31
	xlDateOrder	32
	xl24HourClock	33
	xlNonEnglishFunctions	34
	xlMetric	35
	xlCurrencySpaceBefore	36
	xlCurrencyBefore	37
	xlCurrencyMinusSign	38
	xlCurrencyTrailingZeros	39
	xlCurrencyLeadingZeros	40
	xlMonthLeadingZero	41
	xlDayLeadingZero	42
	xl4DigitYears	43
	xlMDY	44
	xlTimeLeadingZero	45

Category	Constant	Value
Running auto macros	xlAutoOpen	1
	xlAutoClose	2
	xlAutoActivate	3
	xlAutoDeactivate	4
Transition	xlExcelMenus	1
	xlLotusHelp	2

Table C.3 Charting

Category	Constant	Value
Chart types	xlXYScatter	−4169
	xlRadar	−4151
	xlDoughnut	−4120
	xlCombination	−4111
	xl3DSurface	−4103
	xl3DPie	−4102
	xl3DLine	−4101
	xl3DColumn	−4100
	xl3DBar	−4099
	xl3DArea	−4098
	xlArea	1
	xlBar	2
	xlColumn	3
	xlLine	4
	xlPie	5
Axes	xlPrimary	1
	xlCategory	1
	xlSecondary	2
	xlValue	2
	xlSeries	3
Axis crossing point	xlAutomatic	−4105
	xlMinimum	2
	xlMaximum	2
Axis label position	xlNone	−4142
	xlLow	−4134
	xlHigh	−4127
	xlNextToAxis	4
Axis tick mark location	xlNone	−4142
	xlInside	2
	xlOutside	3
	xlCross	4
Blank cell interpretation method	xlNotPlotted	1
	xlZero	2
	xlInterpolated	3

(continues)

Appendixes

Table C.3 Continued		
Category	**Constant**	**Value**
Data label type	xlNone	−4142
	xlShowValue	2
	xlShowPercent	3
	xlShowLabel	4
	xlShowLabelAndPercent	5
Data marker and legend key	xlX	−4168
	xlPicture	−4147
	xlNone	−4142
	xlDot	−4118
	xlDash	−4115
	xlAutomatic	−4105
	xlSquare	1
	xlDiamond	2
	xlTriangle	3
	xlStar	5
	xlCircle	8
	xlPlus	9
Data series range orientation	xlRows	1
	xlColumns	2
Error bar direction	xlX	−4168
	xlY	1
Error bar ends	xlCap	1
	xlNoCap	2
Error bar include types	xlNone	−4142
	xlBoth	1
	xlPlusValues	2
	xlMinusValues	3
Error bar type	xlStDev	−4155
	xlCustom	−4114
	xlFixedValue	1
	xlPercent	2
	xlStError	4
Legend placement	xlTop	−4160
	xlRight	−4152
	xlLeft	−4131
	xlBottom	−4107
	xlCorner	2
Picture type	xlStretch	1
	xlStack	2
	xlScale	3
Trendline type	xlLogarithmic	−4133
	xlLinear	−4132
	xlGrowth	2
	xlPolynomial	3

Category	Constant	Value
Treadline Type	xlPower	4
	xlExponential	5
	xlMovingAvg	6
	xlLinearTrend	9
	xlGrowthTrend	10
Use default style	xlBuiltIn	0

Table C.4 Cut and paste

Category	Constant	Value
Clipboard formats	xlClipboardFormatText	0
	xlClipboardFormatVALU	1
	xlClipboardFormatPICT	2
	xlClipboardFormatPrintPICT	3
	xlClipboardFormatDIF	4
	xlClipboardFormatCSV	5
	xlClipboardFormatSYLK	6
	xlClipboardFormatRTF	7
	xlClipboardFormatBIFF	8
	xlClipboardFormatBitmap	9
	xlClipboardFormatWK1	10
	xlClipboardFormatLink	11
	xlClipboardFormatDspText	12
	xlClipboardFormatCGM	13
	xlClipboardFormatNative	14
	xlClipboardFormatBinary	15
	xlClipboardFormatTable	16
	xlClipboardFormatOwnerLink	17
	xlClipboardFormatBIFF2	18
	xlClipboardFormatObjectLink	19
	xlClipboardFormatBIFF3	20
	xlClipboardFormatEmbeddedObject	21
	xlClipboardFormatEmbedSource	22
	xlClipboardFormatLinkSource	23
	xlClipboardFormatMovie	24
	xlClipboardFormatToolFace	25
	xlClipboardFormatToolFacePICT	26
	xlClipboardFormatStandardScale	27
	xlClipboardFormatStandardFont	28
	xlClipboardFormatScreenPICT	29
	xlClipboardFormatBIFF4	30
	xlClipboardFormatObjectDesc	31
	xlClipboardFormatLinkSourceDesc	32
Copy picture file type	xlPicture	−4147
	xlBitmap	2
Copy picture resolution	xlScreen	1
	xlPrinter	2

Appendixes

(continues)

Table C.4 Continued

Category	Constant	Value
Cut/copy mode	xlCopy	1
	xlCut	2
Paste special	xlFormulas	−4123
	xlFormats	−4122
	xlAll	−4104
	xlContents	2
	xlAdd	2
	xlSubtract	3
	xlMultiply	4
	xlDivide	5
	xlNone	4142

Table C.5 Drawing

Category	Constant	Value
Display	xlAll	−4104
	xlPlaceholders	2
	xlHide	3
Drawing object placement	xlMoveAndSize	1
	xlMove	2
	xlFreeFloating	3
Graphics file converter	xlBMP	1
	xlPICT	1
	xlWMF	2
	xlWPG	3
	xlDRW	4
	xlDXF	5
	xlHGL	6
	xlCGM	7
	xlEPS	8
	xlTIF	9
	xlPCX	10
	xlPIC	11
	xlPLT	12
	xlPCT	13
Line arrow head length	xlMedium	−4138
	xlShort	1
	xlLong	3
Line arrow head style	xlNone	−4142
	xlOpen	2
	xlClosed	3
	xlDoubleOpen	4
	xlDoubleClosed	5

Category	Constant	Value
Line arrow head width	xlMedium	−4138
	xlNarrow	1
	xlWide	3

Table C.6 Files

Category	Constant	Value
File access	xlReadWrite	2
	xlReadOnly	3
File type	xlText	−4158
	xlNormal	−4143
	xlSYLK	2
	xlWKS	4
	xlWK1	5
	xlCSV	6
	xlDBF2	7
	xlDBF3	8
	xlDIF	9
	xlDBF4	11
	xlWJ2WD1	14
	xlWK3	15
	xlExcel2	16
	xlTemplate	17
	xlAddIn	18
	xlTextMac	19
	xlTextWindows	20
	xlTextMSDOS	21
	xlCSVMac	22
	xlCSVWindows	23
	xlCSVMSDOS	24
	xlIntlMacro	25
	xlIntlAddIn	26
	xlExcel2FarEast	27
	xlWorks2FarEast	28
	xlExcel3	29
	xlWK1FMT	30
	xlWK1ALL	31
	xlWK3FM3	32
	xlExcel4	33
	xlWQ1	34
	xlExcel4Workbook	35
	xlTextPrinter	36
Operating system	xlMacintosh	1
	xlWindows	2
	xlMSDOS	3

(continues)

Appendixes

Table C.6 Continued

Category	Constant	Value
Text delimiters	xlDelimited	1
	xlDoubleQuote	1
	xlFixedWidth	2
	xlSingleQuote	2

Table C.7 Form controls

Category	Constant	Value
Edit box input type	xlText	−4158
	xlNumber	−4145
	xlInteger	2
	xlReference	4
	xlFormula	5
List box multi-select	xlSimple	−4154
	xlNone	−4142
	xlExtended	2

Table C.8 Formatting

Category	Constant	Value
AutoFormat types	xlDefaultAutoFormat	−1
	xlClassic1	1
	xlClassic2	2
	xlClassic3	3
	xlAccounting1	4
	xlAccounting2	5
	xlAccounting3	6
	xlColor1	7
	xlColor2	8
	xlColor3	9
	xlList1	10
	xlList2	11
	xlList3	12
	xl3DEffects1	13
	xl3DEffects2	14
	xlLocalFormat1	15
	xlLocalFormat2	16
	xlAccounting4	17

Category	Constant	Value
Border line style	xlNone	−4142
	xlGray75	−4126
	xlGray50	−4125
	xlGray25	−4124
	xlDouble	−4119
	xlDot	−4118
	xlDash	−4115
	xlAutomatic	−4105
	xlContinuous	1
	xlDashDot	4
	xlDashDotDot	5
Border style	xlMedium	−4138
	xlHairline	1
	xlThin	2
	xlThick	4
Cell border	xlTop	−4160
	xlRight	−4152
	xlLeft	−4131
	xlBottom	−4107
Font background	xlNone	−4142
	xlAutomatic	−4105
	xlTransparent	2
	xlOpaque	3
Font underline	xlNone	−4142
	xlDouble	−4119
	xlSingle	2
	xlSingleAccounting	4
	xlDoubleAccounting	5
Interior pattern	xlNone	−4142
	xlGray75	−4126
	xlGray50	−4125
	xlGray25	−4124
	xlAutomatic	−4105
	xlSolid	1
	xlSemiGray75	10
	xlLightHorizontal	11
	xlLightVertical	12
	xlLightDown	13
	xlLightUp	14
	xlGrid	15
	xlGray16	17
	xlGray8	18
Vertical orientation	xlUpward	−4171
	xlDownward	−4170
Visibility	xlVeryHidden	2

Table C.9 Links

Category	Constant	Value
Edition data type	xlBIFF	2
	xlRTF	4
	xlVALU	8
Edition options	xlCancel	1
	xlUpdateSubscriber	2
	xlOpenSource	3
	xlSelect	3
	xlAutomaticUpdate	4
	xlManualUpdate	5
	xlChangeAttributes	6
Link type	xlOLELink	0
	xlExcelLinks	1
	xlOLEEmbed	1
	xlPublisher	1
	xlOLELinks	2
	xlSubscriber	2
	xlPublishers	5
	xlSubscribers	6
Update state	xlUpdateState	1
	xlEditionDate	2
	xlSendPublisher	2

Table C.10 Lists and fills

Category	Constant	Value
AutoFill style	xlFillDefault	0
	xlFillCopy	1
	xlFillSeries	2
	xlFillFormats	3
	xlFillValues	4
	xlFillDays	5
	xlFillWeekdays	6
	xlFillMonths	7
	xlFillYears	8
AutoFill type	xlLinear	−4132
	xlDay	1
	xlWeekday	2
	xlGrowth	2
	xlMonth	3
	xlChronological	3
	xlYear	4
	xlAutoFill	4
AutoFilter criteria	xlAnd	1
	xlOr	2
Filter style	xlFilterInPlace	1
	xlFilterCopy	2

Table C.11 Mail

Category	Constant	Value
Installed system	xlNoMailSystem	0
	xlMAPI	1
	xlPowerTalk	2
Message priority	xlNormal	−4143
	xlLow	−4134
	xlHigh	−4127
Routing delivery order	xlOneAfterAnother	1
	xlAllAtOnce	2
Routing status	xlNotYetRouted	0
	xlRoutingInProgress	1
	xlRoutingComplete	2

Table C.12 Menus and toolbars

Category	Constant	Value
Menu bars	xlWorksheet	−4167
	xlModule	−4141
	xlInfo	−4129
	xlChart	−4109
	xlWorksheet4	1
	xlChart4	2
	xlNoDocuments	3
	xlWorksheetShort	5
	xlChartShort	6
Shortcut menus	xlRowHeader	−4153
	xlModule	−4141
	xlDialogSheet	−4116
	xlColumnHeader	−4110
	xlToolbar	1
	xlWorkbook	1
	xlToolbarButton	2
	xlWorksheetCell	3
	xlWorkbookTab	6
	xlMacrosheetCell	7
	xlTitleBar	8
	xlDesktop	9
	xlWatchPane	11
	xlImmediatePane	12
	xlDebugCodePane	13
	xlDrawingObject	14
	xlButton	15
	xlTextBox	16
	xlChartSeries	17
	xlChartTitles	18
	xlPlotArea	19

(continues)

Appendixes

Table C.12 Continued

Category	Constant	Value
Shortcut menus	xlEntireChart	20
	xlAxis	21
	xlGridline	22
	xlFloor	23
	xlLegend	24
Toolbar position	xlTop	– 4160
	xlRight	– 4152
	xlLeft	– 4131
	xlBottom	– 4107
	xlFloating	5

Table C.13 Pivot tables

Category	Constant	Value
Field calculation	xlRunningTotal	5
	xlDifferenceFrom	2
	xlIndex	9
	xlNormal	–4143
	xlPercentDifferenceFrom	4
	xlPercentOfTotal	8
	xlPercentOfRow	6
	xlPercentOfColumn	7
	xlPercentOf	3
Field data type	xlDate	2
	xlNumber	–4145
	xlText	–4158
Field orientation	xlHidden	0
	xlRowField	1
	xlColumnField	2
	xlPageField	3
	xlDataField	4
Location in table	xlRowHeader	–4153
	xlColumnHeader	–4110
	xlPageHeader	2
	xlDataHeader	3
	xlRowItem	4
	xlColumnItem	5
	xlPageItem	6
	xlDataItem	7
	xlTableBody	8
Position	xlTop	–4160
	xlRight	–4152
	xlLeft	–4131
	xlBottom	–4107
	xlFloating	5

Category	Constant	Value
Sorting	xlSortValues	1
	xlSortLabels	2
Source	xlDatabase	1
	xlExternal	2
	xlConsolidation	3
	xlPivotTable	−4148

Table C.14 Printing

Category	Constant	Value
Orientation	xlPortrait	1
	xlLandscape	2
Page numbering	xlDownThenOver	1
	xlOverThenDown	2
Paper size	xlPaperLetter	1
	xlPaperLetterSmall	2
	xlPaperTabloid	3
	xlPaperLedger	4
	xlPaperLegal	5
	xlPaperStatement	6
	xlPaperExecutive	7
	xlPaperA3	8
	xlPaperA4	9
	xlPaperA4Small	10
	xlPaperA5	11
	xlPaperB4	12
	xlPaperB5	13
	xlPaperFolio	14
	xlPaperQuarto	15
	xlPaper10x14	16
	xlPaper11x17	17
	xlPaperNote	18
	xlPaperEnvelope9	19
	xlPaperEnvelope10	20
	xlPaperEnvelope11	21
	xlPaperEnvelope12	22
	xlPaperEnvelope14	23
	xlPaperCsheet	24
	xlPaperDsheet	25
	xlPaperEsheet	26
	xlPaperEnvelopeDL	27
	xlPaperEnvelopeC5	28
	xlPaperEnvelopeC3	29
	xlPaperEnvelopeC4	30
	xlPaperEnvelopeC6	31
	xlPaperEnvelopeC65	32
	xlPaperEnvelopeB4	33
	xlPaperEnvelopeB5	34
	xlPaperEnvelopeB6	35

Appendixes

(continues)

Table C.14 Continued

Category	Constant	Value
Paper size	xlPaperEnvelopeItaly	36
	xlPaperEnvelopeMonarch	37
	xlPaperEnvelopePersonal	38
	xlPaperFanfoldUS	39
	xlPaperFanfoldStdGerman	40
	xlPaperFanfoldLegalGerman	41
	xlPaperUser	256
Scaling	xlScreenSize	1
	xlFitToPage	2
	xlFullPage	3

Table C.15 Ranges

Category	Constant	Value
Calculation method	xlManual	−4135
	xlAutomatic	−4105
	xlSemiautomatic	2
Cell reference error codes	xlErrNull	2000
	xlErrDiv0	2007
	xlErrValue	2015
	xlErrRef	2023
	xlErrName	2029
	xlErrNum	2036
	xlErrNA	2042
Cell references	xlR1C1	−4150
	xlA1	1
	xlAbsolute	1
	xlAbsRowRelColumn	2
	xlRelRowAbsColumn	3
	xlRelative	4
Name application order	xlRowThenColumn	1
	xlColumnThenRow	2
Precedent type	xlNone	−4142
	xlAll	−4104
	xlDirect	1
Shift cells	xlUp	−4162
	xlToRight	−4161
	xlToLeft	−4159
	xlDown	−4121

Category	Constant	Value
Special cell types	xlNotes	−4144
	xlNumbers	1
	xlConstants	2
	xlTextValues	2
	xlBlanks	4
	xlLogical	4
	xlLastCell	11
	xlVisible	12
	xlErrors	16

Table C.16 Searching and sorting

Category	Constant	Value
Searching	xlValues	−4163
	xlNotes	−4144
	xlFormulas	−4123
	xlWhole	1
	xlByRows	1
	xlNext	1
	xlPart	2
	xlByColumns	2
	xlPrevious	2
Sort direction	xlTopToBottom	1
	xlLeftToRight	2
Sort method (Far East)	xlSyllabary	1
	xlCodePage	2
Sort order	xlAscending	1
	xlDescending	2

Table C.17 Sheets

Category	Constant	Value
Worksheet type	xlExcel4MacroSheet	3
	xlExcel4IntlMacroSheet	4

Appendixes

Table C.18 Subtotals and summaries

Category	Constant	Value
Scenario summary report types	xlPivotTable	−4148
	xlStandardSummary	1
Subtotal position	xlAbove	0
	xlBelow	1
Subtotal/consolidation function	xlVarP	−4165
	xlVar	−4164
	xlSum	−4157
	xlStDevP	−4156
	xlStDev	−4155
	xlProduct	−4149
	xlMin	−4139
	xlMax	−4136
	xlCountNums	−4113
	xlCount	−4112
	xlAverage	−4106

Table C.19 Visual Basic language

Category	Constant	Value
Break mode	xlDisabled	0
	xlInterrupt	1
	xlErrorHandler	2
Data types	vbEmpty	0
	vbNull	1
	vbInteger	2
	vbLong	3
	vbSingle	4
	vbDouble	5
	vbCurrency	6
	vbDate	7
	vbString	8
	vbObject	9
	vbError	10
	vbBoolean	11
	vbVariant	12
	vbDataObject	13
	vbArray	8192
Far East string comparison	vbNormal	0
	vbUpperCase	1
	vbLowerCase	2
	vbProperCase	3
	vbWide	4
	vbNarrow	8
	vbKatakana	16
	vbHiragana	32

Category	Constant	Value
File attributes	vbReadOnly	1
	vbHidden	2
	vbSystem	4
	vbVolume	8
	vbDirectory	16
	vbArchive	32
Message box constants	vbDefaultButton1	0
	vbOKOnly	0
	vbApplicationModal	0
	vbOK	1
	vbOKCancel	1
	vbCancel	2
	vbAbortRetryIgnore	2
	vbYesNoCancel	3
	vbAbort	3
	vbRetry	4
	vbYesNo	4
	vbIgnore	5
	vbRetryCancel	5
	vbYes	6
	vbNo	7
	vbCritical	16
	vbQuestion	32
	vbExclamation	48
	vbInformation	64
	vbDefaultButton2	256
	vbDefaultButton3	512
	vbSystemModal	4096
Excel 4 macro types	xlNone	−4142
	xlFunction	1
	xlCommand	2

Table C.20 Windows

Category	Constant	Value
Display	xlVertical	−4166
	xlHorizontal	−4128
	xlTiled	1
	xlIcons	1
	xlCascade	7
Scroll tabs	xlFirst	0
	xlLast	1
	xlMinimized	−4140
	xlMaximized	−4137

(continues)

Table C.20 Continued

Category	Constant	Value
Window type	xlInfo	−4129
	xlWorkbook	1
	xlClipboard	3
	xlChartInPlace	4
	xlChartAsWindow	5

Appendix D

Style Guidelines for Professional-Quality Code

It is a good idea to have guidelines for naming variables, procedures, constants, and other user-created items in the code you write. Naming these items in a consistent way helps you distinguish between Visual Basic keywords and items that are defined somewhere in code. This is especially useful in large programs or where the code is used, written, or maintained by more than one person.

At first, it may seem like a lot of extra work to follow a set of guidelines. It quickly becomes second nature, however. Style guidelines not only make it easier for others to read your code, they help you remember what you wrote. They also give your work a professional-looking polish. Other programmers will be jealous when they see how consistently you can produce bug-free software just by doing some simple housekeeping.

The guidelines presented here are a good starting point and are used throughout this book in sample code. You may choose to develop your own code or follow someone else's. There are only a few rules that are absolute:

- Use prefixes to identify scope and data type.

- Use descriptive names where possible.

- Indent related blocks of code.

- Precede blocks of code with descriptive comments.

- Note all assumptions in comments at the beginning of procedures.

- Be certain to include comments explaining all complex lines of code.

Identifying Scope

Scope is the range within a code where a variable, constant, or procedure can be used. In Visual Basic there are three levels of scope, as described in the table below.

Scope	Description	Prefix
Local	The variable or constant is valid only within the procedure where it is defined.	*none*
Module	The variable or constant is valid only within the module where it is defined.	m
Global	The variable or constant is valid within any module in a project.	g

Local Scope

Any variable or constant defined in a procedure has a local scope by default. For example:

```
Sub LocalScope()
    ' Define a local variable of data type integer.
    Dim iCount As Integer
    For iCount = 0 to 200
        ' Do something...
    Next iCount
End Sub
```

If another procedure uses the variable iCount, it will be a new variable and won't reflect the value from the procedure LocalScope. Local variables can't be changed outside the procedure.

Constants behave the same way, except that their values never change (hence their name). For example:

```
Sub LocalScope()
    ' Local constants for RGB colors.
    Const RED = &HFF, GREEN = &HFF00, BLUE = &HFF0000
    ' Following code would cause an error, so it's commented out.
    ' RED = 32
End Sub
```

Again, other procedures can't see the value of RED defined in the procedure LocalScope.

> **Note**
>
> The names of constants are usually typed in uppercase characters. The exception to this is a product-defined constant which begins with a product prefix; for example, xlMaximize.

When using local variables, the Dim statement is optional. Visual Basic automatically creates a variable whenever you use a word it does not recognize. For example:

```
Sub AutomaticVariable()
    ' Create a local variable that contains a string.
    vAutoString = "This variable was not explicitly declared"
    ' Create a local variable that contains a number.
    vAutoNumber = 10
End Sub
```

When Visual Basic creates a variable automatically, it uses the default data type. Visual Basic uses the Variant data type as the default, unless you change it using the Deftype statement.

> **Caution**
>
> Automatic variables make it hard to catch spelling errors in variable names. It is safer to turn off this feature by using the Option Explicit statement.

Module Scope

Any variable or constant defined outside a procedure has module scope by default. For example:

```
' Define a module-level variable of data type Boolean (true/false).
Dim mbFlag As Boolean

' Run this procedure to see how module-level variables work.
Sub ModuleVariable()
    ' Assign a value to the module-level variable.
    mbFlag = True
    ' Call another procedure to display the value of the variable.
    DisplayVariable
    ' Displays False in a message box.
    MsgBox bFlag
End Sub

' This procedure is called by ModuleVariable.
Sub DisplayFlag()
```

```
        ' Displays True in a message box.
        MsgBox mbFlag
        ' Change the value to False.
        mbFlag = False
End Sub
```

The `ModuleVariable` and `DisplayFlag` procedures can see and change the `mbFlag` variable. If you move `DisplayFlag` to another module, however, this no longer works—the value `mbFlag` can only be seen in the module where it is declared.

Constants behave the same way. If they are declared outside a procedure, then they can be seen from every procedure in that module.

Global Scope

Variables and constants defined outside a procedure, using the `Public` keyword, have global scope. For example:

```
' Define a global variable of data type Boolean (true/false).
Public gbFlag As Boolean

' Define a global constant for the RGB color red.
Public Const gRED = &HFF
```

The variable `gbFlag` and the constant `gRED` are available to all procedures, in all modules. Notice that you can't use `Public` inside a procedure; this keeps global and module scope declarations together at the beginning of each module.

Identifying Data Types

Data type indicates the kinds of data that a variable can contain. In Visual Basic there are twelve built-in data types, as described in the following table.

Data type	Description	Prefix
Boolean	True or False.	b
Currency	A monetary value within the range +/–9.22E14. Currency values are accurate to the fourth decimal place.	c
Date/time	A date or time expressed in any number of notations.	dt
Double	A decimal value within the range +/–1.798E308.	d
Error	A Visual Basic or user-defined error.	err

Data type	Description	Prefix
Integer	A whole number between −32,768 and 32,767.	i
Long	A whole number between −2,147,483,648 and 2,147,483,647.	l
Object	A reference to an object within an application.	obj
Single	A decimal number between +/−3.402823E38.	sn
String	Text strings can be as many as 2 billion characters long.	s
User-defined	A data type made up of one or more of the above types as described by a Type statement.	u
Variant	Any of the above types, except user-defined.	v

Besides the built-in data types, Visual Basic in Excel defines many types for objects and collections. Variables often refer to objects in Excel, so it is important to use a set of prefixes for object types. The following table shows the object and collection prefixes for Excel objects.

Object type	Object prefix	Collection prefix
AddIn	add	adds
Application	app	N/A
Arc	arc	arcs
Areas	N/A	areas
Axis	ax	axs
AxisTitle	axt	N/A
Border	brd	brds
Button	but	buts
Characters	N/A	chars
Chart	chrt	chrts

(continues)

Object type	Object prefix	Collection prefix
ChartArea	chrta	N/A
ChartGroup	chrtg	chrtgs
ChartObject	chrtobj	chrtobjs
ChartTitle	chrtt	N/A
CheckBox	chk	chks
Corners	N/A	cors
DataLabel	dtl	dtls
Dialog	dlg	dlgs
DialogFrame	dlgf	N/A
DialogSheet	dlgsht	dlgshts
DownBars	N/A	dbars
Drawing	drw	drws
DrawingObjects	N/A	drwobjs
DropDown	ddwn	ddwns
DropLines	N/A	drplns
EditBox	edt	edts
ErrorBars	N/A	errbars
Floor	flr	N/A
Font	fnt	N/A
Gridlines	N/A	grds
GroupBox	gbox	gboxs
GroupObject	grp	grps
HiLoLines	N/A	hls
Interior	interior	N/A
Label	lbl	lbls
Legend	lgd	N/A
LegendEntry	lgden	lgdens

Object type	Object prefix	Collection prefix
LegendKey	lgdkey	N/A
Line	ln	lns
ListBox	lbox	lboxs
Mailer	mail	N/A
Menu	mnu	mnus
MenuBar	mnubr	mnubrs
MenuItem	mnuit	mnuits
Module	mod	mods
Name	name	names
OLEObject	oobj	oobjs
OptionButton	opt	opts
Outline	outline	N/A
Oval	oval	ovals
PageSetup	pgsetup	N/A
Pane	pane	panes
Picture	pict	picts
PivotField	pvtfld	pvtflds
PivotItem	pvtitm	pvtitms
PivotTable	pvt	pvts
PlotArea	plot	N/A
Point	point	points
Range	rng	N/A
Rectangle	rect	rects
RoutingSlip	rslip	N/A
Scenario	scen	scens
ScrollBar	sbar	sbars
Series	series	seriesc

Appendixes

(continues)

Object type	Object prefix	Collection prefix
SeriesLines	N/A	serieslns
Sheets	N/A	shts
SoundNote	sound	N/A
Spinner	spin	spins
Style	style	styles
TextBox	tbox	tboxs
TickLabels	N/A	tlbls
Toolbar	tbar	tbars
ToolbarButton	tbarb	tbarbs
Trendline	trend	trends
UpBars	N/A	ubars
Walls	N/A	walls
Window	win	wins
Workbook	wb	wbs
Worksheet	wsht	wshts

Though some of these may seem long, prefixes for the most commonly used objects have been kept as short as possible.

Choosing Descriptive Names

The names of variables, constants, and procedures should tell you something about them. This is especially important for procedures and variables that refer to objects or that have module or global scope.

For example, a variable that refers to a button with the caption OK should be named butOK. A procedure that sorts arrays should be named SortArray.

It is convenient to use shorter names for frequently used items. For example, iCount is a convenient name for a counter in a For...Next loop. Many people simply use i or j for counters in For...Next loops.

If a name seems too long, it's better to be less descriptive than to use a series of abbreviations. You can always add comments, where the item is declared, to fully describe the item's use.

Difficulty naming a procedure is sometimes a good tip-off that the code is too general or complex. You might consider breaking a procedure into several smaller ones if you can't come up with a descriptive name. The following table shows suggested names to use and avoid in common situations.

Use	Don't use	Reason
iCount, i, j, Index	vCounter, LoopCounter	Counters used in For...Next and Do...Loop statement blocks should be easy to type and identify. Using Integer variables makes loops execute faster.
SortArray, DisplayResult, AdjustMargins	DoThings, ShowIt, FormatOutputForPrinting	Procedure names should be descriptive and specific. Using "It" or "Thing" is far too general. Try to use verb/noun pairs.
butOK, chrtInventory	Button1, chrtInv, rMyData, rngSourceData	Object variables should be consistently named and should clearly identify what they represent. If an object has a descriptive caption or name, include this in the variable name.

Formatting Code

Use tabs to indicate the relationships between blocks of code. For constructions with a beginning and end, such as loops, indent the contents of the construction once for each level of nesting. For example:

```
' Takes a string and reverses it.
Sub ReverseString(vInput)
    ' Begin body of Sub..End Sub, so indent once.
    If TypeName(vInput) = "String" Then
        ' Begin body of If...Then, so indent again.
        Dim sOutput As String, iCount As Integer
        For iCount = Len(vInput) To 1 Step -1
            ' Begin body of For...Next loop, so indent again.
            sOutput = sOutput & Mid$(vInput, iCount, 1)
        Next iCount
        vInput = sOutput
    End If
End Sub
```

Appendixes

In the example, it's easy to see where loops and conditional statements begin and end. This is critical in long passages of conditional code, such as long Select Case statements or a series of If...Then statements.

Commenting Code

Good comments are the most important step in writing code that can be understood and maintained by others. This is crucial if you want to take occasional vacations from work. You can write comments one procedure at a time, using this general form:

1. Procedure description—This tells what the procedure does, mentions any global- or module-level variables it uses, and describes the arguments and return value (if any). You may also consider including the name of the author and the revision history here.

2. Variable declarations—These describe the key variables used in the procedure.

3. Descriptive comments—These narrate what the code is doing. It isn't necessary to explain what every line of code does in English. Simply indicate the actions that are performed and the decisions that are made in the code.

4. Assumption and Undone flags—These are flags that indicate you haven't finished your work yet. You may want to get a procedure up and running before making it bulletproof; when doing this, try to flag the assumptions you are making (you might type these in all uppercase). This makes it easier to get back to work after you've demonstrated the software to your boss.

The code in the following example shows the implementation of the four principles discussed in the preceding list. The bold numbered lines refer to each principle.

```
' (1) Procedure Description
' Adds a button to the Standard toolbar when this workbook is opened.
' Use this commandline to install button:
'       EXCEL.EXE VISIO.XLS
' Make sure "InsertVisioDrawing" macro is available (see VISIO.XLA).
' Written by: A. Wombat
' Revisions: None.
' The bitmap picture embedded on Sheet 1 determines the picture _
  that appears on the button.
Sub Auto_Open()
```

```
' (2) Variable Declarations
Dim tbutCount As ToolbarButton, tbutVisio As ToolbarButton
Application.ScreenUpdating = False
' (3) Descriptive Comments
' Check if toolbar button already exists
For Each tbutCountIn Toolbars("Standard").ToolbarButtons
        If tbutCount.Name = "Insert Visio drawing" Then Exit Sub
Next tbutCount
' Add a blank toolbar button to the Standard toolbar.
Toolbars("Standard").ToolbarButtons.Add Button:=231
' Create an object variable for the button (it is the last _
  button on the toolbar).
Set tbutVisio = Toolbars("Standard").ToolbarButtons _
(Toolbars("Standard").ToolbarButtons.Count)
' Set the macro the toolbar button will run.
tbutVisio.OnAction = "InsertVisioDrawing"
' Give the button a name to display in the Tool Tip balloon.
tbutVisio.Name = "Insert Visio drawing"
' Copy the bitmap.
Sheets("Sheet1").DrawingObjects _
("Visio Toolbar Button").CopyPicture
' Paste it into the button.
tbutVisio.PasteFace
Application.ScreenUpdating = True
' Close this workbook.
(4) Assumptions and Undones.
' UNDONE: Uncomment this line to cause workbook to _
  automatically close.
' Makes it hard to edit this macro, though!
'ActiveWorkbook.Close
End Sub
```

Requiring Variable Declarations

Visual Basic lets you work in a very free-form way. You can start writing code without ever worrying about reserving space for variables or assigning the correct data types. This is a great way to start learning and it means that you can start doing useful work almost immediately. However, it also means that typos in variable names are very hard to catch.

For example, the following code does not display the message box, because bAnswer is misspelled in the If statement. Visual Basic considers "bAnwser" a new variable and initializes it to an empty value:

```
Sub SpellingError()
    bAnswer = True
    If bAnwser = True Then MsgBox("True") ' Oops! Message box _
    never displays.
End Sub
```

If you add an Option Explicit statement to the beginning of a module, Visual Basic checks to make sure that each variable you use has been declared. This is an effective way to check the spelling of variable names throughout your code.

Here's the same code with Option Explicit:

```
Option Explicit

Sub SpellingError()
    Dim bAnswer As Boolean ' This line is now required.
    bAnswer = True
    If bAnwser = True Then MsgBox("True") ' This line causes an _
    error when run!
End Sub
```

You can still have typographical errors, but Visual Basic alerts you that variables have been referenced without being declared when you try to run the code.

Using Option Explicit is more than good form; it is often required by contracts that request software written in Visual Basic.

Summary

Maintain a consistency in the naming conventions used for variables and subroutines. Use prefixes to identify scope and data types where appropriate along with descriptive names. It's easy to guess that iCount is an integer counter from the prefix, but a single x gives no clue to its intended purpose.

Indent all related blocks of code. This simple practice makes it easy to see at a glance which lines belong together. Always precede blocks of code with comments, including subroutines. Also comment any complex logic. Remember, you may have to revisit the code a week, month, or year from now.

Using the Option Explicit statement within a module helps eliminate typographical errors and the logical errors associated with them.

Using Function, Property, and Method Data Types

All functions, properties, and methods return values that have a specific data type. You use this data type when declaring a variable to receive the result from a function, property, or method. Knowing the returned data type is especially important when you use Option Explicit to require variable declaration.

> **Note**
>
> Using Option Explicit in a module tells the compiler that all variables must be declared before use, and prevents variables of one type from being assigned to variables of another type.

Data types can be divided into two categories:

- Fundamental data types
- Variants

The data types in the following table are called *fundamental data types* because they can contain only a specific kind of data that fits within their size in memory.

Data type	Kind of data	Size in memory
Boolean	True/False	2 bytes
Integer	Whole number	2 bytes
Long	Whole number	4 bytes
Single	Real number	4 bytes
Double	Real number	8 bytes
Currency	Scaled integer	8 bytes
Date	Date and time	8 bytes
Object	Reference to any object	4 bytes for the reference, additional space for the object itself
Excel object types (Workbook, Range, etc.)	A reference to a particular type of object	4 bytes for the reference, additional space for the object itself
String	Text	1 byte per character, plus 4 bytes overhead for variable-length strings

Variants are the most general data types available. A Variant can include any of the fundamental types, or it can include an array of data. The Variant data type is as many as 16 bytes long plus additional space if the Variant contains a string or an array. If a Variant contains a string, add 1 byte per character. If a Variant contains an array, add the amount of space required for each element in the array.

The ReturnValues() procedure below shows a procedure with Option Explicit set:

```
'Module-level code.
Option Explicit
Sub ReturnValues()
    Dim sResult As String, dResult As Date
    Dim vResult As Variant
    ' Visual Basic Now function returns a date/time.
    dResult = Now
    ' Visual Basic InputBox function returns a string.
    sResult = InputBox("Enter some data")
    ' Excel properties and methods all return Variants.
    vResult = ActiveSheet
End Sub
```

If the data type of a variable doesn't match the value you try to assign to it, you get a `Type mismatch` error (error code 13). For example, the following line causes an error:

```
sResult = ActiveSheet     ' sResult is declared as a String, error!
```

Advantages of Fundamental Data Types

You can avoid `Type mismatch` errors by declaring all variables as variants. However, fundamental data types have some advantages over variants:

- Fundamental data types use less memory than variants.

- Fundamental data types perform operations slightly faster than variants.

- Fundamental data types help you verify results when programming.

These points are explained in the following sections.

Conserving Memory

Each `Variant` variable uses more memory than its equivalent fundamental data type. This becomes an issue with recursive procedures that may use up all available stack space.

Stack space is the limited amount of memory available for the local variables in a procedure. Stack space is affected by many issues, so it's not possible to list exactly how much stack space is available. You can test for how much stack space is available in a given situation by using the `TestStack()` and `BlowStack()` procedures. If you Run `TestStack()`, you will receive an `Out of Stack Space` error message. Click Debug, and check the value of `i`. This is the number of `Variant` variables that fit on the stack. The following code contains the `TestStack()` and `BlowStack()` procedures:

```
Sub TestStack()
    BlowStack 0
End Sub

Sub BlowStack(i As Variant)
    i = i + 1
    BlowStack i
End Sub
```

Next, change the data type of `i` from `As Variant` to `As Integer` and run `TestStack()` again. More integers fit on the stack than variants. You can try this with other variable types and in different situations to see how the stack is affected.

Improving Performance

Operations with variants are slightly slower than operations with the equivalent fundamental data type. Speed usually is not an issue, because operations occur blindingly fast. Other issues—such as available memory, size of worksheets, and program structure—are more important than this slight difference in speed.

Verifying Results

Fundamental types cause `Type mismatch` errors when you assign the wrong data type. At first this might seem like a disadvantage, but it's actually a good way to catch logic errors in your procedures. Using `Option Explicit` and fundamental data types is sometimes called *type safe programming* because the data types of all items are always compared to make sure that you receive the expected result.

Using Fundamental Data Types with Variants

If the data in a `Variant` fits within a fundamental type, Visual Basic automatically converts the Variant to the fundamental type when you perform an assignment. The following line of code uses a `String` variable to receive the result of the `Path` method, which returns a `Variant`:

```
sResult = Application.Path          ' sResult is a string variable.
```

The preceding line works because the `Variant` returned by `Path` has the subtype `String`. Subtypes are the fundamental type of the data currently in a `Variant`. Use the `VarType` function to get information about a variant's subtype. The following line of code displays a message box if `vResult` contains an `Integer`:

```
If VarType(vResult) = vbInteger Then MsgBox "Integer"
```

Use `TypeName` to get the name of the subtype of a `Variant` as a string. The following line of code displays the name of the type of data `vResult` contains:

```
MsgBox TypeName(vResult)
```

`Variant` variable types allow a great deal of freedom while coding applications, although they consume slightly more memory than fundamental data types. When converting between `Variant`s and other data types, always use the `VarType` function to ensure proper variable assignments.

Function, Property, and Method Data Types

The return values of Visual Basic functions have fundamental data types. Table E.1 lists the return values for the elements in the Visual Basic for Applications type library.

Table E.1 Visual Basic function data types		
Category	**Function**	**Return data type**
Conversion	Asc	Integer
	Hex	String
	Oct	String
	Val	Double
FileSystem	ChDir	String
	ChDrive	None
	EOF	Integer
	FileAttr	Long
	FileCopy	None
	FileDateTime	Variant
	FileLen	Long
	GetAttr	Integer
	Kill	None
	Loc	Long
	LOF	Long
	MkDir	None
	Reset	None
	RmDir	None
	Seek	Long
	SetAttr	None

(continues)

Table E.1 Continued		
Category	**Function**	**Return data type**
	Width	None
Date/Time	DateSerial	Variant
	Day	Variant
	Hour	Variant
	Minute	Variant
	Month	Variant
	Now	Variant
	Second	Variant
	Time	Date
	Timer	Single
	TimeSerial	Variant
	TimeValue	Variant
	WeekDay	Variant
	Year	Variant
Information	Erl	Long
	Err	Long
	Err	None
	IMEStatus	Integer
	IsArray	Boolean
	IsDate	Boolean
	IsEmpty	Boolean
	IsError	Boolean
	IsMissing	Boolean
	IsNull	Boolean
	IsNumeric	Boolean
	IsObject	Boolean

Category	Function	Return data type
	TypeName	String
	VarType	Integer
Interaction	AppActivate	None
	Beep	None
	CreateObject	Object
	DoEvents	Integer
	GetObject	Object
	InputBox	String
	MacScrip	String
	MsgBox	Integer
	SendKeys	Double
Math	Abs	Double
	Array	Variant
	Atn	Double
	Cos	Double
	Exp	Double
	Log	Double
	Randomize	None
	Sgn	Integer
	Sin	Double
	Sqr	Double
	Tan	Double
String	Chr	String
	Date	Date
	LCase	String
	Left	String
	LeftB	String

(continues)

Appendixes

Table E.1 Continued		
Category	**Function**	**Return data type**
	LTrim	String
	Right	String
	RightB	String
	RTrim	String
	Space	String
	Str	String
	String	String
	Trim	String
	UCase	String

Properties and methods of Excel objects always return variants. Table E.2 lists the Variant subtypes of Excel's most common properties and methods. Subtypes are the fundamental type of data contained in a Variant; sometimes there is one (or more) possible subtypes, depending on the situation in which the property or method is used.

Table E.2 Excel's common property and method subtypes	
Property/method	**Returned *Variant* subtype**
Activate	Boolean
Add	Object that was created
Application	String
Border	Border object
BringToFront	Boolean
Caption	String
Copy	Boolean
Count	Integer
Creator	Double

Table E.2 Excel's common property and method subtypes	
Property/method	**Returned *Variant* subtype**
Cut	Boolean
Delete	Boolean
Font	Font object
Height	Double
Index	Integer
Interior	Interior object
Item	Object from the collection
Left	Double
Name	String
Parent	Object
Paste	Boolean
Select	Boolean
SendToBack	Boolean
Text	String
Top	Double
Visible	Boolean
Width	Double
ZOrder	Double

Index

Symbols